Ken Hale

Ken Hale

Ken Hale

A Life in Language

edited by Michael Kenstowicz

The MIT Press
Cambridge, Massachusetts
London, England

This book was set in Times New Roman in '3B2' by Asco Typesetters, Hong Kong, and was printed and bound in the United States of America.

Library of Congress Cataloging-in-Publication Data

Ken Hale : a life in language / edited by Michael Kenstowicz.
    p. cm. — (Current studies in linguistics ; 36)
  Includes bibliographical references and index.
  ISBN 0-262-11257-4 (alk. paper) — ISBN 0-262-61160-0 (pbk. : alk. paper)
  1. Linguistics. I. Hale, Kenneth L. (Kenneth Locke), 1934– II. Kenstowicz,
Michael J. III. Current studies in linguistics series ; 36.
P26.H24 K46   2001
410—dc21   00-061644

Contents

Contributors

Elena Anagnostopoulou   Department of Philology, University of Crete

Noam Chomsky   Department of Linguistics and Philosophy, Massachusetts Institute of Technology

Michel DeGraff   Department of Linguistics and Philosophy, Massachusetts Institute of Technology

Kai von Fintel   Department of Linguistics and Philosophy, Massachusetts Institute of Technology

Morris Halle   Department of Linguistics and Philosophy, Massachusetts Institute of Technology

James Harris   Department of Linguistics and Philosophy, Massachusetts Institute of Technology

Sabine Iatridou   Department of Linguistics and Philosophy, Massachusetts Institute of Technology

Roumyana Izvorski   Department of Slavic Languages and Literatures and Department of Linguistics, University of Southern California

Michael Kenstowicz   Department of Linguistics and Philosophy, Massachusetts Institute of Technology

Samuel Jay Keyser   Department of Linguistics and Philosophy, Massachusetts Institute of Technology

Shigeru Miyagawa   Department of Linguistics and Philosophy and Foreign Languages and Literatures, Massachusetts Institute of Technology

Wayne O'Neil   Department of Linguistics and Philosophy, Massachusetts Institute of Technology

David Pesetsky   Department of Linguistics and Philosophy, Massachusetts Institute of Technology

Hyang-Sook Sohn   Department of English, Kyungpook National University

Kenneth N. Stevens   Department of Electrical Engineering and Com-
puter Science, Massachusetts Institute of Technology

Esther Torrego   Department of Hispanic Studies, University of Massachusetts at Boston

Cheryl Zoll   Department of Linguistics and Philosophy, Massachusetts
Institute of Technology

Preface

Ken Hale is an exceptional man—from many angles.

First, there is Ken Hale the linguistic theorist. It is clear that linguistics at MIT and in the profession as a whole would be quite different today had Ken's father not moved to Arizona to take up ranching (see the following appreciation by Jay Keyser). For, more than any other individual over the past forty years, Ken has broadened the horizons of our field by showing that the lesser-studied languages, particularly Australian Aboriginal and Native American, hold a wealth of phenomena that illuminate Universal Grammar: nonconfigurationality, agreement, ergativity, obviation, switch reference, light verbs, to mention a few. Through Ken's initiative, investigation of these phenomena has shaped most of the basic concepts and principles that inform our current understanding of the way syntax works. Ken's research in phonology has been equally influential. His study of the Maori passive and of Lardil truncations and augmentations was one of the first to conclusively demonstrate how surface phonotactics constrains underlying structure as well as motivates and directs phonological processes. Later, his investigation of Winnebago accent and Ulwa infixation uncovered some of the most stunning evidence found to date for metrical constituency. And with his research on argument structure and thematic roles, Ken essentially inaugurated serious consideration of the lexicon from the generative perspective.

Although his scientific discoveries are of profound and lasting significance, the way Ken Hale does linguistics and why are perhaps even more influential. For Ken, the intricacies and subtleties of language structure are continual sources of wonderment and delight—treasures of the natural world comparable to its flora and fauna—and equally deserving of our respect and, where necessary, protection. Under the ever-increasing threat of extinction, the documentation and analysis of linguistic diversity takes on added significance and urgency. In this area as well, Ken has played a unique role. Building on the Chomskyan insight that language is a type of knowledge, he has always tried to involve his informants directly in the analysis of their languages. Many have gone on to become professional linguists themselves, capitalizing on their native speaker status to make unique contributions to the scientific study of their language as well as to its maintenence and enhancement in community life.

Other facets of Ken Hale's life in language must be mentioned.

There is Ken Hale the linguistic savant. His strange ability to acquire fluency in any language of his choosing seemingly without effort and with great rapidity is legendary. MIT's president Chuck Vest remarked that with Ken's retirement, the number of languages spoken by the Institute's faculty shrinks by 80 percent.

There is Ken Hale the field linguist (regarded by many as the best in the business). He has been to some of the remotest places on earth to observe the communities where the languages are actually spoken. He has collected ream upon ream, reel upon reel of material—enough to fill a small library and to keep him busy until the next turn of the century. Linguistic analysis involves continual guesswork; Ken knows intuitively where to look for the crucial evidence.

Then there is Ken Hale the teacher and colleague. He has prodigious energy—always the first to arrive at the office (to beat the traffic, he says). His enthusiasm for linguistics is infectious. A walking encyclopedia, Ken is the one we turn to for ideas, data, evidence, and encouragement.

Finally, there is Ken Hale the human being. He is one of the kindest, most generous, modest, and decent individuals one is ever likely to encounter. At Ken's retirement party, Howard Lasnik remarked that Ken Hale is his role model—not just for linguistics, but for life.

It is with great affection and admiration that we offer these studies in celebration of Ken Hale's life in language.

Appreciation

Samuel Jay Keyser

*Remarks on the occasion of Ken Hale's
retirement from the linguistics faculty
of the Massachusetts Institute of
Technology at his retirement party held
on 22 April 1999*

Everyone's life has a pivotal moment, a moment when, had things gone otherwise, we would be someone other than who we are. In the case of Ken Hale, that moment may have been in the life, or rather the death, of his grandfather.

Ken's grandfather went to a Dartmouth-Yale football game and never came back. He died of a stroke. The inheritance occasioned by his untimely death enabled Ken's father to exchange commercial banking in Chicago for ranching in Arizona. Anyone who has seen the photograph in Ken's office of the rodeo cowboy caught in midair as he dives from his horse onto a heifer can gauge the impact the move to Canelo, Arizona, had on Ken. That picture, freezing in time as it does a "mad pursuit," is Ken's transmutation of Keats's "Ode to a Grecian Urn."

When Ken was a child, he spent his time trapping, shooting, and riding. He even planned to be a gunsmith. I once asked him if his father was good at ranching. He said his father was good at whatever he turned his hand to. That must be where Ken gets it from. Had he become a gunsmith instead of a linguist, his guns would have ended up behind glass in the Smithsonian.

Ken went to the University of Arizona in 1952 and majored in Anthropology, the closest program to Native Languages of the Southwest he could find. Even so, he divided his undergraduate days between weekend "jackpot" rodeos, studying anthropology, and working on whatever Native American languages he could get his hands on.

In his senior year, he won the bull-riding event at the University of Arizona rodeo. He still wears the trophy belt buckle. That same year, he also entered the bull-riding event in the Tucson rodeo. His ride was immortalized on film in the movie *Arena*. There was a story in the Tucson paper the day after the rodeo. Under a headline that read "Clown Saves

Waddy from Charging Bull," the text began, "Kenneth Hall [*sic*] narrowly escaped serious injury ..." The photograph caught Ken on his back
kicking the bull in the face. That was the first Ken's father heard about it.
He admonished Ken for his foolishness in entering the rodeo. Then he
commiserated with him about the misspelling of his name: "They either
call us Hall, or Hull, or Hole."

Ken was sixteen years old when he had his first experience with an
exotic language. He spent two years at Verde Valley School. He roomed
with a Hopi boy and learned Hopi. Then he roomed with a Jemez boy
and learned Jemez. Since neither language was written at the time, Ken
developed his own system for each. His Spanish teacher wanted him to
concentrate only on Spanish and then French. Ken said she never understood that he learned faster by working on several languages at once.

He resented the time he had to spend on academic subjects other than
languages and talked his parents into allowing him to return home. At
Tucson High School, he was able to add Navajo, O'odam, Pachuco,
Polish, and whatever else came along.

Ken's linguistic ability is legendary. Everybody has a story to tell. In
1978, Ken and I went to the Linguistic Society of America meeting in
New York City. At lunchtime, he had a few errands to run and asked if I
would like to come along. The first stop was the Irish consulate for a visa.
He began the conversation with the receptionist in Gaelic. After five
minutes, the receptionist asked if he spoke English and apologized that
her own Gaelic was not up to his.

I have told this story on other occasions, and people have wondered
why Ken spoke in Gaelic in the first place. The answer is courtesy. Ken
believes it is a mark of respect to speak to someone in his or her own
language. If only we could all be that respectful.

The next stop was an international bookstore where Ken bought a
novel and a dictionary, both in Dutch. He was off to Holland in a few
weeks for a year of teaching and wanted to acquire "a little Dutch" before
he got there. About a year later, Jan Koster told me this story. He was
walking along a corridor at the University of Tilburg when he heard, but
could not yet see, someone lecturing in Dutch. He was surprised that
there was someone on the Tilburg staff who could lecture so authoritatively on the languages of the American Southwest. When he entered the
room, he was astonished to see that it was Ken Hale. Jan told me Ken's
Dutch was flawless.

Ken and Sally have been together for forty-four years. I asked Sally if she would tell me how the two of them met. With her permission, I pass on what she wrote.

I met Ken in 1947 when my mother and I visited friends on a neighboring ranch. I was two years older than Ken and thought him too young and scruffy to merit my attention. He was one of a small flock of little local boys who buzzed around on the ground or on horseback, being "strong silent cowboy types." Generally, to me, they seemed unwashed and fairly inarticulate. I got to know Ken better when we went off together to Verde Valley School in 1948. We were briefly "an item" in 1949 but I was a fickle girl and busily tried out all the older boys in the school, to see what having boyfriends was all about. Ken likes to say I broke his heart. Ah, well. I went off to the University of Arizona and at the beginning of my sophomore year saw a very handsome young cowboy come into the Student Union. To my delight and surprise I realized I knew him! "Ken Hale! My how you've changed!" I decided to give him another try and the rest is history.

Every year, the New Liberty Jazz Band performs in the Patriots' Day parade in the town where Ken and Sally live, Lexington, Massachusetts. We play on a restored 1941 Ford fire engine, and Ken always comes to visit the engine just before the parade begins. At the last parade, I introduced Ken to the other members of the band. When Ken went off to find Sally, the piano player, a retired doctor, asked me who he was. I told him a little about what Ken did and about his stature as one of the foremost linguists in the world. My friend's comment was, "What a modest man he is!"

My friend got it right. The next hour will be a joy for all of us who know and love Ken and want to praise him. But for Ken it will be excruciating. What a modest man he is.

Chapter 1

Derivation by Phase   Noam Chomsky

What follows extends and revises an earlier paper ("Minimalist Inquiries," MI),[1] which outlines a framework for pursuit of the so-called Minimalist Program, one of a number of alternatives that are currently being explored. The shared goal is to formulate in a clear and useful way—and to the extent possible to answer—a fundamental question of the study of language, which until recently could hardly be considered seriously and may still be premature: to what extent is the human faculty of language FL an optimal solution to minimal design specifications, conditions that must be satisfied for language to be usable at all? We may think of these specifications as "legibility conditions": for each language L (a state of FL), the expressions generated by L must be "legible" to systems that access these objects at the interface between FL and external systems—external to FL, internal to the person.

The strongest minimalist thesis SMT would hold that language is an optimal solution to such conditions. The SMT, or a weaker version, becomes an empirical thesis insofar as we are able to determine interface conditions and to clarify notions of "good design." While the SMT cannot be seriously entertained, there is by now reason to believe that in nontrivial respects some such thesis holds, a surprising conclusion insofar as it is true, with broad implications for the study of language, and well beyond.

Note the indefinite article: *an* optimal solution. "Good design" conditions are in part a matter of empirical discovery, though within general guidelines of an a prioristic character, a familiar feature of rational inquiry. In the early days of the modern scientific revolution, for example, there was much concern about the interplay of experiment and mathematical reasoning in determining the nature of the world. Even the most extreme proponents of deductive reasoning from first principles, Descartes for example, held that experiment was critically necessary to discover which of the reasonable options was instantiated in the actual world. Similar issues arise in the case at hand (see MI for discussion).

Tenable or not, the SMT sets an appropriate standard for true explanation: anything that falls short is to that extent descriptive, introducing mechanisms that would not be found in a "more perfect" system satisfying only legibility conditions. If empirical evidence requires mechanisms that are "imperfections," they call for some independent account: perhaps path-dependent evolutionary history, properties of the brain, or some other source. It is worthwhile to keep this standard of explanation in mind whether or not some version of a minimalist thesis turns out to be valid.

These considerations bear directly on parametric variation, in this case yielding conclusions that are familiar features of linguistic inquiry. Any such variation is a prima facie imperfection: one seeks to restrict the variety for this reason alone. The same goal is grounded in independent concerns of explanatory adequacy/learnability, which require further that ineliminable parameters be easily detectable in data available for language acquisition. Both kinds of considerations (related, though distinct) indicate that study of language should be guided by the *Uniformity Principle* (1).

(1) In the absence of compelling evidence to the contrary, assume
     languages to be uniform, with variety restricted to easily detectable
     properties of utterances.

One familiar application is the thesis that basic inflectional properties are universal though phonetically manifested in various ways (or not at all), stimulated by Jean-Roger Vergnaud's influential Case-theoretic proposals 20 years ago. Another is the thesis proposed by Hagit Borer and others that parametric variation is restricted to the lexicon, and insofar as syntactic computation is concerned, to a narrow category of morphological properties, primarily inflectional. These have been highly productive guidelines for research, extending earlier efforts with similar motivation (e.g., efforts to reduce the variety of phrase structure and transformational rules). What counts as "compelling" is, of course, a matter of judgment: there is no algorithm to determine when apparently disconfirming evidence is real or is the effect of unknown factors, hence to be held in abeyance.

On such grounds, we try to eliminate levels apart from the interface levels, and to maintain a bare phrase structure theory and the *Inclusiveness Condition*, which bars introduction of new elements (features) in the course of computation: indices, traces, syntactic categories or bar levels, and so on. The indispensable operation of a recursive system is Merge (or some variant of it), which takes two syntactic objects α and β and forms the new object $\gamma = \{\alpha, \beta\}$. We assume further that γ is of some determinate type: it has label $LB(\gamma)$. In the best case, $LB(\gamma) = LB(\alpha)$ or $LB(\beta)$, determined by general algorithm.[2] Merge yields the relation Immediately-Contain (IC) (equivalently, Is-a-Member-Of), holding of (γ, α) and (γ, β). Iterated Merge, required in any recursive system, yields Contain (equivalently, Term-Of). Arguably Merge also yields a relation between α and β (sister); transitive closure yields C-Command (and also Contain and Identity, presumably available independently).

While (iterated) Merge "comes free," any other operation requires justification. Similarly, any features of lexical items that are not interpretable at the interface require justification. That includes most (maybe all) phonological features; these must be deleted or converted to interface-interpretable form by the phonological component. One might ask to what extent the phonological component is an optimal solution to the requirement of relating syntactic input to legible form, a hard question, not yet seriously addressed. We keep here to *narrow syntax*: computation of LF.

The empirical facts make it clear that there are (LF-)uninterpretable inflectional features that enter into agreement relations with interpretable inflectional features. Thus, the ϕ-features of T (Tense)[3] are uninterpretable and agree with the interpretable ϕ-features of a nominal that may be local or remote, yielding the surface effect of noun-verb agreement. The obvious conclusion, which we adopt, is that the agreement relation removes the uninterpretable features from the narrow syntax, allowing derivations to converge at LF while remaining intact for the phonological component (with language-variant PF manifestation).

We therefore have a relation Agree holding between α and β, where α has interpretable inflectional features and β has uninterpretable ones, which delete under Agree. The relation Agree and uninterpretable features are prima facie imperfections. In MI and earlier work, it is suggested that both may be part of an optimal solution to minimal design specifications by virtue of their role in establishing the property of "displacement," which has (at least plausible) external motivation in terms of distinct kinds of semantic interpretation and perhaps processing. If so, displacement is only an apparent imperfection of natural language, as are the devices that implement it.

Displacement is implemented by selecting a target P and a related category K to be moved to a position determined by P–P a *probe* that seeks K.[4] The target/probe P determines the kind of category that can be moved to this position (a nominal phrase, a *wh*-phrase, etc.). If uninterpretable inflectional features are the devices that implement displacement, we expect to find uninterpretable features of three kinds:

(2) a. To select a target/probe P and determine what kind of category K it seeks
    b. To determine whether P offers a position for movement
    c. To select the category K that is moved

That seems correct. For movement of a nominal to T, for example, the φ-set and EPP-feature of T serve the functions (2a) and (2b), respectively.[5] The category K that is moved has uninterpretable structural Case, serving the function (2c). Agree is the relation between T and the moved category—more precisely, their relevant subparts.[6] Let us say that the uninterpretable features of P and K render their relevant subparts *active*, so that matching leads to agreement. Locality conditions yield an intervention effect if probe P matches inactive K that is closer to P than matching M, barring Agree(P, M), properties that may be nuanced, as we will see.

The picture seems to generalize over an interesting range. To the extent that this is true, uninterpretable features and the Agree relation are not true "imperfections," despite appearances.

Uninterpretability of features—say, of phonological features, φ-features of T or its EPP-feature, or structural Case—is not "stipulated." The existence of these features is a question of fact: does L have these properties or not? If it does (as appears to be the case), we have to recognize the fact and seek to explain it: in the best case, by showing that these are only apparent imperfections, part of an optimal solution to design specifications. Though motivated at the interface, interpretability of a feature is an inherent property that is accessible throughout the derivation. The phonological properties [±continuant], for example, are motivated only at the interface, but these "abstract" features are accessible throughout the derivation, which ultimately eliminates them in favor of narrow phonetic features interpretable at the interface. Similarly, interpretability of φ-features ([+] for N, [−] for T) is accessible throughout the derivation. For convergence, uninterpretable features must be deleted—in narrow syntax, we assume, by the operation Agree, establishing an agreement relation under appropriate conditions.

Suppose that L has generated the syntactic object K with label LB(K). On minimalist assumptions, LB(K) is the only element of K that is immediately accessible to L, so LB(K) must be the element that activates Agree, by virtue of its uninterpretable features: it is these that constitute the probe that seeks a matching *goal*—another collection of features— within the domain of LB(K). What is the relation Match? The optimal candidate is Identity; we therefore take Match to be Identity.

Interpretability of features is determined in the lexicon, by Universal Grammar (UG) we assume, and the distinction must be indicated not only at that stage but throughout the derivation. The natural principle is that the uninterpretable features, and only these, enter the derivation without values, and are distinguished from interpretable features by virtue of this property. Their values are determined by Agree, at which point the features must be deleted from the narrow syntax (or they will be indistinguishable from interpretable features at LF) but left available for the phonology (since they may have phonetic effects). The conclusion is appropriate in other respects: the values of uninterpretable features are redundant, and there is empirical motivation from intervention effects (see MI). Accordingly, Match is not strictly speaking Identity, but Nondistinctness: same feature, independently of value.

The operation Spell-Out removes LF-uninterpretable material from the syntactic object K and transfers K to the phonological component. It must therefore be able to determine which syntactic features are uninterpretable, hence to be removed. Prior to application of Agree, these are distinguished from interpretable features by lack of specification of value. After application of Agree, the distinction is lost. To operate without reconstructing the derivation,[7] Spell-Out must therefore apply shortly after the uninterpretable features have been assigned values (if they have not been assigned values at this point, the derivation will crash, with uninterpretable features at the interface). Spell-Out must be strongly cyclic (as assumed in MI). The conclusion, which follows naturally from examination of feature interpretability, has other desirable consequences. In contrast to Extended Standard Theory–based systems, this system has no overt/covert distinction with two independent cycles; rather, it has a single narrow-syntactic cycle. Furthermore, the phonological cycle is not a third independent cycle, but proceeds essentially in parallel.

I will keep here largely to Case/agreement and related systems: φ-features, structural Case, EPP, A-movement, and the *core functional categories* T, C, *v* (T = tense, C = complementizer, *v* = a light verb that introduces verbal phrases).[8] Within these systems, probe and goal match if features have values for the goal but not for the probe: if φ-features were valued for the probe, it would be inactive and could drive no operation; if they were unvalued for the goal, they would receive no values from the (unvalued) matching features of the probe. If correct, the analysis should generalize to other core syntactic processes. Some extensions to *wh*-movement are suggested in MI, but tentatively, for reasons indicated. This is the easiest case of Ā-movement, since there are grounds to believe that features of probe and goal are involved. In other cases (e.g., topicalization, VP-fronting), postulation of features is much more stipulative; and throughout, questions arise about intermediate stages of successive-cyclic Ā-movement and island conditions.

Matching of probe and goal induces Agree, eliminating uninterpretable features that activate them. A number of questions arise—specifically, with regard to the theses in (3).

(3) a. Goal as well as probe must be active for Agree to apply.
    b. α must have a complete set of φ-features (it must be φ-*complete*) to delete uninterpretable features of the paired matching element β.

Let us tentatively adopt both theses, returning to the matter.[9]

For the Case/agreement systems, the uninterpretable features are φ-features of the probe and structural Case of the goal N. φ-features of N are interpretable; hence, N is active only when it has structural Case. Once the Case value is determined, N no longer enters into agreement relations and is "frozen in place" (under (3a)). Structural Case is not a feature of the probes (T, *v*), but it is assigned a value under agreement, then removed by Spell-Out from the narrow syntax. The value assigned depends on the probe: nominative for T, accusative for *v* (alternatively ergative-absolutive, with different conditions). Case itself is not matched, but deletes under matching of φ-features.

In some cases, an active element E is unable to inactivate a matched element by deleting its unvalued features. E is *defective*, differing in some respect from otherwise identical active elements that induce deletion. The simplest way to express the distinction, requiring no new mechanisms or features, is in terms of (3b): a nondefective probe is φ-complete, a defective one is not.

One case, to which we will return, is participle-object constructions, which may manifest partial φ-feature agreement but without Case assignment to the object, the participle being defective. Other cases, we will assume, are raising constructions and their exceptional-Case-marking (ECM) counterparts, as shown schematically in (4a), where β is the matrix clause, α is an infinitival with YP a verbal phrase (the case most relevant here), and P is the probe: T with a raising verb (case (4b)), *v* with an ECM transitive verb (case (4c)).[10]

(4) a. [$_\beta$ P [$_\alpha$ [Subj [H YP]]]]
   b. i. there are likely to be awarded several prizes
      ii. several prizes are likely to be awarded
   c. i. we expect there to be awarded several prizes
      ii. we expect several prizes to be awarded

The Case/agreement properties of Subj in (4a), and its overt location, are determined by properties of the matrix probe P, not internally to α. α is a TP with defective head T_{def}, which is unable to determine Case/agreement but has an EPP-feature, overtly manifested in (4c). Raising-ECM parallels give good reason to believe that the EPP-feature is manifested in (4b) as well, by trace of the matrix subject; preference for Merge over (more complex) Move gives a plausible reason for the surface distinction between [Spec, T_{def}] in (4b) and in (4c) (see MI). In (4bi) and (4ci), the EPP-feature of T_{def} is satisfied by Merge of expletive; in (4bii) and (4cii), by raising of the direct object.

At this point, there are several ways to proceed.

Alternative 1, the conventional approach adopted in MI (and below), follows the path just outlined. [Spec, T_{def}] of α is filled either by Merge or by Move, then associated to the higher probe. Examples (4bii) and (4cii)[11] illustrate raising to subject, leaving reconstruction sites.[11] T_{def} matches Subj in some of its features (to implement raising) but not all (to preclude inactivation). If P and T_{def} match Subj in the feature [person], then categories with this feature, and only these, can undergo raising (nominals but not adjectivals); on the simplest assumptions, T_{def} has no other φ-features. Expletives too must have the feature [person], since they raise; and pure expletives of the *there*-type should have no other formal features, on the simplest assumptions. In a framework that dispenses with categorial features, as is reasonable on minimalist grounds, [person] plays the role formerly assigned to D- or N-features.[12]

When φ-complete, T values and deletes structural Case for N. The φ-set of N (which is always φ-complete) both values and deletes the φ-features of T (with or without movement). With a defective probe, agreement is not manifested and Case of the matched goal is not assigned a value: raising T exhibits no agreement, and participles lack person; neither determines the Case of matched N, which depends on a higher non-defective probe, T or *v* (see (18)).

Similar properties hold in other constructions, such as attributive adjectival/participial constructions ([*old/smashed*] *car, a car* [*old enough to buy/smashed into pieces*]). Whatever the correct analysis may be, these constructions involve a relation between N and the head of the predicate phrase; the complete φ-set of N values and deletes the matched uninterpretable features of the predicate, but the partial φ-set of the predicate does not value and delete Case in N, which still has to satisfy the Case Filter.

In the MI framework, C is one-to-one associated with φ-complete T (T_{comp}).

(5) C selects T_{comp}; V selects T_{def}.

Control structures and finite clauses have the selectional relation C-T_{comp}, while raising/ECM constructions have the relation V-T_{def}. The reasons given in MI were largely theory-internal, having to do with Case/agreement and related systems. The conclusions are consistent with those reached on other grounds. The earliest straightforward evidence that raising clauses fall together with finite TP, and control clauses with CP, was provided by Luigi Rizzi, who observed that control clauses, like CPs, are phonetically isolable in ways that raising clauses—and of course finite TP (stranding its complementizer)—are not.[13]

These conclusions suggest a possible recasting of the account of defective elements, alternative (2), with the invariant property (6).[14]

(6) C is φ-complete; T is φ-complete only when necessary.

One case in which T must be φ-complete, it could be argued, is selection by φ-complete α with uninterpretable features (specifically, α = C). The selectional property could then be formulated in terms of Match/Agree: the φ-features of α have to be deleted under Agree by T, which therefore must be φ-complete (crash with failure of match is detectable at once); we will return to some problems. It is tempting to associate EPP with φ-completeness: C, and T selected by C, are φ-complete and therefore allow an EPP-feature; T_{def} cannot have an EPP-feature. Accordingly, there is no internal raising to [Spec, T_{def}]; raising takes place "in one fell swoop" in such constructions as (4b), and there are no intermediate reconstruction sites.[15] Case/agreement and EPP proceed as before, with T_{comp}.

The symmetry of raising and ECM constructions suggests that the analysis should be extended to the latter as well.[16] Just as C_{comp} selects T_{comp}, we might expect v_{comp} ($= v^*$; see note 8) to select V_{comp}. Being ϕ-complete, C must select T_{comp} for its unvalued features to delete under Match/Agree, and it allows an EPP-feature. For the same reasons, v^* selects V_{comp} and allows an EPP-feature.

Continuing with alternative 2, unless selected by C or v^*, T and V are defective (raising T and passive/unaccusative V, respectively). They do not enter into Case/agreement and have no EPP-feature. When selected by C or v^*, T and V are ϕ-complete, entering into Case/agreement structures (with raising of associate or not, depending on optionality of the permitted EPP-feature and availability of alternatives to satisfy it). In a transitive construction, the object agrees with V and is assigned accusative Case (raising to [Spec, V] if V has an EPP-feature). There is no internal raising to [Spec, T_{def}] in raising or ECM constructions.[17]

Consider ECM constructions more closely, under alternative 2. The verbal phrase is v-[V-TP]. If the light verb v is ϕ-incomplete (passive), then V is defective, as is T_V selected by V (in raising/ECM constructions). If $v = v^*$, then V must be ϕ-complete for convergence. But (6) does not require that T_V be ϕ-complete in this case, because the ϕ-set of V is valued and deleted independently by the embedded subject. Therefore, T remains defective, and the raising/ECM parallelism remains intact.

The discussion suggests that T should be construed as a substantive rather than a functional category, falling together with N and V, and perhaps others, a possibility that is neutral between alternatives 1 and 2. We can regard T as the locus of tense/event structure (see note 8). The C-T relation is therefore analogous to the v^*-V relation.

Alternative 1 takes the locus of Case/agreement/EPP to be T, v^*; alternative 2 takes it to be T, V. Let us refer to the two alternatives as $Locus_{Tv^*}$ and $Locus_{TV}$, focusing on their basic conceptual difference: the choice of category relevant to Case/agreement/EPP. Much of what follows is neutral among these alternatives or variants that merit consideration as well.[18] I will continue with the conventional choice $Locus_{Tv^*}$, returning to others where appropriate, along with lingering problems.

Suppose that the label LB(K) of K has an uninterpretable selectional feature (by definition, an EPP-feature), which requires Merge in [Spec, LB(K)]. That can be satisfied by Merge of an expletive, in which case long-distance agreement may hold between LB(K) and the goal. Alternatively, an active goal G determines a category PP(G) (pied-piping), which is merged in [Spec, LB(K)], yielding the displacement property; long-distance agreement may still appear, if PP(G) fails to satisfy the φ-features of the probe (e.g., quirky Case subject). The combination of Agree/pied-piping/Merge is the composite operation Move, preempted where possible by the simpler operations Merge and Agree.[19]

FL specifies the features **F** that are available to fix each particular language L. The MI framework takes L to be a derivational procedure that maps **F** to {Exp}, where an expression Exp is a set of interface representations. As a first approximation, take Exp to be {PF, LF}, these being symbolic objects at the sensorimotor and conceptual-intentional interfaces, respectively. We adopt the conventional assumption that L makes a one-time selection [F_L] from **F**. These are the features that enter into L; others can be disregarded in use of L.

Assume further that L assembles [F_L] to lexical items LI of a lexicon Lex, the LIs then entering into computations as units. In the simplest case, Lex is a single collection, but empirical phenomena might call for "distribution" of Lex, with late insertion in the manner of Distributed Morphology (DM).[20] In any case, we can think of Lex as in principle "Bloomfieldian," a "list of exceptions" that provides just the information required to yield the interface outputs and does so in the best way, with least redundancy and complication. In the simplest case, the entry LI is a once-and-for-all collection (perhaps structured) of (A) phonological, (B) semantic, and (C) formal features. The features of (A) are accessed in the phonological component, ultimately yielding a PF interface representation; those of (B) are interpreted at LF; and those of (C) are accessible in the course of the narrow-syntactic derivation. Language design is such that (B) and (C) intersect and are disjoint from (A), though there is some evidence, to which we will return, that presence or absence of features of (A) can have an effect on narrow-syntactic computation. It also seems that FL may retain something like (B)–(C) and the narrow syntax into which they enter while the phonological component is replaced by other means of sensorimotor access to narrow-syntactic derivations, as in sign language. Of particular interest is the subset of (C) that is not in (B):

uninterpretable formal features that appear, prima facie, to violate conditions of optimal design.

For open classes, the simplest picture seems reasonable: LI is a unitary collection, including the phonological matrix. Lex is distributed when departure from the simplest account is warranted in favor of late insertion, typically for inflectional elements and suppletion. Throughout, answers depend on predictability of phonetic outcome by general phonological principles that satisfy UG conditions, and in all cases, the simplest choice should win. For roots and highly predictable inflectional elements (say, English progressive), the distinctions between single-LI and several independent contributions to LI (as in DM systems postulating universal late insertion) seem to have little empirical content, but they might, for example, when an idiosyncratic feature F of a root has syntactic effects. Universal late insertion then requires postulation of a redundant syntactic feature F' as a "placeholder" in narrow syntax for F, with a stipulation that F' must be replaced under late insertion by a root with F (i.e., F' is effectively identical with F).[21] A unitary Lex avoids the redundancy and stipulation. The substantive results of DM remain unchanged.

Narrow syntax maps a selection of choices from Lex to LF; the phonological component, in contrast, has further access to $[F_L]$. Like the extraction of $[F_L]$ from **F**, these assumptions, largely conventional, reduce the computational burden for the procedure L while adding new conceptual apparatus.

More controversially, MI extends the same reasoning to individual derivations: L makes a one-time selection of a lexical array LA, a collection of LIs (a "numeration" if some are selected more than once), and maps LA to Exp. Again, there is a reduction of computational burden, in this case a vast reduction, since Lex, which virtually exhausts L, need no longer be accessed in the derivation once LA is selected. The new concept LA (numeration) is added, while another concept is eliminated: chains are determined by identity, with no need for indices or some similar device to distinguish chains from repetitions, also violating the Inclusiveness Condition. As in the other cases, the tests are ultimately empirical; on purely conceptual grounds, one could argue either way. As noted, the nature of optimal design that is instantiated in FL (if any) is a matter of discovery, within certain guidelines.

Proceeding further, MI proposes another reduction of computational burden: the derivation of Exp proceeds by *phase*, where each phase is determined by a subarray LA_i of LA, placed in "active memory." When the computation L exhausts LA_i, forming the syntactic object K, L returns to LA, either extending K to K' or forming an independent structure M to be assimilated later to K or to some extension of K. Derivation is assumed to be strictly cyclic, but with the phase level of the cycle playing a special role.[22]

A subarray LA_i must be easily identifiable; optimally, it should contain exactly one lexical item that will label the resulting phase. The evidence reviewed in MI suggested that the phases are "propositional": verbal phrases with full argument structure and CP with force indicators, but not TP alone or "weak" verbal configurations lacking external arguments (passive, unaccusative). Assume that substantive categories are selected by functional categories: V by a light verb, T by C. If so, phases are CP and v*P, and a subarray contains exactly one C or v*.

The choice of phases has independent support: these are reconstruction sites, and they have a degree of phonetic independence (as already noted for CP vs. TP). The same is true of vP constructions generally, not just v*P.[23] If these too are phases, then PF and LF integrity correlate more generally.

Suppose, then, we take CP and vP to be phases. Nonetheless, there remains an important distinction between CP/v*P phases and others; call the former *strong* phases and the latter *weak*. The strong phases are potential targets for movement; C and v* may have an EPP-feature, which provides a position for XP-movement, and the observation can be generalized to head movement of the kind relevant here.[24]

The special role of strong phases becomes significant in the light of another suggestion of MI that I will adopt and extend here: cyclic Spell-Out, necessary for reasons already discussed, takes place at the strong phase level. The intuitive idea, to be sharpened, is that features deleted within the cyclic computation remain until the strong phase level, at which point the whole phase is "handed over" to the phonological component. The deleted features then disappear from the narrow syntax, allowing convergence at LF, but they may have phonetic effects.

Spell-Out seeks formal features that are uninterpretable but have been assigned values (checked); these are removed from the narrow syntax as the syntactic object is transferred to the phonology. The valued uninterpretable features can be detected with only limited inspection of the derivation if earlier stages of the cycle can be "forgotten"—in phase terms, if earlier phases need not be inspected. The computational burden is further reduced if the phonological component too can "forget" earlier stages of derivation. These results follow from the Phase-Impenetrability Condition (PIC) (MI, (21)), for strong phase HP with head H,

(7) The domain of H is not accessible to operations outside HP; only H and its *edge* are accessible to such operations.

the *edge* being the residue outside of H′, either specifiers (Specs) or elements adjoined to HP.

H and its edge are accessible only up to the next strong phase, under the PIC: in (8), elements of HP are accessible to operations within the smallest strong ZP phase but not beyond.

(8) [$_{ZP}$ Z ... [$_{HP}$ α [H YP]]]

Local head movement and successive-cyclic A- and Ā-movement are allowed, and both Spell-Out and the phonological component can proceed without checking back to earlier stages. The simplest assumption is that the phonological component spells out elements that undergo no further displacement—the heads of chains—with no need for further specification.[25]

In effect, H and its edge α in (8) belong to ZP for the purposes of Spell-Out, under the PIC. YP is spelled out at the level HP. H and α are spelled out if they remain in situ. Otherwise, their status is determined in the same way at the next strong phase ZP. The question arises only for the edge α, assuming that excorporation is disallowed.

The picture improves further if interpretation/evaluation takes place uniformly at the next higher phase, with Spell-Out just a special case. Assuming so, we adopt the guiding principle (9) for phases Ph$_i$.

(9) Ph$_1$ is interpreted/evaluated at the next relevant phase Ph$_2$.

What are the relevant phases? As noted, because of the availability of EPP, the effects of Spell-Out are determined at the next higher *strong* phase: CP or *v**P. For the same reason, a strong-phase HP allows extraction to its outer edge, so the domain of H can be assumed to be inaccessible to extraction under the PIC: an element to be extracted can be raised to the edge, and the operations of the phonological component can apply to the domain at once, not waiting for the next phase. Keeping to the optimal assumption that all operations are subject to the same conditions, we restate (9) as (10), where Ph$_1$ is strong and Ph$_2$ is the next highest strong phase.

(10) Ph_1 is interpreted/evaluated at Ph_2.

On similar grounds, the PIC should fall under (10). We therefore restate the PIC as (11), for (8) with ZP the smallest strong phase.

(11) The domain of H is not accessible to operations at ZP; only H and its edge are accessible to such operations.

We can henceforth restrict attention to phases that are relevant under (10), that is, the strong phases. For the same reason, we restrict attention to v^* rather than light verb v generally, unless otherwise indicated.

Considerations of semantic-phonetic integrity, and the systematic consequences of phase identification, suggest that the general typology should include among phases nominal categories, perhaps other substantive categories. If categorial features are eliminated from roots, then a plausible typology might be that phases are configurations of the form F-XP, where XP is a substantive root projection, its category determined by the functional element F that selects it. CP falls into place as well if T is taken to be a substantive root, as discussed earlier. Phases are then (close to) functionally headed XPs. Like TP, NP cannot be extracted, stranding its functional head. The same should be true of other nonphases.[26] Some phases are strong and others weak—with or without the EPP option, respectively, hence relevant or not for Spell-Out and the general principle (10).[27]

Let us return to (8), repeated as (12) (HP and ZP strong).

(12) $[_{ZP} Z \ldots [_{HP} \alpha [H \; YP]]]$

Suppose that the computation L, operating cyclically, has completed HP and moves on to a stage Σ beyond HP. L can access the edge α and the head H of HP. But the PIC now introduces an important distinction between $\Sigma = ZP$ and Σ within ZP, for example, $\Sigma = TP$. The probe T can access an element of the domain YP of HP; the PIC imposes no restriction on this. But with $\Sigma = ZP$ (so that $Z = C$), the probe Z cannot access the domain YP.[28]

If Z is C in (12), then its complement TP is immune to extraction to a strong phase beyond CP, and only the edge or head of HP (a strong-phase CP or v^*P) is accessible for extraction to Z. The same holds for $Z = v^*$, and the observations extend to Agree. But T in the domain of Z can agree with an element within its complement, for example, with the in-situ quirky nominative object of its v^*P complement.[29]

If such ideas prove correct, we have a further sharpening of the choices made by FL within the range of design optimization: the selected conditions reduce computational burden for narrow syntax and phonology, and eliminate distinct LF and phonological cycles. Spell-Out (deletion) is determined quickly, under the PIC. The computation is "almost efficient," in something like the sense of Frampton and Gutmann (1999), with bounded memory load, up to the next phase.

Unification of cycles has consequences for semantic interpretation: no level constructed by the phonological component can yield more than very limited semantic interpretation. Phonological rules typically render semantically significant units unrecognizable: they eliminate "trace" so that chains cannot be reconstructed, blur or remove boundaries between units and change their phonetic content, delete semantic features (which would cause PF crash), and so on. Hence, displacement rules interspersed in the phonological component should have little semantic effect. We expect some approximation to (13), if the steps reviewed are on the right track.

(13) Surface semantic effects are restricted to narrow syntax.

As discussed in MI and sources cited, there is mounting evidence that the design of FL reduces computational complexity. That is no a priori requirement, but (if true) an empirical discovery, interesting and unexpected. One indication that it may be true is that principles that introduce computational complexity have repeatedly been shown to be empirically false. One such principle, Procrastinate, is not even formulable if the overt/covert distinction collapses: purely "covert" Agree is just part of the single narrow-syntactic cycle. With the motivation for Procrastinate gone, considerations of efficient computation would lead us to expect something like the opposite: perform computations as quickly as possible, the Earliness Principle of Pesetsky (1989). Thus, if local (P, G) match and are active, their uninterpretable features must be eliminated at once, as fully as possible; partial elimination of features under Match, followed by elimination of the residue under more remote Match, is not an option. In particular, if probe P requires Move (i.e., has an EPP-feature), then the operation must be carried out as quickly as possible. We will return to some illustrations. A natural principle, which has been suggested in various forms, is (14).[30]

(14) Maximize matching effects.

One concern of MI is to show that central properties of inflectional morphology, displacement, and related matters can be accommodated within a framework of the sort just outlined. I will assume that account (modified in accord with revisions here) to be essentially accurate as far as it goes, and turn to some extensions and further modifications.

Consider raising constructions with unaccusatives, abstracting for the moment from English-specific idiosyncrasies so that (15a) converges as (15b).

(15) a. [C [T be likely [Expl to-arrive a man]]]
     b. there is likely to arrive a man

The expletive Expl has the uninterpretable feature *person*. Under local Match, Expl agrees with T and raises to [Spec, T]. The operation deletes the EPP-feature of T and the person feature of Expl, but the ϕ-set of T remains intact because Expl is incomplete (assuming (3b)). Therefore, Agree holds between the probe T and the more remote goal *man*, deleting the ϕ-set of T and the structural Case feature of *man* (assuming, as throughout, George and Kornfilt's (1981) thesis that structural Case is a reflex of agreement). The values assigned under Agree are transmitted to the phonological component: the values of *man* for the ϕ-set of T, nominative for structural Case. Uninterpretable features delete, and the derivation converges as (15b).

Suppose the smallest strong phase is v^*P, not CP.

(16) a. [C [we [$_{v^*P}$ v^*-expect [Expl to-arrive a man]]]]
     b. we expect there to arrive a man

If the derivation is parallel to (15), then Agree holds of (v^*, Expl), deleting the person feature of Expl but leaving v^* intact so that Agree holds of (v^*, *man*). The ϕ-set of v^* deletes; structural Case of *man* is assigned the value accusative and deletes. If v^* lacks an EPP-feature here, then (15) and (16) differ in that there is no raising to [Spec, v^*].[31]

In (15) and (16), no intervention effect is induced by Expl. That follows for (15) under the principle (17), conceptually plausible and empirically supported. (See MI, (51) and discussion; also see (36) below.)

(17) Only the head of an A-chain (equivalently, the whole chain) blocks matching under the Minimal Link Condition (MLC).

For (16), the same principle would suffice if raising takes place in ECM constructions.[32]

The same results hold for both (15) and (16) if matching observes the Maximization Principle (14), which entails that the intervention effect is nullified unless intervention blocks remote matching of all features. That is not the case in these examples: the probe (T or $v*$) matches Expl in one φ-feature (namely, the person feature), but other φ-features of the probe do not match Expl and are therefore free to seek a goal G, establishing (T, DO) or ($v*$, DO) match. In either case, matching values and deletes all features of the probe and goal under (14). That makes sense, and the principle is independently plausible. We will return to evidence that matching should be construed in this way. Note that the locality condition functions independently for distinct features of the probe.

Summarizing, an intervention effect is barred in (15) by principles (14) and (17), and in (16) by (14) and possibly (17), depending on the correct analysis of ECM constructions.[33]

Consider the slightly more complex case of participial passives.

(18) a. C [β T seem ⎫
     b. [β v expect ⎬ [Expl to have been [α caught several fish]]]
                      ⎭

We have the same double agreement as in (15), (16): the probes (T or v) agree with Expl and *fish*. T deletes the uninterpretable feature of Expl (and induces raising) and assigns nominative to *fish*, as in (15); v deletes the uninterpretable feature of Expl (but without raising to [Spec, v]; see note 31), and assigns accusative, as in (16). But in (18) there is another possibility beyond (15) and (16): the participle (Prt) agrees with the direct object (DO) *fish*. In Icelandic, furthermore, Case agreement is manifested: Prt is nominative with probe T, and accusative with probe v.[34]

Note that Case assignment is divorced from movement and reflects standard properties of the probes, indicating that it is a reflex of Agree holding of (probe, goal); the EPP-raising complex is a separate matter. The constructions illustrate both Case assignment without raising to the probe and EPP without Case assignment (namely, Expl in (18b)).[35] Under the Uniformity Principle (1), we conclude that Case is assigned in the same way even where not overtly manifested: structural Case of DO in unaccusative/participial constructions is nominative or accusative depending on the probe (T or v, respectively) in Romance, English, Mainland Scandinavian, and so on, a conclusion with ramified consequences, as recent literature illustrates.

Consider more closely the mechanics of (18). The first stage of the cycle that concerns us is α, articulated further as follows:[36]

(19) [$_\alpha$ Prt [catch [$_{DO}$ several fish]]]

Prt is adjectival: its φ-set may therefore consist of (unvalued) number, gender, and Case, but not person. The φ-sets of Prt and DO match, inducing Agree. DO is φ-complete. Hence, for Prt, number and gender receive the values of DO and delete (maximally, under (14)). But Case is unvalued for both Prt and DO, so neither can assign a Case value to the other.[37]

Next we turn to stage β of the cycle. Here again there is double agreement: (probe, Expl) and (probe, DO). Case of DO is nominative with probe T and accusative with probe v. Probe and DO goal lose uninterpretable features.

What about Prt? Its φ-features are deleted at stage α and should therefore be invisible to Match by the probe. Case of Prt cannot be valued and the derivation crashes, contrary to fact.

The problem is overcome if Spell-Out takes place at the strong-phase level. Then the φ-features of Prt are still visible at stage β of the cycle, though deleted; they disappear at the strong-phase level CP or vP, as the phase is transmitted to the phonological component. At stage α of the cycle, the φ-features of Prt are valued by Prt-DO matching, as just discussed. At the next stage, the probe T/v matches the (still visible) goal Prt, valuing its Case feature; and the probe matches the goal DO, valuing the Case feature of DO as well as its own features (since DO is φ-complete). At the phase level CP-vP, the (now valued) uninterpretable features are eliminated from the narrow syntax as the syntactic object is handed over to the phonological component.

The result, then, is that we have triple matching/agreement: (probe, Expl), (probe, DO), and (probe, Prt). Prt and DO agree with one another: directly for number/gender, indirectly for structural Case (since each agrees with the probe).

Once again no intervention effect is induced by Expl, or in this case by Prt either. In the case of (16), there were two possible reasons: principle (17) (assuming raising of Expl to within matrix VP) or principle (14), which requires maximal (probe, goal) effects. In (18), there is no raising of Prt, so we must resort to principle (14), which is therefore available for (16) as well. The number and gender features of the probe bypass Expl, and its person feature bypasses Prt, allowing probe-DO match. The locality condition again functions independently for distinct features of the probe, but more intricately than in the simpler case of (15), (16); note also that it is essential that Prt lack person, or the structure would always crash because of unvalued structural Case for the object (violation of the Case Filter).

The same reasoning extends to more complex cases—for example, (20), with probe T or v in a raising or ECM construction.

(20) a. probe ... Expl ... Prt$_1$ believe t_{Expl} to have been Prt$_2$ caught [$_{DO}$ several fish]
   b. there were believed (we expected there to have been believed) to have been caught several fish

Here Prt$_1$, Prt$_2$, and DO agree fully for number, gender, and Case (indirectly for Case via agreement with the probe). How the features of Prt are manifested phonetically is in part a language-particular matter.[38]

Looking back at the assumptions that enter into this account, we find only one that goes beyond what seems fairly uncontroversial on minimalist grounds: the special role of the strong-phase level in narrow-syntactic computation and Spell-Out. We therefore have good additional evidence that phases exist within the framework of cyclic derivation and that evaluation/interpretation takes place only at the strong-phase level.[39]

In these constructions, another possible derivation has so far been ignored. Consider the passive counterpart (21) of (16), and suppose that Agree holds of (T, Expl) while Move applies to (T, DO), giving (21c).

(21) a. C [T be expected [Expl to-arrive [$_{DO}$ a man]]]
   b. there is expected to arrive a man
   c. *a man is expected there to arrive

We have just seen that deleted features remain visible until the strong-phase level; hence, the person feature of Expl is visible throughout the computation of (21). The agreement facts show that Expl does not induce an intervention effect, blocking Match of (T, *man*); but Expl does intervene to bar raising of DO. The apparent contradiction is resolved by the Maximization Principle (14). The first matching pair detected in the computation is (T, Expl). The pairing matches the person feature of Expl and the EPP-feature of T; and under (14) it therefore must do both, inducing raising of Expl and hence allowing (T, DO) Match/Agree under (17), as discussed.

For English, the unwanted raising of DO in (21) is barred for idiosyncratic reasons that I have so far put aside (also in MI, n. 40). As is well known, unaccusative constructions such as (15)–(16) and (18)–(21) are awkward in English. More accurately, they are barred, as constructions like (22a–e) show.[40]

(22) a. *there came several angry men into the room
     b. *there arrived a strange package in the mail
     c. *there was placed a large book on the table
     d. *how many packages did there arrive in the mail
     e. *how many packages were there placed on the table

Comparable constructions are grammatical in similar languages, for example, Italian (where the in-situ position of the DO is also revealed by *ne*-cliticization) and Dutch, which has an overt Expl and offers word-by-word translations of ungrammatical English cases.

(23) hoeveel   mensen zijn er   aangekomen
     how-many men   have there arrived

The gap in the English paradigm is filled by idiosyncratic constructions such as (24) that are either fully or partially acceptable ((24a) and (24b), respectively).

(24) a. there were several packages placed on the table
     b. there were placed on the table several (large) packages

Examples (15)–(16) and (18)–(21) are presumably of the same type as (24b), with invisible extraposition. Constructions of type (24a) run counter to a general tendency among the Germanic languages: at one extreme, English permits few word order options, while at the other, Icelandic permits many; but English permits (24a) while Icelandic does not.

It seems, then, that English bars surface structures of the form [V-DO], where the construction is unaccusative/passive. In such cases, DO is extracted to the edge of the construction by an obligatory thematization/extraction rule Th/Ex. The operation is reminiscent of normal displacement of subject and of object, both to edge positions, but it differs in not yielding the usual surface-semantic effects (specificity, etc.).

The phenomenon may be more general. As has occasionally been discussed, there seems to be some condition that has the consequence (25).

(25) In transitive constructions, something must escape the vP.

Furthermore, as Richard Kayne has observed, English marginally allows a kind of transitive expletive construction if the subject is displaced to the right, as in (26).

(26) a. there entered the room a strange man
    b. there hit the stands a new journal

The idiosyncratic properties of Th/Ex might lead us to suspect that (27) holds.

(27) Th/Ex is an operation of the phonological component.

At the relevant stage of the cycle, the syntactic object α so far constructed is transferred to the phonological component for application of Th/Ex. The narrow-syntactic computation then proceeds on course with α unchanged except that the base position is phonologically empty even prior to the strong-phase level, at which point the position would have become phonologically empty even if not subject to Th/Ex.[41]

The constructions reach LF in the same form in English as in similar languages, as we would expect if LF-external systems of interpretation are essentially language-independent and prefer the LF interface to be as uniform as possible across languages—a particularly natural case of the general Uniformity Principle (1), given the virtual absence of evidence about these systems for language acquisition.

A closer look tends to support (27). One relevant consideration is that Th/Ex, leftward or rightward, is incompatible with independent movement of the extracted nominal EN, as we see in (28) ((28a–b) = (22d–e)).

(28) a. *how many packages did there arrive in the mail
    b. *how many packages were there placed on the table
    c. *how many men did there enter the room
    d. *how many journals did there hit the stands

(24) and (26) must be incompatible with *wh*-movement; otherwise, (28) would be permitted.[42] Similarly, (29a) is much worse than (29b), indicating that (29a) has undergone (invisible) rightward extraposition, again barring *wh*-movement.

(29) a. *how many men did there arrive
    b. ?there arrived three men

The incompatibility is not between Th/Ex and *wh*-movement. Thus, in (30) both operations apply.[43]

(30) a. to whom was there a present given
    b. ?at which airport did there arrive three strange men

Rather, the two operations cannot apply to the same phrase.

Why does the English-specific rule Th/Ex, which extracts DO either to the left or to the right, bar *wh*-movement? A preliminary question is whether the position of EN (= DO) is immune to all syntactic operations, for example, *wh*-movement from within EN. Compare the examples in (31).

(31) a.   what are they selling books about *t* (in Boston these days)
     b.   *what are there books about *t* being sold (in Boston these days)

The contrast rules out one pattern of derivation for (31b): given the base form (32), apply *wh*-movement to *what* within EN (as in (31a)) and then apply Th/Ex to EN including the trace of *what*, yielding (31b).

(32) there are being sold [$_{EN}$ books about what] (in Boston these days)

If that were possible, the two cases of (31) would be on a par. We conclude that the base position of EN is completely inaccessible to *wh*-movement, either as a whole or in part.

It remains to determine whether the EN output of Th/Ex is accessible to *wh*-movement. We know that the whole EN is not. The natural expectation is that no part of EN is either, in which case the contrast in (31) cannot be attributed simply to the degradation of movement from an internal phrase (see note 42). The examples in (33) provide some evidence that the expected conclusion is correct.

(33) a.   ?who did they deliver to your office a picture of *t*
     b.   *who was there delivered to your office a picture of *t*
     c.   ?there arrived in the mail some books about global warming
     d.   *what did there arrive in the mail some books about *t*
     e.   ?what topics were there some books about *t* selling in Boston stores
     f.   *what topics were there some books about *t* (being) sold in Boston stores
     g.   ?he's the guy there were lots of songs about *t* playing on the radio
     h.   *he's the guy there were lots of songs about *t* (being) played on the radio

The data are less sharp than one would like, but the differences between ENs and their non-EN counterparts seem fairly clear. A reasonable conclusion, then, is that the output of Th/Ex is inaccessible to syntactic rules entirely, just as the input is—either prior to Th/Ex or by application to the trace of this operation.

Other operations are not barred for EN. Thus, EN still has to satisfy the Case Filter, which in present terms means that it is accessible to Agree, in either its base or its extracted position. And it is accessible to operations that are plausibly regarded as interpretation at the interface (binding theory, absorption).

(34) a. *he thought there were songs about John being played on the radio (*he = John*)
   b. they thought there were songs about each other being played on the radio
   c. who thought there were songs about what being played on the radio

This might mean that the EN output of Th/Ex, while immune to Move (either of the whole EN, or of part of it), is accessible to other operations. A simpler alternative is that the EN output of Th/Ex is immune to all narrow-syntactic or LF interface operations and that the operations that apply (Agree, or those at the LF interface) are accessing the trace left by Th/Ex. It is not easy to distinguish these alternatives on empirical grounds. I will assume the simpler alternative to be correct. We are then led to the conclusions in (35) ((35a) = (27)).

(35) a. Th/Ex is an operation of the phonological component.
   b. Traces are inaccessible to Move, but accessible to some other operations.

Still adopting the simplest principle of a single cycle, with phonology and narrow syntax proceeding in parallel, we conclude that Th/Ex applies at the level of the verbal phrase, which we may presume to be *v*P (*v* a light verb marking unaccusative/passive), a weak phase only; the smallest relevant strong phase is the next higher CP or *v**P. Th/Ex moves EN rightward or leftward, leaving a copy without phonological features, presumably adjunction to *v*P and substitution in [Spec, *v*], respectively, if a weak phase has a phonological counterpart to EPP.

The next task is to sharpen (35b). Why is trace inaccessible to Move, and what other operations can access trace? Recall that the "trace" of XP is XP without its uninterpretable features, including its phonological features, these having been stripped away at Spell-Out, either in the normal course of derivation or by a language-specific rule such as Th/Ex, applying prior to the strong-phase level. Trace is thus an empty category (EC). The compound operation Move consists of Agree, pied-piping, and Merge.

Hence, traces must be inaccessible to one of its three components. Other ECs are accessible to Merge (e.g., first Merge of PRO or pro). Therefore, trace must be inaccessible to Agree or pied-piping. We have just seen that active trace is accessible to Agree (since EN has to satisfy the Case Filter). Therefore, its head must disallow pied-piping, preventing Move.[44] The same is true, vacuously, of inactive trace, but this element might satisfy an even stronger condition: if inactive trace is invisible not only to Agree (like other inactive elements) but even to Match (unlike others), then the principle (17), which restricts intervention to the head of a chain, would follow.

Principle (35b), then, seems to have case (36a) and possibly (36b).

(36) a. EC disallows pied-piping.
      b. Inactive trace disallows Match.

Apart from these restrictions, traces should be subject to operations freely; and (36) ought to hold of ECs generally, not just trace, unless trace has to be distinguished from other ECs by virtue of its relational properties, an unwanted complexity. Such extension of (36) raises various questions. Lexical ECs undergo Move as well as Merge, unlike trace; but they are X^0s, so pied-piping does not apply. And (36) holds only if no XP consists solely of several merged lexical ECs.[45] Inactive argument EC (PRO, pro) raises problems for (36b) with regard to intervention effects. We would also expect that there is a more unified version of (36), if case (b) holds.

Putting these concerns aside, the properties bearing specifically on Th/Ex are these:

(37) a. Th/Ex is an operation of the phonological component.
      b. Pied-piping requires phonological content.

(37a) is an idiosyncratic rule of English, (37b) (= (36a)) a principle of UG, if valid. From (37a), it follows that the output of Th/Ex is immune to all but phonological operations. From (37b), it follows that the trace left by Th/Ex is immune to Move but allows Agree and LF-interpretive operations, as required.

The conclusion supports the picture of Lex outlined earlier and modifies slightly the standard assumption that phonological features do not enter into narrow-syntactic derivations. They do not do so individually, but their absence or presence makes a difference if (37b) is correct.

The rightward variant of Th/Ex is like extraposition in that it does not iterate, perhaps a more general property of operations not driven by uninterpretable features, and/or phonological operations. We would expect the same to be true of the leftward counterpart. But alongside (20) and (38a), the latter surfacing as (38b) after application of Th/Ex, we also find (38c) and (38d).

(38) a. there are expected to be caught many fish
     b. there are expected to be many fish caught
     c. there are many fish expected to be caught
     d. many fish are expected to be caught

(38d) is the unproblematic result of successive-cyclic A-movement with the intermediate stage (39).

(39) are expected [many fish to be caught *t*]

But (38c) is unexplained. It does not result from (39) by leftward Th/Ex, if iterated Th/Ex is barred, as expected for such rules. And both (39) and (38c) should be barred if Merge preempts Move.

We therefore ask whether there might be a different source for (38c). The obvious suggestion is a true existential construction *there be NP*, where NP includes a reduced relative. The conclusion is supported by the semantics of (38). Examples (38a–b) and (38d) have no existential import, but (38c) does: it states that there are many fish such that they are expected to be caught.[46] The same conclusions are illustrated in (40).

(40) a. there are expected to be found many flaws (→ many flaws found) in the proof
     b. #there are many flaws expected to be found in the proof
     c. many flaws are expected to be found in the proof
     d. there are likely to be baked many cakes (→ many cakes baked) in that oven
     e. #there are many cakes likely to be baked in that oven
     f. many cakes are likely to be baked in that oven
     g. there is likely to be taken umbrage (→ umbrage taken) at his remarks
     h. #there is umbrage likely to be taken at his remarks
     i. umbrage is likely to be taken at his remarks

Examples (40b,e,h) have existential import, but the others do not; hence the oddity of (40b) and (40e), presupposing that the flaws and the cakes independently exist (the cakes have already been baked), and of the idiom chunk in (40h). Syntactic tests yield the same conclusion. Thus, constructions of the form (38c) are islands for extraction, but the others are not; (41c) can be derived from (41a), but not (41d) from (41b).[47]

(41) a. there is likely to be demolished a building ($\rightarrow$ a building demolished)
    b. there is a building likely to be demolished
    c. how is there likely to be demolished a building ($\rightarrow$ a building demolished)
    d. *how is there a building likely to be demolished

Leftward Th/Ex is distinct from object shift (OS), a phenomenon whose status and scope are open to many questions. One distinction, already noted, has to do with semantic consequences: the semantic neutrality of Th/Ex is one of the reasons to believe that it falls within the phonological component; but as is well known, that is not true of OS, which we therefore expect to fall (at least in part) within narrow syntax, given the simplifications that led to (13). Continuing to assume cyclicity, the PIC, and preference for Merge over Move, OS must involve raising to the outer edge of the phase v*P, outside the merged subject in [Spec, v*]. Let us examine a few possibilities.

Languages differ with regard to the OS option: for example, Icelandic allows it freely and Mainland Scandinavian partially, while standard English/Romance do not. But if the PIC holds, the picture is a little different: every language allows OS, but in languages of the English/Romance types, the object must move on beyond the position of OS. There is no other way to derive such expressions as (42a).

(42) a. (guess) what$_{Obj}$ [John$_{Subj}$ T [$_{vP}$ t_{Obj} [t_{subj} read t_{obj}]]]
    b. John$_{Subj}$ T [$_{vP}$ that$_{Obj}$ [t_{Subj} read t_{Obj}]]

Here the DO (*what, that*) raises by OS, satisfying the Case Filter and erasing the uninterpretable features of v. In (42a), the shifted DO moves on to [Spec, CP]. In (42b), the DO remains below [Spec, TP]—allowed in an OS language, disallowed in English/Romance. The same holds for topicalization and other forms of $\bar{\text{A}}$-movement.[48]

Let us put aside the language variation for a moment and ask how the non-OS languages work, allowing (42a) but not (42b).

The first thought that comes to mind is that the Equidistance Principle (43) (= (41) of MI) should be reconsidered.

(43) Terms of the minimal domain of H are equidistant from probe P.

The relevant part of (43) has to do with the edge of H. Insofar as this is true, we can restate (43) as (44).

(44) Terms of the edge of HP are equidistant from probe P.

In the vP of (42), the shifted object (*what* in (42a), *that* in (42b)) and the in-situ subject *John* (at t_{Subj}) are equidistant from the probe T, which selects the subject as its goal, inducing Agree. But only in (42a), with OS moving on to [Spec, C], can Move apply, raising the subject to [Spec, T].

In both (42a) and (42b), the shifted object in OS position is inactive,[49] hence not able to agree with T or to move to [Spec, T]. But that is unlikely to be the reason for allowing the probe to pass over it to find in-situ *John*: inactive nominals induce intervention effects. Another consideration is that shifted object apparently may agree with T and nevertheless allow subject extraction, as in the Icelandic counterpart to (45), with shifted DO in a nontransitive strong verbal phase, DO with quirky Case, and V raised to T.[50]

(45) [many students.DAT]$_{\text{Subj}}$ [find.PL]$_{\text{Vb}}$ [the computers.PL.NOM]$_{\text{DO}}$ not
        ugly.PL

It seems, then, that the distinction between (42a) and (42b) lies in the fact that the *wh*-phrase moves on, leaving the position "empty" (i.e., void of phonological features).

The problem we now face is that the argument seems to require countercyclic operations: assuming strict cyclicity, the subject *John* raises to [Spec, T] before the operation is authorized by vacating the outer edge of vP, at the subsequent CP phase. The problem we face is to show that the countercyclicity is only apparent, by recasting it in a framework that keeps to the strict cycle and allows no backtracking to recover crashed derivations along a different path: specifically, canceling OS if the position is not later evacuated.

Optimally, the operations Agree/Move, like others, should apply freely. Let us assume that they do, raising the in-situ active subject freely to [Spec, T] in the course of the derivation. The probe-goal relation must be evaluated for the Minimal Link Condition (MLC) at the strong-phase level after it is known whether the outer edge of vP has become a trace, losing its phonological features. Assume so, setting aside for the moment the apparent countercyclicity. That appears to leave all other consequences unchanged, with (44) restricted to the *phonological edge* of a category—

that is, an edge element with no phonological material c-commanding it within the category.[51]

(46) The phonological edge of HP is accessible to probe P.

In the structure (47), XP prevents Match of probe P and Spec, under the MLC, only if XP has phonological content.

(47) $[_{ZP} \dots P \dots [_{HP} XP [Spec [H YP]]]]$

The background assumption is that the lexicon Lex is only partially distributed, namely, when optimal encoding of information justifies that complication of Lex; see text at note 20. Also presupposed is that Spell-Out takes place at the next higher strong phase ZP and that the MLC too is evaluated at this stage of the derivation under the general principle (10)—a reasonable conclusion, as discussed earlier.[52] It is only at ZP that the phonological content of XP (hence the phonological-edge status of Spec) is determined.

In these terms, we dispense with the notion of equidistance and the principle (44) in which it enters. Operations are strictly cyclic, but the problem of backtracking to recover a failed derivation along a different path remains.

We can improve the picture further by relating these conclusions to earlier ones about traces—namely, (36), repeated as (48).

(48) a. EC disallows pied-piping.
       b. Inactive trace disallows Match.

If XP with phonological content remains at the edge of (47), then it intervenes to prevent Match(P, Spec), hence Agree or Move of Spec. If XP moves on to [Spec, Z], its trace, being inactive with respect to T (see note 49), is invisible to Match by (48b), so Spec, now at the phonological edge, is accessible to the probe P. That suffices to establish (46), which is therefore not needed as an independent principle. (48a) suggests another way of thinking about (46): lacking phonological content, the trace of XP is not even a candidate for Move (under (48a)), so that Spec is the closest "competitor" for the operation, under a natural version of the MLC.

We might raise a more subtle question, which might have some bearing on these issues: is there any difference between Move and Agree with regard to the intervention effect of a trace in the outer edge?[53] Suppose that Move is permitted but Agree alone is barred; the phonological-edge condition of (46) frees Move but not Agree alone. That would raise inter-

esting questions (e.g., about the locality of the postraising ([Spec, T]) relation as a factor), but it is not easy to find relevant facts. To test this possibility, we would want to investigate a language with subject-in-situ
constructions (SSCs) but no OS of type (42b), so as to determine whether
the pure-Agree analogue of (42a) is permitted with SSCs, as in (49).

(49) (guess) what$_{Obj}$ [there T [$_{vP}$ t_{Obj} [a man read t_{Obj}]]]

In Icelandic, with OS and SSCs,[54] the constructions are permitted, as
expected. Thus, Icelandic has the counterpart of (50).

(50) a. there painted probably the house some students red
     b. which house painted probably some students red

In English, (49) and (50) are barred, but for independent reasons. We
would have to investigate the marginal constructions such as (26) in which
English has something like abstract SSCs.

(51) a. there entered the room a strange man
     b. which room did there enter t_{wh} a man

Case (51b) seems considerably worse, which might suggest that only
Move is freed from an intervention effect when at the phonological edge.
But the data are too marginal for any confidence, and the degradation of
(51b), if real, might be attributed to internal-extraction constraints (see
note 42). Mainland Scandinavian should be a better case, because it lacks
the obligatory Th/Ex rule of English. Here we find the configuration (52).

(52) a. *?there painted some students the house red
     b.   *there painted the house some students red
     c. *?which house painted there some students red
     d.   which house painted probably some students red

Case (52a) illustrates the marginality of the construction, carried over in
(52c). Case (52b), with OS as well, is much worse. Case (52d) is fine,
which would be unsurprising and irrelevant if *some students* is in [Spec, T]
and *probably* is in a TP-external position. But Holmberg points out that a
definite pronoun cannot be substituted for *some students*, suggesting that
it may be in its in-situ position in a kind of SSC construction, in which
case the contrast between (52b) and (52c) seems problematic.

Pending better evidence and understanding, I will put aside the question of a possible Move/Agree distinction under (46).

On the assumption that OS is a free option, what distinguishes OS from
non-OS languages—say, Icelandic versus English/Romance? The distinc-

tion might lie in intervention effects applying to the output of OS, or in the option of applying OS in the first place. Let's begin by exploring the first alternative, then turning to the second (concluding finally that they can be unified).

One possibility is that the OS/non-OS distinction has to do with evaluation of the probe-goal relation: the relation of T and in-situ subject. OS languages allow association of T and in-situ subject (effectively, (43)); non-OS languages allow such association only under (46), at the phonological edge. The parameter might be related to "richness of T," a richer T allowing a deeper search of the category including the goal.

What seems a more plausible possibility is that there are no differences with regard to intervention effects and that OS languages have a dislocation rule Disl that raises OS to a higher position, possibly a phonological rule similar to English Th/Ex. Then Icelandic, for example, also excludes OS without further raising of the object, either Ā-movement or Disl. Perhaps supporting that conclusion are some properties of Mainland Scandinavian, which permits object fronting for pronouns but only partially for full noun phrases.[55] Holmberg points out that the fronted pronoun is not at the edge of v*P but in a position higher than the auxiliary, indicating that it raised there from the v*P-edge position, perhaps by a phonological operation, or perhaps by a rule of the kind that has been proposed for clitic movement. If the former, we have an explanation for the fact that the pronoun does not bind anaphors, as Holmberg observes, citing Holmberg and Platzack 1995; similarly, a nominal in this position will not induce an intervention effect, blocking subject raising. One might then ask whether a similar rule Disl raises the full Icelandic shifted object (though to a different higher position). Constructions of the kind illustrated by (45), repeated as (53), provide additional support for this conclusion.

(53) [many students.DAT]$_{Subj}$ find.PL$_{VB}$ [the computers.PL.NOM]$_{DO}$ not ugly.PL

Here we have Agree(T, DO) but it cannot induce Move, raising DO rather than Subj to [Spec, T]. If Disl applies (as a phonological rule), then DO cannot raise to [Spec, T] for the reasons discussed in connection with Th/Ex, even when it agrees with matrix T.[56]

Consider now the backtracking problem. Under the "richness of T/ deeper search" alternative, the problem remains: if OS has produced vP with multiple Spec, as in (42), then search will fail in a non-OS language if the raised object has not moved on, and the derivation must return to the pre-OS stage and proceed without application of OS. Under the Disl alternative, that may not be necessary. If Disl applies, it can be followed unproblematically by raising of subject to [Spec, T], from the phonological edge. If Disl does not apply, the subject can still raise to [Spec, T], but the derivation will crash by evaluation of the MLC at the CP phase unless the outer Spec has been evacuated by raising to [Spec, C] (see note 8). That raises no new problems if the object is a *wh*-phrase, as in (42a); then it can move to [Spec, C]. If the object is not a *wh*-phrase, as in (42b), it can be raised to [Spec, C] by topicalization. If that is a free option, then backtracking will never be necessary in this category of constructions.[57]

We will return directly to the second alternative: that the OS/non-OS distinction lies in the option of applying OS in the first place.

Still another question has to do with Holmberg's Generalization (HG): to a first approximation, OS is permitted only if V has raised to T. The principle is countercyclic, hence problematic. One might seek to reformulate it in terms of phase-level evaluation of optional OS, along lines suggested above for trace at the outer edge. A number of problems then arise, among them the fact that Ā-movement to the outer edge of v*P does not observe HG: *wh*-movement of (or from within) the direct object, for example, does not require V-raising in OS or non-OS languages. Also pertinent is the fact that some form of phonological adjacency seems to be involved in OS:[58] "verb topicalization" (raising of V to [Spec, C], Holmberg argues) frees OS even when an auxiliary verb blocks V-raising to T, making the countercyclic property even worse. Furthermore, not just an in-situ verb, but any element (say, a preposition) bars Mainland Scandinavian shift of object pronouns, which, Holmberg argues, should be assimilated to Icelandic OS, despite some differences, primarily because both fall under HG. Particularly striking is the comparative Scandinavian evidence that Holmberg reviews concerning extraction from verb-particle constructions: just in the cases where the pronominal object precedes the verb particle (perhaps by raising) can OS apply.

Holmberg suggests that HG be reformulated along the following lines:

(54) a. OS is a phonological operation that satisfies condition (54b) and is driven by the semantic interpretation of the shifted object (new/old information, specificity-definiteness, focus or topic, etc.; call the interpretive complex *Int*).[59]

b. OS cannot apply across a phonologically visible category (except adjuncts) asymmetrically c-commanding the object position.

The basic idea is persuasive, but the implementation raises a number of questions. It requires countercyclic operations, and unlike Th/Ex, it violates the semantic expectations for phonological rules (see (13)). It is also necessary to find some different way to handle "invisible" OS in Ā-movement in OS and non-OS languages and visible OS in Icelandic-type languages (both violating (54b)). Also problematic is the way the operation is driven by semantic properties of the XP that is raised, interweaving with phonological properties of the construction. Note that the proposed rule does not fall together with other cases plausibly accounted for in terms of phonological adjacency, such as, T-V assimilation.[60]

The countercyclicity of the proposed operation, and the introduction in (54b) of a property similar to "phonological edge," suggest that the phenomena may fall under principles of phase-based derivation. Let us ask, then, whether the basic content of Holmberg's (1999) revision of HG can be derived in these terms, appealing as much as possible only to plausible general principles, along with a simple parameter that keeps intact the leading intuition: that both phonological and semantic properties are involved in HG.

Consider first the semantic properties Int of the object Obj that undergoes OS (see (54a)). Sometimes the operation is described as driven by these properties of Obj, perhaps by features of Obj that bear the interpretation Int. That is a questionable formulation, however. A "dumb" computational system shouldn't have access to considerations of that kind, typically involving discourse situations and the like. These are best understood as properties of the resulting configuration, as in the case of semantic properties associated with raising of subject to [Spec, T], which may well be related to those of OS constructions. One might also say informally that in (55), the phrase *the men* is raised in order to bind the anaphor.

(55) the men seem to each other to be intelligent

But the mechanisms are blind to those consequences, and it would make no sense to assign the feature "binder" to *the men* with principles requiring that it raise to be able to accommodate this feature. We may also say informally that someone is running to the left to catch the ball, but such functional/teleological accounts, while perhaps useful for motivation and formulation of problems, are not to be confused with accounts of the mechanisms of guiding and organizing motion. The same approach seems sensible in the case of OS. The computational system presumably treats it as an option—if the MI approach is on the right track, feature-driven by properties of $v*$, with the option expressed as optional choice of an EPP-feature. The resulting configuration has particular properties, as in the case of raising to subject (or catching a ball). These properties may have internal inconsistencies, posing interpretive problems—for example, a definite pronoun left in a position that assigns nonspecific interpretation. If so, the expression is deviant.

The general configuration we are considering is (56).

(56) $[_\beta$ C [Spec T ... $[_\alpha$ XP [Subj $v*$ $[_{VP}$ V ... Obj]]]]]

The position [Spec, T] is created by merging the surface subject (by pure Merge or by Move); the XP position is created by OS (perhaps later vacated by $\bar{A}$-movement or Disl). We are concerned with two properties of (56): the interpretations assigned to the configuration, and the phonological adjacency properties that enter into the formation of the (XP, Obj) chain.

Let us adopt the general background assumption that at the interface, arguments are A-chains (with one or more members).[61] The θ-role of the argument is determined by the position of first Merge—the configuration in which it takes place, within Hale and Keyser's (1993) framework for θ-theory. "Surface interpretation" is determined by the position of the head of a chain; see (13).

In (56), the θ-role is determined by the configuration of Obj. If OS does not apply and Obj remains in situ in a trivial A-chain, then the same configuration is freely interpreted at LF, taking account of inherent properties of the lexical items and the θ-role: in particular, it may have the "surface" interpretation Int or its complement Int'. If OS does apply, forming the two-membered chain ⟨XP, Obj⟩, the surface semantic role of the chain is determined by the peripheral EPP position occupied by XP, the raised object. We assume that Int is assigned to the peripheral configuration universally, adopting (57), probably a subcase of a more general principle governing peripheral non-θ (EPP) positions including [Spec, T]—a traditional idea, still somewhat obscure.

(57) The EPP position of $v*$P is assigned Int.

Let us now return to the parameter that distinguishes OS and non-OS languages, adopting the second of the two perspectives mentioned earlier: that the distinction lies in the option of applying OS. Two factors enter into OS: assignment of Int-Int', and phonological adjacency. Suppose the parameter is (58).

(58) At the phonological border of v*P, XP is assigned Int'.

By the "phonological border" of HP, we mean a position not c-commanded by phonological material within HP (see note 51). The concept is broader than "phonological edge," which holds only of edge elements (and is now only an expository device, with the reduction to (48)). For example, in (59), if H and the edge (Spec) of HP are vacated by raising, then Comp is at the border but not the edge.

(59) HP = [Spec [H Comp]]

As throughout, we assume that (58) is evaluated at the next higher strong phase, in accord with (10): at the stage β in (56).

OS languages observe (58), non-OS languages do not. In the construction (56) in an OS language, if Obj is at the phonological border of v*P and resists interpretation Int' (say, a definite pronoun), it must undergo OS to avoid a deviant outcome, raising to the EPP position so that the chain will be assigned Int. It need not undergo OS in a non-OS language, or in an OS language if it is v*P-internal—by which we mean *not at the phonological border*.

That is a start, but more is needed. We have to guarantee that OS applies just in the right places. In the worst case, these effects are specified by particular conditions; a much better result would be that they follow from a general principle applying to optional rules, which captures the functional/teleological intuition about rule application. The natural suggestion, based on ideas of Reinhart (1993 [1997]) and Fox (1995, 2000), is a general economy principle: an optional rule can apply only when necessary to yield a new outcome.

Within the current framework, the optional rule in these constructions assigns an EPP-feature to v*, thus allowing (and requiring) OS. The guiding intuition is formulated in MI as (60).[62]

(60) Optional operations can apply only if they have an effect on
        outcome: in the present case, v* may be assigned an EPP-feature to
        permit successive-cyclic Ā-movement or Int (under OS).

The proposal we are considering, then, is that OS reduces to (61), where (61a) and (61b) are invariant principles—special cases of more general principles governing optionality and interpretation of peripheral positions, respectively—and (61c) is the parameter that distinguishes OS and non-OS languages.

(61) a. $v*$ is assigned an EPP-feature only if that has an effect on outcome.

   b. The EPP position of $v*$ is assigned Int.

   c. At the phonological border of $v*$P, XP is assigned Int'.

Under (10), principle (61a) is evaluated at the next strong phase, where the interpretive operation (61c) also applies: CP containing $v*$P, in the cases under consideration. At that point, it is known whether $v*$-V has raised (to T or to C/[Spec, C]).

Suppose L is a non-OS language, not observing (61c) (e.g., Romance). Then interpretations can be assigned freely in the position of first Merge, including Int or Int'. Under the economy principle (61a), $v*$ may have an EPP-feature, inducing OS, only if that is required in order to yield some outcome other than Int-assignment (which is already free without the EPP-feature and resulting OS): for example, successive-cyclic $\bar{\text{A}}$-movement. Otherwise, Obj remains in situ, whether $v*$P-internally or at the phonological border.

Suppose that L is an OS language observing (61c) (Icelandic, and following Holmberg, Mainland Scandinavian as well, with somewhat different conditions). Suppose Obj is $v*$P-internal, c-commanded by unraised $v*$-V, preposition, particle, and so on. Then the situation is exactly as in non-OS languages: interpretation can be assigned freely, and $v*$ may have an EPP-feature, forcing OS, only to yield some new outcome other than Int-assignment (already available in situ)—$\bar{\text{A}}$-movement, for example. Suppose Obj is at the phonological border of $v*$P. If it remains in that position, the (one-membered) chain will be assigned Int' under (61c); if it raises by OS, the (two-membered) chain will be assigned Int. Under principle (61a), $v*$ may have an EPP-feature, forcing OS and the new interpretation Int. The choice is optional. If Obj resists Int' (say, a definite pronoun), failure to exercise the option yields extreme deviance; if Obj resists Int, exercising the option has the same effect. But the internal semantic properties of Obj are not part of the mechanism of the rule, just as the intention of binding an anaphor is not part of the mechanism of raising.

To illustrate, in Icelandic or Mainland Scandinavian, the counterpart of (62a) is not well formed but the counterpart of (62b) is.

(62) a. *I have her$_{\text{Obj}}$ not [seen t_{Obj}]

   b. I saw$_v$ her$_{\text{Obj}}$ not [t_v t_{Obj}]

In (62a), the trace t_{Obj} of *her* is in a v*P-internal position: the v*-V complex has not raised. The parameter (61c) is inapplicable, and therefore v* cannot have an EPP-feature (as in English/Romance). Accordingly, (62a) cannot be generated: the pronoun remains in situ, free to receive Int (or, deviantly, Int'). In (62b), the trace t_{Obj} is at the phonological border of v*P after verb raising. Accordingly, parameter (61c) permits the option of an EPP-feature for v* under principle (61a), allowing assignment of Int to the pronoun chain.[63]

For an English-type language L lacking V-raising, the parameter is inapplicable: the condition in (61c) never holds, so L is necessarily non-OS. Suppose L is an OV language, the order base-generated or derived by object raising. If L is an OS language, then shift is always possible, whether or not V raises. Parameter (61c) distinguishes Romance from Germanic (Standard English aside), while the OV/VO parameter distinguishes Dutch-German from Scandinavian.

Ignored so far is the case of Icelandic OS crossing the subject, for example, constructions of the form (50a) and (63), where α is the original v*P, t_{Vb} the trace of the raised v*-V complex, and t_{Obj} the trace of the shifted pronominal object (see note 54).

(63)   there read it (never) [$_\alpha$ any students t_{Vb} t_{Obj}]

Though the verb has raised, its object remains in v*P-internal position because the subject has not raised, so that OS should not be permitted under (61). The problem could be overcome by restricting the notion v*P-internal to the domain of v*, but that might not be necessary. Consider again the principle (25): something must be raised from transitive v*P. Hence, if the subject remains in situ, the object must escape v*P. Therefore, v* is permitted to have an optional EPP-feature under the economy principle (61a), allowing OS in this case.

Returning to the basic configuration (56), repeated as (64), we have the two strong phases α and β: v*P and CP, respectively.

(64)   [$_\beta$ C [Spec, T ... [$_\alpha$ XP [Subj v* [$_{VP}$ V ... Obj]]]]]

OS takes place within the v*P phase α, but the conditions (61) that apply to it are evaluated only at the next higher CP phase β, when V-raising may have taken place: to T, or to C/[Spec, C] under V-topicalization. This is in accord with the principle (10) that all evaluation/interpretation takes place at the next higher strong phase, including Spell-Out.

If tenable, these proposals yield the essential conclusions of HG on the basis of general principles and a simple parameter, capturing Holmberg's intuition that the rule of OS involves a kind of phonological adjacency but is motivated by semantic requirements.[64] There is no recourse to countercyclic operations violating the Extension Condition. Nothing need be said about violations of phonological adjacency: specifically, Icelandic OS and the first stage of Ā-movement.[65] The function of the rule is expressed without teleological devices or special features on Obj to drive the derivation, questionable in any event and also invoking Greed with its attendant computational complexity. We can keep to the interpretive principle (13) for "surface interpretation," and the simplifications of general architecture that underlie it. The only features involved are the familiar ones: EPP, and Case/agreement features, functioning in accord with independently motivated principles. Icelandic and Mainland Scandinavian OS are partially unified, with differences remaining to be explained; for both, OS satisfies the revised version of HG.

The account so far leaves open the possibility that V-raising is comparable to Th/Ex and Disl: not part of the narrow-syntactic computation but an operation of the phonological component. Either way, the phonological content of base V is determined prior to Spell-Out at the strong-phase level, so that the effects of the revised HG are determined as well.

There are some reasons to suspect that a substantial core of head-raising processes, excluding incorporation in the sense of Baker (1988), may fall within the phonological component. One reason is the expectation of (near-)uniformity of LF interface representations, a particularly compelling instance of the methodological principle (1), as in the case of Th/Ex (see (27) and comment). The interpretive burden is reduced if, say, verbs are interpreted the same way whether they remain in situ or raise to T or C, the distinctions that have received much attention since Pollock 1989. As expected under (1), verbs are not interpreted differently in English versus Romance, or Mainland Scandinavian versus Icelandic, or embedded versus root structures. More generally, semantic effects of head raising in the core inflectional system are slight or nonexistent, as contrasted with XP-movement, with effects that are substantial and systematic. That would follow insofar as head raising is not part of narrow syntax.

A second reason has to do with what raises. Using the term *strength* for expository purposes, suppose that T has a strong V-feature and a strong nominal feature (person, we have assumed; D or N in categorial systems).

It has always been taken for granted that the strong V-feature is satisfied by V-raising to T (French vs. English), not VP-raising to [Spec, T], and that the strong nominal feature is satisfied by raising of the nominal to [Spec, T] (EPP), not raising of its head to T. But the theoretical apparatus provides no obvious basis for this choice. The same is true of raising to C and D. In standard cases,[66] T adjoins to C, and an XP (say, a *wh*-phrase) raises to [Spec, C], instead of the *wh*-head adjoining to C while TP raises to [Spec, C]. And N raises to D, not NP to [Spec, D]. These conclusions too follow naturally if overt V-to-T raising, T-to-C raising, and N-to-D raising are phonological properties, conditioned by the phonetically affixal character of the inflectional categories (see note 60). Considerations of LF uniformity might lead us to suspect that an LF-interpretive process brings together D-N and C-T-V (see note 8) to form wordlike LF "supercategories" in all languages, not only those where such processes are visible.

Other considerations have to do with the nature of the head-raising rule, which differs from core rules of narrow syntax in several respects. It is an adjunction rule; it is countercyclic in ways that are not overcome along the lines discussed earlier; the raised head does not c-command its trace;[67] identification of head-trace chains raises difficulties similar to those of feature movement, since there is no reasonable notion of occurrence; it observes somewhat different locality conditions. All of this is unproblematic if overt adjunction is a phonological process reflecting affixal properties.

Note further that if excorporation is excluded, head movement is not successive-cyclic, like the rules Th/Ex and Disl discussed earlier, which are plausibly assigned to the phonological component. It could be, in fact, that iterability is a general property of operations of narrow syntax, but these alone.

Boeckx and Stjepanović (1999), extending and modifying work by Lasnik (1999, chap. 7), argue that some problems of pseudogapping can be accounted for by the assumption that head movement is a phonological process, also citing other recent work that finds differences between head movement and XP-movement.

The same conclusion is suggested in recent work on aphasia by Grodzinsky and Finkel (1998), extending earlier work of Grodzinsky's. They argue that a range of symptoms can be explained in terms of inability to identify XP chains, but they note that the results do not carry over to X^0 chains; the result is expected if head raising is a phonological process, creating no chains.

A few final comments of a more general nature.

In considering these issues, we want to be careful to distinguish terminological artifacts from what may be substantive matters. The question commonly arises with regard to the status of entities introduced in linguistic description and theoretical exposition, raising issues often regarded as controversial. Let us turn to a few of these.

Consider the notion of chain. In MI and earlier work, a chain is understood to be a sequence of identical elements—more precisely, a set of *occurrences*, where an occurrence of K is taken to be its sister (not an entirely innocuous proposal, as noted in MI). Thus, in (65a) we have the chain (65b) consisting of two occurrences of K = *John*, K_1 being the syntactic object corresponding to *T-be killed John* and K_2 corresponding to *kill*.

(65) a. John was killed
     b. $\{K_1, K_2\}$

Several aspects of this description have been regarded as problematic under minimalist assumptions, among them (1) the fact that an occurrence of K is an X' category, neither X^0 nor X^{max}, hence arguably invisible, and (2) the very notion of a chain as a set of occurrences formed by multiple merger, not a "syntactic object" susceptible to computational operations as the concept is recursively defined (see Epstein and Seely 1999).

It is not clear, however, that the issues are real. Take the notion of occurrence as X' sister. The conceptual and empirical arguments for X' invisibility are slight. The conceptual argument relies on the assumption that X' is not interpreted at LF, which is questionable and in fact rejected in standard approaches. The empirical argument is that it allows incorporation of (much of) Kayne's (1994) Linear Correspondence Axiom within an impoverished (bare) phrase structure system.[68] But that result, if desired, could just as well be achieved by defining "asymmetric c-command" to exclude (X', YP) (a stipulation, but not more so than X' invisibility).

Furthermore, even if X' were shown to be an inappropriate choice for "occurrence," nothing much seems to follow. Recall that the relation provided most directly by Merge is Immediately-Contain (set membership). Suppose we define "occurrence" in terms of Immediately-Contain, taking an occurrence of K to be not its sister but its "mother," the category immediately containing it, a terminological device that also has the advantage of rendering the notion "occurrence-of " asymmetric. We then replace the chain (65b) by $CH = \{K_3, K_4\}$, where K_3 is the syntactic object corresponding to the TP (65a) and K_4 to the VP *kill John*, CH a proper chain because there is a single XP (here *John*) of which both K_3 and K_4 are occurrences.[69]

Consider the status of chains and the operation multiple Merge, constructing chains. It is not clear that these are more than terminological conveniences. No operations of L apply to chains. Principles holding of chains can be expressed directly in terms of occurrences (e.g., the uniformity condition on bar level), as can interpretive operations referring to chains: for example, principles of θ-role assignment and surface interpretation discussed earlier, or conditions on reconstruction. Some heads H have a property P that determines that H heads an occurrence; P is the EPP property of H, commonly taken to be a selectional feature satisfied by merging K. K may be an expletive or a category determined by probe-goal agreement and pied-piping; the latter is the case of multiple Merge. With no apparent substantive change, we may dispense with multiple Merge and reconstrue Move as the operation Agree/pied-piping/Mark, where Agree holds of (probe H, goal G) as before, and Mark identifies H as the head of an occurrence HP of the pied-piped category K determined by G. How Mark identifies H is a terminological matter: it could be, for example, by constructing an "occurrence list" to which we add the pair $\langle K, HP \rangle$. K now appears only once in the syntactic object formed, in the position of initial Merge, a θ-configuration if K is an argument.[70] Under the simplest assumptions, a principle of phonology spells K out at its highest (i.e., maximal) occurrence in the course of the cyclic derivation, as already discussed; and surface interpretation attends (at least) to the highest occurrence as well.[71]

Under the conventional interpretation, satisfaction of EPP (by Merge or Move) forms the new category $H^{max} = \{K, H'\}$ with label H and an H projection HP as occurrence of K. Under the interpretation just outlined, satisfaction of EPP adds the new item $\{K, HP\}$ to the occurrence list. The two approaches are essentially the same, virtually down to notation. There are differences in the computational operations, but they seem insignificant. And sharpening of the concepts does not seem to raise very serious difficulties.

As for EPP, under the former interpretation, but not the latter, it is a selectional feature. In either case, it is an uninterpreted feature (*feature*, as usual, meaning just linguistic property), an apparent imperfection, which we hope to show is not real by appeal to design specifications (perhaps along lines sketched in MI and elsewhere). Resort to an uninterpreted feature is inescapable. Something distinguishes among heads H that require, allow, or disallow that H head an occurrence of K. And while there may be semantic consequences to displacement, these are surely not properties of an interpretable feature of the head. Expletive constructions do not have the semantic properties of overt-subject constructions, and similar considerations hold for OS, as discussed; the semantic properties of in-situ versus displaced *wh* are not plausibly expressed as properties of the interrogative head; and so on.

If this analysis is correct, then we can proceed freely to use the conventional chain notation with all of its conveniences, understanding that it is reducible to the sterner "official" theory with no chains or multiple Merge. There are further ramifications, but I will put the matter aside.

A broader category of questions has to do with the "internalist" conception of language adopted in this discussion, and in the line of inquiry over the past 40 years from which it derives, a branch of what has been called "biolinguistics" (see Jenkins 1999). FL is considered to be a subcomponent of Jones's mind/brain; Jones's (I-)language L is the state of his FL, which he puts to use in various ways. We study these objects more or less as we study the system of motor organization or visual perception, or the immune or digestive systems. It is hard to imagine an approach to language that does not adopt such conceptions, at least tacitly. So we discover, I think, even when it is strenuously denied, but I will not pursue the matter here. Internalist biolinguistic inquiry does not, of course, question the legitimacy of other approaches to language, any more than internalist inquiry into bee communication invalidates the study of how the relevant internal organization of bees enters into their social structure. The investigations do not conflict; they are mutually supportive. In the case of humans, though not other organisms, the issues are subject to controversy, often impassioned, and needless.

We also speak freely of derivations, of expressions Exp generated by L, and of the set of such Exps—the set that is called "the structure of L" in Chomsky 1986, where the I/E terminology is introduced.[72] Evidently, these entities are not "internal." That has led to the belief that some externalist concepts of "E-linguistics" are being introduced. But that is a misconception. These are not entities with some ontological status; they are introduced to simplify talk about properties of FL and L, and they can be eliminated in favor of internalist notions. One of the properties of

Peano's axioms PA is that PA generates the proof P of "$2 + 2 = 4$" but not the proof P' of "$2 + 2 = 7$" (in suitable notation). We can speak freely of the property "generable by PA," holding of P but not P', and derivatively of lines of generable proofs (theorems) and the set of theorems, without postulating any entities beyond PA and its properties. Similarly, we may speak of the property "generable by L," which holds of certain derivations D and not others, and holding derivatively of an expression Exp formed by D and of the set {Exp} of those expressions. No new entities are postulated in these usages beyond FL, its states L, and their properties. Similarly, a study of the solar system could introduce the notion HT = {possible trajectories of Halley's comet within the solar system}, and studies of motor organizaton or visual perception could introduce the notions {plans for moving the arm} or {visual images for cats (vs. bees)}. But these studies do not postulate weird entities apart from planets, comets, neurons, cats, and the like. No "Platonism" is introduced, and no "E-linguistic" notions: only biological entities and their properties.

Notes

1. Chomsky (2000). For background, see references cited there and Lasnik 1999b, among many others.

2. In what follows, there is no use of labels except for the new object γ, which has the label of either α or β, determined (in the best case) by algorithm. This item is similar to the *locus* that determines the next operation in the system developed by Collins (1999), who proposes that labels be eliminated more generally.

3. Alternatively, associated with T as an Agr node, a collection of uninterpretable ϕ-features selecting T that can also appear elsewhere, selecting a different element; this more complex alternative may be justified, but will be put aside here. Some problems it raises are mentioned in note 12. Others have to do with selection: it is unclear how a collection of such features (unvalued, it will be argued) can have the required selectional properties.

4. Terminology is often metaphoric here and below, adopted for expository convenience.

5. EPP = Extended Projection Principle. Note that the EPP-feature alone is not sufficient to identify a target; the ϕ-set (or comparable features, for other probes) is required to determine what kind of category K is sought.

6. There is presumably a similar but distinct agreement relation, Concord, involving Merge alone.

7. And without recourse to some such device as the distinction between erasure and deletion, invoked in Chomsky 1995 to deal with a paradox of Extended Standard Theory–based systems with a single position for Spell-Out: the "overt" part of the narrow-syntactic computation eliminates uninterpretable features, but

they have to remain until the stage of Spell-Out of the full syntactic object, because of their phonetic reflexes.

8. For expository purposes, I take the nominal with structural Case to be N and use T and C as cover terms for a richer array of functional categories, as in MI. On light verbs, see among others Hale and Keyser 1993, Harley 1995. Call *v* with full argument structure *v**: transitive *v* or experiencer. Only *v* was considered in MI, and I will largely keep to it below. Where assigned by V, not *v*, Case is inherent. Quirky Case largely falls under general Case assignment principles if understood to be inherent Case with an additional structural Case feature (as in MI). We will return to examples.

9. One question is whether (3a) and (3b), if valid, follow from other properties of FL. That seems plausible, but there are many factors to be considered.

10. In English, the expected form *awarded several prizes* surfaces more naturally as *several prizes awarded*. We will return to the matter.

11. Reconstruction for trace of A-movement, as distinct from PRO, was discovered (to my knowledge) by Luigi Burzio, a discovery later published in Burzio 1986: for example, such distinctions as *one interpreter each* (*was assigned* t, **planned PRO to speak*) *to the visiting diplomats*. For extensive review of these topics, see Fox 2000, Sauerland 1998. For a different approach, see Lasnik 1999a. With P = T + raising verb, [Spec, T_{def}] may apparently be manifested: for example, in Icelandic defective infinitivals, possibly reflecting the transitive expletive construction option (see MI).

12. On eliminating categorial features in favor of root structures with functional heads, see Marantz 1997, MI. Functional categories lacking semantic features require complication of phrase structure theory (see MI), a departure from good design to be avoided unless forced. Agr elements, for example, should arouse skepticism (see also note 3). Similarly, D—or at least one variant of D—might be associated with referentiality in some sense, not just treated as an automatic marker of "nominal category"; nonreferential nominals (nonspecifics, quantified and predicate nominals, etc.) need not then be assigned automatic D (at least, this variant of D).

13. For example, *it is to go home* (*every evening*) *that John prefers* (**seems*) (Rizzi 1982). Other early evidence involved reconstruction effects (see note 11). Rizzi explained the distinction in terms of government, a notion not readily available in the framework presented here.

14. Some related ideas are developed by Pesetsky and Torrego (this volume).

15. See Epstein and Seely 1999 for proposals to this effect.

16. The extension is suggested by proposals of Koizumi (1995), Lasnik (1999a,b), and Epstein and Seely (1999), differing from one another and from the version here, which is, furthermore, oversimplified. Second Merge of first-merged object of V makes little sense. The account should be restated, as in the sources cited, in terms of an Agr node selecting V and, by symmetry, selecting T (Agr in turn selected by appropriate *v* and C). It is, then, Agr and not T/*v* that is the locus of ϕ-features,

Case, and EPP, in the version presented here. Since I will not be pursuing this course, in part for reasons discussed later, I will keep to the simplified exposition.

17. For T_{comp}, the EPP-feature is apparently obligatory; for V_{comp} as well, for the sources cited in note 16.

18. One variant might supplement (6) by taking T (and substantive categories generally, including V) to be always defective, so that the locus of nominative Case and subject-verb agreement is C, not T (see Pesetsky and Torrego, this volume, for related ideas). In the notation just used, this alternative falls under $Locus_{Cv^*}$.

19. It has occasionally been suggested that the EPP-feature of the probe P is a Case-assigning feature F_C. If correct, that would leave the basic picture intact: F_C is an uninterpretable selectional feature inducing Merge (sometimes Move), distinct from the features of P that enter into Agree. But it does not seem to be correct. There is good reason to believe that structural Case correlates with agreement, hence also long-distance agreement (without raising to Spec), and accordingly that EPP is satisfied without Case assignment (see (18) and discussion). If either is correct (both seem to be), Case assignment and EPP are independent phenomena.

20. On the current state of DM, see Harley and Noyer 1999. The idea of late insertion derives from Beard 1995.

21. For an illustration in the case of Latin deponent verbs, see Embick 2000.

22. LA_i is a subset of LA, drawn from Lex, but the objects it makes available are those labeled by elements of LA_i, perhaps complex objects already constructed in the course of the derivation, which proceeds in parallel. Suppose that LA is eliminated in favor of iterated selection of LA_i from Lex. The cost is that reduction of computational burden is far less and that search of arbitrary depth is needed to determine whether an item selected from Lex is new. Suppose that LA_i is eliminated and phases are constructed from LA (or the entire Lex). The cost is greater computational burden, in a certain sense. Again, the conceptual arguments are not decisive.

23. See Legate 1998 and, for the broader picture with regard to reconstruction in such cases, Fox 2000.

24. Namely, head movement involving inflectional categories: to C, or to T (hence to a position between the vP and CP phases; see note 8). We will return to the status of head movement.

25. The idea that the phonological component can choose which element of a chain to spell out has been investigated since Groat and O'Neil 1996. Any such approach requires either new UG principles or language-specific rules to determine how the choice is made.

26. For VP, testable only with a nonaffixal light verb. One might consider treating preposition stranding within the same context.

27. Head movement aside; see note 24. For conclusions about next-higher-phase evaluation drawn from the theory of control, see Landau 1999.

28. It is accessibility of the domain of weak phases at Σ, under (10), that permits the extension of phases to weak phases, yielding the preferred result of relative phonetic-semantic integrity of phases, an extension barred in MI.

29. The consequences include some barrier/Relativized Minimality–type phenomena (Empty Category Principle, Subjacency, and Head Movement Constraint effects). They extend partially to Huang's (1982) Condition on Extraction Domain if phases include DPs, as just suggested. For A-movement, (3a) is not obviated; thus, the PIC prevents access to an inactive subject of CP from the next strong phase, but not from a higher T with no intervening strong phase (as in *T be believed [that John is intelligent], with Agree(T, John) barred by (3a) but not the PIC). For Ā-movement, questions arise of the kind mentioned earlier, along with others, among them the issue of Slavic-style multiple wh-movement violating Subjacency.

30. It follows that the computation cannot ignore matching of (P, G), ultimately crashing because of cyclicity and intervention effects. Not to be confused with such reduction of complexity (very limited, because of the PIC) is backtracking of the kind associated with the principle Greed, which allows recovery of a derivation along a more complex path. Other false starts are still not barred. For example, suppose that α, T, V are available and the first choice selects T as the complement of α. Cyclicity prevents selection of V by T, and the derivation crashes. On maximization principles of the kind (14), see among others a preliminary version of McGinnis 1998.

31. A separate question is whether Expl raises to a position within the v^* complement. See note 16. The proposed raising of object does not have the syntactic and semantic properties of raising to [Spec, v^*] (object shift) and therefore presumably is raising internal to the v^* complement, distinct from the kind of raising in (15). Lasnik (1999b) and Epstein and Seely (1999) take Case of a man to be determined in situ, along the lines suggested by Belletti (1988): an inherent Case in present terms, perhaps partitive, but in any event independent of agreement and distinct from nominative/accusative. This seems questionable, in part for reasons that appear directly.

32. The observation is irrelevant if Case is assumed to be assigned to the object in situ, as in the proposals cited (see notes 16, 31).

33. Another possibility is that probe-goal match is evaluated first for the most local pair, subjecting deleted features to Spell-Out, then for the most local remaining pair, and so on. Thus, the first step deletes the single φ-feature of Expl, rendering it invisible for the next step relating (probe, DO). The proposal would not, however, yield other consequences of (14) and (17).

34. On manifestation of agreement and its relation to raising, see Guasti and Rizzi 1999.

35. Consider alternative 2, with EPP a property of the matrix transitive verb (expect in (18b)), however the idea is implemented (see notes 16, 31; also 19). The EPP property should be independent of the embedded clause: whether it is transitive (with the subject raising into the expect-phrase) or nontransitive (as in (18));

whether the language always exhibits Expl overtly (as in English) or only in certain contexts (as in Icelandic). If so, the matrix verb in (18b) has an EPP-feature, but assigns Case independently of that, to the embedded object *fish*, just as T assigns Case to *fish* in (18a) independently of its EPP-feature. Similarly, the EPP-feature of the probe is independent of Case assignment to Prt.

36. To simplify, take Prt to be a light verb distinct from v^*. Here T is ϕ-complete, selected by C. If C is missing and T defective, then the same analysis just transfers to the first ϕ-complete probe. If the proposal of note 18 is tenable, then C is within β, extending the parallelism of (18a) and (18b).

37. Furthermore, Prt is ϕ-incomplete (hence unable to value features), and both Prt and DO lack the (structural) Case-assigning property of T, v.

38. See note 34. In these terms, we can partially overcome a problem that arises within the $Locus_{TV}$ framework (alternative 2, above), if selection is reduced to Match/Agree. The ϕ-features of T_{comp} and V_{comp} are unvalued until they function as probes, then deleting. But they must be available to delete the ϕ-features of C and v^*, which select them. That is unproblematic if Spell-Out takes place at the strong-phase level, though another problem remains: the final operation, capturing selection, violates (3a). It seems questionable, however, that alternative 2 can be sustained, in the light of the considerations just reviewed.

39. To sharpen the issues, one would like to find a language with overt nonclitic expletives, ECM, free use of unaccusatives, and a rich enough manifested morphology to tell whether verb-object agreement holds uniformly between the probe and DO of the lower verb, as in Icelandic. Among unresolved questions are the reasons for Romance-style participial agreement contingent on movement, as discussed in Kayne 1989 and subsequent work. It is simple enough to state the parameter ("Spell out ϕ-features of Prt-goal only if probe induces Move"), but there should be a more principled account, perhaps related to the manifestation-move correlations discussed by Guasti and Rizzi (1999). In any approach in the neighborhood of those surveyed here, movement to [Spec, Prt] (specifically, in nontransitive constructions) would be an additional stipulation, hence no improvement over the straightforward description in terms of probe-goal match; the idea faces other problems, noted by Philip Branigan and Dominique Sportiche (see Chomsky 1995, (132)).

40. On the English-Italian contrast with regard to (22c), see Lasnik 1999b, where a different approach is developed.

41. Note that this amounts to highly limited access of narrow syntax to effects of the phonological component.

42. Compare (28b) with *how many packages were there lying on the table*, much more acceptable (as is (28b), if interpreted as involving stative/adjectival passive), indicating that the status of (28b) is not simply the result of incomplete internal constituent constraints on movement (Kuno 1973). Note that after displacement to the right or left, the trace/copy cannot move; if it did, (28a) and (28b) would be essentially the LF forms of (i) and (ii), respectively.

(i)   there arrived *t* in the mail [how many packages]
(ii) there were [how many packages] placed *t* on the table

The LF forms are permissible, as counterparts in other languages illustrate (e.g., (23)); and (i), (ii) are permissible, on a par with (24a–b).

43. Extraction from within PP is of course barred here (*which airport did there arrive at* t *three strange men* vs. *which airport did three strange men arrive at*), presumably an illustration of constraints mentioned in the preceding note. If Th/Ex belongs to the phonological component, then these effects hold within that component, a conclusion about "surface effects" that is consistent with (13).

44. A consequence, Luigi Rizzi points out, is that null Op cannot pied-pipe (*the man* [Op *I spoke to*] vs. *the man* [[to Op] *I spoke*]).

45. There are other assumptions, among them, that in structures relevant for pied-piping, roots will have at least some phonological specification in the optimal encoding of Lex; very radical allomorphic variation is unexpected for open classes, as noted earlier.

46. Existential import is not a simple matter. For example, *there are steps missing in that proof* does not presuppose that the steps exist and can be filled in to complete the proof; and *there is something lacking in his novel* (a spark, vitality, humor, the characters are wooden, . . .) presupposes nothing about the possibility of overcoming the defect. But in *there are steps expected to be missing in that proof* and *there is something expected to be lacking in his novel*, the existential import returns. Note that the contrast in existential import between (40a) and (40b) indicates that constructions of the form (24a) are not to be construed as *there be NP* constructions, unlike (38c).

47. Examples from Lasnik 1999b, within a somewhat different framework of assumptions.

48. Nothing here turns on the question whether OS is substitution in outer Spec or adjunction; in either case, it is to the edge of the construction, invoking the PIC. It is sometimes supposed that multiple Spec is a stipulation, but that is to mistake history for logic.

49. Irrelevantly, in (42a) the *wh*-phrase is active, having an unvalued uninterpretable feature *wh*; but the probe T does not seek that feature.

50. Examples provided by Anders Holmberg and Thorbjörg Hróarsdóttir, who also point out surprising and unexplained complexities about intervention effects in such cases, apparently turning on matching of quirky Case number and raising of subject to transitive expletive construction position. See also note 56 below.

51. Perhaps "c-commanding from the left," depending on the proper treatment of such matters as rightward adjunction and questions raised by Kayne (1994) about linear ordering.

52. The effect on the MLC is limited under the PIC, which bars "deep search" by the probe.

53. The question is suggested by problems raised by Susi Wurmbrand.

54. See Jonas 1996. Many questions about the data remain obscure, but not in ways relevant here, it appears. Icelandic and Mainland Scandinavian data presented here are provided by Anders Holmberg (personal communication).

55. See Holmberg 1999, on which I am relying for data here and below, along with personal communication.

56. Unexplained is why shifted quirky DO can remain active, unlike shifted structural accusative DO. One can think of possible answers related to the default versus T_{comp} options of quirky Case in [Spec, T] and other options available to quirky Case; or it might be necessary to weaken (3a), which requires that goal as well as probe be active for Agree to hold. The cases reviewed so far (see notes 29, 38) are consistent with the assumption that (3a) holds only for (P, G) pairs in different phases, with G in the domain (not the edge) of the lower phase. But unresolved factual questions make suggestions premature (see note 50).

57. Free topicalization may produce expressions with deviant interpretations, but that is not a problem. The *wh*-phrase case depends on how the operation is to be understood: Is there an uninterpretable *wh*-feature? Is there matching with an appropriate C = Q? What is the status of *wh*-in situ in typologically different languages? And other questions, including some mentioned earlier.

58. See Holmberg 1986, Bobaljik 1995, observations extended in Holmberg 1999.

59. See Diesing 1992, Rizzi 1997. Condition (54b) is (38) of Holmberg 1999.

60. Raising or lowering. See Lasnik 1981, 1999b, and Bobaljik 1994.

61. We take a chain to be a set of occurrences of the first-merged XP, as in MI, returning to the matter below. The discussion can easily be revised for other formulations of LF-interpretive operations.

62. Discussion of (24) and notes 50, 52 of MI, paraphrased here. I restrict attention here to LF outcome.

63. The tacit assumption is that the object pronoun first moves to the outer edge of v*P (as required by (13)), then on to its surface position, whatever the latter operation may be.

64. Consider the issue of intervention effects discussed earlier, with the "richness of T" and Disl alternatives. Neither alternative introduces further parametric variation. For non-OS languages, an extra EPP-feature is permitted for v* under (61a) only with *wh*-movement and Topicalization. The "richness of T" alternative (invoking equidistance, otherwise perhaps unnecessary) applies only in OS languages. Under the more natural Disl alternative (without equidistance), the phonological rule Disl is a universal option, vacuous for non-OS languages.

65. In the latter case, interpretation depends on how *wh*-constructions and the like are construed. Holmberg observes that *it*-type expletives may undergo OS; whether this obviates Int depends on how we understand the expletive-associate relation in such cases.

66. The qualification is intended to leave open other possibilities: for example, TP-raising to [Spec, C] in accord with Kayne's (1994) theory of linearity, head

raising versus XP-raising as a possible distinction between *wh*-in-situ and overt raising (see MI and sources cited, particularly Watanabe 1992 and Hagstrom 1998). The N → D rule developed in Longobardi 1994 and subsequent work has crucial semantic consequences, but it seems that these might be reformulated in terms of the properties of D that do or do not induce overt raising.

67. Commonly, head movement is held to observe c-command, but with a stipulated disjunctive definition for this case, which does not fall under the "free" relation of c-command derived from Merge (see MI). The Head Movement Constraint has been assimilated to general locality conditions in various ways, but special features remain, it seems.

68. Other apparent distinctions between X′ and XP dissolve—largely or completely—with more systematic reinterpretation of relations and operations in terms of labels rather than phrasal categories, as in MI and here.

69. An occurrence defined in terms of IC is an X^{max} except in the case of multiple Spec. If necessary for some reason, the notion could be modified to require it to be an X^{max} here as well (perhaps taking the occurrence to be a pair (K, XP), XP the smallest X^{max} containing K). But sharpening may be superfluous. Occurrences are significant only for moved elements, chains are properly distinguished on independent grounds, and the arguments for invisibility are by now so weak that there is no compelling reason to pursue the matter.

70. This is the θ-theoretic principle (6) of MI, a direct consequence of Hale and Keyser's (1993) conception of θ-theory adopted there. The added assumption is that violation of the principle, which is detectable at once, causes crash.

71. Consider successive-cyclic movement that begins by forming an A-chain and then proceeds to form an Ā-chain—standard *wh*-movement of HP, for example. It is not necessary to think of the single chain as broken up into two for the purposes of interpretation. Rather, there are two sets of occurrences for HP, which is merged just once: the set of occurrences of H (the A-chain) and the set of occurrences of *wh* (the Ā-chain).

72. The purpose was to avoid consistent misunderstanding of the technical usage of the notion "grammar" and others, but the proposed terminology was further misunderstood as suggesting that there are two topics, I- and E-linguistics (I- and E-languages, etc.), the latter concerned with utterances, corpora, behavior, Platonic objects, and so on. The E-concepts, however, were defined as "anything else," intended to identify no coherent object or study. Furthermore, utterances and behavior are no more or less a concern of I-linguistics than of studies of language that might be called (misleadingly, I think) varieties of E-linguistics.

References

Baker, M. 1988. *Incorporation*. Chicago: University of Chicago Press.

Beard, R. 1995. *Lexeme-morpheme-based morphology*. Albany, N.Y.: SUNY Press.

Belletti, A. 1988. The Case of unaccusatives. *Linguistic Inquiry* 19, 1–34.

Bobaljik, J. 1994. What does adjacency do? In H. Harley and C. Phillips, eds., *The morphology-syntax connection*. MIT Working Papers in Linguistics 22. MITWPL, Department of Linguistics and Philosophy, MIT, Cambridge, Mass.

Bobaljik, J. 1995. Morphosyntax. Doctoral dissertation, MIT, Cambridge, Mass.

Boeckx, C., and S. Stjepanović. 1999. Head-ing toward PF. Ms., University of Connecticut, Storrs.

Burzio, L. 1986. *Italian syntax*. Dordrecht: Reidel.

Chomsky, N. 1986. *Knowledge of language*. New York: Praeger.

Chomsky, N. 1995. Categories and transformations. In *The Minimalist Program*. Cambridge, Mass.: MIT Press.

Chomsky, N. 2000. Minimalist inquiries: The framework. In R. Martin, D. Michaels, and J. Uriagereka, eds., *Step by step: Essays on minimalist syntax in honor of Howard Lasnik*. Cambridge, Mass.: MIT Press.

Collins, C. 1999. Eliminating labels. Ms., Cornell University, Ithaca, N.Y.

Diesing, M. 1992. *Indefinites*. Cambridge, Mass.: MIT Press.

Embick, D. 2000. Features, syntax, and categories in the Latin perfect. *Linguistic Inquiry* 31, 185–230.

Epstein, S., and D. Seely. 1999. SPEC-ifying the GF "subject": Eliminating A-chains and the EPP within a derivational model. Ms., University of Michigan, Ann Arbor.

Fox, D. 1995. Economy and scope. *Natural Language Semantics* 3, 283–341.

Fox, D. 2000. *Economy and semantic interpretation*. Cambridge, Mass.: MIT Press.

Frampton, J., and S. Gutmann. 1999. Cyclic computation: A computationally efficient minimalist syntax. *Syntax* 2, 1–27.

George. L., and J. Kornfilt. 1981. Finiteness and boundedness in Turkish. In F. Heny, ed., *Binding and filtering*. Cambridge, Mass.: MIT Press.

Groat, E., and J. O'Neil. 1996. Spell-Out at the LF interface. In W. Abraham, S. Epstein, H. Thráinsson, and J.-W. Zwart, eds., *Minimal ideas*. Amsterdam: John Benjamins.

Grodzinsky, Y., and L. Finkel. 1998. The neurology of empty categories: Aphasics' failure to detect ungrammaticality. *Journal of Cognitive Neuroscience* 10, 281–292.

Guasti, M. T., and L. Rizzi. 1999. Agreement and tense as distinct syntactic positions: Evidence from acquisition. Ms., University of Siena.

Hagstrom, P. 1998. Decomposing questions. Doctoral dissertation, MIT, Cambridge, Mass.

Hale, K., and S. J. Keyser. 1993. On argument structure and the lexical expression of syntactic relations. In K. Hale and S. J. Keyser, eds., *The view from Building 20*. Cambridge, Mass.: MIT Press.

Harley, H. 1995. Subjects, events, and licensing. Doctoral dissertation, MIT, Cambridge, Mass.

Harley, H., and R. Noyer. 1999. Distributed Morphology. *Glot International* 4.4.

Holmberg, A. 1986. Word order and syntactic features in the Scandinavian languages and English. Doctoral dissertation, University of Stockholm.

Holmberg, A. 1999. Remarks on Holmberg's Generalization. *Studia Linguistica* 53, 1–39.

Holmberg, A., and C. Platzack. 1995. *The role of inflection in Scandinavian syntax*. Oxford: Oxford University Press.

Huang, C.-T. J. 1982. Logical relations in Chinese and the theory of grammar. Doctoral dissertation, MIT, Cambridge, Mass.

Jenkins, L. 1999. *Biolinguistics*. Cambridge: Cambridge University Press.

Jonas, D. 1996. Clause structure and verb syntax in Scandinavian and English. Doctoral dissertation, Harvard University, Cambridge, Mass.

Kayne, R. 1989. Facets of past participle agreement in Romance. In P. Benincà, ed., *Dialect variation in the theory of grammar*. Dordrecht: Foris.

Kayne, R. 1994. *The antisymmetry of syntax*. Cambridge, Mass.: MIT Press.

Koizumi, M. 1995. Phrase structure in minimalist syntax. Doctoral dissertation, MIT, Cambridge, Mass.

Kuno, S. 1973. Constraints on internal clauses and sentential subjects. *Linguistic Inquiry* 4, 363–385.

Landau, I. 1999. Elements of control. Doctoral dissertation, MIT, Cambridge, Mass.

Lasnik, H. 1981. Restricting the theory of transformations. In N. Hornstein and D. Lightfoot, eds., *Explanation in linguistics*. London: Longmans.

Lasnik, H. 1999a. Chains of arguments. In S. Epstein and N. Hornstein, eds., *Working minimalism*. Cambridge, Mass.: MIT Press.

Lasnik, H. 1999b. *Minimalist analysis*. Oxford: Blackwell.

Legate, J. 1998. Verb phrase types and the notion of a phase. Ms., MIT, Cambridge, Mass.

Longobardi, G. 1994. Reference and proper names: A theory of N-movement in syntax and Logical Form. *Linguistic Inquiry* 25, 609–665.

Marantz, A. 1997. No escape from syntax: Don't try morphological analysis in the privacy of your own lexicon. In A. Dimitriadis, L. Siegel, C. Surek-Clark, and A. Williams, eds., *Proceedings of the 21st Annual Penn Linguistics Colloquium*. Pennsylvania Working Papers in Linguistics 4.2. Penn Linguistics Club, University of Pennsylvania, Philadelphia.

McGinnis, M. 1998. Locality in A-movement. Doctoral dissertation, MIT, Cambridge, Mass.

Pesetsky, D. 1989. Language-particular processes and the Earliness Principle. Ms., MIT, Cambridge, Mass.

Pollock, J.-Y. 1989. Verb movement, Universal Grammar, and the structure of IP. *Linguistic Inquiry* 20, 365–424.

Reinhart, T. 1993. *Wh*-in-situ in the framework of the Minimalist Program. Ms., Tel Aviv University. [Published in *Natural Language Semantics* 6, 29–56 (1997).]

Rizzi, L. 1982. Comments on Chomsky's chapter "On the representation of form and function." In J. Mehler, E. Walker, and M. Garrett, eds., *Perspectives on mental representation*. Hillsdale, N.J.: Lawrence Erlbaum.

Rizzi, L. 1997. The fine structure of the left periphery. In L. Haegeman, ed., *Elements of grammar*. Dordrecht: Kluwer.

Sauerland, U. 1998. On the making and meaning of chains. Doctoral dissertation, MIT Cambridge, Mass.

Watanabe, A. 1992. Subjacency and S-Structure movement of *wh*-in-situ. *Journal of East Asian Linguistics* 1, 255–291.

Chapter 2

Morphology in Creole Genesis: Linguistics and Ideology

Michel DeGraff

What matters is eventual success, and that will be measured by the extent to which work on the language is integrated in a meaningful way into the life of the community of people who speak it. Ken Hale

2.1 A Prolegomenon

In a forthcoming handbook on morphology, Pieter Muysken writes,

[C]reole morphology is a sorely neglected area of study (due to the widespread belief that creoles have no morphology to speak of) . . . (Muysken, in press)

That is, Creole morphology has often been taken to represent nothing new or substantial. This "widespread belief" is at the core of the age-old orthodoxy that Creole affixes, if any exist, are either (fossilized or relexified) versions of source language forms and/or semantically transparent grammaticalizations of lexical items. This belief is most prevalent in "classic" Creole genesis scenarios that postulate the prior existence of a virtually affixless pidgin. This chapter, especially sections 2.2–2.5, is one small step—a prolegomenon—toward redressing the state of affairs deplored by Muysken, with focus on Haitian Creole (HC). In section 2.6, I peek at methodology and at history to try to understand why Creole morphology came to be "sorely neglected" and why Creoles are often believed to "have no morphology to speak of." I argue that this belief is empirically and conceptually ill founded while showing that "radical" Creoles need not emerge via pidginization qua a "radical break of transmission" that in the limit eliminates all morphology. I suggest that certain methodological aspects of Creole studies are ultimately rooted in the colonial and neocolonial ideologies that characterize the genesis and development of Creole languages. In section 2.7, I find inspiration in Ken Hale's research and ethos for "integrat[ing work on the language] in a meaningful way into the life of the community of people who speak it" (Hale 2001). Lessons from history can be used toward improving the future of Creolophones and of Creole studies, as we try to liberate this future from the legacies of the (neo)colonial past.

2.2   Creole Morphology: A "Solid Datum" for Manufacturing "Consensus"?

Over the last three and a half centuries (starting at least as early as Pelleprat 1655) and continuing into the present (as recently as Lefebvre 1998, McWhorter 1998, and Seuren 1998), most descriptions of Creole morphology have become repeated variations on five main themes: (1) incipience, (2) (near) absence, (3) lapidescence, (4) transparence, and (5) exclusive substrate correspondence. These themes have been handed down by representatives of nearly every intellectual circle interested in Creole languages: first the European colonists, adventurers, missionaries, and polymaths, followed by a series of amateur and bona fide ethnographers, philologists, and linguists—Creolophones and non-Creolophones, creolists and noncreolists, descriptivists and theoreticians, and so on.[1] I illustrate these themes with relevant quotations. (Throughout this chapter, italic type indicates my own emphasis, not that of the quoted author—except where indicated.)

Incipience In this view, Creoles are linguistic neonates whose morphologies lack the features that characterize "older," more "mature" languages. McWhorter (1998) claims that the alleged morphological features of prototypical Creoles (i.e., absence of tone and inflection, and semantically opaque derivation) are

clear results of a break in transmission followed by a *development period too brief* for the [prototypical Creole] traits to be undone as they have in *older* languages. (McWhorter 1998, 788)

Among the other features alleged to be the exclusive province of "older languages" are the following (overlapping) characteristics: "rich paradigms of derivational affixes [which are] alien to any language known as a creole," "idiosyncratic lexicalizations," "semantically evolved derivation," and "evolved idiosyncrasy" whose interpretation requires "a certain degree of metaphorical imagination" and "metaphorical inference" (McWhorter 1998, 796–798, 812, etc.). The traits that McWhorter attributes to "older languages" are reminiscent of those argued by Seuren and Wekker (1986, 68) to belong to "older or more advanced" languages.

Such traits constitute what Seuren and Wekker consider to be lexical "luxuries"—namely, "idiosyncratic exceptions," "highly specialized lexical items," and "richer expressive means." Seuren and Wekker (1986, 66, 68) explicitly contrast the "younger or less advanced" (Creole) languages with the "older or more advanced" (non-Creole) languages. McWhorter (1998, 793, 798–799, 809–812, etc.) contrasts Creole languages with "regular" languages. And Seuren (1998, 292) contrasts Creole languages with "sophisticated" languages:

Creole grammars ... are, in a sense, simplified in that they lack the more sophisticated features of languages backed by a rich and extended cultural past and a large, well-organized literate society.

Furthermore, Whinnom (1971, 110) considers it likely that Creole languages, because of the limited expressiveness of their postpidgin (non) morphology, "constitute a handicap to the creole-speaker's personal intellectual development."

[O]ne feature [of Creole languages] which appears to be seriously impaired by pidginization is the capacity for word-coinage from within the resources of the language: *in the European-"based" pidgins and creoles, derivational affixes and suffixes seem to have lost their original conceptual content and become fossilized.* Obviously there are other devices for word-formation [e.g., periphrases] ... but *what cannot be generated very successfully by the combination of concrete words is abstract terms,* in which it is notorious that pidgins and creoles are deficient. And there are probably upper limits to the number and length of such periphrases.

In other words, there may be some reason to suspect that *the creole-speaker is handicapped by his language.* (Whinnom 1971, 109)

McWhorter's, Seuren's and Whinnom's views are vaguely reminiscent of nineteenth-century (quasi-)Schleicherian/Darwinian notions of language evolution whereby languages "naturally progress" across a simple-to-complex hierarchy of morphological types (e.g., from monosyllabic to isolating to agglutinative to inflectional). In "modern" versions of Schleicherian linguistics, it is Creole languages that are equated to the young, primitive, and structurally simplest linguistic species. In effect, Creole languages are singled out as living fossils—observable instances of Language at its evolutionary incipience.

(Near) absence This is the point critiqued by Muysken above, namely, the claim that "creoles have no morphology to speak of." Such (near) absence is an alleged consequence of incipience. Perhaps the most explicit proposal along such lines is found in Seuren and Wekker's (1986) essay on semantic transparency in Creoles; also see Jespersen 1922, 233–234, on Creoles' morphological "vanishing point."[2]

[T]here is *consensus* [among creolists] on at least one point. It is generally agreed that creole languages have little or no morphology.... [T]he *absence (or extreme poverty) of morphology in creole languages* seems to be a *solid datum* and a *highly significant* one. (Seuren and Wekker 1986, 61)

[M]orphology [is] *essentially alien* to creole languages. (Seuren and Wekker 1986, 66)

This is reminiscent of an earlier claim by D'Ans (1968, 26) in the particular context of HC: "[I]t is *logically impossible* for [Haitian] Creole to manifest [derivational] processes."

Seuren (1998, 292–293) raises (near) absence of morphology to the status of a "historical universal":

Historical universal I: If a language has a Creole origin it is SVO, has TMA [tense-mood-aspect] particles, has *virtually no morphology*, etc.

Lapidescence Lapidescence is related to (near) absence: Creole morphology is (nearly) absent because (most of) the affixes in the source languages have been reduced to "fossils." Therefore, Creoles are by and large morphologically unproductive. In the case of HC, the claim is that morphologically complex words in French were adopted in the incipient Creole as morphologically simplex words that have since remained permanently unanalyzed—what Hall (1953) calls *Gallicisms.*

The three processes of derivation (prefixation, suffixation and compounding) are for the most part *rare* and are found but *scatteringly* in creole, and to a large extent only in *learnèd* words *borrowed* from standard French.... Suffixation is *particularly* scattering, and occurs *chiefly* in Gallicisms. (Hall 1953, 34, 36)

Aspects of Hall's view have been repeatedly put forward by Valdman, who limits the HC affix set to two productive affixes (1978, 148) and concludes:[3]

[Derivation] plays only a minor role in the creation of new words. We have noticed only two affixes that are used today for the renewal of the lexical inventory [in HC] ... (Valdman 1978, 148; my translation)

Such claims are echoed by Samarin's (1980, 221) argument that "[t]he greatest handicap that creoles have in morphosemantic adaptation is their morphological simplicity."

Transparence Alongside (near) absence of (inflectional) morphology (see note 2), transparence is viewed as a consequence of alleged incipience. For example, in McWhorter's (1998) view, one exclusive property of "older" (i.e., non-Creole) languages is semantic *ir*regularity in derivational morphology (pp. 798, 812). Given the incipience of Creoles, derivational affixes (should a Creole have any) must be the product of recent grammaticalization of erstwhile freestanding lexical items. Because of their youth, these recently grammaticalized affixes still conserve the transparent semantics of their unbound ancestors. As a result, Creole derivational affixes cannot manifest the sort of idiosyncratic lexicalizations that are commonplace in "older" languages. Such reasoning leads McWhorter (1998, 809) to argue that, as a radical Creole, HC has "derivational affixes whose semantic contribution is *consistently* transparent." (The determining role of morphological transparency in shaping the "young" Creole lexicon goes back at least to Saint-Quentin 1872 and Hjelmslev 1938; also see Seuren and Wekker 1986.)

Exclusive substrate correspondence In this view, the inventory and characteristics of HC morphological processes are bounded by substrate morphology. Lefebvre (1998, chap. 10) explicitly argues that HC affixes are by and large inherited from, and identical to, Fongbe affixes, modulo pronunciation.

[T]he inventory of productive affixes in [HC] reduces to ten or eleven. (Lefebvre 1988, 311)

[T]here is a [virtual] one-to-one correspondence between [HC] and Fongbe affixes. (Lefebvre 1988, 333)

Creole studies are usually rife with debates. But morphology may constitute one domain of rare consensus. Indeed, if there is any semblance of a consensus on Creole synchrony and diachrony among the five tenets above, it is that Creoles are, at best, morphologically simple to an exceptional degree (when Creole morphology is productive, it is consistently and optimally transparent) and/or relatively simple to account for from a diachronic perspective (Creole morphology derives most of its combinatoric substance from the substrate).

Given these tenets, pieces of HC morphology (if any) must fall into one of four classes: they are (1) (nearly) absent: "no morphology to speak of," in Muysken's (in press) words; (2) virtually "invisible" (i.e., transparent): all derivational affixes combine with transparent (presumably, compositional) semantics; (3) Gallicisms qua fossilized inheritances from French; (4) Africanisms qua substrate retentions with lexifier-derived phonetics (via relexification).

In each case, Creole morphology is argued to be a structural reflex of the short history (the "incipience") of Creole languages and/or the sui generis sociohistorical context of Creole genesis. It is along such lines that "creole morphology [has become] a sorely neglected area of study" (Muysken, in press).[4] Yet, note that such reductive views of Creole morphology lead to the following paradox: either Creole creators have the exceptional capacity to create languages with "perfect" (i.e., optimally transparent) morphology or they are incapable of going beyond the word structure of some subset of ancestral languages or etymological fossils thereof.

2.3 Haitian Creole Morphology: Facts versus Myths

Do the claims in section 2.2 reach any level of observational adequacy? In DeGraff 2000b, I offer a representative HC sample for an affix set that is more elaborate than Lefebvre's "ten or eleven" affixes and Valdman's "two affixes." The sample suggests that the orthodoxy expressed in section 2.2—that Creole morphology is absent, extraordinarily reduced, simple, and/or substrate-bound—is empirically unsubstantiated. For the purposes of this chapter, I present a sample of the data and discussion from DeGraff 2000b. I show that the received theories on Creole morphology in no way describe HC.

What might HC morphology *really* look like? The short passage in (1b) is a fictitious monologue based on the plot in (1a). This monologue was written to realistically and economically illustrate a sample of HC derivational processes within a suitable discourse context. The narrative is imaginary, but it strikes me as conversationally natural and ethnographically appropriate. Furthermore, each of the derivational processes in (1b) is robustly instantiated in HC dictionaries (e.g., Valdman et al. 1981; Freeman and Laguerre 1996 [1998]) and word lists (e.g., Freeman 1989). In particular, see the monumental etymological database in Fattier's (1998) six-volume dialect atlas; Fattier's work is precious because it is not only based on spontaneous data from monolingual HC speakers, but also rich in Creole neologisms illustrating productive word formation patterns of the sort exemplified below.[5]

(1) a. *Plot*

We're on a deserted sidewalk, near a cockfight stadium, in Wanament, a Haitian town near the border with the Dominican Republic. Ti-Yèyèt is a pretty girl from across the border. Ti-Sonson is her Haitian lover. They live together in Wanament, in *plasay* ('concubinage'). Something upsetting just happened. A terrible affront has been committed against Ti-Yèyèt's favorite fighting-cock. The culprit is Ti-Jan, the town's best-known griper and most infamous braggart. Ti-Sonson exhorts his Haitian buddies to revenge against Ti-Jan. Ti-Yèyèt's honor must be restored and the offender must pay dearly for his insults—in a Creole version of Corneille's *Le Cid.*

b. *Segment of Ti-Sonson's exhorting monologue*

Mezanmi wo! Gade yon bòlèt.
my-friends oh look-at a lottery

Ti-Jan, babyadò enkoutab sa a, derespekte Ti-Yèyèt.
Ti-Jan griper foolhardy that the disrespect Ti-Yèyèt

Ti-chouchou m lan se yon bèl dominikèn ki
little-darling 1SG the RES-PRON a pretty Dominican+FEM who
gen yon bèl kòk-batay.
have a beautiful fighting-cock

Se pa ti admire Ti-Yèyèt admire
RES-PRON NEG little-bit admire Ti-Yèyèt admire
kòk-kriyadò li sa a!
experienced fighting-cock 3SG this

Men admirasyon mennen tribilasyon.
but admiration bring tribulation

Ti-Jan dekreta kòk la
Ti-Jan cut-off-crest cock the

epi vantadò a mache-mache grennen kozman sa a.
and braggart the walk-walk shell-out gossip that

Fòk n al debaba djòlè sa a—kòrèkteman!
must 1PL go mow-down boaster that correctly

'Oh, my friends! What nonsense! Ti-Jan, that foolhardy griper,
has disrespected Ti-Yèyèt. My sweetheart is a lovely Dominican
woman with a splendid fighting-cock. Ti-Yèyèt so much admires
her experienced fighting-cock. But admiration brings tribulation.
Ti-Jan has chopped off its crest. And that braggart has been
going around and around spreading gossip. Let's go mow him
down—absolutely!'

Here is a sketch of the derivational processes in (1):

(2) a. Prefixation with *de-*, as in *derespekte* 'to disrespect, to insult'
(cf. *respekte* 'to respect'), *dekreta* 'to cut off the crest' (cf. *krèt* n.
'crest'), and *debaba* 'to mow down' (cf. *baba* adj. 'mute'; variant
of *bèbè*).

b. Prefixation with *en-*, as in *enkoutab* adj. 'foolhardy' (cf. *koute* 'to
listen').

c. Prefixation with *ti-*, as in *Ti-Yèyèt*, *Ti-Sonson*, and *ti-chouchou* n.
'little darling'.

d. Suffixation with *-ab*, as in *enkoutab* (cf. (2b)).

e. Suffixation with *-adò*, as in *babyadò* n. 'griper' (cf. *babye* 'to whine'), *vantadò* n. 'braggart' (cf. *vante* 'to brag'), and *kriyadò* adj. 'old, experienced' (see Spanish *criado* 'experienced' and *criador* n. 'one who trains, breeds, raises, nurtures', as in *criador de gallos* n. 'trainer of (fighting-)cocks'; cf. *criar* 'to train, breed, raise, nurture'). Also see *kriyadò* n. 'chronic weeper' (cf. *kriye* 'to weep').

f. Suffixation with *-ay* (variant: *-aj*), as in *plasay* (variant: *plasaj*) n. 'concubinage' (cf. *plase* 'to live in concubinage').

g. Suffixation with *-è*, as in *djòlè* n. 'boaster' (cf. *djòl* n. 'mouth').

h. Suffixation with (verbal marker) *-e(n)*, as in *gade* 'to look', *admire* 'to admire', *mennen* 'to bring', *mache* 'to walk' (cf. *mach* n. 'march, step (stairs)'), *grennen* 'to shell out' (cf. *grenn* n. 'grain').

i. Suffixation plus gender inflection with *-en/-èn*, as in the pair *Dominiken/Dominikèn* n. (cf. *Dominikani* n. 'Dominican Republic').

j. Suffixation with *-èt*, as in *bòlèt* n. 'lottery' (cf. *bòl* 'bowl, lottery number formed by two identical digits' (Freeman and Laguerre 1996 [1998]) and *boul* (*bòlèt*) 'lottery number, ball'; also see Spanish *boleto/boleta* '(lottery) ticket, ballot' and *bola* 'ball'; cf. the lottery balls used in determining winning numbers).

k. Suffixation with *-man*, as in *kozman* n. 'talk, gossip' (cf. *koze* 'to talk').

l. Suffixation with *-man*, as in *kòrèkteman* adv. 'correctly' (cf. *kòrèk* adj. 'correct').

m. Suffixation with *-syon*, as in *admirasyon* n. 'admiration' (cf. *admire* 'to admire') and *tribilasyon* n. 'tribulation' (cf. *?tribile*: there is no actual word *tribile*, at least not in the dialects that I am familiar with).

n. Compounding, as in *kòk-batay* n. 'fighting-cock'.

o. Reduplication, as in *Ti-Yèyèt, Ti-Sonson, ti-chouchou* n. 'little darling' (affectionate), and *mache-mache* 'to walk a lot' (intensifying).

p. Apocope, as in *gen*, which is the short form of *genyen*.

Ti-Sonson's speech in (1) and the preliminary sampling of HC affixes in (2) contradict the oft-repeated claims that HC morphology is either virtually absent (e.g., Hall 1953, 34, 36; D'Ans 1968, 26; Whinnom 1971, 109–110; Seuren and Wekker 1986; Seuren 1998, 292–293; McWhorter

1998, 810), consistently transparent (e.g., McWhorter 1998, 809, 812), limited to two productive affixes (e.g., Valdman 1978, 148), reducible by and large to unproductive Gallicisms or "pseudo-French" hypercorrections (e.g., Hall 1953, 34, 36; Valdman 1978, 23; 1979, 99; 1987, 120; 1988, 75; 1989, 59), or limited to 10 or 11 affixes that are mostly inherited from the substrate (e.g., Lefebvre 1998, 311, 333). In this 58-word speech plus the word *plasay* in (1a), we find at least 16 different types and about 30 examples (word tokens) of derivational processes (see underlined strings in (1b)). So, roughly speaking, every other HC word in (1) is morphologically complex, including a fair number of lexical-innovation candidates, that is, HC words with no apparent counterparts in French.[6] HC is obviously not on a morphological par with Bantu or Algonquian, but then again neither are English, French, and Fongbe; and the latter are all non-Creole languages (i.e., languages considered to be "regular," "normal," "old," and "advanced" in Valdman's, Seuren and Wekker's, and McWhorter's terminologies).

Let us now revisit previous conclusions on HC morphology, starting with those of Lefebvre (1998, chap. 10).[7] Out of the 16 derivational processes illustrated in (1)–(2), Lefebvre addresses only about half in her pro-relexification arguments; also see pages 65–66 and note 18 for two other HC suffixes missing from Lefebvre's treatment, namely, *ès* as in *titès* 'childhood' (cf. *ti* 'small') and -*te* as in *bèlte* 'beauty' (cf. *bèl* 'beautiful'). (Chaudenson (1996) provides a critique of Lefebvre's general methodology.) Regarding the data in (1)–(2) and in note 18, Lefebvre has no account for the *productive* affixes *en-, -ab, -adò, -èt,* (nominalizing) -*man, -syon, -ès, -te,* reduplication, gender inflection. In fact, Lefebvre explicitly states that, other than the 11 affixes treated in her chapter on morphology, she considers all HC candidate affixes to be fossilized. That is, any candidate affix that is not one of the 11 affixes she has identified as "native" is actually part of a simplex HC word. Lefebvre (1998, 311) claims, for example, that all HC words with *yon* endings, which correspond to "derived words in French, have entered Haitian as simplexes and are therefore listed individually" (p. 311). As I will show, Lefebvre's argument is somewhat related to Valdman's discarding various affixation instances from HC grammar as "nonexistent derivatives formed by adjoining occurring French suffixes to the 'wrong' [HC] stems" (1988, 75)—what Valdman calls "pseudo-French hypercorrections" (see section 2.4 below).

In section 2.4, I address the specifics of Valdman's claims, then critique both his and Lefebvre's arguments on what counts as a "native" HC suffix. In section 2.5, I turn to McWhorter's (1998) claims about a structurally defined Creole prototype. The combined result of these case studies is to show that the "solid datum" alleged in section 2.2 about Creole morphology is actually nonexistent; thus, the points of "consensus" outlined in section 2.2 are empirically untenable. In section 2.6, I also show that, once examined in light of their methodology and history, these points of "consensus" seem related to a particular ideology with well-established antecedents that go back to the very inception of Creole studies.

2.4   Haitian Creole Morphology in the Creole Life Cycle: On Decreolization and Relexification

Let us look at the details of the repeated claims that HC derivational morphology has few productive affixes (see, e.g., Valdman 1978, 148). According to superficial analyses of HC morphology, when an HC word has a potentially affixal ending (*-syon*, say, as in *adorasyon* 'adoration') with an existing French counterpart (e.g., French *adoration*), then the corresponding HC word is considered an unanalyzed simplex loanword from French (Valdman 1978, 131, 139, 142, etc.). In other words, HC *adorasyon*, unlike French *adoration* (and unlike English *adoration*), is understood to lack internal structure. Similar arguments are advanced by Hall (1953, 34, 36), D'Ans (1968, 26), and Lefebvre (1998, 311).

What about HC words ending in *syon* that have no French counterparts? Valdman counts such HC *Xsyon* words (e.g., *vivasyon* 'subsistence' and *desidasyon* 'decision' in (3a)) as "pseudo-French." Not only does Valdman (like Samarin (1980, 221)) consider that HC morphology (or lack thereof) is a structural "obstacle" to HC's "lexical enrichment"; he has repeatedly argued (e.g., 1978, 144, 148, 293; 1987, 111, 120; 1988, 75; 1989, 59) that one of the structural symptoms of the monolingual HC speaker's "diglossic fantasy" and of HC's decreolization is the use of hypercorrective "pseudo-French" forms. These forms, as produced by non-Francophone HC speakers, mimic various kinds of French derivational processes that are not productive in HC. Valdman's examples of hypercorrections via "pseudo-French" affixation include the following words, (affix string underlined):[8]

(3) a. desida<u>syon</u> 'decision'   cf. deside 'to decide'
        viva<u>syon</u> 'subsistence'   cf. viv 'to live'
     b. ajout<u>man</u> 'addition'   cf. ajoute 'to add'
        finis<u>man</u> 'completion'   cf. fini 'to finish'
        remesis<u>man</u> 'thanks'   cf. remèsye 'to thank'

   c. esklava<u>j</u> 'slavery'   cf. esklav 'slave'
   d. edika<u>syone</u> 'to educate'   cf. edika<u>syon</u> 'education', edike 'to
                                                                educate'
   e. an jeneral<u>man</u> 'generally'   cf. an jeneral 'in general'
      fin<u>man</u> 'completely'   cf. fen 'end', fini 'to end',
                                                                'completed'
      souva<u>man</u> 'often'   cf. souvan 'often'
      toujou<u>man</u> 'always'   cf. toujou 'always'

Valdman claims that the forms in (3) "sound more like French than their authentically Haitian counterparts" (1987, 111); in other words, the "pseudo-French" forms in (3) are "nonexistent derivatives formed by adjoining occurring French suffixes to the 'wrong' [HC] stems" (1988, 75). The implication is that HC's productive morphology is "very weak" (Valdman 1978, 144); HC is thus bound to remain dependent on French for its lexical expansion.

The French influence in Haiti, like that of Latin in Francophone countries, manifests itself by its effect on the vernacular lexicon: French is the source of most HC neologisms. (Valdman 1979, 99; my translation)

In effect, such a perspective erroneously confuses etymology and morphology: the diachronic/etymological source of much of HC morphology is localized in the seventeenth- and eighteenth-century French lexicon, but HC synchronic morphology (e.g., as part of the idiolects of monolingual HC speakers with no exposure to French) functions independently of French. Furthermore, Hall's, D'Ans's and Valdman's positions are straightforwardly disconfirmed by morphologically complex *Haitianisms* —HC morphological innovations with no cognates in the source languages—which cannot be "loaned" from French since, by definition, they have no counterparts in French. The same is true with respect to HC affixes that are etymologically related to, say, Spanish (e.g., in (2e)). In fact, Haitianisms are quite common, and many of them are listed in HC dictionaries, including Valdman et al. 1981 and Valdman, Pooser, and Jean-Baptiste 1996. There, they are not flagged as "pseudo-French"; instead, they are correctly acknowledged as bona fide HC words.

Let us now turn to further preliminary data. Consider for example HC *Xsyon* words, which both Valdman (1978, 139) and Lefebvre (1998, 311) take to be simplex in HC (I come back to Lefebvre's empirical claims below). HC has scores of *Xsyon* words that are morphologically *and* semantically related to their stem *X*, often with a high degree of transparency, as in French (and as in English, for that matter), as shown in (4).

(Here and throughout, I give only the meanings that are relevant to establishing the (degree of) semantic relationship. The reader is invited to consult HC native speakers and/or Freeman and Laguerre 1996 [1998] for additional meanings and/or phonological variants.)

(4) administrasyon 'administration' cf. administre 'to administer'
  admirasyon 'admiration'   cf. admire 'to admire'
  adorasyon 'adoration'   cf. adore 'to adore'
  aplikasyon 'application'   cf. aplike 'to apply'
  debakasyon 'disembarkation' cf. debake 'to disembark'
  diskisyon 'discussion'   cf. diskite 'to discuss'
  dominasyon 'domination'   cf. domine 'to dominate'
  edikasyon 'education'   cf. edike 'to educate'
  esplikasyon 'explanation'   cf. esplike 'to explain'
  enpòtasyon 'importation'   cf. enpòte 'to import'
  enskripsyon 'registration'   cf. enskri 'to register'
  entwodiksyon 'introduction' cf. entwodi 'to introduce'
  fòmasyon 'training'   cf. fòme 'to train'
  fòmasyon 'puberty'   cf. fòme 'to undergo puberty'
  imigrasyon 'immigration'   cf. imigre 'to immigrate'
  imitasyon 'imitation'   cf. imite 'to imitate'
  kalkilasyon 'calculation'   cf. kalkile 'to calculate'
  òganizasyon 'organization'   cf. òganize 'to organize'
  ogmantasyon '(pay) raise'   cf. ogmante 'to increase'
  operasyon 'surgery'   cf. opere 'to perform surgery'
  otorizasyon 'authorization' cf. otorize 'to authorize'
  patisipasyon 'participation' cf. patisipe 'to participate'
  pinisyon 'punishment'   cf. pini 'to punish'
  plantasyon 'plantation'   cf. plante 'to plant'
  pwopozisyon 'proposition'   cf. pwopoze 'to propose'
  reyalizasyon 'achievement' cf. reyalize 'to achieve'

The examples in (4) suggest that *-syon* affixation in HC is both productive and by and large regular: witness the transparency of the morphophonological and semantic relationship between the members of the *X/Xsyon* pairs in (4). This is in opposition to Valdman's (1978, 131, 139, 142) and Lefebvre's (1998, 311) claims that *-syon* is not productive in HC. Their argument goes like this: since the *-syon*-ending forms they examine tend to have close French analogues, it can, and should, be argued that they have all been inherited directly from French as unanalyzed simplex words. As already mentioned, this argument constitutes an erroneous conflation of etymology and morphology: the synchronic morphological processes in the minds/brains of HC speakers cannot be explained away by invoking HC-French etymological links. Morphologically transparent cases of -*syon* suffixation are rather frequent in HC; for example, they number about 3 pages in Freeman's (1989) 87-page inverse word list. Therefore, the null hypothesis is that the data in (4) reflect a productive relation between *Xsyon* and *X* in the minds/brains of HC speakers. This relation extends to the formation of words such as those in (5), which may count as Haitianisms (see note 6).[9]

(5) dekoupasyon 'dividing wall,   cf. dekoupe 'to cut up, to carve'
        screen'
      eklerasyon 'enlightenment'   cf. eklere 'to enlighten'
      levasyon 'education, upbringing'   cf. leve 'to educate, to rear'
      pansyon 'anxiety'   cf. panse 'to think'
      pèdisyon 'false pregnancy,   cf. pèdi 'to lose'
        menorrhagia'
      vivasyon 'conviviality'   cf. viv 'to live'

Many of these (dialectal) Haitianisms are documented in Freeman 1989, Freeman and Laguerre 1996 [1998], and Fattier 1998, 242, 250–251, 320. *Vivasyon* in (5) is kindly reported by Yves Dejean (personal communication) among other data that attest to the formation of morphologically complex neologisms in (monolingual) HC with -*syon* and other suffixes (but see note 6). According to Y. Dejean, *vivasyon* is a very common HC word in Fort-Royal, used among Haitians who have no French input whatsoever.[10] For the residents of Fort-Royal, *vivasyon* means 'conviviality', which is a distinct meaning from the one reported by Valdman as the "pseudo-French" rendition of 'subsistence'. Both 'conviviality' and 'subsistence' are semantically related to their stem *viv* 'to live': both meanings are concerned with "support" for life, either physical or emotional, in some extended sense of "support." Thus, both Y. Dejean's *vivasyon* 'conviviality' and Valdman's *vivasyon* 'subsistence' are manifestations of productive derivation with the "authentically Haitian" suffix -*syon*. (Y. Dejean also reports the use of HC *vitès* as a synonym of *vivasyon* in the South, outside of Fort-Royal. Another meaning of *vitès* is 'speed', from *vit* 'fast' (cf. *delika/delikatès* 'delicate/delicateness', *gwòs/gwòsès* 'pregnant/pregnancy', *laj/lajès* 'generous/generosity', *ti/titès* 'small/childhood', etc.). As Y. Dejean reminds me, *titès* is a bona fide

Haitianism that attests to the productivity of yet another HC suffix, contra Valdman and Lefebvre; also see note 18.)

The data in (5) directly contradict Lefebvre's (1998, 311) claim that "-*yon* is *only* found in Haitian words that correspond *exactly* to French words." In fact, Haitianisms with -*syon* are also found in Freeman's (1989) inverse word list and in Freeman and Laguerre's (1996 [1998]) HC-English dictionary. Lefebvre (1998, 311) labels both *admirasyon* and *adopsyon* as ungrammatical. She assigns them "*" because they are not found in Valdman et al.'s (1981) dictionary; the latter is thus erroneously taken as an exhaustive listing of the mental lexicons of HC speakers. Yet both words not only are common in HC, but in fact are listed both in Freeman's (1989) inverse word list and Freeman and Laguerre's (1996 [1998]) dictionary. (Strangely enough, Lefebvre (1998, 311) writes that "[a]n examination of the list of Haitian nouns ending in -*yon* in Freeman's (1988) inverse dictionary supports [her] claims.")[11]

In any case, the presence of neologisms formed with -*syon* is clear evidence that -*syon* is productive in the mental lexicons of HC speakers. Fattier (1998, 250–251, etc.) provides further support for the morphological productivity of HC, including Haitianisms with -*syon*, contra Valdman and Lefebvre. Fattier's data essentially come from monolingual HC speakers who have had little or no contact with French. Therefore, the abundant and diverse attestation of morphologically complex Haitianisms in her data lay to rest the oft-repeated claim that HC is dependent on French when it comes to "lexical enrichment."

Let us return to the list of alleged "pseudo-French" hypercorrections in (3). As for *edikasyone* in (3d), this neologism (or perhaps hapax legomenon) enlists two "authentically Haitian" suffixes: the nominal suffix -*syon*, as in (4) and (5), and the verbal marker -*e(n)*, as in (2h). *Edikasyone* is constructed exactly like other "authentically Haitian" complex words.

(6) estas<u>yone</u> 'to park'   cf. estasyon 'station'
    keks<u>yone</u> 'to question'   cf. keksyon 'question'
    koleks<u>yone</u> 'to collect'   cf. koleksyon 'collection'
    komis<u>yone</u> 'to commission'   cf. komisyon 'commission'
    pans<u>yone</u> 'to think, to ponder' cf. pansyon 'thought, anxiety'

Interestingly, Fattier (1998, 242) mentions *pansyone* as a dialectal case of a doubly suffixed (recursive) neological formation: the verb *pansyone* is a Haitianism that is derived from the noun *pansyon*, which in turn is a Haitianism derived from the verb *panse* 'to think'.[12] Thus, the verb *panse* in (6) recursively gives rise to the neological verb *pansyone* the same way the verb *edike* in (3d) gives rise to the neological verb (or hapax legomenon) *edikasyone*. Both *pansyone* and *edikasyone* are "authentically Haitian" neologisms that conform to HC word formation processes.

In DeGraff 2000b, I give data and arguments in favor of the productivity of other HC affixes, including all those claimed by Valdman to constitute "pseudo-French" affixation (see (3)). Fattier's (1998) corpus of monolingual HC contains similar data. Such data falsify the claims that HC is by and large morphologically unproductive and that many morphologically complex words "sound more like French than their authentically Haitian counterparts" (Valdman 1987, 111). I would argue that, on the contrary, the HC suffixes in (1)–(6) *are* all "authentically Haitian," notwithstanding their etymological links to and other surface similarities with other languages (for the most part, French). Morphology is not reducible to etymology and/or sociolinguistics. The *socially oriented uses* of superficially French-related neologisms and hapax legomena may well implicate etymological and sociolinguistic factors of the sort discussed by Valdman, but at the level of *grammatical competence*, the language-internal combinatorial properties of these derivations are "authentically Haitian."

In fact, that words "borrowed" from French into HC would also give rise to productive affixation should come as no surprise: processes of language contact do not exclude morphological (re)analysis of cognate forms (see, e.g., Weinreich 1953, 31ff.). In English, too, we find words adopted from French (perhaps as simplex, unanalyzed wholes) that have given rise to productive morphological processes that are divorced from the morphosyntax of the French etymological cognates. This is, for example, the case with the English *-ee* suffix (in, e.g., *payee*), originally from the French (feminine) past participle (e.g., *payé(e)*). French *-é(e)* was most likely borrowed as a "fossilized" form into English. Note that English, unlike French, does not mark gender agreement on its participles. French *-é(e)* may have entered English as *-ee* in sixteenth-century English legal documents, as in *appelee* (see, e.g., Barker 1998, 699). Here we may be dealing with the influence on English *-ee* of the (purely orthographic) marking of feminine gender on the past participle of French verbs in *-er*: masculine *appelé* and feminine *appelée* are both pronounced /apəle/. Yet, notwithstanding its *etymology* (and sociohistorical derivation) from French words borrowed into sixteenth-century legal texts as fossilized (i.e., simplex and unanalyzed) units, English *-ee* has since become autonomously productive in English *morphology* and gives rise to neologisms such as English *vendee* ('purchaser'; cf. French *vendu* 'sold'), *nominee, electee, biographee, plannee, tutee, expellee, abusee, asylee* (see Barker 1998, 699).

A similar situation is expected to obtain in other cases of language contact, as in the genesis of HC. The data above tell us that French complex words, even if inherited as simplexes from very specific lexical domains, can in principle give way to morphological (re)analysis. Such (post-borrowing) morphological (re)analysis is obviously subject to complex language-internal and language-external conditions, but it is always likely to take place given the right structural and ecological conditions. The data in (1)–(2) even include one HC suffix with Spanish etymology, namely -*adò* (cf. the Spanish agentive suffix -*dor*). Yet one would not want to claim that *babyadò* 'griper' and *vantadò* 'braggart' manifest "pseudo-Spanish hypercorrections" or that all Haitians have "relative proficiency" in Spanish; compare Valdman's (1988, 73) claim about every Haitian's "relative proficiency" in French. Notwithstanding its Spanish etymology, in the minds/brains of HC speakers -*adò* is an "authentically Haitian" productive suffix. The suffix -*adò* has its diachronic origins in cockfighting arenas near the Haitian-Dominican border (see, e.g., Faine 1936, 45–46), but it has now become fully integrated into the HC lexicon and its scope includes concepts that are not at all related to cockfighting: for example, *petadò* 'farter' (cf. *pete* 'to fart') and *mantadò* 'liar' (cf. *manti* 'to lie'). Furthermore, synchronically HC -*adò* is structurally distinct from Spanish -*dor*. The latter attaches to a verbal root with an intervening theme vowel, as for example in *luchador* 'fighter' and *mentidor* 'liar'. The corresponding verbs, *luchar* 'to fight' and *mentir* 'to lie', have distinct theme vowels, *a* and *i*. As HC *babyadò* from *babye* and *mantadò* from *manti* show, HC -*adò* does not manifest theme-vowel distinctions. Spanish's most common theme vowel has been reanalyzed as an integral part of the agentive suffix, leading to the creation of HC -*adò* with its own combinatorial properties: -*adò* attaches to appropriate verbal stems, independently of their verbal markers. (I thank Karlos Arregi for pointing out to me the HC-Spanish -*adò*/-*dor* differences.) In the relevant respects, the etymology of HC -*adò* resembles that of English -*ee*: borrowing followed by reanalysis, then productive affixation, all in a relatively short diachronic span.

Are the other affixes in (1)–(2) as productive as -*syon* and -*adò*? Advocates of morphologically reduced Creole prototypes may argue that the above sample is only an illusion and that the (alleged?) morphological processes in (2) are not all productive. As noted, I argue elsewhere

(DeGraff 2000b) that HC word formation processes of the sort sketched in (1)–(2) are, to various degrees, truly productive. My claims receive much empirical support from the data in Fattier 1998. Here I will simply note that many of the complex words in (2) are HC neologisms (Haitian-isms), formally and/or semantically, with no apparent cognate in the source languages (e.g., *dekreta* and *debaba, enkoutab, babyadò* and *van-tadò*; also see *safte* 'greed' in note 18). Thus, we really are in the presence of creative word formation patterns that can be reduced neither to relexi-fication as Lefebvre claims, nor to simplex unproductive fossilizations (e.g., Hall's "Gallicisms"), nor to Valdman's "pseudo-French hyper-corrections" or borrowings.

In summary, this first case study tells us that what Valdman calls "pseudo-French" words in HC are actually morphologically complex words built according to word formation processes that are productive in (monolingual) HC. In some cases, such "pseudo-French" words, like *ajoutman* 'addition' (cf. French *ajoutement* in Rey 1995, 41), may have entered the HC lexicon at its very inception, via the regional varieties of French spoken in colonial Saint-Domingue (as Haiti was known until it gained independence in 1804). Such synchronic and diachronic consider-ations cast further doubt on Valdman's diagnostics for "pseudo-French" decreolization. In fact, HC manifests a robust set of productive affixes that allow lexical expansion from HC's internal morphological resources. The data surveyed here also cast doubt on Lefebvre's arguments regard-ing a virtual one-to-one isomorphism between HC and Fongbe affixes (also see notes 7 and 18).

2.5 On Prototypes and Stereotypes: Haitian Creole as a "Regular" Language

The "simple Creole morphology" orthodoxy illustrated in section 2.4 also manifests itself in proposals for Creole prototypes. Such a prototype is delineated most saliently in McWhorter 1998. Like the analyses in section 2.4 in which Creole morphology is deemed underproductive, McWhorter's prototype is straightforwardly disconfirmed by samples of HC data.

In McWhorter 1998, a relatively well defined type of "simple mor-phology" is said to be a criterion for Creoleness, and is viewed as the direct result of Creole genesis and of Creoles' status as young languages. It is worth quoting McWhorter's article at length, as his are currently the most explicit, articulate, and categorical statements regarding the typological profile of Creole morphology in diachrony and synchrony. Yet, it must also be noted that the basic tenets of McWhorter's prototypes are not original: as documented in section 2.6, these tenets find antecedents in previous claims going back to Saint-Quentin 1872, Jespersen 1922, Hjelmslev 1938, 1939, and Seuren and Wekker 1986.[13]

Throughout the history of Creole studies, the characterization of prototypical Creole morphology has opposed Creoles to an alleged class of "regular" or "normal" languages. McWhorter characterizes "simple Creole morphology" as follows (as elsewhere in this chapter, emphasis is added for expository purposes):

[R]ich paradigms of derivation affixes[, as exemplified by Mon-Khmer languages, are] *alien* to any language known as a creole. (McWhorter 1998, 796)

[C]reoles are the *only* natively spoken languages in the world that combine all three of the following traits:

1. little or no inflectional affixation
2. little or no use of tone to lexically contrast monosyllables or encode syntax
3. semantically regular derivational affixation. (McWhorter 1998, 798)

Among McWhorter's (1998) claims regarding the cognitive roots and diachronic path of Creole morphogenesis are these:

[T]he rapid non-native adoption of a language as a lingua franca entails stripping down a system to its essentials, for *optimal learnability and processibility*. The natural result is *the virtual or complete elimination of affixes, sometimes replaced by more immediately transparent analytic constructions*. (p. 793)

[Inflection, lexically contrasting tone, and semantically irregular derivation] *only* develop internally as the result of gradual development over long periods of time [over millennia]. (pp. 792–793; also see pp. 798, 812)

[D]iachronically, inflectional morphology typically results from *gradual processes of reanalysis such as the grammaticalization of erstwhile lexical items*. (p. 793)

Derivational apparatus ... tends to be *eschewed* by creole creators or incorporated in *fossilized* form. Meanwhile, the way derivation typically emerges in language is via *gradual grammaticalization*. (p. 798; also see p. 793)

The semantic irregularity of derivation arises from the inevitable process of semantic drift and metaphorical inference ... (p. 798)

Over millennia, [prototypical Creole] traits will certainly gradually disappear, rendering [Creole] languages indistinguishable from others synchronically. (p. 812)

It is HC that McWhorter regards as one of the "most creole of creoles" and one of "the 'pure' [prototypical] cases," claiming that HC "fulfill[s] all three [prototype] qualifications"—in fact, that it "display[s] *all three* prototype traits in their *purest* form" (pp. 809, 812):

1. *no* use of tone to contrast monosyllables or encode syntax;
2. *no* inflectional affixes; [and]
3. derivational affixes whose semantic contribution is *consistently transparent.*
(McWhorter 1998, 809)

McWhorter is correct in stating that HC does not make use of tone, although it is not theoretically clear why loss of lexical tone should be a defining characteristic of creolization: does lexical tone in, say, Chinese languages "combine low perceptual saliency with low import to basic communication" (McWhorter 1998, 792)? What is the independent measure of "perceptual saliency"? What is "basic communication"? Can "basic communication" in Chinese (interlanguage) bypass the use of tonal distinctions? The latter are at the core of lexical distinctions in Chinese in the same way a (toneless) phonemic inventory is at the core of lexical distinctions in HC—say, between *manman* /mãmã/ 'mother' and *chwal* /ʃwal/ 'horse'. In China, as in Haiti, 'mother' and 'horse' are concepts that may need to be carefully distinguished, even in "basic communication." In Chinese, such lexical contrasts enlist tonal distinctions, which, in McWhorter's (1998, 794) words, require "subtlety of perception unlikely to develop amidst the rapid, utilitarian acquisition typical of settings which give birth to a contact language." In this vein, it must be noted that there exist HC phonemic distinctions which, like Chinese tone, apparently require "subtlety of perception" to the extent that they have gone undetected, not only by naive nonnative speakers "amidst ... rapid, utilitarian acquisition," but even by expert linguists deliberately collecting data in the slow and controlled settings typical of informant sessions (for an overview, see Y. Dejean 1977, 316–326; 1980, 89–94; 1999). This seems rather unexpected if Creoles must develop phonemic inventories that combine high "perceptual saliency" with high "import to basic communication."

When we look at inflection, things get murkier for the prototype proposal. "Loss" of overt inflectional distinctions is not exclusive to creolization, but seems generally symptomatic of language acquisition under "duress" as in various cases of language contact. This was noted long ago by, for example, Meillet (1919, 201) and Weinreich (1953, sec. 2.3); see note 2. In DeGraff 1999a,b,d, 2000a,b, I compare the status of inflection and of some of its syntactic correlates in creolization, language change, and language acquisition, and I conclude that creoles are no more and no less than the result of extraordinary external factors coupled with ordinary internal factors; that is, creoles, alongside language change, are the result of particular types of language contact whose effects on attained grammars are mediated by the contact situation's unstabilizing influence on the triggering experience. (DeGraff 1999b, 477)

In fact, this conclusion is inescapable within a Cartesian, Universal Grammar (UG)–based approach to language contact, as "creolization and language change ultimately reduce to universal mental processes taking place in individual speakers acting as language acquirers and language users" (DeGraff 1999b, 524). In this vein, UG implements what Meillet (1906 [1958, 17]) refers to as "the general conditions of development from a purely linguistic point of view"; that is, UG provides patterns in creolization, language change, and language acquisition, with a cognitive and grammatical "tether" of just the right length (cf. Weinreich, Labov, and Herzog 1968, 139, 176). It is thus not surprising that we find that the "erosion" of inflectional morphology and/or the regularization of morphological distinctions recur in the history of *any* language (whether "old" or "new"); this is standard fare in historical linguistics. Of course, "simplification" in one domain entails "complexification" in others (see below), while processes such as grammaticalization (e.g., of free morphemes into bound morphemes) may offset the results of morphological erosion—recall Givón's popular phrase, "Yesterday's syntax is today's morphology," which goes back to traditional insights from (e.g.), Bopp, Humboldt, and Meillet.

What about the functional teleology of inflectional loss? As with tone, it is not clear that "virtual or complete elimination of [inflectional] affixes" is necessarily correlated with *maximum* "processibility," pace McWhorter (1998, 793); also see Hjelmslev's (1938, 1939) "Creole optimum." One can reasonably make the following argument: if inflection is the morphological encoding of morphosyntactic features and relations, then having inflection *overtly* manifested at PF does contribute to, say, the preservation of overt contrasts and the recoverability of underlying semantics, which is surely a boon for the online decoding of abstract morphosyntactic and semantic features and relations. In fact, given the competing need for perceptual (vs. production) processibility, one could as easily wonder why—or to what extent—inflectional morphology is, as a rule, diachronically subject to erosion despite its apparent parser-friendly "redundancy" (see, e.g., Labov 1994, 586–599; DeGraff 1999b, 523, 534 n. 47). Then again, the increased "form-function opacity" due to case syncretism, as for example in the history of English and Romance, is somewhat compensated by increased rigidity in word order, which serves to encode (some of) the function of moribund case affixes. (Joan Bresnan's recent formalist/functionalist work within Optimality Theory comes to mind as one explicit implementation of similar questions regarding competing factors in morphosyntactic change (see, e.g., Bresnan, to appear). In Bresnan's words, "Markedness of course has many conflicting dimensions" (cf. Mufwene 1991 on markedness conflicts in specific language contact cases: "[G]iven the diversity of factors determining markedness, such conflicts are to be expected"; p. 138).)

On the terminological/conceptual side, the very notion of inflection is theory-internal, and the boundaries between pieces of inflection and pieces of derivation vary from framework to framework; indeed, there are frameworks in which such boundaries dissolve altogether (see Stump 1998, 18–19, for an overview). When the inflection-versus-derivation distinction is relevant (or, rather, the distinction between the inflectional/ syntactic and derivational/lexical *functions* of morphology), its applicability should depend on the precise lexicosemantics and morphosyntactic facts of the language(s) at hand (see, e.g., Stump 1998). No (theoretically usable) definition is given in McWhorter 1998. Thus, the label *inflection* is used here pretheoretically (cf. the analyses of further relevant facts in DeGraff 2000b). This said, HC does have a certain amount of productive and systematic morphological marking for natural gender. In some cases, this morphology is contextually determined. In (7), I give a small sample from DeGraff 2000b.

(7) a. Ameriken/Amerikèn 'American+masc/fem'
      Ayisyen/Ayisyèn 'Haitian+masc/fem'
      Fransè/Fransèz 'French+masc/fem'
      Kapwa/Kapwaz '(person+masc/fem) from Cape Haitian'
      wangatè/wangatèz 'man/woman who believes in and/or makes magical fetishes'

   b. Manman m se   yon Ayisyèn/*Ayisyen.
      mother 1SG RES-PRON a   Haitian+FEM/*Haitian+MASC
      'My mother is a Haitian.'

   c. Manman m se   Ayisyèn/Ayisyen.
      mother 1SG RES-PRON Haitian+FEM/Haitian+MASC
      'My mother is Haitian.'

   d. ... fanm   Ayisyèn/*Ayisyen
        woman Haitian+FEM/*Haitian+MASC
      '... Haitian women ...'

The last pair in (7a), *wangatè/wangatèz*, is one of the Haitianisms that testify to the productivity of HC gender marking: the stem *wanga* is etymologically Bantu, from Kikongo (P. Baker 1993, 145–146; Fattier 1998, 599), and the inflected suffix *-è/èz* is etymologically French. Other cases of neological formations with gender marking are documented in DeGraff 2000b. In (7b), gender inflection on the nominal head of the nonbare predicate (masculine /ajisjẽ/ vs. feminine /ajisjɛn/) is determined via obligatory agreement with a governing subject. In (7c), gender inflection appears optional when the predicate is bare. In (7d), gender agreement is obligatory. Thus far, the facts are preliminary and ill understood, but it appears that the obligatory/optional marking of gender is related to both the semantic class of the predicate head and the structure of the predicate projection. That is, the contrast between (7b) and (7c) and the apparent "optionality" in (7c) seem lexically and syntactically driven. It goes without saying that only an explicit theory of morphology can spell out the conditions under which the pieces of HC gender inflection relate to the lexicon and/or the syntax.

Verbal truncation (or apocope) is another manifestation of inflectional morphology in HC. Like other French-lexifier Creoles (see, e.g., Syea 1992), HC has a class of verbs that are truncated in certain environments (see Hall 1953, 30, for a sample).

(8) a. Konbyen dan   Tonton Bouki gen*(yen)?
       how-many tooth Uncle   Bouki has
       'How many teeth does Uncle Bouki have?'
    b. Tonton Bouki gen(*yen) 32 dan   l.
       Uncle   Bouki has   32 tooth 3sg
       'Uncle Bouki has (all of) his 32 teeth.'

In (8a), the object *konbyen dan* 'how many teeth' is *wh*-moved, which makes the verb the last overt element in the VP. In this case, the long form, *genyen*, surfaces *obligatorily* in my idiolect. In (8b), where the verb is followed by its object, *32 dan l* '(all of) his 32 teeth', truncation is strongly preferred, at least in the dialects I am familiar with where *gen* usually surfaces when the object remains in situ. (In my idiolect, *genyen* in (8b) would be interpreted as the HC form for 'to win', which need not undergo apocope.) There are additional facts that complicate the picture. For example, pronominal objects, unlike full NP objects, do not force truncation. Emphasis disfavors truncation even when a full NP follows a verb. In addition, there is much dialectal variation that I cannot address here. This said, in pursuing a theoretical treatment of the apocope illustrated in (8), one can reasonably hypothesize that *genyen* 'to have' decomposes morphologically as *gen-yen*, *-yen* being an inflectional morpheme (a verbal marker or a *v* head?) whose realization is regulated by subtle morphosyntactic and/or morphophonological factors.

Yet another (overt) inflectional contrast exists in HC, namely, between the transitive and intransitive forms of certain predicates such as *fè/fèt* 'make/made' and *kowonp/kowonpi* 'corrupt/corrupted'.

(9) a. Mwen fè/*fèt kabann lan rapid-rapid maten   an.
       1SG   make bed   the fast-fast   morning the
       'I made the bed very quickly this morning.'
   b. Kabann lan fèt/*fè rapid-rapid maten   an.
       bed   the made fast-fast   morning the
       'The bed was made very quickly this morning.'

The "displaced" position of *kabann lan* in (9b) mirrors that of *John* in the English passive *John was seen*; likewise, the morphological contrast between *fè* /fɛ/ in (9a) and *fèt* /fɛt/ mirrors that between the English active *see* and passive *seen*. The contrast between HC *fè* and *fèt* in (9) is another potential counterexample to the alleged absence of inflectional morphology in HC. With *fè* in (9a), the theme is in object position; with *fèt* in (9b), the theme is in subject position. Assuming that the alternation in (9) is derived in the syntax (contra, e.g., Ritter 1991) and assuming M. Baker's (1988) Mirror Principle, the grammatical-function change in (9) is "signaled" by morphology "in" the syntax. The overt morphological alternation in *fè/fèt* as in (9) is relatively rare. Nonetheless, given the systematicity of HC clauses that are syntactically similar to the pair in (9), inflectional morphology would mark all such grammatical-function changes, whether or not the morphological exponent of this inflection is overt (see M. Baker 1988, 284; also see DeGraff 1994, 1997, 1999b,d, 2000a,b, for further remarks on HC verbal morphology, and Damoiseau 1988, 1991, and Ritter 1991 for more extensive discussion, alternative analyses, and further references).

The use of reduplication to mark intensification (e.g., *mache-mache* 'to walk a lot' and *bèl-bèl* 'very beautiful'; see (2o)) may also count as an example of inflectional morphology: in such cases, "aspect" is marked, not by a freestanding preverbal morpheme, but by reduplication of the predicate. (Thanks to Benjamin Bruening for pointing out the relevance of HC reduplication vis-à-vis the status of Creole inflectional morphology.)

That the above instances of inflectional marking in HC target specific word classes while showing apparent "gaps" (e.g., vis-à-vis gender, apocope, grammatical-function change, and intensifiability) is not surprising. Even in its most robustly overt instantiations, inflection need not apply uniformly to stems of a given category; witness, for example, Russian "indeclinable nouns"—borrowings that do not inflect for morphological case (Halle 1994, 39).

Now, what about transparency? In principle, any Creole prototype with "derivational affixes whose semantic contribution is consistently transparent" constitutes an *un*natural (i.e., artificial) language that contradicts the *universal* Saussurean arbitrariness of the lexical sign (see note 26 on Creoles as "artificial languages"). Given Saussure's notion of the *arbitraire du signe*, *any* natural language should be expected to manifest opaque lexicalizations. There is a priori no reason why Creole creators and Creole speakers should be unable to create and store as independent units derivationally complex words with idiosyncratic (i.e., nontransparent and noncompositional) semantics. Such opaque lexicalizations apply, not only at the level of syntax (e.g., phrasal idioms), but also at the level of the word (e.g., "idiosyncratic lexicalizations," which we may call "word-level idioms"). Saussure's *arbitraire du signe* and recent results in (psycho)linguistics (see below) suggest that speakers of any language should be able to store morphologically and syntactically complex forms in their mental lexicons. The relevant properties of word-level and phrasal idioms are stored in the mental lexicon, alongside simplex lexemes (see, e.g., Aronoff 1976; Jackendoff 1995; Marantz 1997; Pinker 1999; and references therein). Saussure's *arbitraire du signe*—the arbitrary and holistic relationship between "signifié" and "signifiant"—applies both to formally simplex units and to formally complex combinations. The latter are composed by merging the former at either the word or the phrase level.

The processes underlying the (opaque) lexicalization of morphologically complex items (see, e.g., Aronoff 1976, 10ff.) are not fundamentally separate from those underlying the storage of syntactically complex idioms (see, e.g., Jackendoff 1995 and Marantz 1997; also see note 19). As Saussure argued, both word-level lexicalizations and phrase-level lexicalizations ("idiom formation") instantiate the *arbitraire du signe*. That is, both kinds entail the lexical association of formally complex signs with arbitrary (i.e., nonpredictable and noncompositional) semantics. As far as I can tell, the *arbitraire du signe* can be expected to hold of *all* human speakers—human long-term memory does not appear to be short on neurons for the storing of "idiosyncratic" information. The ability to store formal and semantic idiosyncrasies at both the word and the phrase level is (by definition) at the very root of our language faculty, especially the lexicon.

Let us, furthermore, assume that the creation of idioms is part and parcel of human cognition via, say, associative memory and the universal human capacity for metaphorical reasoning, as manifested for example in children's "fast mapping" and lexical innovations (see Clark 1993 and references therein). If so, idiom formation can, in principle, apply to the results of morphological derivation—hence the universal capacity for what McWhorter (1998, 797) calls "endless idiosyncratic lexicalizations." The latter are not the exclusive province of "old" languages since semantic opacity can develop even in the absence of semantic drift and inference "over millennia" (contra McWhorter 1998, 798, 812). As Stump (1998, 17) writes, "[t]he semantic 'drift' typical of derivation need not be understood in diachronic terms."

Take *going postal* (i.e., the sudden manifestation of homicidal rage toward one's coworkers), *Monica-gate* (the political turmoil surrounding Bill Clinton and Monica Lewinsky's sexual relationship), and *red-eye* (in the sense of "overnight flight"). These are "catastrophic" neologisms that seem to have developed "overnight" (no puns intended). They require a fair amount of encyclopedic and cultural inference for interpretation, although they occupy different regions on the continuum of metaphorical drift and semantic opacity. However, the point is that their respective opacity seems to bear little relation to the length of their diachronic life span. The semantic unpredictability of *some* complex words does arise via diachronic grammaticalization and gradual metaphorical drift, but this is not the exclusive source of noncompositionality in the lexicon.

Similar "instantaneously" neological and semantically idiosyncratic derivations both exist in HC (DeGraff 2000b) and arise through acquisition (Clark 1993). In fact, Creole languages are well known for the multifunctionality of their lexicon. Such multifunctionality arises for example via zero-derivation, which is the semantically "vague" derivational process par excellence (Clark and Clark 1979). As Stump (1998, 17) notes:

The semantic idiosyncrasy of many derived lexemes follows not from the fact that their meanings are lexically listed, but from the fact that their meanings are inevitably shaped by pragmatic inferences at the very outset of their existence (and are therefore in *immediate need* of lexical listing).

As expected, semantically opaque zero-derivation is also productive in HC, with the concomitant nontransparent lexicalization occurring rather rapidly.

(10) CIA ta   vle   Noriega Aristide.
     CIA would want Noriega Aristide
     'The CIA would want to [ᵥ *Noriega*] Aristide.' (i.e., bring Aristide to jail in the U.S.)

Recall that, in Saussure's view, all languages are expected to manifest "idiosyncratic lexicalizations" at both the word and the phrase level. Speakers of Creoles are like speakers of any other "regular" languages in terms of cognitive capacities: they have at their disposal both associative memory for lexical storage and combinatorial rules for morphological and syntactic parsing. There is (thus far) no theoretical principle that requires Creoles (qua "regular" languages) to manifest "consistent transparency" in their inherited and innovated morphology in any fashion that would *qualitatively* distinguish them from non-Creole languages. A brief inspection of the examples in (1)–(6) readily suggests that HC suffixation is not consistently transparent to a degree that would radically distinguish it from non-Creole suffixation. HC *-syon*, for example, seems as (non)-transparent as English (or French) *-tion*. For semantically nontransparent *-syon* affixation, see for example *dekoupasyon* 'dividing wall, screen' (cf. *dekoupe* 'to cut up, to carve'), *pansyon* 'anxiety' (cf. *panse* 'to think'), *pèdisyon* 'false pregnancy, menorrhagia' (cf. *pèdi* 'to lose'), and *vivasyon* 'conviviality, subsistence' (cf. *viv* 'to live'). Such semantically opaque derivations are straightforward instantiations of lexical Saussurean arbitrariness, which is naturally expected in Creoles as in any other "regular" languages.

Similarly, cases of semantic opacity are found with most other affixes in HC. Take for example HC *de-*. McWhorter (1998, 797) cites the following four cases from Brousseau, Filipovich, and Lefebvre 1989, 9 (also see Lefebvre 1998, 305–306).

(11) a. pasyante 'to be patient' vs. de-pasyante 'to be impatient'
     b. respekte 'to respect' vs. de-respekte 'to insult'
     c. grese 'to put on weight' vs. de-grese 'to lose weight'
     d. mare 'to tie' vs. de-mare 'to untie'

McWhorter's claim that the entire HC lexicon is consistently transparent is based on just these four pairs of second-hand examples.

Let us first ask whether *de-* is consistently and transparently "inversive" (Brousseau, Filipovich, and Lefebvre 1989; Lefebvre 1998; McWhorter 1998). Actually, McWhorter's claim that *X* and *de-X* are "precise opposites" does not hold of the exceedingly small data set taken from Brousseau, Filipovich, and Lefebvre 1989. The latter authors' claims about HC *de-*, which form the core of McWhorter's argument, are themselves questionable, as work by Damoiseau (1991) and Chaudenson (1996) shows.

First, Damoiseau (1991, 33) has convincingly shown that *derespekte* and *respekte* fall into distinct aspectual and thematic classes. Damoiseau carefully notes that *respekte* is a psychological predicate while *derespekte* denotes an action—an instance of what he (1991, 32) calls a "static" versus "dynamic" contrast. Furthermore, from a θ-role perspective, the θ-role of the subject of *respekte* in a two-argument clause can be described as "experiencer" while the θ-role of the subject of *derespekte* in the same configuration can be described as "agent." Finally, from a tense/aspect perspective, *respekte* without any tense-mood-aspect marking holds of a present situation while *derespekte* in the same environment holds of a nonpresent, completed state of affairs—a situation often referred to in the Africanist and creolist literature as the *factative* effect. In order to achieve a present (imperfective) interpretation, *derespekte* requires the aspect marker *ap*, as shown in the following example from Damoiseau 1991, 33:

(12) a. Ou respekte m.
     2SG respect 1SG
     'You have respect for me.'
   b. Apa w   ap   derespekte m.
     here 2SG PROG disrespect me
     'Now you're "dissing" me!' (i.e., you're showing me disrespect—you're insulting me)

Again, these examples show that HC *respekte* and *derespekte* belong to distinct aspectual and thematic classes. Assuming that these aspectual and thematic classes do not "oppose" each other, then it seems that *respekte* and *derespekte* can hardly quality as "precise opposites," once their semantics are made "precise" enough. Also note that *derespekte* (unlike *demare* 'to untie' in (11d)) is not the kind of action the results of which can be undone; that is, *derespekte*, in its "dynamic" sense, is irreversible (see Horn 1989 for much relevant discussion of the reversibility of the stem to which English *de-* attaches).

There are also empirical problems with respect to *degrese* in (11c) as inversive. As Chaudenson (1996, 27ff.) points out, *degrese* is actually ambiguous between an inversive intransitive reading ('to lose weight' as in (11c)) and a privative transitive reading ('to remove fat'): for example, *degrese vyann* 'to remove the fat from meat'. It is worth noting that these two senses are sometimes expressed by different prefixes in English: *un-* and *de-*. English *un-* in (e.g.) *to uncover* and *to untie* is inversive (cf. *cover* and *tie*) whereas *de-* in *to decaffeinate* ('to remove caffeine from') is privative (cf. *?caffeinate*, which may not even occur, although it is an interpretable potential word).[14] With HC privative *degrese*, the privative reading is hardly inversive at all: there was no previous *grese* action the result of which is inverted/undone by *degrese*, and once the fat is removed from meat to be cooked, it cannot be put back (at least not in the reversible sense).

Neither is *de-* consistently and transparently inversive in (1); see (2a). Take *dekreta* 'to remove the crest'. It is constructed from the nominal base *krèt* 'crest' and there is no **kreta*; *de-* in *dekreta* 'to remove the crest from' is privative/ablative. As for *debaba* 'to mow down', its semantics exhibits the sort of "evolved idiosyncrasy" typical of (word- and phrase-level) idioms: relating the semantics of *debaba* to that of its stem does require "a certain metaphorical imagination," pace McWhorter (1998, 797) (cf. *baba* 'barbaric, idiotic'; *baba* is also a dialectal variant of *bèbè* 'mute'; Yves Dejean, personal communication). In any case, the prefix *de-* in *debaba* does not have any inversive meaning. With the right amount of "metaphorical imagination," *de-* in *debaba* may perhaps be taken as a (quasi-) causative marker, but the overall meaning of *debaba* is unrecoverable from the semantic composition of its morphemes. Further examples of "endless idiosyncratic lexicalizations" abound in, for instance, Valdman et al. 1981; Valdman, Pooser, and Jean-Baptiste 1996; Freeman 1989; Freeman and Laguerre 1996 [1998].

It is notable that HC *de-* even has an intensifying function in some cases, as in *derefize* 'to refuse emphatically' in (13) (cf. *refize* 'to refuse')— this is the quasi inverse of inversive. The list in (13) also includes near-synonymous pairs with subtle semantic and syntactic differences; here too *de-* is not transparently inversive (see DeGraff 2000b for details).

(13) debat 'to struggle, to try'   cf. bat 'to beat; to struggle; etc.'
      dechire 'to tear apart, to tear   cf. chire 'to tear (apart), to
      up'   tear (up)'

defile 'to parade'	cf. file 'to dash away, to flee'
defripe 'to beat, to thrash'	cf. fripe 'to mess up'
degaye 'to mess up'	cf. gaye 'to disperse, to scatter'
degrennen 'to separate 1 by 1, to shell (out)'	cf. grennen 'to shell (out); to scatter'
dekale 'to chip off, to peel off'	cf. kale 'to peel, to skin, to scrape'
dekoupe 'to cut up'	cf. koupe 'to cut'
delage 'to loosen, to untie'	cf. lage 'to release, to give up'
delibere 'to free (a prisoner)'	cf. libere 'to free'
demegri 'to lose weight (emphatic)'	cf. megri 'to lose weight'
depale 'to ramble'	cf. pale 'to speak'
depase 'to exceed, to overtake'	cf. pase 'to pass'
depati 'to stop associating with'	cf. pati 'to depart'
deperi 'to waste away'	cf. peri 'to perish'
derefize 'to refuse (emphatically)'	cf. refize 'to refuse'
detire 'to stretch'	cf. tire 'to pull'
devide 'to empty out'	cf. vide 'to empty'
devire 'to go on a detour'	cf. vire 'to go on a drive, stroll'

Borrowing some turns of phrase from McWhorter (1998, 803–804), it can be said that once the HC data are "viewed more liberally" beyond the "highly selective presentation of data" in McWhorter 1998, 797 (and in Brousseau, Filipovich, and Lefebvre 1989, 9; Lefebvre 1998, 305), various claims on Creole morphology "take on a different perspective."[15] Indeed, contrary to McWhorter's (1998, 797) claim, it is certainly *not* the case that "the [HC] inversive prefix *de-* ... *with few exceptions* transforms a word into its *precise* opposite." A scan of the 24 pages of entries starting with *de* in Freeman and Laguerre's (1996 [1998]) dictionary suggests that cases of inversive *de-* where X and *de-X* are "precise opposites" are not the majority among the reported *de-X* types. That is, *de-* has inversive semantics in only a subset of *de-X* words. In most instances, the "core meaning of the inversive prefix *de-* ... is obscured," as for the Romanian *de-* prefix that McWhorter (1998, 809) takes to illustrate semantically opaque derivation in non-Creole languages. Given such facts, HC *de-* behaves very much like its Romanian counterpart, contrary to the structural divide that McWhorter posits between Creole ("consistently transparent") morphology and non-Creole ("semantically evolved") morphology.

A similar case against "consistent transparency" of Creole morphology can be made with the other derivational processes in (1)–(2). Consider reduplication, illustrated in (2o). It can be semantically transparent, as in its affective use (with proper names: e.g., *Mimich* for *Michèl*) and its intensifying use (e.g., *mache-mache* 'to walk a lot' or *bèl-bèl* 'very beautiful'). (As already noted, this may be yet another example of inflectional— in this case, aspect-marking—morphology, pace McWhorter 1998, 792, 809.) Reduplication can also be semantically opaque (i.e., with unpredictable, noncompositional semantics) as in (e.g.) *youn-youn* '(a) few' from the numeral *youn* 'one' (see Faine 1936, 103; Fattier 1998, 2:843). Next, consider the agentive nominalizer *-adò*, illustrated in (2e). It is semantically transparent in *babyadò* 'griper' (cf. *babye* 'to gripe') and *vantadò* 'braggart' (cf. *vante* 'to brag') but semantically opaque in *kòk-woutchadò*, which overlaps in semantics with *kòk-kriyadò*. *Woutchadò*, for which there is no existing HC stem, presumably derives etymologically from Spanish *luchador* 'fighter'. In a similar vein, *kòk-kriyadò* 'experienced cock' is also opaque, *kriyadò* having been borrowed from Spanish *criado* 'experienced' or from *criador* 'one who trains, breeds, raises, nurtures'.[16] As noted in (2e), the semantically opaque *kriyadò* in *kòk-kriyadò* exists alongside a semantically transparent neologism *kriyadò* 'chronic weeper' (cf. *kriye* 'to weep'). Yet another example among many others where HC manifests "endless idiosyncratic lexicalizations" is *enkoutab* 'foolhardy' in (2b), from *koute* 'to listen'.

Thus, it does seem that HC productive affixes are by and large no more and no less transparent than affixes in other languages. When the database in McWhorter 1998 is expanded, it becomes clear that HC exhibits endless cases of semantically *non*transparent morphology alongside inflectional morphology, thus disconfirming the notion that HC is a "pure case" of the latest Creole prototype.

Do McWhorter's criteria make accurate predictions regarding non-Creole languages? That is, do they prevent non-Creole languages from falling under the classificatory umbrella of the Creole prototype? In fact, there are non-Creole languages that seem closer than HC to the Creole prototype outlined by McWhorter, at least according to the descriptions of Cambodian/Khmer, Chrau, and Palaung in Huffman 1970, Ehrman 1972, Jenner and Pou 1982, Milne 1921, and Thomas 1971. In these descriptions, Cambodian/Khmer, Chrau, and Palaung show no (productive) tone, no (productive) inflection, and mostly moribund derivation.[17] In addition, Chrau manifests other morphosyntactic characteristics that are somewhat reminiscent of familiar "Creole" traits: "zero copula" (Thomas 1971, 75), "verbal adjectives" (Thomas 1971, 110, 148), no overt nominal inflection (Thomas 1971, chap. 8), no overt verbal inflection, tense-mood-aspect and negation morphemes as preverbal unbound markers (Thomas 1971, chap. 9).

That Mon-Khmer manifests "prototypical Creole" properties is not surprising: Creole languages are natural languages acquired by children like any other natural languages. There are surely some tendencies that Creoles as a class may exhibit given their history of formation in abrupt conditions of language contact. However, language contact is not exclusive to Creole genesis, and there is no reason why Creoles qua *regular* natural languages should collectively and exclusively bear a common set of structural features that reflect their history (see note 13). After all, many contingent factors are involved in Creole genesis, including the diverse linguistic ecologies in each contact situation. Beyond broad tendencies toward various degrees of inflectional erosion cum semantic transparency (as noted in, e.g., Meillet 1919 and Weinreich 1953; also see Mufwene 1991; DeGraff 1994, 1997, 1999a,b,d, 2000a,b; and note 2), no set of exclusively Creole prototypical features has been empirically confirmed. Again, this is not surprising once we assume that languages express properties of their speakers' minds/brains: if it could be claimed that Creole languages across time and space constitute a class that can be defined purely structurally so that this class excludes non-Creole languages, then it could be claimed that Creole speakers across time and space also constitute a class of human beings that can be defined *purely* on biological/cognitive grounds, on the basis of mental properties that all and only Creole speakers have (i.e., properties not shared by other human beings). Given what we seem to know about the general uniformity of the species with respect to brain structure, this would be a strange scientific conclusion indeed. This conclusion is also problematic methodologically given Lyell's (1830–1833) Uniformitarian Principle that laws of nature should be assumed to work the same in the present as in the past (also see Labov 1994, 21–24); this is a point I return to in section 2.6 and take up in DeGraff 2000b,c).

What about McWhorter's general diachronic claims that HC (like other prototypical Creoles) developed via an affixless pidgin (i.e., via a "radical break in transmission" that in the limit "eschews" all affixal morphology in the contact languages) and that prototypical Creole affixes develop internally via "gradual grammaticalization" (McWhorter 1998,

788, 792–793, 798, 808, 812)? Such claims are, again, robustly contra-dicted by the available HC data, including the data in McWhorter 1998, 798. In fact, given the linguistic evidence in this chapter, it seems doubtful that the prior existence of a pidgin with drastically reduced morphology is central to the formation of "radical" Creoles such as HC (pace, e.g., Schuchardt 1914; Jespersen 1922; Bloomfield 1933; Hjelmslev 1938; Hall 1953; Valdman 1978; Samarin 1980; Bickerton 1988; Seuren and Wekker 1986; McWhorter 1998; Seuren 1998, 292–293; P. Baker 1999).

Let us reexamine the *de*- prefix mentioned in (11), in particular *de-grese* 'to lose weight, to remove fat/grease'. Chaudenson (1996, 27ff.) points out that seventeenth-century French *dégraisser* is also ambiguous, like its HC descendent. This casts doubt on McWhorter's scenario that HC, as a prototypical Creole, originated from a purely affixless (thus *de*-less) pidgin. In McWhorter's scenario, neither the form nor the (ambiguous) semantics of the French prefix *de*- in *dégraisser* could have been passed down to HC *de*- in *degrese*. At best, HC *degrese* would have been inher-ited as a simplex form. But this is contradicted by the fact that HC *de*- in *degrese* is a productive affix whose form and (ambiguous) semantics in the particular case of *degrese* closely match those of its (seventeenth-century) French counterpart (recall from section 2.4 that affix borrowing does not exclude productivity of the nativized form).

More generally, HC *de*- is etymologically related to the French affix *de*-. There is no sense in which HC *de*- could be argued to have evolved via grammaticalization "over millennia," contra McWhorter (1998, 793, 798, 812). There is no documented unbound cognate for *de*- in (the diachrony of) the HC lexicon. In addition, given the form and semantics of French *de*-, there is no need to postulate such a HC unbound *de*—most of the HC lexicon is etymologically related to seventeenth- and eighteenth-century French (see, e.g., Fattier 1998), and there is no principle that would make derivational affixes immune to this etymological relation. In fact, virtually all HC affixes find their etymological root in morphemes that are affixes in other languages—mostly French, although HC also has affixes with non-French cognates (e.g., *-adò* from Spanish *-dor* illustrated in (2e)). See the discussion on pages 68 and 82 (also see DeGraff 2000b for more extensive details).

Pro-prototype creolists could respond that the bulk of HC productive affixes entered the language via late borrowings owing to heavy lexifier contact postcreolization. But such an argument strikes me as ahistori-cal given that, in Saint-Domingue/Haiti, contact with French was much greater in the seventeenth and eighteenth centuries than after Haiti gained its independence in 1804. As a matter of fact, during the years following the initial European-African contact, the Africans and their descendants became increasingly numerous and increasingly distant from the French speakers. After Haiti gained its independence, the French presence was virtually eliminated in Haiti, except among the tiny bilingual élite whose speech is in general inaccessible to the vast monolingual majority. Therefore, claiming that HC productive morphology is a result of "late, post-creolization borrowing" (cf. Valdman's decreolization) implies that such "borrowing" of morphology could take place only after the relevant sociolinguistic and historical factors made it more difficult for such "borrowing" to occur—"borrowing" is presumably easier when the "lenders" are more numerous and more accessible. On the empirical side, Fattier (1998) documents a substantial set of seventeenth- and eighteenth-century French "survivances" in HC; some of these "survivances" robustly illustrate the use of morphologically complex words at the earliest stages of HC (also see Chaudenson 1996, 27ff.).

Furthermore, the "affixless pidgin" scenario is anti-Uniformitarian. For such a prototypical "affixless pidgin" to emerge, the pidgin creator would have to filter out or reanalyze *all* morphologically complex words from the primary linguistic data. For example, *pini* 'to punish' would enter the incipient Creole, but *pinisyon* 'punishment' could not enter the language as a complex formation built from the stem *pini*. In the "prototypical" Creole genesis situation, all complex words are adopted by the substrate speakers as simplex words and remain simplex for a long period of time. *Pinisyon*, if it existed in the pidgin and early Creole, would have no internal structure and would bear no relationship to *pini* (see section 2.4 for somewhat similar arguments toward different theoretical ends). But the latter assumption makes early "prototypical" Creole speakers unlike any other speakers. That is, such speakers are incapable of pattern matching and of detecting morphological and semantic relationships in the primary linguistic data; for example, they cannot relate *pini* to *pinisyon* despite the systematicity and overall transparency of *-syon* affixation, as in the examples in (4) and their French counterparts. Neither can these early (affixless) Creole speakers generate and decompose transparently derived ordinal numbers such as HC *dezyèm, twazyèm, katriyèm, senkyèm, . . . , santyèm*, and so on '2nd, 3rd, 4th, 5th, . . . , 100th, and so on'. (Both the forms and the combinatorics of HC ordinal numbers are diachronically related to French *deuxième, troisième, quatrième, cin-*

quième,..., *centième*, and so on, contra the empirical and theoretical claims in Lefebvre 1998, 310–311.)

This "prototypical" scenario is not only weakened by the available diachronic and synchronic evidence (see, e.g., morphologically complex "survivances" and neologisms in Fattier 1998), but in fact disconfirmed by what we know about the development of morphology; witness, say, the evidence for "fast mapping" in the acquisition of derivation (see, e.g., Clark 1993) and the status of derivational morphology in language contact and change (see, e.g., Weinreich 1953). Such observations, coupled with the Saussurean quality and the storage-cum-parsing capacities of the human mind (Pinker 1999), makes the consistently transparent Creole prototype with affixless-pidgin ancestry intrinsically anti-Uniformitarian: the prototypical Creole lexicon defies basic properties of human cognition.

In order to save McWhorter's diachronic scenario from total failure, it could perhaps be assumed that the Creole prototype makes "inherently gradient," not categorical, predictions about Creole morphology (see, e.g., McWhorter 1998, 811–812). In any case, given HC's well-established sociohistorical profile as a bona fide Creole, McWhorter's scenario leads us to expect that at least a fair number of HC affixes would betray their origins in a (gradiently) affixless pidgin. Such affixes would still show signs of having developed internally from "erstwhile lexical items," assuming as McWhorter does that there was a (gradiently) affixless pidgin in HC's ancestry. However, by and large HC inflectional and derivational affixes show *no* evidence of erstwhile unbound ancestors that have been reanalyzed as affixes via "gradual grammaticalization."

Not only does HC, as a radical Creole, challenge McWhorter's claims about how "young" languages develop their morphology (via grammaticalization); HC morphology as sketched above also undermines McWhorter's (1998) fundamental opposition between "young" and "old" languages. By McWhorter's own criteria, HC does not count as a "young" language. HC affixes are by and large etymologically related to French affixes (not surprisingly, since most of the HC lexicon is etymologically related to French; see Fattier 1998), and in turn, French affixes often have cognates in Latin. Thus, unlike (hypothesized) "young" languages whose affixes have recently evolved via grammaticalization, HC has affixes with a long etymological ancestry (no less than millennia).

This brings to mind Saussure's sociohistorically related observation that, within the documentable past, every language has an ancestor. Keeping Creoles in mind, I would like to add that, within the documentable past, every language has *at least* one ancestor (also see note 27 regarding the ancient "ancestors" of Caribbean cultures). From a language-internal perspective that takes into account the neological aspects of HC morphology, one can also recall Meillet's (1929 [1951, 74]) observation that every language is repeatedly created anew via acquisition (see DeGraff 1999a, 14, for discussion). Thus, from either an E-language or an I-language perspective, one could argue that each language is as "old" or as "new" as every other: most (I-)languages (including "proto-typical Creoles" such as HC) are cases of language (re-)creation with contingent primary linguistic data provided by speakers of some parent language(s). In Creole genesis cases, these data, alongside UG, may underdetermine the attained grammar to an extent greater than in the case of non-Creole languages, but the difference is one of degree, not one of quality.

Sign languages like the one currently developing in Nicaragua may be one example of "pure" language creation without any previous ancestry in a stable communal (E-)language. Interestingly, such "young" sign languages manifest the sorts of morphological distinctions—for example, "rich" agreement morphology—lacking in many "old" languages such as English and Chinese (see Kegl, Senghas, and Coppola 1999). This may be a modality-specific effect (see, e.g., Kegl, Senghas, and Coppola 1999, 213–214, 223). Be that as it may, the recent emergence in Nicaragua of (sign) languages with extensive morphological paradigms provides yet other examples of "young" languages that robustly disconfirm the predictions of the Creole prototype (also see note 2).

To sum up regarding the Creole prototype proposed in McWhorter 1998 and its antecedents in traditional Creole genesis scenarios that allege a prior pidgin with little or no morphology (see, e.g., Jespersen 1922, 233–234): Its basic generalizations and predictions are disconfirmed by the available diachronic and synchronic evidence from HC, a "most creole of creoles." Furthermore, it is theoretically problematic: there is no a priori reason why prototypical pre-Creole pidgins—qua (conventionalized) interlanguages—should be virtually affixless as envisaged by the traditional catastrophic scenarios. As for "optimal learnability and processibility" and "consistently transparent" semantics, these are only some of the factors driving the acquisition/creation of I-languages, and they are therefore not expected to be the sole determinant in the development of Creole morphology and lexical semantics. Given Saussurean arbitrariness, Creole languages (e.g., HC, Sranan (Wekker 1996, 95), and

Saramaccan (Norval Smith, personal communication)), like any other natural languages, are expected to, and do, manifest semantically opaque derivations in the form of word-level morphologically complex idioms. This is as expected: in any natural language, derived words, like simplex words, can function as Saussurean signs (see, e.g., Aronoff 1976; Jackendoff 1995; Marantz 1997; Stump 1998; Pinker 1999; also see note 19). These observations cast further doubt on the morphological distinction that McWhorter posits between "young" and "old" languages (also see Seuren and Wekker 1986; Seuren 1998, 292–293). The notions "old" and "new" as applied to language types may be yet another intuitively attractive taxonomy with various sociohistorically and/or sociological motivations, but with no basis in linguistic theory—somewhat on a par with the distinction between "dialect" and "language." In other words, UG does not seem to encode specific information about the ancestry of individual languages.

2.6   Creole Morphology and the Morphology of an Ideology

Thus far, we have seen that the "simple morphology" orthodoxy in Creole studies fails both empirically and theoretically, and that it does so conclusively once we go beyond "highly selective presentation of data" and once we incorporate "data [that] are viewed more liberally" (cf. McWhorter's (1998, 803–804) own methodological exhortations in note 15). As I have shown here and in DeGraff 2000b,c, the "simple Creole morphology" orthodoxy illustrated in sections 2.2–2.5 is more a myth than a scientific conclusion based on observable facts. In the case studies at hand, the perennial Creole prototypes—with "little or no morphology," with "substrate-bound morphology," and/or with "semantically transparent morphology"—could not be further from the true nature of HC qua prototypical Creole, once a truly representative empirical sample is brought to bear on the implementation of the relevant proposals. Particularly striking is the quality of data that have been enlisted to support these proposals—data that are either flawed or too limited (or both). Yet these proposals are widely believed. It is as if their empirical claims were self-evident.

Furthermore, the evidence disconfirming the analyses by Hall, D'Ans, Whinnom, Valdman, Samarin, Seuren and Wekker, McWhorter, Lefebvre, and others, not only is readily available from published sources and from native speakers, but sometimes is found in these authors' own work as well as in references they cite to support the empirically untenable orthodoxy.

In the most notable cases, the only "solid datum" leading to "consensus" is the virtual absence of data: for example, Whinnom (1971), Seuren and Wekker (1986), and Seuren (1998, 292–293)—the defenders of the no-morphology model of the Creole lexicon—present not one piece of supporting evidence (i.e., not one example of periphrastic constructions in lieu of morphologically complex words) and not one supporting reference.

For instance, Whinnom (1971, 109–110) claims that, because bound morphemes are lacking in Creoles, the Creole speaker may be "handicapped by his language": Creole morphology is "deficient" and prevents Creole speakers from forming "abstract terms" (see section 2.2).

On the empirical side, the HC lexicon does include both morphologically simplex "abstract" words such as *chagren* 'sorrow', *kòlè* 'anger', *lanmou* 'love', and *lapenn* 'grief' and morphologically complex "abstract" words such as *titès* 'childhood' (cf. *ti* 'small'; see pp. 65–66) and *bèlte* 'beauty' (cf. *bèl* 'beautiful'). All these existing HC words are abstract terms, I presume, and directly contradict Whinnom's claim.[18]

On the theoretical side, even if one were to assume total absence of bound morphemes (purely for the sake of argumentation), it is not clear why Creoles could not express abstract concepts via morphologically simplex terms and periphrases built from such terms; Whinnom does not investigate the availability of such means. In any case, bound morphemes (or the relevant properties thereof), like unbound morphemes, are listed in the mental lexicon. Periphrases may thus be considered the syntactic analogues of morphologically complex words. As with affixed words, it is pieces (and/or processes) from the mental lexicon that enter into the composition of periphrases. The difference is that periphrases are put together with "syntactic glue" whereas complex words are put together with "morphological glue."[19] Therefore, another problem for Whinnom's position is that size limits (due, e.g., to short-term memory and on-line processing capacities) would apply equally to morphologically complex words, periphrases, sentences, and other outputs of the combinatorial rules of language. Yet no one would claim that abstract propositions (e.g., related to beliefs) cannot be expressed via sentences because of size limits. Finally, if morphology has any more expressive power than syntax, then English speakers would look greatly "handicapped" when compared with Algonquian or Bantu speakers. Wouldn't the latter "result" be considered undesirable or intolerable?[20]

I have now established that one common feature of various "simple Creole morphology" claims is that they are falsified by data that were readily available to their authors. On the larger empirical/methodological front, I must ask, how do creolists claim that inflection or (semantically opaque) derivation is absent or posit the inventory and nature of derivational processes without consulting, or while contradicting, the appropriate sources on Creole lexicons? The proponents of the "simple Creole morphology" orthodoxy seem to manifest a strong belief that Creoles *must* at all costs conform to particular synchronic and/or diachronic assumptions about Creole morphology: these assumptions are recurrently raised to the level of generalizations independently of straightforwardly available counterevidence.

In what follows, I do not wish to ascribe unconscious motives to certain creolists. It would be simplistic to assume that these creolists (across time and space) are all driven by similar motivations. I am also convinced that most of us creolists try our very best to come up with what we believe are valid scientific hypotheses about the diachrony and synchrony of Creole languages. But, as I cannot look inside researchers' minds, the best I can do is inspect the textual evidence and relate specific claims to one another and to prevalent attitudes of their times. It is this textual evidence and the corresponding empirical claims and (in)adequacy thereof that establish the particular patterns I would like to elucidate. These patterns have permeated creolistics since its very genesis as a recognizable field of inquiry.[21]

I thus examine the historiographical roots and the historical development of the conventionalized wisdom about Creole morphology (see DeGraff 2000c for further details). As early as in Pelleprat 1655 and through Saint-Quentin 1872, Baissac 1880, Adam 1883, Jespersen 1922, Bloomfield 1933, Hockett 1958, Whinnom 1971, Valdman 1978, McWhorter 1998, and so on, the one preconceived notion that has permeated Creole studies is the assumption that Creoles are "inferior dialects" or non-"normal"/non-"regular" languages intrinsically marked by one or both of the following related genetic factors: (1) their catastrophic genesis as emergency (thus "simple" and "optimal") solutions to communicative problems in plurilingual communities; (2) their genesis as failures on the part of "inferior" beings to acquire "superior" languages.

Assumption (2) is clearly racist, and both assumptions are non-Uniformitarian, therefore methodologically problematic. According to the Uniformitarian Principle (Lyell 1830–1833), laws of nature should be assumed to work the same in the present as in the past—for example, in the domain of geology, Lyell's title speaks for itself: *Principles of Geology; Being an Attempt to Explain the Former Changes of the Earth's Surface, by Reference to Causes Now in Operation*. The implication is clear: measurable evidence from the present (e.g., from observable phenomena in conjunction with current scientific results) should constrain our theories about past events, lest we lose the possibility of explaining the past in ways that are falsifiable within known and testable principles. In the case of Creole genesis, I find it reasonable to assume that there are no radically different mental processes and/or substances that distinguish the "Creole mind" from the "non-Creole mind." We should then assume that the creators of Creole languages are biologically similar to other humans and that Creole genesis at the level of the individual speaker reduces to cognitive processes that are common to the entire species. Therefore, measurable evidence within our best theories of acquisition, language contact, comparative morphosyntax, and so on, must impose limits on (the postulated mental bases of) Creole genesis scenarios.

In this vein, Alleyne (1994) makes some particularly perceptive observations that touch on non-Uniformitarian assumptions in Creole studies; these observations are worth quoting at length.

One of the most important, if not the most important, factor in the existence and preservation of the stigmatization of creole languages is the uncertainty of the tradition to which these languages might be attached. This is the central problem of genesis, and it plays a fundamental role in the development of the generally negative social psychological attitudes and interpretations that have emerged in opposition to any notion of standardization. In this regard it is very interesting to observe how hypotheses about genesis impinge on and affect social psychological attitudes. Those hypotheses ... continue to link creole languages definitionally to pidgins and thereby ... account for them fundamentally through the process of simplification. *The simplification assigned to creoles is not the form sometimes inferred in the process of change from Anglo-Saxon to English or from Latin to French, but some kind of drastic, extreme, extraordinary, or unnatural simplification.* Thus the teleological model on which Indo-European language families are based ignores linguistic convergence as a natural development or the possibility that fundamental change may occur through language contact situations typical of creole languages.... *[T]hese ideological assumptions about natural language change have come to support and fuel those social psychological attitudes that are based on the perception that [creole] languages are corrupt, deviant derivatives within the Western linguistic tradition and, concomitantly, on the notion of their inadequacy.* (Alleyne 1994, 8–9)

In the sort of catastrophic scenarios criticized by Alleyne, the sociohistorical context of Creole genesis gives rise to a class of languages that can be *structurally* distinguished from the class of "regular" languages. In other words, not only do Creoles form a (non-"normal") sociolinguistic class of their own (see, e.g., Valdman 1978, 345–346; 1992, 81); they also form a (non-"regular") *typological* class of their own, independent of the typology of their respective source languages.

McWhorter 1998 (sketched in section 2.5) is the most recent prominent representative of a family of scenarios in which Creole languages arise, in Alleyne's phrase, via "drastic, extreme, extraordinary, or unnatural simplification." The sort of simplification postulated in McWhorter's analysis would count as "unnatural" insofar as it presupposes "a radical break in transmission" that would have "eschewed" or "fossilized" all affixal morphology in the contact languages (McWhorter 1998, 788, 792–793, 798, 804, 808); such simplification is claimed to exist exclusively in the history of Creole languages and serves as a litmus test to distinguish Creoles from "regular" languages.

From a Cartesian (i.e., internalist/mentalistic) perspective, the (non-"regular"/non-"normal") Creole prototypes imply that Creole speakers dispersed across history and geography also form a biological/cognitive class of their own. This biological/cognitive class shares certain (non-Saussurean) morphological and lexical characteristics. The latter differ from proposal to proposal; contrast, for example, D'Ans 1968, Whinnom 1971, Valdman 1978, Samarin 1980, Seuren and Wekker 1986, Seuren 1998, and McWhorter 1998 as quoted in this chapter. In each case, though, the characteristics delineated for Creoles make Creole speakers' linguistic profiles look "simple"/"simplified" in a way similar to the prototypes envisaged in the writings of early creolists from the (post)colonial period, during which the intellectual inferiority of Creole speakers was taken for granted.

I now sketch how particular strands of the "simple Creole morphology" orthodoxy have been woven into the history of Creole studies, from its onset as part of Europe's imperialist enterprise in Africa and in the Americas.

Let me first succinctly evoke the very beginning of Creole studies through the writings of the Jesuit missionary Father Pelleprat (1606?–1667), one of the earliest commentators on Caribbean society and Caribbean Creole speech. For Father Pelleprat, the Africans slaves' "mode of speaking" is defined as failure on their part to acquire the French grammar of the colonists.

We wait until they learn French before we start evangelizing them. It is French that they try to learn as soon as they can, in order to communicate with their masters, on whom they depend for all their needs. We adapt ourselves to their mode of speaking. They generally use the infinitive form of the verb [instead of the inflected forms] ... adding a word to indicate the future or the past.... With this way of speaking, we make them understand all that we teach them. This is the method we use at the beginning of our teaching.... Death won't care to wait until they learn French. (Pelleprat 1655 [1965, 30–31], my translation)

Thus, Pelleprat in 1655 may have been among the first to consider (Caribbean) Creole languages as simplified speech varieties resulting from "failure" to acquire the corresponding European lexifier, announcing the view to be defended in a long series of publications across more than three centuries (see Holm 1988, 22ff., for a review). In this "creolization as failure" scenario, "*de*creolization" is an "improvement" for Creole communities (see, e.g., Jespersen 1922, 228, 235; Bloomfield 1933, 474).

In the seventeenth century, Pelleprat's attitude was representative of larger trends in intellectual thought surrounding the twin genesis of (Caribbean) Creole languages and Creole studies. Let us now consider two representatives of eighteenth-century scholarship in colonial Saint-Domingue. Michel Étienne Descourtilz (1775–1835), a Frenchman who traveled through colonial Saint-Domingue from 1799 to 1803, notes that, in reporting "Creole" speech samples between two slaves, he "did his best to correct their ... conversations" (1809, 3:135). Here the one "correcting" Saint-Domingue Creole—or early HC—speech does not even speak it fluently. The same was true for another European traveler to the Caribbean: Justin Girod-Chantrans (1750–1841). After spending one year in Saint-Domingue (1782–1783), he published one of the earliest known texts in Saint-Domingue Creole (Y. Dejean 1977, 13). In his (1785 [1980]) travelogue, Girod-Chantrans calls early HC "weak," "dull," "unclear," "insipid" (p. 158), an "imbecile jargon"—contrast this with Saint-Quentin's (1872) description of Cayenne Creole as "clear," "consistent," and "logical," even though both Girod-Chantrans and Saint-Quentin ultimately adopt a similar outlook that Creoles are imperfect languages. Girod-Chantrans, like many of his contemporaries in Europe, found French-lexifier Creoles to be "nothing but French back in infancy" (p. 157).[22] Expressions of ridicule like Girod-Chantrans's were all too common—see Y. Dejean 1977 for an overview of early reports on HC.

Given the logic of the "founders" of Creole studies and, more generally, of Europe's *mission civilisatrice*, it was logically and pragmatically impossible for early creolists to consider Creoles as "normal" or "regular" languages, in Valdman's and McWhorter's parlance. European observers and their local counterparts could not but interpret Creole structures as validation of their belief that non-Europeans were inferior, taking "divergences [between European and Creole languages] as proof of the Blacks' incapacity to learn languages properly" (Holm 1988, 22). In the case of French colonies, these divergences were taken to attest to the cognitive inferiority of the Africans and their Creole descendants and the cognitive superiority of the European colonizers. Throughout, European languages (and other biological and cultural phenomena viewed as European) were held as the standard against which to measure their non-European counterparts. Anything other than this Eurocentric classificatory stance would have defied the (necessary) ideological order of the colonial moment. Holm (1988, 2, 22) mentions that European scholars' traditional fascination with classical languages such as Latin and with flexional morphology as a linguistic canon of excellence also played against Creole (and African) languages. This is related to Bloomfield's (1933, 8) observation that eighteenth-century language scholars "forc[ed] their descriptions into the scheme of Latin grammar."

In any case, at the onset of Creole studies, it was perhaps Europe's material interest in Africa and the Caribbean that would ultimately induce European intellectuals to (in Chomsky's words) "disguise reality in the service of external power" (1979, 5). Early creolists may have participated in what Chomsky (1975, 130, citing Bracken 1973) calls "the expression of the racist ideology that came naturally enough to philosophers who were involved in their professional lives in the creation of the colonial system." As Meijer and Muysken (1977, 21) sum up the matter: "Most of the nineteenth-century views on creoles were shaped by the same racism that characterized slavery."

In the nineteenth century, the "simple morphology" disguise is elevated to a criterion of Creoleness, as in Pierre Larousse's (1869) entry for *Creole* in the *Grand dictionnaire universel du XIX siècle*.

The Creole language, in our colonies, in Louisiana and Haiti, is a *corrupted French* in which several Spanish and Gallicized words are mixed. This language, often unintelligible when spoken by an old African, is extremely sweet when spoken by white Creole women. (Larousse 1869; my translation)

A somewhat similar definition is found in Vinson's (1882) entry for *Creole* in the *Dictionnaire des sciences anthropologiques*.

Creole languages result from the adaptation of a language, especially some Indo-European language, to the (so to speak) phonetic and grammatical genius of *a race that is linguistically inferior*. The resulting dialect is composite, truly mixed in its vocabulary, but its grammar remains essentially Indo-European, albeit *extremely simplified*. (Vinson 1882, 345, cited in Baggioni 1988, 87; my translation)

Let us now look at some of the first detailed descriptions of French-lexicon Creoles and recall the details of Saint-Quentin's (1872) Rousseauistic hypothesis regarding the cognitive basis for his Creole prototype (some of these details—for example, Creole languages as "infantile jargon"—are found in much of the creolistics literature of the time; the "universality" of such concepts is noted explicitly by Adam (1883, 3)).[23]

[Creole morphosyntax] is, therefore, *a spontaneous product of the human mind, freed from any kind of intellectual culture....* But when one studies its structure, one is so very surprised, so very charmed by its *rigor and simplicity* that one wonders if the creative genius of the most knowledgeable linguists would have been able to give birth to anything that so completely reaches its goal, *that imposes so little strain on memory and that calls for so little effort from those with limited intelligence.* An in-depth analysis has convinced me of something that seems paradoxical. Namely: *if one wanted to create ab ovo an all-purpose language that would allow, after only a few days of study, a clear and consistent exchange of simple ideas, one would not be able to adopt more logical and more productive structures than those found in Creole syntax.* (Saint-Quentin 1872 [1989, 40–41]; my translation)

Aspects of Saint-Quentin's "simple Creole morphology" argument (italicized in the quotation) reappear throughout Creole studies in various theoretical and/or sociolinguistic guises, as in Adam's (1883, 4–5) Rousseauistic concept of Creoles as *langues naturelles* (as opposed to *langues cultivées*); Jespersen's (1922, 228) idea that the creators of Creole languages, from both the superstrate and the substrate languages, spoke "as if their minds were as innocent of grammar as those of very small babies ... [thus, Creoles'] inevitable naïveté and ... childlike simplicity..."; Hjelmslev's (1938, 1939) "optimum"; Whinnom's (1971, 109–110) morphological "handicap"; D'Ans's (1968, 26), Valdman's (1978, 375–376), and Samarin's (1980, 221) derivational deficiency vis-à-vis "lexical enrichment" and "morphosemantic adaptation"; Seuren and Wekker's (1986) Creole "semantic transparency"; Bickerton's (1988, 276) radical Creole showing "the loss [of] all bound morphology"; and McWhorter's (1998) toneless, inflectionless, and semantically transparent Creole morphology.

The sustained attraction of the "simple Creole morphology" orthodoxy can be sampled through the writings of a famous quartet of linguists with infamous sound bites on Creole languages: Antoine Meillet (1866–1936), Leonard Bloomfield (1887–1949), Suzanne Sylvain (1898–1975),[24] and Charles Hockett (1916–2000).

[W]e also need to take into account the sort of changes occurring in languages that are *imperfectly* used by speakers who do not try to speak them *normally.* Thus, the

black slaves in the colonies did not try to make *normal use* of their masters'
French or Spanish: their "Creole" modes of speaking—Spanish Creole or French
Creole—thus constitute *varieties of Spanish or French that are deprived of almost
all their grammar, weakened in their pronunciation, reduced to a small lexicon.*
(Meillet 1924 [1951, 68]; my translation)

Speakers of a *lower* language may make so little progress in learning the dominant
speech, that the masters, in communicating with them resort to *"baby-talk."* This
"baby-talk" is the masters' *imitation* of the subjects' *incorrect speech.* There is
reason to believe that it is by no means an exact imitation, and that some of its
features are based not upon the subjects' mistakes but upon grammatical relations
that exist within the upper language itself. The subjects, in turn, deprived of the
correct model, can do no better now than to acquire the *simplified* "baby-talk"
version of the *upper* language. The result may be a conventionalized *jargon*
[Bloomfield's emphasis]. During the colonization of the last few centuries, Europeans have repeatedly *given* jargonized versions of their language to slaves and
tributary peoples.... When the jargon has become the only language of the subject group, it is called a *creolized language* [Bloomfield's emphasis]. The creolized
language has the status of an *inferior* dialect of the masters' speech. It is subject to
constant leveling-out and *improvement* in the direction of the latter.... With an
improvement of social conditions, this leveling is accelerated. (Bloomfield 1933,
472, 474)[25]

At the time of [HC] genesis, there was, on one side, the powerful and feared
master speaking with a small and invariant set of French words, and, on the other
side, there were slaves speaking a great diversity of African dialects. It is thus
expected that most of the [HC] lexicon is drawn from French. The genesis of [HC]
morphosyntax has a different status: on one side, there was the simplified French
used by the colonists, and, on the other side, there was *the multitude of African
languages all with nearly the same grammatical structure—a structure that, like the
colonist's simplified French, was very simple.* As for these African languages, M.
Migeod writes: "The complete dissimilarity of vocabulary but *uniformity of syntax
is often most striking, and the reason may perhaps fairly safely be ascribed to the
early crystallization of the mental powers of the black race."* Therefore, the African, in order to communicate, was able to adopt the basic patterns of French
morphosyntax, but he was also able to retain his old speech habits according to his
emotional and cogitative modes. (Sylvain 1936, 36–37; my translation)

Haitian Creole is *highly aberrant,* and yet is properly classified as a variety of
North French.... One simple test of this [i.e., of the hypothesis that Creoles are
aberrant types of their lexifier languages] is the relative ease with which different
people can learn a given pidgin or creole. (Hockett 1958, 423—in a section entitled
"Pidgins, Artificial Languages, and Creoles")[26]

To recapitulate, the "simple Creole morphology" orthodoxy has ancient
antecedents in Creole studies, starting with Pelleprat 1655 and later in the
dictionary and encyclopedia definitions in Larousse 1869 and Vinson
1882 and in the descriptive grammars of Saint-Quentin (1872) and Baissac

(1880). Adam (1883, 7, 11, etc.) and, to a lesser extent, Sylvain (1936, 36–37) took the simplicity of Creole morphosyntax to derive from the non-Indo-European substrate. Schuchardt (1914 [1980, 91–92]) and especially Jespersen (1922, 233–234) talked about a morphological "vanishing point" in the diachronic path of Creole languages. Regarding (alleged) Creole transparency, Hjelmslev (1938, 1939), in advance of McWhorter (1998), posited that Creole morphology is "optimal" insofar as it establishes a one-to-one relationship between morphemes and formants. This is reminiscent of Saint-Quentin's (1872 [1989, 40–41]) aforementioned claim that Creole morphosyntax is completely rigorous, simple, clear, consistent, and logical. (Also see the references in note 1.)

It thus can be safely asserted that, if there is any long-reigning orthodoxy and alleged truism in Creole studies, it indeed has to do with the oft-repeated claim that Creole morphology is *maximally simple and/or simplified and/or simple to account for* from a diachronic and/or synchronic perspective. In fact, this orthodoxy is empirically untenable, theoretically unfounded, and methodologically bizarre. Yet, notwithstanding modern advances in linguistics and our current understanding of UG, this anti-egalitarian myth has continued unabated for the past three and a half centuries with sociologically and scientifically dismal consequences (for Creolophones and Creole studies), specifically in the domains of language planning, education, and linguistic description (DeGraff 2000b,c).

I thus consider suspect any description of Creole languages that claims that these languages a priori lack certain linguistic structures—for example, semantically opaque derivation qua "evolved idiosyncrasy" as in McWhorter's (1998) Creole prototype. Regarding the latter, I fail to see any reason why such processes should be consistently absent in a given language grouping. A language that admits derivation only if semantically transparent entails that its speakers never lexicalize the result of morphological combination, no matter how often the word is derived. This is a strange assumption indeed: there is no known memory limitation that a priori excludes the lexical and idiomatic storage of derivationally complex words and phrases (see discussion in section 2.5).

Descriptions of Creole languages that make such peculiar antiuniversal assumptions become even more suspect when they adduce little or no evidence to support claims that are made about entire linguistic domains (e.g., morphology and lexicon). And my suspicion turns into complete mistrust when Creole languages are systematically contrasted with "regular"/"normal" languages. For instance, in a peculiar terminological twist, one hallmark of "regular" (i.e., non-Creole) languages is the presence of semantically *ir*regular morphology (McWhorter 1998). Creole languages have also been claimed to constitute sociolinguistically and structurally non-"normal" languages whose fate, when coexisting with their lexifiers, is extinction via *de*creolization qua merger into the next available European "normal" language (Valdman 1978, 345ff.; 1992): "Creole languages differ from other languages along many dimensions and these differences entail certain limits with respect to their development" (1978, 345). Seuren and Wekker (1986, 66) put Creole languages in the class of "younger or less advanced" and "beginning" languages, which is contrasted with a class of "more advanced" languages. For Seuren (1998, 292), "Creole grammars ... lack the more sophisticated features of languages backed by a rich and extended cultural past and a large, well-organized literate society." Such views are reminiscent of Schleicherian/Darwinian distinctions between primitive and civilized languages (see, e.g., Adam 1883, 4–5). As I have argued, various diagnoses for the morphological "limits" of Creoles are empirically unfounded and seem ideologically driven.[27]

2.7 Toward a New Perspective on Creole Studies

Going beyond linguistics per se, there is a twin paradox in Creole studies that I have not yet addressed: namely, that the negative attitudes and the writings of educated Creolophones (say, in Haiti) often reflect the attitudes and writings of creolists who (either explicitly or implicitly) devalue their objects of study. HC, spoken by all Haitians and the only language of the vast majority, is central to Haitian life. HC is at the core of the everyday and productive lives of at least the six million Haitians for whom it is the only language they efficiently speak and understand. Yet HC and other Creoles remain among the most stigmatized and undervalued languages of the world, even among self-styled progressive intellectuals, including linguists. And educated Creolophones too are often among those who stigmatize and devalue Creole languages (for overviews and critiques, see, e.g., Bebel-Gisler and Hurbon 1975; Y. Dejean 1975, 1993; Prudent 1980; Devonish 1986). Perhaps owing to the context of Haiti's violent past as a French colony based on slavery and its even more violent metamorphosis from Europe's cash cow to a defiant free Black republic, the cognitive and cultural parity of Haitians and Europeans was (and, for many in Haiti and elsewhere, remains) an "unthinkable"; see DeGraff 2000c.

The following comments by Haitian historian Hénock Trouillot are typical of the attitude toward HC among the dominant classes:

[HC] facilitates mediocrity in many ways.... [HC] closes itself in structures that are narrow and limited, with the heavy disadvantage that it is a language that has not been systematized, a language with a syntax and orthography that are not yet part of a grammar with broad recognition in the intellectual world.... [HC] has no fixed orthography and no fixed syntax. Worse yet, it is (nearly) unreadable for many Francophone readers. (Trouillot 1980, 12, 15, 22; my translation)

A related sentence of insignificance is passed by Jean Métellus, a well-known Haitian scholar, who speaks with the voice of apparent authority as a neurologist, novelist, poet, and linguist.

[W]ith [HC] one can do many things, but one can do neither physics, nor chemistry, nor mathematics, nor medicine, nor biology.... I think that with [HC] one can only do poetry.... But this is not a language that can be used for basic science or that can be used in the advancement of knowledge. (Métellus 1997–1998, 18; my translation)

The point should be clear: there still exist influential scholars and writers for whom HC does not qualify as a "regular"/"normal" language, even though the vast majority of Haitians are monolingual Creolophones and HC is the native tongue of virtually all Haitians (see Y. Dejean 1993; also see note 28 for somewhat similar attitudes outside the HC context). This disdain for Creole languages has its counterpart in the creolists' views critiqued above. Even French-born creolist and language-teaching expert Albert Valdman is among those who consider HC to belong to a class of non-"normal" languages; his views are clearly stated in his much-quoted 1978 book (pp. 345ff.) and in many articles written thereafter (see quotations above). Valdman (in an article that otherwise seems to promote HC) even casts doubt on the *intrinsic* necessity to elevate HC—qua the "mother tongue" of the vast *monolingual* majority of Haitians—to language of instruction and official language:

Notwithstanding the fact that [HC] is the only language shared by all Haitians, there is no inherent principle of language planning that compels its use as the primary school vehicle or as the official language. Nor, contra the celebrated UNESCO article of faith ... has it been convincingly demonstrated that in a multilingual country, in all situations, literacy is most effectively imparted in a child's mother tongue. (Valdman 1984, 84)

Here Valdman seems opposed to UNESCO's basic principle of universal education, a pedagogically sound principle according to which "education is best carried on through the mother tongue of the pupil," and in support of which "every effort should be made to provide education in the mother tongue" (see, e.g., UNESCO 1953, 6, 47). Green and Hale (1998, 198) paraphrase this truism as "the unimpeachable rationale ... to facilitate a child's overall education by carrying it out in his or her own language."

Thus, there still exist deeply negative attitudes about Creole languages, on the part of both Creolophones and creolists. These two sets of historically rooted attitudes interact in subtle and pernicious ways that often cast long shadows on descriptions of Creole languages and on Creolophones' (self-)images and socioeconomic prospects. These attitudes systematically devalue Creole languages and their speakers in favor of European languages and their speakers. In the case of Haiti (and other Creolophone communities), such attitudes have had devastating effects on social reform and education. For instance, Creole languages are still underused and/or misused in the schools, and their very use by (monolingual) Creole speakers is often misperceived as an indelible marker of lower class and inferior intellect. Such factors have contributed to blocking the upward mobility and political empowerment of (monolingual) Creole speakers— keeping them, in effect, in a situation of "linguistic apartheid" (as decried by P. Dejan/Dejean 1988, 1989, 1993; also see Bebel-Gisler and Hurbon 1975 and Y. Dejean 1975). What can be done? I would like to argue that (apparent?) neocolonial intellectual imperialism in Creole studies, coupled with the typical ambivalence toward Creoles among many educated Creolophones, must be vigorously critiqued in order to further scientific and social progress in and about Creole communities. Modern linguistic theory provides needed arguments to critique antiegalitarian stances among both creolists and Creolophones. And there is much to learn from Ken Hale's "life in language," especially from his life as linguist *engagé*.

The title of this section, "Toward a New Perspective on Creole Studies," is inspired by Hale 1972a: "A New Perspective on American Indian Linguistics." Hale's "new perspective" is straightforward: linguistic research must become "research on, for and with" the speaker (Cameron, Frazer, and Harvey 1992, 22). In other words, our work as linguists must also involve our political commitment to social and economic justice in the communities we work in. This political commitment, whenever possible, must involve the training, hence "empowerment," of the native-speaker informant as bona fide native-speaker linguist. This position has informed Hale's fieldwork for some forty years, and it is in this sense that he has collaborated, and continues to collaborate, with speakers of indigenous languages: many among his teachers/collaborators/students/consultants are Native and Central Americans and Australian Aborigines. Hale imposes no prerequisites for linguistic training (see, e.g., Hale 1972a, 95–96; 1972b, 391ff.; 1973, 205). Through this collaboration, the indigenous speakers work toward becoming full-fledged partners in linguistics research and applied linguistics. In turn, they have contributed to theoretical developments as they elaborate accurate descriptions of their native languages (see, e.g., Hale 1965, 1972a,b). In some cases, these indigenous speakers are or become activists who work toward rescuing their native or ancestral languages from a (quasi-)moribund state (see, e.g., Hale 1972b, 1992, 1993; Green and Hale 1998; Fermino 2000). This is where theoretical linguistics meets "language rescue" and where field linguistics meets political activism, with native speakers becoming linguists *engagé(e)s* fighting for respect for and the survival of their own language and culture.

How is this relevant to Creole studies and Creolophone communities? To use HC as an example: I would like to believe that much of the current ambivalence toward HC among Haitians is not only rooted in history, but also conditioned by a high degree of ignorance about what constitutes knowledge of language and about how Haiti's history has paradoxically, if inevitably, contributed to the debasement of its national culture. Indeed, there are specific historical events that lie at the root of widespread ambivalence toward Creole culture: historical events such as slavery, colonization, postcolonial class struggles, and "surrealist appropriations" in academic discourse (as defined by anthropologist Drexel Woodson (1992)) have conspired to deprive HC and other authentically Haitian phenomena (e.g., Vodou) of much symbolic capital. The Haitian revolution is one of history's events that, to Haitian historian Michel-Rolph Trouillot, may still constitute an "unthinkable," given the then prevalent racism of Western thought and the contemporary remnants thereof.

[Afro-Caribbean cultural practices] were not meant to exist. . . . [They] emerged on the edges of the plantation system, gnawing at the logic of an imposed order and its daily manifestations of dominance. (Trouillot 1998, 28)

The linguist *engagé(e)* will thus use both history and linguistics to demystify current attitudes about HC. History will teach the creolist and the Creolophone about the origins of their respective prejudices (if any). As for Cartesian UG-based approaches to language, they are intrinsically egalitarian: all languages are "regular"/"normal," contra the antiegalitarian approach illustrated by Pelleprat (1655), Saint-Quentin (1872),

Baissac (1880), Jespersen (1922), Bloomfield (1933), D'Ans (1968), Whinnom (1971), Valdman (1978), Samarin (1980), Seuren and Wekker (1986), McWhorter (1998), Seuren (1998), and others. In Cartesian thought, the concept of (inferior) "coloured minds" is a "logical embarrassment" (Bracken 1974, 158, cited in Chomsky 1975, 130). The UG-based approach to linguistics will teach Creolophones, and remind creolists, that the biological cognitive basis of language is a precious genetic heirloom universally inherited by every healthy member of the human species, each of whom is endowed with an equally precious language faculty. It is this heirloom that defines the humanity and the individuality of every human being, including Creole speakers. As Sapir (1933 [1963, 7]) succinctly put it, "[L]anguage is an essentially perfect means of expression and communication among every known people." More explicitly:

[A]ll attempts to connect particular types of linguistic morphology with certain correlated stages of cultural development are vain. Rightly understood, such correlations are rubbish. Both simple and complex types of language of an indefinite number of varieties may be found spoken at any desired level of cultural advance. When it comes to linguistic form, Plato walks with the Macedonian swineherd, Confucius with the head-hunting savage of Assam. (Sapir 1921, 219)

Sapir's view and the available evidence on crosslinguistic morphology (in, e.g., English, Chinese, Wampanoag, Kivunjo, and Nicaraguan Sign Language) contradict the persistently popular view championed by (e.g.) Seuren (1998, 292) that "the more sophisticated features of languages [are] backed by a rich and extended cultural past and a large, well-organized literate society" (see note 27).

My perhaps naive hunch is that the practice of Cartesian theoretical linguistics *by Creolophones* has much to contribute to eliminating the apparent ideological "handicap" manifested by creolists and Creolophone scholars commenting on the alleged nonviability of Creole languages. Having Creolophones read what creolists write will provide useful checks and balances, and so will having Creolophones write what creolists read. Such collaboration is beneficial to the international linguistics community. This is illustrated by Dominique Fattier's recent collaboration with linguists at Haiti's Faculté de Linguistique Appliquée. This collaboration was central to the empirical reliability of Fattier's (1998) outstanding description of HC dialects. I also trust that promoting HC and other Creole languages as valid objects of scientific study in the eyes of Creole speakers themselves may go some way in providing correctives to the current role—or, rather, nonrole—of Creole languages in the (mis)education of Haitians and of creolists.

Another step toward increasing the participation of Creolophones in linguistics is to get young Creole speakers interested in their own languages in ways that are educationally and scientifically constructive. This may be hard to do given the socioeconomic realities facing Creole communities and the status of linguistics as a less than lucrative field. But from my own interaction with Haitian students, I am confident that HC speakers would relish the opportunity to participate in greater numbers in the scientific study of their language, especially when they realize that Creole languages (qua "regular"/"normal" languages) have contributed great insights to the scientific study of the mind, as practiced in respectable research centers throughout the world.

Exposure to HC linguistics can start at the earliest possible age. Indeed, searching for the rules of one's native language simply amounts to apprenticeship in scientific discovery (see, e.g., Honda and O'Neil 1993). Hale (1973) discusses the cognitive, intellectual, and scientific benefits of engaging schoolchildren in linguistics research, with their native languages supplying the "raw" data for scientific experiments.

It makes extremely good sense to engage school-age children in the study of their own language—it is perhaps one of the very best ways of enabling them to become familiar with certain basic principles of scientific inquiry. It has an advantage over other sciences in that the school-age child comes prepared with an extremely large body of data (in the form of intuitions about the sentences of his language).... [H]e comes equipped with the primary data of linguistics, the science which seeks to explain the fantastically complicated ability which human beings have which enables them to speak and to understand the indefinitely many sentences of their native languages. Since primary data are so readily available, they provide an excellent opportunity for teachers to engage their students in the process of making observations about language, observations which are similar in nature to the kinds of observations that any scientist makes in relation to the phenomena he studies.... [S]kills which are developed and exercised in making and reporting linguistic observations are of a kind which can be of great use to students in many phases of their lives, both academic and non-academic. (Hale 1973, 205)

I would surely ensconce myself (deeper) in some academic utopian exile if I believed that linguistics could suddenly reverse widespread negative attitudes about Haiti and its people, attitudes deeply rooted in (post)-colonial history and in socioeconomics and politics.[28] Ultimately, HC will gain due respect in all sectors of Haitian life and beyond only when it too can accumulate real and symbolic "capital" (see Bourdieu 1991) and become wedded to sources of true power. This can only happen if HC starts at last to function as a true official language, not only on paper, but also in practice. As P. Dejan/Dejean (1988, 59; 1989, 27) reminds us, such changes require nothing less than political reform toward full defense of the human rights of Creole speakers. Devonish (1986) makes similar arguments.

The function of an official language in any country, particularly in an under-developed ex-colonial country ..., ought to ... involve the mass of the population in the decision-making processes of their society, as well as in its economic development. (Devonish 1986, 32)

The language variety spoken as the language of everyday communication by the ordinary members of a community is the most effective language medium for releasing creativity, initiative and productivity among the members of such community. Such a language is also the most effective means of promoting popular participation in, and control of, the various decision-making bodies within the state. A revolutionary official language policy would, therefore, have to be committed to the creation of a unity between the language variety or varieties used for everyday communication among the mass of the population, and the language variety or varieties used for official purposes. (Devonish 1986, 35)

Yet my goal in this chapter, although scientific *and* political, is much more modest than Devonish's. Attainment of socioeconomic and political power by larger numbers of HC speakers (e.g., via adequate education in the language that all Haitians speak and via increased use of HC at all levels of socioeconomic and political life) is made even more elusive by the following fact, which I'd like more linguists to do something about: among the *only* professional corps that is qualified to scientifically, thus authoritatively, document the linguistic viability of Creole languages (i.e., linguists), there exist influential figures who continue upholding mythical hierarchies among human languages, with Creoles consistently ranked at the bottom. Such hierarchies are maintained, for example, when our most respected publications carry articles that relegate Creole languages to some non-"regular," non-"normal," and/or "deficient" typology with properties that seem unexpected from any natural language: for example, (1) absence of morphology, (2) inability to express abstract notions, and (3) affixation that is always semantically transparent. (Do Creole speakers lack the necessary neurons for morphology, for abstract thought or for lexical storage of complex words?) Such stereotypes actually reinforce the status of Creoles as languages that are unfit for education and for general use in Creolophone communities (or any human society whatsoever). If such Creole stereotypes/prototypes were to exist (contra the data), they would not meet human linguistic needs. The extreme Creole prototype—such as McWhorter's—would not even be usable for metaphors, idioms, puns, proverbs, poetry, charades, folk tales, and so on. Indeed, how could such forms of verbal art ever exist in any language that lacks the Saussurean structural means for noncompositional lexical semantics?

2.8   Envoi

The scientific investigation of a given language cannot be understood in isolation. In carrying out field research, linguists are inevitably responsible to the larger human community which its results could affect.... What matters is eventual success, and that will be measured by the extent to which work on the language is integrated in a meaningful way into the life of the community of people who speak it. (Hale 2001, 76, 100)

Notes

This study in pursuit of "reflexive" linguistics (in the sense of Pierre Bourdieu) would not have been possible without the invaluable reflections of colleagues and friends: Jean Robert Cadely, Noam Chomsky, Paul Dejean, Yves Dejean, Dominique Fattier, Ken Hale, Morris Halle, Dimitri Hilton, Tometro Hopkins, Michael Kenstowicz, Antonia MacDonald-Smythe, Alec Marantz, Heliana Mello, Salikoko Mufwene, Wayne O'Neil, Marilene Phipps, Geneva Smitherman, and Adrienne Talamas.

Ken's "life in language" requires insight, dedication, and courage. To me, it is an endless source of inspiration.

1. See, for example, Pelleprat 1655 [1965, 30–31, 34]; Saint-Quentin 1872 [1989, 172–173]; Baissac 1880, 23, 30; Schuchardt 1909 [1980, 69–70, 97], 1914 [1979, 74, 91–92; 1980, 92]; Jespersen 1922, 233–234; Bloomfield 1933, 471–475; Sylvain 1936, 27, 31, 37–38, 48–49; Faine 1936, 93, 126; Hjelmslev 1938, 286, and 1939; Hall 1953, 28, 34; D'Ans 1968, 26; Tinelli 1970, 2ff.; Férère 1974, 88ff.; Valdman 1978, 130, 149–152; Y. Dejean 1977, 390ff., 423–424, and 1980, 138, 160; Seuren and Wekker 1986, passim; Bickerton 1988, 272–276; Lefebvre 1998, chap. 10; McWhorter 1998, passim; Seuren 1998, 292–293; P. Baker 1999, 17, 19.

2. Morphological reduction of a more restricted sort—namely, absence of certain inflectional affixes (see, e.g., DeGraff 1994, 1997, 1999a,b,c, 2000a,b; Déprez 1999)—must be distinguished from total absence of affixation. Inflectional "erosion" seems typical of language contact in general and applies to *both* "old" and "young" languages (see, e.g., Meillet 1919 [1958, 201]; Weinreich 1953, sec. 2.3; Givón 1979, 20ff.) Weinreich (1953, 41ff.) writes about "grammatical systems [showing preference for] relatively free and invariant morphemes in [their] paradigm," about "the disappearance of grammatical categories," and about "highly hybridized makeshift trade languages [in which] most obligatory categories

expressed by bound morphemes are well known to be abandoned." (Weinreich dutifully notes possible exceptions, for example on page 42.) Givón (1979, 20–21) reminds us that the "reduction of inflections" in Caribbean Creoles should not be surprising given that the most influential substrate languages (e.g., Kwa in the case of HC) were themselves noninflecting. In the VP domain, Sylvain (1936, 138–139), Goodman (1964, 81), Chaudenson (1979, 80ff.), Chaudenson, Mougeon, and Beniak (1993), DeGraff (1997, 1999b, 2000a,b), and many others have pointed out that most of the preverbal nonaffixal markers in HC (and other French-lexifier Creoles) find cognates in the verbal periphrastic constructions manifested in earlier stages of French, with contemporary counterparts in regional French dialects (e.g., in Québécois; see Gougenheim 1971 for an inventory of such periphrastic constructions in French diachrony.

In certain writings, the empirical divide between derivation and inflection seems blurred. One case in point is McWhorter 1998. With respect to HC, McWhorter's claims vacillate at times between absence of inflectional morphology (i.e., HC has "no inflectional affixes"; e.g., pp. 792, 809), absence of "rich paradigms of derivational affixes" (p. 796), and complete absence of morphology (i.e., HC is one of the languages "eliminating [morphological paradigms] entirely"; p. 810, also see p. 799).

3. Hall's reasoning is also echoed by, among others, Tinelli (1970, 2ff.) and Y. Dejean (1977, 423–424; 1980, 160). Yves Dejean (personal communication) now agrees that he had underestimated the inventory and productivity of HC morphological processes.

4. Dijkhoff's (1993) treatment of Papiamentu compounding is a notable exception, perhaps among others that I am not yet aware of.

5. I use the following abbreviations:

(i) adj.   adjective
    adv.   adverb
    ANT   anterior
    FEM   feminine
    MASC   masculine
    n.   noun
    NEG   negative
    PROG   progressive marker
    RES-PRON   resumptive pronoun (see DeGraff 1992, 1993, 1995)
    v.   verb
    1SG ... 3PL   1st person singular ... 3rd person plural

6. One cannot be totally certain that particular forms were/are absent from the *mental* lexicons of (French) speakers at any particular time. Then and now, dictionaries are only imperfect inventories of speakers' mental lexicons. Hence the need for caution in determining neologisms; *Haitianisms* may be a more appropriate term to distinguish such well-established "neologisms" from recent (and truly *neo*-logical) lexical innovations.

7. To some extent, I agree with Lefebvre (1998), and also with Adam (1883) and Sylvain (1936): I too am convinced that various aspects of HC grammar are

somewhat in "correspondence" with substrate grammar; this is hardly surprising given what we know about native language influence on the results of second language acquisition by adults. But it is certainly inaccurate to posit as Adam and Lefebvre do that Creole morphosyntax is virtually isomorphic with that of its substrate. For example, the inventory and properties of HC morphological processes, once carefully studied, robustly contradict the claim that HC affixes are mostly in a "one-to-one correspondence" with Fongbe affixes (see main text). In other words, Lefebvre's "relexification" hypothesis cannot even account for the genesis and structure of the HC lexicon—the latter is where "relexification" may be expected to apply most straightforwardly.

Suzanne Sylvain, the Haitian-born linguist who is often hailed as an early HC "relexificationist" in contrast to her "superstratist" compatriot and contemporary Jules Faine, was actually very careful in showing, throughout her book, that HC grammar was substantially influenced by *both* the lexifier and the substrate.

HC also displays patterns that distinguish it both from the lexifier and from the (major) substrate (see, e.g., DeGraff 1992, 1993, 1994, 1995, 1997, 1999b,c, 2000a,b).

8. Valdman takes most of his examples from Orjala 1970, 154–155. Orjala, like Valdman, calls such forms "Gallicisms." Unlike Valdman, though, Orjala considers such examples to demonstrate *productive* word formation processes in rural (i.e., monolingual) HC. For Valdman, the examples in (3) do not count as evidence for productive suffixation; instead, they count as evidence that HC derivation is "very weak," which in turn makes HC's "lexical enrichment" dependent on "pseudo-French" affixation. The latter is claimed to be symptomatic of decreolization.

9. *Eklerasyon* in (5) is also found in Valdman 1978, 139, with the French translation 'conscience éclairée' (i.e., 'enlightened conscience'). Valdman writes that, notwithstanding morphophonological and semantic similarities between stem and derived form, "it is difficult to extract from [*eklerasyon*] a suffix that has the same semantics elsewhere." This statement contradicts the stable paradigm of semantically transparent derivations in (4); furthermore, some of the pairs in (4)–(5) and many other such examples are found in Valdman et al. 1981 and Valdman, Pooser, and Jean-Baptiste 1996; also see note 18.

10. Fort-Royal is a small, rural, totally monolingual Haitian community (of about 300 households) near Petit-Goâve, 70 kilometers west of the capital Port-au-Prince. Fort-Royal is also where Y. Dejean directs Sant Twa Ti Flè ('Three Little Flowers Center'), a small school where HC is the only language of instruction.

11. Lefebvre gives "1988" and "Lawrence, KS" as the year and place of publication for Freeman's inverse word list. The version I consulted was published in 1989 in Port-au-Prince. It seems unlikely that *adorasyon* and *admirasyon* and the HC -*syon* neologisms were all post-1988 additions to the Port-au-Prince edition.

12. HC *pansyon* also has the sense of 'boardinghouse, pension' (cf. French *pension*), but this is not the relevant meaning for the derived verb *pansyone*. Throughout this text, I mention only the senses that are relevant for the points being made.

13. Whether Creole languages can be defined in terms of a purely structural prototype has been debated many times before. The antiprototype view has proposed
that creolization is defined by sociohistorical factors such as massive language
contact, abrupt emergence of a new variety as a contact language distinct from the
languages (previously) in contact, and so on (see DeGraff 1999a,b,d for an overview). For example, for Schuchardt (1909), the structural output of language
contact is partly determined by language-external factors that belong to (e.g.)
sociology and history. Similarly, Meillet (1906 [1958, 17]) observes that "social
change" is the ultimate, "most often mediated and indirect" root of linguistic
change. In Hall's (1966, 123) words, "There are no structural criteria which, in
themselves, will identify a creole as such, in the absence of historical evidence." In
Hoenigswald's (1971, 473, 479) words, Creoles "furnish the theory of linguistic
change—so largely speculative in character—with quasi-empirical foundation"
and "[p]ossibly all change processes partake of the characteristics of creolization,
with the *particular* historical circumstances making the crucial, but essentially
quantitative, difference." In a related vein, Mufwene (1998) argues that "creolization is a social, not a structural, process." In so doing, he joins Hall, Givón (1979),
and Muysken (1988), among others, in arguing that there may be no coherent
typological and theoretical basis for a Creole prototype in purely linguistic terms.
As Muysken (1988, 300) states, "The very notion of a 'creole' language from the
linguistic point of view tends to disappear if one looks closely; what we have is just
a language." Elsewhere I too have argued that, within mentalist approaches to
language creation and language change, "the notion of 'creolization' as a unitary
and distinct linguistic phenomenon evaporates" (DeGraff 1999b, 477).

14. Also see *to delouse* 'to remove lice from'. There is no *to louse* with the meaning 'to add lice to'; *to louse*, in one of its senses, is actually synonymous with *to
delouse*. But see *to louse up*, which does mean 'to infect with lice'—though apparently there is no **to delouse up* or **to unlouse*. Contrast *to delouse/*to unlouse/
to louse with *to degrease/to ungrease/to grease*. The semantics of English *de-* (and
HC *de-*) are obviously much more complicated than they appear at first sight,
perhaps having intricate causative and/or aspectual properties. But the central
point here is that *de-* (in HC and English—and also in Romance) cannot be said
to be transparently and consistently inversive. See Horn 1989 for a range of fascinating facts concerning the semantics and pragmatics of *de-* and its congeners.

15. McWhorter (1998, 803–804) warns against "highly selective presentation of
data" and encourages creolists to view "creole data ... more liberally."

16. I am thankful to Calixto Agüero-Bautista for discussion of cockfighting
practices and terminology in the Dominican Republic.

17. It is puzzling that Ehrman 1972, Jenner and Pou 1982, Milne 1921, and
Thomas 1971 are enlisted in McWhorter 1998 to support the claim that Mon-
Khmer languages have "rich paradigms of morphological affixes alien to any
language known as creoles" (p. 796). These authors explicitly state that derivation
in Cambodian, Chrau, and Palaung is by and large "moribund" and "seldom used
in new combinations" (see, e.g., Ehrman 1972, 3; Jenner and Pou 1982, xxxiv;

Milne 1921, 6; and Thomas 1971, 19–20, 56, 152–153, 235 (also chaps. 8–9); also see Huffman 1970, 16, 311).

18. As it turns out, the "abstraction" suffix -*te* is commonly found in HC, as in the following sample of straightforwardly compositional adjective-to-noun derivations:

(i) ansyen 'old'   ansyennte 'seniority'
    bon 'good'   bonte 'goodness'
    brav 'brave'   bravte 'bravery'
    fèm 'firm'   fèmte 'firmness'
    frekan 'insolent'   frekanste 'insolence'
    fyè 'proud'   fyète 'pride'
    klè 'bright'   klète 'brightness'
    lach 'cowardly'   lachte 'cowardice'
    lèd 'ugly'   lèdte 'ugliness'
    mal 'miserable'   malsite 'misery'
    malpwòp 'unclean'   malpwòpte 'uncleanliness'
    mechan 'mean'   mechanste 'meanness'
    pwòp 'clean'   pwòpte 'cleanliness'
    saf 'greedy'   safte 'greed'
    sal 'dirty'   salte 'dirtiness'

The semantically transparent paradigm in (i) also speaks against the analysis in Valdman 1978, 139, where *bèl* and *bèlte*, like *eklere* and *eklerasyon* (see note 9), are claimed to constitute one of those morphophonologically and semantically related pairs where "it is difficult to extract from the derived member of the pair a suffix that has the same semantics elsewhere." Furthermore, HC -*te* is productive, as attested by Haitianisms such as *malsite* and *safte*. *Safte* is included in Valdman et al. 1981, along with some of the other examples in (i); also see the variant *safrite* in Fattier 1998, 393.

Recall that as productive HC suffixes, -*te* in (i) and -*ès* on pp. 65–66 also contradict the affix set postulated in Lefebvre 1998, chap. 10. The latter excludes both -*te* and -*ès*, along with many of the derivational processes illustrated in this chapter (see note 7).

19. In theories like Distributed Morphology (see, e.g., Halle and Marantz 1993; Halle 1994; Marantz 1997), the theoretical distinction between "morphological glue" and "syntactic glue" does not have primitive status, as it is claimed that the syntax is the unique "combinatoric engine" in the grammar (Marantz, Miyashita, and O'Neil, 2000). In such a framework, it is impossible to draw a conceptual boundary between the sort of meaning expressed by 'morphological" combination of bound morphemes and the sort of meaning expressed by "syntactic" combination of words. There is also evidence that precludes a strict separation between the two modules; witness the well-known example *better* vs. **more good*, which suggests that blocking can apply across morphology and syntax.

20. Also see Rickford 1980 for a solid rebuttal of related claims about the expressive adequacy of Creole discourse. Rickford analyzes Guyanese greole narratives

that cast doubt on Creoles' putative inadequacy. Yet Rickford does not refute the alleged structural bases of Whinnom's (1971, 109–110) claims, namely, the limitations on Creole morphology and the implications thereof for Creole speakers' intellectual capacities.

There is a certain irony in the fact that Whinnom's unsubstantiated statement on the inherent intellectual "handicap" of Creole languages is in the same volume where one can read, "[P]idgin-creole studies have become a respectable field. No longer are young linguists advised not to waste their time on such peripheral subjects but to study 'real' languages if they wish to get on in the academic world" (DeCamp 1971, 13). Whinnom's arguments make Creole languages look quite un-'real'.

21. Here I also follow Chomsky's (1979, 31) advice in trying to go beyond "local exception[s]" that instantiate "ideological control" toward uncovering "the overall pattern [that] remains hidden"; also see Chomsky's (1993) exhortation to address the reality and causes of the "overall pattern." This "overall pattern" is also what Smitherman (2000, 67) addresses in her critique of a particular "tradition, qua tradition" in the context of prejudices in academia toward African-American speech.

For it is this tradition, qua tradition, rather than the work of any single scholar, that sets the stage for public decision making and social policy formulation that govern the lives and ultimately the survival of black Americans.

My sketch below is not fully representative; Goodman (1964), Y. Dejean (1977), Prudent (1980), Holm (1988), and the papers in Arends, Muysken, and Smith 1995 provide more comprehensive surveys. The case studies and quotations in this chapter are meant as an illustration of my thesis regarding the negative impact of certain age-old preconceptions in Creole studies.

22. M. L. E. Moreau de Saint-Méry (1750–1819), himself born in Martinique of European descent, sharply critiqued his Swiss contemporary Girod-Chantrans's "Creole" data, calling it "Swiss Creole." About one of Girod-Chantrans's "Creole" letters, he wrote:

[Girod-Chantrans's] jargon [*baragouin*] will pass for [Saint-Domingue] Creole only for our scientists, who in turn introduce a similar sort of "Creole" in the theater, and persuade Parisians that their "Creole" is the real one. [Girod-Chantrans's alleged Creole] letter could only have been written by himself, or by someone who wanted to make fun of his naivete ... (1797 [1958, 81]; my translation)

Moreau de Saint-Méry's allusion to "Creole' in the theater" strikes me as uncannily prescient given the abundance of fanciful descriptions of HC in past and present Creole studies (for recent critiques, see Chaudenson 1996; DeGraff 1999c; Y. Dejean 1999).

Also noteworthy is the fact that most early creolists (with exceptions such as Moreau de Saint-Méry, Ducœurjoly, and Saint-Quentin) could hardly qualify as Creole speakers. The situation has hardly changed since; but see section 2.7.

23. What Saint-Quentin (1872) calls "syntaxe" (which is the topic of his description of the French-lexifier Creole of Cayenne, Guyane) is roughly what we would today call morpho(phono)logy with basic aspects of word order.

24. Suzanne Sylvain is perhaps the earliest bona fide Haitian-born creolist.

25. Throughout Bloomfield 1933, 471–475, Creoles are viewed as (originating from systems that are) "aberrant," "substandard," "baby-talk," "simplified," "imperfect," "reproductions [of some European language]," "incorrect," "inferior dialects," "subject to improvement in the direction of [masters' speech]." This stands in sharp contrast to Bloomfield's (1925) progressive, egalitarian, and eloquent manifesto "Why a Linguistics Society?" where he promotes the study of "dialects," unwritten languages, and Native American languages.

The layman usually ... believes that languages which possess no written literature are mere "dialects" or "jargons," of small extent and subject to no fixed rule. Quite by contrast, linguistics finds ... a similarity, repugnant to the common-sense view, between the languages of highly civilized people and those of savages, a similarity which disregards the use or non-use of writing.... [S]tandard and literary languages are not original forms from which dialects faultily deviate ... but are only secondary creations on the basis of dialects, which latter root far more deeply in the past.

Yet Bloomfield (1933) himself applies the "layman['s] ... common-sense view" to Creoles, removing them from the scope of his own egalitarian credo. Such ambivalence and contradictory pronouncements are still common among contemporary creolists and Creolophones (for further discussion, see, e.g., Bebel-Gisler and Hurbon 1975; Y. Dejean 1975, 1993; Prudent 1980; Devonish 1986; Zéphir 1996; DeGraff 2000c).

26. The *Library of Congress Classification Schedule 1998* classifies Creole-related books under the "PM" category, which is misleadingly synopsized as "Hyperborean, [American] Indian, and Artificial Languages"! (I thank Theresa Tobin for an enlightening tour through the arcane "ontology" of the Library of Congress.)

27. It also seems that Seuren (1998, 292) would take, say, Caribbean Creole culture—for example, its linguistic, religious, social, artistic, and culinary practices —to bear no historical connection to the "rich and extended cultural past" of Africa, Europe, Asia, and the (pre-Columbian) Americas. If so, Seuren must in turn deny, for example, the well-documented symbolic and theological complexity of Haitian Vodou, much of which has deep roots in, inter alia, Christianity and, especially, ancient traditional religions from the Gulf of Guinea in Africa (see Hurbon 1987; Desmangles 1992; and references therein). In effect, Seuren may be adopting the still popular bias according to which no Caribbean phenomenon can be related to any "rich and extended cultural past," the available evidence notwithstanding.

Interestingly, Seuren's devaluation of Caribbean languages and cultures is found in the same book where Seuren accuses Wilhelm von Humboldt (1767–1835) of exhibiting "basic Eurocentrism," "cultural prejudice," and "cultural arrogance" and of having "a fundamentally chauvinist mind," all of which, according to Seuren, is related to "racial and nationalist prejudices [that] were rife in the western world of the early 19th century" (p. 111). As evidenced here and in the main text, such prejudices still exist even as we near the twenty-first century, and even in the "polite society" of respectable linguistic publications.

28. Linguistic prejudices and myths surrounding "minority languages" persist on a large scale even in the most literate and economically advanced societies and even among the latters' political, academic, and intellectual elites (see, e.g., O'Neil's (1998), Rickford's (1999), and Smitherman's (2000) critiques of the most recent "Ebonics debate" following the 1996 Oakland, California, school board's resolution recognizing African-American English as a valid "primary language"). In the case of HC in Haiti, the stigmatized "minority language" happens to be the *first* and *only* language of the vast majority of the population. This point often goes unappreciated, not only among casual observers, but also among scholars, educators, and administrators directly concerned with Haiti (for sociolinguistic and political analyses, see, e.g., Bebel-Gisler and Hurbon 1975; Y. Dejean 1975, 1993; P. Dejan/Dejean 1988, 1989, 1993).

References

Adam, Lucien. 1883. *Les idiomes négro-aryen et maléo-aryen: Essai d'hybridologie linguistique*. Paris: Maisonneuve.

Alleyne, Mervin. 1994. Problems of standardization of creole languages. In Marcyliena Morgan, ed., *Language and the social construction of identity in creole situations*, 7–18. Center for Afro-American Studies, University of California, Los Angeles.

Arends, Jacques, Pieter Muysken, and Norval Smith, eds. 1994. *Pidgins and creoles: An introduction*. Amsterdam: John Benjamins.

Aronoff, Mark. 1976. *Word formation in generative grammar*. Cambridge, Mass.: MIT Press.

Baggioni, Daniel. 1988. L'histoire de la créolistique et ses rapports à l'histoire de l'anthropologie. De Lucien Adam (1883) à Louis Hjelmslev (1938). *Études Créoles*, 11, 82–93.

Baissac, Charles. 1880. *Étude sur le patois créole mauricien*. Nancy: Imprimerie Berger-Levrault.

Baker, Mark. 1988. *Incorporation: A theory of grammatical function changing*. Chicago: University of Chicago Press.

Baker, Philip. 1993. Assessing the African contribution to French-based creoles. In Salikoko Mufwene, ed., *Africanisms in Afro-American language varieties*, 123–155. Athens: University of Georgia Press.

Baker, Philip. 1999. Theories of creolization and the degree and nature of restructuring. Ms., University of Westminster. Paper presented at the International Symposium on Degrees of Restructuring in Creole Languages, Regensburg, June 1998.

Barker, Chris. 1998. Episodic -*ee* in English: A thematic role constraint on new word formation. *Language* 74, 695–727.

Bebel-Gisler, Dany, and Laënnec Hurbon. 1975 [1987]. *Cultures et pouvoir dans la Caraïbe*. 3rd ed. Paris: L'Harmattan.

Bickerton, Derek. 1988. Creole languages and the bioprogram. In Frederick Newmeyer, ed., *Linguistics: The Cambridge survey*. Vol. 2, *Linguistic theory: Extensions and implications*, 268–284. Cambridge: Cambridge University Press.

Bloomfield, Leonard. 1925. Why a linguistics society? *Language* 1, 1–5.

Bloomfield, Leonard. 1933. *Language*. New York: Henry Holt.

Bourdieu, Pierre. 1991. *Language and symbolic power*. Cambridge, Mass.: Harvard University Press.

Bracken, Harry. 1973. Essence, accident and race. *Hermathena* 116, 88–95.

Bracken, Harry. 1974. *Berkeley*. London: Macmillan.

Bresnan, Joan. To appear. The emergence of the unmarked pronoun. In Géraldine Legendre, Sten Vikner, and Jane Grimshaw, eds., *Optimality-theoretic syntax*. Cambridge, Mass.: MIT Press.

Brousseau, Anne-Marie, Sandra Filipovich, and Claire Lefebvre. 1989. Morphological processes in Haitian Creole: The question of substratum and simplification. *Journal of Pidgin and Creole Languages* 4, 1–36.

Cameron, Deborah, Elizabeth Frazer, and Penelope Harvey. 1992. *Researching language: Issues of power and method*. London: Routledge.

Chaudenson, Robert. 1979. *Les créoles français*. Paris: Fernand Nathan.

Chaudenson, Robert. 1996. Petit sottisier glané dans les recherches sur l'origine des systèmes grammaticaux créoles. In Daniel Véronique, ed., *Matériaux pour l'étude des classes grammaticales dans les langues créoles*, 17–37. Aix-en-Provence: Publications de l'Université de Provence.

Chaudenson, Robert, Raymond Mougeon, and Édouard Beniak. 1993. *Vers une approche panlectale de la variation du français*. Aix-en-Provence: Institut d'Études Créoles et Francophones. Diffusion: Didier Érudition.

Chomsky, Noam. 1975. *Reflections on language*. New York: Pantheon.

Chomsky, Noam. 1979. *Language and responsibility*. Sussex, England: Harvester Press.

Chomsky, Noam. 1993. *Year 501: The conquest continues*. Boston: South End Press.

Clark, Eve. 1993. *The lexicon in acquisition*. Cambridge: Cambridge University Press.

Clark, Eve, and Herbert Clark. 1979. When nouns surface as verbs. *Language* 55, 767–811.

Damoiseau, Robert. 1988. Éléments pour une classification des verbaux en créole haïtien. *Études Créoles* 11, 41–64.

Damoiseau, Robert. 1991. Exemples de procédures de réinterprétation d'un lexique français en créole haïtien. *Études Créoles* 14, 1–43.

D'Ans, André-Marcel. 1968. *Le créole français d'Haïti*. The Hague: Mouton.

DeCamp, David. 1971. The study of pidgin and creole languages. In Dell Hymes, ed., *Pidginization and creolization of languages*, 13–39. Cambridge: Cambridge University Press.

DeGraff, Michel. 1992. The syntax of predication in Haitian. In *NELS 22*, 103–117. GLSA, University of Massachusetts, Amherst.

DeGraff, Michel. 1993. A riddle on negation in Haitian. *Probus* 5, 63–93.

DeGraff, Michel. 1994. The morphology-syntax interface in creolization (and diachrony). *Studies in the Linguistic Sciences* 24, 115–132.

DeGraff, Michel. 1995. On certain differences between Haitian and French predicative constructions. In Jon Amastae, Grant Goodall, Mario Montalbetti, and Marianne Phinney, eds., *Contemporary research in Romance linguistics*, 237–256. Amsterdam: John Benjamins.

DeGraff, Michel. 1997. Verb syntax in creolization (and beyond). In Liliane Haegeman, ed., *The new comparative syntax*, 64–94. London: Longman.

DeGraff, Michel. 1999a. Creolization, language change, and language acquisition: A prolegomenon. In Michel DeGraff, ed., *Language creation and language change: Creolization, diachrony, and development*, 1–46. Cambridge, Mass.: MIT Press.

DeGraff, Michel. 1999b. Creolization, language change, and language acquisition: An epilogue. In Michel DeGraff, ed., *Language creation and language change: Creolization, diachrony, and development*, 473–543. Cambridge, Mass.: MIT Press.

DeGraff, Michel. 1999c. Empirical quicksand: Probing two recent articles on Haitian Creole. *Journal of Pidgin & Creole Languages* 14, 1–12.

DeGraff, Michel. 1999d. Parameter-setting in acquisition and through creolization and language change. In Rob Wilson and Frank Keil, eds., *The MIT encyclopedia of the cognitive sciences*, 624–627. Cambridge, Mass.: MIT Press.

DeGraff, Michel. 2000a. À propos des pronoms objets dans le créole d'Haïti: Regards croisés de la morphologie et de la diachronie. *Langages* 38, 89–113.

DeGraff, Michel. 2000b. Morphology in language creation and language change: Haitian Creole as "prototypical" case study. Ms., MIT.

DeGraff, Michel. 2000c. Toward a new perspective on Creole studies. Ms., MIT.

Dejan, Pòl. 1988. *Ki sa gouvènman peyi a janm fè ant 1943 ak 1988 pou l regle koze pa konn li ak pa konn ekri ann Ayiti*. Port-au-Prince, Haïti: Sekreteri d Eta pou Alfabetizasyon.

Dejean, Paul. 1989. *Survol des tentatives d'alphabétisation en Haïti par les services gouvernementaux, 1943–1988*. Port-au-Prince, Haïti: Groupe d'Action et de Recherche pour l'Éducation.

Dejean, Paul. 1993. *Haïti: Alerte, on tue!* Montréal: CIDIHCA.

Dejean, Yves. 1975. *Dilemme en Haïti: Français en péril ou péril français?* New York: Éditions Connaissance d'Haïti.

Dejean, Yves. 1977. Comment écrire le créole d'Haïti. Doctoral dissertation, Indiana University.

Dejean, Yves. 1980. Comment écrire le créole d'Haïti. [Abridged and revised version of Dejean 1977.] Outremont, Québec: Collectif Paroles.

Dejean, Yves. 1993. An overview of the language situation in Haiti. *International Journal of the Sociology of Language* 102, 73–83.

Dejean, Yves. 1999. L'archipel nous revient: Créolistes et données. *Études Créoles* 22, 85–114.

Déprez, Viviane. 1999. The roots of negative concord in French and French-lexicon Creoles. In Michel DeGraff, ed., *Language creation and language change: Creolization, diachrony, and development*, 375–427. Cambridge, Mass.: MIT Press.

Descourtilz, Michel Étienne. 1809. *Voyages d'un naturaliste et ses observations faites sur les trois règnes de la nature, dans plusieurs ports de mer français, en Espagne, an continent de l'Amérique septentrionale ...* 3 vol. Paris: Dufart, père.

Desmangles, Leslie. 1992. *The faces of the gods: Vodou and Roman Catholicism in Haiti*. Chapel Hill: University of North Carolina Press.

Devonish, Hubert. 1986. *Language and liberation: Creole language politics in the Caribbean*. London: Karia Press.

Dijkhoff, Marta. 1993. Papiamentu word formation: A case study of complex nouns and their relation to phrases and clauses. Doctoral dissertation, University of Amsterdam.

Ehrman, Madeline. 1972. *Contemporary Cambodian: Grammatical sketch*. Washington, D.C.: Foreign Service Institute.

Faine, Jules. 1936. *Philologie créole: Études historiques et étymologiques sur la langue créole d'Haïti*. Port-au-Prince, Haïti: Imprimerie de l'État.

Fattier, Dominique. 1998. Contribution à l'étude de la genèse d'un créole: L'atlas linguistique d'Haïti, cartes et commentaires. Doctoral dissertation, Université de Provence. (Distributed by Presses Uninversitaires du Septentrion, Villeneuve d'Ascq, France.)

Férère, Gérard. 1974. Haitian Creole: Sound-system, Form-classes, texts. Doctoral dissertation, University of Pennsylvania.

Fermino, Jessie Little Doe. 2000. An introduction to Wampanoag grammar. Master's thesis, MIT.

Freeman, Bryant. 1989. *Dictionnaire inverse de la langue créole haïtienne*. Centre de Linguistique Appliquée, Université d'État d'Haïti, Port-au-Prince.

Freeman, Bryant, and Jowel Laguerre. 1996 [1998]. *Haitian-English dictionary*. 2nd ed.: 1998. Institute of Haitian Studies, University of Kansas.

Girod-Chantrans, Justin. 1785 [1980]. *Voyage d'un Suisse dans différentes colonies d'Amérique ...* Neuchâtel: Imprimerie de la Société typographique. [1980 edition: Paris: Libraire Jules Tallandier.]

Givón, Talmy. 1979. Prolegomena to any sane creology. In Ian Hancock, ed., *Readings in Creole studies*, 3–35. Ghent: E. Story-Scientia.

Goodman, Morris. 1964. *A comparative study of Creole French dialects*. The Hague: Mouton.

Gougenheim, Georges. 1971. *Étude sur les périphrases verbales de la langue française*. Paris: Nizet.

Green, Thomas, and Ken Hale. 1998. Ulwa, the language of Karawala, eastern Nicaragua: Its position and prospects in modern Nicaragua. *International Journal of the Sociology of Language* 132, 185–201.

Hale, Ken. 1965. On the use of informants in field-work. *Canadian Journal of Linguistics* 10(2–3), 108–119.

Hale, Ken. 1972a. A new perspective on American Indian linguistics. In Alfonso Ortiz, ed., *New perspectives on the pueblos*, 87–110. Albuquerque: University of New Mexico Press.

Hale, Ken. 1972b. Some questions about anthropological linguistics: The role of native knowledge. In Dell Hymes, ed., *Reinventing anthropology*, 382–397. New York: Pantheon.

Hale, Ken. 1973. The role of American Indian linguistics in bilingual education. In Paul Turner, ed., *Bilingualism in the Southwest*, 203–225. Tucson: University of Arizona Press.

Hale, Ken. 1992. Language endangerment and the human value of linguistic diversity. *Language* 68, 35–42.

Hale, Ken. 1993. On the human value of local languages. In André Chrochetière, Jean-Claude Boulanger, and Conrad Ouellon, eds., *Proceedings of the 15th International Congress of Linguists, vol. I*, 17–31. Québec: Les Presses de l'Université Laval.

Hale, Ken. 2001. Ulwa (Southern Sumu): The beginnings of a language research project. In Paul Newman and Martha Ratliff, eds., *Linguistic fieldwork*, 76–101. Cambridge: Cambridge University Press.

Hall, Robert, Jr. 1953. *Haitian Creole: Grammar, texts, vocabulary. The American Anthropologist. Memoir 74*. Washington, D.C.: American Anthropological Association.

Hall, Robert, Jr. 1966. *Pidgin and Creole languages*. Ithaca, N.Y.: Cornell University Press.

Halle, Morris. 1994. The Russian declension: An illustration of the theory of Distributed Morphology. In Jennifer Cole and Charles Kisseberth, eds., *Perspectives in phonology*, 29–60. Stanford, Calif.: CSLI Publications.

Halle, Morris, and Alec Marantz. 1993. Distributed Morphology and the pieces of inflection. In Kenneth Hale and Samuel Jay Keyser, eds., *The view from Building 20: Essays in linguistics in honor of Sylvain Bromberger*, 111–176. Cambridge, Mass.: MIT Press.

Hjelmslev, Louis. 1938. Relation de parenté des langues créoles. *Revue des Études Indo-Européennes* 1, 271–286.

Hjelmslev, Louis. 1939. Caractères grammaticaux des langues créoles. In *Congrès International des Sciences Anthropologiques et Ethnologiques; Compte-Rendu de la Deuxième Session*, 373. Copenhagen: Einar Munksgaard.

Hockett, Charles. 1958. *A course in modern linguistics*. New York: Macmillan.

Hoenigswald, Henry. 1971. Language history and Creole studies. In Dell Hymes, ed., *Pidginization and creolization of languages*, 473–480. Cambridge: Cambridge University Press.

Holm, John. 1988. *Pidgins and Creoles*. Cambridge: Cambridge University Press.

Honda, Maya, and Wayne O'Neil. 1993. Triggering science-forming capacity through linguistic inquiry. In Kenneth Hale and Samuel Jay Keyser, eds., *The view from Building 20: Essays in linguistics in honor of Sylvain Bromberger*, 229–255. Cambridge, Mass.: MIT Press.

Horn, Laurence. 1989. Morphology, pragmatics, and the *un*-verb. In Joyce Powers and Kenneth de Jong, eds., *ESCOL '88: Proceedings of the Fifth Eastern States Conference on Linguistics*, 210–233. Department of Linguistics, The Ohio State University.

Huffman, Franklin. 1970. *Modern spoken Cambodian*. New Haven, Conn.: Yale University Press.

Hurbon, Laënnec. 1987. *Dieu dans le Vaudou haïtien*. Port-au-Prince, Haïti: Éditions Henri Deschamps.

Jackendoff, Ray. 1995. The boundaries of the lexicon. In Martin Everaert, Erik-Jan van der Linden, Andre Schenk, and Rob Schreuder, eds., *Idioms: Structural and psychological perspectives*, 133–165. Hillsdale, N.J.: Lawrence Erlbaum Associates.

Jenner, Philip, and Saveros Pou. 1982. *A lexicon of Khmer morphology*. Honolulu: University Press of Hawaii.

Jespersen, Otto. 1922. *Language: Its nature, development and origin*. London: G. Allen & Unwin.

Kegl, Judy, Ann Senghas, and Marie Coppola. 1999. Creation through contact: Sign language emergence and sign language change in Nicaragua. In Michel DeGraff, ed., *Language creation and language change: Creolization, diachrony, and development*, 179–237. Cambridge, Mass.: MIT Press.

Labov, William. 1994. *Principles of linguistic change*. Oxford: Blackwell.

Larousse, Pierre. 1869. *Grand dictionnaire universel du XIX siècle*. Paris: Larousse.

Lefebvre, Claire. 1998. *Creole genesis and the acquisition of grammar: The case of Haitian Creole*. Cambridge: Cambridge University Press.

Lyell, Charles. 1830–1833. *Principles of geology; Being an attempt to explain the former changes of the earth's surface, by reference to causes now in operation*. London: J. Murray.

Marantz, Alec. 1997. No escape from syntax. In Alexis Dimitriadis, Laura Siegel, Clarissa Surek-Clark, and Alexander Williams, eds., *Proceedings of the 21st Annual Penn Linguistics Colloquium*, 201–225. Pennsylvania Working Papers in Linguistics 4.2. Penn Linguistics Club, University of Pennsylvania.

Marantz, Alec, Yasushi Miyashita, and Wayne O'Neil. 2000. Introduction: Mind articulation. In Alec Marantz, Yasushi Miyashita, and Wayne O'Neil, eds.,

Image, language, brain: Papers from the First Mind Articulation Project Symposium. Cambridge, Mass.: MIT Press.

McWhorter, John. 1998. Identifying the creole prototype: Vindicating a typological class. *Language* 74, 788–818.

Meijer, Gus, and Pieter Muysken.1977. On the beginnings of pidgin and creole studies: Schuchardt and Hesseling. In Albert Valdman, ed., *Pidgin and creole linguistics*, 21–45. Bloomington: Indiana University Press.

Meillet, Antoine. 1906 [1958]. L'état actuel des études de linguistique générale. Opening lecture for the course on comparative grammar at the Collège de France. [Reprinted in Antoine Meillet, *Linguistique historique et linguistique générale, vol. I*, 1–18. Paris: Honoré Champion. (1958).]

Meillet, Antoine. 1919 [1958]. Le genre grammatical et l'élimination de la flexion. *Scientia (Rivista di Scienza)* 25(86). [Reprinted in Antoine Meillet, *Linguistique historique et linguistique générale, vol. I*, 199–210. Paris: Honoré Champion (1958).]

Meillet, Antoine. 1924 [1951]. Introduction à la classification des langues. Introductory chapter of *Les langues du monde*. [Reprinted in Antoine Meillet, *Linguistique historique et linguistique générale, vol. II*, 53–69. Paris: Klincksieck (1951).]

Meillet, Antoine. 1929 [1951]. Le développement des langues. In *Continu et discontinu*, 119ff. Paris: Bloud & Gay. [Reprinted in Antoine Meillet, *Linguistique historique et linguistique générale, vol. II*, 71–83. Paris: Klincksieck (1951).]

Métellus, Jean. 1997–1998. What is an intellectual? (Interview.) *Haïtiens aujourd'hui*, 12/97–1/98, 2, 1, 11–26.

Milne, Mary. 1921. *An elementary Palaung grammar.* Oxford: Clarendon Press.

Moreau de Saint-Méry, M. L. E. 1797 [1958]. *Description topographique, physique, civile, politique et historique de la partie française de l'Isle Saint Domingue.* 3 vols. Philadelphia: Chez l'Auteur. [1958 edition: Paris: Société de l'Histoire des Colonies Françaises.]

Mufwene, Salikoko. 1991. Pidgins, creoles, typology, and markedness. In Francis Byrne and Thom Huebner, eds., *Development and structures of creole languages: Essays in honor of Derek Bickerton*, 123–143. Amsterdam: John Benjamins.

Mufwene, Salikoko. 1998. Creolization is a social, not a structural, process. Paper presented at the International Symposium on Degrees of Restructuring in Creole Languages, Regensburg, June 1998.

Muysken, Pieter. 1988. Are Creoles a special type of language? In Frederick Newmeyer, ed., *Linguistics: The Cambridge survey.* Vol. 2, *Linguistics theory: Extensions and implications*, 285–301. Cambridge: Cambridge University Press.

Muysken, Pieter. In press. Pidginization, creolization and language death. In Geert Booij and Christian Lehmann, eds., *Handbook of morphology.* Berlin: Mouton de Gruyter.

O'Neil, Wayne. 1998. Ebonics in the media. *Radical Teacher* 54, 13–17.

Orjala, Paul. 1970. A dialect survey of Haitian Creole. Doctoral dissertation, Hartford Seminary Foundation.

Pelleprat, Father Pierre. 1655 [1965]. *Relation des missions des Pères de la Compagnie de Jésus dans les iles et dans la terre ferme de l'Amérique méridionale.* Paris: Chez Sébastien Cramoisy & Gabriel Cramoisy. [Translated and reprinted in 1965 as *Relato de las misiones de los Padres de la Compañía de Jesús en las islas y en tierra firme de América meridional.* Caracas: Fuentes para la Historia Colonial de Venezuela.]

Pinker, Steven. 1999. *Words and rules: The ingredients of language.* New York: Basic Books.

Prudent, Lambert-Félix. 1980. *Des baragouins à la langue antillaise: Analyse historique et sociolinguistique du discours sur le créole.* Paris: Éditions Caribéennes.

Rey, Alain. 1995. *Dictionnaire historique de la langue française.* Paris: Le Robert.

Rickford, John. 1980. "Me Tarzan, you Jane!" Adequacy, expressiveness, and the creole speaker. *Journal of Linguistics* 22, 281–310.

Rickford, John. 1999. The Ebonics controversy in my backyard: A sociolinguist's experiences and reflections. *Journal of Sociolinguistics* 3, 267–275.

Ritter, Elizabeth. 1991. Déplacement de NP en haïtien: Oui ou non? *Recherches Linguistiques de Vincennes* 20, 65–86.

Saint-Quentin, Alfred de. 1872 [1989]. *Introduction à l'histoire de Cayenne*, with *Étude sur la grammaire créole* by Auguste de Saint-Quentin. Antibes: J. Marchand. [1989 edition: Cayenne: Comité de la Culture, de l'Éducation et de l'Environnement, Région Guyane.]

Samarin, William. 1980. Standardization and instrumentalization of creole languages. In Albert Valdman and Arnold Highfield, eds., *Theoretical orientations in Creole studies*, 213–236. New York: Academic Press.

Sapir, Edward. 1921. *Language: An introduction to the study of speech.* New York: Harcourt, Brace and Company.

Sapir, Edward. 1933 [1963]. Language. In *Encyclopaedia of the social sciences* 9, 155–169. New York: Macmillan. [Reprinted in *Selected writings of Edward Sapir*, 7–32. Berkeley and Los Angeles: University of California Press (1963).]

Schuchardt, Hugo. 1909 [1980]. Die Lingua Franca. *Zeitschrift für romanische Philologie* 33, 441–461. [Translated in Glenn Gilbert, ed., *Pidgin and Creole languages: Selected essays by Hugo Schuchardt*, 65–88. Cambridge: Cambridge University Press (1980).]

Schuchardt, Hugo. 1914. *Die Sprache der Saramakkaneger in Surinam.* Verhandelingen der Koninklijke Akademie van Wetenschappen te Amsterdam. Afdeeling Letterkunde. Nieuwe Reeks. 14(6). Amsterdam: Johannes Müller. [Preface translated in T. L. Markey, ed., *The ethnography of variation: Selected writings on pidgins and creoles*, by Hugo Schuchardt; edited and translated by T. L. Markey, 73–108. Ann Arbor, Mich.: Karoma (1979) and in Glenn Gilbert, ed., *Pidgin and*

Creole languages: Selected essays by Hugo Schuchardt, 65–88. Cambridge: Cambridge University Press (1980).]

Seuren, Pieter. 1998. *Western linguistics: An historical introduction*. Oxford: Blackwell.

Seuren, Pieter, and Herman Wekker. 1986. Semantic transparency as a factor in creole genesis. In Pieter Muysken and Norval Smith, eds., *Substrata versus universals in creole genesis*, 57–70. Amsterdam: John Benjamins.

Smitherman, Geneva. 2000. *Talkin that talk: Language, culture and education in African America*. London: Routledge.

Stump, Gregory. 1998. Inflection. In Andrew Spencer and Arnold Zwicky, eds., *The handbook of morphology*, 13–43. Oxford: Blackwell.

Syea, Anand. 1992. The short and long form of verbs in Mauritian Creole: Functionalism versus formalism. *Theoretical Linguistics* 18, 61–97.

Sylvain, Suzanne. 1936. *Le créole haïtien: Morphologie et syntaxe*. Wetteren, Belgium: Imprimerie de Meester.

Thomas, David. 1971. *Chrau grammar*. Honolulu: University of Hawaii Press.

Tinelli, Henri. 1970. Generative phonology of Haitian Creole. Doctoral dissertation, University of Michigan.

Trouillot, Hénock. 1980. Les limites du créole dans notre enseignement. Port-au-Prince, Haïti: Imprimerie des Antilles.

Trouillot, Michel-Rolph. 1998. Culture on the edges: Creolization in the plantation context. *Plantation Society in the Americas* 5, 8–28.

UNESCO. 1953. *The use of vernacular languages in education*. Monographs on Fundamental Education 8. Paris: UNESCO.

Valdman, Albert. 1978. *Le créole: Structure, statut et origine*. Paris: Klincksieck.

Valdman, Albert. 1979. La situation linguistique en Haïti. *Études Créoles* 2, 95–106.

Valdman, Albert. 1984. The linguistic situation of Haiti. In Charles Foster and Albert Valdman, eds., *Haiti—Today and tomorrow: An interdisciplinary study*, 77–99. Lanham, Md.: University Press of America.

Valdman, Albert. 1987. Le cycle vital créole et la standardisation du créole haïtien. *Etudes Créoles* 10, 107–125.

Valdman, Albert. 1988. Diglossia and language conflict in Haiti. *International Journal of the Sociology of Language* 71, 67–80.

Valdman, Albert. 1989. Aspects sociolinguistiques de l'élaboration d'une norme écrite pour le créole haïtien. In Ralph Ludwig, ed., *Les créoles français entre l'oral et l'écrit*, 43–63. Tübingen: G. Narr.

Valdman, Albert. 1992. Aspects de l'enseignement du créole comme langue étrangère et langue seconde. *Etudes Créoles* 15, 81–94.

Valdman, Albert et al. 1981. *Haitian Creole-English-French dictionary*. 2 vols. Creole Institute, Indiana University.

Valdman, Albert, with Charles Pooser and Rozevel Jean-Baptiste. 1996. *A learner's dictionary of Haitian Creole*. Creole Institute, Indiana University.

Vinson, Julien. 1882. Créole. In *Dictionnaire des sciences anthropologiques*. Paris.

Weinreich, Uriel. 1953. *Languages in contact: Findings and problems*. New York: Linguistic Circle of New York.

Weinreich, Uriel, William Labov, and Marvin Herzog. 1968. Empirical foundations for a theory of language change. In W. P. Lehmann and Yakov Malkiel, eds., *Directions for historical linguistics*, 95–195. Austin: University of Texas Press.

Wekker, Herman. 1996. Creole words. In Jan Svartvik, ed., *Words: Proceedings of an international symposium, Lund, 25–26 August 1995*, 91–104. Stockholm: Kungl. Vitterhets Historie och Antikvitets Akademien.

Whinnom, Keith. 1971. Linguistic hybridization and the "special case" of pidgins and creoles. In Dell Hymes, ed., *Pidginization and creolization of languages*, 91–115. Cambridge: Cambridge University Press.

Woodson, Drexel. 1992. Which beginning should be hindmost? Surrealism in appropriations of facts about Haitian "contact culture." Paper read at special session, Contact Culture: In Search of Hemispheric Americana, meeting of the American Anthropological Association, San Francisco.

Zéphir, Flore. 1996. *Haitian immigrants in Black America: A sociological and sociolinguistic portrait*. Westport, Conn.: Bergin & Garvey.

Chapter 3

Counterfactuals in a Dynamic Context

Kai von Fintel

3.1 Introduction

A primary goal of research in the semantics/pragmatics interface is to investigate the division of labor between the truth-conditional component of the meaning of an expression and other factors of a more pragmatic nature. One favorite strategy, associated foremost with Grice (1967, 1989), is to keep to a rather austere semantics and to derive the overall meaning of an utterance by predictable additional inferences, called "implicatures," which are seen as based on certain principles of rational and purposeful interaction. In this chapter, I will explore a different way in which the truth-conditional component is complemented in context.

Imagine that we have persuasive evidence that an expression α in context c expresses a proposition p. The straightforward way of capturing this in a semantic system is to attribute to α a context-dependent meaning that maps c to p in a systematic and adequate way.

(1) *Analysis A*
$$[\![\alpha]\!]^c = p$$

A logically possible alternative attributes to α a meaning that has two aspects: it alters the initial context c to a new context c' (2a) and maps c' to the proposition p in a systematic and, importantly, simpler way than under analysis A (2b).[1]

(2) *Analysis B*
    a. $c|\alpha| = c'$
    b. $[\![\alpha]\!]^{c'} = p$

I will argue for analysis B in the case of counterfactual conditionals. But this is not easy. It should be clear that this kind of proposal cannot claim any conceptual advantages.[2] Even if analysis B succeeds in making step (2b), the truth-conditional component of the meaning of α, admirably austere, it still appears to be disfavored in matters of overall complexity. Furthermore, it involves a somewhat strange conception of context change. The usual kind of context change contemplated in dynamic systems for natural language interpretation concerns the effect successful assertions have on the "conversational record" (introduction of new discourse referents, elimination of alternatives under consideration, etc.). What is going on according to analysis B is that even before we compute the denotation of an expression, it is able to change the input context. We will see that there is nevertheless a perfectly reasonable perspective on the context change posited here: context repair in the face of presupposition failure. We will also see a way of implementing the proposal in a dynamic semantics.

Critical support for the analysis has to come from empirical arguments. Perhaps, we have direct evidence for the reality of the austere semantics, so that the context-changing part is a necessary evil. Perhaps, we can find evidence that the context changes posited by the analysis are in fact going on.

3.2 The Nonmonotonicity of Counterfactuals

We will be concerned with examples like these:

(3) a. If kangaroos had no tails, they would topple over.
    b. If Hoover had been a Communist, he would have been a traitor.
    c. If Oswald hadn't killed Kennedy, someone else would have.

A pleasingly simple analysis of such counterfactuals with the schema *if ϕ, (then) would ψ*, from now on symbolized as $\phi > \psi$, would say that they are true at a world w iff all ϕ-worlds accessible from w are ψ-worlds.

(4) $[\![\phi > \psi]\!]^{f}(w) = 1$ iff $\forall w' \in f(w): [\![\phi]\!]^{f}(w') = 1 \rightarrow [\![\psi]\!]^{f}(w') = 1$
    f: an accessibility function from worlds to sets of worlds

This strict conditional analysis of counterfactuals runs into all kinds of trouble (for a classic discussion of some of the issues, see Goodman 1947). In particular, it turns out to be impossible to maintain a stable view of what accessibility function is needed in a given context. The problem can be illustrated by looking at the inference pattern of Strengthening the Antecedent.

(5) *Failure of Strengthening the Antecedent (Downward Monotonicity)*
If kangaroos had no tails, they would topple over.
$\not\Rightarrow$ If kangaroos had no tails but used crutches, they would topple over.

If one were in a somewhat silly frame of mind, one would presumably accept as true David Lewis's classic example *If kangaroos had no tails, they would topple over*. According to the strict conditional analysis, this sentence claims that all of the worlds accessible from our world where kangaroos have no tails are worlds where they topple over. Imagine that a useful notion of accessibility here is the one that relates to our world all the worlds that share with it certain facts of a biological nature (and some laws of physics such as gravity)—but only certain ones: there must be worlds where kangaroos can live without tails. Among those "biologically accessible" worlds, all the ones where kangaroos have no tails are worlds where they chronically topple over. Since the claim is made about *all* such worlds, it is implicitly made also about those among the accessible worlds where kangaroos use crutches. Thus, it should a fortiori be accepted as true that *If kangaroos had no tails but used crutches, they would topple over*. This however is an eminently debatable claim, even if one accepts the initial counterfactual. The strict conditional analysis incorrectly predicts the validity of Strengthening the Antecedent.

By now, it is well known what the solution to this puzzle has to be (Stalnaker 1968, 1975, 1981, 1984; Stalnaker and Thomason 1970; Lewis 1973a,b, 1981).[3] The strict conditional analysis is wrong about the truth-conditions expressed by a counterfactual conditional. Instead, the semantics of the counterfactual must be stated so as to select the worlds quantified over in a way that is sensitive to the antecedent proposition. The first counterfactual makes a claim only about those accessible worlds that are as similar to our world as is possible while making the antecedent true. Arguably, in such worlds kangaroos would not use crutches; hence, they topple over. On the other hand, the antecedent of the second counterfactual forces us to look at worlds where tailless kangaroos use crutches. We again will focus on those worlds among these oddities that are as similar *as possible* to our beloved actual world. The two conditionals thus make claims about two entirely different sets of worlds, which means it is not surprising that Strengthening the Antecedent is not an inference pattern to put any trust in.

One well-known variant of this by now standard possible-worlds semantics for counterfactuals states the truth-conditions relative to a relation of comparative similarity between worlds. The central notion is $w' \leq_w w''$, which says that w' is more similar to w than w'' is to w. A counterfactual quantifies over a selected subset of the antecedent ϕ-worlds, namely, those ϕ-worlds that are at least as similar to the evaluation world w as any other ϕ-world.[4] In addition to similarity, we also speak interchangeably of "closeness" or "nearness" to the evaluation world.

(6) For any proposition p, any similarity relation $\leq$, and any world w:

$$\max_{\leq,w}(p) = \{w': p(w') = 1 \ \& \ \forall w'': p(w'') = 1 \rightarrow w' \leq_w w''\}$$

(7) $[\![\phi > \psi]\!]^{\leq}(w) = 1$ iff $\forall w': w' \in \max_{\leq,w}([\![\phi]\!]^{\leq}) \rightarrow [\![\psi]\!]^{\leq}(w') = 1$

Counterfactual conditionals attempt to maximize similarity with the actual world to the degree that that is possible in view of the counterfactual antecedent, so the worlds quantified over are those antecedent worlds that are maximally similar to the actual world. Since similarity is obviously a context-dependent and vague notion, counterfactuals will inherit these characteristics.

A crucial property of this semantics is that the conditionals are correctly predicted to be *nonmonotonic*. In addition to the failure of Strengthening the Antecedent, here are two more failures of monotone inferences:

(8) *Failure of Hypothetical Syllogism (Transitivity)*
   If Hoover had been a Communist, he would have been a traitor.
   If Hoover had been born in Russia, he would have been a
   Communist.
   $\not\rightarrow$ If Hoover had been born in Russia, he would have been a traitor.

(9) *Failure of Contraposition*
   (Even) if Goethe hadn't died in 1832, he would still be dead now.
   $\not\rightarrow$ If Goethe were alive now, he would have died in 1832.[5]

Hypothetical Syllogism (Transitivity) fails because even if all the closest ϕ-worlds are ψ-worlds and all the closest ψ-worlds are χ-worlds, we are not necessarily speaking about the same ψ-worlds (the ψ-worlds that ϕ takes us to may be rather remote ones). So in (8), we get the following picture: The closest ϕ-worlds in which Hoover was born in Russia (but where he retains his level of civic involvement) are all ψ-worlds in which he becomes a Communist. On the other hand, the closest ψ-worlds in which he is a Communist (but where he retains his having been born in the United States and being a high-level administrator) are all χ-worlds in which he is a traitor. The closest φ-worlds do not include the closest ψ-worlds, so Transitivity does not go through.

Contraposition fails because the assumption that the closest φ-worlds are ψ-worlds does not preclude a situation where the closest non-ψ-worlds are also φ-worlds. The selected φ-worlds in which Goethe didn't die in 1832 are all ψ-worlds where he dies nevertheless (well) before the present. But of course, the closest (in fact, *all*) non-ψ-worlds (where he is alive today) are also φ-worlds where he didn't die in 1832.

3.3 The Alternative

We will take it for granted from now on that the standard nonmonotonic semantics for counterfactuals correctly describes the truth-conditions of a counterfactual uttered in an initial context. The counterfactual is true at a world w iff all of the φ-worlds closest to w are ψ-worlds.

What we will explore is the possibility of an analysis of the B type sketched in section 3.1. Do we arrive at these truth-conditions in a way that is more complex than assumed by the standard theory? The idea would be that a counterfactual $\phi > \psi$ has two aspects to its meaning: (1) it shifts the input context to one where the accessibility function f, one of the contextual parameters, has been altered so as to assign to any world at least some φ-worlds, namely, the closest ones; (2) with respect to the newly altered context, the counterfactual will then be evaluated as true at a world w iff all of the φ-worlds accessible via f from w are ψ-worlds.

This alternative account treats the selection of the domain of quantification as the outcome of a process separate from the quantificational claim expressed by the counterfactual modal operator. I claim that counterfactuals both change and make use of a contextual parameter that I will call the "modal horizon." This parameter is simply the accessibility function appealed to by the simple strict conditional analysis, but it is now subject to evolution throughout a discourse. The modal horizon gradually widens as more and more (counterfactual) possibilities are considered. The evolution of the modal horizon is governed by the same kind of similarity measure that is employed by the standard account. Counterfactuals assert that all φ-worlds assigned to the evaluation world by the current modal horizon are ψ-worlds. With respect to an initial, null context, my counterfactuals will have exactly the same truth-conditions as those of the standard analysis. The crucial difference between the analyses surfaces only when we consider sequences of counterfactuals. In my account, the modal horizon evolves and is kept track of during such a sequence. In the standard account, counterfactuals are considered in splendid isolation from surrounding discourse.

As I hinted in section 3.1, this kind of account needs strong supporting evidence. Two properties of my account turn out to be of particular empirical value. (1) There are essentially dynamic facts concerning the way the order of counterfactuals in a sequence matters to the coherence of the sequence and to the plausibility of arguments. These facts demonstrate the need for context change in the semantics of counterfactuals. (2) The modal horizon–based analysis allows a restricted notion of entailment (which I call "Strawson entailment") that involves the assumption of a constant horizon. According to this notion, patterns like Strengthening the Antecedent, Hypothetical Syllogism, and Contraposition (for which there are spectacular counterexamples) turn out to be valid inference patterns. I will suggest that there is empirical evidence for the limited kind of validity of these patterns.[6]

Again, on purely conceptual grounds, this kind of analysis has no particular attraction. It may be hard to appreciate why such a project would be of any interest. The suspicion may be that either these are mere notational variants or that the analysis, by moving to an ill-understood pragmatic component, will lose some of the rigor and explicitness of the standard approach. Before I move on to the empirical evidence, let me quote two masters who are somewhat skeptical of "pragmatic" solutions. But keep in mind that they may not have been thinking of the kind of analysis explored here.

Lewis wrote (1973a, 13):

It is still open to say that counterfactuals are vague strict conditionals based on similarity, and that the vagueness is resolved—the strictness is fixed—by a very local context: the antecedent itself. That is not altogether wrong, but it is defeatist. It consigns to the wastebasket of contextually resolved vagueness something much more amenable to systematic analysis than most of the rest of the mess in that wastebasket.

Stalnaker also saw a "pragmatic" option (in fact, his analysis of indicative conditionals in Stalnaker 1975 is a precedent for my analysis of counterfactuals) but was more open to this possibility than Lewis in the passage above. Stalnaker wrote (1984, 125–126):

One can defend a strict conditional account of conditionals against the counter-examples and arguments we have given by emphasizing the context-dependence of conditionals. One may argue that the conditional is *semantically* a fixed strict conditional but that the domain of possible worlds relative to which it is defined varies with context. Apparent failures of hypothetical syllogism and contra-position are to be explained as fallacies of equivocation caused by shifts in context. For example, one may say of a counterexample to hypothetical syllogism that the first premise seems true because it suggests one context, while the second seems true because it suggests a different context. Perhaps no single plausible context will be one relative to which both premises are true. Therefore, it is argued, the counterexamples do not defeat the claim that the inference is, within any single context, valid.... A suitable elaboration of this reply would build into the *pragmatics* of conditionals an apparatus similar to what is built into the *semantics* in the kind of theory I am defending.... Despite the differences in logic, the difference between a strict conditional theory and a theory of the general kind I am defending might be more superficial than it seems. The principal difference might be in where the line between semantics and pragmatics is drawn, which will determine at what level of abstraction one's notion of validity is defined. But the question is not arbitrary. If one draws the line in the wrong place, one may not only give a less efficient and perspicuous description of the phenomena, one may miss some significant generalizations. In general, if contexts shift too easily and often, then semantic validity will have little to do with the persuasiveness of arguments. Generalizations about the structure of arguments may be missed. On the other hand, if a simple semantics for a specific kind of construction, combined with general pragmatic principles governing the structure of discourse, can account for the complexities of the context shifts, one may have a better overall theory even if a purely semantic concept of validity loses its close connection with the phenomena of argument.

3.4 Evidence

The alternative analysis will start earning its keep when we consider sequences of counterfactuals. A crucial feature of the account is that the modal horizon is passed on from one counterfactual to the next and that it continually evolves to include more and more possibilities. Where the analyses will crucially differ is in cases where a counterfactual early in a sequence has brought into play some remote possibility. According to the type B account defended here, a later counterfactual cannot ignore any possibilities as far out as the possibilities considered earlier. According to the standard account, the later counterfactual is allowed to just make a claim about the closest antecedent worlds and ignore any more remote possibilities.

One case in point comes from Lewis-Sobel sequences. Lewis argued against the view that in his counterexamples to Strengthening the Antecedent the context is subtly shifted. He in fact maintained that the pertinent examples are cases where the context (that is, the selection function or similarity measure) remains relevantly the same throughout the examples. He attempted to demonstrate this with the following kind of example (based on examples he attributed to Sobel):

(10) If the USA threw its weapons into the sea tomorrow, there would be war; but if all the nuclear powers threw their weapons into the sea tomorrow, there would be peace.

This speaker "simultaneously" asserts a counterfactual conditional and the negation of a counterfactual conditional derived from it by Strengthening the Antecedent. Lewis deliberately put this example in the form of a single run-on sentence, with the counterfactuals conjoined by semicolons and *but*. This was meant to ensure that the context stays constant throughout, an assumption that in our more dynamic days seems rather naïve.

Similarly, Edgington (1995, 252–253) presents the following scenario: "[A] piece of masonry falls from the cornice of a building, narrowly missing a worker. The foreman says: 'If you had been standing a foot to the left, you would have been killed; but if you had (also) been wearing your hard hat, you would have been alright.'" Edgington says, quite correctly, that the building foreman's remarks constitute "a single, pointful piece of discourse." One can easily read them as a shrewd way of putting the suggestion that the worker should wear her hard hat at all times.

Consider now the clear contrast between Lewis's example and a variant presented by Irene Heim in an MIT seminar in the spring of 1994.

(11) ??If all the nuclear powers threw their weapons into the sea tomorrow, there would be peace; but if the USA threw its weapons into the sea tomorrow, there would be war.

In (11), the two counterfactuals claimed to be consistent by Lewis are reversed in order and the sequence does not work as before. The reason seems intuitively clear: once we consider as contextually relevant worlds where all nuclear powers abandon their weapons, we cannot ignore them when considering what would happen if the USA disarmed itself. We seem to be in need of an account that keeps track of what possibilities have been considered and does not allow succeeding counterfactuals to ignore those possibilities. An account according to which the context remains constant throughout these examples would not expect a contrast between these two orders.[7]

The fact that (10) and Edgington's example are "single pointful pieces of discourse" argues against attempts at dismissing them as cases of illicit equivocation. But there is no argument here against the idea that the context can and does change over the course of simple pointful discourses. The proper diagnosis would seem to be that over the course of (10), the set of worlds quantified over properly expands, but that over the course of (11), it cannot shrink. This asymmetry is unexpected if one maintains there is no context change.

Note also that if someone utters (10), someone else can then rejoin that the initial conditional is "no longer" true.[8]

(12) A: If the USA threw its weapons into the sea tomorrow, there would be war; but if all the nuclear powers threw their weapons into the sea tomorrow, there would be peace.

   B: But that means that if the USA threw its weapons into the sea tomorrow, there wouldn't NECESSARILY be war.[9]

   B′: But that means that if the USA threw its weapons into the sea tomorrow, there might NOT be war.

This is unexpected under a static approach. If we go back to the simpler antecedent, the domain of quantification should shrink back to the closest worlds where just the USA disarms, ignoring the far-fetched worlds where all the nuclear powers become meek. But that does not seem to happen.[10]

The same kind of sensitivity to the order in which conditionals are presented that we observed in (10) versus (11) can be detected when we examine the Hoover counterexample to Hypothetical Syllogism, (8).

(8) If Hoover had been a Communist, he would have been a traitor.
   If Hoover had been born in Russia, he would have been a Communist.
   $\not\Rightarrow$ If Hoover had been born in Russia, he would have been a traitor.

Now note what happens when we reverse the order in which the premises are presented.

(13) If Hoover had been born in Russia, he would have been a Communist.
   ??If Hoover had been a Communist, he would have been a traitor.
   $\not\Rightarrow$ If Hoover had been born in Russia, he would have been a traitor.

We are not at all tempted to admit both premises as true. The natural way of reading the second premise is as taking into account a set of Communist scenarios *including* those introduced by the first premise. With respect to the active context, then, the second premise is naturally read as expressing a proposition that is in fact false.

We have now seen some indication that the continual context changes posited by my account are in fact observable. The other kind of evidence for the analysis comes from arguments that the austere statement of the truth-conditions is supported by facts about grammar. Consider negative polarity items (NPIs), expressions that are prototypically allowed in the semantic scope of negation but not in "positive" environments. Two examples are *any* and *ever*.

(14) a.   I don't think we have any potatoes.
            *I think we have any potatoes.
      b.   I don't think there will ever be another Aristotle.
            *I think there will ever be another Aristotle.

Ladusaw (1979) showed that NPIs are licensed in downward monotone positions. The most spectacular illustration can be found in quantified sentences.

(15) a.   *Some (student who has ever been to Rome) (has liked it there).
      b.   No (student who has ever been to Rome) (has liked it there).
      c.   Every (student who has ever been to Rome) (has liked it there).

The determiner *some*, which is not downward monotone in either argument, does not license NPIs. The determiner *no*, which is downward monotone in both its arguments, licenses NPIs in both positions. The determiner *every* is downward monotone in its first argument and licenses NPIs there, but is upward monotone in its second argument and does not license NPIs there. Now, NPIs *are* licensed in the antecedent of conditionals.[11]

(16) If you had left any later, you would have missed the plane.

This fact has always been problematic from the point of view of Ladusaw's generalization, since it was also accepted that conditional antecedents are not downward monotone contexts (Strengthening the Antecedent is after all invalid). Kadmon and Landman (1993) suggest that conditionals are in fact downward monotone, as long as we keep the context constant for the whole stretch of the argument. The same idea is advocated by Katz

(1991). These authors fail to address the fact that the Stalnaker-Lewis analysis (and Kratzer's (1978, 1979, 1981a,c) variant, which those authors primarily refer to) actually does claim to keep the value of contextually supplied parameters constant. The similarity measure is the same for both premise and conclusion. Strengthening the Antecedent is invalid because the measure can react very differently to the two antecedents (the original one and the strengthened one). It would be nice if we had a semantics of conditionals that gave us some kind of limited monotonicity to plug into the general theory of NPI licensing. I suggest that the analysis I am exploring here is up to this task: we will be able to formulate a limited kind of entailment, with respect to which counterfactual antecedents will be downward monotone environments hospitable to NPIs.[12]

This concludes the initial review of the kind of evidence that supports an analysis that combines automatic context change with a strict conditional statement of the truth-conditions of counterfactuals. I turn now to the formal development of the analysis.

3.5   Warmbrod's Proposal

Our starting point comes from the work of Warmbrod (1981a,b), who formulates his proposal in terms of a strict conditional analysis that interprets counterfactuals relative to a contextually given accessibility relation R.

The particular relation R that we use in deciding on the truth-value of a given conditional may be thought of as varying from one occasion of speech to another. So it is immediately apparent that a large task remains for pragmatic theory. Listeners usually seem to know how to interpret the conditionals of everyday discourse, and hence we must assume that they know what accessibility relation is to be used in interpreting conditionals. Hence, we need a pragmatic theory of interpretation to explain how they manage to identify the right relation. (Warmbrod 1981a, 279)

Determining the accessibility relation is a task that needs to be done once and for all for all the conditionals in a piece of coherent discourse. A conditional is always evaluated relative to a whole piece of discourse rather than in isolation. "When several conditionals appear together in a single corpus, it seems ... reasonable that we identify a single relation ... early in the corpus. That relation is then held constant until the corpus ends" (1981a, 281). Based on an early (I guess, ideally, the first) conditional in a discourse, a "standard" accessibility relation is chosen as follows:

(17) An accessibility relation R results from a *standard interpretation* of
an antecedent ϕ in w relative to a comparative similarity
relation $\leq$ iff

$w R w'$ iff $\forall w'' \in [\![\phi]\!]$: $w' \leq_w w''$.

The accessibility relation should only get us to worlds that are at least
as similar to w as the most similar antecedent worlds. Warmbrod's "formalism captures the same basic intuition (for isolated counterfactuals)
that Stalnaker and Lewis have in mind" (1981a, 280). For discourses
containing more than one counterfactual, Warmbrod imposes a condition
of "normality."

(18) An accessibility relation R is *normal* for a body of discourse D
relative to a world w iff for every antecedent ϕ in D, there is some
ϕ-world w' such that $w R w'$.

Warmbrod's "pragmatic theory of interpretation embodies two claims.
First, a relation R used to interpret a body of discourse D must result
from standard interpretation of some antecedent or hypothesis advanced
early in D. Second, R must be normal for D relative to the actual world"
(1981a, 282).

This analysis has some of the ingredients of the approach we are planning to develop. It combines a strict conditional analysis with a view of
the context that admits that the context may change. Warmbrod does not
give a compositional procedure for context change. What he does is state
a global condition under which a context does *not* change in a sequence
of counterfactuals. He requires the context to stay constant for a well-
behaved, "normal" discourse. The global nature of his normality condition prevents him from dealing with embedded conditionals (as he readily
admits in a footnote). While assigning an important role to context
change in the analysis, Warmbrod puts the emphasis on defending the
strict conditional semantics.

3.6 Heim's Proposal

Some of the technical deficiencies of Warmbrod's proposal are not found
in a system sketched by Irene Heim in an MIT seminar presentation in the
spring of 1994 (her goal was to put on firmer ground the idea found in
Katz 1991 that conditionals are downward monotone *if* one keeps the context constant). Heim adopts a strict conditional semantics as far as truth-

conditions are concerned but adds to this a semantic presupposition about the contextually supplied accessibility function: f has to assign to the evaluation world a set of worlds containing at least some antecedent worlds.[13]

(19) *Heim's semantics for counterfactuals*
  f is an accessibility function and $\leq$ a comparative similarity order.
  a. Compatibility presupposition
    $[\![\phi > \psi]\!]^{f, \leq}$ is defined at w only if $\exists w' \in f(w)$: $[\![\phi]\!]^{f, \leq}(w') = 1$.
  b. Truth-conditions
    If defined at w,
    $[\![\phi > \psi]\!]^{f, \leq}(w) = 1$ iff $\forall w' \in f(w)$: $[\![\phi]\!]^{f, \leq}(w') = 1 \rightarrow [\![\psi]\!]^{f, \leq}(w')$
    $= 1$.

Two important issues are left open by this semantics: (1) how is the accessibility function initially identified? and (2) what happens when an initially identified accessibility function does not include accessible antecedent worlds for some counterfactual later on? These issues need to be addressed in a separate part of the theory. Heim herself, in her class handout, merely stated that the accessibility function needs to deliver a similarity-based Lewis sphere around the evaluation world.

(20) *Admissible contexts (Lewis sphere condition)*
  A context with the parameters f and $\leq$ is only admissible if
  $\forall w$: $\forall w' \in f(w)$: $\forall w''$: $w'' \leq_w w' \rightarrow w'' \in f(w)$.

I would like to propose that we add two further ingredients to the theory of contextually supplied accessibility functions: (1) Initially, we assume a trivial accessibility function that assigns to any evaluation world w merely the singleton set of that world itself $\{w\}$. (2) Any time the compatibility presupposition fails (which will be the case for any initial counterfactual under the previous assumption), the context is adjusted by minimally expanding the accessibility function so as to satisfy the compatibility function. The role of the similarity measure will crucially lie in controlling the initial identification of the accessibility function and its subsequent evolution. Instead of formalizing this here, I will do so in the next section in a more fully dynamic system.

Before I take on that task, let me assess whether this semantics is monotonic or nonmonotonic. In fact, adding a compatibility/normality presupposition to a strict conditional semantics makes it just as nonmonotonic as the standard account. For example, Strengthening the Antecedent is invalid: for a given world w, the premise $\phi > \psi$ may be true (with respect to the contextual parameter f) while the conclusion ϕ & $\chi > \psi$ may be undefined (because f might assign to w a set of worlds none of which is a ϕ & χ–world).

But the new semantics allows us to formulate a special notion of entailment according to which counterfactuals are monotonic. Heim, who wanted to make counterfactuals monotonic enough to license NPIs, suggested that if one requires a constant context and requires all the propositions in the argument to be defined (all presuppositions have to be satisfied), one validates (e.g.) Strengthening the Antecedent in a limited way. This is parallel to Warmbrod's requirement that the context be "normal" for a whole sequence.

(21) *Strawson entailment*

$\phi_1, \ldots, \phi_n \models_{\text{Strawson}} \psi$ iff for all $f, \leq, w$ such that
$[\![\phi_1]\!]^{f, \leq}, \ldots, [\![\phi_n]\!]^{f, \leq}$, and $[\![\psi]\!]^{f, \leq}$ are all defined at w
if $[\![\phi_1]\!]^{f, \leq}(w) = 1, \ldots, [\![\phi_n]\!]^{f, \leq}(w) = 1$, then $[\![\psi]\!]^{f, \leq}(w) = 1$.

The definedness condition here is what forces the accessibility function to be lax enough to accommodate all the antecedents considered in the sequence of counterfactuals, in particular the conclusion.

Here is why I have called this notion "Strawson entailment." In a famous passage, Strawson (1952) discussed the possibility of making the traditional "subaltern" inference from *Every S is P* to *Some S is P* valid within a modern logical framework. He essentially proposed that natural language quantifiers carry an existence presupposition with respect to their domain. He understood this presupposition to be what is now called a semantic or logical presupposition: if the presupposition is not satisfied, the sentence will be neither true nor false. The subaltern inference is straightforwardly valid in this system: whenever *Every S is P* is true, its existence presupposition, that there are Ss, must be satisfied, but then *Some S is P* will have to be true as well. Unfortunately, some other traditional inferences will now be invalid. For example, the traditional simple conversion of negative universal statements will fail. *No S is P* may be true (there are Ss but none of them are Ps) while *No P is S* may be neither true nor false (there are no Ps). Strawson then suggested that when in traditional logic the above inference is called valid, what is meant is this: "We are to imagine that every logical rule of the system, when expressed in terms of truth and falsity, is preceded by the phrase 'Assuming that the statements concerned are either true or false, then ...'" (Strawson 1952, 176). There we are. This will indeed solve Strawson's problem.

If Strawson was right, this notion of entailment is natural enough to have engendered an entire tradition of logic (the one that assumed existential import for natural language quantifiers). And if Heim is right, this notion of entailment underlies grammatical NPI licensing. Of course, one may well be skeptical of Strawson's own reason for adopting this notion while following Heim in taking it to be operative in cases where it enforces constancy of a particular contextual parameter. The latter is surely a feature often assumed to be essential for proper logical argumentation.[14]

We will now explore the possibility of incorporating what for Heim is a task for pragmatics (the selection of a new context once the current one has led to presupposition failure) into the "context change potential" of counterfactuals.

3.7 Dynamic Implementation

The story in Heim's sketch is that counterfactuals presuppose that the contextually supplied accessibility function contains worlds at which the antecedent is true. Whenever a previously uncontemplated antecedent possibility is introduced, there is presupposition failure and a decision has to be made whether the context should be adjusted by adding the novel antecedent to the set of relevant possibilities. If the decision is made to adjust the context, this is most economically done by "expanding" the accessibility function just enough to encompass some worlds at which the antecedent is true.

What is done in a dynamic semantic system is to encode the effect a successful assertion of a sentence has on the context in the "dynamic meaning" of the sentence. Well-known dynamic effects concern the progressive elimination of worlds from the context set (the set of worlds that according to the common ground of the conversation are still viable candidates to be the actual world) and the addition of discourse referents to the domain of entities that can be referred to anaphorically. What we are concerned with here is the gradual "expansion" of the accessibility function, which is a contextual parameter of evaluation for counterfactual sentences. As mentioned earlier, to have a more evocative name for this evolving contextual parameter, I will call it the "modal horizon."

The procedure will be this: If a conditional is accepted as an assertion, the context will first be changed to expand the modal horizon if the antecedent wasn't already considered a relevant possibility. Then, the conditional will be interpreted in the new context. What we would like to do then is to assign to the counterfactual $\phi > \psi$ a context change potential, a function from contexts to contexts that changes the context so as to add the antecedent to the modal horizon. The proposition expressed by the conditional is then computed with respect to the already updated context. Somewhat formally:

(22) *Dynamic semantics for counterfactuals (rough)*
   a. Context change potential
      $$f|\phi > \psi|^{\leq} = \lambda w.\,f(w) \cup \{w': \forall w'' \in [\![\phi]\!]^{f,\leq}: w' \leq_w w''\}$$
   b. Truth-conditions
      $$[\![\phi > \psi]\!]^{f,\leq}(w) - 1 \text{ iff}$$
      $$\forall w' \in f|\phi > \psi|^{\leq}(w): [\![\phi]\!]^{f,\leq}(w') = 1 \rightarrow [\![\psi]\!]^{f|\phi>\psi|^{\leq},\leq}(w') = 1$$

We pretend that the modal horizon f is the only contextual parameter that evolves in the course of a sequence. The context change potentials of sentences are conceived as functions from input modal horizons to new potentially updated modal horizons. The only sentences that effect any context change are counterfactuals (we pretend that apart from atomic sentences, negated sentences, and conjunctions, we have only counterfactuals). These update f by adding to it for any world w the closest antecedent worlds. Of course, if such worlds are already assigned by f to w, the new f will be the same as the old f. To assess the truth of a counterfactual at a world w with respect to an initial f and a similarity relation $\leq$, we first update f with the context change potential of the counterfactual. We then check whether all of the worlds assigned to w by the updated f that are ϕ-worlds are also ψ-worlds.

This rough first attempt has no provision for embedded conditionals. If the antecedent contains a conditional, we should presumably allow the embedded conditional to update the accessibility function before we look for the worlds quantified over by the containing conditional. If the consequent contains a conditional, we will have to pass on to subsequent discourse the update that this embedded conditional effects. We revise and clean up the proposal as follows:

(23) *Dynamic semantics for counterfactuals (revised)*
   a. Auxiliary notion: Update of f by a sentence ϕ
      For any sentence ϕ, any accessibility function f, and similarity relation $\leq$:
      $$f^{\phi,\leq} = \lambda w.\,f(w) \cup \{w': \forall w'' \in [\![\phi]\!]^{f,\leq}: w' \leq_w w''\}$$

b. Context change potential of counterfactuals

$$f|\phi > \psi|^{\leq} = f^{\phi, \leq} |\phi|^{\leq} |\psi|^{\leq}$$

c. Truth-conditions

$$[\![\phi > \psi]\!]^{f, \leq}(w) = 1 \text{ iff}$$

$$\forall w' \in f^{\phi, \leq} |\phi|^{\leq}(w): [\![\phi]\!]^{f, \leq}(w') = 1 \rightarrow [\![\psi]\!]^{f^{\phi, \leq} |\phi|^{\leq}, \leq}(w') = 1$$

Over the course of a piece of reasoning/discourse in which a number of conditionals are asserted, the context will naturally evolve so as to expand the modal horizon. If the semantics in (23) is all there is, we have a one-way street: more and more possibilities are introduced. One can think of the modal horizon f as a discourse referent but one that continues to be updated throughout a discourse. It is like a mailbox into which more and more items are stuffed. It is in this respect that the present account differs from the standard account in which the set of worlds selected by the similarity measure shrinks and expands according to the whim of the antecedent.

The relocation of nonmonotonicity from the semantics of the modal operator to the contextual evolution of the modal horizon does not lead to a difference in the truth-conditions derived for an isolated counterfactual. Assume that initially, f is trivial in that it assigns to each world w only $\{w\}$. Now, $\phi > \psi$ is offered. f needs to be expanded. Apart from w, we need to have in $f(w)$ the closest ϕ-worlds and all additional non-ϕ-worlds that are closer to w than the closest ϕ-worlds. The conditional now claims that all of the ϕ-worlds in $f(w)$ are ψ-worlds. The ϕ-worlds in $f(w)$ at this point are exactly the closest ϕ-worlds to w.

It is once we move beyond isolated conditionals uttered in a null context that the approaches will begin to diverge. The central point of this chapter is that we now have an explanation both of the Stalnaker-Lewis counterexamples to the classic inference patterns and of the data discussed earlier. Before we turn to judgments and intuitions about coherence and entailment, we will have to question the one-way nature of the evolution of the modal horizon.

3.8 One-Way Street?

One-way expansion in modalized arguments is discussed in Lewis's seminal paper on scorekeeping (Lewis 1979b [1983, 247]):

Suppose I am talking with some elected official about the ways he might deal with some embarrassment. So far, we have been ignoring those possibilities that would be political suicide for him. He says: 'You see, I must either destroy the evidence or else claim that I did it to stop Communism. What else can I do?' I rudely reply: 'There is one other possibility—you can put the public interest first for once!' That would be false if the boundary between relevant and ignored possibilities remained stationary. But it is not false in its context, for hitherto ignored possibilities come into consideration and make it true. And the boundary, once shifted outward, stays shifted. If he protests 'I can't do that', he is mistaken.

In the same article, Lewis also made a similar observation about rapid context shifts in the analysis of statements about knowledge, which then became the topic of a more recent work (Lewis 1996). Note that Lewis clearly articulates the one-way nature of the context shift (more possibilities come into consideration; no shrinking back is allowed).[15]

Is the expansion of the modal horizon really irreversible? It seems that there should be procedures for "resetting" of the context. Imagine a speaker deliberating as follows:

(24) If the USA threw its weapons into the sea tomorrow, there would be war. Well, if all the nuclear powers threw their weapons into the sea tomorrow, there would be peace. But of course, that would never happen. So, as things stand, if the USA threw its weapons into the sea tomorrow, there would be war.

It appears that this resetting of the context has to rely on explicit indications, whereas expansion occurs silently and smoothly. Consider the interpretation of the crucial resetting sentence.

(25) But of course, that would never happen.

I take it that the most natural way of reading this sentence is that it asserts that the actual world w is such that no worlds in $f(w)$ are worlds where all the nuclear powers throw their weapons into the sea tomorrow. So, the claim is that this is not a relevant possibility. Now, by the time the second counterfactual in (24) is processed and accepted, the modal horizon f is such that it assigns to any world a set of worlds some of which are in fact such worlds. So, the claim made by (25) would be blatantly false in that context. There are two obvious ways of incorporating the resetting effect of (25): (1) one could posit a reset operator that is prefixed to such sentences and provide it with a semantics that has it eliminate possibilities from the modal horizon, or (2) one could treat resetting as a pragmatic operation that occurs at a higher level than the dynamic semantics, essentially as a repair mechanism. Perhaps, it is the fact that (25) is in blatant contradiction with the preceding discourse that will trigger a contraction of the modal horizon.

One piece of evidence that at least sometimes resetting is a rather indirect pragmatic mechanism comes from examples like this one:

(26) A: If John had been at the party, it would have been much more fun.
     B: Well, if John had been at the party and had gotten into a fight with Perry, that wouldn't have been any fun at all.
     A: Yes, but Perry wasn't there. So, if John had been at the party, he wouldn't have gotten into a fight with Perry.

Here, the factual assertion that Perry wasn't there seems to trigger a resetting of the context (or serve as a reason for not admitting in the first place the expansion proffered by B). Of course, factual assertions cannot in general have such a disruptive effect on counterfactual reasoning, which precisely serves to abstract away from (certain) facts. The following is a case in point:

(27) A: If John had been at the party, it would have been much more fun.
     B: But John wasn't at the party.
     A: Yes. I said if he *had* been there, it would have been more fun.

For the time being, I do not have a theory of when and how the modal horizon can be expanded and contracted by expressions other than conditionals. I need to leave this interesting topic for some other occasion.[16]

3.9   Inferences and Validity

In classic logic, it is considered imperative that in the assessment of arguments the context remain stable. But once we recognize the dynamic character of language—the fact that the context changes all the time and that language is one of the driving forces of this context change—this changeability of the context may need to be taken into account when we talk about the validity of inferences.[17]

A dynamic notion of entailment already appears in "Indicative Conditionals" (Stalnaker 1975), one of the founding papers of dynamic semantics. Stalnaker argues that the inference from ϕ *or* ψ to *if not* ϕ, *then* ψ (indicative), which is invalid in his semantics, is nevertheless a "reasonable inference" as he defines that notion. We can translate his notion into the present system as follows:

(28) *Dynamic entailment*

$\phi_1, \ldots, \phi_n \models_{\text{dynamic}} \psi$ iff for all contexts c,

$$[\![\phi_1]\!]^c \cap \cdots \cap [\![\phi_n]\!]^{c|\phi_1|\ldots|\phi_{n-1}|} \subseteq [\![\psi]\!]^{c|\phi_1|\ldots|\phi_n|}$$

For any starting context it has to hold that when the premises are successively asserted and accepted, the context evolves into one whose context set is included in the proposition expressed by the conclusion in that resulting context. There is a corresponding notion of dynamic consistency.

(29) *Dynamic consistency*

A sequence $\phi_1, \ldots, \phi_n$ is dynamically consistent iff there is a context c such that

$$[\![\phi_1]\!]^c \cap \cdots \cap [\![\phi_n]\!]^{c|\phi_1|\ldots|\phi_{n-1}|} \neq \varnothing$$

Consider as a useful application of this dynamic notion of consistency the difference between the Lewis-Sobel sequence and Heim's variant, repeated here.

(10) If the USA threw its weapons into the sea tomorrow, there would be war; but if all the nuclear powers threw their weapons into the sea tomorrow, there would be peace.

(11) ??If all the nuclear powers threw their weapons into the sea tomorrow, there would be peace; but if the USA threw its weapons into the sea tomorrow, there would be war.

The Lewis-Sobel sequence is dynamically consistent because we can start with a context whose modal horizon is just wide enough to include those ϕ-worlds that are ψ-worlds; this horizon is then widened by the second sentence, which may well be true if all of the closest ϕ & χ–worlds that now come into vision are non-ψ-worlds. The Heim sequence is dynamically inconsistent, because we have no automatic mechanism that would allow the horizon to shrink between the addition of the first sentence and the assessment of the second sentence. As a result, the first sentence makes the claim that the ϕ & χ–worlds in the set of accessible worlds are all non-ψ-worlds, while the second sentence makes the claim that all the ϕ-worlds in the very same set of accessible worlds are ψ-worlds: a straightforward contradiction.

The notion of dynamic entailment is one that replicates in my system most of the logical assessments made by the standard theory. Most of the classic monotonic inference patterns are dynamically invalid. There is one notable exception. Hypothetical Syllogism is dynamically invalid when the premises are ordered in one way: $\psi > \chi$, $\phi > \psi \therefore \phi > \chi$; but it is dynamically valid when the premises are ordered in the other way: $\phi > \psi$, $\psi > \chi \therefore \phi > \chi$. In effect, then, exactly those patterns are dynamically invalid for which we can find intuitive counterexamples. While this seems nice, there is reason to think that dynamic entailment is in fact not the notion that we use to assess logical arguments. Consider the following sequence as an example of dynamic entailment:

(30) If the USA threw its weapons into the sea tomorrow, there would be war; but if all the nuclear powers threw their weapons into the sea tomorrow, there would be peace. So, if the USA threw its weapons into the sea tomorrow, there might not be war.

This argument uses as the sequence of premises the same Lewis-Sobel sequence that we saw to be dynamically consistent. By the time the second premise has widened the modal horizon, the conclusion will be true with respect to that newly expanded context. So, the argument in (30) is dynamically valid.

But of course, (30) is quite weird when seen not as coming from a speaker whose mind is evolving but as a deliberate argument for a particular conclusion.[18] This suggests to me that while the dynamic notion of consistency is quite the correct tool for assessing evolving discourse, for assessing *logical arguments* for a particular conclusion the fully dynamic notion of entailment is not adequate. For logical argumentation, we take speakers to be committed to a stable context. Someone who makes a logical argument gives an implicit promise that the context is not going to change during the argument. We should say that a speaker who presents a sequence as an attempt to argue for a particular conclusion has to be assuming a context that is such that the argument does not change the modal horizon.

This introduces in the context of our dynamic system a notion of entailment corresponding to Strawson entailment as discussed earlier.

(31) *Strawson entailment*

$\phi_1, \ldots, \phi_n \models_{\text{Strawson}} \psi$ iff for all contexts c such that

$c = c|\phi_1|\ldots|\phi_n||\psi|$,

it holds that

$[\![\phi_1]\!]^c \cap \cdots \cap [\![\phi_n]\!]^{c|\phi_1|\ldots|\phi_{n-1}|} \subseteq [\![\psi]\!]^{c|\phi_1|\ldots|\phi_n|}.$

Consider as an example the validity of Strengthening the Antecedent. Under the *assumption* that a context is already such that *if* φ and *if* φ & χ will not further expand the accessibility function, the inference is fine: thus, it is Strawson-valid. It appears to me that speakers can reasonably offer arguments of the form of Strengthening the Antecedent. What should we say about such behavior? Do they commit a fallacy? More likely, what we want to say is that they must be making tacit additional assumptions that make their inference valid. According to my account, the additional assumption that they are making is that the accessibility function is such that it remains constant throughout the inference.

As we saw earlier, there is another reason to explore the usefulness of "Strawson entailment." There is a well-established account according to which the validity of "downward" inferences such as Strengthening the Antecedent is the factor that governs the appearance of negative polarity items (NPIs) in various environments. The antecedent of conditionals is a well-known problem case for this account. If we could pursue an account according to which Strawson entailment is the operative notion in NPI licensing, we might get somewhere interesting (see von Fintel 1999).

3.10 Outlook

In this chapter, I have presented a sketch of an alternative implementation of the standard possible-worlds semantics of counterfactuals. I would like to end by briefly pointing out some respects in which the account sketched here should be further investigated. (1) I have kept away from exploring the internal compositional semantics of conditionals. Kratzer (1977, 1978, 1979, 1981a,b,c, 1986, 1991) has convincingly argued that we need to derive the meaning of conditionals from independently motivated analyses of modal operators (such as *would*) in combination with *if*-clauses. It remains to be seen how to best translate my sketch into her richer system. (2) One important extension would be to apply the system to indicative/epistemic conditionals. This will be more complex than what I did here because there will have to be some tighter interaction between the evolution of the context set and that of the modal horizon; see von Fintel 1998 for some initial ideas about the indicative/subjunctive distinction, without context-dynamics however. (3) One should explore the connections to other dynamic or Discourse Representation Theory–based approaches to modality (especially Roberts 1986, 1989, 1995; Kasper 1992; Kibble 1994, 1996; Geurts 1995; Frank 1997; Stone 1997). (4) My system does not incorporate provisions for presupposition projection. One should try to see how many of Heim's suggestions can be carried over (Heim 1992).

Notes

In a joint seminar at MIT in the spring of 1994, Irene Heim presented an idea from which I started developing the material in this chapter and in related papers. Ever since then, she has helped me sustain my enthusiasm for this project. My debt to her is immeasurable. I further benefited from helpful discussion with and criticism by Angelika Kratzer, Bob Stalnaker, Sabine Iatridou, Renate Musan, Roger Schwarzschild, Larry Horn, Joe Moore, Chris Gauker, Manfred Krifka, and Jeroen Groenendijk, and from class discussions at MIT and at ESSLLI 99 in Utrecht, where Gianluca Storto spotted a typo in the machinery in (23). Some of the material in this chapter was presented in talks on various occasions: the LSA Annual Meeting in San Diego on January 6, 1996, a colloquium at the University of Massachusetts at Amherst on March 29, 1996, and SALT VI at Rutgers University on April 28, 1996. The audiences at these occasions helped me along quite a bit. Thanks especially to Jim McCawley, Angelika Kratzer, Maribel Romero, Satoshi Tomioka, and Cleo Condoravdi. Of course, none of the people mentioned are even remotely responsible for any errors that remain.

1. I will adopt the perhaps risky strategy of supplementing the discussion in the text with sketches of formal machinery without commenting much on the technicalities. I hope that the formally adept readers won't need much commentary, while others will be able to grasp what is going on without studying the formalism. I will use the familiar notation $[\![\alpha]\!]^c$ for the denotation of α with respect to the contextual parameter c. The context change potential of α is written as $|\alpha|$ and is a function from contexts to contexts. I follow common practice in dynamic semantics by writing the function to the right of its argument to symbolize the sequential nature of discourse.

2. The Gricean strategy mentioned at the outset is sometimes claimed to have a conceptual advantage (Grice speaks of a "modified Occam's razor" that prefers an austere semantics). But I fail to understand why a two-factor analysis should be methodologically preferred over a one-factor analysis. The substantial support for Gricean analyses comes from empirical arguments that show the different behavior of truth-conditional aspects and "pragmatic" aspects (implicatures, etc.).

3. For two useful overviews on conditional semantics, see Nute 1984 and Edgington 1995.

4. Formulating the semantics of counterfactuals in these terms is only possible under what Lewis calls the Limit Assumption (that there will always be such a set of closest antecedent worlds), which Lewis in fact rejects. Stalnaker, on the other hand, defends the assumption against Lewis's arguments by saying that in actual practice, in actual natural language semantics, and in actual modal/conditional reasoning, the assumption is eminently reasonable. I side with Stalnaker, not the least because it makes life easier. For discussion, see Lewis 1973a and Stalnaker

1984, chap. 7, esp. 140–142. Further arguments *against* the Limit Assumption can be found in Herzberger 1979 and Pollock 1976, 18–20. Further arguments *for* the Limit Assumption can be found in Warmbrod 1982.

5. From Kratzer 1979.

6. My analysis belongs to the ever-growing body of work concerned with the interaction of semantics with facts about context dependence and mechanisms of context change. The importance of these aspects of linguistic meaning was urged on us by the same authors who pioneered the possible-worlds semantics for counterfactuals: Stalnaker (1972, 1973, 1974, 1975, 1978, 1988, 1998) and Lewis (1979a,b). Semantic theories that give prominence to the context-changing potential of linguistic expressions have since then been developed by Heim (1982, 1983, 1992), Veltman (1981, 1985, 1986, 1996), Landman (1986), Barwise (1987), Groenendijk and Stokhof (1991), and many other researchers.

There is a (not very close) affinity between the dynamic analysis of counterfactuals explored here and pragmatic defenses of material implication analyses of indicative conditionals, such as the one presented by Grice (1967, 1989) and refined especially in Jackson's work (1979, 1984, 1987, 1990). Other pragmatically informed analyses of indicative conditionals include those of Veltman (1986) and McCawley (1993, 548ff.). There is also a (somewhat closer) affinity with pragmatic defenses of strict implication analyses of subjunctive conditionals or variants thereof, such as the ones presented by Warmbrod (1981a,b, 1983), Wright (1983), and Lowe (1990, 1995). Warmbrod's proposal in particular will be discussed as a precedent for my account.

7. There are apparently some speakers who do not find a problem with example (11). Such speakers seem to rescue the example by putting exhaustive focus on *the USA* in the second counterfactual. In effect, they interpret the second counterfactual as saying through exhaustive focus, "If only the USA threw its weapons into the sea tomorrow, there would be war." Under this interpretation, of course, there is no conflict between the two conditionals. I would therefore urge caution: the example is to be read without exhaustive focus on the subject.

It is possible to circumvent this issue by moving to examples where there is no interference from focus. David Beaver (personal communication) has suggested the following contrasting pair to me:

(i)   If I went to the store, it would be closed by the time I got there. But if I ran really fast to the store, it might of course still be open.

(ii) ??If I ran really fast to the store, it might still be open. But if I went to the store, it would be closed by the time I got there.

Beaver's example contains no NP that could be exhaustively focused to rescue the sequence. The effect Heim detected can therefore be observed without interference.

8. What I mean by "no longer true" is not that the objective facts have changed. It is the parameters of the discourse that have changed so that the proposition expressed by the first counterfactual in the initial context can no longer be expressed by the same linguistic expression in the new context. Compare the fact that the claim that *France is hexagonal* may be true in a context where it is pre-

ceded by *Italy has the shape of a boot*, but may cease to be true in a later context where the standards of precision have been sharpened.

9. Note that the stress on *necessarily* is required. B cannot say (i) or (ii).

(i) But that means that if the USA threw its weapons into the sea tomorrow, there would NOT be war.

(ii) But that means that it is not TRUE that if the USA threw its weapons into the sea tomorrow, there would be war.

The reason for this is investigated in a separate paper (von Fintel 1997). The idea is that bare conditionals obey the Excluded Middle and that therefore negating them either has a very strong meaning or needs to be done by using an explicit operator that does not obey the Excluded Middle.

10. Note that B′ in her reply to A seems to rely on an inference from *if p and r, would q* to *if p, might q*. This pattern is invalid in the standard system, but will be valid in mine (if we bothered to introduce *might*-counterfactuals explicitly).

11. Partee (1993) shows that the licensing of NPIs in *if*-clauses is not some dumb mistake of the grammar. If the *if*-clause restricts a nonuniversal quantifier, where it is uncontroversial that there is no downward monotonicity, NPIs are not allowed.

(i) *Sometimes, if a man feeds a dog any bones, it bites him.

12. Heim (1984) presents an attempt at defining a limited kind of downward monotonicity to license NPIs, but Kadmon and Landman (1993) show this proposal to be insufficient.

13. This analysis turns Warmbrod's global normality requirement into a semantic presupposition of the counterfactual and will therefore be able to deal with embedded conditionals.

14. Elsewhere, I explore Strawson entailment and NPI licensing in detail (von Fintel 1999).

15. Of course, we have to note that the expansion in this example is not one we can account for here. Lewis's example involves a modal statement ("You can put the public interest first for once"), which goes beyond the simple system discussed here. One obvious way of incorporating such sentences would be to have *can* ϕ claim that there are ϕ-worlds in the current modal horizon. If the current horizon does not in fact support this claim, one way of repairing the situation is to expand the horizon. Further development of this idea will have to await a future occasion.

16. Context resetting will presumably be more pervasive when we try to apply the methods developed here to indicative/epistemic conditionals. I hope to turn to this task soon in a companion paper. Both Jeroen Groenendijk and Manfred Krifka have urged me to think more about cases of contraction of the modal horizon.

17. There has been some technical discussion of various possible notions of validity in dynamic systems (see especially van Benthem 1995; Dekker 1996; Muskens, van Benthem, and Visser 1997; Veltman 1996.

18. Thanks to Jeroen Groenendijk for this observation and example (30).

References

Barwise, Jon. 1987. Noun phrases, generalized quantifiers, and anaphora. In Peter Gärdenfors, ed., *Generalized quantifiers*, 1–29. Dordrecht: Reidel.

Benthem, Johan van. 1995. *Language in action: Categories, lambdas, and dynamic logic*. Cambridge, Mass.: MIT Press.

Dekker, Paul. 1996. The values of variables in dynamic semantics. *Linguistics and Philosophy* 19, 211–257.

Edgington, Dorothy. 1995. On conditionals. *Mind* 104, 235–329.

von Fintel, Kai. 1997. Bare plurals, bare conditionals, and *only*. *Journal of Semantics* 14, 1–56.

von Fintel, Kai. 1998. The presupposition of subjunctive conditionals. In Uli Sauerland and Orin Percus, eds., *The interpretive tract*, 29–44. MIT Working Papers in Linguistics 25. MITWPL, Department of Linguistics and Philosophy, MIT, Cambridge, Mass.

von Fintel, Kai. 1999. NPI licensing, Strawson entailment, and context dependency. *Journal of Semantics* 16, 97–148.

Frank, Annette. 1997. Context dependence in modal constructions. Doctoral dissertation, Universität Stuttgart.

Geurts, Bart. 1995. Presupposing. Doctoral dissertation, Universität Stuttgart.

Goodman, Nelson. 1947. The problem of counterfactual conditionals. *Journal of Philosophy* 44, 113–128.

Grice, Paul. 1967. Logic and conversation. Ms.

Grice, Paul. 1989. *Studies in the way of words*. Cambridge, Mass.: Harvard University Press.

Groenendijk, Jeroen, and Martin Stokhof. 1991. Dynamic predicate logic. *Linguistics and Philosophy* 14, 39–100.

Heim, Irene. 1982. The semantics of definite and indefinite noun phrases. Doctoral dissertation, University of Massachusetts, Amherst.

Heim, Irene. 1983. On the projection problem for presuppositions. In Michael Barlow, Daniel P. Flickinger, and Michael T. Wescoat, eds., *Proceedings of the 2nd West Coast Conference on Formal Linguistics*, 114–125. Stanford Linguistics Association, Stanford University, Stanford, Calif.

Heim, Irene. 1984. A note on polarity sensitivity and downward entailingness. In Charles Jones and Peter Sells, eds., *Proceedings of NELS 14*, 98–107. GLSA, University of Massachusetts, Amherst.

Heim, Irene. 1992. Presupposition projection and the semantics of attitude verbs. *Journal of Semantics* 9, 183–221.

Herzberger, Hans. 1979. Counterfactuals and consistency. *Journal of Philosophy* 76, 83–88.

Jackson, Frank. 1979. On assertion and indicative conditionals. *Philosophical Review* 88, 565–589.

Jackson, Frank. 1984. Two theories of indicative conditionals. *Australasian Journal of Philosophy* 62, 67–76.

Jackson, Frank. 1987. *Conditionals.* Oxford: Blackwell.

Jackson, Frank. 1990. Classifying conditionals. *Analysis* 50, 134–147.

Kadmon, Nirit, and Fred Landman. 1993. *Any. Linguistics and philosophy* 16, 353–422.

Kasper, Walter. 1992. Presuppositions, composition, and simple subjunctives. *Journal of Semantics* 9, 307–331.

Katz, Graham. 1991. The downward entailingness of conditionals and adversatives. In Matt Alexander and Monica Dressler, eds., *Papers from the Second Annual Meeting of the Formal Linguistics Society of Midamerica (FLSM 2)*, 217–243. University of Michigan, Ann Arbor.

Kibble, Rodger. 1994. Dynamics of epistemic modality and anaphora. In Harry Bunt, Reinhard Muskens, and Gerrit Rentier, eds., *Proceedings of the International Workshop on Computational Semantics.* ITK, University of Tilburg.

Kibble, Rodger. 1998. Modal subordination, focus, and complement anaphora. In Jonathan Ginzburg, Zurab Khasidashvili, Carl Vogel, Jean-Jacques Levy, and Enric Vallduví, eds., *The Tbilisi Symposium on Logic, Language and Computation: Selected papers*, 71–84. Stanford, Calif.: CSLI Publications.

Kratzer, Angelika. 1977. What *must* and *can* must and can mean. *Linguistics and Philosophy* 1, 337–355.

Kratzer, Angelika. 1978. *Semantik der Rede: Kontexttheorie, Modalwörter, Konditionalsätze.* Königstein/Taunus: Scriptor.

Kratzer, Angelika. 1979. Conditional necessity and possibility. In Rainer Bäuerle, Urs Egli, and Arnim von Stechow, eds., *Semantics from different points of view*, 117–147. Berlin: Springer-Verlag.

Kratzer, Angelika. 1981a. Blurred conditionals. In Wolfgang Klein and Willem Levelt, eds., *Crossing the boundaries in linguistics: Studies presented to Manfred Bierwisch*, 201–210. Dordrecht: Reidel.

Kratzer, Angelika. 1981b. The notional category of modality. In H. J. Eikmeyer and H. Rieser, eds., *Words, worlds, and contexts: New approaches in word semantics*, 38–74. Berlin: Walter de Gruyter.

Kratzer, Angelika. 1981c. Partition and revision: The semantics of counterfactuals. *Journal of Philosophical Logic* 10, 201–216.

Kratzer, Angelika. 1986. Conditionals. In A. M. Farley, P. Farley, and K.-E. McCullough, eds., *CLS 22: Papers from the Parasession on Pragmatics and Grammatical Theory*, 1–15. Chicago Linguistic Society, University of Chicago, Chicago, Ill.

Kratzer, Angelika. 1991. Modality. In Arnim von Stechow and Dieter Wunderlich, eds., *Semantik: Ein internationales Handbuch der zeitgenössischen Forschung*, 639–650. Berlin: Walter de Gruyter.

Ladusaw, William. 1979. Polarity sensitivity as inherent scope relations. Doctoral dissertation, University of Texas, Austin.

Landman, Fred. 1986. *Towards a theory of information: The status of partial objects in semantics*. Dordrecht: Foris.

Lewis, David. 1973a. *Counterfactuals*. Oxford: Blackwell.

Lewis, David. 1973b. Counterfactuals and comparative possibility. *Journal of Philosophical Logic* 2, 418–446.

Lewis, David. 1979a. A problem with permission. In Esa Saarinen, Risto Hilpinen, Ilkka Niiniluoto, and Merril Provence Hintikka, eds., *Essays in honour of Jaako Hintikka: On the occasion of his fiftieth birthday on January 12, 1979*, 163–175. Dordrecht: Reidel.

Lewis, David. 1979b. Scorekeeping in a language game. *Journal of Philosophical Logic* 8, 339–359.

Lewis, David. 1979b [1983]. Scorekeeping in a language game. *Journal of Philosophical Logic* 8, 339–359. Reprinted in David Lewis, *Philosophical papers: Volume I*, 233–249. Oxford: Oxford University Press (1983).

Lewis, David. 1981. Ordering semantics and premise semantics for counterfactuals. *Journal of Philosophical Logic* 10, 217–234.

Lewis, David. 1996. Elusive knowledge. *Australasian Journal of Philosophy* 74, 549–579.

Lowe, E. J. 1990. Conditionals, context, and transitivity. *Analysis* 50, 80–87.

Lowe, E. J. 1995. The truth about counterfactuals. *Philosophical Quarterly* 45, 41–59.

McCawley, James. 1993. *Everything that linguists have always wanted to know about logic but were ashamed to ask*. Chicago: University of Chicago Press.

Muskens, Reinhard, Johan van Beethem, and Albert Visser. 1997. Dynamics. In Johan van Benthem and Alice ter Meulen, eds., *Handbook of logic and language*, 587–648. Amsterdam: Elsevier.

Nute, Donald. 1984. Conditional logic. In Dov Gabbay and Franz Guenthner, eds., *Handbook of philosophical logic, vol. II*, 387–439. Dordrecht: Reidel.

Partee, Barbara. 1993. On the "scope of negation" and polarity sensitivity. In Eva Hajičová, ed., *Functional description of language: Proceedings of the conference, Prague, November 24–27, 1992*. Faculty of Mathematics and Physics, Charles University, Prague.

Pollock, John. 1976. *Subjunctive reasoning*. Dordrecht: Reidel.

Roberts, Craige. 1986. Modal subordination, anaphora, and distributivity. Doctoral dissertation, University of Massachusetts, Amherst.

Roberts, Craige. 1989. Modal subordination and pronominal anaphora in discourse. *Linguistics and Philosophy* 12, 683–721.

Roberts, Craige. 1995. Domain restriction in dynamic semantics. In Emmon Bach, Eloise Jelinek, Angelika Kratzer, and Barbara Partee, eds., *Quantification in natural languages*, 661–700. Dordrecht: Kluwer.

Stalnaker, Robert. 1968. A theory of conditionals. In Nicholas Rescher, ed., *Studies in logical theory*, 98–112. Oxford: Blackwell.

Stalnaker, Robert. 1972. Pragmatics. In Donald Davidson and Gilbert Harman, eds., *Semantics of natural language*, 380–397. Dordrecht: Reidel.

Stalnaker, Robert. 1973. Presuppositions. *Journal of Philosophical Logic* 2, 447–457.

Stalnaker, Robert. 1974. Pragmatic presuppositions. In Milton Munitz and Peter Unger, eds., *Semantics and philosophy*, 197–213. New York: New York University Press.

Stalnaker, Robert. 1975. Indicative conditionals. *Philosophia* 5, 269–286.

Stalnaker, Robert. 1978. Assertion. In Peter Cole, ed., *Syntax and semantics 9*, 315–322. New York: Academic Press.

Stalnaker, Robert. 1981. A defence of conditional excluded middle. In William Harper, Robert Stalnaker, and Glenn Pearce, eds., *Ifs: Conditionals, belief, decision, chance, and time*, 87–104. Dordrecht: Reidel.

Stalnaker, Robert. 1984. *Inquiry*. Cambridge, Mass.: MIT Press.

Stalnaker, Robert. 1988. Belief attribution and context. In Robert Grimm and Daniel Merrill, eds., *Contents of thought*, 140–156. Tucson: University of Arizona Press.

Stalnaker, Robert. 1998. On the representation of context. *Journal of Logic, Language, and Information* 7, 3–19.

Stalnaker, Robert, and Richmond Thomason. 1970. A semantic analysis of conditional logic. *Theoria* 36, 23–42.

Stone, Matthew. 1997. The anaphoric parallel between modality and tense. IRCS report 97, University of Pennsylvania, Philadelphia.

Strawson, P. F. 1952. *Introduction to logical theory*. London: Methuen.

Veltman, Frank. 1981 [1984]. Data semantics. In Jeroen Groenendijk, Theo Janssen, and Martin Stokhof, eds., *Formal methods in the study of language*. Amsterdam: Mathematical Centre. Reprinted in Jeroen Groenendijk. Theo Janssen, and Martin Stokhof, eds., *Truth, interpretation, information*, 43–63. Dordrecht: Foris (1984).

Veltman, Frank. 1985. Logics for conditionals. Doctoral dissertation, University of Amsterdam.

Veltman, Frank. 1986. Data semantics and the pragmatics of indicative conditionals. In Elizabeth Traugott, Alice ter Meulen, Judy Reilly, and Charles Ferguson, eds., *On conditionals*, 147–168. Cambridge: Cambridge University Press.

Veltman, Frank. 1996. Defaults in update semantics. *Journal of Philosophical Logic* 25, 221–261.

Warmbrod, Ken. 1981a. Counterfactuals and substitution of equivalent antecedents. *Journal of Philosophical Logic* 10, 267–289.

Warmbrod, Ken. 1981b. An indexical theory of conditionals. *Dialogue: Canadian Philosophical Review* 20, 644–664.

Warmbrod, Ken. 1982. A defense of the limit assumption. *Philosophical Studies* 42, 53–66.

Warmbrod, Ken. 1983. Epistemic conditionals. *Pacific Philosophical Quarterly* 64, 249–265.

Wright, Crispin. 1983. Keeping track of Nozick. *Analysis* 43, 134–140.

Chapter 4

Infixation versus Onset　　　Morris Halle
Metathesis in Tagalog,
Chamorro, and Toba Batak

4.1　Introductory Remarks

According to Bloomfield (1933, 218), the relationship between such Tagalog forms as /sulat/ 'a writing', on the one hand, and /sumulat/ 'one who writes' and /sinulat/ 'that which is written', on the other, is one of infixation, where the sequences /um/ and /in/, respectively, are "added before the first vowel of the underlying form." This account of the Tagalog facts, which can be found in most treatments of the language, is however not the only logically possible one. Identical results are obtained if we posit that the affixes are prefixes of the form /mu/ and /ni/, respectively, and that words with these prefixes are subject to Onset Metathesis, which permutes the onsets of the first two syllables of the words; that is, /mu-sulat/ → /su-mulat/ and /ni-sulat/ → /si-nulat/.

I begin by noting that from the point of view of syntax, morphemes are indivisible, atomic pieces. The syntax is systematically oblivious of phonological aspects of the morphemes. In the theory of Distributed Morphology (Halle and Marantz 1993) this obliviousness is formally reflected by the absence—in syntactic representations—of the phonetic exponents of the morphemes. In the syntax proper, morphemes are nothing but complexes of syntactic and semantic features; their phonetic exponents are inserted by Vocabulary Insertion, which is part of the morphology. Since the phonetic exponents of morphemes are thus not present in the syntax, it is literally impossible within the syntax to infix /um/ or /in/ before the first vowel of the Tagalog stem. This can only be done in the morphology or phonology, after the phonetic exponents of the morphemes have been spelled out.

Morphologically, Tagalog *sumulat* and *sinulat* are composed of the verb base (VBase) *sulat* and the affixes *um*/*mu* and *in*/*ni*, respectively. The words thus differ from English *writer* and *writing* primarily in that the affix is a suffix in English, but a prefix in Tagalog. What needs to be determined in addition is whether the morphophonology of Tagalog infixes these prefixes before the first vowel of the stem, as Bloomfield and others have thought, or whether the onset of the prefix and that of the following syllable undergo metathesis, as suggested above.

Metathesis operations are well attested in the phonology of different languages. Among the better-known metathesis phenomena are the *liquid metathesis* of the Slavic languages (for some discussion, see Breuer 1961, 76ff.; Blevins and Garrett 1998); the metathesis in the Tiberian Hebrew *hitpaʕe:l*, which affects stems beginning with a coronal continuant or affricate (e.g., /hit-sadde:r/ → /his-tadde:r/ 'to arrange oneself', but/hit-raxe:c/ 'to wash oneself'); and the /y-C/ → /C-y/ permutation in Zoque discussed at length in Dell 1973.

Onset metathesis, such as the one proposed below for Tagalog and Chamorro, is less widely attested in the phonology of ordinary languages, but has been found in various language games, which Bagemihl (1989, 1995) refers to as *ludlings*. Bagemihl (1989, 490) cites two ludlings—one in Javanese and the other in Chasu—where onsets of consecutive syllables are permuted, as illustrated in (1).

(1) a. *Javanese*
         sa.tus → ta.sus 'one hundred'
         ḍu.wit → wu.ḍit 'money'
     b. *Chasu*
         na.so → sa.no 'five'
         ke.nda → nde.ka 'nine'

Since Onset Metathesis is thus an attested phenomenon in actually spoken languages, Universal Grammar (UG) must include devices that permute the linear order both of consecutive phonemes and of onsets of consecutive syllables. The precise nature of the formal mechanism involved in these operations is yet to be established definitively (for some proposals, see Kenstowicz and Kisseberth 1979, 370; Bagemihl 1989; and especially Raimy 1999). In (2), I show the different effects produced by the two processes. In (2a), I illustrate the effects of Infixation—that is, of preposing the onset of the stem before the vowel-initial prefix. In (2b), I illustrate the effects of Onset Metathesis—that is, of a process that permutes the phonetic features linked to the onsets of two consecutive morphemes.

(2) a. *Infixation (Stem Onset Preposing)*

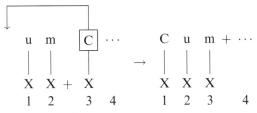

    b. *Onset Metathesis*

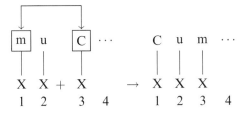

I will show that Onset Metathesis rather than Infixation applies in Tagalog (section 4.2) and Chamorro (section 4.3), whereas both Infixation (Stem Onset Preposing) and Onset Metathesis apply in Toba Batak (section 4.4).

The interest of these results is twofold. On the one hand, they imply that the widely held view about the centrality of infixation in the morphophonology of Tagalog and Chamorro is mistaken, and they suggest that accounts of infixation processes in some other languages might need to be similarly revised. On the other hand, they raise questions about the validity of the inferences for phonological theory that have been drawn from the supposition that the Tagalog facts are instances of infixation. For example, Prince and Smolensky (1993, 34) adopt the popular functionalist explanation that "infixation after a word-initial C results in a considerably more satisfactory syllable structure than prefixation would" and claim as one of the virtues of Optimality Theory that it "allows us to make this insight the keystone of a significantly improved theory of edge-oriented infixation." If the Onset Metathesis alternative illustrated in (2b) is correct, this supposed advantage of Optimality Theory vanishes, for, on that account, the syllable structure of the output form does not differ from that of the input; instead, what changes is the sequential order of the onsets, for which Prince and Smolensky's functionalist explanation is clearly irrelevant.

4.2 Tagalog

In discussing the facts of Tagalog, it is important to keep in mind that most studies, including such excellent scientific descriptions of the language as Schachter and Otanes (S&O) 1972, represent most words in conventional Tagalog spelling, which systematically omits the glottal stop /ʔ/ and represents /h/ only in syllable onsets. S&O write:

> The phoneme /ʔ/ is not represented in conventional spelling.... When /ʔ/ occurs word initially, however, its presence may be inferred from the conventional spelling, which, in such cases, always begins with a vowel letter.... When a syllable-initial glottal stop occurs after a prefix that ends in a consonant, a hyphen is placed after the prefix ... (1972, 57; see also 19)

Failure to note this simple fact leads to misunderstandings of various sorts. For example, Crowhurst (1998, 590) states that in Tagalog, "a verbal morpheme *um* surfaces as prefix before V-initial stems (e.g., *um-asim* 'turn sour'), but as an infix with C-initial stems (e.g., *t-um-awag* 'call')." Once the actually occurring stem-initial glottal stop is restored, the distinction between prefixed and infixed *um* vanishes. Crowhurst's special treatment of putatively vowel-initial stems thus does not reflect a phonological fact of the language; it reflects only a confusing aspect of Tagalog orthography.

The omission of /h/ in non-onset position leads to different distortions of the phonological data. S&O write:

> Word final /h/ is lost in the middle of a phrase. Thus, *baga* /baːgah/ 'ember', but *Bagah ba?* /baːga bah/ '(Is it) an ember?' Before the suffixes *-an* and *-in*, however, final /h/ is retained.... [A]lthough neither word-final /h/ nor word-final /ʔ/ is retained in the middle of a phrase, the contrast between them is preserved, /h/ being lost altogether, but /ʔ/ being replaced by vowel length ... (1972, 23)

Moreover, they observe that

> since neither /ʔ/ nor word-final /h/ is represented in conventional spelling, pairs of words that differ only in that one of them ends in /ʔ/ and the other in /h/ are spelled in the same way. (1972, 57)

For example, orthographic *bata* stands for both phonological /bataʔ/ 'child' and /batah/ 'bathrobe', and orthographic *vaya* stands for both phonological /vayaʔ/ 'invitation' and /vayah/ 'nurse'. In the transcriptions of Tagalog forms below, both the glottal stop and the /h/ that are omitted in the official orthography have been restored.

4.2.1   The [+realis] Morpheme /ni/

Tagalog verb forms consist of a verb base (VBase), a topic marker (TM), and a number of other affixes reflecting tense, aspect, mood, transitivity, and so on. Of particular interest here is the exponent of the [+realis] mood, which distinguishes the imperfective and perfective forms of the verb from their [−realis] counterparts, the contemplative mood and the neutral basic form. The exponent of the [+realis] mood appears in absolute initial position of the word, with one important exception: it may be preceded by the benefactive TM /ʔi/. In the literature, the [+realis] exponent is said to have the form /in/ and to be subject to infixation. This is illustrated with the perfective forms in (3) (examples from S&O 1972, 370).

(3) in-ʔawit → ʔ-in-awit 'sang'
     in-bigy-an → b-in-igy-an 'gave to'
     ʔi-in-bilih → ʔi-b-in-ilih → 'bought for'
     ʔi-in-ka-takboh → ʔi-k-in-a-takboh 'caused to run for'

As noted in section 4.1, if we assume that the [+realis] exponent is of the form /ni/ and is subject to Onset Metathesis (2b), rather than to Infixation (Stem Onset Preposing) (2a), we obtain outputs that are phonologically identical, but that differ in their effects on both the morphological structure and the syllable structure of the strings. This is illustrated in (4).

(4) ni-ʔawit → ʔi-nawit 'sang'
     ni-bigy-an → bi-nigy-an 'gave to'
     ʔi-ni-bilih → ʔi-bi-nilih 'bought for'
     ʔi-ni-ka-takboh → ʔi-ki-na-takboh 'caused to run for'

S&O (1972, 365) remark that Infixation/Metathesis is optional where the [+realis] morpheme is followed by a nonnasal sonorant, that is, /ʔ h r l w y/. This exceptional treatment is obligatory in cases where /ni/ is preceded by the benefactive TM /ʔi/ and is followed by /ʔ/ or /h/. Importantly, in all cases where the process does not take place, the [+realis] morpheme surfaces not as /in/, but as /ni/. This is illustrated in (5).

(5) a. ni-ligaw-an *or* li-ni-gaw-an 'paid court to'
         ʔi-ni-yam-an *or* ʔi-yi-nam-an 'caused to get rich'
         ʔi-ni-regalo *or* ʔi-ri-negalo 'gave as a present'
         ni-hatid *or* hi-natid 'delivered' ⟨absence of /ʔi/ TM⟩
     b. ʔi-ni-hatid 'delivered to'
         ʔi-ni-ʔuwi 'took home'

As shown in (5), if the morpheme is assumed to be of the form /ni/, we need to state only that these forms are exceptions to Onset Metathesis. If, on the other hand, the morpheme is assumed to be of the form /in/, it is necessary to stipulate in addition that in cases where infixation is blocked, the morpheme /in/ changes shape to /ni/.[1] The need for this additional stipulation constitutes a compelling argument against positing /in/ as the underlying form of the [+realis] morpheme and consequently also against infixation as a process accounting for the output forms reviewed here.

4.2.2   The Agent Topic Marker /mu/

As observed in section 4.1, infixation has been posited not only for the [+realis] morpheme in Tagalog, but also for the agent topic marker /mu/ (respectively /um/). The evidence against infixation given just above is an a priori reason for assuming that the agent TM is underlyingly /mu/ and that it, like the [+realis] morpheme /ni/, is subject to Onset Metathesis. Additional considerations for this proposition are presented below.

An important phonological process involving the /ni/ morpheme concerns its effect on a following morpheme beginning with /m/. According to S&O (1972, 364), "[w]hen present in a formation whose basic form begins with a prefix with initial /m/, N is realized as a replacement of this /m/ by /n/. Thus, ... N + *mag-* /mag/ → *nag-* /nag/ ...," where N is S&O's symbol for the [+realis] morpheme. This is illustrated in (6) (cf. S&O 1972, 364, 367), where S&O's abstract N has been replaced with its phonological exponent /ni/.

(6) ni-ma-ʔintindih-an → n-a-ʔintindih-an 'understood' (367)
    ni-mag-ʔaral → n-ag-ʔaral 'studied' (367)
    ni-ma-ka-gawa → n-a-ka-gawa 'was/were able to do' (367)

To account for the forms in (6), I propose that such forms are subject to the two simple rules in (7).

(7) a. V → ∅ in the morpheme /ni/
    b. [+cons] → ∅ in env. [+cons] + ____

I assume that (7a) is a readjustment rule that applies to the prefix /ni/ (and, as I will argue directly below, also to /mu/) in certain morphologically restricted contexts. By contrast, (7b) is a phonological rule, which applies across morpheme boundaries but not morpheme-internally and is subject to further restrictions. Since (7a) is part of the Readjustment component, it precedes all phonological rules, including in particular

Onset Metathesis, which therefore can never affect forms subject to (7a). The effects of the rules in (7) are illustrated in (8).

(8) a. ni-ma-ka-ʔaral $\xrightarrow{(7a)}$ n-ma-ka-ʔaral $\xrightarrow{(7b)}$ n-a-ka-ʔaral
    b. ni-ma-ʔinitindih-an $\xrightarrow{(7a)}$ n-ma-ʔinitindih-an $\xrightarrow{(7b)}$ n-a-ʔinitindih-an

A Tagalog verb form has exactly one TM, which may be (1) a suffix of the VBase, as in /bigy-an/ 'give to' ← /bigy/ 'give' + /an/ locative TM, or as in /bilh-in/ 'buy' ← /bilih/ 'buy' + /in/ object TM, or (2) a prefix, as in /ʔi-bilih/ 'buy for' ← /ʔi/ benefactive TM + /bilih/ 'buy', or as in /ʔu-malis/ 'leave' ← /mu/ agent TM + /ʔalis/ 'leave', where /mu/ undergoes Onset Metathesis.

According to S&O (1972, 364), the [+realis] /ni/ prefix is deleted before /mu/, and, as shown in (9), the contrast between the [+realis] perfective form and the [−realis] base form of the verb is then lost.

(9) a. /ni/ [+realis] + /mu/ agent TM + /ʔalis/'leave' → mu + ʔalis →
       ʔu + malis
    b. NULL [−realis] + /mu/ agent TM + /ʔalis/ 'leave' → ʔu + malis

The deletion of an affix in morphologically defined contexts (as in (9a)) is not uncommon. For example, in Russian, the perfective suffix /nu/ is deleted—obligatorily or optionally—in the past tense as well as in the active participle and gerund of many verbs (e.g., *po-gib-nu-t'* (inf.) vs. *po-gib-l-a* (past), *po-gib-š-ij* (act. part.) 'perish'; *ot-verg-nu-t'* (inf.) vs. *ot-verg-l-a* or *ot-verg-nu-l-a* (past), *ot-verg-š-ij* or *ot-verg-nu-v-š-ij* (act. part.) 'reject'). In parallel fashion, the Tagalog /ni/ prefix is deleted before verbs with the TM /mu/.[2]

There is, however, an important exception to the deletion of /ni/ before /mu/: deletion does not take place if /mu/ is followed by /pag/ (transitivizer). The preservation of /ni/ before /mu/ in these forms immediately explains the contrast between the forms in (10) and those in (11), which I have copied from Maclachlan 1989, 71.

(10) n-ag-lutoʔ 'cooked'
     n-ag-tipon 'collected'
     n-ag-rayos 'arranged'
     n-ag-banat 'stretched'
     n-ag-tunaw 'dissolved'

(11) du-mating 'arrived'
     ku-maway 'waved at'
     du-maʔing 'complained'

gu-malaw 'wandered'
lu-mangoy 'swam'

As shown in the derivations in (12), when /ni/ does not delete, it undergoes rule (7a), which in these forms also applies to /mu/. These forms are
then subject to rule (7b), which deletes all but the last in a string of consecutive consonants.

(12) a. [+realis] + AGENT TM + TRANS? + Verb
        ni   + mu   + pag   + luto? $\xrightarrow{\text{(7a)}}$
        n   + m   + pag   + luto? $\xrightarrow{\text{(7b)}}$
        n   + Ø   + Øag   + luto?
     b. [+realis] + AGENT TM + INTRANS + Verb
        ni   + mu   + NULL   + dating $\xrightarrow{\text{/ni/ Del/}}$
        Ø   + mu   + dating $\xrightarrow{\text{Ons Met}}$
                    du   + mating

This account depends crucially on the assumption that the exponent of
the agent TM is /mu/ rather than /um/, for rule (7a) would fail to apply
to /um/, resulting in the output /n-um-ag-luto?/, which is evidently wide
of the mark. I conclude that the exponent of the agent TM is of the form
/mu/ and that like the [+realis] morpheme /ni/, /mu/ is subject to Onset
Metathesis rather than Infixation (Stem Onset Preposing).

4.3 Chamorro

Chamorro, as described by Topping (1973), presents additional evidence
for Onset Metathesis and against Infixation (Stem Onset Preposing). Like
Tagalog, Chamorro has traditionally been said to have the two infixes
-um- and -in-, which in Chamorro have a variety of morphological functions. However, Topping (1973, 170ff.) has argued compellingly that these
morphemes must be treated as the prefixes /mu/ and /ni/, just like their
counterparts in Tagalog. Even though Topping's book is a main source
for most subsequent work on Chamorro, all writers—including Topping
himself in other parts of his book—maintain the traditional infixation
analysis. Below I restate Topping's arguments against infixation.

Topping writes:

It is interesting that the canonical form of both of these affixes is just the opposite
of what one would expect in a language that is basically CVCV. It is tempting to
posit underlying prefixes *mu-* and *ni-* for these infixes with appropriate rules of
metathesis. There appears to be some evidence to support such a hypothesis.
(1973, 170)

According to Topping, in Chamorro, *mu-/-um* is the exponent of an "action" morpheme "because whenever it is used the emphasis is on the actor or the action" (1973, 184). The morpheme appears as /mu/ if the following stem begins with a nasal; elsewhere, /mu/ undergoes Onset Metathesis. This is illustrated by the contrast between the forms in (13a) that have nasal-initial stems and do not undergo Onset Metathesis and the forms in (13b) that have stems beginning with nonnasal phonemes and do undergo Onset Metathesis.[3]

(13) a. mu-ŋeloʔ 'peeps'
       mu-naŋo 'swims'
       mu-naʔ 'causes'
    b. gu-mupu 'flew' (gupu 'fly')
       tu-mohge 'stoop up' (tohge 'stand')
       du-mankolo 'became big' (dankolo 'big')

On the Infixation (Stem Onset Preposing) account, it would be necessary to posit two exponents for this morpheme (/mu/, before stems beginning with nasals, and /um/, elsewhere), and it would have to be stipulated that Infixation applies only in the latter case. The facts can also be accounted for by positing just one prefix, /mu/, which is subject to Infixation before an obstruent or nonnasal consonant, but not elsewhere. Strings undergoing Infixation would in addition be subject to a metathesis rule that turns /mu/ into /um/. Both of these Infixation alternatives involve extra complications that do not arise in the Onset Metathesis proposal.

Topping's argument for preferring /ni/ over /in/ as the representation of this morpheme concerns the interaction of Onset Metathesis with two other rules of Chamorro phonology: Nasal Place Assimilation and Deletion of postnasal obstruents. As illustrated in (14) (from Topping 1973, 173), Nasal Place Assimilation (NPA) applies before Deletion (Del).

(14) fan-chommaʔ $\xrightarrow{\text{NPA}}$ fañ-chommaʔ $\xrightarrow{\text{Del}}$ fañ-ommaʔ
     fan-chupa $\xrightarrow{\text{NPA}}$ fañ-chupa $\xrightarrow{\text{Del}}$ fañ-upa 'tobacco field'
     man-pokkat $\xrightarrow{\text{NPA}}$ mam-pokkat $\xrightarrow{\text{Del}}$ mam-okkat 'walk'

Now consider the word *chinemmaʔ* 'forbidden thing', which contains the VBase *chommaʔ* 'forbid'. The vowel change /o/ → /e/ is the result of vowel harmony, which applies to a stressed back vowel "preceded by one of several particles that has a front vowel" (Topping 1973, 52). Among the particles that trigger fronting is the /ni/ ~ /in/ affix, which in the construction under discussion functions as a nominalizing morpheme.

The plural of *chinemma* 'forbidden thing' is formed by prefixing *fan*, which is phonetically identical with the prefix in (14), but has a different function. In this case, the prefix + noun combination surfaces as *fan-chinemma?*, without undergoing either Nasal Place Assimilation or Deletion. As Topping points out, this can be readily accounted for if we assume that the underlying form has the prefix *ni*, which—as already established—is subject to Onset Metathesis. That is, *fan-ni-chemma?* → *fan-chi-nemma?*, without undergoing either Nasal Place Assimilation or Deletion. This is achieved by ordering Nasal Place Assimilation and Deletion before Onset Metathesis (OM), as shown in (15).

(15) fan-ni-chemma? $\xrightarrow{\text{NPA}}$ DNA $\xrightarrow{\text{Del}}$ DNA $\xrightarrow{\text{OM}}$ fan-chi-nemma?

QED

If instead we had assumed that Infixation (Stem Onset Preposing) was at work here and that it was ordered before Nasal Place Assimilation and Deletion, the incorrect output *fan-iñ-emma?* would have been generated. This is shown in (16).

(16) fan-in-chemma? $\xrightarrow{\text{NPA}}$ fan-iñ-chemma? $\xrightarrow{\text{Del}}$ fan-iñ-emma? $\xrightarrow{\text{Inf}}$

DNA $\longrightarrow$ ***fan-iñ-emma?

Things are not improved by ordering Infixation before Nasal Place Assimilation and Deletion, as shown in (17a), or between Nasal Place Assimilation and Deletion, as shown in (17b).

(17) a. fan-in-chemma? $\xrightarrow{\text{Inf}}$ fan-ch-in-emma? $\xrightarrow{\text{NPA}}$

fañ-ch-in-emma? $\xrightarrow{\text{Del}}$ ***fañ-in-emma?

b. fan-in-chemma? $\xrightarrow{\text{NPA}}$ fan-iñ-chemma? $\xrightarrow{\text{Inf}}$

fan-ch-iñ-emma? $\xrightarrow{\text{Del}}$ ***fan-iñ-emma?

4.4   Toba Batak

The fact that Infixation (Stem Onset Preposing) must be ruled out in Chamorro and Tagalog does not rule out Infixation as a morphophonological process in other languages. In particular, as shown below, in Toba Batak /um/-Infixation is a bona fide morphophonological process.

In Toba Batak, both /ni/ and /um/ figure as independent morphemes, which occur as prefixes in some contexts and as infixes elsewhere. In addition, the nominalizing morpheme /al/ shares with /um/ and /ni/ the property of appearing as a prefix in some contexts and as an infix elsewhere. The distributions are reviewed below.[4]

An important difference between Tagalog and Chamorro, on the one hand, and Toba Batak, on the other, is that Tagalog and Chamorro have no vowel-initial syllables, whereas Toba Batak admits vowel-initial syllables freely.

Like Tagalog and Chamorro, Toba Batak has a /ni/ morpheme, which in certain environments undergoes Onset Metathesis. Toba Batak /ni/'s primary function is that of exponent of the passive completive mode (N74). As illustrated in (18), before vowel-initial stems, the morpheme appears in its underlying /ni/ form; before consonant-initial stems, /ni/ is subject to Onset Metathesis.

(18) ni-ulÓs-an 'have been covered' ((completive passive) from *úlOs* 'blanket') (N69)
      bi-núat 'has been taken' ((completive passive) from *ni + búat* 'take' (N69))
      ji-noú-an 'have been called repeatedly' ((completive passive) from *ni + jóu* 'call' + *an*) (N71)

As in Tagalog and Chamorro, the argument for viewing these alternations as the result of Onset Metathesis rather than of Infixation (Stem Onset Preposing) is that the Infixation analysis requires stipulating in addition that the prefix is subject to the change /ni/ → /in/, whereas the Onset Metathesis account does not.

Unlike /ni/, the morpheme /al/ is a bona fide infix. As illustrated in (19), it appears in that shape as a prefix before vowel-initial roots, but as an infix before consonant-initial roots (see also (20a)).

(19) b-al-átuk 'ladder' (N94)
      al-ógo 'wind' (N94)

The prefix /um/ is the phonetic exponent of a number of apparently diverse grammatical morphemes. On the one hand, /um/ functions as the exponent of the completive active-participial mode of the verb (N74) (see (20a)). But it also serves as the exponent of the comparative marker in adjectives (see (20b)) and of the primary derivational affix of some intransitive stems (see (20c)).

(20) a. j-um-óu-i 'have called repeatedly' ((completive active) from *jóu* 'call') (N71)
          up-pásak 'has beaten' ((completive active) from *um-pásak*) (N74)
          g-um-al-útcan 'be in violent wavy motion' ((intransitive) from [um-[al-[gutcan]]]) (N92) (with repeated cyclic application of Infixation (Stem Onset Preposing))

   b. d-um-áo 'farther' (from *daó* 'far') (N72)
     up-padditá 'more preacherlike' (from *padditá* 'preacherlike')
     (N72)
     umm-úli 'more beautiful' (from *ulí* 'beautiful') (N64)
   c. h-um-Órdit 'make slight movement' (from root *hÓrdit*) (N98)
     g-um-ÓrsiN '(has) become brown' (from gOrsíN 'brown')
     (N100)

As illustrated in (2a), Infixation is the result of Onset Preposing. The
preposed onset need not be part of the verb root; it can instead come from
a prefix, as shown in (21b). As illustrated in (21a), /ha/ is a prefix used in
forming nouns. Noun stems formed with /ha/ may in turn take the prefix
/um/, which undergoes Infixation as shown in (21b).

(21) a. ha-súbba 'indigo' (N94)
      ha-úma 'rice field' (N94)
   b. [um-[ha-tioN]] → h-um-a-tíoN 'run to and fro excitedly' (N98)
      [um-[ha-tiltal]] → h-um-a-tíltal 'prance about' (N98)

The /um/ prefix triggers two phonological rules. Before vowel-initial
stems, affix-final /m/ is geminated (examples in (20b)). Moreover, before
labial and nasal consonants, affix-final /m/ undergoes full assimilation to
the following stem-initial consonant (e.g., /up-pasak/ 'beat', /up-padditá/
'more preacherlike' (20a–b)). I assume that the assimilation rule has the
form in (22), where the features linked to the timing slot X_3 are spread to
the timing slot X_2.

(22)

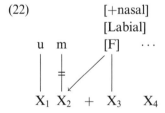

As established by Hayes (1986a,b) and Schein and Steriade (1986),
geminate consonants behave exceptionally with regard to a variety of
processes, a fact Hayes calls "inalterability." As I now show, in the present instance, inalterability is a straightforward consequence of the general
prohibition against the crossing of association lines (Sagey 1988). To see
what is involved, it is necessary to make explicit the effect of Infixation
(Stem Onset Preposing) (2a) on a phoneme sequence that includes a
geminate resulting from assimilation (22).

(23)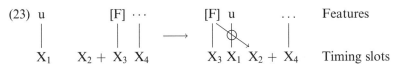

The phonological representation in (23) consists of two autosegmental sequences: one composed of feature bundles and the other, of timing slots. The units in one of the sequences are linked to those in the other by means of "association lines." When Infixation (2a) is applied to the string on the left in (23), both the feature bundle [F] and the timing slot X_3 must be moved to the left of /u/ and its timing slot X_1. As shown in (23), the effect of this is that the line associating the feature bundle [F] to the timing slot X_2 crosses the line associating the features of /u/ to the timing slot X_1. Since this output violates the basic coherence for a notation in which timing slots and their feature composition are projected on separate lines, such representations must be ruled out whenever they arise. A direct consequence of this prohibition is that changes such as those illustrated in (23) are universally excluded. It is this fact that underlies the inalterability of these geminate consonants.

Crowhurst (1998) reports that in recent years, Toba Batak has generalized the assimilation process (22), so that at present /um/ is subject to assimilation before all consonant-initial stems, not only those that begin with labials or nasals, as in (22). Crowhurst reports that this generalization of the assimilation process was already noticed in a 1981 study by Percival, but at that time the generalization was an optional process, as illustrated in (24) with examples from Crowhurst.

(24) ud-dátu, d-um-átu 'wiser'
us-sÓmal, s-um-Ómal 'more usual'
ug-gógo, g-um-ógo 'stronger'
ul-lógo, l-um-ógo 'drier'

According to Crowhurst's informant, in the contemporary language, assimilation is now obligatory, and as a consequence, there is no longer any need for Infixation (Stem Onset Preposing) in Toba Batak. Crowhurst (1998, 595) describes the change as consisting of two independent parts: "first … infixes have been migrating to prefix position in Toba Batak; second, as this happens, the pattern of consonant assimilation observed only with labial- and nasal-initial stems in Nababan's dialect is being extended to consonants at all places of articulation." On this account, in the underlying representation, which was also that found in the output at a historically earlier time, /um/ appeared inside consonant-initial stems. Subsequently, /um/ "migrate[d] to prefix position," first only in labial- and nasal-initial stems and later in all consonant-initial stems. The prefixed /um/ then undergoes assimilation.

Central to Crowhurst's account is the assumption that the infix /um/ appeared inside the adjective stem and subsequently "migrate[d] to prefix position." As noted in section 4.1, a morpheme cannot appear inside another morpheme in underlying representations. In view of this, Crowhurst's account must implicitly assume that at some point, /um/ was infixed into the adjective only to "migrate to prefix position" at a subsequent point. This is highly implausible, and since Crowhurst offers no argument in support of her account, it cannot compete with the straightforward account presented above.

4.5 The Moral

1. Neither Tagalog nor Chamorro is subject to Infixation (Stem Onset Preposing). Instead, both languages are subject to Onset Metathesis (2b). The evidence supporting this conclusion is detailed in sections 4.2 and 4.3.

2. Infixation viewed as Stem Onset Preposing (2a) is—or until recently was—an active process in Toba Batak. Since it changes the phonological exponents of the morpheme to which /um/ is prefixed, Infixation must apply at a point where the morphemes are supplied with phonetic exponents. This cannot be part of the syntax of a language, because the syntax does not have access to the phonological properties of the morphemes.

3. The interaction in Toba Batak between Infixation (Stem Onset Preposing) and the assimilation rule (22) provides a strong argument for ordered rules and derivations. In a derivational account, no restriction needs to be imposed on Infixation, if it is ordered after assimilation. In a nonderivational account without rule ordering, it is necesssary to state either that assimilation takes place before labials and nasals, whereas Infixation affects only nonlabial or nonnasal consonants, or that Infixation affects consonants that are nonnasal and nonlabial, and that assimilation is computed on the surface representation. The first alternative stipulates an aspect of the solution that follows automatically on a derivational account; the second effectively introduces rule ordering into the derivation by stipulating that assimilation is computed on the surface representation.

4. Since it does not alter the syllable structure of the output string, Onset Metathesis (2b) does not affect the syllable structure of the output

string in any significant way. As noted in section 4.1, this conclusion is important in view of the fact that the Tagalog data have been widely cited as an instance where differences between underlying and surface structure are the result of the tendency of language to improve the syllabic well-formedness of surface strings over that of underlying sequences. Since no such difference between underlying and surface strings is involved in the solution that is to be preferred on general grounds, this suggested explanation is not valid.

Notes

I thank Juliette Blevins, François Dell, John Frampton, Bill Idsardi, Michael Kenstowicz, Andrea Rackowski, Bert Vaux, and Cheryl Zoll for helpful comments and advice.

1. The need for an additional rule turning /in/ into /ni/ in these cases was noted specifically by French (1988, 42–43).

2. A similar situation arises in Tagalog, where the object TM suffix /in/ is deleted in all [+realis] forms. For example, the stem /linis-in/ 'clean' has the /in/ suffix in the [−realis] base form /linis-in/ and the contemplative form /lilinis-in/, but deletes /in/ in the [+realis] perfective form /ni-linis/ and the imperfective form /ni-lilinis/.

3. Topping states that /mu/ appears only before nonlabial nasals. As Michael Kenstowicz has observed (personal communication), the exclusion of labial nasals is unnecessary since Onset Metathesis is vacuous before labial nasals: for example, *mu-metgot* 'become big' (*metgot* 'big').

4. The discussion below is based on the somewhat sketchy information in Nababan 1981 and must therefore be taken as less than fully reliable. Numbers in parentheses preceded by *N* refer to pages in Nababan 1981 (e.g., (N74) = Nababan 1981, 74).

References

Bagemihl, Bruce. 1989. The Crossing Constraint and "backward languages." *Natural Language & Linguistic Theory* 7, 481–549.

Bagemihl, Bruce. 1995. Language games and related areas. In John Goldsmith, ed., *The handbook of phonological theory*, 697–712. Oxford: Blackwell.

Blevins, Juliette, and Andrew Garrett. 1998. The origins of consonant-vowel metathesis. *Language* 74, 508–556.

Bloomfield, Leonard. 1933. *Language*. New York: Henry Holt.

Breuer, Herbert. 1961. *Slavische Sprachwissenschaft*. Berlin: Walter de Gruyter.

Crowhurst, Megan. 1998. Suffixation and prefixation in Toba Batak. *Language* 74, 590–604.

Dell, François. 1973. *Les règles et les sons*. Paris: Hermann.

French, Koleen Matsuda. 1988. Insights into Tagalog. Dallas, Tex.: The Summer Institute of Linguistics.

Halle, Morris, and Alec Marantz. 1993. Distributed Morphology and the pieces of inflection. In Kenneth Hale and Samuel Jay Keyser, eds., *The view from Building 20*, 111–176. Cambridge, Mass.: MIT Press.

Hayes, Bruce. 1986a. Assimilation as spreading in Toba Batak. *Linguistic Inquiry* 17, 467–499.

Hayes, Bruce. 1986b. Inalterability in CV phonology. *Language* 62, 321–351.

Kenstowicz, Michael, and Charles Kisseberth. 1979. *Generative phonology*. New York: Academic Press.

Maclachlan, Anna. 1989. The morpho-syntax of Tagalog verbs. In Benjamin Shaer, ed., *McGill working papers in linguistics 6*, 65–84. Department of Linguistics, McGill University.

Nababan, P. W. J. 1981. *A grammar of Toba Batak*. Pacific Linguistics, Series D, No. 37. Canberra: Australian National University.

Percival, W. K. 1981. *A grammar of the urbanised Toba Batak of Medan*. Pacific Linguistics, Series B, No. 76. Canberra: Australian National University.

Prince, Alan S., and Paul Smolensky. 1993. Optimality Theory: Constraint interaction in generative grammar. Ms., Rutgers University and University of Colorado.

Raimy, Eric. 1999. Representing reduplication. Doctoral dissertation, University of Delaware.

Sagey, Elizabeth. 1988. On the ill-formedness of crossing association lines. *Linguistic Inquiry* 19, 109–118.

Schachter, Paul, and Fe T. Otanes. 1972. *Tagalog reference grammar*. Berkeley: University of California Press.

Schein, Barry, and Donca Steriade. 1986. On geminates. *Linguistic Inquiry* 17, 691–744.

Topping, Donald. 1973. *Chamorro reference grammar*. Honolulu: University of Hawaii Press.

Chapter 5

Spanish Negative _in-_:	James Harris
Morphology, Phonology,	
Semantics	

5.1 Introduction

At the descriptive level, this is a case study of the Spanish negative prefix _in-_, of which a few examples are given in (1).[1]

(1) a. in-estabilidad   'instability'
      in-necesario   'unnecessary'
      in-admisible   'inadmissible'
      im-posible   'impossible'
      in-justo   'unjust'
    b. in-defenso   'defenseless'
      in-édito   'unpublished'
      in-somne   'sleepless'
      im-pune   'unpunished'
    c. i-legal   'illegal'
      i-rreal   'unreal'

The investigation provides an analysis of the morphological (e.g., types of bases the prefix attaches to), phonological (e.g., deletion and assimilation of prefix-final /n/), and semantic (e.g., scope) properties of this prefix. I make crucial use of data not taken into account in extensive descriptive studies like Narváez 1970, Urrutia Cárdenas 1978, Varela Ortega 1983, and Lang 1990 or in theoretically more sophisticated work like Varela Ortega 1992 and Peperkamp 1997.

At a more general level, this is a study of the relationship between form and meaning in words. Certain details of the phonological form of words like those in (1) provide valuable clues to nonobvious properties of their morphological structure. At the same time, semantic and morphological structures of particular words, though related in some way, are far from isomorphic to each other; thus, neither is a reliable guide to, or diagnostic of, the other. Familiar phenomena of semantic drift or blurry connotations of words are not the issue; rather, the morphologically complex words examined reveal numerous instances of radical lack of correspondence in the elementary units of semantic and overt morphological structures and in the relationships among these units.

5.2 Morphology

Spanish negative *in-* is extremely productive; dictionaries give long lists of words that contain it. Moreover, *in-* meets a more stringent test of true productivity, namely, that neologisms with this prefix are readily coined and accepted as natural and well formed. For example, a few years ago Spanish-speaking phonological feature theorists created the neologisms *inestridente* 'nonstrident' and *inestridencia* 'nonstridency', which are now indispensable though (unlike *estridente* and *estridencia*) not found in standard dictionaries.

What kinds of morphological constituents does *in-* take as its bases? As can be inferred from the examples in (1a), this prefix most commonly attaches to adjectives that exist as independent words. Additional examples are given in (2).

(2) i-rrecuperable   'unrecoverable'
     in-frecuente   'infrequent'
     i-rrefutable   'irrefutable'
     in-oportuno   'untimely'
     in-elegante   'inelegant'
     i-rracional   'irrational'
     im-besable   'unkissable'
     i-limitado   'unlimited'
     in-tocable   'untouchable'
     i-rregular   'irregular'
     in-maduro   'immature'
     in-seguro   'unsure'
     in-grato   'ungrateful'
     in-capaz   'incapable'
     in-moral   'immoral'
     i-lícito   'illicit'

Negative *in-* can also attach to independent nouns. A few examples are given in (3).

(3) in-composición   'lack of proportion'
    in-certidumbre   'uncertainty'
    in-advertencia   'negligence'
    in-disciplina   'lack of discipline'
    i-rresolución   'indecision'
    in-digestión   'indigestion'
    i-rreflexión   'impetuosity'
    in-fidelidad   'infidelity'
    i-rreligión   'impiety'
    in-ecuación   'inequality'
    in-decoro   'indecorousness'
    im-pudor   'immodesty'

Although examples are not common, *in-* even attaches to verb stems, as illustrated in (4).[2]

(4) in-comunicar   'to isolate'
    in-disponer   'to indispose'
    in-cumplir   'to fail to fulfill'

I conclude from examples like those in (2) through (4) that *in-* is transparent with respect to morphological category. That is, unlike most derivational affixes, *in-* has no category of its own but rather assumes the category of the base to which it attaches: attached to an adjective, it forms an adjective; attached to a noun, it forms a noun; attached to a verb, it forms a verb. This property is noted for future reference as in (5).

(5) $_\alpha[\text{in} \ _\alpha[\text{base}]]$
    $\diagdown...\diagup$

I reject the view that the examples under discussion contain three unrelated prefixes that attach to and form adjectives, nouns, and verbs, respectively. On this view, it would be sheer accident that these three prefixes happen to have both the same phonological form /in/ and the same negative meaning. The generalization embodied in (5) is obviously preferable a priori. The possibility that *in-* always attaches to an adjectival constituent is examined below and found untenable.

I have tacitly assumed so far that *in-* attaches to "words" not only in the intuitive sense but also in the technical sense of *word* as opposed to *stem* or *root*. That is, I have taken for granted that, say, *intocable* 'untouchable' in (2) has the morphological structure (6a), not (6b) or (6c).

(6) a. yes: $_{word}[in\ _{word}[toc+a+ble]_{word}]_{word}$

　　b. no: $_{word}[_{stem}[in\ _{stem}[toc+a]_{stem}]_{stem}\ ble]_{word}$

　　c. no: $_{word}[_{stem}[_{root}[in\ _{root}[toc]_{root}]_{root}\ a]_{stem}\ ble]_{word}$

In the presumably correct structure (6a), *in-* takes the word *tocable* 'touchable' as its base; while in incorrect (6b), it takes the stem *toca* as its base, forming the negative stem *intoca-*; and in (6c), it takes the root *toc* as its base, forming the negative root *intoc-*. The technical sense of *word* used here is provided by the post–Lexical Phonology theory of rule domains articulated in Halle 1990a,b, Halle and Vergnaud 1987, Halle, Harris, and Vergnaud 1991, Harris 1993, and other work, in which morphological domains are classified as "cyclic" or "noncyclic."[3] We will see that negative *in-* appears in both "cyclic" and "noncyclic" constituents. I argue that the word domain illustrated in (6a) is a "noncyclic" one, while the stem and root constituents are "cyclic."

Confirmation that (6a) is the correct structure is provided by examples like those in (7).

(7) [in $_A$[estridente]$_A$]　　'nonstrident'
　　[in $_A$[escrutable]$_A$]　　'inscrutable'
　　[in $_N$[estabilidad]$_N$]　　'instability'[4]

These words manifest the familiar obligatory epenthesis of *e* in Spanish before an otherwise unsyllabifiable /s/.[5] As has long been established, *e*-epenthesis is seen word-initially but not stem- or root-initially when /s/ can be syllabified as a coda of the final syllable of the preceding morpheme: *es.fera* 'sphere' but *hemis.ferio* 'hemisphere' (not *hemies.ferio*), *es.cribir* 'to write' but *ins.cribir* 'to inscribe' (not *ines.cribir*), and scores of similar examples, such as those in (12) below. There is thus no doubt that negative *in-* can take word-level constituents as its base, technically as well as intuitively.

There are, however, clear cases like those in (1b), in which *in-* appears on a base that does not exist as an independent word with the appropriate form and/or meaning. Additional examples are given in (8).

(8) a. *Adjective*

　　　in-alámbrico　　'wireless'　　　(cf. alambre 'wire')
　　　*alámbrico　　 'wired'

in-defenso	'defenseless'	(cf. defensa 'defense')
*defenso	'defendable'	
in-número	'uncountable'	(cf. número 'number (N)')
*número	'countable'	
in-doloro	'painless'	(cf. dolor 'pain')
*doloro	'painful'	
in-édito	'unpublished'	(cf. editar 'to publish')
*édito	'published'	
in-somne	'sleepless'	(cf. insomnia 'insomnia')
*somne	'sleepy'	
in-forme	'shapeless'	(cf. forma 'shape')
*forme[6]	'shapely'	
im-pune	'unpunished'	(cf. punitivo 'punitive')
*pune	'punished'	

b. *Noun*

im-properio	'insult'	(cf. propio 'proper')
*properio	'compliment'	

Since the appropriate unsuffixed adjectival (8a) or nominal (8b) bases do not exist in cases like these, we must conclude that the lexicon of Spanish contains some entries that have at least as much structure as that illustrated in (9).[7]

(9) $_a$[in $_A$[$_A$[$_N$[alambr]$_N$ ic]$_A$ o/a]$_A$]$_a$

No less structure can adequately reflect the knowledge of native speakers, which includes the following facts (among others) in the case at hand: (1) there is a stem *alambr-* as in the noun *alambre*, (2) the suffix *-ic-* can attach to noun stems to form adjective stems, (3) this suffix takes the class vowel *-o* for masculine and *-a* for feminine,[8] and (4) *in-* is the negative prefix under discussion. The fact that the adjective *alámbrico* happens not to exist is registered by the absence of an entry for this word in the lexicon (see note 7) of Spanish, which does however have an entry for *inalámbrico*.

In this example, the suffix *-ico/-ica* identifies *alámbrico* as a well-formed though accidentally unused adjective. Other cases, like those in (10), are less straightforward.

(10) a. $_A$[in $_?$[[numer] o]$_?$]$_A$ or $_A$[$_?$[in [numer]]$_?$ o]$_A$

          $_A$[in $_?$[[pun] e]$_?$]$_A$ $_A$[$_?$[in [pun]]$_?$ e]$_A$

    b. $_N$[in $_?$[$_?$[[prop] eri]$_?$ o]$_?$]$_N$ $_N$[$_?$[in $_?$[[prop] eri]$_?$]$_?$ o]$_N$

In (10), we see the roots *numer-* as in the noun *número* 'number' (and other words), *pun-* as in the adjective *punitivo* 'punitive' (and other words), and *prop-* as in *propio* 'proper' (and other words). These roots—like all roots but unlike stems and words—have no specification for morphological category. The final vowels *-o* and *-e* in (10a) and the sequence *-eri-* in (10b) are not identifiable as derivational suffixes that can bestow stemhood and/or morphological category on the elements *numero, pune,* and *properio.* Given that the category of negative *in-* is provided as suggested in (5), there is no source for the category label Adjective for *innúmero* and *impune* or the label Noun for *improperio.* Moreover, no independent evidence is available for these particular cases regarding the level of attachment of the prefix, that is, whether it attaches to the highest/outermost constituent as shown on the left in (10) or to the next lowest constituent as shown on the right. We must evidently conclude that the lexicon (Encyclopedia) of Spanish contains entries in which the negative prefix *in-* carries its own category label and is attached to an element that is not a "word" in any relevant sense. The exact morphological status of these stem- or rootlike elements is not clear; however, the word-final vowels *-o* and *-e* in (10) are normal "class markers" of Spanish nouns, adjectives, and adverbs (see references in note 8).

To summarize up to this point, negative *in-* must be the leftmost overt constituent in a word, but it is otherwise morphologically promiscuous: this prefix doesn't care what it attaches to. Evidently, negative *in-* can appear in both "cyclic" and "noncyclic" domains.

It is instructive to examine the prefixes *in-* (not negative) and *con-* illustrated in (11).

(11) a. in-tención   'intention'   (cf. a-tención 'attention')
        in-yección   'injection'   (cf. pro-yección 'projection')
        in-clusivo   'inclusive'   (cf. ex-clusivo 'exclusive')
        in-herente   'inherent'   (cf. co-herente 'coherent')
        in-vertir   'to invest'   (cf. per-vertir 'to pervert')
        im-primir   'to print'   (cf. re-primir 'to repress')
        im-poner   'to impose'   (cf. su-poner 'to suppose')
        in-cluir   'to include'   (cf. ex-cluir 'to exclude')
     b. con-clusivo   'conclusive'   (cf. in-clusivo 'inclusive')
        con-tener   'to contain'   (cf. de-tener 'to detain')
        con-cluir   'to conclude'   (cf. in-cluir 'to include')
        con-ducir   'to lead'   (cf. pro-ducir 'to produce')
        com-poner   'to fix'   (cf. re-poner 'to recover')

Meaning is noncompositional in all of the examples in (11). In many cases, the prefix attaches to a base that does not exist independently, for example, **yección*, **herente*, **primir*, **cluir*, **ducir*. Moreover, even in cases in which an independent word with the appropriate phonological form exists, it may have little or no semantic relation to the corresponding prefixed word, for example, *poner* 'to put, to lay (eggs)' versus *im-poner* 'to impose', *tener* 'to have' versus *de-tener* 'to detain'. These are earmarks of affixation at the "root/stem level" as opposed to the "word level," and of "cyclic" domains in Halle/Harris/Vergnaud terms. Confirmation of this fact is provided by examples like the following:

(12) con-streñir   'to constrict'   (cf. estreñir 'to constipate')
      in-scribir   'to inscribe'   (cf. escribir 'to write')
      in-spirar   'to inhale'   (cf. espirar 'to breathe')
      in-struir   'to instruct'   (cf. con-struir 'to construct')

In contrast to the stems in (7), the stems in (12) do not undergo epenthesis of *e* before syllabically stray /s/, a word-level/"noncyclic" phenomenon. We conclude that nonnegative *in-* and *con-* always attach to stems, not words, as registered in (13).

(13) a. yes: $_{word}[_{stem}[in/con \ _{stem}[clus+ión]_{stem}]_{stem}]_{word}$
             $_{word}[_{stem}[in/con \ _{stem}[clus+iv]_{stem}]_{stem} \ o]_{word}$
    b. no: $_{word}[in/con \ _{word}[clus+ión]_{word}]_{word}$
            $_{word}[in/con \ _{word}[clus+iv+o]_{word}]_{word}$

In sum, negative *in-* usually takes freestanding words as its bases, thus forming a "noncyclic" domain, but in some cases it takes bound stems (or roots) in "cyclic" domains. On the other hand, nonnegative *in-* (11a) and *con-* (11b) take only stems.[9]

5.3 Phonology

For the most part, the /n/ of negative *in-* displays the expected phonological properties of any underlying /n/ (Harris 1984, in preparation). This is illustrated in (14).[10]

(14) a. in-*V*
       i[n]-accesible   'inaccessible'
       i[n]-eficiente   'inefficient'
       i[n]-imitable   'inimitable'
       i[n]-oxidable   'rustproof'
       i[n]-útil   'useless'

   b. in-*nasal*

i[n]-movilizarse	'to become immobilized'
i[n]-noble	'ignoble'

   c. in-*obstruent*

i[m]-posible	'impossible'	
i[m]-besable	'unkissable'	
i[ɱ]-frecuente	'infrequent'	([ɱ] = labiodental)
i[ŋ]-capaz	'incapable'	(c = /k/)
i[ŋ]-grato	'ungrateful'	
i[ŋ]-justo	'unjust'	(j = /x/)

As shown, the /n/ of *in-* is realized phonetically as coronal [n] before a vowel (14a) and before another nasal consonant (14b), and undergoes Place assimilation before an obstruent (14c).[11]

Before stems that begin with one of the liquids /l/ or /r/, however, the /n/ of negative *in-* displays the special behavior illustrated in (15), which is invariable over tempi and registers.[12]

(15) a. /n/-/l/

i-legítimo	'illegitimate'
i-limitado	'unlimited'
i-legible	'illegible'
i-lógico	'illogical'
i-legal	'illegal'

     b. /n/-/r/

i-rreconocible	'unrecognizable'
i-rresolución	'indecision'
i-rrebatible	'irrefutable'
i-rreligión	'impiety'
i-rregular	'irregular'

Prefix-final /n/ of nonnegative *in-* and *con-* in (11) displays the same special phonological behavior.

(16) a. /n/-/l/

i-luminación	'illumination'	(cf. luminoso 'luminous')
i-lustración	'illustration'	(cf. lustre 'gloss')
i-lusorio	'illusory'	(cf. de-lusorio 'delusive')
i-lativo	'illative'	(cf. re-lativo 'relative')
co-loquio	'colloquium'	(cf. soli-loquio 'soliloquy')
co-lindar	'to abut'	(cf. linde 'boundary')

co-ligar	'to amalgamate'	(cf. ligar 'to bind')
co-locar	'to place'	(cf. local 'site')
co-legir	'to collect'	(cf. e-legir 'to elect')
co-ludir	'to collude'	(cf. e-ludir 'to elude')

  b. /n/-/r/

i-rradiación	'irradiation'	(cf. radiación 'radiation')
i-rrisible	'laughable'	(cf. risible 'laughable')
co-rresponder	'to correspond'	(cf. responder 'to answer')
co-rrupción	'corruption'	(cf. e-rupción 'eruption')
co-rrosión	'corrosion'	(cf. e-rosión 'erosion')
co-rromper	'to corrupt'	(cf. romper 'to break')
co-rrecto	'correct'	(cf. e-recto 'erect')

Though /nl/ and /nr/ are disallowed in the environments/domains shown in (15) and (16), they are valid phonological sequences in larger domains, as illustrated in (17).

(17) a. *Prefix-stem*

      /n-l/

en-ladrillar	'to lay bricks'	(cf. ladrillo 'brick')
en-loquecer	'to go crazy'	(cf. loco 'crazy')
en-lejiar	'to apply lye'	(cf. lejía 'lye')
en-lodar	'to smear with mud'	(cf. lodo 'mud')
en-lutar	'to dress in mourning'	(cf. luto 'mourning')
en-lazar	'to connect'	(cf. lazo 'tie, bond')

      /n-r/

en-ratonarse	'to get sick from eating mice'	(cf. ratón 'mouse')
en-riquecer	'to enrich'	(cf. rico 'rich')
en-rojecer	'to turn red'	(cf. rojo 'red')
en-rejar	'to put up bars'	(cf. reja 'bar')
en-redar	'to enmesh'	(cf. red 'web, mesh')

  b. *Verb-clitic*

cánten-les	'sing to them'
hágan-lo	'do it'

All of the prefixed bases in (17a) conspicuously contain the stems of independent words, shown at the far right.[13] We may thus assume that the prefix *en-* in (17a) is a "word-level" suffix, or more technically that *en-* forms a "noncyclic" domain in terms of the Halle/Harris/Vergnaud theory. Consequently, words in the class illustrated in (17a) do not undergo the processes that affect prefix-final /n/ if these are assigned to a pre-"word-level" morphological stratum and/or if these processes are triggered by "cyclic" morphemes. Moreover, the examples in (17b) show that the processes at issue do not occur at the verb-clitic boundary, which follows from the proposals just advanced.

We have seen in section 5.2—especially (6), (10), and (13)—that negative *in-* attaches to both words and stems (or roots) while nonnegative *in-* and *con-* attach to stems (or roots) rather than words.[14] Combining these data with those illustrated in (15)–(17), I propose the two-part generalization formulated in (18).[15]

(18) a. Negative *in-* attaches to *stems* in (15), as do both prefixes in (16); these prefixes form "cyclic" domains.
    b. Special prefix-final /n/ behavior results from *stem-level* processes; this behavior is due to "cyclic" rules.

Our next topic is the nature of the processes that account for the special behavior of prefix-final /n/ illustrated in (15) and (16). Let us consider the prelateral context first. The basic observation is that underlying bisegmental /nl/ has the surface realization [l], a single segment, not a geminate. It is thus inescapable that deletion is involved in some way. The simplest possible statement of this deletion is shown in (19).

(19) $[+\text{nasal}] \rightarrow \varnothing\ /\ \underline{\quad}\ [+\text{lateral}]$

Rule (19) applies only in the stem-level/"cyclic" phonology, where it accounts for the *n*-$\varnothing$ alternation in *i-legal* versus *in-admisible*, *i-luminación* versus *in-scribir*, *co-loquial* versus *con-struir*, and so on.[16] Since (19) is a "stem-level" or "cyclic" rule, it correctly leaves the cases of "word-level" or "noncyclic" affixation in (17) untouched.

It is not a viable alternative to consider the variants *in-/i-* (negative), *in-/i-* (nonnegative), and *con-/co-* as strictly morphological allomorphy rather than as controlled by phonological rule. On the allomorphy proposal, it is accidental that three distinct and otherwise unrelated prefixes end in /n/ and that this /n/ alternates with zero. (Why not, say, negative **in-/is-*, nonnegative **il-/id-*, and **cog-/co-*?) The generalization embodied in (19) is obviously preferable a priori.

At this point the morphological proposals made in the previous section converge with the phonological proposals made here to find joint support in the examples in (20).

(20) a. legible   'legible'
       ilegible   'illegible'
       *inlegible
    b. leíble   'readable'
       inleíble   'unreadable'
       *ileíble

Although dictionaries generally list *legible* and *leíble* as interchangeable, these words are not synonyms for any Spanish speaker I have consulted. It is not surprising therefore that the same speakers don't find *ilegible* and *inleíble* to be synonymous either. *Legible* and *ilegible* (like their English glosses) have an idiosyncratically narrow meaning: they describe something that can(not) be read because its written characters are (not) decipherable. *Leíble* and *inleíble* (like their English glosses) have a broader meaning (which properly includes that of *(i)legible*): they describe something that can(not) be easily read for any of a number of reasons or combinations of reasons—for example, because the style is (not) clear, the concepts are (not) easy to grasp, the subject matter is (not) palatable, the written characters are (not) decipherable, and so on. *(I)legible* belongs to the erudite Latinate stratum of the vocabulary.[17] *Leíble*, on the other hand, is a transparent and productive deverbal derivation from the modern native stem *le+e-/le+i-* 'read', whose ancestors enjoy unbroken vernacular transmission through proto-Romance back to Latin and beyond. Negative *inleíble* is not listed in any dictionary that I have searched, but native speakers accept it without qualms as a well-formed and natural neologism.[18] Crucially, *inleíble* does not undergo nasal deletion (19): **ileíble* is no less ill formed than **inlegible*. This array of facts is exactly what the proposals above lead us to expect: the narrow idiosyncratic meaning and special phonological behavior of *ilegible* are characteristic of relatively fossilized lexical items that have a morphological analysis at the stem level (a "cyclic" domain) but are not productively derived from the root up; the fully compositional meaning and lack of phonological peculiarity of *inleíble* are characteristic of productive and transparent morphological derivation from the root through the word level (the last a "noncyclic" domain).[19]

We turn now to the prerhotic context in (15)–(17). What happens here is phonologically more complicated than rule (19) in the prelateral environment. In order to understand the present phenomena, it is necessary to be aware of the peculiarly skewed obligatory surface distribution of the alveolar trill and its numerous dialectal and stylistic variants, all of which I transcribe henceforth with the cover symbol [Ř].[20] Relevant underlying sources of these segments are listed in (21). Keep in mind that (21) is a nonexhaustive statement of *sources* of surface [Ř], not a formal statement of *rules* (see references in note 20 for the latter).

(21) a. /$_{word}$[____   [Ř]ompe   'it breaks'
                              [Ř]abí   'rabbi'
     b. /[+cons] $_σ$[____   al.[Ř]e.de.dor   'around'
                              Is.[Ř]a.el   'Israel'
                              hon.[Ř]a   'honor'
                              que/rr/é → que.[Ř]é   'I'll want'
                              pe/rr/o → pe.[Ř]o   'dog'

Word-initial environment (21a) is found not only in unprefixed words like *[Ř]ompe* and *[Ř]abí* but also in cases of word-level prefixation like *en[Ř]edar*, *en[Ř]iquecer* (17a), and others such as *auto-[Ř]etrato* 'self-portrait', *pre-[Ř]omano* 'pre-Roman', and so on.

Now consider the examples in (22) in the light of (21). The symbol [ř] represents an alveolar flap whose articulation and auditory impression are markedly different from those of the trill and variants transcribed as [Ř]. Both [ř] and [Ř] are in syllable onsets in all the examples in (22).

(22)   *[ř]*   *[Ř]*
     a. e-[ř]up+ción 'eruption'   co-[Ř]up+ción 'corruption'
                                          i-[Ř]up+ción 'invasion'
     b. e-[ř]os+ión 'erosion'   co-[Ř]os+ión 'corrosion'
     c. di-[ř]ec+to 'direct'   co-[Ř]ec+to   'correct'
         e-[ř]ec+to   'erect'

Examples like those in (11), (12), and (16) establish that the prefixes in the right column of (22) end in /n/ in underlying representation. In contrast, the prefixes in the left column end in a vowel. This is established for /e-/ by examples like those in (23a) and for /di-/ by examples like those in (23b).

(23) a. e-[ř]izar   'to bristle'   (cf. [Ř]izo 'tight curl')
        e-migrar   'to emigrate'   (cf. migrar 'to migrate')
        e-mitir   'to emit'   (cf. re-mitir 'to remit')
     b. di-vertir   'to divert'   (cf. per-vertir 'to pervert')
        di-famar   'to defame'   (cf. in-fame 'infamous')
        di-ferir   'to differ'   (cf. in-ferir 'to infer')
        di-gerir   'to digest'   (cf. in-gerir 'to ingest')

There is a striking difference between the examples in (22) and the case of prelateral *n*-deletion illustrated in (15)–(16). In the prelateral case, the prefix has no phonological effect on the stem: the stem has initial [l] with or without a prefix. In (22), on the other hand, whether a given stem surfaces with initial flap [ɾ́] or trill [Ř] is determined by the prefix. Moreover, /nr/ surfaces as one segment [Ř] in *in*-stem ((15), (16b), (22)), in contrast to the two-segment realization [nŘ] both morpheme-internally (21b) and in *en*-word (17a). These data can be accounted for straightforwardly if we postulate a stem-level/"cyclic" domain rule of total assimilation that can be formulated essentially as in (24).

(24) ____]pfx

Illustrative derivations are given in (25).

(25) | /onra/ | /in-real/ | underlying representations |
|---|---|---|
| – | r | (24) |
| on.ra | ir.re.al | syllabification |
| Ř | Ř | in environment (21b) |
| [on.Řa] | [i.Ře.al] | surface representations |

Rule (24) applies to prefixed /in-real/ but not to unprefixed /onra/. In the prefix-stem case, the geminate /rr/ produced by rule (24) is realized, as /rr/ always is, as monosegmental [Ř], as indicated in (21b). Rule (24) is inapplicable to unprefixed /onra/, to the word-level/"noncyclic"-domain case illustrated in (17), and to novel inventions like *inredactable* (note 18). In these three cases, /nr/ is realized as [n.Ř] as expected in environment (21b), which crucially refers to syllabic constituency.[21]

5.4 Semantics

The meaning of negative *in*-word is usually compositional, that is, a regular function of the meaning of its morphological constituents. For example, *in-* plus *móvil* means 'not *móvil*'. As illustrated in (26), ambiguities in the semantic scope of *in-* are straightforwardly attributable in some cases to the point of attachment of the prefix in overt morphological structure.

(26)   *Overt form*   *Meaning*
   a. $_A[$in-$_A[_V[_A[$util$]_A$ iza$]_V$ ble$]_A]_A$ not-$_A$utilizable$_A$
   b. $_A[_V[_A[$in-util$]_A$ iza$]_V$ ble$]_A$ [not-$_A$util$_A$] izable

According to Varela Ortega (1992, 21), *inutilizable* can mean either *que no puede ser utilizado* 'which can't be used, unusable'—where *in-* has semantic scope over the adjective *utilizable* 'usable'—or *que puede ser inutilizado* 'which can be put out of action, made useless'—where *in-* has semantic scope over the adjective (stem) *util* 'useful'. These scope relationships correspond directly to the overt morphological bracketings (26a), where *in-* attaches to the constituent $_A[$utilizable$]_A$, and (26b), where *in-* attaches to the constituent $_A[$util$]_A$.

A similar case is shown in (27), in which *in-*word is a noun.

(27) *Overt form*   *Meaning*
   in-$_N[_A[$estabil$]_A$idad$]_N$ property/state = [not-stable] (i)
                                           $_N[_A[$in(estable)$]_A$ idad$]_N$
                                           not-[property/state = stable] (ii)
                                           $_N[$in($_N[$estabil+idad$]_N$)$]_N$

According to Moliner (1994), the noun *inestabilidad* has meaning (i) shown on the right, namely, *cualidad o estado de inestable* 'the property or state of being [not-stable]'. In this case, *in-* takes semantic scope over an adjective stem embedded inside a noun, as indicated in meaning (i). Native speakers whom I have consulted agree with Moliner that *inestabilidad* has meaning (i). They contend furthermore that it can also have meaning (ii), where *in-* takes semantic scope over the entire noun *estabilidad*, that is, 'not the property of being stable' or, in more natural English, 'lack of stability'. Moreover, we find an interesting complication in examples like those in (28).

(28)   *Overt form*   *Meaning*
   a. i-$_N[$religión$]_N$ property = [not-religious] (i)
                                           $_N[_A[$i(religioso)$]_A$ ión$]_N$
                                           not-[property = religious] (ii)
                                           $_N[$i($_N[$religioso$]_N$ ión)$]_N$
   b. in-$_N[$acción$]_N$ state = [not-active] (i)
                                           $_N[_A[$in(activo)$]_A$ ión$]_N$
                                           not-[state = active] (ii)
                                           $_N[$in($_N[$activo$]_N$ ión)$]_N$
   c. in-$_V[$comunicar$]_V$ cause state = [incommunicado] (i)
                                           $_V[_A[$in(comunicado)$]_A$ ar$]_V$

Again according to Moliner, *irreligión* means *cualidad de irreligioso* 'the property of being [not-religious]', *inacción* means *estado de inactivo* 'the state of being [not-active]', and *incomunicar* means *dejar incomunicado algo o a alguien* 'to make something or someone incommunicado' or, put more simply, 'to isolate' (see note 2). In each case, the meanings are those marked (i) in the right column. Again my consultants accept these meanings, and again they contend that a second meaning, (ii) in the right column, is also available except for verbs like *incomunicar*.[22]

The problem is obvious: in meaning (i) in all cases—often the primary interpretation or indeed the only interpretation available for some words —negative *in-* takes semantic scope over a property or state expressed by an adjective stem. But, as illustrated in (29), whatever the sister constituent of *in-* may be, no adjective stem is present in the overt morphological form of any of these examples or in many others like them.

(29) *i- $_A$[[religi] <u>os</u>]$_A$ -ión
   *in- $_A$[[act] <u>iv</u>]$_A$ -ión
   *in- $_A$[[comunic] <u>ad</u>]$_A$ -ar

The variety of "missing" adjectival morphemes (*-os* '-ous' in *irreligión*, *-iv* '-ive' in *inacción*, *-ad* '-ate' in *incommunicar*, and others in other examples) rules out the possibility that a process of morphological deletion is at work here, as Aronoff (1976) proposes for cases like English *nomin+ate/nomin+ɖ/ɖ+ee*, for example. An additional layer of complexity is implied by the fact that the meanings of adjectives like *religioso* and *activo*—semantically present but morphologically absent in *irreligión* and *inacción*—themselves seem to be built on elementary units that correspond to the meanings of *religión* and *acción*—morphologically absent in *religioso* and *activo*.[23] It is also worth noting that despite words like *activo*, *actividad* 'activity', and *acción*, Spanish has no simple stem *act-* corresponding to the basic verb and noun 'act' in English (roughly *obrar* and *hecho*, respectively, in Spanish).

Cases like *inestabilidad* (27) bear on the familiar notion of "bracketing paradoxes." As shown in (7), the evidence of *e*-epenthesis indicates that the bracketing of overt morphological structure is (30a). On the other hand, both of the semantic scope relations in (30b) are available, though only structure (ii) matches the overt bracketing (30a).

(30) a. *Overt morphological constituent structure*
   $_N$[in $_N$[$_A$[<u>e</u>stab(i)l]$_A$ idad]$_N$]$_N$

b. *(Covert) semantic constituent structure*
   $_N[_A[in \ _A[stab(i)l]_A]_A \ idad]_N$ (i)
   $_N[in \ _N[_A[stab(i)l]_A \ idad]_N]_N$ (ii)

Furthermore, overt structure (30a) is motivated on morphological grounds, independently of *e*-epenthesis, namely, by the allomorphy of the base, notated in (30) by the parenthesized /i/ in the adjectival stem. This /i/ appears always and only before *-idad* '-ity' as in *estabilidad* versus *estable*, not *estabile (cf. *noble* 'noble' and *nobleza*, not *nobileza, and many analogous examples). In the morphological structure (30a)—but not in semantic representation (i) of (30b)—the conditioned allomorph *stabil* and the conditioning environment *-idad* are structurally adjacent; that is, they are sister constituents of the noun *estabilidad*. This constitutes evidence that (30a) and not version (i) of (30b) is the correct constituent structure of the overt form, even though the latter represents the scope relations of the primary meaning of the word.

In studies of Spanish morphology, it is normally assumed without discussion that semantic structure is a reliable guide to, and diagnostic of, morphological structure.[24] For example, Peperkamp (1997, 90) assigns $_N[_A[in-_A[stabl]_A]_A \ idad]_N$ as the unique morphological constituent structure of *inestabilidad*, giving the following "reasons": (1) the "meaning is 'the state of not being stable', rather than 'not the state of being stable'"; (2) "*in-* subcategorizes for adjectives, not for nouns." Both (1) and (2) happen to be observationally faulty, but the point at issue now is that Peperkamp takes it for granted that semantic structure is a clear-cut "reason" to assign a particular morphological structure.[25]

The general lesson from the material examined here is that overt morphological structure is often not isomorphic with semantic structure, or even close to it. Especially instructive in this respect are examples like *irreligión, inacción,* and *incomunicar* (28)–(29). These are worse than mere paradoxes since no amount of rearranging and/or relabeling of brackets over a given string of morphemes can produce compatible semantic, morphological, and phonological representations. This follows from the fact that primary constitutive elements of semantic structure are not present at all in the overt morphological structure of these words. Problematic in a different way are cases like *impune* (8) and others, in which a semantically required adjectival element not only does not appear in the overt string of morphemes in the base of *in-* but moreover does not exist at all as a freestanding word or even as a bound stem in Spanish.

Clearly, we have only begun to scratch the surface of the form-meaning relationship in Spanish words. The modest goal of this chapter is to encourage others to examine the proposals made here in order to correct them where necessary and to extend them where possible.[26]

Notes

I risk embarrassing Ken—gush is not his style—by saying that he has been an extraordinary friend, colleague, and role model for over 30 years. It's a terrible thing to have Ken as role model: you know for sure that you will never come near measuring up.

Many people have helped me with this chapter. I can't mention everyone by name, but I would like to single out Calixto Agüero, Karlos Arregi, Jorge Guitart, Antonia Lema, Isabel Oltra, Margarita Suñer, and Soledad Varela for special thanks. The usual disclaimers apply.

1. For the sake of readability, I often write a hyphen (not used in standard orthography) between prefix and base. Orthographic *rr* (last example in (1)) represents an alveolar trill (and stylistic/dialectal variants) whose underlying sources are described in section 5.3.

2. See Varela Ortega 1992, 53–54, for discussion of verbs of this type.

3. Caveat lector: I write these terms in quotation marks to emphasize that the meaning given to them by Halle/Harris/Vergnaud cannot be assumed to be identical to traditional usage. Halle, Harris, and Vergnaud (1991) and Harris (1993) present novel results for Spanish that remain a challenge for other approaches.

4. Dictionaries give *instable* and *instabilidad* as variants of *inestable* and *inestabilidad*. My consultants know that the former words exist, but they use only the latter. Discussion of the types of bases to which *in-* can attach continues below.

5. In the examples in (7), the epenthesis-triggering /s/ is followed by another [+consonantal] segment, a disallowed syllable-onset cluster in Spanish. Technically outdated but detailed discussion of *e*-epenthesis and of onset clusters can be found in Harris 1983, 13–14, 20–22, 26–31.

6. Irrelevantly, there is a verb *forme* 'form(s)' (first or third person singular present subjunctive).

7. For the sake of the exposition, I use *lexicon* in the standard sense here and below. The grammatical component that I am referring to, however, is the Encyclopedia of Distributed Morphology (see Halle and Marantz 1993, 1994, and much related work, especially the Distributed Morphology website: http://www.ling.upenn.edu/~rnoyer/dm/).

8. For class vowels ("class markers") see Harris 1991a,b, 1996, 1999.

9. Some readers may find it fun as well as instructive to verify that these claims correctly predict the well-formedness of such forms as *inescrible* 'unwritable', *inscribible* 'inscribable', *ininscribible* 'uninscribable' versus the ill-formedness of *ininescrible*, *ininescribible*, and so on.

10. The facts in (14) are slightly different in certain so-called velarizing dialects, which I do not have space to discuss. These differences do not affect the argument. Crucially, the data in (15) and (16) are valid for all dialects.

11. Partial or total labialization of /n/ before /m/ is possible depending on dialect, tempo, and register; /n/ may be deleted before continuants (with nasalization of the preceding vowel) in some dialects/styles.

12. Prefixal /i/ is not nasalized as a concomitant of the obligatory disappearance of /n/ in (15) and (16). This phenomenon is thus distinct from the variable nasal deletion cum vowel nasalization mentioned in the previous note.

13. There is some dialect variation in these forms. For example, some speakers use *ladrillar* instead of *en-ladrillar*, though no speaker uses **lejiar* or **lutar* instead of *en-lejiar* and *en-lutar*, so far as I know.

14. There happens to be an independent word or words (adjective or noun) *recto* with the various meanings 'straight, literal (meaning), right (angle), rectum'— obviously not the base of *correcto* or *erecto* at the end of (16b).

15. In (18) and subsequently, I use the traditional term *stem* in its traditional sense. In some versions of Distributed Morphology, however, "stem" has no theoretical status. Harris 1999 contains discussion with specific reference to Spanish.

16. The sequence /nl/ does not occur inside morphemes (though /nr/ does). Thus, we must ask whether (19) is responsible for this gap—that is, whether (19) applies morpheme-internally as well as over the prefix-stem/root boundary. I leave this issue open here; it is taken up in Harris, in preparation.

17. Corominas (1961) gives 1495 as the date of first written attestation of *legible*; no date is given for *ilegible*.

18. The same goes for *inlavable* 'unwashable', *inredactable* 'uneditable', and other words that can be made up on the spot. Unlike the pair *(in)leíble/(i)legible*, however, these are not involved in interesting semantic contrasts.

19. English speakers may gain an intuitive foothold on the differences between *(i)legible* and *(in)leíble* by reflecting on English *(il)legible* and *(un)readable*: the verb *read* is patently present in the latter but there is no corresponding verb **lege* /leǰ/ in the former.

20. Descriptions can be found in many sources; for early generative treatments, see Harris 1969, 46–56, and Harris 1983, 62–71. The most recent explicit analysis I know of is Bonet and Mascaró 1997.

21. Readers have suggested an alternative that seeks to eliminate rule (24) by generalizing the environment of (19) to both /l/ and /r/. I see no way to implement this suggestion without losing the contrast illustrated in (25) and/or losing other generalizations regarding the distribution of [ř] and [Ř].

22. To be sure, for particular words in particular contexts, native speakers find it difficult to distinguish among potential readings and thus to decide which is the relevant one.

23. Thanks to Ken Hale for this observation.

24. Varela Ortega 1992 is a conspicuous exception.

25. Peperkamp does not account for the allomorphy of *stabl/stabil*, a consequential descriptive gap. In general, however, her analysis is rich in data and carefully argued.

26. It would be difficult to find a better model or a higher standard of quality in this field than the pioneering and insightful work on lexical semantic structure by Ken Hale and coauthors (see Hale and Keyser 1992, 1993; Jeanne and Hale 1998).

References

Aronoff, Mark. 1976. *Word formation in generative grammar.* Cambridge, Mass.: MIT Press.

Bonet, Eulàlia, and Joan Mascaró. 1997. On the representation of contrasting rhotics. In *Issues in the phonology and morphology of the major Iberian languages,* edited by Fernando Martínez-Gil and Alfonso Morales-Front, 103–126. Washington, D.C.: Georgetown University Press.

Corominas, Joan. 1961. *Breve diccionario etimológico de la lengua castellana.* Madrid: Gredos.

Hale, Kenneth, and Samuel Jay Keyser. 1992. The syntactic character of thematic structure. In *Thematic structure: Its role in grammar,* edited by I. M. Roca, 107–144. Berlin: Foris.

Hale, Kenneth, and Samuel Jay Keyser. 1993. On argument structure and the lexical expression of syntactic relations. In *The view from Building 20,* edited by Kenneth Hale and Samuel Jay Keyser, 53–109. Cambridge, Mass.: MIT Press.

Halle, Morris. 1990a. An approach to morphology. In *Proceedings of NELS 20,* edited by Juli Carter, Rose-Marie Déchaine, Bill Philip, and Tim Sherer, 150–184. GLSA, University of Massachusetts, Amherst.

Halle, Morris. 1990b. Respecting metrical structure. *Natural Language & Linguistic Theory* 8, 149–176.

Halle, Morris, James Harris, and Jean-Roger Vergnaud. 1991. A reexamination of the Stress Erasure Convention and Spanish stress. *Linguistic Inquiry* 22, 141–159.

Halle, Morris, and Alec Marantz. 1993. Distributed Morphology and the pieces of inflection. In *The view from Building 20,* edited by Kenneth Hale and Samuel Jay Keyser, 111–176. Cambridge, Mass.: MIT Press.

Halle, Morris, and Alec Marantz. 1994. Some key features of Distributed Morphology. In *Papers on phonology and morphology,* edited by Andrew Carnie and Heidi Harley, with Tony Bures, 275–288. MIT Working Papers in Linguistics 21. MITWPL, Department of Linguistics and Philosophy, MIT, Cambridge, Mass.

Halle, Morris, and Jean-Roger Vergnaud. 1987. *An essay on stress.* Cambridge, Mass.: MIT Press.

Harris, James W. 1969. *Spanish phonology.* Cambridge, Mass.: MIT Press.

Harris, James W. 1983. *Syllable structure and stress in Spanish*. Cambridge, Mass.: MIT Press.

Harris, James W. 1984. Theories of phonological representation and nasal consonants in Spanish. In *Papers from the XIIth Linguistic Symposium on Romance Languages*, edited by Philip Baldi, 153–168. Amsterdam: John Benjamins.

Harris, James W. 1991a. The exponence of gender in Spanish. *Linguistic Inquiry* 22, 27–62.

Harris, James W. 1991b. The form classes of Spanish substantives. *Morphology Yearbook* 1, 65–88.

Harris, James W. 1993. Integrity of prosodic constituents and the domain of syllabification rules in Spanish and Catalan. In *The view from Building 20*, edited by Kenneth Hale and Samuel Jay Keyser, 177–193. Cambridge, Mass.: MIT Press.

Harris, James W. 1996. The syntax and morphology of Class Marker Suppression in Spanish. In *Grammatical theory and Romance languages*, edited by Karen Zagona, 99–122. Amsterdam: John Benjamins.

Harris, James W. 1999. Nasal depalatalization *no*, morphological wellformedness *sí*: The structure of Spanish word classes. In *Papers on morphology and syntax, cycle one*, edited by Karlos Arregi, Benjamin Bruening, Cornelia Krause, and Vivian Lin, 47–82. MIT Working Papers in Linguistics 33. MITWPL, Department of Linguistics and Philosophy, MIT, Cambridge, Mass.

Harris, James W. In preparation. The skewed distribution of Spanish nasals: Morpheme-internal generalizations, full specification and filters. Ms., MIT, Cambridge, Mass.

Jeanne, LaVerne, and Ken Hale. 1998. Transitivización en hopi. Paper presented at the Encuentro Internacional de Lingüística en el Noroeste, Universidad de Sonora, Hermosillo, México. November 1998.

Lang, Mervyn L. 1990. *Spanish word formation*. London: Routledge.

Moliner, María. 1994. *Diccionario del uso del español*. Madrid: Gredos.

Narváez, R. A. 1970. *An outline of Spanish morphology*. St. Paul, Minn.: EMC Corporation.

Peperkamp, Sharon. 1997. Prosodic words. Doctoral dissertation, Universiteit van Amsterdam. The Hague: Holland Academic Graphics.

Urrutia Cárdenas, H. 1978. *Lengua y discurso en la creación léxica*. Madrid: Planeta.

Varela Ortega, Soledad. 1983. Lindes entre morfemas: el prefijo negativo *in-*. In *Serta Philologica F. Lázaro Carreter*, 637–648. Madrid: Cátedra.

Varela Ortega, Soledad. 1992. *Fundamentos de morfología*. Madrid: Síntesis.

Chapter 6

| **Observations about the Form and Meaning of the Perfect** | Sabine Iatridou, Elena Anagnostopoulou, and Roumyana Izvorski |

Για τον Κεν, με αγαπη και ευγνωμοσυνη
За Кен, с любов и благодарност

6.1 Goal

The goal of this chapter is to establish how certain aspects of the meaning of the perfect are composed from the elements present in its morpho-syntactic representation.

Not all languages have a present perfect that is structurally and interpretationally distinct from a simple past. We will only be looking at languages that make the distinction.[1] In languages that have a perfect, there is variation with respect to the range of meanings associated with it. There are certain meaning components that are always found with a perfect and there are others that vary depending, as we will show, on several factors.

6.2 Background

6.2.1 Common Characterizations

There are a number of intriguing issues surrounding the perfect that have drawn considerable attention in the literature, among the most commonly discussed ones being that the perfect shares properties with both temporal and aspectual forms, and that certain adverbials that one would expect to be possible with the perfect are actually disallowed. In this section, we will briefly present the central points concerning these common characterizations.

Similarly to the tenses, the perfect temporally locates an eventuality relative to some reference point. Thus, the perfect is often described as expressing anteriority. Consider, for example, sentence (1).

(1) Petros has visited Thailand.

Sentence (1) asserts that there is an eventuality of Petros's visiting Thailand that occurred before the moment of utterance. This common and intuitive characterization brings the present perfect very close to the meaning of the simple past, and for this reason, the two have often been discussed in opposition to each other (McCoard 1978 and many others).

The literature on the distinction between the present perfect and the simple past usually revolves around the following points.

While both the present perfect and the simple past express temporal precedence or anteriority (which is why the perfect is often called a tense), it has often been pointed out that they do so in different ways. In Reichenbachian terms, for example (as in Hornstein 1990), it has been said that while the simple past expresses a temporal precedence between the Speech time and the Reference time (R__S), the perfect expresses a temporal precedence between the Event time and the Reference time (E__R).[2]

Another much-discussed difference between the present perfect and the simple past regards compatibility with different adverbial classes. There are two subcases of this. In some (though not all) languages, certain past-oriented adverbs like *yesterday* or *in 1959* cannot appear with the present perfect but can with the simple past (McCoard 1978; Klein 1992; Giorgi and Pianesi 1998; and many others). It is obviously surprising that past-oriented adverbs would not be compatible with a temporal configuration expressing anteriority (dubbed the "present perfect puzzle" by Klein (1992)), and this question has received a fair amount of attention. On the other hand, there are also adverbs (e.g., *since*) that are compatible with the (present) perfect but not with the simple past. McCoard (1978) provides an extensive list of adverbs that are compatible only with the perfect or only with the simple past, as well as of adverbs that are compatible with both.[3]

A third way of characterizing the perfect in opposition to the simple past has to do with aspect (which is the reason why the perfect is often called an aspect). The perfect is said to describe (or focus on) a state that follows from a prior eventuality (e.g., Parsons 1990; Vlach 1993; Giorgi and Pianesi 1998).[4] On this view, (1) says that Petros is in the/a state that results from an eventuality of visiting Thailand. This has been taken to mean that sentences containing a perfect are stative sentences. On the other hand, sentences containing a simple past inherit the aspectual properties of the main predicate and can therefore be statives or nonstatives (accomplishments, achievements, or activities).

6.2.2   Uses of the Present Perfect

In the literature, four major uses of the present perfect have been identified (see, e.g., McCawley 1971; Comrie 1976; Binnick 1991).

The *universal perfect* (U-perfect) conveys the meaning that the predicate holds throughout some interval stretching from a certain point in the past up to the present (e.g., McCoard 1978; Dowty 1979; Mittwoch 1988; Vlach 1993). It has been noted that the U-perfect can be formed only if the "underlying eventuality" (the eventuality referred to by the syntactic material occurring just below the perfect) is a stative verb or adjective or a progressive. As we will show later, what is required is *unboundedness*, a notion related to but not identical with stativity. An eventuality is described as unbounded when it is ongoing at an interval (and is therefore not asserted to have reached an endpoint—achievement of the goal, in the case of telics; termination for atelics). An eventuality is described as bounded when it is contained in an interval (i.e., when it is asserted to have completed/terminated). The syntacticosemantic feature [unbounded] is realized by progressive or imperfective morphology, the feature [bounded] by the perfective.[5] (We will return to the issue of stativity and unboundedness in section 6.4.)

(2) a. I have been sick since 1990.
   b. <u>1990   NOW</u> (= time of utterance)

On the U-perfect reading, (2a) is understood to mean that there is a sickness eventuality that holds throughout the named interval, that is, a period extending from 1990 up to now. The U-perfect has often been claimed not to be a core meaning of the perfect because many languages do not have a U-perfect (Jespersen 1924; Comrie 1976).

The *experiential perfect* asserts that the subject has a certain experience. Unlike the U-perfect, the experiential perfect can be formed from an underlying eventuality of any Aktionsart.

(3) a. I have read *Principia Mathematica* five times.
   b. I have been sick since 1990.
   c. 1990   ____   NOW (= time of utterance)

(3a) asserts that I have had the experience of reading *Principia Mathematica* five times. On the other hand, (3b) is ambiguous. On the experiential reading, it says that within the interval that extends from 1990 till now there is some (at least one) interval in which I was sick. On this reading, (3b) can be continued by *I was sick for three months in the fall of 1993*. This reading is indicated in (3c). However, the string also has the U-perfect reading, as in (2a–b).

The *perfect of result* is said to be possible only with telic predicates and only for as long as the effect of the underlying eventuality holds.

(4) I have lost my glasses.

Sentence (4) can be a resultative perfect only if said while the glasses are still lost. As soon as the glasses are found, (4) can only be uttered as an experiential perfect.

Finally, the *perfect of recent past* is used to report an eventuality that just happened.

(5) He has just graduated from college.

Sometimes, the term *existential perfect* is used as a cover term for the last three uses (McCawley 1971; Mittwoch 1988), but the prototypical existential perfect is often taken to be the experiential (McCawley 1971). We will have a few things to say about the perfect of recent past and nothing about the perfect of result, whose status as an independent category is unclear to us.[6] The chapter will focus mostly on the universal/experiential distinction and its crosslinguistic parameterization.

6.3   The Universal/Existential Ambiguity Debate

The distinction between universal (U-) and existential (E-) perfect has been the subject of much discussion in the literature. In fact, the very nature of the distinction has been a matter of considerable debate. One view holds that we are dealing not with a true semantic ambiguity but with a pragmatic one, the U-perfect being just the limiting case of the E-perfect (Bauer 1970; Inoue 1978; McCoard 1978; Heny 1982; Klein 1992, 1994). Another view holds that the U/E distinction is a genuine semantic ambiguity (Dowty 1979; Richards 1982; Mittwoch 1988; Abusch and Rooth 1990; Vlach 1993).

Pragmatic accounts of the U/E distinction in the perfect (e.g., Klein 1992, 1994) attribute the U-reading to a vagueness with respect to the actual duration of the underlying stative predicate. They argue that the semantic contribution of the perfect is to assert that the underlying eventuality precedes the reference time, without specifying its exact temporal location or duration. Whether or not, in the case of states, the eventuality continues to hold *at* and possibly *after* the reference time is left unspecified; it is sufficient that some time span, during which the eventuality holds, precedes the reference time.

What about the view that the U/E distinction is part of the semantics? As pointed out by Dowty (1979), when the adverb in an ambiguous sentence like *Mary has lived in Boston for three years* is preposed, only the U-reading survives. This shows that the U-perfect is not just a special case of the E-perfect, as pragmatic accounts would have it.[7] Indeed, if the U-perfect were a subcase of the E-perfect, then the former would entail the latter and we would never find a case where only the U-reading is available. Other arguments come from Mittwoch (1988). She observes that, on the E-reading, in a sentence like *Sam has been in Boston since Tuesday*, Tuesday is not included in the set of possible intervals at which the state of Sam's being in Boston holds. On the U-reading, however, Tuesday is asserted to be part of the interval throughout which Sam is in Boston. Clearly, then, it cannot be the case that the U-reading is a subcase of the E-reading.

Another argument for a semantic treatment of the U/E distinction comes from the temporal interpretation of clauses embedded under present perfect predicates. This issue is discussed by Brugger (1997), who points out that in English, the existential present perfect behaves like the simple past in terms of the range of interpretations it allows to embedded past tense clauses. Matrix past tenses can license a purely morphological past (i.e., a past that is not interpreted as such) in their embedded clause; this is what happens under the simultaneous reading of a sentence like *John claimed that Mary was sick*. The E-perfect allows the same simultaneous interpretation (in addition to the shifted reading); for example, in *Since Christmas, John has claimed on several occasions that Mary was sick*, the two eventualities of John's claiming and Mary's being sick can be contemporaneous. The exact explanations for these sequence-of-tense facts need not concern us here; what is important for our purposes is that the U-perfect does not license the simultaneous interpretation of an embedded past tense. A sentence like *Since Christmas, John has been claiming that Mary was sick* or a sentence like *John has always claimed that Mary was sick* only has the interpretation that Mary's sickness is prior to John's claiming. The explanation, given by Brugger, is that in the U-perfect the underlying eventuality continues at the utterance time and thus semantically, the U-perfect behaves like a present tense.[8] This would be another argument in favor of viewing the distinction between the U-perfect and the E-perfect as a semantic one.

Other arguments have been proposed in favor of a semantic treatment of the U/E distinction.[9] If the arguments made here are correct, they constitute additional evidence for the semantic view.

The points we would like to contribute to the U/E-perfect debate are these (not in order of significance):

1. The U-reading asserts that the underlying eventuality holds throughout the interval specified by the adverbial *and* at its endpoints. In case of the present perfect, this means that the utterance time is included by assertion.
2. The U-reading is never available to a perfect unless the latter is modified by certain adverbials. We will discuss what contribution the adverbials make.
3. The E__R interval does not have a distinguished status in the perfect.
4. The crosslinguistic distribution of the U-reading is not quirky, as is often assumed, but can be predicted by the morphosyntactic features that enter into the composition of the perfect participle.
5. Anteriority is not part of the meaning of the perfect (participle).

From these points, it is clear that we are in the so-called semantic camp. That is, we do not believe the difference between the U- and the E-perfect is one of pragmatics; instead, we believe it is one of meaning, determined by the morphosyntactic content of the sentence. We will explicate each point in turn, with an emphasis on 2–5.

6.3.1   Point 1: Inclusion of the Utterance Time by Assertion

In the U-reading of a sentence like (2a), the meaning is conveyed that the speaker is still sick at the moment of utterance.[10] Is this an implicature or an assertion of (2a)?

For pragmatic accounts of the U/E distinction, clearly it is not a matter of assertion.[11] But even semantic accounts of the U/E distinction do not always take the position (at least explicitly) that in the U-reading, the reference time is included in the underlying eventuality by assertion. Mittwoch (1988) argues that the reading that the eventuality holds at the utterance time is not part of the main assertion of the U-reading of the present perfect but an implication stemming from the fact that the underlying predicate is a state and, although the interval denoted by the adverbial has ended, the interval at which the eventuality holds need not have ended.[12] Abusch and Rooth (1990) similarly take the interval denoted by the adverbial to extend "up to now" without discussing whether the underlying eventuality is asserted to hold at the utterance time or not.

Our position is that the U-perfect asserts that the underlying eventuality holds throughout the interval specified by the adverbial *and* at its endpoints. Let us take as example the present perfect in (2a) on the U-perfect interpretation. There is an interval that we will call the *perfect time span*, which starts with 1990.[13] The *left boundary* (LB) of the perfect time span is specified by the argument of the adverbial. The *right boundary* (RB) is set by tense. This means that in the present perfect, RB is at (i.e., includes) the utterance time. In the past perfect, RB precedes the utterance time; in the future perfect, RB follows the utterance time.[14] Recall that for a U-perfect like (2a), 1990, or a final subinterval of 1990, is included in the sickness eventuality by assertion, as shown by Mittwoch (1988). In other words, at LB, the predicate holds by assertion. We propose that the same holds for RB. That is, in the U-perfect reading of the present perfect, the underlying eventuality holds at the utterance time by assertion. This can be seen in the following sentences, which contain claims that the eventuality does not hold at the utterance time and are therefore contradictions:

(6) a. *She has been sick at least/ever since 1990 but she is fine now.
    b. *She has always lived here but she doesn't anymore.

Effectively, in the U-perfect, the underlying eventuality holds throughout the entire perfect time span and since RB is part of the perfect time span, the eventuality holds at RB as well. On the U-perfect reading of the present perfect, the underlying eventuality holds at the utterance time, since RB is the utterance time. This fact results from a combination of the perfect and the meaning of the present tense. On the U-perfect reading of the past perfect (or pluperfect), the underlying eventuality is again asserted to hold at RB of the perfect time span, but now RB is in the past with respect to the utterance time, owing to the past tense component of the pluperfect. The same consideration applies to the future perfect: in this case, RB is in the future with respect to the utterance time. Consider the following discourse:

(7) a. Mary visited Peter last week.
    b. A strange bug had bitten him a week before
    c. and he had been very sick since then.
    d. Mary will visit Peter again in two weeks.
    e. At that point, he will have been sick for a month.

According to (7a–c), Peter got a bug-bite two weeks before the utterance time; his ensuing sickness started at the time of the bug-bite and continued up to and including the time of Mary's visit, which happened a week before the utterance time. Whether it continued beyond that is not indicated in (7c). What is relevant is that at the time specified by the past tense (when Mary's visit took place), the eventuality is asserted to have held.

This is similar to the eventuality's being asserted to hold at the utterance time in the U-reading of the present perfect. The same holds for the future perfect, as is illustrated in (7d–e). At the time when Mary's visit will take place (i.e., two weeks after the utterance time), the eventuality will still hold. Thus, the eventuality of Peter's being sick will have held throughout a period of one month starting two weeks before the utterance time (LB) and extending up to and including two weeks after the utterance time (RB).

As we said earlier, previous views on this point have held that the U-perfect reading of the present perfect asserts only that the underlying state holds up till now, and it is left to the pragmatics to determine whether the state holds at the utterance time or not. Indeed, one can say while sipping a cup of coffee *I have been digging in the yard for two hours.* The context of utterance makes it clear that no digging is actually happening at the utterance time. However, this is not a counterexample to point 1 since one can say *I am (busy) digging in the yard* while sipping a cup of coffee during a break in the digging. The progressive (which can be used only with nonstatives) seems to allow assertions about subeventualities of the underlying eventuality. This "flexibility" remains when the predicate is part of a perfect sentence. Stative predicates do not allow the same leeway as nonstatives. That is, one cannot say *He is in the room* during even a short absence from the room. Nor can one say *He has been in the room ever since this morning* (as a U-perfect) when he is not in the room anymore. This asymmetry between statives and nonstatives exists outside the perfect and is inherited in the perfect, creating the illusion that in the U-perfect reading, the eventuality does not hold at the utterance time.

From now on, we will use the noncancelable inclusion of RB in the predicate as a diagnostic for the U-perfect reading. However, we will use only stative adjectives, to avoid the aforementioned difficulties.

In summary, in the U-perfect reading, the underlying eventuality holds by assertion at all the points of the perfect time span, including its endpoints (LB and RB). As we have shown, LB is set by the argument of the perfect adverbial and RB by tense.

6.3.2　Point 2: U-Perfect and Adverbial Modification
First, we will show that truly unmodified perfects are never U-perfects.[15] Later, we will return to why this may be so.

6.3.2.1　Unmodified Perfects Are Never U-Perfects　To demonstrate that the U-reading is never available to a perfect unless it is modified by cer-

tain adverbials, we have to look at predicates that in principle can yield the U-perfect. We will look in turn at individual-level predicates, stage-level statives, and progressives.

Individual-level statives that hold throughout an individual's life and cannot be coerced into stage-level statives, like *be tall* and *have brown eyes*, are ungrammatical in the perfect without adverbials. The unacceptability of such sentences shows a fortiori that the U-perfect is missing.[16]

(8) He has had brown eyes *(since he was born).

Next, consider the perfect of stage-level statives (and individual-level predicates that can be coerced into stage-level predicates). Stage-level predicates are possible in the perfect without adverbials.

(9) Mary has been sick.

Does this sentence have a U-reading? It can certainly have an experiential reading, but there is also a context in which it can appear where the reading is clearly not experiential. We have to consider this context, shown in (10), to see whether we are dealing with a U-reading.

(10) A: I haven't seen Mary in a while. Where is she?
     B: She has been sick.

Is B's utterance (*She has been sick*) a U-perfect? It is at least compatible with (10B) that Mary is still sick at the utterance time (the sentence can be continued with *and she still is and so she hasn't been coming to the office*), which raises the suspicion that we are, in fact, dealing with a U-reading.[17] However, unlike a U-perfect, (10B) is also compatible with Mary's not being sick at the utterance time; (10B) could also be continued with *but she is fine now and she will come to the office soon*. In other words, *She has been sick* is simply silent about whether Mary is sick at present and this is precisely not how the U-perfect behaves.

What type of perfect is (10B), then? We argue that (10B) has the range of meanings found with (11).

(11) She has been sick lately.

Sentence (11) says nothing about whether Mary is sick at the present time.

(12) She has been very sick lately. I don't know how she is now.

In other words, there is a covert *lately* in (10B), or, possibly, there is an anaphoric reference to something with that interpretation, provided by the context in (10A). From the nature and meaning of this adverbial it follows that (10B) is an example of the perfect of recent past.

There is also crosslinguistic evidence showing that (10B) is not a U-perfect and that it most likely is a perfect of recent past. Some languages, such as Bulgarian, have a U-perfect but not a perfect of recent past. In Bulgarian, the discourse in (10) cannot be rendered with a perfect in B's answer at all.

(13) A: I haven't seen Mary in a while. Where is she?
    B: #Tja e bila bolna.
       she is been sick
       'She has been sick.'

In Bulgarian, there are two possibilities. Either B's utterance can contain a present tense, in which case it is asserted that Mary is still sick, just as it would be in English; or it can contain a simple past, leaving the context to determine whether Mary is still sick or not or whether the speaker is just ignorant about this matter (i.e., exactly the meaning of the simple past). We conclude that (9)/(10B) is not a U-perfect.

Why should English and Bulgarian differ with respect to having the perfect of recent past? Whatever the ultimate answer is, at a first level it is that the two languages differ in the temporal morphology that accompanies *lately*. In English, this adverbial must take the present perfect; in Bulgarian, it takes the past tense.

(14) a. She has been sick lately.
    b. *She was sick lately.
    c. *Tja e bila bolna naposledûk.
       she is been sick   lately
       Literally: 'She has been sick lately.'
    d. Tja beše bolna naposledûk.
       she was sick   lately
       Literally: 'She was sick lately.'

This correlates with the fact that English but not Bulgarian has a perfect of recent past in the absence of an overt adverbial. An English present perfect can "pick up" a *lately* in the discourse, but a Bulgarian present perfect cannot. This possibly points to a lexical idiosyncrasy.[18]

Finally, this brings us to the perfect of the progressive. It is sometimes said that the perfect of the progressive has only the U-reading (Vlach 1993).[19]

(15) I have been cooking.

However, in fact (15) is not a U-perfect, as nothing is asserted about the utterance time (the sentence can be continued by *but I'm done now*), but it can be an experiential perfect or a perfect of recent past. As before, then, we conclude that the perfect of the progressive in isolation does not have the U-perfect reading.[20] Other examples pointing to this conclusion are found in Mittwoch 1988 (e.g., *He has been eating your porridge; it's all gone/I have been writing a difficult letter; thank goodness it's finished*).

6.3.2.2 So What Do Adverbials Do?   We have shown that the U-reading is possible only when the perfect is modified by an adverbial. Of the adverbials that trigger a U-reading, there are some with which the U-reading is simply possible and some with which it is obligatory.

(16) a. U-reading possible: since, for five days
    b. U-reading required: at least since, ever since, always, for five days now

With Dowty (1979), Vlach (1993), and others, we assume that there are at least two levels of adverbials, perfect-level and eventuality-level, "level" here corresponding to scope.[21] We take perfect-level adverbials to be situated higher than eventuality-level adverbials. This simply reflects the fact that the perfect morphology is higher in the tree than the part describing the eventuality. The perfect adverbial is below Tense, whose [+/−past] feature can appear on the perfect, yielding present, past, or infinitival perfects. In the addendum, we address issues pertaining to the order of functional categories in the perfect and to the placement of adverbs.

   One diagnostic for whether an adverbial is perfect-level is whether the perfect morphology is obligatory.[22] For example, *since*-adverbials require perfect morphology.[23]

(17) a. I have been sick since yesterday.
    b. *I am sick since yesterday.
    c. *I was sick since 1990.

There are also adverbials that are perfect-level but appear not to require perfect morphosyntax (e.g., *for*-adverbials). However, the appearance that perfect morphology is optional with these adverbials is only an illusion. In fact, such adverbials are ambiguous; they can be either perfect-level or eventuality-level. As the latter, they do not require perfect morphosyntax;

as the former, they do. We will return to more details of this issue when we discuss *for*-adverbials.

Not all perfect-level adverbials are capable of forming a U-perfect. For example, *lately* and *five times before* require perfect morphology and hence are perfect-level—but they do not form a U-perfect.

When there is perfect morphology but no overt perfect-level adverbial, we argue (with Vlach (1993)) that there is a covert adverbial. (We will return to the nature of this covert adverbial). When there is no overt eventuality-level adverbial, the context (possibly as a default mechanism along the lines of existential closure (Heim 1982)) provides one with roughly the meaning '(at least) once' (henceforth, *ONCE*) (see also Bennett 1977; Bäuerle 1979).[24]

Adverbials that relate to intervals can have either a "durative" or an "inclusive" interpretation (e.g., Dowty 1979; Mittwoch 1988; Vlach 1993). The same holds for perfect adverbials. If the perfect-level adverbial is durative, the underlying predicate must hold of every subinterval of the perfect time span (universal quantification over the points of the interval); that is, the perfect time span must be "filled up" with a homogeneous predicate. On a durative interpretation, since LB and RB belong to the perfect time span, the predicate holds of them too. This is how the U-perfect is derived.

If the perfect-level adverbial is inclusive, then the perfect sentence asserts that a particular eventuality is properly included in the perfect time span (existential quantification over the points of the interval). In other words, neither of the boundaries is asserted to be part of the eventuality (see Mittwoch 1988 for a detailed discussion of this point with respect to LB). This is how the E-perfect is derived.

Let us now discuss some perfect-level adverbials in more detail.

***Since*-adverbials**   For *since*-adverbials, LB is set by the argument of *since* and RB is set by tense. *Since*-adverbials are ambiguous between being durational and being inclusive. When *since* is durational, it yields the U-perfect only. When *since* is inclusive, it yields the E-perfect (Vlach 1993; see also Bennett and Partee 1972; Dowty 1979). Alternatively (Arnim von Stechow, personal communication), *since* can be described as being neither durational nor inclusive, but as being the *default* perfect-level adverbial in the sense that it merely sets the LB of the perfect time span denoted by the perfect; therefore, all possible readings are permitted with *since*-adverbials. Either characterization is compatible with our proposal, though we will use the former terms in what follows.

The adverbial *ever since* has only the U-perfect reading, most likely because of the universal association of *ever*, which indicates universal quantification over the points of the perfect time span.

The adverbial *at least since* also has only the U-perfect reading. Without going into details, we will sketch what may be going on here. Addition of *at least* to other adverbials also forces the durative reading. For example, *He was in his office between 3 and 4* permits both the durative and the inclusive interpretation of the adverbial. But *He was in his office at least between 3 and 4* has only the durative interpretation.[25]

We have said that *since* is both durative and inclusive. But in order to obtain the U-perfect reading, it is not enough to access the durative reading of *since*. We also need a predicate that can satisfy the subinterval requirements of the durative side of *since*, in other words, a homogeneous predicate (later, we will show some effects of this requirement). Such a predicate is available in (18a) but not in (19a). This is why the U-perfect reading is possible in (18a), as illustrated in the interpretation in (18b) and the logical form in (18c), alongside the E-reading (see (18d) and (18e)), whereas it is not possible in (19a), which has only the E-reading (see (19b) and (19c)). In other words, the eventuality denoted by *be sick* but not the one denoted by *read "The Book of Sand" five times* is such that it satisfies the requirements of the universal quantifier provided by durative *since* (as in the logical form in (18c)). The E-perfect is derived by replacing the universal quantifier with an existential quantifier, as in (18e) and (19c). We will show later that there are languages and environments that have all the elements of the perfect but not the right type of eventuality to plug into (18c).

(18) a. Since 1990 I have been sick.

   b. *U-reading*

   There is[26] a time span (the perfect time span) whose LB is in 1990 and whose RB is the utterance time, and throughout[27] that time span I was sick.

   or

   There is a time span (the perfect time span) whose LB is in 1990 and whose RB is the utterance time, and all the points of that time span are points of my being sick.

or

There is a time span (the perfect time span) whose LB is in 1990 and whose RB is the utterance time, and that entire time span is filled with one eventuality of my being sick.

c. $\exists i \ (LB = 1990 \ \& \ RB = Now \ \& \ \forall t \in i \ (Eventuality \ (t)))$

d. *E-reading*

There is a time span (the perfect time span) whose LB is in 1990 and whose RB is the utterance time, and in that time span is an eventuality of my being sick.

e. $\exists i \ (LB = 1990 \ \& \ RB = Now \ \& \ \exists t \in i \ (Eventuality \ (t)))$

(19) a. Since 1990, I have read "The Book of Sand" five times.

b. There is a time span (the perfect time span) whose LB is in 1990 and whose RB is the utterance time, and in that time span is an eventuality of my reading "The Book of Sand" five times.[28]

c. $\exists i \ (LB = 1990 \ \& \ RB = Now \ \& \ \exists t \in i \ (Eventuality \ (t)))$

For-adverbials (following Vlach 1993)   *For*-adverbials can be perfect-level or eventuality-level. We conclude the latter since a *for*-adverbial does not require the perfect (*I was sick for five* days). *For*-adverbials are only durational (Dowty 1979).[29] When a *for*-adverbial is perfect-level, LB is calculated backward from RB. Being durational, *for*-adverbials, when they are perfect-level, can only yield the U-perfect.

(20) a. I have been sick for five days.

b. For five days, I have been sick.

c. There is a time span (the perfect time span) whose LB is five days before RB and whose RB is the utterance time, and throughout that time span I was sick.

When the *for*-adverbial is eventuality-level and it is in a perfect sentence (i.e., when we are dealing with the perfect version of the sentence *I was sick for five days*), it co-occurs with a (covert or overt) perfect-level adverbial.

(21) a. Since 1970, I have been sick for five days.

b. There is a time span (the perfect time span) whose LB is in 1970 and whose RB is the utterance time, and in that time span is an eventuality of my being sick for five days.[30]

When a perfect sentence contains no overt perfect-level adverbial, what is missing is only the LB of the perfect time span, since RB is set by tense.

In such a case, LB can be set contextually or by other interpretive elements; for example, the scene set by present tense would be the existence of the subject.[31] Consider a sentence like (22a). If the *for*-adverbial is perfect-level, the U-perfect results as in (22b) in the way already described. But when the *for*-adverbial is eventuality-level, there is no overt perfect-level adverbial. RB of the covert perfect-level adverbial is set by tense. In the absence of any information (contextual or otherwise) about LB, present tense also affects LB, since present tense is relevant over the entire existence of the individual.[32] So when the *for*-adverbial is eventuality-level, the interpretation of (22a) is an E-perfect along the lines of (22c).

(22) a. I have lived in Thessaloniki for 10 years.
   b. There is a time span (the perfect time span) whose LB is 10 years ago and whose RB is the utterance time, and throughout that time span I lived in Thessaloniki.
   c. There is a time span (the perfect time span) whose LB is when I was born and whose RB is the utterance time, and in that time span there is an eventuality of my living in Thessaloniki for 10 years.

Recall that sentence-final *for*-adverbials yield sentences that are ambiguous between the U-perfect and the E-perfect while sentence-initial *for*-adverbials yield only the U-perfect reading (e.g., Dowty 1979; Mittwoch 1988).

(23) a. John has been in Boston for two weeks. (*Ambiguous: E- and U-perfect*)
   b. For two weeks, John has been in Boston. (*Unambiguous: U-perfect only*)

From the above contrast, the general conclusion is often drawn that sentence-initial adverbials yield U-perfects and sentence-final adverbials yield U-perfects and E-perfects. This is wrong, however. Sentence-initial adverbials can also yield E-perfects.

(24) Since 1990, I have read "The Book of Sand" five times. (*E-perfect*)

The difference in what readings they permit when sentence-initial is a function of how the adverbials in question yield the U/E-perfects. *Since*-adverbials are always perfect-level, while *for*-adverbials can be either perfect-level or eventuality-level. The readings that a *for*-adverbial (which is always durative) permits are a direct result of whether it is perfect-level (yielding U-perfect only) or eventuality-level (yielding E-perfect only). On the other hand, the readings that a *since*-adverbial permits are a function of whether the durative or the inclusive persona of the adverbial has been chosen.

For a *since*-adverbial, position in the syntactic tree is irrelevant; it combines with other elements of the sentence to yield a U-perfect or an E-perfect in the manner described above.

For a *for*-adverbial, on the other hand, position in the syntactic tree does matter. The fact that a sentence-final *for*-adverbial can yield an E-perfect or a U-perfect means that a sentence-final *for*-adverbial can be either eventuality-level or perfect-level. The fact that a sentence-initial *for*-adverbial yields only the U-perfect in turn means that a sentence-initial *for*-adverbial can only be perfect-level.

Why should sentence-initial position determine that *for*-adverbials are necessarily perfect-level? The answer is that perfect-level adverbials attach higher than eventuality-level adverbials, as we suggested at the beginning of this section.

A distinctive property of adverbial modification is that it is highly local. An adverbial cannot modify parts of a clause that are more deeply embedded than itself. The domain of an adverbial's modification is determined by its surface position—that is, the position of Merge.[33] Now *for*-adverbials that appear in sentence-final position may have been merged lower down (in the VP domain, or, as we will argue, in the domain including grammatical aspect), in which case they are eventuality-level, or they may have been merged later, higher in the structure, where the perfect resides (perfect-level). But a *for*-adverbial that appears on the left has necessarily been merged late, outside the VP domain. Thus, this adverbial cannot be eventuality-level; it can only be perfect-level. Alternatively, if it is assumed that temporal adverbials in sentence-initial position are topicalized (see note 35), the lack of ambiguity with *for*-adverbials follows from Shortest Move. If it is assumed, as we argue here, that in a perfect sentence, there are always two levels of (overt or covert) adverbials, eventuality-level and perfect-level, then an eventuality-level adverbial will not be able to skip an (overt or covert) perfect-level adverbial.[34] A similar though not identical argument is presented in Thompson 1995.[35] We leave this issue since it has little effect on our main proposals.

Always   *Always* can also be either perfect-level or eventuality-level,[36] and different meanings arise in the two cases. Individual-level predicates can take *always* only in the perfect.

(25) a.   Emma has always been tall.
    b.   *Emma is/was always tall.

From (25b), we conclude that *always* cannot be an eventuality-level adverbial with individual-level predicates and that when individual-level predicates appear with *always* in perfect sentences, *always* is a perfect-level adverbial. More evidence for this comes from the fact that *always* cannot co-occur with other perfect-level adverbials when an individual-level predicate appears.

(26) *Since 1990, I have always been tall.

On the other hand, with eventives or stage-level statives, *always* can occur in nonperfect sentences (27a) and it can co-occur with perfect adverbials (27b–c), showing that with such predicates, it can be eventuality-level.

(27) a.   I always give/gave him a dime when he asks/asked me for
        money.
    b.   Since 1990, I have always given him a dime when he (has) asked
        me for money.
    c.   Since 1990, I have always been sick when he (has) visited me.

In summary, *always* can be eventuality-level with stage-level predicates but not with individual-level predicates. It can be perfect-level with individual-level predicates and with stage-level predicates.

What does perfect-level *always* mean? It means 'throughout the perfect time span'; that is, there is universal quantification over the points of the perfect time span, therefore including the boundaries—the meaning, in other words, of a U-perfect. Since there is no space for another perfect-level adverbial, there is no further indication about LB (RB being the utterance time in the present perfect). And as before, in the absence of any overt information, either LB is contextually determined or the meaning of tense kicks in; for example, in the present perfect, the perfect time span starts with the beginning of the existence of the subject.

Covert perfect-level adverbial   What is the nature of the covert perfect-level adverbial? Since the presence of the covert perfect-level adverbial precludes a U-perfect, we must conclude that the covert adverbial is not durative but inclusive. Though we have no more to say about this here, this conclusion may not be surprising, given that existential quantification is the nature of default closure and that universal quantification requires lexical specification.

6.3.3   Point 3: The E__R Interval Does Not Have a Distinguished Status in the Perfect

It is very important not to confuse the perfect time span with the E__R interval, which is a common representation of the perfect in Reichenbachian frameworks (e.g., Hornstein 1990). RB may be reminiscent of Reichenbach's R, but LB of the perfect time span is not E; LB is set by the adverbial. Consider the following sentence:

(28) Since 1991, I have been to Cape Cod only once, namely, in the fall of 1993.

(29) 1991 . . . . ._____. . . . . NOW
              (fall 1993)

In (28), E is temporally located in the fall of 1993, which means that the E__R span starts with the fall of 1993 and continues until the utterance time. On the other hand, the perfect time span starts in 1991.

Neither should the perfect time span be confused with the interval in which the state resulting from the underlying eventuality holds, for example, the "poststate" or the "result state," both of which are also common descriptions of the perfect. In (28), for example, the poststate holds from (after) the fall of 1993 and stretches indefinitely into the future.[37] On the other hand, the perfect time span starts earlier (1991) and ends earlier (utterance time).

6.3.4   Point 4: (Im)perfective Morphology and the U-Perfect

As mentioned earlier, because the U-perfect is restricted crosslinguistically, it has been claimed to be a language-specific, unpredictable quirk, not a central use of the perfect. Indeed, standard means that yield the U-perfect in English, such as modification by *always* or *since*-adverbials, result in ungrammaticality in, for example, Greek.

(30) *Εχο   panta zisi stin   Athina.
      have-1SG always lived in-the Athens
      'I have always lived in Athens.'

We propose that the availability of the U-perfect is fully predictable from the morphological composition of the perfect participle. Specifically, we argue that grammatical aspect—imperfective or perfective specification of the participle—determines whether or not the U-perfect is possible.

Before we explicate this further, let us briefly consider the meaning contribution of the (im)perfective outside the perfect. *Perfective aspect* conveys the meaning that the eventuality in question is completed, which for telics means achievement of the goal, and for atelics, termination. The effect of the perfective is illustrated in (31), which asserts that the eventuality of building a house is completed; that is, the goal has been achieved and the house has been built. Typically, the perfective on telics can be accompanied by *in*-adverbials but not *for*-adverbials (see note 29).

(31) Eχtisa   ena spiti (mesa se ena χrono/*γ_1a ena χrono).
     build-PAST.PERF-1SG a house (in one year/*for one year)
     'I built a house (in a year/*for a year).'

We will call the feature that appears as perfective morphology *[bounded]*.

On the other hand, *imperfective aspect* presents a situation as ongoing,[38] without including the endpoints. When the imperfective appears on telics, the achievement of the goal is not included in the assertion. Typically, the imperfective (on both telics and atelics) can be accompanied by *for*-adverbials but not by *in*-adverbials.

(32) Eχtiza   to spiti   (*mesa se ena χrono/γ_1a ena χrono).
     build-PAST.IMPERF-1SG the house (*in one year/for one year)
     'I was building the house (*in a year/for a year).'

We will call the feature that appears as imperfective morphology *[unbounded]*.

Let us return now to the perfect and to the role of the (im)perfective in the availability of the U-perfect reading. In order for an eventuality to hold throughout an interval, it must be homogeneous; that is, the subinterval property must hold of it (recall (18a–c)). Perfective morphology on the predicate describing the eventuality blocks the subinterval property. It presents the eventuality as bounded, and bounded eventualities are not homogeneous since any interval including the completion/termination differs in nature from the preceding intervals. We will demonstrate the relevance of perfective and imperfective aspect for the readings of the perfect by looking at Greek, Bulgarian, and English.

6.3.4.1 Greek In Greek, the perfect participle is based only on the perfective stem, even though Greek verbs show a perfective/imperfective distinction outside the perfect.[39] On telics, the perfective, and therefore the perfect participle, asserts the achievement of the goal. As a result, the U-perfect, which requires the subinterval property, is not possible. We will return later to activities. On statives, it happens that in Greek, as in many other languages, the perfective yields an inchoative reading (though we do not know why).

(33) O $\gamma_1$annis aγapise   tin Maria to 1981.
the Jannis love-PAST.PERF-3SG the Maria in 1981
'Jannis started loving/fell in love with Maria in 1981.'

This sentence does not mean that there was an eventuality of loving that lasted for some interval in 1981 or throughout 1981, the way the English *John loved Mary in 1981* could be interpreted. Instead, it means that Jannis fell in love with Maria in 1981. An inchoative is a change-of-state (i.e., telic) eventuality. Therefore, the perfect of a stative Greek verb will lack the U-perfect reading. It is possible to form the present perfect of a stative, but the resulting sentence has only an E-reading.

(34) O $\gamma_1$annis eχ_1i aγapisi   tin Maria.
the Jannis has-3SG loved the Maria
'Jannis has started loving/fallen in love with Maria.'

6.3.4.2 Bulgarian   In Bulgarian, the perfective has a similar effect. With telics, it asserts achievement of the goal and therefore the U-perfect is precluded. And as in Greek, the perfective on statives turns them into inchoatives. For example, 'love' in the perfective means 'come to love', and the perfect based on the perfective participle lacks the U-perfect reading. The perfect formed from this participle is grammatical, but only with an E-perfect reading, as the gloss in (35) indicates.

(35) Marija (*vinagi) e obiknala   Ivan (*ot   1980 nasam).
Maria (*always) is love-PERF.PART Ivan (*from 1980 till-now)
'Maria has fallen in love with Ivan.'

However, unlike Greek, Bulgarian also has a perfect participle that is based on the imperfective stem. The imperfective does not present the eventuality as completed; in other words, it does not describe it with a distinct final subinterval. Therefore, the predicate can satisfy the sub-interval requirements of a durative adverbial and this perfect can have the U-perfect reading.

(36) Marija vinagi e običala   Ivan.
Maria always is love-IMPERF.PART Ivan
'Maria has always loved Ivan.'

Since the imperfective participle of any Aktionsart presents that eventuality as homogeneous (i.e., without a distinguished final subinterval of termination or completion), the imperfective will permit a U-perfect reading.

In addition to having perfect participles based on the perfective and on the imperfective, Bulgarian has a participle based on another aspect, which we will call *neutral*.[40] This term has been used by Smith (1991)—though not for Bulgarian—to mean that only LB (i.e., the beginning point) and some of the internal process of the eventuality is talked about. Crucially, according to Smith, the neutral differs from the perfective in that it allows reference to the internal temporal structure of the eventuality, and in that no RB is asserted.[41]

The relevance of the neutral to our discussion is that there is a perfect participle based on it and that this participle can yield a perfect with the U-perfect reading. What is crucial in the present context, then, is to show that the neutral is unbounded (i.e., it does not assert the achievement of the goal when it takes telic predicates), so that its behavior is predicted to differ from that of the perfective in Bulgarian and in Greek.

The desired distinction clearly exists. The perfective asserts the achievement of the goal, but the neutral is silent about it, just as the imperfective is.

(37) a. Maria izpi   vinoto   (#no ne znam   dali   go
       Maria drink-PERF.PAST the-wine   but not know-1sG whether it
       izpi   cjaloto).
       drink-PERF.PAST all
       'Maria drank up the wine (#but I don't know whether she finished it).'

    b. Maria pi/pieše   vinoto   (no ne znam   dali
       Maria drink-NEUT/IMPERF the-wine but not know-1sG whether
       go izpi   cjaloto).
       it drink-PERF.PAST all
       'Maria was drinking the wine (but I don't know whether she finished it).'

Sentence (37a), with the perfective, asserts that the wine was finished. Sentence (37b), with the neutral, says nothing about whether the wine was finished but simply asserts that an activity of wine drinking took place, and in this respect, it is similar to the expansion with the imperfective.

Thus, we can conclude that the neutral asserts unboundedness (i.e., lack of RB), or at least, it does not assert boundedness. This is retained in the perfect that uses the participle based on the neutral, as one would expect.

Compare the perfect based on the perfective participle with the perfect based on the neutral participle.

(38) a. Tja e izpila   vinoto   (#no ne znam
       she is drink-PERF.PART the-wine   but not know-1SG
       dali   go e izpila   cjaloto).
       whether it is drunk-PERF all
       'She has drunk the wine (#but I don't know whether she
       finished it).'

   b. Tja e pila   vinoto (no ne znam   dali   go
       she is drink-NEUT.PART the-wine but not know-1SG whether it
       e izpila   cjaloto).
       is drunk-PERF all
       'She has been drinking the wine (but I don't know whether she
       finished it).'

Given the facts in (38), we expect the perfect formed from the neutral participle to have a U-reading. This is indeed the case, as (39) illustrates.

(39) Az šum pila   vinoto   ot   sutrinta   nasam.
     I   am drink-NEUT.PART the-wine from the-morning till-now
     'I have been drinking the wine since this morning.'

A final point concerning the neutral and the U-perfect is that although, in principle, the imperfective participle can be formed for all verb classes, only verbs denoting accomplishments and activities have a neutral participle.[42]

6.3.4.3 English   Now let us examine the English perfect. Given that the perfect asserts the achievement of the goal of a telic predicate, it seems that the syntacticosemantic features below the perfect contribute boundedness.

(40) He has read the book #but he didn't finish it.

With activities, there is no achievement of goal that can be tested for, but let us assume on the basis of the above that boundedness is contributed. If the perfect indeed incorporates boundedness, then it follows that the U-perfect will not be possible with the perfect of telics and activities.

(41) a. *He has danced ever since this morning.[43]
   b. *He has drawn a circle ever since this morning.

However, if we follow the above reasoning and conclude that the morphology of the English perfect participle incorporates boundedness, we have created a problem. We would expect that boundedness would also be contributed to the perfect of statives. Consequently, we would expect the U-perfect to not be possible there either. In other words, we would expect the English perfect to behave like the Greek or Bulgarian perfect with the perfective participle. But the U-perfect *is* possible with English statives, as shown in section 6.1. In light of this, we must refine our earlier remarks. What we need to be able to derive is that the perfect of telics and activities is interpreted as incorporating boundedness, whereas the perfect of statives is not.

There is a way to achieve this goal. Telics and activities (i.e., nonstatives) can carry either progressive or nonprogressive morphology, the choice between the two corresponding to unbounded versus bounded interpretation. We take this to mean that when a nonstative has the feature [unbounded], the morphological component will make it appear in the progressive; when a nonstative has the feature [bounded], it will appear as nonprogressive. Statives, on the other hand, appear only as nonprogressive.[44] This is not because they can only have the feature [unbounded], however. Statives can be either [bounded] or [unbounded], but independent properties preclude the expression of [unbounded] with the progressive morphology.[45] But, of course, regardless of the overt signal, the specification of [bounded]/[unbounded] is visible to the semantics. In summary:

(42) a. nonstative, [unbounded] $\rightarrow$ progressive
    b. nonstative, [bounded] ⎫
    c. stative, [unbounded]   ⎬ $\rightarrow$ nonprogressive
    d. stative, [bounded]   ⎭

It now follows that when the underlying eventuality is nonstative, only the perfect of the progressive will permit the U-perfect, because the perfect of the nonprogressive incorporates boundedness. With statives, the U-perfect will always appear to be possible, because a stative can always be interpreted as unbounded, the bounded/unbounded aspectual distinction never being expressed overtly with English statives.[46]

6.3.4.4 Aspectual Morphology and the Interpretations of the Perfect
Let us recapitulate. On the basis of data from Greek, Bulgarian, and English, we propose that (un)boundedness is contributed by syntactico-semantic features of the verb that are retained when the verb becomes

a participle. The perfect itself does not contribute (un)boundedness. In other words, when a perfect sentence conveys the meaning of completion, this meaning comes from features asserting boundedness that are embedded below the perfect and not from the perfect itself. The perfect merely sets up a time span, in which an (un)bounded eventuality occurs. In other words, the meaning of the perfect is roughly as in (43), with the possible expansions in (44a–d).

(43) There is an interval (the perfect time span) in/throughout which there is a bounded/unbounded eventuality.

(44) a. ... throughout ... unbounded   →   universal perfect
     b. ... in ... unbounded ...   →   experiential perfect
     c. ... in ... bounded ...   →   experiential perfect
     d. ... throughout ... bounded   →   depends on Aktionsart

Let us start with expansion (44a). The U-perfect is obtained when a predicate holds throughout the perfect time span. Given the durative interpretation of the interval and the unbounded eventuality in (44a), the U-perfect is possible here. The cases we have illustrated are statives and progressives in English and the perfect based on the imperfective and neutral participles in Bulgarian.

Next, consider expansion (44b). Since *inclusive* means 'properly included', the boundaries of the perfect time span will not by assertion be part of the eventuality; therefore, the U-perfect is not possible. The cases we have illustrated are all the cases mentioned in the previous paragraph but on the experiential reading.

Similarly in expansion (44c): the proper inclusion requirement precludes the U-perfect reading.

Finally, consider expansion (44d). If the predicate is telic, boundedness asserts achievement of the goal. Therefore, the subinterval requirement of *throughout* cannot be satisfied. But what if the predicate is an activity? Can we "fill up" the perfect time span with an activity that happens to terminate exactly at RB, so that the requirements of both *throughout* and boundedness are satisfied?

One Greek adverbial that can bring this situation about (possibly the only one, in fact) is *apo ... meχri* 'from ... to'.[47] We can obtain truth-conditions similar to those of a U-perfect by making 'now' the second argument of the adverbial. This permits us to include the utterance time in the eventuality (as long, of course, as the underlying eventuality is not a telic or stative, the latter because it would turn into a telic owing to the perfective component of the perfect participle).

(45) $E\chi_1 i$ kivernisi apo to 1990 meχri tora.
     has-3SG governed from the 1990 until now
     'She/He has governed from 1990 to now.'

6.3.5   Point 5: Anteriority Is Not Part of the Meaning of the Perfect (Participle)

We have argued that the notions of completion and boundedness, which are often associated with the perfect, are not part of the meaning of the perfect at all, but a reflex of the aspectual morphology ((un)boundedness) that is embedded below the perfect.

At the outset, we mentioned that the present perfect is said to express anteriority or some type of pastness. How does the anteriority/pastness of the present perfect come about? First of all, in the U-perfect reading of the present perfect, the underlying predicate holds at the utterance time as well. This means that the anteriority/pastness is related to the experiential reading (recall Brugger's independent argument for this based on sequence of tenses), in other words, to the inclusive interpretation of the perfect time span. And now it should be obvious how (and why) the anteriority comes about: since in the present perfect, RB of the perfect time span is the utterance time and since the underlying eventuality happens in the perfect time span, it follows that the eventuality will occur before RB/utterance time. Similarly in the pluperfect, since RB is before the utterance time and the eventuality happens before RB (since it happens *in* the perfect time span), the eventuality will happen before the utterance time. Finally, in the future perfect, RB is in the future with respect to the utterance time. Since the eventuality happens in the perfect time span (i.e., before RB), it can happen before or after the utterance time, which is exactly the under-specified meaning of the future perfect. In other words, we can derive the fact that the present perfect can express anteriority and that the U-Perfect cannot. This is possible owing to the meaning of the perfect together with the fact that when tense combines with the perfect, it situates RB with respect to the utterance time.

To summarize and highlight: There is no component of the perfect that directly expresses anteriority; that is, one should not look at the mor-phology of (e.g.) the participle and postulate a morpheme or an operator whose meaning is anteriority. Postulating such a morpheme or operator is unnecessary since anteriority can be derived as just described—but it would also be wrong, as then the U-perfect would be impossible to derive, given that it asserts that at the utterance time, the eventuality still holds.

6.4   Stativity versus Unboundedness

We said earlier that morphology that marks unboundedness on the underlying eventuality is a necessary condition for the formation of a U-perfect. An eventuality is described as unbounded when it is not asserted to have reached an endpoint (achievement of the goal, for telics; termination, for atelics). How does our position relate to the claim that for English, a stative or a progressive is required in order to yield a U-perfect (e.g., Dowty 1979; Mittwoch 1988; Vlach 1993)?

Stativity has been defined in different ways. According to Smith (1991, 67) (along with many others who follow Vendler's (1957) original description), "[Dynamism and agency], which are closely related, distinguish non-statives from statives." Crucially, for Smith, the progressive and statives differ because the progressive, unlike statives, is dynamic and agentive. In Smith's system, we can classify a predicate for situation aspect in the absence of any inflectional morphology; that is, we can classify what Smith calls the verb constellation, the verb plus its arguments. Grammatical aspect ((im)perfective) is on a different tier, so to speak, not affecting situation aspect (to which stativity belongs).

Vlach (1981) defines stativity as follows:

(46) A sentence F is stative if and only if the truth of (Past F) *when I arrived* requires that F was true for some period leading up to the time of my arrival.

It is clear that unlike Smith's definition of stativity, Vlach's definition is applicable only after inflectional morphology has applied since the test requires interpretation in a particular sentential context. For Vlach, then, stativity is characterized by a combination of situation aspect and grammatical aspect.

The rationale behind Vlach's proposal is basically that predicates that are readily agreed to be statives behave a certain way in his schema, and everything that behaves the same way must also be a stative. Take for example the predicate *be asleep*, which is [−dynamic], and so on, a stative by anyone's definition.

(47) John was asleep when I arrived.

Vlach, like many others who investigate English, assumes that *was asleep* in (47) is a state, pure and simple. However, *was asleep* in (47) is not just an uninflected stative predicate. Basically, *was asleep* in (47) has the feature [unbounded], as shown by the obligatory use of the imperfective in languages with richer morphology than English. So one could say that Vlach's test actually checks for stative + [unbounded] or just plain [unbounded]. Indeed, the latter is the case, as we can show by adding the feature [unbounded] contributed by imperfective/progressive morphology on a predicate that is clearly not stative (i.e., [−dynamic], etc.) in Vendler's or Smith's sense.

(48) John was lifting weights/building a rocket/throwing bricks/...
      when I arrived.

The predicates in (48) all pass Vlach's test for stativity, and indeed Vlach argues that the progressive is stative (unlike Smith, who explicitly argues that progressives and statives are different). However, if we draw the conclusion with Vlach that *lifting weights/building a rocket/throwing bricks/...* are statives, we have clearly left behind the idea that statives are [−dynamic], [−agentive], and so on.

Clearly, the predicates that pass Vlach's test are not the same as Vendler's [−dynamic] states or predicates that Smith's system would classify as statives.[48]

In effect, Vlach described the effects of imperfective marking. One can call it "stativity," but this can be misleading, as this term is also used to refer in the Vendlerian sense to [−dynamic] predicates. We are using the term *statives* in the Vendlerian way and the term *unbounded* for bigger parts of the syntactic tree that satisfy Vlach's diagnostic. As noted earlier, this terminology is used because on some tests, English statives behave like progressives/imperfectives and because on English statives, the imperfective is not visible.[49]

One final but important point. One might say that regardless of the terminology issue, Vlach's test does correctly isolate the crucial property that is required for the U-perfect. That is, one might be tempted to argue that the predicates that pass the test are the ones that yield the U-perfect. But this is not so. As noted earlier, the Bulgarian neutral yields the U-perfect. Moreover, consistent with the crosslinguistic picture, the neutral marks unboundedness; that is, it does not describe an eventuality as terminated/completed. However, the neutral, unlike the imperfective, does not pass Vlach's test.

(49) a. *Ivan pisa   pismoto kogato Maria vleze   v
     Ivan write-NEUT.PAST the-letter when   Maria entered in
     stajata.
     the-room
     'Ivan was writing the letter when Maria entered the room.'
   b. Ivan pišeše   pismoto kogato Maria vleze   v
     Ivan write-IMPERF.PAST the-letter when   Maria entered in
     stajata.
     the-room
     'Ivan was writing the letter when Maria entered the room.'

In other words, we have not been using the term *stative* because on the
one hand, the term is used in different ways, and on the other hand, certain tests for stativity (e.g., Vlach's) do not yield the appropriate class for
the U-perfect.

Most researchers take Dowty's test (the subinterval property) and
Vlach's test to yield the same class of predicates. As indicated, though,
predicates marked with the Bulgarian neutral satisfy the subinterval property but do not pass Vlach's test.

6.5   Conclusion

We have argued for a version of the Extended-Now Theory as well as for
the role of adverbials in the interpretation of the perfect and the universal/
existential ambiguity. We have also demonstrated that the crosslinguistic
availability of the universal perfect can be explained on principled grounds
once the morphosyntactic composition of the perfect participle is taken
into account. In turn, the fact that the availability of the universal perfect
is dictated by morphosyntactic factors shows that the universal/existential
distinction is not a pragmatic distinction (the universal being a subcase of
the existential) but one generated by different (morpho)semantic compo-
sitions. In the addendum, we discuss certain syntactic issues that arise in
conjunction with the semantic issues examined so far.

Addendum

A.1   Functional Heads and Their Order
We are now in a position to draw preliminary conclusions about the order
of the syntactic heads in a perfect sentence. In Greek and Bulgarian, the

participle is specified for (im)perfective, which we take to mean that the functional head that corresponds to the perfect (i.e., the node that contains features of the perfect itself) is above the (im)perfective head, which we will refer to as *Asp(ect)*. Also, in English, the perfect is above the progressive and not the reverse, as the relative order of auxiliaries shows (i.e., *He has been singing*, not **He is having sung*). In addition, the T(ense) node is clearly above Perf. As for passive/active specification, we assume that if Voice is projected as a separate node, it is below Perf. In perfect passive constructions, the perfect is above the passive in all the languages we have examined (e.g., in English, *He has been arrested*, not **He was had arrested*). This result is not surprising given that the passive is related to the argument structure of the eventuality whereas the perfect relates the eventuality as a whole to the temporal domain. When the progressive and the passive co-occur, their relative order is Asp > Voice (*The house was being built*). By putting the pieces together (leaving aside for the time being the issue of the auxiliary), we arrive at the tree in (50), fully instantiated by the sentence in (51) from Chomsky 1957.

(50)

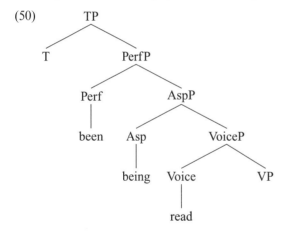

(51) These books have been being read all year.

As discussed in section 6.3.2, there are at least two levels of adverbials in a perfect sentence, and their syntactic ordering correlates with semantic scope. Depending on whether temporal adverbials are eventuality-level or perfect-level, they attach to AspP/VP or PerfP, respectively. Hence, the order of morphemes or auxiliaries correlates with the order of adverbials, as expected given our assumptions (see also Alexiadou 1997 and Cinque 1999 for a broader claim along these lines).

A.2   Where Does the Meaning of the Perfect Reside?

A natural question is how the meaning of the perfect is distributed over the auxiliary and the participle in languages with a periphrastic perfect.[50] This question can be investigated by separating the participle from the auxiliary and examining what aspects of the meaning survive.

Reduced relatives represent one environment where a participle can occur without an auxiliary. In Bulgarian, it is possible to form a reduced relative with perfects of all verb classes.

(52) Zapoznah se   sûs ženata   napisala   knigata.
     met-1SG   REFL with the-woman written-ACT.PART-FEM-SG the-book
     Literally: I met the woman written the book.
     (= 'I met the woman who has written the book.')

In Bulgarian, the meaning components discussed earlier—namely, the role of the (im)perfective in the U/E-perfects—remain with the participle. This is shown in (53)–(54).

(53) a. ženata   pročela   knigata
        the-woman read-PERF.PART the-book
        'the woman who has read the book'
     b. ženata   čela   knigata
        the-woman read-NEUT.PART the-book
        'the woman who has read the book'

(54) a. *ženata   pročela   knigata ot   sutrinta   nasam
        the-woman read-PERF.PART the-book from the-morning till-now
        'the woman who has read the book since this morning'
     b. ženata   čela   knigata ot   sutrinta   nasam
        the-woman read-NEUT.PART the-book from the-morning till-now
        'the woman who has read the book since this morning'
     c. ženata   običala   Ivan ot   1980 nasam
        the-woman love-IMPERF.PART Ivan from 1980 till-now
        'the woman who has loved Ivan since 1980'
     d. ženata   celuvala   Ivan ot   sutrinta   nasam
        the-woman kiss-IMPERF.PART Ivan from the-morning till-now
        'the woman who has been kissing Ivan since this morning'

The reduced-relative perfect in (53a) employs a perfective participle and as a result asserts the achievement of the goal (i.e., asserts that the book is finished). This is not the reading contributed by the neutral participle in (53b); here, it is only asserted that the woman has engaged in book-reading at some point. Just as in the case of the present perfects discussed earlier, the perfective participle precludes the U-reading (54a). The perfect in reduced relatives can have a U-reading only when the participle is neutral (54b) or imperfective (54c–d). We conclude that in Bulgarian, there is no semantics exclusively related to the perfect that is contributed by the auxiliary, at least not from the aspects of meaning associated with the perfect that we have investigated in this chapter.

Duplicating the above test in English, however, proves impossible; reduced relatives containing a perfect are not allowed.

(55) a. I saw the boy *(who has) eaten the fish.
     b. I saw the boy *(who has) left on time.
     c. I saw the boy *(who has) walked through the park.

On the other hand, reduced relatives containing other participles are possible.

(56) a. The boy (who is) singing the "Marseillaise" is my brother.
     b. I saw a house (which was) built in 1925.

The property that correlates with the ability to form a reduced relative containing a perfect is the type of auxiliary. A reduced relative can contain a perfect, if the missing auxiliary is 'be'. (This is the essence behind "whiz-deletion" accounts; also see Pesetsky 1995, 295–296 n. 19.) A reduced relative cannot contain a perfect if the missing auxiliary is 'have'. We have found this to hold throughout the European Indo-European languages. As just noted, reduced relatives with a perfect are impossible in English, where the auxiliary is *have*. In Bulgarian, on the other hand, the auxiliary is always 'be' (Bulgarian does not have a null copula, unlike other Slavic languages) and therefore reduced relatives with a perfect are always possible.

As one might expect at this point, in auxiliary selection languages (e.g., Italian), reduced relatives containing perfect participles are possible with verbs whose participles in the perfect combine with 'be' (supposedly unaccusatives) but impossible with verbs whose participles combine with 'have' (supposedly transitives and unergatives; Burzio 1981, 1986).

(57) a. Il treno [arrivato entro le 3] è ripartito subito.
         the train [arrived by 3]   left again immediately
         'The train which had arrived by 3 left again immediately.'
     b. *Un ragazzo [ballato nella stanza] sembrava conosciuto.
         a boy   [danced in the room] looked familiar

    c. *Una donna [mangiata/o un panino] fu avvelenata.
       a woman   [eaten a sandwich]   was poisoned

And as in Bulgarian, we can construct a U-perfect for a reduced relative that contains a perfect.

(58) Le attrici   [piaciute   a mia madre fin dal 1970] ...
     the actresses [pleased-FEM.PL to my mother since 1970]
     'The actresses that have appealed to my mother since 1970 ...'

On the basis of these facts, we conclude that in the cases where the participle can be separated from the auxiliary (all of Bulgarian, perfects of unaccusatives in auxiliary selection languages), the participles alone incorporate sufficient content to generate sentences with the range of perfect-related meanings discussed here. But the participle cannot be separated from the auxiliary in 'have'-perfects. Why should this be so? Is it the semantics or the syntax that blocks the separation of 'have' from the perfect participle?

The impossibility of separating perfect participles from *have* reduces to the question of the difference between 'have' and 'be' and/or to the question of the difference between the participles in 'have'-perfects and 'be'-perfects. It might be argued that separation is impossible because in 'have'-perfects, the features of the perfect partly reside on 'have'; on this view, the participle by itself is simply not sufficient to "bring about" the perfect. We cannot give an exhaustive answer to this question here; we will only discuss the issue in the context of some existing theories of the 'have'/'be' relation and auxiliary selection.

Consider first Burzio's (1981, 1986) analysis of 'have' and 'be' in Italian. Burzio proposes the following rule for assigning *essere* 'be'.

(59) Essere-*assignment*
    a. The auxiliary is realized as *essere* whenever a "binding relation" exists between the subject and a "nominal contiguous to the verb."
    b. A "nominal contiguous to the verb" is a nominal that is either part of the verb morphology (i.e., a clitic) or a direct object.

Rule (59) allows two subcases of *essere*-assignment.

(60) Essere-*assignment*
    a. NPcl-V   (the subject binds a clitic)
    b. NP V NP   (a binding relation between the subject and the direct object)

This captures the main environments where auxiliary 'be' is found in Italian, namely, contexts of *si*-cliticization (60a) and contexts of NP-movement (i.e., passives and unaccusatives, (60b)).

Implicit in Burzio's analysis is that 'have' is the canonical realization of an auxiliary. The special case is 'be', which requires a construction-specific rule. The environments in which the special rule applies are defined on purely formal syntactic grounds. Meaning does not play a role. In such an analysis, there is no reason to expect that 'have' will have more perfect-related semantic content than 'be'.

Another type of approach to the 'have'/'be' relationship takes 'have' to be closer to a main verb than 'be' is, in that 'have' has a basically transitive syntax. Hoekstra (1984), Roberts (1986), and Cowper (1989a,b), among others, propose that 'have' has an external θ-role and a Case feature to assign. In languages in which the passive and the perfect participle coincide morphologically (Romance, Germanic), participles always have the syntax of a passive. In the perfect of transitive verbs, 'have' combines with the (passive) participle and, by doing so, it "restores" the transitivity of the predicate. In other words, approaches like this one are tailor-made for languages where the perfect and passive participles are identical in form (except for agreement). This makes such approaches unworkable in the present context because in the languages discussed here, such homophony/syncretism does not occur. In Greek, for instance, the passive is synthetic; and in Bulgarian, the perfect and passive participles differ.

Still other accounts of the 'have'/'be' relationship take 'be' to be the canonical realization of an auxiliary and 'have' to be the special case—that is, exactly the reverse of what Burzio (1981, 1986) proposes. Here we will discuss one influential proposal of this type: the idea that 'have' is the lexicalization of 'be' + head X—that is, 'be' plus an incorporated head (Freeze 1992—though only for possessive 'have'/'be'; Kayne 1993).[51] But within such assumptions as well, it seems that auxiliary 'have' differs from 'be' only syntactically. More specifically, in Kayne's work, the variation between 'have' and 'be' is argued to be sensitive to morphosyntactic factors like first and second person versus third person, verb class, and so on. It is clear that for Kayne the 'have'/'be' variation does not result in or depend on a difference in the semantics of the auxiliaries or the participles.

So from these approaches to the 'have'/'be' relationship, nothing follows that would dictate a semantic difference between 'have' and 'be' or the corresponding participles. This provides a potential answer to the original question of how the semantics of the perfect are distributed over auxiliaries and participles. However, it does not answer the question we encountered along the way, namely, why is a reduced relative with a perfect participle impossible when the missing relative would have been 'have'? We will conclude the chapter with a possible answer. We do not want to commit ourselves to any particular theory of auxiliary selection. The main idea can be expressed with different background assumptions. We will cast our suggestion in the framework according to which 'have' is 'be' with an incorporated head, but we do so for illustrative purposes only. Because the letter of Kayne's (1993) proposal cannot be transferred to the present discussion,[52] we will switch to an adaptation of Kayne's analysis due to Peter Svenonius (personal communication).

Svenonius's adaptation capitalizes on the fact that in 'be'-perfects, the participle agrees with the subject, while in 'have'-perfects, it does not.[53] This generalization also holds within reduced relatives containing a perfect; that is, when the missing auxiliary is 'be'—the only type of reduced relative possible, after all—the participle shows the agreement it does in a full perfect. This can be made to follow from the derivations in (61) and (62).

(61)

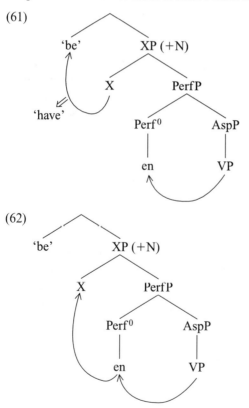

(62)

The part of the tree below PerfP was discussed in section A.1. X is a nominal head that may incorporate to 'be', resulting in 'have'. In (61), X incorporates to 'be', giving 'have'. In such a case, the participle stays where it is and does not show agreement. In (62), the participle raises to X and therefore shows nominal inflection (number, gender).[54] In such a case, the auxiliary remains 'be'. In languages like English, (61) is the only possible derivation for the perfect. In languages like Bulgarian, (62) is the only possibility. And there are languages in which both derivations are possible, namely, auxiliary selection languages. This Kayne-like analysis maintains the derivational relationship between 'be' and 'have' and also derives the complementarity between 'have' and participle agreement.

How do derivations (61) and (62) account for the distribution of reduced relatives based on perfect participles? The generalization that reduced relatives with perfect participles are possible if and only if the missing auxiliary is 'be' now translates into the question of why participles can be isolated from auxiliaries only when they move to X as in (62) and not when X moves to 'be' as in (61).[55]

We have already encountered a reason to assume that X is nominal in nature. If the participle moves to it, the complex declines in the nominal paradigm. If the participle does not move up, and X incorporates to 'be', the resulting complex is not nominal, since the host of the incorporation is the auxiliary verb.

If indeed X is nominal, we can say that the reason that the reduced relative can contain a perfect in the 'be'-cases but not in the 'have'-cases is that the reduced relative is nominal in the former but not in the latter. This means that a reduced relative is possible only as long as it is nominal. Why should this be so? Possibly all categories whose meaning intersects with the meaning of a head that they modify must be of the same categorial type as the head (or weaker, there should be no mismatch). This explains why adjectives cannot modify verbs, nor adverbs nouns. This means that everything that modifies a noun must be nominal. This is certainly clear for adjectives. Perhaps it also holds for relative clauses. Then reduced relatives must be nominal.

That the availability of reduced relatives correlates with the nominal nature of the participle is supported also by data from Spanish, a language with only 'have'-perfects. Consistent with what we have said so far, reduced relatives containing a perfect are largely impossible in Spanish. But there is an exception: reduced relatives with a perfect are possible for (possibly a subset of) unaccusatives. Crucially, the participle in such reduced relatives shows subject agreement.

(63) Las chicas [recen   llegadas   a la estacion] son mis
      the girls [recently arrived-FEM.PL at the station] are my
      hermanas.
      sisters
      'The girls who have just arrived at the station are my sisters.'

Such subject agreement is impossible in a full perfect.

(64) Las chicas han llegado/*as.
      the girls have arrived/*FEM.PL

We do not know what licenses a construction like (63), but the obligatorily nominal nature of the participle, evidenced by its agreeing in the
nominal paradigm, shows that the correlation between the availability of
reduced relatives with a perfect participle and the nominal nature of the
latter is on the right track.

If modification of a nominal requires that the modifier be nominal, an
obvious question is how full relative clauses can modify nominals, if they
are CPs. There are two possible answers. First, one could stipulate that
there is no mismatch between a CP and a noun. Second, one could say
that relative-clause CPs are also nominal. This may not be as outlandish
as it initially seems if one takes into account the existence of free relatives,
which look like CPs but have the category of the *wh*-word. That is, free
relatives whose *wh*-word is nominal can themselves be shown to be
nominal (Bresnan and Grimshaw 1978; Groos and Van Riemsdijk 1981).
How can we derive the nominal nature of relative-clause CPs? Chomsky
(1995) assumes that the category resulting from Move/Merge is the category of the host. What if this weren't necessarily so? In certain cases, it
would be forced because the alternative (i.e., the category of the whole
being the category of the moved element) would give uninterpretable
results or (e.g.) violate selectional restrictions of a higher node.[56] However, if there are no such restrictions, then the category of the moving
element may be able to determine the category of the whole. This would
derive free relatives, but it would also be a possibility for relative-clause
CPs. After all, being adjuncts, the latter have no selectional restrictions
imposed on them, so that if the relative pronoun determines the category
of the whole, no problem is created for a higher projection. In addition, if
modification of the noun by the relative clause requires the relative clause
to be nominal, then category determination by the moving element will
even be forced.

Incidentally, this might also explain why there is movement in relative-clause CPs in languages with overt Ā-movement. This movement is not triggered by what triggers Ā-movement in questions, since there is no [+Q] feature to worry about. In other words, movement of the relative pronoun is triggered by the need to make the entire clause nominal. This also might account for why inversion does not take place in relative clauses. If inversion is movement of the verb to C in order to check a feature on C, then we do not expect it in relative clauses. There is no feature on C in such cases; the relative pronoun moves to change the category of the relative clause. Bhatt (1999) implements within a head-raising framework (Brame 1968; Vergnaud 1974; Kayne 1994) the idea that relative clauses are a case of movement that projects.

Notes

Ken Hale was part of the beginnings of this project and we benefited a great deal from discussions with him. We also learned much from Rajesh Bhatt, Noam Chomsky, Memo Cinque, David Embick, Kai von Fintel, Alessandra Giorgi, Irene Heim, Richard Larson, Julie Legate, Alec Marantz, David Pesetsky, and Arnim von Stechow. Finally, we thank the audiences at NELS 28, the University of Massachusetts at Amherst, the University of Pennsylvania, and the University of Tübingen for comments and discussions. Many thanks to Anne Mark for making the chapter readable. The research for this project was supported by NSF grant NYI SBR-9458319 to Sabine Iatridou.

1. There are even languages that have a perfect that is distinct from a simple past only in the passive and not in the active (Russian, Irish; Comrie 1976, 63, 84). We will not be looking at such languages either.

2. We refer here to the Reichenbachian parameters E, R, and S, with respect to which the meaning of the various tenses is described. E is the point (or interval, depending on the framework) at which the eventuality holds, S is the utterance time, and R is a reference point/interval. Klein (1992, 1994) (among others) also proposes a three-way composition of tenses, although somewhat different from Reichenbach's; when cast in Klein's terms, the distinction between the present perfect and the simple past is quite similar to that described in the main text. For McCawley (1993), who is otherwise writing within Reichenbachian assumptions, the perfect does not specify an E__R relationship; rather, the R interval coincides with an extended-now interval (see McCoard 1978) and the E interval is a subinterval of the R interval. In that sense, McCawley's treatment is similar to Dowty's (1979), as well as to ours, neither of which relies on the Reichenbachian parameters, as we will show.

3. In addition to the crosslinguistic parameterization of the present perfect puzzle (e.g., English has it, Italian and Dutch do not), there is variation within the same language. In Modern Greek, for example, one cannot say *Mary has built this house in 1963*, but one can say *This house has been built in 1963*.

(i) *I Maria   eχ$_1$i χtisi   to spiti   to 1963.
the Maria-NOM has built-ACT the house-ACC the 1963

(ii) To spiti   eχ$_1$i χtisti   to 1963.
the house-NOM has built-NONACT the 1963

4. Others, such as Klein (1992, 1994), propose that the perfect has a tense part and an aspect part, but for Klein both tense and aspect are relations between time spans. So, for Klein the aspect part of the perfect is that the topic time is "in posttime" of the situation time, while the tense part of the perfect concerns the relation between the topic time and the utterance time.

5. The contribution of the features [unbounded] and [bounded] can be said to be as in (ia) and (ib), respectively (representations in the spirit of Klein's (1994) characterization of the imperfective/perfective distinction).

(i) a. $\lambda P.\ \lambda t. \exists e[t \subseteq \text{Time}(e)\ \&\ P(e)]$
    b. $\lambda P.\ \lambda t. \exists e[\text{Time}(e) \subseteq t\ \&\ P(e)]$

These aspectual features have the effect of turning properties of events into properties of interval (von Stechow 1999). We should emphasize, though, that nothing in (ia) predicts the obligatory property of framing, exhibited by the English progressive and other imperfectives (*He was reading the book *#(when the bomb exploded/when I saw him/etc)*). We will show later that there are aspects that do not describe an eventuality as terminated/ completed, and yet they do not have the framing property (e.g., the Bulgarian neutral).

Since they do not contain a completion/termination interval, unbounded eventualities are homogeneous. This means that putting the issue of granularity aside, unbounded eventualities correspond to intervals having the subinterval property (Dowty 1979 and section 6.4 below).

(ii) *Subinterval property*
    The subinterval property holds of an interval iff the eventuality that holds at that interval holds of every subinterval of that interval.

The notion of granularity was meant to further subdivide between activities and statives, but that has been notoriously hard to achieve.

See Bennett and Partee 1978, Dowty 1979, Hinrichs 1983, Parsons 1990, Smith 1991, and Landman 1992, among many others, for discussion of (im)perfectiveness, its relation to boundedness, and its effect on (a)telics.

6. Brugger (1997) makes a proposal that formally distinguishes between the experiential perfect and the perfect of result. Moreover, Kratzer (1994) develops a semantic treatment of the perfect of result in terms of the notion of "target state" (Parsons 1990). She argues that as a semantic category, the perfect of result is encoded in the meaning of the adjectival suffix in adjectival participles. In her proposal, the verbs that can form adjectival participles are those that comfortably allow the perfect of result in that they are easily conceptualized as having target states.

7. Dowty (1979, 343) points out that the lack of ambiguity when the adverb is preposed is evidence that a true syntactic ambiguity underlies the two readings. We will come back to this later.

8. Brugger also points out that the present perfect in Portuguese has only the U-reading. If this is so, then it cannot be that the U-perfect is just a special case of the E-perfect.

9. As Richard Larson (personal communication) points out, traditional parallelism tests suggest that the U/E distinction is not a matter of vagueness. For example, in *John has been sick since 1990, and Mary has too*, it is not possible to get a U-reading for one of the conjuncts and an E-reading for the other. Either both are U or both are E.

10. Von Stechow (1999) argues that in German, the U-perfect does not assert that the utterance time is included in the underlying eventuality. Thus, a sentence like *Ich habe hier schon immer gewohnt* 'I have always lived here' can be followed by *... bis vor kurzem* 'until recently' without leading to a contradiction. This is different in, for example, English and Bulgarian. Arnim von Stechow (personal communication) suggests that the German facts can be taken to show that whether or not the U-perfect asserts inclusion of the utterance time is open to parametric variation, possibly related to the properties of the present tense in the languages in question. On this view, the present tense has a more extended function in German than in English and for this reason, only the present asserts inclusion of the utterance time in the eventuality. Von Stechow further suggests that this might also explain why sentences with *seit* 'since' in German are in many cases more natural in the present than in the perfect (contrary to English, where *since* requires the perfect).

11. In the case of perfects modified by *for*-adverbials, Klein (1992, 1994) takes the adverbial to be modifying the underlying eventuality. Thus, for him, a sentence like *Mary has lived in Boston for three years* asserts that the state of Mary's living in Boston for three years has ended without making any assertion about whether Mary continues to live in Boston at the utterance time or not, leaving it to discourse to specify. However, Klein does not discuss U-readings with *since*-adverbials, and we believe that they provide the crucial evidence regarding the interpretation of the perfect because they can never modify the underlying eventuality. So, for a sentence like *Mary has lived in Boston since 1990*, it is not clear how Klein would justify that a particular subinterval of the state of Mary's living in Boston is identified as having ended.

12. Mittwoch conjectures that if a state has obtained for some time and still obtains at the utterance time, there is no reason for using the perfect; rather, Gricean principles would favor use of the present tense. She notes that in response to *I haven't seen John lately*, one would say *He is ill* (and not *He has been ill*) if John is known to be ill at the utterance time. However, we argue later that present tense would be preferred in this case because a sentence like *He has been ill (lately)* is not a U-perfect and thus is compatible with John's not being ill at the utterance time. Therefore, such sentences do not provide an argument against the position that the U-perfect *asserts* that the underlying eventuality holds at the utterance time.

13. In effect, this is a version of the Extended-Now Theory (McCoard 1978; Vlach 1993), even though we do not take it either to be a pragmatic theory of the perfect or to be restricted to the present perfect (see also Dowty 1979).

14. In Reichenbachian terms, this means that RB is representable by R.

15. By *truly unmodified*, we mean to exclude those perfect sentences that do not themselves contain an overt adverb but are part of a discourse where one is present. For example:

(i) A: What has he been doing since yesterday at 5 p.m.?
    B: He has been writing a paper.

B's utterance contains no overt adverb, but it is clear that it means *Since yesterday at 5 p.m., he has been writing a paper.*

16. The unacceptability of such sentences also shows that the experiential reading is absent. This is probably due to a combination of factors. If the subject is alive and therefore still has brown eyes, then the simple present tense must be used. If the subject is dead, then the sentence cannot be used because of the present tense part of the present perfect (see note 33).

17. One could actually argue that there is no reason to suspect that (9) is a U-perfect, exactly because one can continue it with *and she still is.* If (9) were a U-perfect, it would assert that Mary is still sick and the continuation would therefore feel redundant. There is a feeling of such redundancy in *Mary has lived here ever since 1990 and she still does.* This indeed would be one more argument for the conclusion we are drawing in the main text, namely, that (9) is not a U-perfect.

18. Note that in English, the adverb *lately* takes the present perfect only, while *recently* can take either the perfect or the past tense. Thus, lexical idiosyncrasy of the sort we are discussing is found not only crosslinguistically, but also within one and the same language.

19. This is said because it is assumed that the perfect of the progressive does not have the experiential reading. However, this seems to be inaccurate, as (i) illustrates.

(i) Have you ever been watching TV when the tube exploded? (Comrie 1976)

Why should there have been difficulty in detecting the experiential reading of the perfect of the progressive? Possibly the reason is that we need to control for the factors that justify the presence of the progressive to begin with. One such factor is that the progressive in isolation (e.g., as a conversation starter) is infelicitous (maybe even ungrammatical) if it does not frame an adverbial clause. The progressive does frame such a clause in Comrie's example and therefore the sentence is fine. One might ask whether the progressive's need to frame is satisfied in the reading of the recent past. It probably is in (15), if we take the progressive to frame the recent past adverbial *just*, with the reading that the interval denoted by *just* is inside an interval of cooking. But see the next note on a related matter.

20. Interestingly, *I have been cooking lately* can be uttered by someone who used to eat in restaurants a lot but has recently changed habits. It is not exactly clear to us how the progressive functions here, given that it is normally not compatible with habitual contexts. Possibly, something like this is going on. We know that there are local effects that appear to override larger constraints. For example, the existential *there is* construction is supposed to not take definites, yet one can easily

say *There is the tallest girl you have ever seen in the room next door*. Superlatives require the definite article and so the latter appears in an environment where one would not expect it (though it does appear without the discourse-oldness that the *there is* construction cannot tolerate). Similarly in the case under discussion, progressives and habituals usually do not mix; but since *lately* requires the progressive on nonstative underlying predicates (something reminiscent of the U-perfect; see just below), the latter appears in a habitual environment with *lately*, overriding the usual incompatibility between the habitual and the progressive.

Moreover, in the case of the habitual reading, an assertion is made about the utterance time, namely, that the habit still holds. This is, of course, reminiscent of the U-perfect (which however is not restricted to habitual contexts). An additional reason to believe there is a connection between this habituality/*lately* reading and the U-perfect is that in languages that can use the present tense with adverbs to convey what the U-perfect does, it is also the present tense that is used with recent past adverbials to convey a recently formed habit. On the other hand, if this habituality/*lately* reading of the perfect were a subcase of the U-perfect, we would expect it to be present in other languages that have the U-perfect. However, we have found no such language. We leave the resolution of this issue for a future occasion. As this reading of the perfect progressive is not an instance of a perfect that is unmodified by adverbials (since there is either an overt or a covert 'lately' that is recoverable from the context), its existence does not impinge on the discussion in the main text.

21. According to Vlach, among others, there is an additional level of adverbial modification, namely, the one that relates to the present/past tense specification of a sentence.

22. This reflects the idea that temporal morphology is just an instance of agreement between the verb and adverbs (in all sentences, not just ones with the perfect). This view of tense morphology as agreement permits a parallel with subject agreement. When the subject is *Peter* and the verb is inflected, the morphology that appears must be third person singular. When the verb is not inflected, as in *I consider Peter to be the best candidate*, *Peter* can still be the subject. What is not possible is for *Peter* to be the subject of a verb that is (e.g.) second person plural. Similarly in the domain of temporal interpretation: the adverbial determines the meaning and if the verb inflects, it must do so appropriately. If it does not inflect, then there is no mismatch in features and the adverbial interpretation goes through. For example, even though *by*-adverbials in a pluperfect require a past tense on the auxiliary when the latter is inflected, the adverbial can also appear with infinitival perfects: *He must have left by 3 o'clock*. Tense is [+/−past] to reflect the overt or covert presence of a past- or present-oriented adverb. This position, which is also taken in Vlach 1993, is the topic of some debate (see, e.g., Dowty 1979; Partee 1984).

23. There is only one case in which *since* is allowed without perfect morphology:

(i) It is two years since he died.

See Mittwoch 1988, 219, for discussion of this construction.

24. Another possibility would be existential closure over intervals filled by an eventuality. This might be better, but we will keep on talking about *ONCE* closing over eventualities.

25. This holds only when the alternatives are superset intervals of the interval between 3 and 4. When the alternatives are disconnected, as when the interval between 3 and 4 is being compared with the intervals between 11 and 12 and between 7 and 8 as in (i), things are different.

(i) A: Was he in his office between 11 and 12, between 3 and 4, and between 7 and 8?

    B: Well, he was in his office at least between 3 and 4. I don't know about the other times.

B's statement can be uttered truthfully if the subject was in his office for 10 minutes between 3 and 4. In the case of *at least since*, the alternative intervals are supersets of the perfect time span. The is because RB is fixed (set by tense) and so only LB can be made to vary.

26. Ever since Partee 1973, whether tense is a definite or existentially quantified expression, appropriately restricted, has been a matter for debate. Similarly, in our case, the perfect time span could be expressed as a definite. We have nothing further to say here about the larger debate; we will continue to use existential quantification, but we do not believe that any crucial element of our proposal would change if the perfect time span were expressed as a definite.

27. The prepositions *throughout* and *in* are meant to indicate the durative and inclusive readings, respectively.

28. Not surprisingly, it is possible to have complex eventualities that consist of subeventualities. We will argue later that notions like "poststate" do not have any distinguished status in the perfect; however, if we were to revert to this terminology for a moment, the relative scope of the perfect- and eventuality-level adverbs would also explain why a sentence like (i) cannot be paraphrased with (ii).

(i) I have read "The Book of Sand" five times.

(ii) I have been five times in the poststate of reading "The Book of Sand."

29. *For*-adverbials are durative, which means that the predicate they modify must be homogeneous/have the subinterval property. It follows that *for*-adverbials cannot appear when a telic eventuality is asserted to culminate because of the distinguished final subinterval of culmination. It is very often said that *in*-adverbials test for telicity and *for*-adverbials for atelicity, but this is an oversimplification.

(i) He walked to the park in/*for an hour.

(ii) He walked in the park for/*in an hour.

The oversimplification is due to a common jump in the logic: we think we are testing for Aktionsart, but what we are really examining is a particular Aktionsart + grammatical aspect ((im)perfective) combination. So we do not a priori know whether what we are diagnosing is the result of Aktionsart, grammatical aspect, or their combination. The fact that we can have an *in*-adverbial in (i) and not in (ii) means that *in*-adverbials go with the telicity + perfectivity combination. This is even clearer in languages other than English. In effect, *in*-adverbials tell us when the (inherent) endpoint/goal has been achieved. This means that we need an Aktionsart that has such an inherent endpoint (i.e., telics) and a grammatical aspect that asserts that the eventuality has culminated.

When a telic predicate is put in the imperfective, nothing is asserted about the achievement of the goal and *in*-adverbials are not possible. (The imperfectivity + telicity combination is exactly the domain of the imperfective paradox. See Dowty 1979; Landman 1992; and others.)

In other words, *in*-adverbials test for achievement of the goal (telicity + perfectivity), not just telicity (i.e., not just existence of an inherent endpoint).

We can also explain why *for*-adverbials are not possible in (i). What we actually see is that *for*-adverbials are incompatible with the telicity + perfectivity combination. That is, they are incompatible not with the existence of an inherent endpoint but with the assertion of culmination (i.e., the assertion that the inherent endpoint has been achieved). In other words, *for*-adverbials test not for atelicity but for the absence of culmination (i.e., the complement set of the telicity + perfectivity combination).

30. This correctly says nothing about whether the five days were contiguous or not. Here is one place where having *ONCE* close over time intervals rather than eventualities might offer an advantage (see the discussion in note 25). Even if the five days are disconnected, their sum still forms an interval (since it is just the result of adding smaller intervals). Instead of (21b), we could have (i).

(i) There is a time span (the perfect time span) whose LB is in 1970 and whose RB is the utterance time, and in that time span is a five-day interval of my being sick.

31. This comes close to saying that when there is no overt perfect-level adverbial, the sentence contains enough interpretive elements to bring about a perfect interpretation and that therefore no covert perfect-level adverbial is needed. But even if this is the case, the major question (why there is no U-perfect reading in the absence of an overt perfect-level adverbial) remains.

32. This is the domain of Chomsky's (1970, 85) famous "Einstein sentences," which have become the topic of considerable debate in studies of the perfect. The issue is that *Einstein has visited Princeton* cannot be uttered after Einstein's death if *Einstein* is the topic of the sentence. However, it can be uttered after Einstein's death in the context of (e.g.) listing famous people who have visited Princeton.

33. To account for the restriction on an adverbial's interpretational "reach," Hornstein (1990) proposes that adverbs can modify only those elements that they govern. To account for the fact that the modification domain of adverbs is determined at Spell-Out, Thompson (1995) proposes that adverbials are barred from A-movement since they do not have features to check, unlike DPs (see also Chomsky 1995). This does not preclude movement of adverbials in constructions like *wh*-movement, topicalization, and focus movement (see also Alexiadou 1997 for discussion).

34. Why would a Tense-level adverbial not cause a Shortest Move violation? If Tense-level adverbs do not exist (Hornstein 1990), then of course there is no issue; but if they do (Vlach 1993), then something needs to be said. Possibly Tense-level adverbials are not attractable? Possibly they are analogous to the case of subjects, which although topiclike do not count as interveners for topicalization of the object? Since we have not committed ourselves to the existence of Tense-level adverbials, we leave this question for a different occasion.

35. Thompson discusses the syntactic behavior of adverbials in sentences like *The secretary had eaten at 3 p.m.*, which can mean either 'The time that the secretary actually ate was 3 p.m.' (eventuality-level) or 'The secretary had already eaten by 3 p.m.' (perfect-level). She demonstrates that the meaning of the adverbials (i.e., whether they are eventuality-level or perfect-level—what she calls the R point reading) interacts with binding. For example, in (i), the adverbial can only be perfect-level under coreference. On the eventuality-level reading, a Principle C violation arises.

(i) Mary had seen him$_i$ at the time that John$_i$ presented his paper.

However, with respect to Thompson's other tests, we have reached a different conclusion. Thompson claims that when the VP is isolated via pseudoclefting, *though*-movement, or VP-fronting, only the eventuality-level reading of the adverbial survives. This would support her position that perfect-level adverbials are attached higher than the VP. But our informants judge that the following sentences are acceptable:

(ii) Work at MIT since 1990 though he has, he still doesn't know where Building 20 is.

(iii) John claims he has worked at MIT since 1990 and work at MIT since 1990 he has.

(iv) What he has done is work illegally as a doctor since 1990.

Given that *since*-adverbials are necessarily perfect-level, the fact that they can appear when the verb is used in isolation shows that in these environments, it is at least the Perf(ect) node that has been topicalized and not just the VP. This is a problem for Thompson's account because she assumes that because the verb is not participial, only the VP is topicalized. However, our test (basically the permissibility of the *since*-adverbial) shows that the syntacticosemantic features of the perfect are there, though something has inhibited the morphological formation of the participle. See Urushibara 1997 for a discussion of facts similar to the ones Thompson addresses and for a morphological account of the appearance of the bare forms in (ii)–(iv).

36. When *always* is eventuality-level, it is an adverbial of quantification placed within the perfect time span.

37. This is related to the frequent description of the experiential perfect as an individual-level type of property of the subject, since once one participates in an eventuality, one forever has the experience of having done so (see, e.g., Smith 1991).

38. On one of its uses. The imperfective has a wider distribution than is discussed here.

39. Certain stative verbs like 'have', 'be', and 'know' do not have a perfective form at all. These verbs also do not have a perfect participle and do not form a perfect.

40. Traditional Bulgarian grammars do not make a distinction between perfective and neutral, calling both the "past completed" form. Not all verbs have a morphological distinction between neutral, imperfective, and perfective forms. Moreover, morphological neutral is available only for the past tense forms.

41. Smith characterizes neutral as "default with a specific positive value" (1991, 119), a definition that is unclear to us. She also says that neutral is found in languages that have no aspectual distinctions or that neutral is the absence of aspectual morphology in languages that do make an imperfective/perfective distinction. However, she also notes (1991, 133, fn. 3) that in principle, a language could have neutral in contrast to perfective and imperfective.

42. Regarding the distribution of imperfective and neutral perfect participles, the following generalization holds: when both an imperfective and a neutral participle are available, it is the neutral participle that is used in forming the U-perfect, and not the imperfective one. The imperfective participle is used in forming a U-perfect only for those verbs that do not mark the neutral. To account for this distribution, we propose that the neutral is more specified than the imperfective and that this is why it is chosen in the relevant environments. In particular, the neutral has the feature [unbounded] (or it lacks the feature [bounded]) and it requires the features [dynamic] and [durative]. See Smith 1991 for definition of the primitive features [dynamic] and [durative]. The feature [dynamic] separates statives from nonstatives; the feature [durative] separates statives, activities, and accomplishments from achievements and semelfactives. The neutral is precluded on statives, achievements, and semelfactives. The less marked imperfective has only the feature [unbounded] (or it lacks [bounded]). Thus, as far as the U-perfect is concerned, both the neutral and the imperfective have the relevant feature, [unbounded]. However, the neutral is chosen over the imperfective when it is applicable because it is the more specified form with respect to the features of the underlying eventuality. The question then arises why the simple past allows either the Neutral or the imperfective. We argue that this optionality is only apparent and that the imperfective is chosen for framing purposes (see section 6.5).

43. A sentence like (i) should not be taken as a counterexample to the claim that the perfect of activities does not permit the U-perfect reading.

(i) He has worked here ever since he was a child.

In (i), the predicate is interpreted as 'be a worker' or 'be an employee', which is not an activity but a generic/habitual predicate that patterns with statives.

44. This has been expressed in various ways; for example, it is said that the progressive requires something like [dynamic] or that the progressive contributes [dynamic], this feature not being compatible with statives.

45. Actually, it is unclear whether [bounded] can appear on English statives. As noted earlier, this feature on statives in certain languages makes the predicate inchoative, but there are languages in which statives simply cannot appear with perfective morphology (Comrie 1976). Possibly English is such a language. If so, then statives will only be marked [unbounded]. This would also provide a possible alternative explanation for why statives do not have the progressive/nonprogressive opposition in English.

46. One should not be misled into believing that the experiential reading requires boundedness. In Bulgarian, the experiential reading is possible with the imperfective and neutral participles. A similar situation holds for English, as in Comrie's (1976) (i).

(i) Have you ever been watching TV when the tube exploded?

47. When it accompanies a present tense, RB can be left out and it is automatically taken to be the utterance time.

48. In our opinion, Vlach overinterpreted one particular behavioral pattern. There are other tests that make progressives and statives look similar and still others that make them look different.

Both progressives and statives can appear in the present tense in English without being generics or sportscasters' speech.

(i) a. He is lifting weights.
    b. He is sick.
    c. He lifts weights. (only generic)

The fact that (ic) does not have an episodic interpretation can be made to follow from the fact that on nonstatives, activities come in the progressive and nonprogressive forms and therefore the bare (nonprogressive) verb is interpreted perfectively. And recall that there is no such thing as present perfective.

One difference between progressives and statives is that progressives can take agentive adverbials like *carefully*, *deliberately*, and *conscientiously*, whereas statives cannot.

Imperatives (both imperfective and perfective) and pseudoclefts are often used as tests for stativity, but what they really test for is agentivity.

49. Dowty (1979) calls the predicates that satisfy the subinterval property "statives." Again, we do not adopt this terminology for the reasons given in the main text. (See also note 5.)

50. As is well known, there are two major classes of perfect formation. Class I languages do not use an auxiliary to form the perfect, but the matrix verb contains one or more morphemes that are associated with the perfect (synthetic perfects; e.g., Classical Greek, Latin, Turkish). Class II languages use an auxiliary to form the perfect (analytic/periphrastic perfects). This auxiliary may end up incorporated in the verb (e.g., Tajik) or it may be a separate lexical item (Romance, Slavic, Germanic, (Modern) Greek). Here we discuss only analytic perfects.

51. Benveniste (1966) is often cited in this context. However, this is a misreading of Benveniste's discussion. He says that possessive 'have' replaced possessive 'be to' in many languages, but he does not say that the one shaped the other.

52. In Kayne's system, participle agreement is a function of a local relationship obtaining or not obtaining between a DP object and the participial Agr_O. When 'be' selects for D/PP, participle agreement is the result of the derived subject's passing through the participial Agr_O. When 'be' selects for $Agr_O P$, the obligatoriness of participial agreement reduces to the obligatoriness of adjectival agreement. So, Kayne's account has two different mechanisms to derive participle agreement with 'be', depending on whether 'be' subcategorizes for D/PP or $Agr_O P$. The complementarity between 'have' and participle agreement follows from the assumption that a major source of participle agreement ('be' + $Agr_O P$) is a source that could never yield 'have'.

However, Kayne does not consider languages in which the perfect auxiliary is always 'be'. In such languages, it is incorrect to attribute participle agreement to Agr_O. In languages like Bulgarian where the perfect auxiliary is invariably 'be', the perfect participle *always* agrees with the subject, as in (i). (Siloni (1997) discusses a similar pattern found in Hebrew, though not specifically for perfect participles; Siloni's discussion covers participles found with all complex tenses.)

(i) Maria e̲ pisal-a̲   (knigata).
    Maria is write-PERF.PART-FEM.SG the-book
    'Maria has worked on the book.'

Obviously, we cannot appeal to Agr_O to account for these cases of participle agreement. We therefore conclude that the source of participle agreement with participles combining with 'be' is not Agr_O, contra Kayne (1993). The same conclusion is drawn by Siloni (1997) on the basis of the Hebrew facts mentioned above.

53. Kayne (1993) mentions three counterexamples to this: a dialect area in central France where agreement appears on the participle of 'be' when it combines with 'have' (e.g., 'Mary has been'), the dialect of Cori described by Chiominto (1984), and the Aquila dialect in Abruzzo. In the latter two cases, agreement on the participle combining with 'have' is found only with unaccusatives.

54. This nominal head X is reminiscent of Siloni's (1997) AgrP(article), which yields participle agreement with the DP that passes through it.

55. Burzio (1986), Williams (1980), Chomsky (1981), and Stowell (1981) assume that the grammatical subject of the participle in reduced relatives is PRO. Siloni (1997) argues that even though the subject is grammatically present, it is not PRO but a variable bound by a null operator. Kayne (1994) and Bhatt (1999) propose a head-raising analysis for reduced relatives. For our purposes, it is sufficient to assume that reduced relatives are formed on the basis of the smallest projection that can be lexicalized and can serve as a relative modifier at the same time.

56. For example, if the direct object moves in front of the verb (overtly or covertly), the resulting category should still be verbal in order to be able to successfully interact with higher nodes (e.g., T).

References

Abusch, D., and M. Rooth. 1990. Temporal adverbs and the English perfect. In J. Carter, R.-M. Déchaine, B. Philip, and T. Sherer, eds., *NELS 20*, 1–15. GLSA, University of Massachusetts, Amherst.

Alexiadou, A. 1997. *Adverb placement: A case study in antisymmetric syntax.* Amsterdam: John Benjamins.

Bauer, G. 1970. The English "perfect" reconsidered. *Journal of Linguistics* 6, 189–198.

Bäuerle, R. 1979. Temporale Deixis, temporale Frage: Zum propositionalen Gehalt deklarativer und interrogativer Sätze. Tübingen: Narr.

Bennett, M. 1977. A guide to the logic of tense and aspect in English. *Logique et Analyse*, n.s., 80, 491–517.

Bennett, M., and B. Partee. 1972. Toward a logic of tense and aspect in English. Ms., System Development Corporation, Santa Monica, Calif.

Bennett, M., and B. Partee. 1978. Toward the logic of tense and aspect in English. (Revision of 1972 ms.) Indiana University Linguistics Club, Bloomington.

Benveniste, É. 1966. *Problems in general linguistics.* Coral Gables, Fla.: University of Miami Press.

Bhatt, R. 1999. Covert modality in non-finite contexts. Doctoral dissertation, University of Pennsylvania.

Binnick, R. 1991. *Time and the verb.* Oxford: Oxford University Press.

Brame, M. 1968. A new analysis of the relative clause: Evidence for an interpretive theory. Ms., MIT.

Bresnan, J., and J. Grimshaw. 1978. The syntax of free relatives in English. *Linguistic Inquiry* 9, 331–391.

Brugger, G. 1997. Event time properties. In A. Dimitriadis, L. Siegel, C. Surek-Clark, and A. Williams, eds., *Proceedings of the 21st Annual Penn Linguistics Colloquium*, 51–63. Pennsylvania Working Papers in Linguistics 4.2. Penn Linguistics Club, University of Pennsylvania.

Burzio, L. 1981. Intransitive verbs and Italian auxiliaries. Doctoral dissertation, MIT.

Burzio, L. 1986. *Italian syntax: A Government-Binding approach.* Dordrecht: Reidel.

Chiominto, C. 1984. *Lo parla forte della pora gente.* Rome: Bulzoni.

Chomsky, N. 1957. *Syntactic structures.* The Hague: Mouton.

Chomsky, N. 1970. Deep structure, surface structure and semantic interpretation. In R. Jacobson, ed., *Studies in general and Oriental linguistics presented to Shiro Hattori on the occasion of his sixtieth birthday*, 52–91. Tokyo: TEC.

Chomsky, N. 1981. *Lectures on government and binding.* Dordrecht: Foris.

Chomsky, N. 1995. *The Minimalist Program.* Cambridge, Mass.: MIT Press.

Cinque, G. 1999. *Adverbs and functional heads*. Oxford: Oxford University Press.

Comrie, B. 1976. *Aspect*. Cambridge: Cambridge University Press.

Cowper, E. A. 1989a. Perfective *-en* IS passive *-en*. In J. Fee and K. Hunt, eds., *Proceedings of the Eighth West Coast Conference on Formal Linguistics*, 85–93. Stanford, Calif.: CSLI Publications.

Cowper, E. A. 1989b. Thematic underspecification: The case of *have*. In B. Brunson, S. Burton, and T. Wilson, eds., *Toronto working papers in linguistics* 10, 85–94. Department of Linguistics, University of Toronto.

Dowty, D. 1979. *Word meaning in Montague Grammar*. Dordrecht: Reidel.

Freeze, R. 1992. Existentials and other locatives. *Language* 68, 553–595.

Giorgi, A., and F. Pianesi. 1998. *Tense and aspect: from semantics to morphosyntax*. Oxford: Oxford University Press.

Groos, A., and H. van Riemsdijk. 1981. Matching effects in free relatives: A parameter of core grammar. In A. Belletti, L. Brandi, and L. Rizzi, eds., *Theory of markedness in generative grammar*, 176–216. Scuola Normale Superiore, Pisa.

Heim, I. 1982. The semantics of definite and indefinite noun phrases. Doctoral dissertation, University of Massachusetts, Amherst.

Heny, F. 1982. Tense, aspect and time adverbials. Part II. *Linguistics and Philosophy* 5, 109–154.

Hinrichs, E. 1983. The semantics of the English progressive: A study in situation semantics. In A. Chukerman, M. Marks, and J. F. Richardson, eds., *CLS 19*, 171–182. Chicago Linguistic Society, University of Chicago.

Hoekstra, T. 1984. *Transitivity: Grammatical relations in Government-Binding Theory*. Dordrecht: Foris.

Hornstein, N. 1990. *As time goes by: Tense and Universal Grammar*. Cambridge, Mass.: MIT Press.

Inoue, K. 1978. How many senses does the present perfect have? In D. Farkas, W. Jacobsen, and K. Todrys, eds., *Papers from the 14th Regional Meeting, Chicago Linguistic Society*, 167–178. Chicago Linguistic Society, University of Chicago.

Jespersen, O. 1924. *The philosophy of grammar*. Reprint, New York: Norton (1965).

Kayne, R. 1993. Toward a modular theory of auxiliary selection. *Studia Linguistica* 47, 3–31.

Kayne, R. 1994. *The antisymmetry of syntax*. Cambridge, Mass.: MIT Press.

Klein, W. 1992. The present perfect puzzle. *Language* 68, 525–552.

Klein, W. 1994. *Time in language*. London: Routledge.

Kratzer, A. 1994. The event argument and the semantics of voice. Ms., University of Massachusetts, Amherst.

Landman, F. 1992. The progressive. *Natural Language Semantics* 1, 1–32.

McCawley, J. 1971. Tense and time reference in English. In C. Fillmore and D. T Langendoen, eds., *Studies in linguistic semantics*, 96–113. New York: Holt, Rinehart and Winston.

McCawley, J. 1993. *Everything that linguists have always wanted to know about logic but were ashamed to ask.* 2nd ed. Chicago: University of Chicago Press.

McCoard, R. W. 1978. *The English perfect: Tense choice and pragmatic inferences.* Amsterdam: North-Holland.

Mittwoch, A. 1988. Aspects of English aspect: On the interaction of perfect, progressive, and durational phrases. *Linguistics and Philosophy* 11, 203–254.

Parsons, T. 1990. *Events in the semantics of English: A study of subatomic semantics.* Cambridge, Mass.: MIT Press.

Partee, B. 1973. Some structural analogies between tenses and pronouns in English. *Journal of Philosophy* 70, 601–609.

Partee, B. 1984. Nominal and temporal anaphora. *Linguistics and Philosophy* 7, 243–286.

Pesetsky, D. 1995. *Zero Syntax.* Cambridge, Mass.: MIT Press.

Richards, B. 1982. Tense, aspect, and time adverbials, part I. *Linguistics and Philosophy* 5, 59–107.

Roberts, I. 1986. *The representation of implicit and dethematized subjects.* Dordrecht: Foris.

Siloni, T. 1997. *Noun phrases and nominalizations: The syntax of DPs.* Dordrecht: Kluwer.

Smith, C. 1991. *The parameter of aspect.* Dordrecht: Kluwer.

Stechow, A. von 1999. Eine erweiterte Extended Now-Theorie für Perfekt und Futur. *Zeitschrift für Literaturwissenschaft und Linguistik* 113, 86–118.

Stowell, T. 1981. Origins of phrase structure. Doctoral dissertation, MIT.

Thompson, E. 1995. The structure of tense and the syntax of temporal adverbs. In R. Aranovich, W. Byrne, S. Preuss, and M. Senturia, eds., *Proceedings of the Thirteenth West Coast Conference on Formal Linguistics*, 499–514. Stanford, Calif.: CSLI Publications.

Urushibara, S. 1997. Facets of the English past participle. In M. Kajita et al., eds., *English linguistics: A festschrift for Akira Ota on the occasion of his 80th birthday*, 130–146. Tokyo: Taishukan.

Vendler, Z. 1957. Verbs and times. *The Philosophical Review* 66, 143–160. Reprinted in *Linguistics in Philosophy*. Ithaca, N.Y.: Cornell University Press (1967).

Vergnaud, J.-R. 1974. French relative clauses. Doctoral dissertation, MIT.

Vlach, F. 1981. The semantics of the progressive. In P. Tedeschi and A. Zaenen, eds., *Syntax and semantics 14: Tense and aspect*, 271–292. New York: Academic Press.

Vlach, F. 1993. Temporal adverbials, tenses, and the perfect. *Linguistics and Philosophy* 16, 231–283.

Williams, E. 1980. Predication. *Linguistic Inquiry* 11, 203–238.

Chapter 7

Accentual Adaptation in North Kyungsang Korean

Michael Kenstowicz and
Hyang-Sook Sohn

7.1 Introduction

The North Kyungsang (NK) dialect of Korean is a pitch accent system in which one or in certain cases two syllables in every freestanding lexical item are the locus of a pitch peak. The position of the accent is in general unpredictable: witness the minimal triple *káci* 'kind', *kací* 'eggplant', *ká:cí* 'branch'. When foreign words are adapted into this dialect of Korean, they must be assigned a pitch peak. Since any syllable of the word can be accented in the native lexicon, one might expect the accent of the donor language (typically English) to be copied more or less faithfully. It therefore comes as a surprise that this is not what happens. Instead, accent is assigned to one of three locations (initial, penultimate, or final) according to general principles. We have collected a corpus of some 600 words; the vast majority have predictable accent. We are aware of one other comparable finding. Shinohara (1997a,b, 2000) has investigated the locus of accent in Japanese adaptations of words from English and French. As is well known, in Japanese nouns (as opposed to verbs) the locus of accent varies: for an *n*-syllable noun, there are $n + 1$ patterns, as witnessed by the series *i'noti* 'life', *koko'ro* 'heart', *atama'* 'head', *miyako'* 'capital city' (cf. *miyako-ga'*) from McCawley 1965. Shinohara finds that when a word is adapted from English, the locus of the English accent is by and large respected. But words adapted from French follow a quite different path. Their accent is assigned according to the Latin stress rule: the final syllable is disregarded and a bimoraic trochaic foot is placed at the right edge of the remainder. The result is that the antepenult is accented if the penult is light; otherwise, the penult is accented: *masi'kuri* < *mâchicoulis*, *aNta'Ndju* < *entendu*. This "default" accent pattern is also regularly applied to limited sectors of the native vocabulary such as certain compounds and proper names. Our findings for NK are similar to Shinohara's for Japanese: a bimoraic trochee is assigned at the right edge of the word (with no extrametricality). But this generalization is overlaid by another, NK-specific pattern (detailed below).

Shinohara's study and comparable results from our investigation pose an interesting theoretical problem: given that the native words the NK-learning child hears in first language acquisition have unpredictable accent, why is the right-edge-oriented bimoraic foot analysis chosen in the adaptation situation? What evidence could lead the child to discover penultimate accent as the default accent so that this is the accentuation that emerges in adaptation? Why is the place of accent in English by and large respected in Japanese adaptations but not in NK adaptations? Or is what happens in adaptation largely independent of the native system and a more direct reflection of Universal Grammar (UG)? If so, are there other factors about NK (and Japanese) that cue a trochaic foot at the right edge of the word as the "default" accentuation? These are some of the questions that our results lead us to pose for future research.

This chapter is organized as follows. In section 7.2, we outline the accent patterns of the native NK lexicon. We then review N.-J. Kim's (1997) arguments that penultimate accent should be singled out as predictable. In section 7.3, we present the results of our study and the principles that govern the location of accent in the adaptation data. In section 7.4, we discuss three aspects of the segmental phonology of NK that impinge on the analysis in various ways. In section 7.5, we examine several alternations that are suspended in adapted forms under the influence of the citation form. In section 7.6, we show that adaptations corroborate a constraint on input items. The chapter concludes with a summary of the results.

7.2   NK Accent Patterns

In (1), we list noun stems of one to three syllables to demonstrate the point that accent falls unpredictably on any syllable of the stem in the native NK vocabulary. The data are tabulated in terms of "doubled-" versus "single-" accent words. Items in the former category have a pitch peak (high tone) over their first two syllables; items in the latter category have a pitch peak over just one syllable. The doubled- versus single-accent contrast even exists for monosyllables: it shows up when a suffix such as the nominative-i is added. In the transcriptions that follow, gemination marks tense (glottalized) consonants, *Ch* marks an aspirated stop, *i* is the high central/back unrounded vowel, and ə stands for its mid counterpart. For most NK speakers, the contrast between these two vowels is neutralized phonetically. Our transcriptions do not indicate the automatic voicing of intersonorant plain stops and the palatalization of *s* before *i*.

(1) σ   múl   'water'
             (cf. múr-í
             nom.)
      súl   'wine'
             (cf. súr-i
             nom.)

σσ   cákí   'self'   ká:má   'palanquin'
      kɨrím   'picture'   sá:rám   'person'

      káci   'kind'   kɨcí   'eggplant'
      mánɨl   'garlic'   namúl   'vegetable'
      kúksi   'noodle'   nempí   'pot'
      yəcun   name   toŋsén   'younger sibling'

σσσ múcíke   'rainbow'   hó:ráŋi   'tiger'
      hárépi   'grandfather'   kó:kúma   'sweet potato'

      kámani   'rice bag'   kurúma   'cart'
      tóksuli   'eagle'   camcári   'dragonfly'
                                pitúlki   'dove'
                                halmáŋku   'old woman'

                   satarí   'ladder'
                   mintɨllé   'dandelion'
                   pusirəm   'abscess'
                   pilumppák   'wall'

It is clear that whether a word belongs to the doubled-accent class or not—and if not, then which syllable of the word is accented—is in general unpredictable. However, this statement must be qualified by the fact that words in which the first syllable contains a long vowel are systematically assigned to the doubled-accent class (Chung 1991, 99). Furthermore, aside from a handful of cases in which a long vowel appears in the final syllable of the stem, long vowels are restricted to the word-initial syllable in the NK native lexicon—a property that is true for the Seoul dialect as well (Ahn 1998, 68). But the doubled-accent class also contains many words with an initial short vowel: *sé* 'bird' (cf. *sé-ká* nom.), *cákí* 'self'. For words in the single-accent class, accent falls unpredictably on the first, second, or third syllable.

However, N.-J. Kim (1997) presents several arguments that penultimate accent is the regular pattern for words without a long vowel. First, he cites a sample of 34 loanwords, 30 of which have penultimate accent (2a); the remaining 4 have a final syllable with a long vowel that takes the accent (2b). These data are consistent with an analysis that assigns a bimoraic foot at the right edge of the word.[1]

(2) a. kítha   'guitar'
       théksi   'taxi'
       thókhən   'token coin'
       puráca   'brassiere'
       wasíŋthon   'Washington'
       thenísɨ   'tennis'
       ameríkha   'America'
       hirosíma   'Hiroshima'
       khelliphonía   'California'
       parusellóna   'Barcelona'
    b. utó:ŋ   'Japanese noodle'
       oté:ŋ   'Japanese-style sausage'

Our more extensive corpus of adaptations (see below) shows that this interpretation, while essentially correct, is an oversimplification. Second, as Chung (1991, 74) observes, native NK stems longer than three syllables consistently have penultimate accent. Most of these terminate in the vowel -*i* (*mikkuráci* 'mudfish', *ttakttakúri* 'woodpecker', *heparáki* 'sunflower'), but not all do so (*isusíke* 'toothpick', *acupánim* 'elder brother-in-law'). Chung refers to a similar state of affairs in Kimatuumbi (Odden 1996) where the number of accent patterns for words with four syllables or more is severely restricted compared with the number for shorter words. Evidently, accentual contrasts have a secondary status compared with segmental contrasts, perhaps because the primary function of the former is prosodic integration. Third, as also observed by Chung (1991, 85), when words vacillate in accent pattern, one variant is always penultimate: *tóksuri* ≈ *toksúri* 'eagle', *therepí* ≈ *therépi* 'TV' (Japanese), *múcíke* ≈ *mucíke* 'rainbow'. In other words, penultimate accent acts like a magnet that attracts lexical items from the initial, final, and doubled classes. Fourth, stems with final accent shift the accent to the right under suffixation/encliticization: the shifted accent is realized on the penultimate syllable of the enclitic unless the final syllable contains a long vowel: for example, *kací* 'eggplant' but *kaci-meŋkúro* 'like an eggplant', *kaci-potá*: 'than an eggplant'. Finally, penultimate accent is the most frequent type in the shorter native stems: out of 218 polysyllabic nouns in N.-J. Kim's sample, 133 (61%) have penultimate accent; out of 107 polysyllabic verbs, 52 (49%) are in the penultimate class. These results are comparable to our own: in our corpus of adaptations, 60% of the items belong to the penultimate class; the remaining 40% are divided almost equally between the doubled- and final-accent classes.

7.3 The Corpus

Our corpus consists of some 600 items—almost all nouns. Shinohara (1997a) distinguishes between "on-line adaptations" and "loanwords." The former are more or less spontaneous renderings of a foreign word in the target language—for example, when an interpreter must pronounce a foreign word such as a name for a monolingual client. Our data for the most part fall between fully integrated loanwords and novel renditions of foreign words: the corpus consists of words the second author has either adapted herself or heard used by other NK speakers either in Korea or in the United States. As far as accent is concerned, on-line adaptations and more fully integrated borrowings seem to be treated the same way. See Paradis and LaCharité 1997 for cases where this distinction is crucial.

We begin with several preliminary observations. First, the adapted word almost always falls into one of the three NK accent classes: doubled, final, penultimate. There are cases of antepenultimate accent, but these are limited to situations where a final cluster is broken by two epenthetic vowels (see section 7.4.3). Second, assignment to the three accent classes is made on a principled basis according to the weight of the relevant syllables. The basic generalization can be stated in terms of the disjunctions in (3).

(3) a. If the initial syllable of the output is heavy, then the word falls into the doubled-accent class.
   b. Otherwise, if the final syllable is heavy, the word falls into the final-accent class.
   c. Otherwise, the word falls into the penultimate class.

In terms of weight, the hierarchy of syllable rimes in (4) is relevant.

(4) $V: > VC_{son} > VC_{obstr} > V > V_{epen}$

7.3.1 Doubled versus Final Accent

Let us examine the first disjunction in (3)—competition between doubled and final accent—in terms of the weight hierarchy in (4). In (5), we show cases from the corpus where the initial vowel is long—all fall into the doubled-accent class. This is an invariant regularity: if the initial syllable contains a long vowel, then it always carries the doubled accent. This regularity accords with the generalization mentioned above that holds over the native lexicon as well.

(5) a. pí:nə́si   'Venus'
       ó:thó   'auto'
       pyú:thí   'beauty'
       ró:má   'Rome'
       yú:thóphia   'utopia'
    b. phéjphə́   'paper'
       péjpí   'baby'
    c. pá:kén   'bargain'
       thá:két   'target'
       phá:khíŋ   'parking'
       má:málleiti   'marmalade'
       ká:tín   'garden'

The source of the long vowel can be a tense vowel (5a), a diphthong (5b), or a long vowel arising from loss of preconsonantal /r/ (5c). Since in general final long vowels are avoided in our corpus (see below), there is no conflict between the doubled- and final-accent classes with respect to a long vowel.

A second, smaller subclass of doubled-accent words comprises items whose initial syllable is closed by a consonant—usually a sonorant. We sample these items in (6), arranged in terms of the weight of the final syllable. In (6a), the final syllable is closed by a sonorant; in (6b), it is closed by an obstruent; in (6c), it terminates in a vowel; and in (6d), it terminates in an epenthetic vowel.

(6) a. rə́ntə́n   'London'   amsitherídám   'Amsterdam'
       syámphéin   'champagne'   piltíŋ   'building'
       éncín   'engine'   khonthiról   'control'
       cénthílmen   'gentleman'
       héntíl   'handle'
       hə́nthíŋ   'hunting'
       réŋkhíŋ   'ranking'

séntál	'sandal'
phéntíum	'Pentium'
ménsyə́n	'mansion'

b. ínthə́net   'Internet'
   mémpə́sip   'membership'

c. ántánthe   'andante'
   khóntó   'condo'
   ínphílle   'inflation'
   símphóni   'symphony'

d. khə́mphékthɨ   'compact'
   áŋkhórɨ   'encore'

e. khépthín   'captain'   nepkhín   'napkin'
   phápsóŋ   'pop song'   khakthéjl   'cocktail'
   syópphíŋ   'shopping'
   syókkhíŋ   'shocking'

Here competition with the final-accent class is possible. When a tie occurs and both the initial and the final syllables are closed by a sonorant, initial accent predominates: our corpus has just the three items listed in (6a) ('Amsterdam', 'building', and 'control') where accent falls on the final syllable.

When the initial syllable is closed by an obstruent (6e), competition with final accent is greater (though the number of examples in our corpus is so small that it is unclear how much stock can be placed in this particular case): 'captain' and 'pop song' have doubled accent, while 'napkin' and 'cocktail' have final accent. Finally, when the initial syllable is open CV or epenthetic, the word never falls into the doubled class.

To summarize: The rule that words with an initial-syllable long vowel fall into the doubled-accent class is automatically extended to the adaptation data. The doubled-accent pattern is never applied to words with an initial light open syllable even though words with this accentual structure form a substantial part of the NK native lexicon. For example, N.-J. Kim (1997, 108–109) lists 80 monosyllabic words belonging to the doubled-accent class. Sixty of these contain a short vowel (e.g., *kí* 'ear', *kí-ká* nom.; *kót* 'place', *kós-í*, nom.), while only 20 have a long vowel (e.g., *mé:* 'falcon', *mé:-ká* nom.; *pé:m* 'snake', *pé:m-í* nom.). Thus, in terms of frequency, there are many more instantiations of the doubled accent in words with a short vowel. But this accent pattern is never extended to the adaptation data: only the pattern of the numerically smaller class of long-vowel stems

is. Why this discrepancy? The answer presumably is that accent is predictable for the long-vowel words. Given that the lexicon only records
unpredictable, distinctive information, the language learner is forced to
posit a rule (or constraint ranking in Optimality Theory (OT)) that will
assign an accent to long-vowel words. On the other hand, short-vowel
words bearing the doubled-accent pattern will have to be indicated lexically (the tonal analyses of Chung (1991) and N.-J. Kim (1997) posit a
floating high tone, while the accentual analysis of Idsardi and S.-H. Kim
(1997) proposes a metrical bracket) since they contrast in accent with
other short-vowel words: *múl, múl-i* 'water' versus *súl, súl-i* 'wine'. However, there is one aspect of the doubled-accent pattern that does not
directly reflect the grammar of NK. The rule assigning heavy initial syllables to the doubled class is extended down the weight hierarchy to include syllables closed by a sonorant (and some but not all cases of closure
by an obstruent). In the native lexicon, there is no evidence that such
CVR syllables are targeted by the doubled-accent pattern. For example,
disyllables with an initial CVR seem to be equally distributed across the
three accent types: initial (*páŋku* 'rock', *kímchi* 'pickled cabbage', *mánthe*
'net bag'), final (*tanchú* 'button', *nempí* 'pot', *kamcá* 'potato'), doubled
(*táncí* 'jug', *cáŋnán* 'joke', *nálké* 'wing'). The extension of the doubled
accent to CVR syllables thus appears to be an "emergent" phenomenon.[2]
Perhaps this phenomenon indicates that the default UG setting for the
weight of CVC syllables counts them as heavy.[3]

7.3.2 Final versus Penultimate Accent

We now turn to the competition between final and penultimate accent.
Languages in which accent is located in a two-syllable window at the right
edge of the word are quite common. They fall into two principal types:
languages such as Chukchee (Kenstowicz 1997) and Uyghur (Comrie
1997) where the final syllable is accented unless it is light and the penult is
heavy (LL', LH', H'L, HH') and languages such as Tahitian (Bickmore
1995) where the penult is stressed unless the final syllable is heavy (L'L,
LH', H'L, HH'). Let us examine the four possible combinations of light
and heavy syllables in the NK adaptation corpus to see which type better
matches our data.

   The vast majority of items in the final-accent class have a penultimate
light and a final closed syllable (as well as a light initial syllable that
exempts them from the doubled-accent pattern). We cite just a few examples in (7a). The number of words of this syllabic structure with penulti-

mate accent is much smaller. We list all those we have found in (7b). Some but not all (e.g., 'festival') tend to match the accent of the English source.

(7) a.   allatín   'Aladdin'
         pɨracíl   'Brazil'
         khepinét   'cabinet'
         kharamél   'caramel'
         ticithál   'digital'
         chenə́l   'channel'
         khɨllarinét   'clarinet'
         khecháp   'ketchup'
    b.   eərópik   'aerobic'
         éphɨl   'apple'
         otísyən   'audition'
         kháthɨn   'cotton'
         phesɨthípal   'festival'
         mécik   'magic'

Final long vowels are quite unusual in our corpus. This gap may reflect a constraint of the language (*papekhyú:* 'barbecue' is an isolated example and has the alternant *pá:pékhyu*). For example, compensatory lengthening from loss of coda [r] is blocked word-finally, as in *apsó:pa* 'absorber', *kharénta* 'calendar'. But the constraint against final long vowels may itself be trumped by minimality: monosyllables seem to systematically lengthen, as in *sɨphá:* 'spa', *sikhí:* 'ski', *sɨthá:* 'star'. If this conjecture is true, such lengthening would be another "emergence of the unmarked" phenomenon since words of the form CV are not uncommon in the native lexicon: *cí* 'rat', *pé* 'boat', *khó* 'nose'. Also, the epenthetic vowel apparently fails to make weight. More study of this point is clearly required.

When the penult is heavy and the final syllable is light, penultimate accent is regular.

(8)   orénci   'orange'
      théksi   'taxi'
      thémpho   'tempo'
      inphulluénca   'influenza'
      hellikhóptha   'helicopter'
      kharénta   'calendar'
      anaúnsə   'announcer'
      apsó:pa   'absorber'

We now turn to cases where the final and the penultimate syllables have the same weight. The number of items in our corpus in which both of the last two syllables are heavy is limited. Both the final-accent and the penultimate-accent patterns are represented.

(9) *Final*   *Penultimate*
    khakthéjl 'cocktail'   ollímphik   'Olympic'
    nepkhín   'napkin'   wasíŋthon   'Washington'
    khəmpék 'comeback'   éksyən   'action'
                            khonéksyən 'connection'
                            sɨkhéntal   'scandal'

When both the final and the penult are light CV, penultimate accent predominates. Some cases with final accent may be early loanwords from French that have been integrated into the native system (10b). In opposition to this handful of LL# adaptations with final accent, our corpus includes 26 cases with penultimate accent (10a).

(10) a. aphɨríkha   'Africa'
        ameríkha   'America'
        khelliphonía 'California'
        sikháko   'Chicago'
        kholloráto   'Colorado'
        phɨlloríta   'Florida'
        miccupísi   'Mitsubishi'
        aksesári   'accessory'
        sinéma   'cinema'
        khokhóa   'cocoa'
        khúkhi   'cookie'
        hwemíri   'family'
        héphi   'happy'
        hisɨthéri   'history'
        airóni   'irony'
        masɨkhára   'mascara'
        míni   'mini'
        misɨthéri   'mystery'
        phophúri   'potpourri'
        phothe.ítho 'potato'
        sophɨráno   'soprano'
        sɨphakéthi   'spaghetti'

thɨróphi	'trophy'
thəksíto	'tuxedo'
enə́ci	'energy'
purápo	'bravo'
b. pallé	'ballet'
pananá	'banana'
khamerá	'camera'
opherá	'opera'
khometí	'comedy'
phianó	'piano'
saikhó	'psycho'

The preponderance of penultimate accent for the LL# cases argues that NK has the bimoraic parse of languages like Tahitian. This agrees with the default status accorded to the penultimate-accent class in the native lexicon by N.-J. Kim (1997).

To summarize: When an adapted word does not fall into the doubled-accent class for lack of an initial heavy syllable, it is assigned a bimoraic foot at its right edge. The rule or constraint ranking introducing this accent is independently motivated in NK grammar by accentual alternations that arise when a polysyllabic suffix/enclitic is added to a noun stem with final accent. Also, as observed earlier, penultimate accent is invariably assigned to longer stems—stems of four or more syllables—where accent ceases to play a distinctive role. Although it may be non-distinctive here, every lexical item is nevertheless required to bear an accent for reasons of culminativity. The default accentuation thus emerges in such longer words that step out from under the control of a distinctive lexical accent. Given that the English inputs are perceived to lack an accentual specification, the default accent will be assigned by the NK grammar. As is well known, "tip of the tongue" and other psycholinguistic phenomena suggest that accent plays a role in lexical storage and retrieval (Cutler 1989). If experiments can be designed to detect lexical accent, it would be exceedingly interesting to bring them to bear on the accentuation of such "long words" as well as on the penultimate accent of shorter words like *káci* 'kind, sort' that contrast with final-accent and doubled-accent forms such as *kací* 'eggplant' and *ká:cí* 'branch'. N.-J. Kim (1997) derives the penultimate accents of both long and short words from inputs that lack an accent. But given that accent helps to distinguish short words (cf. *káci* 'sort, kind', *kací* 'eggplant'), we would not be surprised if this accent were in fact recorded in the lexicon. The issue is essentially one of radical versus contrastive underspecification; see Steriade 1995 for a recent review.

7.4 Additional Complications

In this section, we examine three factors that impinge on the basic accent principles that apply to NK adaptations: the behavior of liquids, the treatment of diphthongs, and epenthetic vowels.

7.4.1 Liquids

Korean has only one liquid phoneme, realized as a lateral in the coda and as a rhotic elsewhere. These phonotactic constraints give rise to regular alternations between [l] and [r]: *mál* 'horse', *már-i* nom. In our data, the adaptations of the English liquid phonemes /l/ and /r/ do not violate these constraints on the distribution of the allophones comprising the Korean liquid phoneme. But it is also clear that the adaptation is not simply a matter of identifying English /l/ and /r/ with the liquid phoneme of Korean and then redistributing the sounds in accord with Korean allophonic norms. Rather, in certain cases it appears that English /l/ and /r/ are matched with phones that fall outside the spectrum of the Korean liquid phoneme. The data are summarized in (11).

(11)

	/l/		/r/	
Initial	ra.ín	'line'	ra.ísɨ	'rice'
	ré:cə́	'leisure'	ró:.yálthi	'royalty'
Final	séntál	'sandal'	ó:nə́	'owner'
	hosɨthél	'hostel'	meníce	'manager'
Preconsonantal	piltíŋ	'building'	pá:kén	'bargain'
Intervocalic	céri	'jelly'	a.iróni	'irony'
	célli			
	phɨlloríta	'Florida'	phɨráŋsɨ	'France'

Initial /l/ is systematically realized as [r]: compare *ra.ín* 'line' and *ré:cə́* 'leisure'. The adaptation of English /l/ makes one maneuver in order to remain faithful to the source language but still respect NK phonotactics: intervocalic /l/ is often preserved by gemination (cf. *phaillóthi* 'pilot', *pɨllaínti* 'blind', *kɨllə́pɨ* 'glove' and *céri* ≈ *célli* 'jelly', *kɨrásɨ* ≈ *kɨllásɨ* 'glass'). It is interesting that the closed syllable resulting from liquid gemination does not contribute to weight. There are no cases in our corpus in which a word is assigned to the doubled-accent class in virtue of its initial syllable being closed by a geminate [ll]. All words of this structure have final (*khallə́m* 'column', *halloké́n* 'halogen, *sillikhó́n* 'silicon', *allatín* 'Aladdin') or penultimate (*ollímphik* 'Olympic', *kholloráto* 'Colorado') accent. On the other hand, coda [l] counts as heavy for the final-accent class, as expected (*ticithál* 'digital', *isiraél* 'Israel', *piracíl* 'Brazil', *phisithól* 'pistol'). There is thus a mismatch between the phonotactically and prosodically motivated syllabifications: the closed syllable arising from gemination of the intervocalic lateral does not count for weight.

When the English source word has a rhotic in a closed syllable, it is realized as lengthening of the preceding vowel. This length normally counts for weight in the assignment of the doubled accent: *pá:kén* 'bargain', *khá:ti* 'card', *ká:tin* 'garden', *há:móni* 'harmony', *má:kárin* 'margarine' versus *pə́:ti* 'birdie' (golf). A few items have doublets: 'mark' belongs to either the doubled (*má:khi*) or the penultimate (*má:khi*) class; in 'carpet' when the /r/ is realized as length the accent is doubled (*khá:pét*), otherwise it is penultimate (*khaphéthi*). These data indicate that to Korean ears, English coda /r/ (an approximate) sounds closer to zero than to /l/. Given the absence of falling-sonority diphthongs in the language, a glide-like realization is precluded, making zero the closest option. This interpretation is supported by the few examples in our corpus of coda rhotics from other languages with different, more salient realizations. They are realized as onset [r]: *raríko* 'largo', *perisaíyu* 'Versailles', *koripachóphi* 'Gorbachev'. In the light of the "phonemic"-level adaptation of French liquids into Arabic reported in Paradis and LaCharité 1997, the matter clearly merits further study.

One final point. In NK, a long vowel occurs only under accent; in cases where coda /r/ deletes but accent falls elsewhere, the syllable is realized with a short vowel. Thus, in *khalliphonía* 'California', there is no lengthening by /r/ since it appears neither in the initial syllable nor inside the disyllabic window at the right edge of the word; compare the length in *sikhá:phi* 'scarf' and *sikhə́:thi* 'skirt', where penultimate accent may reach the syllable with an underlying /r/.

7.4.2 Diphthongs
Korean lacks falling-sonority diphthongs with an off-glide (except possibly for [ij]). In general, English diphthongs of this structure are realized as two separate syllabic nuclei. The normal accent assignment then takes place. We illustrate first with [ai], [au], and [oi] diphthongs.

(12) a.i.ró.ni   'irony'
     ma.i.ná.sɨ   'minus'
     ra.i.ón   'lion'
     ma.í.khɨ   'mike'
     ma.ú.sɨ   'mouse'
     o.íl   'oil'

An exception is the diphthong [ej]. In many cases, it is realized as a diphthong in our data (in which case it counts as a long vowel for the doubled-accent pattern); in other cases, it is treated heterosyllabically.

(13) péj.pí   'baby'   che.ín.ci   'change'
     théj.pɨl   'table'   te.í.thɨ   'date'
     phéj.phɔ́   'paper'
     khéj.pɨl   'cable'
     khe.í.pɨl

7.4.3 Epenthetic Vowel

Next, we turn to the epenthetic vowel. It is well known that epenthetic vowels often shun accent (Broselow 1982) but may count for defining a disyllabic window (Alderete, to appear; Shinohara 1997a,b, 2000). Let us survey the NK adaptation data with this phenomenon in mind. First, the maximal syllable template in Korean is CVC—the language scrupulously avoids complex onsets or codas. Initial and final clusters are broken with epenthetic vowels. Furthermore, there are rigid restrictions on codas: in the adaptation process, these coda conditions may force a preconsonantal or word-final consonant that would otherwise enter the coda into the onset by epenthesis, where it can be pronounced. For example, coda consonants are unreleased and exclude a [+continuant] (C.-W. Kim 1970). Thus, underlying /s/ is realized as a stop [t]: /nas/ *nát* 'sickle', but *nás-il* acc. In order to preserve the [+continuant] of the source word, foreign words ending in [s] are systematically adapted with an epenthetic vowel: *cú:sɨ* 'juice', *kɨrásɨ* 'glass', *pósɨ* 'boss'.

An epenthetic vowel occupying the initial syllable never takes the accent. But in order to know whether it is actively avoided by the accent, we need to make it the target of penultimate accent. (It can't be the target of the doubled accent since it is not long.) But to make this test, the final syllable must be light. Unfortunately, because of the minimality phenomenon, words such as 'ski', 'spa', and 'star' have a final long vowel that takes the accent: *sɨkhí:*, *sɨphá:*, *sɨthá:*. Thus, we cannot tell if initial-syllable epenthetic vowels avoid the accent on purpose. In any case, they do count for licensing the doubled accent because a long vowel that would otherwise willingly enter the doubled class cannot do so when it is displaced from the left edge of the word by epenthesis: compare *kirí:si* 'Greece' with *ré:cə́* 'leisure'.

A final epenthetic vowel never takes the accent, but it may serve as the second member of the doubled accent when the first syllable is long (14a); a medial epenthetic vowel behaves the same way (14b).

(14) a. cú:sɨ   'juice'
        kó:ltɨ   'gold'
        khá:tɨ   'card'
        wɔ́:ltɨ   'world'
     b. sɔ́ŋkɨrasɨ   'sunglasses'
        ó:síthɨria   'Austria'

Consequently, if the doubled accent is the product of a rule or constraint associating a [HH] pitch accent from the left edge of the word with an initial-syllable long vowel, then epenthesis must apply prior to this process for two reasons: it displaces a long vowel from the left edge of the word (*kirí:si* 'Greece') and it supplies a vowel that may carry the second high tone (*cú:sɨ* 'juice').

Finally, there are cases of a medial cluster where the penultimate vowel is epenthetic. Here we find mixed behavior. In some cases, the accent fails to land on the epenthetic vowel and targets the final vowel instead (15a); but in others, the epenthetic vowel is accented (15b). We suspect that many of the latter are older loanwords that have been more fully integrated into the system. Their vowel may no longer be treated as inserted and hence they naturally take penultimate accent.

(15) a. nikɨró   'negro'
        methɨró   'metro'
     b. allekɨro   'allegro'
        kharisɨma   'charisma'
        pakɨna   'Wagner'
        kɨrisɨto   'Christ'

If more cases like (15a) can be identified, then we will apparently have the phenomenon identified by Shinohara (1997a,b, 2000) for Japanese adaptations where an epenthetic vowel counts for defining the disyllabic window necessary for accent but itself repels the pitch peak. Further study of this point is clearly necessary.

An additional complication is presented by cases in which the foreign source ends in an /st/ or /ft/ cluster (16).

(16) thósithi   'toast'
       pésithi   'best'
       réphithi   'left'
       théksithi   'text'
       kíphithi   'gift'
       phásithi   'first'

Here two vowels are inserted: one to realize the fricative in an onset and the other to realize the following stop. In this case, the accent rejects both epenthetic vowels and shifts leftward outside the final disyllabic window in order to find an underlying vowel. This suggests that while epenthetic vowels count for determining the window in which accent is realized, they are avoided as bearers of accent in favor of underlying vowels—a phenomenon more robustly attested in Japanese adaptations.

In sum, our data conform to Shinohara's (1997a) and Steriade's (1999) hypothesis that as a repair strategy, epenthesis typically chooses the vowel from the phonemic inventory that is perceptually least salient. The principle of minimal saliency explains why epenthetic vowels (employed in adaptations) are typically those with the shortest duration and most overlap of other vowels in acoustic space. This holds for Japanese (Keating and Huffman 1984) and presumably for Korean as well. The principle also explains why epenthetic vowels tend to coarticulate with adjacent (especially preceding) consonants rather than augmenting syntagmatic contrasts: witness *pí:chí* 'beach' and *pirá[ši]* 'brush' with epenthetic [i] after palatals. It also seems clear that accent increases the saliency of a vowel and hence is incompatible with epenthesis. Finally, we observed two cases of epenthesis that do not contribute to prosodic weight and hence also conform to the principle of minimal saliency. First, the epenthetic vowel breaking initial *s*C clusters in monosyllables fails to suppress lengthening of final vowels to satisfy minimality: *sikhí:* 'ski'. Second, the closed syllable that arises from the gemination of laterals does not count as heavy for the doubled-accent assignment: *khallám* 'column'.

7.5 Role of the Citation Form

Kenstowicz (1996) calls attention to asymmetries in the phonology of nominal versus verbal forms in Korean. In particular, nominal stems ending in a cluster are being reanalyzed by the younger generation of Korean speakers as terminating in a single consonant (*tak* 'chicken', *tak-i* < *talk-i* nom.) while verb stems exhibit no tendency to restructure (cf. *palk-ass-ə* 'was bright'). The different phonological behavior of nouns and verbs is to be traced to the morphology of Korean. Nouns may occur in isolation without a Case marker, in the citation form; they may also omit structural Case markers in the sentence under poorly understood conditions. When they do so, they are subject to various phonological neutralizations that bring them in line with the language's CVC maximal syllable template. The phonological simplifications in inflection such as *tak-i* < *talk-i* nom. arise from analogizing the inflected form to the citation form of the noun for various structural properties—an effect dubbed "base-identity" and conceived of as an output-output faithfulness constraint active in the grammar (as opposed to a principle of the learning system formally unconnected to the computation of input-output mappings). Verb roots do not behave in the same way because they require an inflection and hence are not subject to the neutralizing effects arising in the bare citation form. Owing to this difference in the morphology, gross disparities are being introduced into the phonological structure of noun versus verb roots. In the traditional generative model, the only tool available for expressing systematic relations between one word and another is the phonological cycle. But in this case, the cycle is of no use because there is no motivated way in which the root can anticipate whether or not it will occur without a suffix. Consequently, no formal connection can be drawn between differences in the shape of noun versus verb roots and the parallel difference in morphological structure. Kang (1992) documents additional nominal versus verbal disparities of this form. See also Lee 1999 for recent discussion.

7.5.1 Accentual Alternations

In our accentual data, there are a couple of circumstances in which alternation is eliminated in order to remain faithful to the citation form. To understand their significance, we must consider them in the light of accentual alternations occurring in the native system. The latter are usefully tabulated in terms of the three categories nonfinal, final (oxytone), and doubled accent.

(17) *Nonfinal*   *Final*

núna	'older sister'	toŋséŋ	'younger sibling'
mánɨl	'garlic'	namúl	'vegetable'
nára	'country'	yurí	'glass'
mə́ri	'head'	namú	'tree'

Doubled
óppá   'older brother'
kɨrím   'picture'
á:nkyɔ́ŋ   'eyeglasses'

The data in (18) show the accentual alternations that arise when words from the various accentual categories are combined into phonological phrases (for recent discussion of Korean phrasal accent, see Kenstowicz and Sohn 1997; N.-J. Kim 1997; S.-H. Kim 1999). We mark the locus of the phrasal accent with underlining. Lexically accented syllables that do not fall under the phrasal accent have small F0 perturbations that speakers are normally unaware of (Kenstowicz and Sohn 1997). The phrasal peak extends over both components of the double accent.

(18) n<u>ú</u>na mánɨl   'sister's garlic'
      n<u>ú</u>na namúl   'sister's vegetable'
      n<u>ú</u>na kɨrím   'sister's picture'

      <u>óppá</u> mánɨl   'older brother's garlic'
      <u>óppá</u> namúl   'older brother's vegetable'
      <u>óppá</u> kɨrím   'older brother's picture'

      toŋséŋ m<u>á</u>nɨl   'younger sibling's garlic'
      toŋséŋ nam<u>ú</u>l   'younger sibling's vegetable'
      toŋs<u>é</u>ŋ kɨrím   'younger sibling's picture'

In general, the accent of the phrase (line-2 grid mark) is projected from the first member of the phrase (in OT terms, LEFTMOST ≫ RIGHTMOST). But words such as *toŋséŋ* 'younger sibling' with final accent in their bare form yield the phrasal accent to the following member of the phrase: *toŋséŋ m<u>á</u>nɨl* 'younger sibling's garlic', *toŋséŋ nam<u>ú</u>l* 'younger sibling's vegetable'. In other words, a word-final phrase accent is only licensed at the right edge of the accentual phrase. From a crosslinguistic perspective, we might make better sense of this alternation as follows (Kenstowicz and Sohn 1997). In pitch accent systems such as NK, the locus of accent is cued by a drop in pitch (phonologized as a [IIL] pitch accent). A word-final (monomoraic) syllable is not the optimal site to realize such an accent (recall that Japanese speakers fail to interpret French words as having a final accent). We will assume here that this phenomenon can be subsumed under the familiar NONFINALITY constraint of Prince and Smolensky (1993) that bars word-final accent but that NONFINALITY is overridden before a stronger prosodic boundary where juncture lengthening adds a (silent) beat (Selkirk 1984), rendering the accent nonfinal.[4]

(See Côté, to appear, for discussion of such boundary effects.) The following tableaux indicate the intended analysis. The x denotes the phrase-final juncture beat.

(19) a.

/núna mánɨl/	LEFTMOST	RIGHTMOST
☞ nú̲na mánɨl x		*
núna má̲nɨl x	*!	

b.

/toŋséŋ mánɨl/	NONFINALITY	LEFTMOST
toŋsé̲ŋ mánɨl x	*!	
☞ toŋséŋ má̲nɨl x		*

c.

/toŋséŋ namúl/	NONFINALITY	LEFTMOST
toŋsé̲ŋ namúl x	*!	
☞ toŋséŋ namú̲l x		*

There is one exception to the avoidance of word-final phrase-medial accent, however. When the following word in the phrase belongs to the doubled-accent class, it throws the phrasal accent back to a preceding oxytone: *toŋsé̲ŋ kɨrím* 'younger sibling's picture'. We see this alternation as a clash resolution strategy invoked when a final accent is followed by the doubled accent. There are various ways in which the resolution can be expressed depending on how the doubled accent is represented. For concreteness, we will assume here that it is a [HH] pitch accent. Nonfinal pitch accents on words such as *mánɨl* 'garlic' are [HL], while the pitch accent associated with a phrase-medial oxytone such as *namúl* 'vegetable' is just [H] (Kenstowicz and Sohn 1997). The combination of an oxytone plus a doubled accent thus creates three successive Hs. Evidently, the clashing H#HH is resolved by switching the second H to L with repulsion of the phrasal prominence. The intended analysis is sketched in (20).

(20)

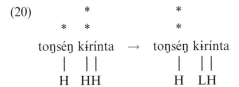

The alternations in (18) are the by-products of a complex diachronic evolution (Ramsey 1975). In general, the locus of accent retracted one syllable in the evolution of NK from Middle Korean (MK). The South Hamkyung (SH) dialect of North Korea more faithfully reflects the original place of accent: compare SH *kamakwí* 'raven', *atíl* 'son', and *kamúlchi* 'mullet' with NK *kamákwi*, *átɨl*, and *kámulchi*. Accent retraction should have merged the distinction between original initial σ'σσ ... and peninitial σσ'σ ... accent. However, the contrast was preserved by assigning the former class of words to the doubled-accent category: compare SH *móki* 'mosquito' and *tókkepi* 'spirit' with NK *mókí*, *tókképi*. The doubled accent, which is an innovation of NK, had an independent development form initial long vowels: compare NK *sá:rám* 'person' with (conservative) Seoul *sa:ram*. The latter is the source of the synchronic NK implicational relation between length and the doubled accent. Finally, the NK oxytones correspond to MK unaccented forms. Being unaccented, they naturally escaped accent retraction. Our synchronic analysis outlined above rests on the assumption that there has been considerable restructuring of the diachronic source grammar.

7.5.2 Accentual Stability

We now turn to the behavior of accentual adaptations with respect to the system just outlined. In general, adapted forms behave parallel to native ones—with two interesting exceptions.

First, final-accented words in our corpus systematically fail to shift their accent to the right in the phrase;[5] compare the forms in (21b) with those in (21a). This phenomenon was observed independently by M. Kim (1997).

(21) a. kharamél   'caramel'
         kharamér-i   nom.
         kharamél#cócha   'even a caramel'
         kharamél məknɨnta   'eats caramel'

         pél   'bell'
         pér-i   nom.
         pél#cócha   'even a bell'
         pél sóri   'bell's sound'
                                     (cf. sóri 'sound')

         allatín   'Aladdin'
         allatín-i   nom.
         allatín#meŋkúro   'like Aladdin'
         allatín núna   'Aladdin's sister'

b. namúl   'vegetable'
   namúr-i   nom.
   namúl#cócha   'even a vegetable'
   namúl məkní̱nta   'eats vegetable'

   súl   'wine'
   súr-i   nom.
   súl#cócha   'even wine'
   súl#cíp   'wine house'
                             (cf. cíp 'house')

   toŋséŋ   'younger sibling'
   toŋséŋ-i   nom.
   toŋséŋ#meŋkú̱ro   'like younger sibling'
   toŋséŋ nú̱na   'younger sibling's sister'

In order to explain this phenomenon, we speculate that in the process of adaptation, the citation form has a special status as the gateway through which lexical items enter the native system. In effect, the NK grammar cannot parse English sentences to extract English words. Foreign words can only enter the NK system if they are preparsed in the citation form. If this point is granted, then the otherwise peculiar behavior of the adapted forms in (21) begins to make some sense. In the case of the oxytones, we recall that they were claimed to escape NONFINALITY at the end of the phonological phrase in virtue of the junctural beat that renders them nonfinal. The citation form is a phonological phrase unto itself and so can be expected to inherit characteristics of phrase-terminal position. The citation form lacks Case marking and the copular verb is normally omitted as well, so that the noun stem appears flush against the edge of the phrase. We suggest that an output-output faithfulness constraint analogizing adaptations with respect to the junctural beat buffers the accent of *kharamél* from the end of the word, allowing it to satisfy NONFINALITY. In effect, it passes into the nonfinal-accent class of (17a). If two adaptations with final accent form a phrase, then lower-ranked LEFTMOST ≫ RIGHTMOST selects the candidate with initial accent: *allatí̱n kharamél* 'Aladdin's caramel'. The tableau in (22) indicates the intended analysis.

(22)	/pél sóri/	BASE-IDENTITY	NONFINALITY	LEFTMOST
☞ pé̱l x sóri x				
pél só̱ri x	*!			*

The second case in which the base-identity phenomenon affects accentual adaptations concerns the doubled-accent pattern. We first examine the phrasal behavior of native items in this category and then look at adaptations.

In the native NK system, monosyllables readily populate the doubled-accent class, which, as noted earlier, contains specimens with both long and short syllables. They regularly realize their second tone on the following syllable in the phrase, be that an inflection, an enclitic, or another freestanding word.

(23) tó:n   'money'
      tó:n-í   nom.
      tó:n#méŋkúro   'like money'
      tó:n cúntá   'give money'
                        (cf. cúntá 'give')

      má:l   'word'
      má:l-í   nom.
      má:l#póta   'than a word'
      má:l hántá   'make word (speak)'
                        (cf. hántá 'make')

      múl   'water'
      múr-í   nom.
      múl#méŋkúro   'like water'
      múl məknínta   'consumes water'
                        (cf. məknínta 'eats')

      són   'hand'
      són-í   nom.
      són#póta   'than a hand'
      són cápnínta   'hold hands'
                        (cf. capnínta 'holds')

Several other tonal processes diagnose nouns in the doubled pattern. The most interesting is the accent shift from oxytones mentioned earlier. As we noted, it is suspended before a doubled accent—both polysyllabic ones such as kírím 'picture' (which display their doubled accent overtly) and monosyllabic ones such as tó:n 'money' and múl 'water' (which display their doubled accent covertly).

(24) toŋsɛ́ŋ kɨrím   'younger sibling's picture'
                       (cf. kɨrím 'picture')
     toŋsɛ́ŋ tón   'younger sibling's money'
                       (cf. tó:n-í 'money')
     toŋsɛ́ŋ múl   'younger sibling's water'
                       (cf. múr-í 'water')
cf. toŋsɛ́ŋ súl   'younger sibling's wine'
                       (cf. súr-i 'wine')

The behavior of doubled-accent monosyllables such as *tó:n* 'money' and *múl* 'water' in (24) is puzzling. If we are correct that the retraction of the phrasal accent to the oxytone in *toŋsɛ́ŋ kɨrím* 'younger sibling's picture' is due to the deletion of the second of three successive H pitch accents (recall (20)), then how can a monosyllable contribute two accents? One possibility is that the silent beat posited at the end of the phonological phrase supports the floating accent. However, we prefer to see this as a parallelism effect. In all other contexts, *tó:n* and *múl* display two accents and hence create the clashing environment H#HH when preceded by an oxytone. Evidently, this property is carried over to phrase-final position by analogy—a uniformity effect discussed under the label of metrical consistency by Burzio (1994), paradigm uniformity by Flemming (1995), uniform exponence by Kenstowicz (1996), and lexical conservatism by Steriade (1998).

Let us now consider how adaptations fare with respect to these native patterns for the doubled accent. Adaptations with an overt doubled accent behave in totally parallel fashion, blocking the shift of accent from an oxytone by clash resolution: H#HH → H#LH. (Long vowels are only realized in the initial syllable of the phonological phrase, hence the shortening of *ó:thó* 'car' in *toŋsɛ́ŋ óthó* 'younger sibling's car'.)

(25) toŋsɛ́ŋ khóntó   'younger sibling's condo'
                       (cf. khóntó 'condominium')
     toŋsɛ́ŋ péjpí   'younger sibling's baby'
                       (cf. péjpí 'baby')
     toŋsɛ́ŋ óthó   'younger sibling's car'
                       (cf. ó:thó 'car')

But adapted monosyllables with a long vowel systematically fail to double their accent before an inflection or in the phrase.

(26) thí:m   'team'
     thí:m-i   nom.
     thí:m≠meŋkúro   'like a team'
     thí:m mantínta   'make a team'

     thí:p   'tip'
     thí:p-i   nom.
     thí:p≠meŋkúro   'like a tip'
     thí:p cúntá   'give a tip'

     pú:m   'boom'
     pú:m-i   nom.
     pú:m≠meŋkúro   'like a boom'
     pú:m mantínta   'create a boom'

This behavior suggests that *thí:m* belongs to the single-accent class of *cíp* 'house' and *pél* 'bell' discussed earlier despite the long vowel that should otherwise place it in the doubled-accent class of *tó:n* 'money'. This interpretation is confirmed by the failure of these words to repel the accent of an oxytone (27a).

(27) a. toŋséŋ thím   'younger sibling's team'
        yəŋhwá púm   'movie boom'
                          (cf. yəŋhwá 'movie')
     b. toŋséŋ cíp   'younger sibling's house'
     c. toŋséŋ tón   'younger sibling's money'
        toŋséŋ múl   'younger sibling's water'

Why should *thí:m* 'team' be assigned to the *cíp* 'house' class in spite of the long vowel that should otherwise place it in the doubled-accent class of *tó:n* 'money'? If the monosyllables *tó:n* and *múl* display the "covert" double accent by analogy to their phrase-internal form (the uniformity phenomenon), as proposed above, then adaptations can be expected to behave differently precisely because they lack a phrase-internal counterpart (at least on initial exposure) and so there is no overt double accent for them to be faithful to. So long as Uniformity dominates the constraint that assigns a doubled accent to an initial-syllable long vowel, *thí:m* will be adapted with a single accent H and hence display the behavior of *cíp* 'house' and *pél* 'bell'.

To summarize the results of this section: While in general foreign adaptations are well integrated into the NK accent system, we have examined two situations in which the accentuation of the adapted form fails to follow the patterns expected on the basis of the native system. Both seem to involve the analogical influence of the citation form of a noun on its accentual shape under inflection, cliticization, or phrasal complementation. In the case of *kharamél* 'caramel', the phrase-medial form mimics the silent beat of the phrase-final form, rendering the accent nonfinal. In the case of *thí:m* 'team', the otherwise regular uniformity effect that supplies a double accent to a final monosyllable on the basis of its phrase-medial form is inapplicable because for adaptations, the phrase-medial forms are faithful to the citation form and not vice versa.

An alternative interpretation of these facts attributes the special behavior of *thí:m* 'team' and *kharamél* 'caramel' to their underlying representation. On this scenario, the speaker will posit the covert double accent for a monosyllable like *thí:m* only if there is direct support from a paradigmatically related form. Since this evidence is lacking in the case of "on-line" adaptations, the underlying form is taken at face value from the citation form, contravening the otherwise unviolated phonotactic constraint that long initial syllables have the doubled accent. In order to extend this line of reasoning (essentially Kiparsky's (1968) well-known Alternation Condition) to oxytones, we might treat this class as underlyingly unaccented (following the apparent Middle Korean source). The idea would then be that in the face of a final accent, the speaker has two choices: take it as underlyingly unaccented (whence, on this analysis, the apparent shift of accent in inflection) or treat it as accented. The former analysis requires a departure from the surface shape of the citation form and hence, on this scenario, is only motivated by positive evidence from alternations in inflection. But one again such evidence is precisely what is missing from the adaptation situation; hence, *kharamél* is taken at face value and treated as accented.

While we believe that this line of reasoning has some merit, it fails to provide a general account of the adaptation situation. In the next section, we examine two cases from the segmental phonology of Korean adaptations that are problematic for this point of view.

7.6   The Adaptation of Stops

In the adaptation of English words, the voiced versus voiceless contrast in stops is treated as a plain versus aspirated distinction in Korean: *pə́si* 'bus' versus *phési* 'pass'. Korean stops contrast for [±aspiration]; unaspirated stops are regularly voiced in intersonorant position (though native speakers are normally unaware of this allophonic change). The opposition for aspiration is neutralized in syllable codas, which are unreleased (C.-W. Kim's (1970) "principle of closure"): *íp*, *í[b]-i* 'mouth' but *áp*, *áph-i* 'inside'. When faced with an English word ending in a stop, the Korean speaker has two options. The [±voice] opposition can be preserved and expressed as [±aspiration] by placing the stop in the onset of an epenthetic syllable. Alternatively, the gross syllabic profile of the source word can be maintained at the cost of neutralizing the voicing distinction. For many words, both options are available; for others, the choice seems to be lexicalized in favor of one option or the other.[6]

(28) *Citation form*   *Nominative*
    khe.í.khɨ   khe.í.khɨ-ka, *khe.í.ki-ka   'cake'
    khe.ík   khe.í.k-i, *khe.í.kh-i   'cake'
    thók   thók-i, *thókɨ-ka, *thókh-i 'talk'
    mə́kɨ   mə́kɨ-ka, *mə́k-i   'mug'

The significant point for our purposes is the following. Once a choice has been made for the citation form, the inflected and phrasal forms must follow suit. Thus, given *thók* 'talk', aspiration may not be restored in **thókh-i* or **thókhɨ-ka*. And given *mə́kɨ* 'mug', the inflected form must be faithful to the bare form and retain the epenthetic vowel: *mə́kɨ-ka*, **mə́k-i*. Finally, in adaptations such as 'cake' that allow both options, a mixed form that lacks the epenthetic vowel but restores the aspiration is judged as sharply ungrammatical: **khe.í.kh-i*.

In this case, appeal to a learning strategy requiring positive evidence from alternations to justify an underlying representation that departs from the surface citation form is inadequate as an explanation for the base-identity effect. While positive evidence from alternation might be required in order to assign the doubled accent to *thí:m* 'team', as described above, the Korean speaker adapting 'cake' clearly already knows that the final stop is voiceless—equated with aspiration. Nevertheless, it can only be realized, via the citation form, in the onset of an epenthetic syllable; and it is this realization that is the basis for extension to inflection and phrasal modification via BASE-IDENTITY.

A second case in which taking the isolation form as equivalent to the input fails to provide the proper coverage concerns nouns that end in a coronal stop. Like the standard Seoul dialect, NK contrasts coronal stops and affricates for glottalization and aspiration. As mentioned earlier, coda consonants in Korean are unreleased, leading to neutralization of laryngeal distinctions as well as change of the continuant [s] to [t].

(29)   *Citation*
                        form   *Accusative*
  /nac/   nát   nác-íl   'daylight'
  /nach/   nát   nách-íl   'face'
  /nas/   nát   nás-íl   'sickle'
  /muth/   mút   múth-il   'earth'

There is an interesting gap in the lexicon with respect to this neutralization: while verbal and adjectival stems ending in /t/ abound (*mit-* 'believe, *tot-* 'rise', *kut-* 'harden'), there are no noun stems whose input form ends in /t/. Stated differently, we know of no Korean noun that ends in [t] in the isolation form and that remains unchanged (except for allophonic voicing) before a vowel-initial inflection.

The absence of nonalternating [t]-final noun stems is unusual. [t] is the unmarked coronal obstruent and hence should be selected before a marked one is. Furthermore, according to the Alternation Condition (Kiparsky 1968), in conditions of neutralization when the inflected form is not known or remembered, the surface form is normally taken at face value and becomes the basis for the underlying representation. One might conclude that the absence of noun stems ending in /t/ reflects an accident of the history of the language that is of no synchronic significance. If this is so, then we have every reason to expect that when nouns are adapted into Korean, stems ending in [t] should readily fill this lexical gap. The surprise is that this is not what happens. Adapted forms respect this restriction on the lexicon too.

(30) *Citation form*   *Nominative*
     khéthi, khét   khéthi-ka, khés-i   'cat'
     thikhéthi, thikhét   thikhéthi-ka, thikhés-i   'ticket'
     phaillóthi, phaillót   phaillóthi-ka, phaillós-i 'pilot'
     sínpáti, sínpát   sínpáti-ka, sínpás-i   'Sinbad'
     halliúti, halliút   halliúthi-ka, halliús-i   'Hollywood'

In these adaptations, the laryngeal features of the final dental stop either are preserved in the onset of an epenthetic vowel (*khéthi*) or are neutralized in order to remain faithful to the gross syllabic profile of the English source (*khét*). When the latter path is chosen, the corresponding inflected form must end in [s]: *khét* (citation), *khét-i* (nom.), *khét-e* (dat.) is strongly rejected as a possible noun inflection. The otherwise peculiar but systematic change of [t] to [s] found in the adaptation of foreign words ending in [t] and [d] in (30) now makes sense if the gap in the native lexicon noted above (no noun stems ending in /t/) is also imposed on adapted forms. Given that /t/ is barred from the input, the closest related sound is substituted: evidently, /s/ is chosen over the affricate /c/ or aspirated /th/ on grounds of markedness. Once again, the Alternation Condition is not respected. It remains to be seen whether the ban on nominal stems ending in /t/ can also be explained in terms of the influence of the citation form. We leave this as a task for future research. See Sohn 1999 for discussion.

7.7 Summary

In this chapter, we have examined adaptations that foreign words (principally of English origin) experience when they are integrated into the lexicon of North Kyungsang (NK) Korean. Our discussion concentrated on changes in accentuation. Two major patterns were distinguished: adaptations in which the initial syllable of the output is heavy (long vowel or closed syllable) are assigned the doubled-accent pattern in which the first two syllables carry a pitch peak. The long-vowel cases conform to a systematic generalization of NK grammar, while the extension to closed syllables is an emergent property that may reflect the UG default status of closed syllables as heavy. Remaining words are assigned a bimoraic trochaic foot at their right edge. Here as well, closed syllables count as heavy (in contrast to NK grammar). As in Japanese, the bimoraic foot at the right edge of the word is the default accent assigned in NK grammar when the word lacks a lexical accent (stems of four or more syllables and enclitics). The discussion then shifted to several factors that impinge on the accent of adapted words: the treatment of liquids, diphthongs, and epenthetic vowels. Next, we considered the special status of the citation form in constraining the accentuation of adapted nominals. Oxytones and monosyllables containing a long vowel fail to alternate in the manner of native words, contravening otherwise exceptionless generalizations. Two explanations were considered: an output-output faithfulness constraint (Base-Identity) analogizing the inflected form to the citation form and Kiparsky's (1968) Alternation Condition requiring the underlying input form to mimic the surface form in the absence of alternations. Finally, we considered the adaptation of final stops in the light of these two proposals. Even though the speaker knows that the adapted form ends in a voiceless aspirated stop in the English source, this sound is barred from surfacing in inflection. This makes sense under an output-output faithfulness constraint but is inexplicable in terms of a constraint on the selection of the input form. In the case of nouns adapted with a final [t] in the citation form, it was found that they systematically alternate with [s] in inflection and thereby conform to a gap in the lexicon: no nominal stems terminating in /t/. This is a striking violation of the spirit of the Alternation Condition. It is unclear whether it makes sense in terms of base-identity, an issue that was left as a challenge for future research.

Finally, a word of caution is in order. The results reported here are preliminary: the study is based on a corpus of 600 items. Further data collection is needed to corroborate our findings and to tie up loose ends. We hope this study will encourage more phonologists to begin investigating adaptations; they provide a potentially rich source of evidence on the language-specific and UG determinants of phonological form. See Paradis and LaCharité 1997 and Paradis and Prunet 2000 for recent discussion of loanword phonology from this perspective.

Notes

We thank Sang-Cheol Ahn, Yoonjung Kang, Sun-Hoi Kim, Shigeko Shinohara, and Cheryl Zoll for helpful comments. The first author has many fond memories of teaching the MIT Field Methods course 24.942 with Ken Hale. One of the most successful classes (1995) was on Korean and stimulated us to begin working on Korean accent. We are especially pleased to be able to offer this chapter in tribute to our esteemed colleague.

1. The second author assigns 'guitar' and token' to the doubled-accent class: *khí:thá, thó:khín*.

2. See Shinohara 1997a,b, 2000, for other examples of such "emergence of the unmarked" effects (McCarthy and Prince 1994) in adaptations and Broselow, Chen, and Wang 1998 for examples from second language acquisition.

3. See Rosenthall and Van der Hulst 1999 for a recent OT proposal on how to represent the weight of CVC syllables.

4. Monosyllabic case suffixes and enclitics preserve accent on the stem, while polysyllabic ones generally attract the accent from the stem: compare *satalí* 'ladder', *satalí-ka* nom., *satalí-təl* pl. with *satali-meŋkúro* 'like a ladder', *satali-potá:* 'than a ladder'. There are additional complexities, discussed in N.-J. Kim 1997, 80–93. We will assume here that the monosyllabic particles are incorporated into the prosodic domain of the stem, rendering the stem's accent nonfinal.

5. The words in (10b) such as *pallé* 'ballet' ending in an accented vowel do shift their accent and hence contrast with cases like *nikɨró* 'negro' and *methɨró* 'metro'

where accent is stable. This contrast supports the idea that the former have been nativized and are no longer recognized as loans.

6. The nominative case suffix has two allomorphs: -*ka* after a stem ending in a vowel and -*i* after a stem ending in a consonant.

References

Ahn, Sang-Cheol. 1998. *An introduction to Korean phonology*. Seoul: Hanshin.

Alderete, John. To appear. Head-dependence in stress-epenthesis interaction. In Ben Hermans and Marc van Oostendorp, eds., *The derivational residue in phonology*. Amsterdam: John Benjamins.

Bickmore, Lee. 1995. Refining and formalizing the Tahitian stress placement algorithm. *Oceanic Linguistics* 34, 410–442.

Broselow, Ellen. 1982. On predicting the interaction of stress and epenthesis. *Glossa* 16, 115–132.

Broselow, Ellen, Su-I. Chen, and Chiling Wang. 1998. The emergence of the unmarked in second language phonology. *Studies in Second Language Acquisition* 20, 261–280.

Burzio, Luigi. 1994. *Principles of English stress*. Cambridge: Cambridge University Press.

Chung, Young Hee. 1991. The lexical tone system of North Kyungsang Korean. Doctoral dissertation, Ohio State University.

Comrie, Bernard. 1997. Uyghur phonology. In Alan Kaye, ed., *Phonologies of Asia and Africa, vol. 2*, 913–928. Winona Lake, Ind.: Eisenbrauns.

Côté, Marie-Hélène. To appear. Edge effects and the prosodic hierarchy: Evidence from stops and affricates in Basque. In *NELS 29*. GLSA, University of Massachusetts, Amherst.

Cutler, Anne. 1989. Auditory lexical access: Where do we start? In William Marslen-Wilson, ed., *Lexical representation and process*, 342–356. Cambridge, Mass.: MIT Press.

Flemming, Edward. 1995. Auditory representations in phonology. Doctoral dissertation, UCLA.

Idsardi, William, and Sun-Hoi Kim. 1997. Metrical tone in North Kyungsang Korean. In Susumu Kuno et al., eds., *Harvard studies in Korean linguistics 7*, 106–120. Department of Linguistics, Harvard University.

Kang, Ong-Mi. 1992. Korean prosodic phonology. Doctoral dissertation, University of Washington.

Keating, Patricia, and Marie Huffman. 1984. Vowel variation in Japanese. *Phonetica* 41, 191–207.

Kenstowicz, Michael. 1996. Base identity and uniform exponence: Alternatives to cyclicity. In Jacques Durand and Bernard Laks, eds., *Current trends in phonology:*

Models and methods, 363–394. European Studies Research Institute, University of Salford, Manchester.

Kenstowicz, Michael. 1997. Quality-sensitive stress. *Rivista di Linguistica* 9, 157–188.

Kenstowicz, Michael, and Hyang-Sook Sohn. 1997. Phrasing and focus in Northern Kyungsang Korean. In Pier Marco Bertinetto et al., eds., *Certamen Phonologicum III: Papers from the Third Cortona Phonology Meeting*, 137–156. Torino: Rosenberg & Sellier.

Kim, Chin-Wu. 1970. Two phonological notes: A-sharp and b-flat. In Michael Brame, ed., *Contributions to generative phonology*, 155–170. Austin: University of Texas Press.

Kim, Michael. 1997. Korean monosyllables: Floating V-slot and edge bracket. In Susumu Kuno et al., eds., *Harvard studies in Korean linguistics* 7, 138–152. Department of Linguistics, Harvard University.

Kim, No-Ju. 1997. Tone segments and their interaction in North Kyungsang Korean: A correspondence theory account. Doctoral dissertation, Ohio State University.

Kim, Sun-Hoi. 1999. The metrical computation in tone assignment. Doctoral dissertation, University of Delaware.

Kiparsky, Paul. 1968. How abstract is phonology? Indiana University Linguistics Club, Bloomington.

Lee, Yongsung. 1999. The noun-verb asymmetry in Korean phonology. Paper presented at the Korean Conference at the summer meeting of the Linguistic Society of America, Urbana, Ill.

McCarthy, John, and Alan Prince. 1994. The emergence of the unmarked: Optimality in Prosodic Morphology. In Mercè Gonzàlez, ed., *NELS 24*, 333–379. GLSA, University of Massachusetts, Amherst.

McCawley, James. 1965. The accentual system of Standard Japanese. Doctoral dissertation, MIT.

Odden, David. 1996. *Phonology and morphology of Kimatuumbi*. Oxford: Oxford University Press.

Paradis, Carole, and Darlene LaCharité. 1997. Preservation and minimality in loanword adaptation. *Journal of Linguistics* 33, 379–430.

Paradis, Carole, and Jean-François Prunet. 2000. Nasal vowels as two segments: Evidence from borrowings. *Language* 76, 324–357.

Prince, Alan, and Paul Smolensky. 1993. Optimality Theory: Constraint interaction in generative grammar. Ms., Rutgers University and University of Colorado.

Ramsey, Samuel. 1975. Accent and morphology in Korean dialects. Doctoral dissertation, Yale University.

Rosenthall, Sam, and Harry van der Hulst. 1999. Weight-by-position by position. *Natural Language & Linguistic Theory* 17, 499–540.

Selkirk, Elisabeth. 1984. *Phonology and syntax*. Cambridge, Mass.: MIT Press.

Shinohara, Shigeko. 1997a. Analyse phonologique de l'adaptation japonaise de mots étrangers. Thèse de doctorat, Université de la Sorbonne Nouvelle, Paris III. [Also available from the Rutgers Optimality Archive, ROA-243-0298, http://ruccs.rutgers.edu/roa.html]

Shinohara, Shigeko. 1997b. Default accentuation and foot structure in Japanese: Analysis of Japanese adaptations of French words. In Benjamin Bruening, Yoonjung Kang, and Martha McGinnis, eds., *Papers at the interface,* 263–290. MIT Working Papers in Linguistics 30. MITWPL, Department of Linguistics and Philosophy, MIT.

Shinohara, Shigeko. 2000. Default accentuation and foot structure in Japanese: Evidence from Japanese adaptations of French words. *Journal of East Asian Languages* 9, 1–42.

Sohn, Hyang-Sook. 1999. Lexicon optimization of word-final coronals in loanword adaptation. Paper presented at the Korean Conference at the summer meeting of the Linguistic Society of America, Urbana, Ill.

Steriade, Donca. 1995. Underspecification and markedness. In John Goldsmith, ed., *The handbook of phonological theory*, 114–174. Cambridge, Mass.: Blackwell.

Steriade, Donca. 1998. Lexical conservatism. Ms., UCLA.

Steriade, Donca. 1999. The phonology of perceptibility effects: The P-map and its consequences for constraint organization. Ms., UCLA.

Chapter 8

Enhancement Revisited

Samuel Jay Keyser and
Kenneth N. Stevens

8.1 Introduction

In Stevens and Keyser 1989, we examined how certain features can be used to enhance the acoustic correlates of other features with which they are associated. For example, if a nonlow back vowel is also rounded, the acoustic correlate of backness is enhanced by rounding. The reason is that rounding lowers the second formant (F2) and positions it closer to the first formant (F1), a configuration characteristic of back vowels. Thus, rounding enables back vowels to sound as if they were even more back. In our earlier work, we took it for granted that rounding was, like backness, a gesture associated with a feature specification. However, this may not always be the case. That is, it is possible for enhancement gestures to be affiliated with feature gestures where those enhancement gestures are not featural in origin.[1]

Let us consider an example of the latter variety. In English and in several other languages as well, including French and Polish, /ʃ/ (Wierzchowska 1980) is typically accompanied by a slight to significant rounding of the lips. The reason for the gesture is, we suggest, acoustic and perceptual. Rounding of the lips lengthens the front cavity between the tongue blade constriction and the lip opening and therefore lowers the resonance of this cavity. The acoustic attribute that distinguishes a [−anterior] consonant like /ʃ/ from a [+anterior] consonant like /s/ is a front-cavity resonance that is in the range of the third formant (F3). Rounding of the lips can be used to guarantee that the frequency of this front-cavity resonance is sufficiently low to be the third formant of the vocal tract. It is not reasonable, however, to associate this rounding with a featural representation. That is, we do not suppose that /ʃ/ in the word /ʃɪp/ *ship* is represented lexically as [+strident, −anterior, +round]. Thus, a gesture normally associated with a distinctive feature representation (e.g., rounding in a high back vowel /u/ as in *soup*) can also occur as an enhancing gesture without featural status. In what follows, we explore this nonfeatural use of vocal tract gestures to enhance the acoustic correlates of distinctive feature representations.

Even a cursory examination of the sound-generating capabilities of the human vocal tract shows that the acoustic properties that result from a manipulation of a single primary articulator can be enhanced or strengthened by recruiting another articulator. This second articulator is manipulated in combination with the primary articulator to strengthen the relevant acoustic property. Thus, while movements of particular articulators and the resulting acoustic properties are to some degree orthogonal, articulators also interact in generating certain acoustic attributes. Below, we provide a general overview of the theoretical framework within which we are working, followed by examples illustrating that theory.

8.2 Overview of the Enhancement Process

Implicit in the enhancement process is a four-way relationship among features, the articulatory correlates of features, the system of contrasts as reflected in the minimal pairs in a given language, and enhancement gestures needed to maximize these contrasts. The flowchart in figure 8.1 summarizes our conceptualization of the relationship between distinctive features and enhancement instructions.

The phonological representations box refers to that portion of the lexical entry of a given language that is phonological in nature. The inventory of features of a specific language is always a subset of a universal register of features. The articulatory gestures arising from an array of features are the result of two inputs. One of these inputs comes directly from the feature representation and is analogous to the phonological tree (see Keyser and Stevens 1994 and references therein). This tree designates a set of articulator-free manner features and a set of articulator-bound features attached to active articulators that are used to produce a segment.

The second input performs an enhancing function. Depending on the contrasts that are used in the language, these enhancement instructions engage additional articulators whose function is to strengthen the acoustic manifestation of a distinction that is not maximally salient as a consequence of direct instructions from the feature representation. This second input is initiated by knowledge of the contrasts in the language and by

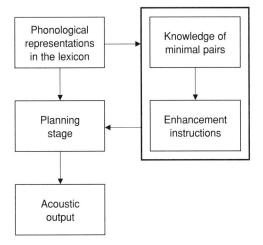

Figure 8.1
Relationship among features, articulatory correlates of features, minimal pairs in a given language, and enhancement instructions needed to maximize the contrasts for these pairs

acoustic knowledge of a rather sophisticated sort. In particular, the second input must have acoustic knowledge of how contrasts are meant to sound and how those contrasts can be enhanced so that a given segment is maximally distinct from its nearest competitors. The addition of enhancement gestures to articulatory gestures is not featurally initiated.

The two kinds of inputs to the articulatory system differ in certain ways. The phonological input is discrete and quantal in nature. The enhancement input is nondiscrete and continuous. To put it in other terms, the former is digital, the latter analog and graded. Within this framework, we speak of [+/−] only when we refer to the featural character of an entry. When we speak of enhancement instructions, the values [+/−] play no role. We represent this distinction orthographically by placing features between brackets when we speak of lexical entries and by omitting brackets and [+/−] values when we refer to gestures as enhancement devices.

While many enhancement instructions use the same articulators as do distinctive feature gestures, some are completely independent of those gestures. For example, the lip spreading used to enhance the acoustic correlate of the feature [−back] for vowels and the mandible lowering used to enhance the acoustic correlate of the feature [+low] for vowels never play a role as gestures associated with distinctive features.

We assume that distinctive feature entries in a mental lexicon are intended as instructions to articulators. However, somewhere in the system attention must be paid to the fact that these articulatory gestures are intended to achieve acoustic and, hence, perceptual targets. This is where enhancement comes in.

Let us see how this enhancement process operates in terms of the above discussion of /ʃ/ and /s/. For the consonant /ʃ/, the distinctive feature [−anterior] requires that the tongue blade be positioned so that the constriction is posterior to the alveolar ridge. The critical acoustic correlate of a [−anterior] obstruent is that the lowest spectral prominence of the frication noise be in the region of F3. This acoustic property may be present only weakly if the tongue blade constriction is behind the alveolar ridge. A mechanism that can strengthen this acoustic property is lip rounding, a gesture that most speakers of English, in fact employ. Thus, we have a situation where implementing the articulatory gestures specified by a feature results in a weak acoustic representation of the feature. Additional gestures that are not part of the original feature specification are brought to bear to strengthen the acoustic contrast between the segment in question and a minimally contrastive segment, in this case /ʃ/ and /s/ or /ʒ/ and /z/.

On the assumption that segments are represented featurally and that features are fundamentally instructions to articulators, enhancement functions as a kind of quality control device that comes into play when the vocal tract is to produce an acoustic output. At that point, the speaker makes a judgment about whether or not the putative acoustic output is sufficiently distinct from a nearest neighbor. If the judgment is positive, no additional shaping of the vocal tract occurs. If the judgment is negative, then additional shaping comes into play, for example, rounding the lips for /ʃ/. In mature speakers, this judgment is presumably not made on-line, as it were; instead, it is part of an internalized model that has knowledge of the relation between articulatory and acoustic patterns (see Jordan 1990, 1996). Thus, rounding is added to /ʃ/ before the sound is produced. However, we also suppose that this knowledge is built up over time and is part of what a child acquires when learning how to speak his or her language.

This model suggests that speakers store two kinds of information relating to how words are represented in memory. The first is purely articulatory in nature. It is the familiar feature-and-tree-geometry representations of segments and larger elements. However, acoustic information must be stored as well: namely, information about how the acoustic output for a particular tree ought to sound in relation to other minimally distinctive trees. These two bodies of information must somehow be linked since both come into play in speech.

8.3 Examples of Some Enhancement Phenomena

We discuss four types of enhancement: (1) voicing for obstruent consonants, (2) nasalization for vowels, (3) place features for tongue blade consonants, and (4) tongue body features for vowels. For each example, there is (a) a primary articulatory gesture associated with the distinctive feature, (b) a primary acoustic output associated with that gesture, and (c) a mechanism for recruiting other articulatory gestures to enhance (b). For example, stiffening or slackening of the vocal folds is a primary articulatory gesture. The absence/presence of glottal vibration is a primary acoustic output for obstruent consonants. And, as we will show, there are several mechanisms that function to enhance the primary acoustic correlate of stiff/slack vocal folds.

8.3.1 Voicing for Obstruent Consonants

8.3.1.1 The Mechanisms We consider first the generation of the sound source at the larynx, and we examine the conditions under which vibration of the vocal folds is facilitated or inhibited during obstruent consonants. When an obstruent consonant is produced, there is a reduced pressure drop across the glottis, and continued vibration of the vocal folds is in jeopardy. Maintenance of vocal fold vibration during an obstruent consonant can be facilitated in several ways: (1) by slackening of the vocal folds (Halle and Stevens 1971; Stevens 1977), (2) by decreasing the stiffness of the walls of the supraglottal airway (Svirsky et al. 1997), (3) by actively expanding the supraglottal volume during the consonantal interval, either by advancing the tongue root or by lowering the larynx, or both (Westbury 1983), and (4) by opening the velopharyngeal port for some period of time during the consonant closure. Likewise, inhibition of vocal fold vibration is facilitated in the opposite way: stiffening the vocal folds, stiffening the vocal tract walls, actively preventing the supraglottal volume from expanding, and maintaining a closed velopharyngeal port. In addition, spreading or constricting of the glottis relative to its normal position for phonation makes it more difficult for the vocal folds to vibrate.

It is proposed that the primary articulatory gesture that contributes to facilitation of glottal vibration is slackening of the vocal folds. The feature has traditionally been called [+slack vocal folds] (Halle and Stevens 1971). We continue to use that designation.

The feature [+slack vocal folds] for obstruent consonants is normally accomplished by lowering the larynx. As the larynx is lowered, the cricoid cartilage slides along the spine. It has been pointed out by Honda, Hirai, and Kusakawa (1993) that owing to a convex curvature of the spine, a change in the tilt of the cricoid cartilage in relation to the thyroid cartilage occurs as the larynx is lowered. As the cricoid cartilage moves downward, the angle between the cricoid and thyroid cartilages increases, leading to a shortening of the vocal folds and a decrease in their stiffness. Lowering of the larynx is accompanied by a general slackening of the walls of the vocal tract. The downward movement of the larynx, then, creates three of the conditions that facilitate vocal fold vibration for obstruents: decreasing the vocal fold stiffness, decreasing the stiffness of the vocal tract walls, and increasing the supraglottal volume. The influence of these movements can be enhanced by advancing the tongue root during the consonantal interval, to further increase the vocal tract volume. Raising the larynx has the opposite effect. It stiffens the vocal folds, decreases the vocal tract volume, increases the stiffness of the vocal tract walls, and therefore inhibits maintenance of vocal fold vibration. The feature in this case is [+stiff vocal folds]. As noted above, this reduction in glottal vibration can be enhanced by spreading the glottis. Glottal vibration is also inhibited by constricting the glottis.

Raising or lowering the larynx, thereby increasing or decreasing vocal fold stiffness, has the effect of increasing or decreasing the fundamental frequency (F0) if these gestures are made during sonorant intervals when there is no increase in the supraglottal pressure. The effect of these movements on F0 in vowels adjacent to voiced and voiceless consonants is well known (see House and Fairbanks 1953; Erickson 1993).

The laryngeal and other adjustments for obstruent consonants to facilitate or to inhibit voicing apply equally to both [−continuant] and [+continuant] consonants, that is, to both stops and fricatives. In the case of fricatives, however, air must continue to flow through the supraglottal constriction, and consequently the default configuration for the glottis is somewhat spread.[2] In the case of a voiceless fricative, the spreading occurs over the length of the glottis. In the case of a voiced fricative, the membranous part of the vocal folds is not spread, since continued glottal

Table 8.1
Contexts for voiceless stops

1	2	3	4	5
rapid	still	p'an	nap	writer
rupee	instill	rep'eat	neck	ricing

vibration is required. Sufficient airflow is presumably achieved by spreading the posterior cartilaginous portion of the glottis.

Let us examine how enhancement of the voiced/voiceless distinction for obstruents works in English. In table 8.1, we list examples containing voiceless consonants, all of which are specified by the phonological feature [+stiff vocal folds]. To begin with, we note that the distinction between /p/ and /b/ in *rapid* and *rabid* or in *rupee* and *ruby* (table 8.1, column 1) does not require enhancement by glottal spreading for /p/ because the distinction is maintained through strong glottal vibration intervocalically for /b/. Similarly, in the environments illustrated in column 2, there is no contrast between voiced and voiceless stops in English, and consequently, no enhancement gestures are needed.

8.3.1.2 Aspiration and Voicing In certain environments, as in column 3 of table 8.1, voiceless stop consonants are produced with spreading of the glottis. These are the so-called aspirated consonants. They occur when the consonant is in onset-initial position pretonically.[3]

All the columns save for 3 contain examples of nonaspirated stop (or in one case fricative) consonants. These forms are in the complement set to those in column 3; that is, they are neither pretonic nor onset-initial. Typically, accounts of English have supposed that voiceless obstruents are aspirated and that a rule of deaspiration applies in the complement set just mentioned. A different interpretation is possible, however. Note first that the feature [spread glottis] is not distinctive for obstruents in English and therefore does not appear in the phonological representation specifying any given English obstruent. Nonetheless, it does accompany the gesture motivated by the feature [+stiff vocal folds] in certain environments, namely, those in column 3. We take this fact to be due to the use of glottal spreading as an enhancement gesture in onset-initial pretonic stop consonants.

What is there about pretonic, onset-initial position that requires enhancement of voicing? Recall that, in our view, enhancement may take place whenever a given distinction can be made more salient than it might otherwise be. In onset-initial pretonic position, the distinction that is threatened is that between voiced and voiceless consonants: for example, /pæn/ versus /bæn/. In English, prevoicing in /bæn/ is weak compared, say, to prevoicing in French: for example, *pain* 'bread' versus *bain* 'bath'. Consequently, in English, the distinction between an unaspirated initial /p/ and /b/ is only weakly represented in the sound. The distinction is enhanced by spreading the glottis for /p/.

8.3.1.3 Word-Final Voicing   In the case of *nap* (table 8.1, column 4), the word-final voicing contrast with *nab* is compromised for two reasons. First, glottal vibration during the closure for /b/ may be weak. Second, the difference in F0 that is normally observed in a vowel following a voiced or voiceless stop is unobservable because there is no following vowel. An enhancement gesture is therefore appropriate. To inhibit glottal vibration for a voiceless stop, the glottis is often constricted immediately preceding the stop closure. A consequence of this glottal constricting movement, when combined with the basic stiffening gesture for the feature [+stiff vocal folds], is a rapid decrease in the amplitude of glottal vibration. This amplitude decrease can occur in advance of the stop consonant closure, resulting in a shortening of the vowel. This shortening can in turn be enhanced by overt reduction of the vowel length. This further reduction in vowel length, then, as well as the constricting of the glottis, enhances the distinction between a voiceless and a voiced stop.

8.3.1.4 Advanced Tongue Root and Voicing   The relevant distinction in column 5 of table 8.1 is the voicing contrast that distinguishes *writer* and *rider* or *ricing* and *rising*. This distinction can be carried in part by the duration of the preceding vowel. However, closer examination of this vowel shows differences in the formant frequencies in the vowel off-glide, depending on whether the following consonant is voiced or voiceless (Kwong and Stevens 1998). Immediately preceding a voiceless consonant, as in *writer* or *ricing*, F1 is frequently lower and F2 higher than for the contrasting voiced consonants, as in *rider* and *rising*, respectively. Furthermore, F1 in the first part of the diphthong is often lower when the following consonant is voiceless than when it is voiced, though this vowel raising is not consistent in American English. From these findings, it can be inferred that the tongue root has been advanced in the vowel that precedes the voiceless consonant. Advancing of the tongue root results in a raising of the tongue body. Consequently, the pharynx is fully extended, and little further expansion is possible during the consonantal portion of the gesture. This fully extended pharynx therefore prevents further airflow through the glottis and consequently inhibits consonantal voicing. This method of enhancing the voicing contrast seems to apply only when the preceding vocalic nucleus consists of a [+low] vowel followed by an off-glide with a high tongue body position. If the vowel is a lax vowel, as in *bitter* or *bidder*, *better* or *bedder*, *latter* or *ladder*, and so on, the voicing distinction is apparently neutralized.

The case of Canadian Raising is relevant to this discussion (see, e.g., Kenstowicz 1994). As just noted, advanced tongue root is responsible for the formant distribution in the off-glide in words like *writer* in American English and presumably in Canadian English as well. A major difference between the two varieties of English has often been noted: namely, that the vowel of the vocalic nucleus in words like *writer* is considerably higher in Canadian than in American English. We have noted, however, that some speakers of American English have a marked tendency—not as prominent as in Canadian English, but discernible nonetheless—to raise the vowel nucleus as well as the glide before voiceless consonants. We conclude that the characteristic formant distribution in glides before voiceless consonants in both varieties of English is due to advancing the tongue root, and that regressive assimilation is responsible for the accompanying raising in a preceding vowel nucleus.

We believe that advancing the tongue root for the glide is intended to enhance the voicelessness of the following consonant. We also believe that enhancement is not a rule-governed phenomenon, but rather occurs at the last stage of vocalization planning—that is, after all rules have applied. When raising occurs in those dialects of Canadian and American English where there is no flapping, enhancement of voicelessness as a postrule phenomenon is possible.[4]

8.3.1.5 Nasalization and Voicing The above examples illustrate enhancement of the voicing feature (i.e., the features [stiff vocal folds] and [slack vocal folds]) by manipulating duration, by spreading or constricting the glottis, by adjusting the stiffness of the vocal tract walls, or by manipulating the vocal tract volume. Another way to maintain vocal fold vibration during an obstruent consonant is to partially open the velopharyngeal port during a portion of the consonant closure interval. This gesture prevents buildup of pressure in the vocal tract and hence permits vocal fold vibration to continue. However, if the consonant is to be an obstruent (in contrast to a sonorant nasal consonant), it is necessary to close the velopharyngeal port a few tens of milliseconds before the consonant is released. The result is a consonant with attributes similar to those of a prenasalized stop.

In Mixtec (Iverson and Salmons 1996), prenasalization occurs optionally before labials in word-initial position and obligatorily before alveolars.

(1) a. $^{(m)}$ bà?à 'good'
       $^{(m)}$ bá?ú 'coyote'
    b. ^{n}da?a 'hand'
       ^{n}dákɨ 'stiff, stale'

Iverson and Salmons argue (p. 170) that these examples "reflect superficial prenasalization as a property of phonetic implementation rather than as a fundamental phonemic feature" and elsewhere (p. 172) that prenasalization is an instantiation of "a low-level phonetic phenomenon serving to help maintain a distinction that is otherwise difficult to produce." In this case, the relevant contrast is that between voiced and voiceless unaspirated stop consonants. While we agree with Iverson and Salmons's assessment of the role of prenasalization in Mixtec, we prefer not to describe it as "low-level" since its implementation involves knowledge of a rather abstract sort. In particular, it involves knowledge of minimal pairs differing in terms of voicing, knowledge of how this distinction should sound, and knowledge of how articulatory gestures need to be modified to maximize the acoustic difference. (See figure 8.1.)

8.3.2   Nasalization and Spread Glottis

Another example illustrating the common acoustic result of two different articulatory gestures is related to nasalization for vowels. The nasalization of a vowel is normally achieved by lowering the soft palate, resulting in acoustic coupling between the main vocal tract and the nasal cavity. The principal consequence of this acoustic coupling is a flattening of the spectrum in the vicinity of F1. This decreased low-frequency prominence is due to increased acoustic losses on the extensive surface area of the nasal cavity as well as to the introduction of additional spectral peaks in the vicinity of F1. One of these peaks, thought to be due to a sinus resonance, is typically at low frequencies in the region 300–400 Hz (Dang, Honda, and Suzuki 1994; Chen 1997). This resonance enhances the amplitude of the first or second harmonic in the spectrum of a nasalized vowel.

An increased F1 bandwidth and a general flattening of the spectrum at low frequencies also occur when there is vocal fold vibration with a spread glottis (Hanson 1997). The glottal opening contributes acoustic losses to the lowest vocal tract resonance, and also enhances the amplitude of the first harmonic in relation to higher harmonics. Thus, some of the acoustic consequences of spreading the glottis are similar to the primary acoustic correlate of nasalization.

The enhancement of the first harmonic in relation to higher harmonics has been reported as a concomitant of vowel nasalization in French (Hattori, Yamamoto, and Fujimura 1958; Chen 1997). Through experiments involving the manipulation of synthetic speech, Klatt and Klatt (1990) have shown that enhancing the amplitude of the first harmonic of a vowel and increasing the F1 bandwidth bias perception of the signal toward nasalization. It is not unreasonable to suppose, then, that a spread glottis is contributing to the relative enhancement of this harmonic for nasal vowels in French.

Ohala (1982) calls attention to an Indo-Aryan phenomenon, first studied by Grierson (1922), in which nasal vowels appear in certain words where the following consonant is voiceless. This process is of interest since these words never had a nasal consonant in their prehistory. One can surmise that the final voiceless consonant induced some spreading of the glottis in the preceding vowel, leading to an increased F1 bandwidth and an enhanced first harmonic. Nasalization of the vowel can be viewed as a process of enhancing this acoustic property by further decreasing the prominence of F1.

8.3.3   Consonantal Place of Articulation: Tongue Blade Features

8.3.3.1   The Feature [anterior]   The fricative consonants /ʃ/ and /ʒ/ are produced by raising the tongue blade against the hard palate and shaping the blade to form a narrow opening, 3–4 cm. long, between the blade and the palate. A narrow cavity is usually formed on the underside of the tongue blade. A turbulence noise source is generated when the airstream emerging from the tongue blade constriction impinges on the lower incisors. The primary acoustic consequence of this source and the surrounding acoustic cavities is that the lowest major spectral prominence in the sound is in the F3 region—about 2800 Hz for female speakers and about 2500 Hz for male speakers. With proper positioning and shaping of the tongue blade, this lowest resonance can usually be adjusted to be in the proper frequency range. However, as noted above, the length of the cavity in front of the tongue tip can be "fine tuned" by adjusting the degree of lip rounding so as to lower the frequency of the lowest resonance until it becomes aligned with the F3 region for the speaker. Measurements made from a database of utterances displaying movements of points on the lips (Westbury 1994) show that protrusion of both upper and lower lips is greater for fricative consonants in words like *ship* than in words like *sit*. Lip rounding, then, can be used to enhance the acoustic property that is characteristic of the [−anterior, +distributed] fricative consonant.

8.3.3.2   The Feature [distributed]   One class of consonants is produced by raising the tongue blade to form a complete or partial constriction in the airway between the blade and the roof of the mouth. Within this class of consonants, one subgroup is produced with this constriction in a more anterior position, in the vicinity of the alveolar ridge or anterior to this ridge. A second subgroup is produced with the constriction posterior to the alveolar ridge. Within each of these consonant groups, [+anterior] and [−anterior], there is a further division into consonants produced with the tip of the tongue, creating a relatively short constriction, and consonants for which a longer constriction is formed with the surface of the tongue blade. This division is represented by the feature [distributed], [+distributed] indicating the longer, laminal constriction and [−distributed] the shorter, apical constriction.

In the case of the [+anterior] consonants, the longer constriction is produced by placing the front of the tongue blade immediately behind the teeth to form a dental, laminal consonant, whereas the tongue tip is on the alveolar ridge for the apical consonant. The length of the cavity behind the constriction is longer for the laminal than for the apical consonant, probably by about 0.5 to 1.0 cm.

Consequently, the half-wavelength resonance of this back cavity for the laminal consonant is about 100–200 Hz below that for the apical consonant. This back-cavity resonance is the starting frequency of the F2 transition as the consonant is released into the following vowel. The decrease in this F2 value or locus for the laminal consonant relative to the apical consonant can be made even greater by narrowing the back cavity near the middle of its length. This narrowing is achieved by backing the tongue body. Consequently, tongue body backing can enhance the acoustic contrast between a dental consonant and an alveolar consonant.

A similar argument can be made for enhancing the contrast between a [+distributed] and a [−distributed] consonant that is [−anterior]. In this case, it is the [−distributed] consonant that has the longer back cavity and hence the lower F2 locus. Backing of the tongue body can further lower this frequency and thereby enhance the contrast between [+distributed] and [−distributed] consonants.

This use of tongue body fronting or backing to enhance the contrast between [+distributed] and [−distributed] consonants appears to operate in Malayalam (see Ladefoged 1971; Stevens, Keyser, and Kawasaki 1986), which has this distinction for [+anterior] consonants. Acoustic data show that the [+distributed] consonant has a lower F2 in the vowel immediately adjacent to the consonant and also well into the vowel. In the case of the [−distributed] alveolar consonant, F2 is higher. We take these acoustic data as evidence for the use of tongue body backing to enhance the feature [+distributed] for the laminal consonant. Details of this example of enhancement can be found in Stevens, Keyser, and Kawasaki 1986.

8.3.3.3 Syllable-Final Nasal Consonants Cues for place of articulation for syllable-final nasal consonants are carried primarily by the transitions of the formants from the vowel into the consonant closure. Normally, the latter part of the vowel in which these transitions occur is nasalized. This vowel nasalization is expected to make the formant movements less distinct and hence to make the distinction between different places of articulation less salient perceptually (Repp and Svastikula 1988).

Hercus (1972)[5] has observed that in the Southern Central Australian languages Arabana, Aranda, and WaNgkaNgurru, medial nasal consonants /m/, /n/, and /n̠/ in poststress position are produced with a brief obstruent interval at the time of consonantal closure. This phenomenon is called prestopping. It occurs in a wide variety of Southern Central Australian languages as well as in Olgolo, a North Queensland language (see Dixon 1970). For these nasal consonants, the soft palate is lowered immediately following the obstruent interval, and the consonant becomes a nasal. In this way, nasalization is postponed until the consonantal closure is complete so that the formant transitions occur while the vowel is still nonnasal. The result is more distinctive formant transitions and hence more salient distinctions between places of articulation for the consonant. We suggest that this denasalization is invoked to enhance the place distinction for the poststress, medial consonants.[6]

Since there can be as many as six places of articulation for nasal consonants in these languages (four of which involve the tongue blade), it is
not surprising that an enhancement gesture like prestopping is invoked.
Prestopping produces formant transitions with greater clarity in a postvocalic, poststress position where the preceding vowel may be heavily
nasalized and where the following unstressed vowel may not carry the
necessary fine distinctions in the formant transitions.

As Hercus shows, there is considerable variation among the languages
of Southern Central Australia with respect to this phenomenon. She
notes, in fact, that /m/, /n/, and /n̠/ are by far the most commonly prestopped nasals, the distribution of the remaining nasals being variable.[7]

It is worth noting that whereas prestopped nasals are in complementary
distribution with non-prestopped nasals in Araban-WaNgkaNgurru, this
is not the case in Aranda. In the latter language, the loss of initial consonants appears to have produced a situation in which prestopped nasals
occurred in vowel-initial words where they contrasted with non-prestopped
nasals. Assuming this to be so, we have a case where what began as an
enhancement phenomenon was elevated to phonological status; that is,
prestopped nasals became distinctive in Aranda while remaining non-
distinctive in Arabana-WaNgkaNgurru and related languages (see Hercus
1972). In Western Aranda, for example, prestopped nasals occur freely in
initial position, a consequence of their becoming distinctive (Ken Hale,
personal communication).

We suspect, though we do not have evidence, that a thorough examination of the languages of the world will show that languages that have
nasal vowels do not have a full array of word-final nasal consonants, since
the nasalization of the vowel would greatly mask the formant transitions
into a following nasal consonant, making it indistinct with respect to
other members of its class.

8.3.3.4 The Liquids   We noted earlier that lip rounding is used in English
and in other languages to enhance the distinction between [+/−anterior]
consonantal fricatives. Lip rounding appears to be used in English in /r/
(see Ladefoged and Maddieson 1996) but not /l/. Our own measurements,
based on data from an x-ray microbeam system (Westbury 1994), support
this observation. We conclude that lip rounding functions to enhance the
difference between the liquids /l/ and /r/ as in *light* and *right*. In the case
of /r/, F3 is low, and it arises from a resonance of the cavity in front of the
constriction formed by the tongue blade. The lowering of F3 is enhanced

if the front-cavity length is increased by rounding the lips. For /l/, on the other hand, F3 is higher and the front-cavity length is shorter. Lip rounding is avoided in order to guarantee a higher F3.

8.3.4   Tongue Body Features

8.3.4.1   Tongue Body Fronting for Vowels and Glides   When the tongue body is raised and fronted, F1 decreases and F2 increases to become close to F3. The raised F2 is a well-known acoustic correlate of the feature [−back]. F2 and F3 can be increased still further by raising the tongue blade so that a long, narrow channel is formed between the blade and the hard palate. Thus, raising the tongue blade can enhance the acoustic correlate of the feature [−back], especially for a [+high] vowel or glide. F2 and F3 can also be raised by spreading the lips, thereby shortening the front cavity and increasing the natural frequency of that cavity. We observe, then, that the acoustic correlates of vowels and glides that are [−back, +high] can be enhanced by raising the tongue blade to shape the front cavity and by spreading the lips. Likewise, for nonlow back vowels, speakers can enhance the feature [+back] by rounding the lips. In many languages, such as Spanish, this rounding gesture is not distinctive and, in our view, is simply a graded gesture.

8.3.4.2   Advanced Tongue Root for Vowels   The articulatory correlate of the feature [+advanced tongue root] ([+ATR]) is a widening of the vocal tract in the pharyngeal region. This widening is accompanied by a reduction in the cross-sectional area of the vocal tract in the oral region. The acoustic consequence of this kind of perturbation in the vocal tract shape is a lowering of F1. (Depending on the vowel, there may also be some lowering or raising of F2.) Likewise, implementation of [−ATR] causes a raising of F1. A decrease in F1 causes a decrease in the amplitudes of the spectral prominences for formants above F1. Measurements of vowels in languages that have a distinction in this feature show a shift in F1 of roughly 100 Hz between a [+ATR] and a [−ATR] vowel. Calculations show that a decrease of 100 Hz in F1 causes a reduction in the amplitudes of higher formant peaks in the range of 2.5 to 5.0 dB, depending on whether the vowel is a low or a high vowel.

It has been reported that vowels with the feature [+ATR] are often produced with a breathy voice quality (Stewart 1971), whereas [−ATR] vowels are produced with a more tense or creaky voice. A breathy glottal

configuration leads to a glottal source with weaker high-frequency amplitude or a spectrum that slopes downward more steeply with increasing
frequency, compared with a modal or pressed voice. A decreased spectrum
amplitude at 3 kHz of 10 dB is not unusual for a breathy voice compared
with a modal voice. Use of this modified glottal configuration for a
[+ATR] vowel, then, would enhance the downward-sloping spectrum that
occurs as a consequence of the low F1 accompanying such a vowel. The
role of the breathy glottal configuration for enhancing the perception of
[+ATR] vowels has been shown by Kingston et al. (1997).

8.4 Some Diachronic Consequences of Enhancement

There appear to be cases in the literature where gestures whose sole
function was to enhance have evolved over time into distinctive features.
For example, Kingston et al. (1997) point out a "historical development
of many Mon-Khmer languages of Southeast Asia, in which higher vowels
have developed diachronically in syllables which originally had breathy or
lax voice, while lower vowels developed in originally tense (or modal)
voiced syllables (see Huffman 1976 for a review)." Enhancement sheds
light on why this might be so. In particular, the gesture that produces
higher vowels (i.e., tongue raising) has the acoustic consequence of an
increased downward tilt of the spectrum at high frequencies. This is
caused by the lowering of F1 that results from tongue body raising.
Breathy voice, which is achieved by spreading of the glottis, has a similar
acoustic consequence. Hence, tongue body raising enhances breathy
voice. The reverse is also possible: as noted in section 8.3.4.2, breathy
voice enhances [+ATR].

We suspect that the Great Vowel Shift in English is the result of the
phonologizing of an enhancement gesture. English philologists have long
supposed that the Great Vowel Shift began with a diphthongization of
high vowels. (See Halle and Keyser 1967 and references therein.) This
gesture would make sense in terms of enhancing the feature [−voice] for a
following consonant. (See section 8.3.1.4 above.)[8]

8.5 General Discussion

In all the examples given here, enhancement applies only to articulator-
bound features. This observation raises the question of whether manner
features like [continuant], [sonorant], and [strident] are enhanceable. We

conclude that they are not. As pointed out in section 8.1, enhancement involves the recruitment of an articulator or articulators that are different from the ones implementing the distinctive feature. Manner features, among the so-called articulator-free features, do not specify an articulator and therefore one cannot speak of recruiting additional articulators to help with their implementation. In terms of our particular view of the phonological tree, only terminal features of such trees are enhanceable (see Keyser and Stevens 1994).

Enhancement of the type we are considering here can be considered as a form of "fine-tuning" of a basic phonological contrast. One might expect, then, that young children acquire the ability to fine-tune only after a basic contrast is in place. For example, young children might be less likely than adults to use lip rounding when producing the palatoalveolar fricative /ʃ/. We do not know whether this prediction is borne out.

Henton, Ladefoged, and Maddieson (1992) note with approval Ohala's (1980) principle that consonants maximally utilize a small number of distinctive features and differ by a "minimum, not a maximum, number of distinctive features." They go on to suggest that this principle is "mitigated somewhat when it is recognized that some contrasts, most notably those for phonation, use a large number of cues for each distinctive feature" (p. 96). We agree with Ohala's principle and suggest that in every case that Henton, Ladefoged, and Maddieson might point to as a mitigating case, enhancement is playing a role. More generally, there has always been a conflict between careful description of sounds on the part of phoneticians, on the one hand, and a desire to simplify phonemic registers on the part of phonemicists, on the other. We believe that this is a case in which both parties are right and that the tension between them can be resolved when enhancement is taken into account.

Notes

In the world of music, the highest praise that can be lavished on anyone is to say that he or she is a musician's musician. Ken Hale is a linguist's linguist. This is apparent to everyone who has ever worked with him, the present authors included. This chapter has benefited from his knowledge of how phonologies work, especially among the languages of Australia. But even beyond, many of the examples discussed here have had their origins in an offhand comment or an e-mail from Ken about something he thought we should look into. This chapter is small recompense for our accumulated debt to him.

1. In this chapter, we treat enhancement as a segmental strategy that enables segments to be maximally distinct where that distinctiveness may be threatened by

saliency. However, we do not think that enhancement is limited to the segmental level. For example, stress and syllable lengthening mark (i.e., enhance) phrase finality. Word-initial marking occurs by means of introducing a glottal stop before a vowel-initial word, as in phrases like *this apple* where one hears a glottal stop before the noun in many English dialects. These types of enhancement at a suprasegmental level are not considered here. (In this and in what follows, we are indebted to Michael Kenstowicz for helpful and clarifying observations.)

2. In a language like English, the spreading of the glottis for fricatives is not regarded as a mechanism for enhancing the feature [+continuant]; rather, it is part of the definition of how that feature is to be implemented. In some languages, however, glottal spreading has the status of a feature, that is, [+spread glottis] (see Vaux 1998).

3. Similar arguments apply in word-initial position, even though the consonant is not pretonic. Thus, the initial /p/ in *Potomac*, *Potemkin*, and *potato* is aspirated despite the following unstressed and reduced vowel. Even though minimal pairs are lacking in these instances, aspiration nonetheless occurs—as a result, we suspect, of a more general phenomenon of English whereby word-initial segments are enhanced whenever possible (Gow, Melvold, and Manuel 1996).

4. In those dialects where flapping has occurred and hence voicing in the consonant itself is neutralized, another explanation is required. In Keyser and Stevens, forthcoming, we argue that flapping is not a rule of either Canadian or American English, but is best viewed as a result of a strategy of rapid speech whereby separate speech gestures overlap whenever possible. In the case of so-called flapping, the closing and the opening gestures of the intervocalic alveolar consonant overlap to such an extent that the voicing distinction cannot be carried in the consonant interval. For details concerning the interaction between enhancement and rapid speech phenomena, see Keyser and Stevens, forthcoming.

5. We are indebted to Andrew Butcher for bringing this reference to our attention.

6. Prestopped laterals also occur in similar environments in these languages although they occur less frequently than prestopped nasals. We assume that prestopping of laterals is, as with nasals, an enhancing gesture.

7. There is one important restriction on prestopping: it does not occur in post-stress position if the prestressed segment is either a vowel or a nasal. It appears that an obstruent in the relevant onset licenses prestopping in a following nasal. We have no explanation for this.

8. Evidence to support this speculation may be found in spelling variations in late Middle English texts (e.g., the Paxton letters). We will address this possibility in a forthcoming publication.

References

Chen, M. Y. 1997. Acoustic correlates of English and French nasalized vowels. *Journal of the Acoustical Society of America* 102, 2360–2370.

Dang, J., K. Honda, and H. Suzuki. 1994. Morphological and acoustical analysis of the nasal and the paranasal cavities. *Journal of the Acoustical Society of America* 96, 2088–2100.

Dixon, R. M. W. 1970. Olgolo syllable structure and what they are doing about it. *Linguistic Inquiry* 1, 273–276.

Erickson, D. 1993. Laryngeal muscle activity in connection with Thai tones. *Annual Bulletin No. 27, Research Institute of Logopedics and Phoniatrics*, 135–149. University of Tokyo.

Gow, D. W., J. Melvold, and S. Manuel. 1996. How word onsets drive lexical access and segmentation: Evidence from acoustics, phonology and processing. In H. T. Bunnel and W. Idsardi, eds., *Proceedings of International Conference on Speech and Language Processing*, vol. 1, 66–69. New Castle, Delaware: Citation Delaware.

Grierson, G. A. 1922. Spontaneous nasalization in the Indo-Aryan languages. *Journal of the Royal Asiatic Society*, 381–388, July.

Halle, M., and S. J. Keyser. 1967. Review of "John Hart's works on English orthography and pronunciation, 1551, 1569, 1579: Part II, phonology, Edited by Bror Danielsson. Pp. 294, Uppsala: Almqvist and Wiksell, 1963." *Language* 43, 773–787.

Halle, M., and K. N. Stevens. 1971. A note on laryngeal features. *MIT Research Laboratory of Electronics Quarterly Progress Report* 101, 198–213.

Hanson, H. M. 1997. Glottal characteristics of female speakers: Acoustic correlates. *Journal of the Acoustical Society of America* 101, 455–481.

Hattori, S., K. Yamamoto, and O. Fujimura. 1958. Nasalization of vowels in relation to nasals. *Journal of the Acoustical Society of America* 30, 267–274.

Henton, C., P. Ladefoged, and I. Maddieson. 1992. Stops in the world's languages. *Phonetica* 49, 65–101.

Hercus, L. A. 1972. The pre-stopped nasal and lateral consonants of Arabana-WaNgaNguru. *Anthropological Linguistics* 14, 293–305.

Honda, K., H. Hirai, and N. Kusakawa. 1993. Modeling vocal tract organs based on MRI and EMG observations and its implication on brain function. *Annual Bulletin No. 27, Research Institute of Logopedics and Phoniatrics*, 37–49. University of Tokyo.

House, A. S., and G. Fairbanks. 1953. The influence of consonantal environments upon the secondary acoustical characteristics of vowels. *Journal of the Acoustical Society of America* 25, 105–113.

Huffman, F. E. 1976. The register problem in fifteen Mon-Khmer languages. In P. N. Jenner, L. C. Thompson, and S. Starosta, eds., *Austroasiatic studies I*, 575–590. Honolulu: University of Hawaii Press.

Iverson, G. K., and J. C. Salmons. 1996. Mixtec prenasalization as hypervoicing. *International Journal of Anthropological Linguistics* 62, 165–175.

Jordan, M. I. 1990. Motor learning and the degrees of freedom problem. In M. Jeannerod, ed., *Attention and performance XIII*, 796–836. Hillsdale, N.J.: Lawrence Erlbaum.

Jordan, M. I. 1996. Computational aspects of motor control and motor learning. In H. Heuer and S. Keele, eds., *Handbook of perception and action*, vol. 2, 71–120. San Diego, Calif.: Academic Press.

Kenstowicz, M. 1994. *Phonology in generative grammar.* Oxford: Blackwell.

Keyser, S. J., and K. N. Stevens. 1994. Feature geometry and the vocal tract. *Phonology* 11, 207–236.

Keyser, S. J., and K. N. Stevens. Forthcoming. The role of enhancement and strategies of conservation in language and speech.

Kingston, J., N. A. Macmillan, L. W. Dickey, R. Thorburn, and C. Bartels. 1997. Integrality in the perception of tongue root position and voice quality in vowels. *Journal of the Acoustical Society of America* 101, 1696–1709.

Klatt, D. H., and L. Klatt. 1990. Analysis, synthesis, and perception of voice quality variations among female and male talkers. *Journal of the Acoustical Society of America* 87, 820–857.

Kwong, K., and K. N. Stevens. 1998. On the voiced-voiceless distinction for *writer/rider*. Ms., MIT.

Ladefoged, P. 1971. *Preliminaries to linguistic phonetics.* Chicago: University of Chicago Press.

Ladefoged, P., and I. Maddieson. 1996. *The sounds of the world's languages.* Oxford: Blackwell.

Ohala, J. J. 1980. Discussion during symposium on phonetic universals in phonological systems and their explanation. In *Proceedings of the 9th International Congress of Phonetic Sciences, No. 3, Copenhagen*, 181ff.

Ohala, J. J. 1982. The phonological end justifies any means. In S. Hattori and K. Inoue, eds., *Proceedings of the XIIIth International Congress of Linguistics*, 232–243. Tokyo.

Repp, B. H., and K. Svastikula. 1988. Perception of the [m]-[n] distinction in VC syllables. *Journal of the Acoustical Society of America* 83, 237–247.

Stevens, K. N. 1977. Physics of laryngeal behavior and larynx modes. *Phonetica* 34, 264–279.

Stevens, K. N., and S. J. Keyser. 1989. Primary features and their enhancement in consonants. *Language* 65, 81–106.

Stevens, K. N., S. J. Keyser, and H. Kawasaki. 1986. Toward a phonetic and phonological theory of redundant features. In J. Perkell and D. Klatt, eds., *Variance and variability in speech processes*, 426–447. Hillsdale, N.J.: Lawrence Erlbaum.

Stewart, J. M. 1971. Niger-Congo, Kwa. In T. Sebeok, ed., *Linguistics in Sub-Saharan Africa*, 179–212. The Hague: Mouton.

Svirsky, M. A., K. N. Stevens, M. L. Matthies, J. Manzella, J. S. Perkell, and R. Wilhelms-Tricarico. 1997. Tongue surface displacement during bilabial stops. *Journal of the Acoustical Society of America* 102, 562–571.

Vaux, B. 1998. The laryngeal specifications of fricatives. *Linguistic Inquiry* 29, 497–511.

Westbury, J. R. 1983. Enlargement of the supraglottal cavity and its relation to stop consonant voicing. *Journal of the Acoustical Society of America* 73, 1322–1336.

Westbury, J. R. 1994. X-ray microbeam speech production database user's handbook. Technical report, Waismann Center, University of Wisconsin, Madison.

Wierzchowska, B. 1980. *Fonetyka i fonologia jezyka polskiego.* Wroclaw, Poland: Zaklad Narodowy Imienia Ossolinskich.

Chapter 9

The EPP, Scrambling, and   Shigeru Miyagawa
***Wh*-in-Situ**

9.1 Introduction

In this chapter, I will take up two issues that originally emerged early in the principles-and-parameters era. The first issue is Hale's (1980, 1983) *configurationality parameter*. Hale proposed that languages divide between those that are configurational and those that are nonconfigurational. A configurational language is associated with the familiar hierarchical structure shown in (1), whereby the subject and the other phrases are in an asymmetrical relation to the verb. In the terminology of the time, a configurational language is one that is associated with a VP node (Saito and Hoji 1983; Whitman 1986).

(1) *Configurational*

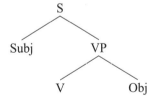

On the other hand, a nonconfigurational language has a flat structure; therefore, all phrases in a sentence are in a symmetrical relation to the verb. A hallmark of a nonconfigurational language is free word order. Hale proposed that all of the possible word orders are base-generated, all being equivalent because every phrase has the same, symmetrical relation to the verb regardless of the word order (see also Farmer 1980). A nonconfigurational language lacks the VP node.[1] Thus, a subject and an object may occur in either order. The structure in (2) instantiates this for a verb-final language such as Japanese.

(2) *Nonconfigurational*

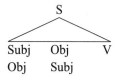

Subj	Obj	V
Obj	Subj	

The first work to challenge Hale's proposal was Saito and Hoji 1983. Using arguments based on weak crossover and Condition C, Saito and Hoji showed convincingly that Japanese, a nonconfigurational language under Hale's conception, is just as hierarchical in structure as configurational languages such as English. They proposed that free word order derives by scrambling, a type of movement found in free-word-order languages. Saito and Hoji's analysis, further developed in Saito 1985, 1989, 1992, is now generally assumed in the field. To go beyond their solution and into the realm of the *explanation* behind the configurationality parameter, we must seek out the nature of scrambling within Universal Grammar. What triggers it? Why, for example, doesn't English allow the same type of scrambling as Japanese?[2]

The second issue I will take up is what might be termed the *wh-parameter*. Huang (1982) argued that languages vary in the level at which *wh*-movement applies. In many languages (e.g., English, Italian, Russian), at least one *wh*-phrasal movement occurs at overt syntax. In the so-called *wh*-in-situ languages (e.g., Chinese, Japanese, Turkish), LF is the sole level at which *wh*-movement takes place. This proposal, which is largely assumed today, provided the first important attempt at a solution to the *wh*-parameter problem. Watanabe (1992), in challenging Huang's analysis, proposes an alternative solution. He argues that overt *wh*-movement occurs in every language; in the so-called *wh*-in-situ languages, what moves is a *wh*-operator that is phonologically null. What differentiates overt *wh*-movement languages from the *wh*-in-situ languages is morphology. In the former, the *wh*-operator cannot be morphologically separated from the rest of the *wh*-phrase; thus, the entire phrase "pied-pipes" to [Spec, CP] (see also Chomsky 1993). But in the latter, the phonologically null *wh*-operator may separate from the rest of the phrase, allowing only the *wh*-operator to move overtly to C.

I will explore an analysis in which certain core cases of both of these parameters derive from one principle of Universal Grammar—the Extended Projection Principle (EPP). The intuition behind this exploration is that these two parameters have to do with movement: the emergence of "scrambling" in the nonconfigurational languages, but not in the configurational ones; and the emergence of overt *wh*-movement in some languages, but its absence in others. The EPP is responsible for inducing overt phrasal movement. For the configurationality parameter, I will focus on a subset of the so-called scrambling phenomenon, specifically, those instances in which scrambling is A-movement. In Miyagawa 1997, following the general framework of Mahajan 1990, I have proposed that A-movement scrambling is due to some feature associated with the local T. As a result, it is an obligatory operation, a notion that goes against nearly every study of scrambling. I will extend this line of investigation, exploring an analysis in which the relevant feature on T is the EPP.[3] Thus, A-movement scrambling is triggered by the EPP. An important result of the analysis is that the A-movement scrambling environment has a "nonconfigurational" form as originally proposed by Hale, but instantiated within a configurational structure, thus capturing his original intuition about free word order and structure. As we will see, on this account, the configurationality parameter reduces to whether a language has a particular type of verbal movement to T at overt syntax.[4] For the *wh*-parameter, I will explore an approach that is based in part on Chomsky (2000) and Hagstrom 1998, with some assumptions also drawn from Watanabe 1992. I will assume that there are two features crucially associated with a *wh*-question, Q and *wh*. I adopt Chomsky's (2000) idea that the EPP-feature is associated with "core functional categories," which are C, T, and *v*. This means that C is associated with an EPP-feature that must be satisfied.[5] The EPP may be satisfied either by moving an appropriate XP to the specfier of the head with the EPP-feature or by raising an appropriate head to the head with the EPP-feature (Chomsky 2000; also see Alexiadou and Anagnostopoulou 1998). In a language such as English, I will assume that the *wh*-phrase is associated with both the Q- and the *wh*-features, one being morphologically inseparable from the other. Thus, the entire *wh*-phrase must pied-pipe to [Spec, CP] to satisfy the EPP-feature on C. In Japanese, along with a *wh*-in-situ, a question particle occurs at the right edge of the question, as shown in (3).

(3) John-ga nani-o   katta no?
    John-NOM what-ACC bought Q-PART
    'John bought what? = What did John buy?'

Hagstrom (1998) argues that this question particle initially occurs by the *wh*-in-situ. The question particle head raises to C, thus ending up at the right edge. Crucially, Hagstrom assumes that the question particle is not *wh*, but an existential quantifier. I will assume that the question particle is associated solely with the Q-feature. I will further assume that the *wh*-phrase is solely associated with the *wh*-feature. Thus, in Japanese, the EPP-feature on C is satisfied by head-raising the question particle to C. Therefore, the *wh*-parameter boils down to morphology, as Watanabe (1992) originally suggested: those languages, like English, in which the Q- and *wh*-features are associated with a single, morphologically inseparable item, and those, like Japanese, in which the two features are distributed on morphologically separate items. The Q- and *wh*-features on the lexical item(s) are "matched" with the same features on a functional head. An issue that I will spend some time on is the identity of the functional head that is associated with the *wh*-feature. It is normally assumed that C is the functional head that carries the *wh*-feature. However, I will give evidence that, at least in Japanese, this *wh*-feature occurs on T intead. On this account, the *wh*-feature is on a par with ϕ-features on T. According to this analysis, the fact that, in the Japanese example (3), the object *wh*-phrase does not move (it is "in situ") has to do with the fact that the subject phrase, *John*, satisfies the EPP-feature on T. The object *wh*-phrase, 'what', need not move, in the same way that a "normal" object in English need not move, as in (4).

(4) John bought <u>a book</u>.

In both the Japanese and the English examples, the subject, *John*, has satisfied the EPP-feature on T, allowing the object to stay "in situ."

It is important to point out that, by combining the two issues mentioned, I do not mean to imply that if a language has one property (e.g., free word order), it must have the other (*wh*-in-situ). There are languages, such as Russian, that have relatively free word order, yet also display overt *wh*-movement. There are also languages, such as Chinese, that have rigid word order, yet belong to the *wh*-in-situ family. In this chapter, I will look extensively at Japanese, which happens to have both the nonconfigurational property of free word order and the *wh*-in-situ phenomenon. The proposed analysis of *wh*-in-situ is informed by the EPP analysis of scrambling, and vice versa. However, the EPP analysis of scrambling is, in principle, applicable to any nonconfigurational language, regardless of whether it is a *wh*-in-situ language or not; and the EPP analysis of *wh*-in-situ is applicable in principle to any language that has this property, whether or not it is also nonconfigurational. I begin with the configurationality parameter.

9.2   The EPP and Scrambling

Ever since Saito and Hoji 1983 and Saito 1985 (also Hoji 1985), the nonconfigurational property of free word order has come to be viewed as a result of the syntactic operation of scrambling.[6] In the Japanese examples in (5), (5a) has the "basic" SOV word order, while (5b), which has OSV word order, derives from moving the object to the head of the sentence.

(5) a. S   O   V
       Taroo-ga piza-o   tabeta.
       Taro-NOM pizza-ACC ate
       'Taro ate pizza.'
    b. O   S   V
       Piza-o$_i$ Taroo-ga t_i tabeta.
       pizza-ACC$_i$ Taro-NOM t_i ate

Mahajan (1990) has shown, on the basis of Hindi, that there are two types of movement of this sort, A-movement and Ā-movement scrambling.[7] A-scrambling, for example, avoids a weak crossover violation; Ā-scrambling, for example, allows reconstruction.[8] Mahajan's findings have been replicated in Japanese by a number of linguists (see Nemoto 1993; Saito 1992; Tada 1993; Yoshimura 1992). A question that immediately arises is, what is the nature of the syntactic movement in (5b)? Given that the two word orders SOV and OSV are in principle always available, those who have worked on this phenomenon have assumed that it is purely an optional operation (see, e.g., Fukui 1993; Kuroda 1988; Saito and Fukui 1998; Takano 1998). In contrast, in Miyagawa 1997, based in part on Mahajan's work, I argued that these two types of scrambling are feature-driven. A-scrambling is triggered by a feature on T, while Ā-scrambling is triggered by focus.

(6) Scrambling is feature-driven, not optional (Miyagawa 1997).
    A-scrambling: some feature on T
    Ā-scrambling: focus

Below, I will give further evidence for the nonoptionality of scrambling. In particular, I will show that the feature on T responsible for A-scrambling is the EPP.

In this chapter, I will focus on *zen'in* 'all' and look at its interpretation relative to negation. If 'all' occurs in object position in the environment of sentential negation, it is interpreted inside the scope of negation (partial negation).

(7) Taroo-ga zen'in-o home-nakat-ta (yo/to omou).[9]
    Taro-NOM all-ACC praise-NEG-PAST (EXCL/COMP think)
    '(I think that) Taro didn't praise all (!).'
    not > all, (*)all > not[10]

In contrast, if 'all' occurs in subject position, it can only be interpreted outside the scope of negation.

(8) Zen'in-ga sono tesuto-o uke-nakat-ta (yo/to omou).
    all-NOM   that test-ACC take-NEG-PAST
    'All did not take that test.'
    *not > all, all > not

To account for this subject/object asymmetry, let us suppose that, in order for 'all' to be in the scope of negation, it must be c-commanded by the negation (Klima 1964). Assuming that negation occurs in the structure above *v*P (e.g., Laka 1990; Pollock 1989), this means that the object 'all' stays in situ in its original complement position, making it possible for 'all' to be in the scope of negation. These structural relations are shown in (9).

(9)

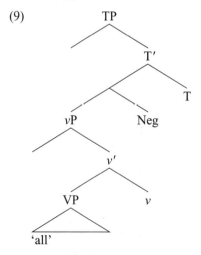

On the other hand, the fact that the subject 'all' cannot be interpreted inside the scope of negation suggests that this 'all' moves to a position

outside the c-commanding domain of negation. A reasonable assumption
is that it moves to [Spec, TP], as shown in (10).

(10)

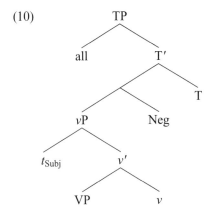

What triggers this movement of the subject DP? There are two possibilities: it is triggered by the EPP-feature on T, or the nominative Case feature is strong.[11]

Evidence that it is the EPP-feature comes from scrambling of the
object. If the object is scrambled, which results in OSV word order, the
subject 'all' can stay in situ in [Spec, *v*P], where it may be interpreted
within the scope of negation. The following is a minimal pair. The
example in (11a) again illustrates that, in the SOV order, the subject 'all'
moves to [Spec, TP]; (11b) shows that in the OSV order, the same subject
'all' need not move.

(11) a. Zen'in-ga sono tesuto-o uke-nakat-ta   (yo/to omou).[12]
          all-NOM   that test-ACC take-NEG-PAST
          'All did not take that test.'
          *not > all, all > not
      b. Sono tesuto-o$_i$ zen'in-ga t_i uke-nakat-ta   (yo/to omou).[13]
          that test-ACC$_i$ all-NOM t_i take-NEG-PAST
          'That test, all didn't take.'
          not > all, (all > not)

Thus, for example, the statement 'Taro and Hanako in fact didn't take it'
(*Taroo-to Hanako-wa zitu-wa ukenakatta*) may follow (11b), but not
(11a).

Given what we have observed to this point, we can make a simple
generalization: one DP must move into [Spec, TP]. Once this happens, the

other DP(s) may stay in situ. In the SOV word order, it is the subject DP that raises to [Spec, TP], while in the OSV order, it is the object DP. The latter is shown in (12) (I will comment on the V-to-T raising below).

(12)

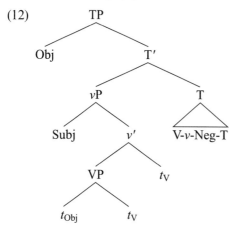

The fact that the nominative subject DP may stay in situ in [Spec, *v*P] in this structure clearly indicates that the nominative Case feature is not strong. Rather, the movement, either the subject in the SOV order or the object in the OSV order, must be due to the EPP.

(13) *The EPP and scrambling*
    A-scrambling is triggered by the EPP-feature on T.

We see, then, that this type of scrambling is no more optional than the EPP. Any movement triggered by the EPP is obligatory.[14]

    An assumption behind the EPP analysis of local scrambling is that the verbal complex (V-*v*) moves overtly to T, as shown in (12). With this head movement, the subject DP and the object DP become equidistant from T. The EPP-feature on T is therefore able to attract either DP to [Spec, TP]. The EPP does not concern itself with particular Case features of a DP; it simply requires that an appropriate DP (or, in some cases, a PP) move to [Spec, TP] to check the EPP-feature on T.[15] This analysis captures directly the intuition behind Hale's (1980, 1983) nonconfigurational analysis of languages such as Japanese. In his original analysis, a nonconfigurational language such as Japanese has a flat phrasal structure; as a result, the subject and the object (and other phrases) are in a symmetrical relationship with the verb. The subject and object may occur in either order, SO or OS, without disturbing the fundamental structural relation they have with the verb. In the EPP analysis, V-to-T raising makes the verbal complex + T equidistant (i.e., structurally symmetrical) relative to the subject and the object (and the other phases), making it possible for either of these DPs to satisfy the EPP requirement.[16] Later, we will look at a construction where verb raising does not occur; we will see that in this construction, only the subject DP can satisfy the EPP.

This EPP analysis of A-scrambling provides a partial answer to the question of why a nonconfigurational language such as Japanese evidences (A-)scrambling, while a configurational language such as English does not. The difference has to do with V-to-T movement. Japanese has V-to-T movement, for which we will see evidence later. Thus, the subject and the object (and other phrases) become equidistant from T, allowing the EPP-feature on T to attract either of these phrases. English does not have V-to-T movement in overt syntax (Emonds 1976; Pollock 1989), so that the subject is the closest phrase to T. Thus, only the subject can satisfy the EPP. I leave open the question of why some languages that have V-to-T movement, such as French (Emonds 1976; Pollock 1989) and other Romance languages, do not have scrambling of the sort found in Japanese.[17]

We saw in (11b) that in the OSV scrambling word order, the subject DP may stay in [Spec, vP], allowing the subject 'all' to be in the scope of negation. However, as indicated for this example, the other reading, in which the subject 'all' is outside the scope of negation, is also possible. This reading results when the subject 'all' moves to [Spec, TP], to satisfy the EPP requirement, and the object then undergoes Ā-scrambling for focus. It is possible to disambiguate the sentence using an appropriate adverb. An adverb such as 'fortunately' occurs high in the projection of T. If the subject 'all' occurs to the left of this adverb, it must be in [Spec, TP], instead of in [Spec, vP], and therefore it cannot be inside the scope of negation.

(14) Kono ronbun-o$_i$ zen'in-ga saiwaini t_i yoma-nakat-ta
     this   article-ACC$_i$ all-NOM   fortunately t_i read-NEG-PAST
     (yo/to omou).
     'This article, all did not fortunately read.'
     *not > all, all > not

In contrast, a VP adverb such as 'happily' in the same position does not force the subject to be in [Spec, TP], as expected, making it possible for the subject 'all' to have scope inside the negation.

(15) Kono ronbun-o$_i$ zen'in-ga yorokonde(wa) t_i yoma-nakat-ta
     this   article-ACC$_i$ all-NOM   happily t_i read-NEG-PAST
     (yo/to omou).
     'This article, all didn't read happily.'
     not > all, all > not

A VP adverb, by nature, occurs in the projection of V, so that the subject
DP that precedes it is not forced to be in [Spec, TP]. This example has the
reading that not all read the article happily (not > all), which is the interpretation relevant to the point at hand. It also has the interpretation that
all did not read the article happily (not > happily). In the latter interpretation, the subject 'all' has moved to [Spec, TP] to satisfy the EPP, and
outside the c-commanding domain of the negation.[18] Changing the sentence from OSV to SOV order allows only the second interpretation, in
which the negation is on 'happily'.

(16) Zen'in-ga yorokonde kono ronbun-o yoma-nakat-ta (yo/to omou).
     all-NOM   happily   this article-ACC read-NEG-PAST
     'All didn't read this article happily.'
     *not > all, not > happily

9.3   The EPP and Long-Distance Scrambling

We have seen that A-scrambling, which is local, is triggered by the EPP-
feature on T. In this section, we will look at long-distance scrambling.
As noted by Mahajan (1990), long-distance scrambling can only be Ā-
scrambling.[19] From the perspective taken here, this means that long-
distance scrambling can never be triggered by the EPP-feature on the
matrix-clause T. This is shown in (17).

(17) Syukudai-o$_i$ zen'in-ga [$_{CP}$ sensei-ga t_i dasu to]
     homework-ACC$_i$ all-NOM   [$_{CP}$ teacher-NOM t_i assign COMP]
     omowa-nakat-ta (yo/to omou).
     think-NEG-PAST
     'Homework, all did not think that the teacher would assign.'
     *not > all, all > not

The matrix subject, 'all', can only be interpreted outside the scope of
matrix negation, showing that it has raised to the matrix [Spec, TP]. This
sentence only means that no one thought that the teacher would assign
homework. This is not at all surprising. There is no point in the derivation

at which the subordinate object and the matrix subject are equidistant from the matrix T. The matrix subject DP is always closest to the matrix T, so that it is the only DP that can satisfy the EPP-feature on the matrix T.

9.4 Subjunctive Verbs

We have seen that in the SOV order, subject 'all' only takes scope outside negation.

(18) Zen'in-ga sono tesuto-o uke-nakat-ta   (yo/to omou).
     all-NOM   that test-ACC take-NEG-PAST
     'All did not take that test.'
     *not > all, all > not

This is true with such sentence endings as the exclamation *yo* and *to omou* '(I) think that ...' However, with a different item at the end of the sentence, namely, *koto* 'fact', we get a very different result.

(19) Zen'in-ga sono tesuto-o uke-nakat-ta   koto.
     all-NOM   that test-ACC take-NEG-PAST
     'All did not take that test.'
     not > all, (all > not)

As shown, with *koto*, it is possible to interpret the subject within the scope of negation, even though the word order is SOV. Why does this happen with *koto*?

Hiraiwa (to appear) argues that a verb that precedes a nominal such as *koto* 'fact' is in what he calls the subjunctive form (see also Watanabe 1996). In modern Japanese, there is no overt difference between the subjunctive form and the finite form; however, in Classical Japanese, there was a difference (cf. Miyagawa 1989 and references therein).

(20) *Classical Japanese for 'eat'*
     subjunctive form: taburu
     finite form: tabu

The finite form may be followed by the complementizer *to*, or the exclamatory particle *yo*, both of which are found in the data presented so far. Even though the inflectional distinction between subjunctive and finite forms has been lost in modern Japanese, Hiraiwa argues that there is still a difference: the subjunctive form must raise to C to be licensed, while the finite form does not. If this is correct, we have an explanation for the availability of partial negation in (19). The verb is at C, along with the negative morpheme suffixed to it; the negative morpheme therefore c-commands the subject 'all' in the [Spec, TP]. Consequently, partial nega-tion is possible regardless of whether the subject moves to [Spec, TP] or stays in situ in [Spec, *v*P]. We find the same result with an unergative verb, which requires the subject to always move to [Spec, TP] to satisfy the EPP-feature on T.

(21) Zen'in-ga asoba-nakat-ta <u>koto</u>.[20]
    all-NOM   play-NEG-PAST
    'All didn't play.'
    not > all, (all > not)

Compare this with (22), which has the exclamatory *yo* or the com-plementizer *to* followed by 'think'.

(22) Zen'in-ga asoba-nakat-ta (yo/to omou).
    all-NOM   play-NEG-PAST
    'All didn't play.'
    *not > all, all > not

As shown, the partial negation is not possible, confirming Hiraiwa's analysis that a finite verb does not raise to C. Finally, the subjunctive form appears in relative clause and complex NPs. Note that the partial negation is possible in this construction as well.

(23) [DP [CP zen'in-ga *e* yoma-nakat-ta] hon]
    [DP [CP all-NOM   *e* read-NEG-PAST] book]
    'the book that all didn't read'
    not > all, (all > not)

Recall that a high adverb such as 'fortunately' forces the subject to its left to be in [Spec, TP]. However, in the case of the relative clause, the high adverb does not exclude the partial negation interpretation.

(24) [DP [CP zen'in-ga saiwaini   *e* yoma-nakat-ta] hon]
    [DP [CP all-NOM   fortunately *e* read-NEG-PAST] book]
    'the book that all fortunately didn't read'
    not > all, (all > not)

'All' in this example is in [Spec, TP] because of 'fortunately' to its right; despite that, partial negation is possible. This is further evidence that the verb form along with the negative morpheme is at C.

9.5 Evidence for Verb Raising

We began this analysis with the observation that either the subject or the object can satisfy the EPP. For the object to satisfy the EPP, it scrambles locally to [Spec, TP]. By so doing, it allows the subject to stay in situ, in [Spec, *v*P]. The fact that either the subject or the object can satisfy the EPP is due to the assumption that the verbal complex (V-*v*) moves to T in overt syntax (see Koizumi 1995), making every phrase in the TP equidistant from T.[21] Thus, the EPP-feature on T can attract either the subject or the object.

Let us now look at evidence for the verb-raising analysis. Japanese has a construction in which the verb stem is separated from the tense marker by an emphatic particle such as *sae* 'even' or *mo* 'even' (see Kuroda 1965). The tense is carried by the light verb *suru* 'do'.

(25) Taroo-ga sensei-o   seme-<u>mo</u>   sita.
      Taro-NOM teacher-ACC blame-even did
      'Taro even blamed the teacher.'

A reasonable assumption is that, because the emphatic particle intervenes, the verb does not raise to T in overt syntax. Thus, "*do*-support" is required, to carry the tense on T. This, in turn, predicts that the EPP can only attract the nominative subject; the accusative object is too far away. This prediction is borne out. If the accusative phrase is scrambled, and, contrary to the prediction, if this counts as satisfying the EPP, the "remaining" subject should be able to stay in [Spec, *v*P]. However, as shown in (26a), scrambling of the object in the emphatic construction does not allow the subject to stay in [Spec, *v*P]. Example (26b) is a "normal" sentence, which shows that scrambling of the object is triggered by the EPP in this case.

(26) a. *Emphatic construction*
          Sensei-o$_i$ zen'in-ga t_i seme-<u>mo</u>   si-nakat-ta (yo/to omou).
          teacher-ACC$_i$ all-NOM t_i blame-even do-NEG-PAST
          'The teacher, all did not even blame.'
          *not > all, all > not
      b. *"Normal" construction*
          Sensei-o$_i$ zen'in-ga t_i seme-nakat-ta   (yo/to omou).
          teacher-ACC$_i$ all-NOM t_i blame-NEG-PAST
          'The teacher, all didn't blame.'
          not > all, all > not

The fact that, in (26a), 'all' in subject position unambiguously takes wide scope over the negation indicates that this subject DP moves to [Spec, TP] to satisfy the EPP. The object DP is scrambled for focus (see Miyagawa 1997). This is an indication that, in the emphatic construction, only the subject DP can satisfy the EPP, because there is no verb raising to T in overt syntax. In contrast, the "normal" construction in (26b) allows the object DP to satisfy the EPP because, in this construction, there is verb raising to T.

9.6 Multiple Agreement

Up to this point, we have focused on the EPP and have ignored the particular formal features associated with T and the various DPs. Given the assumption that the verbal complex raises to T in Japanese, either the subject or the object DP (or some other DP) may raise to [Spec, TP] to satisfy the EPP. But how are the features, such as structural Case, checked? Let us suppose, following Chomsky (2000), that feature checking takes place without feature movement. Rather, the feature(s) on T and the matching feature(s) on a particular lexical item are checked by feature matching, which Chomsky calls "Agree." For example, T is associated with a ϕ-feature that must find a matching ϕ-feature on a DP (the subject DP). The two ϕ-features Agree, and they delete along with the uninterpretable structural Case feature on the DP. By virtue of this feature matching and deletion, an agreement relationship is established between T and the lexical item. This process of Agree takes place prior to any movement. As noted, all instances of Agree delete matching features, including the Case feature. This leaves only the EPP-feature on T to be satisfied. The EPP requires that an XP merge with T, which is commonly accomplished by moving an XP into [Spec, TP]. In Chomsky 2000, it is proposed that such movement must be licensed by agreement. That is, an XP may move and merge with T if it agrees with T. In English, the closest XP that qualifies is the subject DP; thus, the subject DP is raised to [Spec, TP] to satisfy the EPP-feature of T. However, in Japanese, verb raising to T makes both the subject and the object DPs equidistant from T; given that T agrees with both the subject and the object, either of these DPs may raise to [Spec, TP] to satisfy the EPP, as we have seen.[22]

In this section, we will look at an instance of multiple agreement, in which the same formal feature on T agrees with a multiple occurrence of the same structural Case. We will see that, if one of the items with this structural Case is selected for movement to [Spec, TP] to satisfy the EPP, the other phrase must also raise to a [Spec, TP], leading to a multiple-specifier structure (see Ura 1996). This construction gives a striking piece of evidence that agreement licenses movement.

A stative construction in Japanese allows the object to be marked by either the accusative or the nominative case marker. The following is a "potential" construction, which exhibits this double-nominative option (see Kuno 1973):

(27) Taroo-ga sono hon-o/-ga   yom-e-ta.
     Taro-NOM that book-ACC/-NOM read-can-PAST
     'Taro was able to read that book.'

So far, we have seen that, in the SOV order, the subject DP raises to [Spec, TP] to satisfy the EPP. The same is true for the potential construction, but only if the object is marked with the accusative case marker. As shown in (28a), with this "accusative" option, the object DP stays in situ, as evidenced by the fact that the object 'all' is in the scope of negation. However, as shown in (28b), if the object is marked with the nominative case marker, 'all' in the object position cannot stay in situ, instead raising to a projection of T.[23]

(28) a. Taroo-ga zen'in-o osie-rare-nakat-ta   (yo/to omou).
        Taro-NOM all-ACC   teach-can-NEG-PAST
        'Taro wasn't able to teach all.'
        not > all, (*)all > not
     b. Taroo-ga zen'in-ga osie-rare-nakat-ta   (yo/to omou).
        Taro-NOM all-NOM   teach-can-NEG-PAST
        'Taro was not able to teach all.'
        *not > all, all > not

In (28b), why is the nominative object forced to move to the projection of T along with the nominative subject? Let us suppose that, in this example, there is only one agreement feature: it is on T, and it is also on the nominative subject and the nominative object. Thus, the same feature on T establishes a multiple agreement with (the pertinent feature) of both DPs. Thus, as far as agreement is concerned, the nominative subject and the nominative object are "one entity," because they are both linked by agreement to the same formal feature on T. On the assumption that agreement licenses movement, if one DP moves, then both must move.

This is precisely what we see in (28b). Presumably, the subject and the object DPs move into multiple specifiers of TP.

(29)

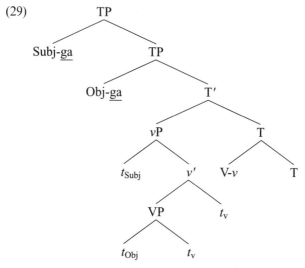

I have assumed that movement of a DP to satisfy the EPP occurs at overt syntax. If the analysis of multiple agreement is correct, and the second of the two nominative phrases (the nominative object DP) is forced to move as part of the EPP movement, the analysis predicts that this movement, too, occurs in overt syntax. There is evidence that this is in fact correct. In (30), 'all' occurs in the goal phrase of a double-object construction. The theme object DP has accusative case marking. As a result, multiple agreement is not triggered, and the object DP may stay in situ, in the VP. Consequently, the 'all' goal phrase, too, stays in situ, where it is able to be interpreted within the scope of negation.

(30) Taroo-ga zen'in-ni sigoto-o atae-rare-nakat-ta (yo/to omou).
     Taro-NOM all-DAT work-ACC give-can-NEG-PAST
     'Taro wasn't able to give work to all.'
     not > all, (*)all > not

However, we get a very different result if the theme object DP is marked with the nominative case marker. As shown in (31), this nominative object DP enters into multiple agreement with the nominative subject, as expected, so that it moves to a [Spec, TP]. As a result, the 'all' goal phrase is "pushed out" of its original position, to a position where it can no longer take scope inside the negation.

(31) Taroo-ga zen'in-ni sigoto-<u>ga</u> atae-rare-nakat-ta (yo/to omou).
     Taro-NOM all-DAT   work-NOM give-can-NEG-PAST
     'Taro was not able to give work to all.'
     *not > all, all > not

If, contrary to assumption, the movement of the second nominative phrase
occurs in covert syntax, instead of overt syntax, there is no reason why the
goal phrase needs to move as well; instead, we would expect the nominative
object to covertly raise across the goal phrase, leaving the goal phrase in the
original, VP-internal position. That this is not the case shows that the
nominative object moves in overt syntax, which is expected if its movement
is triggered by the EPP as licensed by multiple agreement with T.[24]

   This phenomenon of multiple agreement, in which one formal feature
on T agrees with a multiple occurrence of the same uninterpretable feature
on DPs (nominative Case), is not commonly found among the languages
of the world. Why does it emerge at all in Japanese? Let us consider the
agreement system. In Japanese, no distinction is made in verbal inflection
for gender, number, or person. That is, verbal inflection is completely
neutral; overtly it exhibits no agreement at all. Suppose that, in this kind
of language, a formal feature is completely neutral with respect to type of
agreement, paying attention only to the overt manifestation of an uninterpretable feature on a DP, which is the Case feature. This is tantamount
to the idea that, in this type of language, a DP or T does not carry a ϕ-
feature in any relevant sense. The formal feature on T can, in principle,
agree with more than one DP with the same uninterpretable Case feature,
because it is not sensitive to gender, number, or person. In other types of
languages, in which a distinction is made in gender/number/person for
agreement, a ϕ-feature on T is matched with a ϕ-feature on a DP. On the
assumption that each DP carries a distinct ϕ-feature, this means that there
can only be one-to-one agreement between a ϕ-feature on T and a ϕ-feature
on a DP. Thus, we would not expect to find multiple agreement in these
languages.[25]

   Rizzi's (1986) Chain Condition provides independent evidence for the
multiple-agreement analysis. The Chain Condition is a locality condition
on anaphor binding. Note that the following sentence is marginal (Snyder
1992):

(32) ?*[Taroo-to Hanako]-o$_i$ otagai$_i$-ga t_i mita.
     [Taro-and Hanako]-ACC$_i$ each other$_i$-NOM t_i saw
     'Taro and Hanako, each other saw.'

The object, 'Taro and Hanako', which is the intended antecedent of the reciprocal 'each other', has been moved to the head of the sentence. The problem here is that the reciprocal anaphor locally c-commands the trace of its antecedent (t_i), an environment in which the Chain Condition is violated. The sentence becomes acceptable if the anaphor is embedded in a larger DP.

(33) [Taroo-to Hanako]-o$_i$ [otagai$_i$-no   sensei]-ga t_i mita.
     [Taro-and Hanako]-ACC$_i$ [each other$_i$-GEN teachers]-NOM t_i saw
     'Taro and Hanako, each other's teachers saw.'

Here, the anaphor does not locally c-command the trace of its antecedent (t_i).[26]

Turning to multiple agreement, note, first of all, that the potential verb 'can hire' allows the nominative option on the object.

(34) Taroo-ga Hanako-ga/-o   yato-e-ru.
     Taro-NOM Hanako-NOM/-ACC hire-can-PRES
     'Taro can hire Hanako.'

Reciprocal binding is fine if the object has the accusative case marker.

(35) [Taroo-to Hanako]$_i$-ga   otagai$_i$-o   yato-e-ru.
     [Taro-and Hanako]$_i$-NOM each other$_i$-ACC hire-can-PRES
     'Taro and Hanako can hire each other.'

However, if the object takes the nominative case marker, the same sentence becomes highly marginal.

(36) ?*[Taroo-to Hanako]$_i$-ga   otagai$_i$-ga   yato-e-ru.
     [Taro-and Hanako]$_i$-NOM each other$_i$-NOM hire-can-PRES
     'Taro and Hanako can hire each other.'

We can account for this straightforwardly under the multiple-agreement analysis. Both nominative DPs in this example have moved to a [Spec, TP]. As a result, the object reciprocal anaphor c-commands the trace of its antecedent, the subject DP 'Taro and Hanako', thereby violating the Chain Condition.

(37) ?*[[Taro-and Hanako]$_i$ ... each other$_i$ ... t_i ...]

As expected, the sentence improves markedly if the anaphor is embedded in a larger DP.

(38) [Taroo-to Hanako]$_i$-ga [otagai$_i$-no   gakusei]-ga
    [Taro-and Hanako]$_i$-NOM [each other$_i$-GEN students]-NOM
    yato-e-ru.
    hire-can-PRES
    'Taro and Hanako can hire each other's students.'

To summarize: We have seen that A-movement scrambling is triggered by the EPP-feature on T. This is made possible by the fact that the verbal complex raises to T in overt syntax, making the subject and the object (and other phrases) equidistant from T. Thus, either the subject or the object may move to [Spec, TP] to satisfy the EPP. In either case, the movement is obligatory. We also saw that this A-movement undertaken to satisfy the EPP is licensed by agreement. Where there is multiple agreement with a feature on T, all DPs that are part of this multiple agreement must raise to a [Spec, TP] to satisfy the EPP.

In the remainder of the chapter, I will turn to the *wh*-parameter. As I will show, the analysis developed to this point will suggest a very different approach to the *wh*-in-situ phenomenon from those given in the literature.

9.7   The Function of the Question Particle

A *wh*-question in Japanese typically contains a *wh*-phrase in situ and a question (Q) particle at the end.

(39) Taroo-ga nani-o   katta   no?
    Taro-NOM what-ACC bought Q
    'Taro bought what? = What did Taro buy?'

The Q-particle may take the form of *no*, as in this example, or *ka*, in formal style and in all indirect questions.[27] Let us begin by looking at the function of this Q-particle.

Yoshida and Yoshida (1997) note that it is possible to optionally "drop" the Q-particle. Thus, the *wh*-question in (39) may be asked with or without the Q-particle *no*. What Yoshida and Yoshida do not note is that dropping the Q-particle changes the meaning of the *wh*-question. The interpretations in (40)–(43) are possible only with the Q-particle in place.

(40) *Exhaustive interpretation*
    Hanako-ga   pikunikku-ni nani-o   mottekita ???(no)?
    Hanako-NOM picnic-to   what-ACC brought   (Q)
    'Hanako brought what to the picnic?'

(41) *Pair-list interpretation*
    Dare-ga nani-o   katta   *(no)?
    who-NOM what-ACC bought (Q)
    'Who bought what?'

(42) *Functional interpretation*
    Dare-o_i minna-ga t_i aisiteiru *(no)?
    who-ACC_i everyone-NOM t_i love   (Q)
    'Who does everyone love?' Answer: 'His mother'.

(43) *'Why'*
    Hanako-ga   naze iku ?*(no)?
    Hanako-NOM why go   (Q)
    'Why is Hanako going?' (see Yoshida and Yoshida 1997)

The question in (40) has the typical "exhaustive" (or "maximality") inter-pretation for a *wh*-question: it is expected that the answer will exhaustively list all the things Hanako brought to the picnic. However, this exhaustive interpretation is possible only with the Q-particle. Without it, there is no presupposition that the answer needs to list everything that Hanako brought; listing just one item will satisfy the question, even if it is under-stood that Hanako brought more than one thing. With the Q-particle, the question in (41) has a clear pair-list interpretation; but without the Q-particle, the most salient interpretation is that of a single-pair (or echo) question. With the Q-particle, the question in (42) allows a functional interpretation, whereby it can be answered with something like 'His mother'; but without the Q-particle, the question presupposes that there is one person everyone loves. Finally, as (43) illustrates, a 'why' question is marginal without the Q-particle.[28]

These observations point to the fact that the Q-particle contributes a quantificational force to the *wh*-question. In (40), the exhaustive inter-pretation with the Q-particle evidences a quantifier-variable structure, whereby the variable ranges exhaustively over the set of things that Hanako brought to the picnic. It is also well known that pair-list and functional interpretations involve quantification of some sort (see, e.g., Chierchia 1991, 1993; Engdahl 1980, 1986; Groenendijk and Stokhof 1984; May 1985). A 'why' question is, in many ways, comparable to a functional interpretation (Miyagawa 1998).

Hagstrom (1998) in fact proposes that the Q-particle is an existential quantifier. The *wh*-phrase is what is commonly termed the "restriction," which restricts the possible objects in the set (e.g., people, things) (see also Miyagawa 1998). This combination of existential quantifier and restriction directly reflects the analysis of *wh*-questions in the semantics literature (e.g., Hamblin 1973; Karttunen 1973).

Hagstrom's argument that the Q-particle is an existential quantifier comes from "donkey"-type sentences. But first, it is important to point out a distributional property of the Q-particle. As already noted, there are (at least) two Q-particles, *ka* and *no*.[29] Of these, *ka* appears to be the "purer" particle, in that it can occur both in direct (formal-style) and indirect questions. As is well known, the same *ka* also occurs in existential quantifiers, which are composed of a *wh*-phrase and *ka* (see Nishigauchi 1990).

(44) *Wh*   *Existential quantifier*
      dare 'who'   dare-ka 'someone'
      nani 'what'   nani-ka 'something'
      doko 'where'   doko-ka 'somewhere'
      itu 'when'   itu-ka 'sometime'

Hagstrom's argument is based on the behavior of these existential quantifiers that contain *ka*. To begin with, note the following pair, which contain an indefinite expression, not an existential quantifier with *some* or *ka*:

(45) a. If an article$_i$ is published in *LI*, John <u>usually</u> reads it$_i$.
      b. *LI*-ga   ronbun$_i$-o   syuppansureba, John-ga   <u>taitei</u>
          LI-NOM article$_i$-ACC publish-if   John-NOM usually
          sore$_i$-o yomu.
          it$_i$-ACC read
          'If *LI* publishes an article, John usually reads it.' (see Nishigauchi 1990)

Both sentences contain an indefinite expression ('an article') that "binds" a pronoun that it does not c-command. This is a typical "donkey"-type sentence. In Heim's (1982) approach to indefinites, an indefinite does not have an inherent quantificational force; rather, it is simply a restrictive variable. It picks up its quantificational force from its environment; in (45a–b), this quantificational force comes from the adverb 'usually'. The "binding" of the pronoun by the indefinite is made possible by the fact that both are bound by this quantificational adverb, 'usually'. As Hagstrom notes, while indefinite DPs behave alike in English and Japanese, as we just saw, other types of indefinite expressions behave differently. As shown in

(46), the English indefinite expression *something* behaves just like an indefinite DP, showing that *something* lacks inherent quantificational force. However, the same expression in Japanese leads to ungrammaticality.

(46) a.   If something$_i$ is published in *LI*, John <u>usually</u> reads it$_i$.

    b.   *LI-ga   nani-ka$_i$-o   syuppansureba, John-ga   <u>taitei</u>
       LI-NOM what-Q$_i$-ACC publish-if   John-NOM usually
       sore$_i$-o yomu.
       it$_i$-ACC read
       'If *LI* publishes something, John usually reads it.'

Hagstrom accounts for the ungrammaticality of the Japanese example in (46b) by arguing that *ka* in *nani-ka* is an existential quantifier. As such, *nani-ka* 'something' in Japanese, but not the corresponding expression, *something*, in English, has inherent quantificational force. Consequently, *nani-ka* is not bound by the quantificational adverb 'usually', making it impossible for the existential quantifier to "bind" the pronoun.

To capture the distribution of the Q-particle, Hagstrom makes an innovative proposal in which the Q-particle always originates within the same constituent as the *wh*-phrase, which is what happens with existential quantifiers. In a *wh*-question, the Q-particle is raised to C, being attracted by the Q-feature on C. This is why the Q-particle occurs at the right edge of a question construction. What remains is an indefinite expression.[30]

(47) *Japanese*

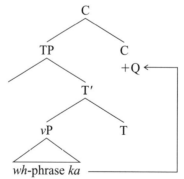

Q-particle movement in Japanese ostensibly unifies Japanese *wh*-questions with English *wh*-questions: both exhibit overt movement, to C (Japanese) or to [Spec, CP] (English). In either case, we might ask, what drives this movement? In Chomsky 2000, it is suggested that it is the EPP-feature on C. Departing from earlier works, Chomsky suggests that the

EPP-feature is associated with what he calls "core functional categories," which are C, T, and *v*. In English, *wh*-phrasal movement to [Spec, CP] is triggered by the EPP, its movement licensed by agreement, as noted earlier.

(48) *English*

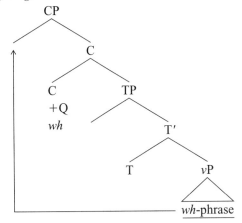

wh-phrase

As shown, in English, C is associated with both Q- and *wh*-features. Presumably, this EPP movement to [Spec, CP] is licensed by the agreement established by the *wh*-feature on C with the uninterpretable *wh*-feature on the *wh*-phrase. What about in the case of Japanese? Chomsky suggests that in certain circumstances, head movement to a category can satisfy the EPP-feature on that category (see also Alexiadou and Anagnostopoulou 1998). Thus, the Q-particle movement proposed by Hagstrom is an instance of satisfying the EPP, presumably licensed by agreement between the Q-feature on C and the matching feature on the Q-particle.[31]

Note, first of all, that the Q-feature occurs on C in both the English type and the Japanese type. I will simply assume that this is universal. In English, the *wh*-feature is also assumed to be on C, and the *wh*- and Q-features both agree with the *wh*-phrase. But in Japanese, it is the Q-feature on C that agrees with a matching feature on the Q-particle. The Q-particle, being an existential quantifier, does not have a matching feature for the *wh*-feature. Presumably, the *wh*-phrase itself has such a feature. But the question arises, on which functional head is the *wh*-feature located in Japanese? A natural assumption is that the *wh*-feature in Japanese is also located on C. This would lead to a type of analysis like Watanabe's (1992) for the *wh*-parameter. In the English type, both the Q-

and the *wh*-features occur on the *wh*-phrase; one cannot be morphologically separated from the other, so that the entire *wh*-phrase must pied-pipe to [Spec, CP], to satisfy the EPP. In contrast, in the Japanese-type, the two features are distributed between two morphologically separate elements, the *wh*-phrase for *wh* and the Q-particle for Q. The Q-particle by itself raises to C to satisfy the EPP-feature on C.

The general approach just outlined provides a straightforward account for an observation made by Cheng (1991) about "clause typing" of *wh*-questions.

(49) *Clause typing of* wh-*questions*
     A *wh*-question has either overt *wh*-phrasal movement or a question particle.

English and Japanese represent the two possibilities. In English, one *wh*-phrasal movement must occur in overt syntax to clause-type the sentence as a *wh*-question. In Japanese, a question particle arises, presumably, for the same purpose. In the latter case, there is no need to move the *wh*-phrase, because the Q-particle by itself fulfills the need for clause typing. On the EPP account, this clause-typing observation boils down to morphology. A language is, in principle, free to have one of two types of morphological arrays. In one type (English), the *wh*-phrase contains both the *wh*- and the Q-features; they are morphologically inseparable. Thus, the entire *wh*-phrase undergoes overt movement. In the second type (Japanese), the two features are distributed on two morphologically separable items. Only the item with the Q-feature needs to raise to C; this is the Q-particle.

This immediately raises the question, why doesn't the Japanese type have the option of raising the *wh*-phrase to [Spec, CP], just as in English, instead of the Q-particle? This question only arises if we assume that the *wh*-feature as well as the Q-feature is on C in Japanese. The *wh*-feature would agree with the *wh*-feature on the *wh*-phrase, and the Q-feature on C would agree with the Q-particle. Thus, in principle, either should be able to move—the *wh*-phrase to [Spec, CP], or the Q-particle to C—to satisfy the EPP. Yet, in actuality it is only the Q-particle that moves. One possibility, suggested by Alexiadou and Anagnostopoulou (1998) in another context, is that, when either phrasal movement or head movement will satisfy the EPP, the head movement option is taken. According to them, head movement is more economical, in that it does not extend the structure, unlike phrasal movement.

I will take a different approach. I will show that the *wh*-feature in Japanese occurs on T, and not on C.[32] If the *wh*-feature is on T, it is correctly predicted that the *wh*-phrase in Japanese can never satisfy the EPP-feature on C, because there is no feature on C that agrees with a feature on the *wh*-phrase. Only the Q-particle can do so. My arguments are based on the type of data considered in sections 9.2–9.6, on scrambling. What I will show is that, in certain cases, the *wh*-feature may enter into an agreement to license movement of a *wh*-phrase to [Spec, TP], thereby satisfying the EPP-feature on T. If this analysis is correct, it means that there is overt *wh*-movement even in Japanese, a point already suggested by Takahashi (1993). Unlike Takahashi, who argued that only long-distance scrambling can count as *wh*-movement and that its landing site is [Spec, CP], I will show that local scrambling has this property and that the landing site is [Spec, TP] instead.

9.8   PP and the EPP: Evidence That the *Wh*-Feature in Japanese Is on T

Let us begin with the question, can a PP satisfy the EPP-feature on T? The following PP-scrambling examples (locative PP and comitative PP) show that these PPs cannot do so. In both cases, the subject 'all' raises to [Spec, TP] to satisfy the EPP, in turn allowing only the wide-scope reading of 'all' relative to negation.

(50) Disuko-de$_i$ zen'in-ga t_i odora-nakat-ta (yo/to omou).
      disco-at$_i$ all-NOM t_i dance-NEG-PAST
      'At the disco, all did not dance.'
      *not > all, all > not

(51) Hanako-to$_i$ zen'in-ga t_i asoba-nakat-ta (yo/to omou).
      Hanako-with$_i$ all-NOM t_i play-NEG-PAST
      'With Hanako, all did not play.'
      *not > all, all > not

These examples indicate that these PPs do not contain a feature with which a feature on T can agree, so that scrambling the PP does not count as A-movement for satisfying the EPP. This is predicted if we assume that, in the domain of T, agreement of the sort that can license movement is the uninterpretable structural Case feature on XP; a PP, by nature, is not associated with structural Case.[33]

In contrast to (50) and (51), in which scrambling a PP does not count as A-movement that satisfies the EPP-feature on T, (52) and (53) with a locative PP and a comitative PP show that a *wh*-PP does fulfill the EPP requirement of T.

(52) Doko-no   disuko-de$_i$ zen'in-ga t_i odora-nakat-ta no?
     where-GEN disco-at$_i$ all-NOM t_i dance-NEG-PAST Q
     'At which disco, all didn't dance?'
     not > all, (all > not)

(53) Dare-to$_i$ zen'in-ga t_i asoba-nakat-ta no?
     who-with$_i$ all-NOM t_i play-NEG-PAST Q
     'With whom, all didn't play?'
     not > all, (all > not)

Given the assumptions made about movement and the EPP, we conclude from these data that a *wh*-PP, but not a "normal" PP, contains a feature that matches a feature on T, and this agreement in turn makes it possible for the *wh*-PP to move to [Spec, TP] as A-movement to satisfy the EPP. Therefore, the *wh*-feature in Japanese is on T.

Another possibility, which does not involve the EPP, is that in these examples, the subject 'all' is satisfying the EPP instead of the *wh*-PP, and the narrow reading of this 'all' relative to the negation is somehow allowed because the sentence is a *wh*-question. For example, we can imagine that in a *wh*-question, the verbal complex raises all the way to C, very much like the subjunctive (or "attributive") form of the verb, as argued by Hiraiwa (to appear). This possibility is made even more plausible by the fact that in Classical Japanese, the verbal form in a question was normally the attributive form, what Hiraiwa calls the "subjunctive." We can dismiss this possibility, however, because, if the *wh*-PP is not scrambled, the subject 'all' has only wide scope relative to the negation. I will illustrate this only for a locative PP, although the result is the same for the comitative PP.

(54) Zen'in-ga doko-no   disuko-de odora-nakat-ta no?
     all-NOM   where-GEN disco-at   dance-NEG-PAST Q
     'All did not dance at which disco?'
     *not > all, all > not

It is possible that the verbal form in a question is "subjunctive"; nevertheless, it fails to raise to C, as we see in (54). On this account, we can surmise that this raising of the verb to C is blocked by the occurrence of the Q-particle at C. I will give other data to show that the verb in a question does not raise to C.

On the basis of the above discussion, it is plausible to assume that a *wh*-phrase can satisfy the EPP-feature on T under the right circumstance. Thus, we have seen that the following items can satisfy the EPP-feature on T in Japanese:

(55) *Items that can satisfy the EPP*
    a. Nominative subject (in the SOV word order)
    b. Accusative object (in the OSV word order)
    c. *wh*-PP (not non-*wh* PP) (in the *wh*-XP SV word order)

Possibilities (55a) and (55b) are due to the fact that there is a formal feature on T that is matched with the uninterpretable structural Case on the DP to establish agreement. Possibility (55c), with a *wh*-PP, suggests that the *wh*-feature occurs on T; there is no other feature that can enter into an agreement with a (*wh*-) PP, as we saw with non-*wh* PP scrambling. Consequently, scrambling a *wh*-phrase is licensed by the *wh*-feature on T, which agrees with the *wh*-feature on the *wh*-phrase. This is tantamount to saying that this scrambling counts as overt *wh*-phrasal movement. This supports Takahashi's (1993) proposal that scrambling of a *wh*-phrase sometimes counts as overt *wh*-movement. While Takahashi assumes that the landing site of this movement is [Spec, CP], and it is only possible for long-distance scrambling, I assume that its landing site is the projection of T instead, and it is possible for local scrambling.

It is important to emphasize that the *wh*-movement found in Japanese is in no way optional. Under the assumptions made here, T in Japanese may be associated with a formal feature that agrees with a structural Case feature on a DP, and also the *wh*-feature.

(56)

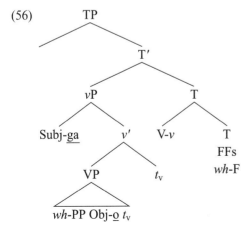

The formal feature agrees with the uninterpretable structural Case feature on a DP (subject, object), which has the effect of deleting the formal feature and the Case feature. In addition, the *wh*-feature on T agrees with the *wh*-feature on the *wh*-PP, again deleting the matching feature on T and on the *wh*-phrase (PP in (56)). All of these feature matchings establish an agreement relation between the DP/PP and T, making the DP/PP a candidate for movement to [Spec, TP] to satisfy the EPP. Because the verbal complex moves to T, all phrases are viable candidates structurally for this movement. It is simply a matter of selecting one for this purpose. One XP *must be* selected, because the EPP is not optional; it must be satisfied. Once it is satisfied, the other XPs stay in situ.

This account provides a simple explanation for the *wh*-in-situ phenomenon, illustrated in (57).

(57) John-ga   nani-o   katta   no?
      John-NOM what-ACC bought Q
      'John bought what? = What did John buy?'

The object *wh*-phrase in (57) need not move, precisely in the same way that an object in English need not move.

(58) John bought *a book*.

In both cases, the subject DP, *John*, moves to [Spec, TP] to satisfy the EPP, allowing the object to stay in situ. In the next paragraph, I will give further evidence that the *wh*-feature in Japanese is on T.

Let us again consider the possibility noted earlier for the range of data we have seen. Suppose that, if a *wh*-phrase is scrambled, it moves to [Spec, CP], as suggested by Takahashi (1993), and the verbal complex, including the negation, raises to C.[34] On this alternative view, scrambling of a *wh*-phrase is exactly like overt *wh*-movement in languages such as English. A *wh*-phrase moves to [Spec, CP], and this movement is accompanied by some verbal element moving to C. If this account is correct, the non-*wh* subject 'all' raises to [Spec, TP], but it can still be in the scope of negation because the negation is at C, having been taken there by the raising of the verb and T to C. However, this approach is not correct, as earlier observations about adverbs indicate. Recall that, in an object-scrambling environment, if a high adverb such as 'fortunately' follows the subject, the subject must be in [Spec, TP], despite the object scrambling. In contrast, a VP adverb such as 'happily' in the same position would allow the subject to be in the original, [Spec, *v*P] position. The examples are repeated here.

(59) Kono ronbun-o$_i$ zen'in-ga saiwaini t_i yoma-nakat-ta
   this   article-ACC$_i$ all-NOM   fortunately t_i read-NEG-PAST
   (yo/to omou).
   'This article, all did not fortunately read.'
   *not > all, all > not

(60) Kono ronbun-o$_i$ zen'in-ga yorokonde(wa) t_i yoma-nakat-ta
   this   article-ACC$_i$ all-NOM   happily t_i read-NEG-PAST
   (yo/to omou).
   'This article, all didn't read happily.'
   not > all, all > not

In (59), the adverb 'fortunately' occurs, by nature, in the projection of
T. As a result, the subject 'all' to its left must be in [Spec, TP]. If a VP
adverb such as 'happily' occurs in this position, as in (60), the subject
that precedes it is able to be in [Spec, vP] because the scrambled object
has satisfied the EPP. Now, note that in the following *wh*-question, the
scrambling of the object *wh*-phrase satisfies the EPP, as expected:

(61) Dono ronbun-o$_i$ zen'in-ga t_i yoma-nakat-ta no?
   which article-ACC$_i$ all-NOM t_i read-NEG-PAST Q
   'Which article, all did not read?'
   not > all, all > not

However, if we place the adverb 'fortunately' after the subject, the subject
cannot be interpreted inside the scope of negation.

(62) Dono ronbun-o$_i$ zen'in-ga saiwaini t_i yoma-nakat-ta no?
   which article-ACC$_i$ all-NOM   fortunately t_i read-NEG-PAST Q
   'Which article, all did not fortunately read?'
   *not > all, all > not

This shows clearly that the verbal complex, including the negation, does
not raise all the way to C under *wh*-phrase scrambling. If it did, the
addition of the adverb should not prohibit the "inside the negation"
interpretation of the subject 'all', since the verbal complex and its negation would be at C, above [Spec, TP]. As expected, if the adverb is of the
VP type, the subject may be interpreted inside the scope of negation.

(63) Dono ronbun-o$_i$ zen'in-ga yorokonde(wa) t_i yoma-nakat-ta no?
   which article-ACC$_i$ all-NOM   happily t_i read-NEG-PAST Q
   'Which article, all did not read happily?'
   not > all, all > not

It is important to note that the fact that the scrambled phrase ('which article') is an argument is irrelevant. The same pattern of judgment emerges with scrambling of adjunct PPs. The following is an instance of *wh*-PP scrambling, repeated from (53):

(64) Dare-to$_i$ zen'in-ga t_i asoba-nakat-ta no?
     who-with$_i$ all-NOM t_i play-NEG-PAST Q
     'With whom, all didn't play?'
     not > all, (all > not)

The *wh*-PP meets the EPP requirement of T, as indicated by the fact that the subject 'all' may be interpreted inside the scope of negation. Now, note that, if we put 'fortunately' to the right of this subject, this 'not > all' interpretation disappears, as predicted. On the other hand, a VP adverb in the same position does not exclude this interpretation, again as predicted.

(65) a. Dare-to$_i$ zen'in-ga saiwaini t_i asoba-nakat-ta no?
        who-with$_i$ all-NOM   fortunately t_i play-NEG-PAST Q
        'With whom, all did not fortunately play?'
        *not > all, all > not
     b. Dare-to$_i$ zen'in-ga yorokonde(wa) t_i asoba-nakat-ta no?
        who-with$_i$ all-NOM   happily t_i play-NEG-PAST Q
        'With whom, all did not play happily?'
        not > all, all > not

This gives further evidence for the proposal that the *wh*-feature in Japanese occurs on T.[35]

9.9 Multiple Agreement and *Wh*

Recall that in a multiple-nominative construction in Japanese, the object as well as the subject must move to a [Spec, TP].

(66) Taroo-ga zen'in-<u>ga</u> osie-rare-nakat-ta (yo/to omou).
     Taro-NOM all-NOM   teach-can-NEG-PAST
     'Taro wasn't able to teach all.'
     *not > all, all > not

This is so because one formal feature on T simultaneously agrees with the two occurrences of the nominative Case feature. The two DPs, subject and object, thus take part in a single instance of agreement. Consequently, when one moves to [Spec, TP], the other must as well, because movement is licensed by agreement.

In contrast to the multiple-nominative example (66), in which the object 'all' cannot be interpreted inside the scope of negation, the *wh*-question version (67) makes this interpretation possible.

(67) Dare-ga zen'in-ga osie-rare-nakat-ta   no?
     who-NOM all-NOM   teach-can-NEG-PAST Q
     'Who wasn't able to teach all?'
     not > all, all > not

This example allows an interpretation in which 'who' taught some/most, but not all. Why is this? In the non-*wh* example (66), the only possible agreement that can be established is between the formal feature on T and the multiple occurrence of the nominative structural Case. This forces both nominative DPs to raise to a [Spec, TP]. However, in the *wh*-question example (67), an additional feature on T is available, namely, the *wh*-feature. Selecting the agreement established by the *wh*-feature as the licensing agreement for movement allows just the *wh*-phrase subject to raise to [Spec, TP], without also triggering the movement of the non-*wh* object DP.

We get the same result in a double-object construction. Recall that if the theme object is marked with the nominative case marker, it moves to a [Spec, TP] in overt syntax, "pushing" the 'all' goal phrase out of its original position and outside the c-commanding domain of the negation. The relevant example, (31), is repeated here.

(68) Taroo-ga zen'in-ni sigoto-ga atae-rare-nakat-ta (yo/to omou).
     Taro-NOM all-DAT   work-NOM give-can-NEG-PAST
     'Taro was not able to give work to all.'
     *not > all, all > not

In this example, the 'all' goal phrase cannot have scope inside the negation, having been pushed out to a position outside the c-commanding domain of the negation by the overt movement of the nominative object DP, 'work'. This movement is triggered by multiple agreement. Now, note that, if the subject is a *wh*-phrase instead, the goal phrase may stay in situ and take scope inside the negation, even though the theme object has the nominative case marker.

(69) Dare-ga zen'in-ni sigoto-ga atae-rare-nakat-ta no?
     who-NOM all-DAT   work-NOM give-can-NEG-PAST Q
     'Who was not able to give work to all?'
     not > all, all > not

Here again, the occurrence of the *wh*-phrase in subject position triggers the EPP movement. If, instead, the multiple agreement involving the two nominative structural Cases is selected as the licensing agreement, the object DP must move to a [Spec, TP].

The proposed account makes a further prediction: namely, that if *both* nominative phrases are *wh*-phrases, the nominative object necessarily moves to a [Spec, TP]. In this case, there are two instances of multiple agreement, one involving the multiple occurrence of nominative structural Case, the other involving multiple *wh*-phrases. Selecting either for the licensing agreement would force both phrases to undergo EPP movement. This is shown in (70), which is identical to (69) except that the object DP has been changed to the *wh*-phrase 'what kind of work'.

(70) Dare-ga zen'in-ni donna   sigoto-ga atae-rare-nakat-ta no?
     who-NOM all-DAT   what:kind work-NOM give-can-NEG-PAST Q
     'Who was not able to give what kind of work to all?'
     *not > all, all > not

In this example, the 'all' goal phrase may not take narrow scope relative to the negation, indicating that it has been pushed out of its original position by the overt movement of the object DP.

If the *wh*-object DP has accusative case marking instead, the goal phrase as well as the accusative phrase may stay in situ, as expected.

(71) Dare-ga zen'in-ni donna   sigoto-o atae-rare-nakat-ta no?
     who-NOM all-DAT   what:kind work-ACC give-can-NEG-PAST Q
     'Who was not able to give what kind of work to all?'
     not > all, all > not

The narrow-scope interpretation of 'all' is made possible by the fact that the licensing agreement here involves the single occurrence of the nominative structural Case on the subject.

9.10   Subordinate Structures

In this section, I will explore some consequences of the proposed analysis for constructions involving a subordinate structure.

9.10.1   Scrambling within the Subordinate Clause

We saw earlier that local scrambling of a non-*wh* PP, such as a comitative PP, does not satisfy the EPP-feature on T. In contrast, a *wh*-PP, when scrambled, is able to do so. On the assumption that the *wh*-feature occurs on T, the matching of this feature and the *wh*-feature on the *wh*-PP serves as the licensing agreement for A-movement. The minimal pair is repeated below.

(72) a. Hanako-to$_i$ zen'in-ga t_i asoba-nakat-ta (yo/to omou).
       Hanako-with$_i$ all-NOM t_i play-NEG-PAST
       'With Hanako, all did not play.'
       *not > all, all > not
   b. Dare-to$_i$ zen'in-ga t_i asoba-nakat-ta no?
       who-with$_i$ all-NOM t_i play-NEG-PAST Q
       'With whom, all didn't play?'
       not > all, (all > not)

In (72a), with the non-*wh* PP 'with Hanako', scrambling of this PP does not satisfy the EPP, so that the subject 'all' raises to [Spec, TP]. In contrast, in (72b), the *wh*-PP is able to satisfy the EPP.

This analysis makes the following prediction. In a direct *wh*-question that has a subordinate clause that contains a *wh*-PP, local scrambling of the *wh*-PP will not satisfy the EPP-feature on the subordinate T. This is because the subordinate T does not contain a *wh*-feature, given that it is a direct question. The *wh*-feature is on the matrix T. Example (73) shows that this prediction is borne out. The comitative *wh*-PP has scrambled locally within the subordinate clause; as shown, the subordinate subject DP raises to the specifier of the subordinate TP, showing that it is the subject DP, and not the *wh*-PP, that can satisfy the EPP-feature on the subordinate T.

(73) Hanako-ga   Taroo-ni [$_{CP}$[$_{TP}$ dare-to$_i$ [$_{TP}$ zen'in-ga t_i
     Hanako-NOM Taro-DAT [$_{CP}$[$_{TP}$ who-with$_i$ [$_{TP}$ all-NOM t_i
     asoba-nakat-ta]] to]   itta no?
     play-NEG-PAST]] COMP] told Q
     'Hanako told Taro that, with whom, all didn't play?'
     *not > all, all > not

In contrast, if the subordinate clause is an indirect question, local scrambling of a *wh*-PP satisfies the EPP-feature on the embedded T, because this T has a *wh*-feature.

(74) Hanako-ga   [$_{CP}$[$_{TP}$ dare-to$_i$ zen'in-ga t_i asoba-nakat-ta] ka]
     Hanako-NOM [$_{CP}$[$_{TP}$ who-with$_i$ all-NOM t_i play-NEG-PAST] Q]
     siritagatteiru   (yo/to omou).
     wants:to:know
     'Hanako wants to know, with whom, all didn't play.'
     not > all, (all > not)

Example (75) excludes the possibility that this narrow reading of 'all' is facilitated by the verbal complex + Neg + T raising all the way to C in an indirect question. In this example, the *wh*-PP has not been scrambled.

(75) Hanako-ga   [cp[TP zen'in-ga dare-to   asoba-nakat-ta] ka]
     Hanako-NOM [cp[TP all-NOM   who-with play-NEG-PAST] Q]
     siritagatteiru   (yo/to omou).
     wants:to:know
     'Hanako wants to know, with whom, all didn't play.'
     *not > all, all > not

If it were the case that the verbal complex + Neg + T raises to C in an indirect question, this sentence should allow the narrow interpretation of 'all' relative to the negation regardless of the fact that the *wh*-PP has not undergone local scrambling. The fact that such an interpretation is impossible confirms that the narrow reading of 'all' relative to negation in the scrambled example in (74) is due to the fact that the *wh*-PP satisfies the EPP, allowing the subject DP, [all], to stay in situ in [Spec, vP].

Finally, we see the "adverb" effect in the indirect question. If a high adverb occurs after the subject in an object-scrambling environment, the subject must be in [Spec, TP] even in an indirect question, as expected.

(76) Hanako-ga   [cp dare-to$_i$ [TP zen'in-ga saiwaini t_i
     Hanako-NOM [cp who-with$_i$ [TP all-NOM   fortunately t_i
     asoba-nakat-ta] ka] siritagatteiru   (yo/to omou).
     play-NEG-PAST] Q] wants:to:know
     'Hanako wants to know, with whom, all did not fortunately play yesterday.'
     *not > all, all > not

On the other hand, a VP adverb allows the 'all' subject to be interpreted inside the scope of negation when the *wh*-PP scrambles.

(77) Hanako-ga   [cp[TP dare-to$_i$ zen'in-ga yorokonde(wa) t_i
     Hanako-NOM [cp[TP who-with$_i$ all-NOM   happily t_i
     asoba-nakat-ta] ka] siritagatteiru   (yo/to omou).
     play-NEG-PAST] Q] wants:to:know
     'Hanako wants to know, with whom, all did not play happily.'
     not > all, all > not

9.10.2   Long-Distance Scrambling of *Wh*

In sections 9.2–9.6, we saw that a formal feature on T may enter into an agreement with the structural Case on an object DP to license A-movement of the object DP to satisfy the EPP. We also saw that this is not possible if the DP undergoes long-distance scrambling. The relevant example (17), is repeated here.

(78) Syukudai-o$_i$ zen'in-ga [$_{CP}$ sensei-ga t_i dasu   to]
     homework-ACC$_i$ all-NOM   [$_{CP}$ teacher-NOM t_i assigned COMP]
     omowa-nakat-ta (yo/to omou).
     think-NEG-PAST
     'Homework, all did not think that the teacher will give.'
     *not > all, all > not

This is expected because agreement involving a formal feature on T and a structural Case is strictly local; it must be implemented within the local TP domain of the participating features.

Likewise, scrambling a *wh*-phrase long-distance does not allow the scrambled phrase to satisfy the EPP-feature on the matrix T.

(79) Donna   seiseki-o$_i$ zen'in-ga [$_{CP}$ sensei-ga t_i dasu   to]
     what:kind grade-ACC$_i$ all-NOM   [$_{CP}$ teacher-NOM t_i assigned COMP]
     omowa-nakat-ta no?
     think-NEG-PAST   Q
     'What kind of grade, the students all did not think that the teacher will give?'
     *not > all, all > not

This is expected because there is no point in the derivation at which the scrambled *wh*-phrase and the matrix subject are equidistant from the matrix T. Before being attracted by the *wh*-feature on the matrix T, the *wh*-phrase is at the left edge of the lower CP. Even with V raising to T in the matrix clause, the matrix subject 'all' is closer to the matrix T than the *wh*-phrase.

9.11   Concluding Remarks

In this chapter, I explored the possibility of deriving aspects of the configurationality parameter and the *wh*-parameter from considerations related to the EPP. For the configurationality parameter, the difference boils down to whether a language has a particular type of V-to-T movement. If it does, as in the case of Japanese, a nonsubject DP, such as the object, can undergo A-movement to [Spec, TP] to satisfy the EPP-feature on T. A similar phenomenon is attested in Finnish (Holmberg and Nikanne, to appear; see note 17). But this, in turn, leaves a "V-to-T parameter." In

Romance languages, for example, V-to-T movement apparently occurs, yet there is no A-scrambling of the sort found in Japanese and Finnish. We are thus left with "types" of V-to-T movement, where one type, found in languages such as Japanese, licenses A-scrambling, while another type, found in languages such as French, does not. I leave this issue open here. For the *wh*-parameter, I argued, along lines pursued by Watanabe (1992), that the difference boils down to morphology. An overt *wh*-movement language has a *wh*-phrase that is associated with both *wh*- and Q-features. These two are morphologically inseparable. As a result, the entire *wh*-phrase must pied-pipe to [Spec, CP] to satisfy the EPP-feature on C. In Japanese, on the other hand, these two features are distributed between two morphologically separate items. The Q-particle, which is the existential quantifier and is associated with the Q-feature, head-raises to C, as argued by Hagstrom (1998). Head movement can satisfy the EPP-feature on C (Chomsky 2000; also see Alexiadou and Anagnostopoulou 1998). A central question in the chapter was why the *wh*-phrase cannot move to satisfy the EPP-feature on C in Japanese, as it does in English. I gave a number of arguments to show that the *wh*-feature in Japanese is on T instead of C. As a result, there are instances in Japanese in which scrambling of a *wh*-phrase within the TP domain counts as overt *wh*-movement.

Notes

I have benefited from discussions of the subject matter in this chapter with Noam Chomsky, Ken Hale, and David Pesetsky. For helpful comments, I am also grateful to Gugliemo Cinque, Paul Hagstrom, Irene Heim, Sabine Iatridou, Daisuke Inagaki, Shin Ishihara, Richie Kayne, Hisa Kitahara, Howard Lasnik, Norvin Richards, Hiromu Sakai, Takae Tsujioka, Asako Uchibori, Tomo Yoshida, and the anonymous reviewer. Earlier versions were presented at MIT's LF Reading Group, the University of Connecticut, the University of Illinois, SUNY Stonybrook, CUNY, the University of Hiroshima, Keio University, and the University of Venice. I thank those in the audiences for helpful comments.

Finally, and most importantly, I wish to express my gratitude to Ken Hale for his lifetime of work with human language, which continues to this day, and for his support and friendship.

1. The idea that Japanese, a stereotypical nonconfigurational language, lacks the VP node was suggested in earlier work by Hinds (1973). Hinds proposed this in response to Nakau's (1973) analysis that assumed the VP node for Japanese.

2. Bošković and Takahashi (1998) and Kitagawa (1990) propose, along the lines of Hale's original idea, that the various word orders may be base-generated within a hierarchical structure. In Miyagawa 1996, 1997, I propose that the VP-internal "free" orders of the arguments of ditransitive verbs are base-generated.

3. McGinnis (1998) also proposes that A-scrambling is triggered by a feature on T; she calls this feature "Scr(ambling)," which occurs apart from the EPP.

4. A question that will remain unresolved is why certain languages that have overt V-to-T movement (e.g., those in the Romance group) nevertheless fail to evidence scrambling of the sort found in nonconfigurational languages.

5. A natural question that arises is, does the EPP-feature on C arise only in questions? I will remain neutral on this question; at the least, I assume that the EPP applies to C in *wh*-questions.

6. Harada (1977) was the first to suggest that the various word order possibilities in Japanese are due to syntactic movement that is now called scrambling, a term introduced by Ross (1967).

7. Webelhuth (1989) was the first to take up the A/Ā distinction in scrambling. He argued that certain scrambling operations in German have both A and Ā properties simultaneously.

8. There is a question about whether reconstruction in fact provides evidence for Ā-movement. If one assumes that A-chains do not reconstruct, then it is evidence for Ā-scrambling. Otherwise, the reconstruction data are neutral to whether the movement is Ā- or A-movement. See Lasnik 1999 for relevant discussion and references.

9. I have provided two possible ways to end the sentence. One is *yo*, which functions as exclamation. The other is *to omou* '(I) think that …', which has the function of making the example into a subordinate clause. As we will see later, another item that is commonly used with Japanese data, *koto* 'fact', has a different effect on the examples we will look at. Henceforth, I will not gloss the two items at the end of each example.

10. The asterisk in parentheses for the 'all > not' reading is intended to indicate that, for some speakers, this reading is possible. I assume that this reading is due to interpreting 'all' collectively (group reading).

11. There is also an assumption that A-movement of 'all' does not leave an accessible copy in [Spec, *v*P]. This is consistent with the idea that A-movement does not leave an accessible copy (Chomsky 1995), or that the copy is deleted (Lasnik 1999). However, as it turns out, whether a(n) (accessible) copy is left or not depends on the type of quantifier involved. In the construction examined here, with 'all', A-movement clearly does not leave an accessible copy. However, in another type, in which 'all' occurs in the modifier position of a DP, it does leave a copy in [Spec, *v*P]. This is shown by the fact that ['all' N] in subject position may be interpreted inside the scope of negation. (Many native speakers do not allow *zen'in* 'all' in the modifier position; for these speakers, replacing it with *subete* 'all' will produce a natural sentence.)

(i) [Zen'in-no gakusei]-ga   sono tesuto-o uke-nakat-ta   (yo/to omou).
    [all-GEN   students]-NOM that test-ACC take-NEG-PAST
    'All students didn't take that test.'
    not > all, all > not

In this example, an accessible copy of the A-moved subject resides in [Spec, *v*P], where it is able to take scope inside the negation. See Miyagawa 1998 for an analysis of quantifiers and (in)accessible copies. Here, I will use 'all', which does not leave an accessible copy under A-movement.

12. This sentence becomes ambiguous—that is, the 'not > all' interpretation becomes possible—if the predicate is formed from a Sino-Japanese nominal and the light verb.

(i) Zen'in-ga sono tesuto-o teisyutu-si-nakat-ta   (yo/to omou).
    all-NOM   that test-ACC turning:in-do-NEG-PAST
    'All didn't turn in that test.'
    (?)not > all, all > not

This suggests that the Sino-Japanese construction has a complex structure, possibly having an external argument position that the overt subject binds. This external position is c-commanded by the negation. In this chapter, I will only use native Japanese verbs.

13. Virtually every native speaker I have consulted agrees with the distinction between the SOV and the OSV orders noted in the text. For the OSV order in (11b), some speakers find the 'not > all' interpretation somewhat weaker than the other one, indicating that these speakers prefer the Ā-scrambling option for the object. For some speakers, the distinction is more easily detected if the tense is nonpast, as in (i).

(i) a. Zen'in-ga sono tesuto-o uke-na-i   (yo/to omou).
       all-NOM   that test-ACC take-NEG-PRES
       'All will not take that test.'
       *not > all, all > not
    b. Sono tesuto-o$_i$ zen'in-ga t_i uke-na-i   (yo/to omou).
       that   test-ACC$_i$ all-NOM t_i take-NEG-PRES
       'That test, all won't take.'
       not > all, (all > not)

14. The idea that the nominative subject in Japanese may stay in situ in the VP-internal position has been suggested in earlier works (e.g., Fukui 1986; Kitagawa 1986; Kuroda 1988). However, these studies do not correlate this possibility with scrambling of a nonsubject DP. Thus, the analysis presented here contrasts sharply with the earlier ones; in the EPP analysis, some XP must move to [Spec, TP]—either the nominative subject, the accusative object, or, as we will see later, some other DP or PP.

15. Later, we will see that, in fact, the movement to satisfy the EPP is sensitive to certain features that enter into an agreement relationship with a feature on T.

16. In Miyagawa 1997, I make the same nonconfigurational proposal within a configurational structure based on assumptions slightly different from those of the present EPP analysis.

17. Holmberg and Nikanne (to appear) note a similar phenomenon in Finnish. In a transitive construction ('Graham Greene has written this book'), the subject

raises to [Spec, TP], as in (ia), or the object may move into this position, as in (iib). In the latter case, the subject stays in situ in [Spec, *v*P].

(i) a. Graham Greene on kirjoittanut tämän kirjan.
  Graham Greene has written   this   book
 b. Tämän kirjan on kirjoittanut Graham Greene.
  this   book has written   Graham Greene

In (ib), the subject ('Graham Greene') stays in [Spec, *v*P], the verb has moved to T, and the object ('this book') has moved to [Spec, TP].

18. It is possible to force this second structure, by requiring reconstruction of the scrambled object. Note, first of all, that example (i) with the VP adverb 'happily' is ambiguous as expected.

(i) Syasin-o_i zen'in-ga yorokonde(wa) t_i tora-nakat-ta (yo/to omou).
 picture-ACC$_i$ all-NOM happily t_i take-NEG-PAST
 'Picture, all didn't take happily.'
 not > all, all > not

However, in (ii), where the scrambled object must reconstruct owing to the presence of the anaphor, the preferred reading is for the subject 'all' to be interpreted outside the scope of negation (not > happily).

(ii) Zibun-zisin$_j$-no syasin-o_i zen'in$_j$-ga yorokonde(wa) t_i
  self-self$_j$-GEN   picture-ACC$_i$ all$_j$-NOM happily t_i
  tora-nakat-ta (yo/to omou).
  take-NEG-PAST
  'Self's picture, all didn't take happily.'
  *not > all, all > not, not > happily

Thanks to the anonymous reviewer for raising this issue.

19. Saito (1992) and Tada (1993) give evidence for the uniformly Ā nature of long-distance scrambling in Japanese. See Yoshimura 1992 for a slightly different analysis.

20. In an earlier version of this chapter, I marked this sentence as not having partial negation. However, a number of native speakers informed me that it is in fact possible to have partial negation. Although I find it somewhat difficult, I will follow these speakers' judgment; there is certainly a contrast between this example, which allows partial negation (for many speakers), and the example in (22), with the *yo/to omou* 'exclamation/Comp think' ending, which clearly does not allow partial negation.

21. Koizumi (1995) in fact proposes that it is possible for the verbal complex to raise all the way to C. This is a possibility I reject, on empirical grounds. If it were possible, there should be no difference between SOV and OSV order. 'All' in subject position in either order should have an interpretation in which it is inside the scope of negation, because, under the "raising to C" analysis, the negation is at C along with the verbal complex. The fact that there is a clear difference between the unscrambled (SOV) and scrambled (OSV) orders suggests that the verbal complex + negation only raises to T. The one exception is with subjunctive verbs.

22. There is a technical issue here regarding the mechanism for checking the structural Case on the object. In Chomsky 1995, it is proposed that this checking is done by *v*, by adjoining the object DP to *v*P. If this is correct, it would be more accurate to state that the V-*v*-T complex, and not just T, agrees with both the subject DP and the object DP, the latter a function of the verbal complex's having moved to T.

23. This is consistent with the observation by Tada (1992) and Koizumi (1995, 1998) that the nominative object of a stative predicate takes scope higher than the VP in which it originates.

24. Two questions arise (at least) for this analysis. First, where is the "external-ized" goal phrase? It is between the two [Spec, TP]s. There are a number of items that can occur in this position, between the nominative subject and the nominative object. I will assume that the goal phrase is adjoined to the lower TP, although there are other possibilities. Second, what is the ordering of the two movements in the multiple-agreement structure? One possibility is that the nominative object phrase first moves to a [Spec, TP] and that the nominative subject then moves into a higher [Spec, TP]. This meets cyclicity straightforwardly. However, there is an alternative analysis based on Richards's (1997) proposal for multiple specifiers for *wh*-movement. Richards argues that at the point where the first movement occurs, there is only one specifier, and the closer XP is attracted to this specifier. Then, a second, "inner" specifier is created, and the second XP "tucks in" to this inner specifier.

(i) [Spec XP [Spec XP [... *t* ... *t* ...]]]

I will not attempt to argue for one analysis or the other.

25. I thank Noam Chomsky for suggesting this possible reason why Japanese, but not, say, English, has multiple agreement.

26. The Chain Condition is a condition on representation, not on derivation. It is difficult to express such a condition on representation in the minimalist model. Hence, it is likely that the Chain Condition has to be reformulated as some con-dition on locality, although the correct formulation is not precisely clear. Thanks to Richie Kayne for noting this point.

27. The particle *ka* is clearly a question particle. Whether *no* is also a question particle is a matter of debate. It may be that *no* "implies" an (empty) question particle. For example, in an indirect question, only *ka* may be used.

(i) Taroo-ga [CP dare-ga   kuru ka/*no] siritagatteiru.
    Taro-NOM [CP who-NOM come Q]   wants:to:know
    'Taro wants to know who is coming.'

However, it is possible for *no* to appear in front of *ka*, as long as *ka* occurs.

(ii) Taroo-ga [CP dare-ga   kuru no ka] siritagatteiru.
     Taro-NOM [CP who-NOM come   Q] wants:to:know
     'Taro wants to know who is coming.'

No is often used to "nominalize" a clause, and that may be what is going on here.

As a final note, *ka* is marginal in a direct question if the verbal inflection is of the informal-speech style. It is fine with the formal style of speech (Miyagawa 1987). Because I am using the informal speech style throughout this chapter (a common practice for Japanese data), I will use *no* for direct questions and will refer to it as a question particle, keeping open the possibility, noted above, that *no* may imply a phonetically null question particle instead.

28. Yoshida and Yoshida (1997) also mention this in a footnote.

29. A third type is *ndai*, which occurs only with *wh*-questions (see Miyagawa 1998).

(i) a. Dare-ga kuru ndai?
        who-NOM come Q
        'Who will come?'
    b. *Taroo-ga kuru ndai?
        Taro-NOM come Q
        'Will Taro come?'

I will not deal with *ndai* here.

30. Kuroda (1965) was the first to note the possibility that the *wh*-phrase in Japanese is an indefinite expression.

31. This way of analyzing the difference between the English type and the Japanese type is compatible with Pesetsky's 2000 study of *wh*-questions. According to Pesetsky, some languages (e.g., English) have a "specifier" requirement on C, so that a *wh*-phrase must move to this specifier. In other languages (e.g., Japanese), C has no specifier requirement, leading to the *wh*-in-situ phenomenon.

32. In a different context, Richards (1997) also argues that the *wh*-feature in Japanese is on T.

33. A locative/goal PP with an unaccusative verb appears to satisfy the EPP, suggesting that Japanese has locative inversion similar to that found in other languages (e.g., *Into the room walked a man*) (see Bresnan and Kanerva 1989).

(i) Yado-ni$_i$ (zikandoori-ni) zen'in-ga t_i tuka-nakat-ta   (yo/to omou).
    inn-at$_i$ (on time)   all-NOM t_i arrive-NEG-PAST
    'At the inn, all didn't arrive (on time).'
    not > all, all > not

In fact, it appears that, even in the "normal" word order, the subject may take scope inside the negation in this type of unaccusative construction.

(ii) Zen'in-ga zikandoori-ni yado-ni tuka-nakat-ta   (yo/to omou).
     all-NOM   on time   inn-at arrive-NEG-PAST
     'All didn't arrive at the inn on time.'
     not > all, all > not

If this judgment is correct, it suggests that there is an empty expletive in [Spec, TP] to satisfy the EPP. I will leave this topic for further research, including a more careful empirical study of the phenomenon.

34. Koizumi (1995) gives evidence that it is possible for the verb to raise to C in Japanese, although his argument does not demonstrate that this movement is always forced.

35. There is an alternative account of the data we have observed that does not involve the *wh*-feature on T. First, in contrast to the earlier examples, in which a non-*wh* PP cannot satisfy the EPP-feature on T, (i) shows that a non-*wh* PP that is marked for contrastive focus with *wa* can indeed satisfy it.

(i) Hanako-to-wa$_i$ zen'in-ga t_i hanasa-nakat-ta (yo/to omou).
    Hanako-with-CNTR$_i$ all-NOM t_i speak-NEG-PAST
    'With Hanako, all did not speak.'
    not > all, all > not

As shown, the subject 'all' may be interpreted inside the scope of negation, suggesting that the contrastive comitative phrase, 'with Hanako', fulfills the EPP requirement. Because a noncontrastive PP does not fulfill the EPP requirement, as we have seen, this suggests that contrastive focus is also a feature that occurs on T. Returning to the *wh*-PP facts, one possibility is that the relevant feature on T for the *wh*-construction is not *wh*, but focus, just as in (i). That is, a *wh*-phrase has a focus feature that agrees with the same feature on T, which makes it possible to establish an agreement relationship. This account has the advantage of collapsing the *wh*-construction with the contrastive focus construction. However, it complicates the picture of A- versus Ā-scrambling. In Miyagawa 1997, I suggested that A-scrambling is triggered by some feature on T, which, in this chapter, I argue to be the EPP. Ā-scrambling is triggered by focus. However, if the remarks in this note are anywhere on the right track, it appears that there is focus movement that is also A-scrambling. A number of conceptual and empirical issues must be investigated for this alternative, "focus" account. I will leave it as an open issue.

References

Alexiadou, Artemis, and Elena Anagnostopoulou. 1998. Parametrizing AGR, word order, V-movement, and EPP-checking. *Natural Language & Linguistic Theory* 16, 491–539.

Bošković, Željko, and Daiko Takahashi. 1998. Scrambling and Last Resort. *Linguistic Inquiry* 29, 347–366.

Bresnan, Joan, and Jonni Kanerva. 1989. Locative inversion in Chicheŵa: A case study of factorization in grammar. *Linguistic Inquiry* 20, 1–50.

Cheng, Lisa L.-S. 1991. On the typology of *wh*-questions. Doctoral dissertation, MIT, Cambridge, Mass.

Chierchia, Gennaro. 1991. Functional WH and weak crossover. In *Proceedings of the Tenth West Coast Conference on Formal Linguistics*, edited by Dawn Bates, 75–90. Stanford, Calif.: CSLI Publications.

Chierchia, Gennaro. 1993. Questions with quantifiers. *Natural Language Semantics* 1, 181–234.

Chomsky, Noam. 1993. A minimalist program for linguistic theory. In *The view from Building 20*, edited by Kenneth Hale and Samuel Jay Keyser, 1–52. Cambridge, Mass.: MIT Press.

Chomsky, Noam. 1995. Categories and transformations. In *The Minimalist Program*, 219–394. Cambridge, Mass.: MIT Press.

Chomsky, Noam. 2000. Minimalist inquiries: The framework. In *Step by step*, edited by Roger Martin, David Michaels, and Juan Uriagereka, 89–155. Cambridge, Mass.: MIT Press.

Emonds, Joseph. 1976. *A transformational approach to English syntax*. New York: Academic Press.

Engdahl, Elisabet. 1980. The syntax and semantics of questions in Swedish. Doctoral dissertation, University of Massachusetts, Amherst.

Engdahl, Elisabet. 1986. *Constituent questions*. Dordrecht: Reidel.

Farmer, Ann. 1980. On the interaction of morphology and syntax. Doctoral dissertation, MIT, Cambridge, Mass.

Fukui, Naoki. 1986. A theory of category projection and its application. Doctoral dissertation, MIT, Cambridge, Mass.

Fukui, Naoki. 1993. Parameters and optionality. *Linguistic Inquiry* 24, 399–420.

Groenendijk, Jeroen, and Martin Stokhof. 1984. *Studies on the semantics of questions and the pragmatics of answers*. Amsterdam: Academisch Proefschrift.

Hagstrom, Paul. 1998. Decomposing questions. Doctoral dissertation, MIT, Cambridge, Mass.

Hale, Ken. 1980. Remarks on Japanese phrase structure: Comments on the papers on Japanese syntax. In *Theoretical issues in Japanese linguistics*, edited by Yukio Otsu and Ann Farmer, 185–203. MIT Working Papers in Linguistics 2. MITWPL, Department of Linguistics and Philosophy, MIT, Cambridge, Mass.

Hale, Ken. 1983. Warlpiri and the grammar of non-configurational languages. *Natural Language & Linguistic Theory* 1, 5–47.

Hamblin, C. L. 1973. Questions in Montague English. *Foundations of Language* 10, 41–53.

Harada, S.-I. 1977. Nihongo-ni henkei-wa hitsuyoo da (Transformations are needed in Japanese). *Gengo* 6, 11–12.

Heim. Irene. 1982. The semantics of definite and indefinite noun phrases. Doctoral dissertation, University of Massachusetts, Amherst.

Hinds, John. 1973. Some remarks on *soo su-*. *Papers in Japanese Linguistics* 2, 18–30.

Hiraiwa, Ken. To appear. On nominative-genitive conversion. In *A few from Building E39*, edited by Elena Guerzoni and Ora Matushansky. MIT Working Papers in Linguistics. MITWPL, Department of Linguistics and Philosophy, MIT, Cambridge, Mass.

Hoji, Hajime. 1985. Logical Form constraints and configurational structures in Japanese. Doctoral dissertation, University of Washington, Seattle.

Holmberg, Anders, and Urpo Nikanne. To appear. Expletives, subjects and topics in Finnish. In *Subjects, expletives and the EPP*, edited by Peter Svenonius. Oxford: Oxford University Press.

Huang, C.-T. James. 1982. Logical relations in Chinese and the theory of grammar. Doctoral dissertation, MIT, Cambridge, Mass.

Karttunen, Lauri. 1973. Syntax and semantics of questions. *Linguistics and Philosophy* 1, 3–44.

Kitagawa, Yoshihisa. 1986. Subjects in Japanese and English. Doctoral dissertation, University of Massachusetts, Amherst.

Kitagawa, Yoshihisa. 1990. Anti-scrambling. Ms., University of Rochester, Rochester, N.Y.

Klima, Edward. 1964. Negation in English. In *The structure of language*, edited by Jerry A. Fodor and Jerrold Katz, 246–323. Englewood Cliffs, N.J.: Prentice-Hall.

Koizumi, Masatoshi. 1995. Phrase structure in minimalist syntax. Doctoral dissertation, MIT, Cambridge, Mass.

Koizumi, Masatoshi. 1998. Remarks on nominative objects. *Journal of Japanese Linguistics* 16, 39–66.

Kuno, Susumu. 1973. *The structure of the Japanese language*. Cambridge, Mass.: MIT Press.

Kuroda, S.-Y. 1965. Generative grammatical studies in the Japanese language. Doctoral dissertation, MIT, Cambridge, Mass.

Kuroda, S.-Y. 1988. Whether we agree or not: A comparative syntax of English and Japanese. *Lingvisticæ Investigationes* 12, 1–47.

Laka, Itziar. 1990. Negation in syntax: On the nature of functional categories and projections. Doctoral dissertation, MIT, Cambridge, Mass.

Lasnik, Howard. 1999. Chains of arguments. In *Working minimalism*, edited by Samuel David Epstein and Norbert Hornstein, 189–215. Cambridge, Mass.: MIT Press.

Mahajan, Anoop. 1990. The A/A-bar distinction and movement theory. Doctoral dissertation, MIT, Cambridge, Mass.

May, Robert. 1985. *Logical Form*. Cambridge, Mass.: MIT Press.

McGinnis, Martha Jo. 1998. Locality in A-movement. Doctoral dissertation, MIT, Cambridge, Mass.

Miyagawa, Shigeru. 1987. LF affix raising in Japanese. *Linguistic Inquiry* 18, 362–367.

Miyagawa, Shigeru. 1989. *Structure and Case marking in Japanese*. New York: Academic Press.

Miyagawa, Shigeru. 1996. Word order restrictions and nonconfigurationality. In *Formal Approaches to Japanese Linguistics 2*, edited by Masatoshi Koizumi, Masayuki Oishi, and Uli Sauerland, 117–141. MIT Working Papers in Linguistics 29. MITWPL, Department of Linguistics and Philosophy, MIT, Cambridge, Mass.

Miyagawa, Shigeru. 1997. Against optional scrambling. *Linguistic Inquiry* 28, 1–26.

Miyagawa, Shigeru. 1998. *Wh* chains and quantifier induced barriers. Ms., MIT, Cambridge, Mass.

Nakau, Minoru. 1973. *Sentential complementation in Japanese.* Tokyo: Kaitakusha.

Nemoto, Naoko. 1993. Chains and Case positions: A study from scrambling in Japanese. Doctoral dissertation, University of Connecticut, Storrs.

Nishigauchi, Taisuke. 1990. *Quantification in the theory of grammar.* Dordrecht: Kluwer.

Pesetsky, David. 2000. *Phrasal movement and its kin.* Cambridge, Mass.: MIT Press.

Pollock, Jean-Yves. 1989. Verb movement, Universal Grammar, and the structure of IP. *Linguistic Inquiry* 20, 365–424.

Richards, Norvin. 1997. What moves where when in which language? Doctoral dissertation, MIT, Cambridge, Mass.

Rizzi, Luigi. 1986. On chain formation. In *Syntax and semantics 19: The syntax of pronominal clitics*, edited by Hagit Borer, 65–95. New York: Academic Press.

Ross, John R. 1967. Constraints on variables in syntax. Doctoral dissertation, MIT, Cambridge, Mass.

Saito, Mamoru. 1985. Some asymmetries in Japanese and their theoretical implications. Doctoral dissertation, MIT, Cambridge, Mass.

Saito, Mamoru. 1989. Scrambling as semantically vacuous A′-movement. In *Alternative conceptions of phrase structure*, edited by Mark Baltin and Anthony Kroch, 182–200. Chicago: University of Chicago Press.

Saito, Mamoru. 1992. Long distance scrambling in Japanese. *Journal of East Asian Linguistics* 1, 69–118.

Saito, Mamoru, and Naoki Fukui. 1998. Order in phrase structure and movement. *Linguistic Inquiry* 29, 439–474.

Saito, Mamoru, and Hajime Hoji. 1983. Weak crossover and Move α in Japanese. *Natural Language & Linguistic Theory* 1, 245–259.

Snyder, William. 1992. Chain-formation and crossover. Ms., MIT, Cambridge, Mass.

Tada, Hiroaki. 1992. Nominative objects in Japanese. *Journal of Japanese Linguistics* 14, 91–108.

Tada, Hiroaki. 1993. A/A′ partition in derivation. Doctoral dissertation, MIT, Cambridge, Mass.

Takahashi, Daiko. 1993. Movement of *wh*-phrases in Japanese. *Natural Language & Linguistic Theory* 11, 655–678.

Takano, Yuji. 1998. Object shift and scrambling. *Natural Language & Linguistic Theory* 16, 817–889.

Ura, Hiroyuki. 1996. Multiple feature-checking: A theory of grammatical function splitting. Doctoral dissertation, MIT, Cambridge, Mass.

Watanabe, Akira. 1992. Subjacency and S-Structure movement of *wh*-in-situ. *Journal of East Asian Linguistics* 1, 255–291.

Watanabe, Akira. 1996. Nominative-genitive conversion and agreement in Japanese: A cross-linguistic perspective. *Journal of East Asian Linguistics* 5, 373–410.

Webelhuth, Gert. 1989. Syntactic saturation phenomena and the modern Germanic languages. Doctoral dissertation, University of Massachusetts, Amherst.

Whitman, John. 1986. Configurationality parameters. In *Issues in Japanese linguistics*, edited by Takashi Imai and Mamoru Saito, 351–374. Dordrecht: Foris.

Yoshida, Keiko, and Tomoyuki Yoshida. 1997. Question marker drop in Japanese. *International Christian University Language Research Bulletin* 11, 37–54.

Yoshimura, Noriko. 1992. Scrambling and anaphora in Japanese. Doctoral dissertation, University of Southern California, Los Angeles.

Chapter 10

Grammar Games:	Wayne O'Neil
Unscrambling Skaldic	
Syntax	

10.1 Introduction

Ken Hale, writing about creativity in Aboriginal verse, points out that the "wealth possessed by a human community . . . is in great measure 'mental' or 'intellectual.'" He goes on to note that although "Aboriginal Australia has produced a good number of true monuments to the human intellect, [they] have gone unnoticed and unappreciated by non-Aboriginal observers precisely because they are products of the mind, accessible only through the language in which they are expressed and often requiring strenuous effort on the part of the learner who seeks to uncover or to master the principles which inhere in them" (Hale 1984, 284).

In the research presented here, although I cannot claim to have mastered them, I have uncovered what I believe to be some of "the principles which inhere in" another "monument to the human intellect": the syntactically intricate skaldic poetry of medieval Scandinavia, chiefly of Iceland—an intellectual endeavor nearly as far removed from Aboriginal Australia by temperament, by place, and by climate as is possible, but (like Aboriginal verse) one that clearly reveals the intellectual "wealth possessed by a human community" living under severely limited material conditions.

10.2 Skaldic Poetry Itself

Skaldic poetry has the characteristics of a language game as outlined by Hale and Nash (1997, 248) in their discussion of Damin, a language auxiliary to Lardil (invented, perhaps):

• "in a number of ways it is dependent on the 'everyday language' . . .";
• "it shows a degree of consciousness of linguistic elements for which evidence is quite poor or lacking in everyday language";

• "apart from the specific ways in which it is distinguished from the everyday language of its speakers, the special language shares its remaining regularities."

The language game that is skaldic poetry—focusing here on the *dróttkvætt* ("court-meter") stanza, the most popular and widely used of the verse types—exhibits the following properties, the first four formal and more or less required, the other three optional:

• each stanza consists of eight lines made up of syntactically and semantically complete four-line half stanzas (*helmingar*);
• each line consists of six syllables, with three main stresses, and ends in a trochee;
• pairs of lines are bound together by alliteration on three stressed syllables (two in odd-numbered lines, one in even-numbered lines);
• each line contains internal rimes on two stressed syllables (near rime in odd-numbered lines, perfect rime in even-numbered lines);
• the poetry often contains elaborate figures of speech (*kennings*) of up to seven terms, based in Scandinavian and Germanic mythology and elite social convention;
• word order may be quite free compared with that of everyday language;
• the several clauses of a stanza may be intercalated, or interlaced.

Because of these rigid formal requirements, skaldic verse is somewhat impervious to corruption in its textual transmission, although it is also important to realize that skaldic poetry—surviving only in written form, of course—was composed, presented, received, and transmitted orally.

The seven characteristics of skaldic poetry are illustrated in the first *helmingr* of the following *dróttkvætt* stanza, *Grettis saga Ásmundarsonar 9* (Jónsson 1936, 39), where the rimes—near and perfect—are indicated by underlining, alliteration by double underlining, and intercalated clauses by parentheses. The figures of speech are made clear in the translation.

(1) M̲i̲k vill m̲enja st̲økkvir
      Me will treasures' dispenser
      (m̲jök k̲e̲nnik þess) br̲e̲nna,
      (greatly feel-I this) burn,
      h̲odda gr̲u̲nd, á h̲ön̲dum
      treasures' field, on hands
      (h̲öfugt r̲á̲ð es þat) b̲á̲ðum.
      (heavy matter is that) both.

'A man [= treasures' dispenser] wishes to burn me on both my hands, woman [= treasures' field]. I feel this greatly. That is a serious matter.'

In addition to the conventional kennings in *Grettis saga 9* (reflecting a world in which men dispense treasures that women then display), we see that the narrative clause of this *lausavísa* (occasional verse) is interrupted three times: the infinitive *brenna* is separated from its object *mik*, the modal *vill*, and the subject *menja støkkvir* by an exclamatory clause; the adjunctive PP is separated from the rest of the main clause by the vocative *hodda grund*; and the two-part NP of the adjunctive PP *á höndum báðum* is broken up by a second exclamatory clause. However, abstracting away from these interruptions (none of which is itself exceptional syntactically) and ignoring the figurative language, we see that the several parts of the narrative clause fall into one of the possible word orders of everyday Old Icelandic (insofar as that can be determined):

- the modal *vill* has been raised to C^0;
- the pronoun *mik* has been raised to [Spec, CP];
- both the subject *menja støkkvir* and the infinitive *brenna*—the main verb of the clause—remain in their underlying positions,
- the PP *á höndum báðum* having been adjoined to the right.

Only the inversion of *báðum höndum* to *höndum ... báðum*, satisfying the alliteration on /h/ and the rimes of lines three and four (/Vnd/, /áð/), is slightly exceptional—more about this below.

Taking all these characteristics of skaldic poetry together, Lee Hollander asserted that "we have in it a formal artificiality not found to this degree elsewhere in world literature" (Hollander 1965, 636). Whatever the status of its complexity in world literature, it is certainly the case that skaldic poetry is "accessible only through the language in which [it is] expressed" and requires "strenuous effort on the part of the [person] who seeks to uncover or to master the principles which inhere in [it]." Snorri Sturluson, in his *Edda* (Jónsson 1935)—in part a thirteenth-century handbook of eddic and skaldic poetics, explicated many of the most striking characteristics of skaldic poetry, but as Hollander has pointed out (with respect to the last of the seven characteristics listed above), Snorri "lends us no hand here. . . . He merely furnishes us the technical term *stál* (pl. *stælir*) for the phenomenon . . ." (Hollander 1965, 636). Edwards, on the basis of her exhaustive examination of the entire corpus of skaldic poetry (from the ninth through the fourteenth centuries), also notes that "the skalds them-selves, despite their taste for exultant comment on their own art, make no proven references to clause arrangement or syntax" (Edwards 1983, 173).

In the present chapter, I offer an explanation of these two phenomena (clause intercalation and word order—what we might think of as phrase intercalation), their appearance in the poetry driven to a certain extent by the formal conditions that a well-formed verse is required to meet. The surprisingly simple conclusions are that a perceptual constraint on clause intercalation more or less follows from the finiteness of memory of a sort specific (perhaps) to language processing, and that skaldic word order fol-lows from a simple relaxation of the constraints on the ordinary syntactic movement possible in Old Icelandic, thus allowing *parts* of a constituent, rather than the whole constituent, to raise to the left and right edges of a construction.

10.3   Clause Intercalation

In the 1920s, Konstantin Reichardt described the basic constraint on clause intercalation in skaldic poetry: "Bevor der zweite Satz nicht abgeschlossen ist, kann ein dritter Satz nicht gespalten eingeschoben werden" ('A third split sentence cannot be inserted before the second sentence is concluded'; Reichardt 1928, 80). In other words, there is a limit of two on how many incomplete, suspended clauses the composer/listener can be required at any one time to carry in his head, or hers (for there *were* woman skalds; see Helgadóttir 1961). The suspension of three clauses moves the task beyond some more or less well defined perceptual limit. Thus, if we let A, B, C,... stand for the several clauses of a *helmingr*, and $A_1, A_2, \ldots, B_1$, $B_2, \ldots$, and $C_1, C_2, \ldots$ be the clauses partitioned into their several parts, then (2) is a possible intercalation of these clauses,

(2) $A_1, B_1, A_2, C_1, B_2, C_2$

while (3) is not.

(3) *$A_1, B_1, C_1, A_2, B_2, C_2$

In (1), for example, the intercalation pattern (not counting the vocative *hodda grund*) is much simpler than allowed:

(4) $A_1, B, A_2, (\textit{hodda grund}), A_3, C, A_4$

For in this verse, the main clause is parceled out in four parts across the full length of the *helmingr*, the two exclamatory clauses and the vocative phrase coming in syntactically complete and themselves uninterrupted.

Egils saga Skalla-grímssonar 46 (Nordal 1933, 227) exhibits a more complex two-clause intercalation, in both its *helmingar:* A_1, B_1, A_2, B_2; C_1, D_1, C_2, D_2.

(5) Drekkum ór, þótt Ekkills
    (A₁) Let-us-drink fully, (B₁) although Ekkill's
    eykríðr beri tíðum
    horse-rider bear often
    horna sund at hendi,
    horns' sound to,
    hvert full, bragar Ulli;
    (A₂) each toast, (B₂) poetry's Ullr;
    leifik vætr, þótt Laufa
    (C₁) leave-I nought, (D₁) although Laufi's
    leikstœrir mér fœri,
    spear-advancer me bring,
    hrosta tjarnar horni,
    (C₂) mash's lake (in) the horn,
    horn til dags at morni.
    (D₂) horns until dawn tomorrow.
    'Let us drink every draught fully even though [Ekkill's horse = ship; a ship's rider =] the man should bring the poet [= bragar Ulli] ale [i.e., horns' sound] without stop; I will leave no ale [= mash's lake] in the horn even though the man [= Laufi's spear-advancer] bring me horns until dawn tomorrow.'

And the first *helmingr* of *Egils saga 51* (Nordal 1933, 269) is an example of three-clause intercalation within four lines of poetry (A_1, B_1, A_2, C_1, B_2, C_2), more or less the outer limit of permissible and possible complexity, given the four lines and 24 syllables at the poet's disposal.

(6) Þverra nú, þeirs þverrðu,
    (A₁) Grow-fewer now, (B₁) those-who decreased,
    þingbirtingar Ingva,
    (A₂) assembly-luminaries Ingvi's,
    hvar skalk manna mildra,
    (C₁) where shall-I men munificent,
    mjaðveitar dag, leita. . .?

(B₂) mead-carving's day, (C₂) look-for...?
'Now chieftains [= Ingvi's assembly-luminaries] grow fewer in
number, who squandered gold [= mead-carving's day]. Where am I
to find munificent men...?'

While Reichardt provides a useful descriptive account of clause intercalation in skaldic poetry of this sort (see more recently Bach 1972;
Edwards 1983, 1984), we would like to have an explanation of it.

An explanation cannot lie in the grammar of the language, for the
grammar does not allow for clauses other than relative clauses to repeatedly break into the flow of a sentence (e.g., nesting and self-embedding),
and even given these possibilities, there is a strong tendency for relative
clauses to be right-adjoined in Old Icelandic prose as in Old Germanic
generally (see O'Neil 1977)—an observation about performance, perhaps,
not about grammar. If, however, we take clause intercalation to be playing with or seeking to challenge perceptually constrained but relative
limits on nesting and self-embedding, then we can begin to see what might
account for Reichardt's condition on clause intercalation: it could simply
follow from the fact that memory for such things is indeed short, brought
close to its limits if required to store more than one incomplete syntactic
structure while dealing with a second of the same or similar type. Matters
of this sort were dealt with long ago by Chomsky and Miller (1963, 471ff.)
and Chomsky (1965, 10–15). (For recent, detailed discussion, see Gibson's
(2000) distance-based theory of linguistic complexity.) Chomsky, for
example, after observing that "repeated nesting contributes to unacceptability" and that "self-embedding contributes still more radically to unacceptability," concludes (1965, 13–14):

To account for the greater unacceptability of self-embedding ..., we must add
other conditions on the perceptual device beyond mere limitation of memory. We
might assume, for example, that the perceptual device has a stock of analytic
procedures available to it, ... and ... that it is unable (or finds it difficult) to utilize
a procedure φ while it is in the course of executing φ.

If skaldic clause intercalation is indeed held in check by a relative limit
on processing space, then it should be possible in this skaldic world of
artifice and virtuosity to find verses that try to go further beyond understanding than the constraint already given by Reichardt. *Egils saga 45*
(Nordal 1933, 226) is one example, having the pattern in (7),

(7) A_1, B_1, C_1, B_2, C_2, A_2

though it is interesting to note that this crude verse is generally considered spurious—not composed by Egill, a written composition perhaps.

(8) Títt erum verð at vátta,
     (A₁) Eager am-I meal to witness,
    vætti berk, at hættak,
     (B₁) witness bear-I, (C₁) that ventured-I,
    þung, til þessar göngu,
     (B₂) heavy, (C₂) on this journey,
    þinn kinnaló minni. . . .
     (A₂) your spew my. . . .
    'I am eager to witness your meal with my vomit. I bear heavy witness that I ventured on this journey.'

There are a few other such examples in the corpus, but very few. The data (in schematic form) are fully presented in both Reichardt 1928 and Edwards 1983.

To conclude the discussion of clause intercalation: intercalation at this level of syntax, by Edwards's count (1983, 144) characteristic of about 20 percent of the extant *dróttkvætt* verse, is constrained by the finiteness of grammatical memory—that is, by performance factors and not by the grammar of the language. Clearly this is a relative rather than an absolute constraint, one that might be the target of poetic license and/or challenged once written composition became possible. Edwards notes, however, a countervailing fourteenth-century development "towards the simpler patterns of clause arrangement," which she suggests "undoubtedly reflects the changed role of skaldic poetry—now much less an élitist medium for the praise of princes or the display of personal virtuosity than a vehicle for Christian devotional and didactic material, especially hagiography" (1984, 138).

10.4 Word Order: Poetic Scrambling

At first glance, the word order of skaldic poetry seems unprincipled and thus a mystery. However, in the standard editions of the Icelandic sagas (where much of the extant skaldic poetry is found), difficult verses are explicated in a way that allows a second glance and provides an approach to explaining the intricacies of skaldic poetic word order. From this point of view, consider *Egils saga 51*, given in (6) above. In a footnote to this verse, Nordal (1933) places the words, phrases, and clauses in an order that we can take to be their order in everyday Old Icelandic—with some influence from the syntax of his Modern Icelandic.

(9) Þverra nú Ingva þingbirtingar (a), þeirs þverrðu mjaðveitar dag (b); hvar skalk leita mildra manna ...?

Each of the kennings (marked (a) and (b) in (9)) is then glossed—(a), for example.

(10) a) *Ingva* (sækonungs) *þing:* orusta; *birtingr* (bjartur, frægur maður?) smbr. *rógbirtingr:* hermaður ...

That is, Ingvi is the king of the sea; his assembly is battle, the luminaries of battle being chieftains; *þingbirtingr* is to be compared (*smbr.*) with the compound noun *rógbirtingr* 'strife-luminary', which is taken to mean 'warrior'; and so on. Finally, Nordal gives a Modern Icelandic translation of the verse, to which I have added an English translation.

(11) Nú fækkar þeim höfðingjum, sem sóuðu gulli; hvar á eg að leita hinna örlátu manna ...?
'Now the chieftains grow fewer in number, who squandered gold; where am I to find munificent men ...?'

If we take seriously the notion that the word order given to the verse by Nordal is characteristic of everyday Old Icelandic, then we see that in composing his verse, Egill has in this case "simply" done the following:

• suspended the main clause after a normal tensed-V, adverbial opening;
• suspended the relative clause after a normal relative subject, tensed-V opening;
• completed the main clause by providing its subject;
• suspended the next main clause (a question) after giving the question word, the modal with a cliticized subject, and the object;
• completed the relative clause by providing its object;
• finally completed the question by providing its main verb—the infinitive *leita*—clause-finally.

Note that in this verse, basic constituents are not themselves broken up and distributed through the clause; it is simply "the audience's grammatical sense [that is] called into play by the suspended constructions" (Edwards 1983, 166) as it works to match the clause parts up in order to perceive the whole.

But matters can be much more difficult, and as Edwards correctly concludes, "further assessment of the potential 'difficulty' of skaldic poetry would need to embrace other aspects of composition including internal word order and diction" (1983, 144). For it is at the level of word order that not only is "the audience's grammatical sense called into play by the suspended constructions but also their semantic sense...: [for example,] given a suspended clause-part containing a word for 'fire' and certain semantic clues, an alert audience might listen for a word meaning 'of water/the sea' in the completion in order to form a kenning for 'gold'" (Edwards 1983, 166). Though the parts of a constituent may be dispersed, the conventionality of the kennings aids in reconstructing it, as we see below. (Enjambment also helps the audience; see the appendix.)

We now turn to an explication of the complexities of "[clause-] internal word order"—first to a relatively simple but instructive example, a two-constituent, three-word clause from *Grettis saga 4* (Jónsson 1936, 20), itself broken up by parts of another clause (a matter not relevant to the analysis).

(12) Skáldi sígr ... þvísa.
   Poet slides ... this.
   'This poet is going downhill.'

From underlying [NP V_{tensed}] (syntactic representations simplified here and below for ease of explication), the everyday language would allow, by raising the tensed V to C^0 and the NP (optionally) to [Spec, CP], both structures (13) and (14).

(13) [V_{tensed} [NP t_V]]

(14) [NP [V_{tensed} [t_{NP} t_V]]]

But in the poem, just the N of the NP has been raised to [Spec, CP], leaving the demonstrative in place and thus violating a constraint on XP-movement.

(15) [N [V_{tensed} [[D t_N] t_V]]]

This partial relaxation of the constraint on constituent movement, together with clause intercalation, is basic to an explanation of skaldic word order, which when iterated leads to greater and greater complexity and artifice. Consider *Gunnlaugs saga ormstungu 14* (Nordal and Jónsson 1938, 90), for example, which takes matters a step further.

(16) Fold nemr flaum af skaldi
     Earth takes joy from poet
     flóðhyrs, . . .
     sea-fire's, . . .
     'The woman [sea-fire's earth: sea-fire = gold—a reference to the
     Rhine gold; gold's earth = woman] deprives the poet of joy.'

In this case, we begin with at least this (somewhat simplified) underlying
structure,

(17) [[NP] [NP PP V_{tensed}]]

which then requires V-raising to C^0 and allows the raising of any one of
the other major constituents to [Spec, CP]. But instead we find this:

(18) [[N [V_{tensed} [[$t_N t_D$] [NP PP t_V]]]] flóðhyrs]

That is, in addition to the tensed V raising to C^0, the subject of the clause
has raised out of its underlying position, but in two pieces, moving in
opposite directions to the separate edges of the clause: the N to [Spec,
CP], the genitive determiner (*flóðhyrs*) to right-adjoined position.

   A rough formulation of this basic principle of skaldic scrambling goes
as follows:

(19) Raising proper parts of a constituent is allowed, but only to the
     edges of the clause, either to [Spec, CP] or to a right-adjoined
     position.

(It is in fact possible to break up a compound noun in this way as well;
see Reichardt 1969 on tmesis.)

   Grettis saga 19 (Jónsson 1936, 70) provides an example of one way in
which a three-part constituent can be distributed.

(20) Tolf höfum gröf hjá gjalfri
     twelve have-we grave by sea
     gunnelds búit runnum.
     war-fire's prepared trees.
     'I have prepared a grave by the sea for twelve warriors [= war-fire's
     trees].'

In this case, two of the three parts of the NP have raised to opposite edges
of the clause, leaving one of its parts in place. The underlying structure
in (21)

(21) [[gröf hjá gjalfri] [tolf gunnelds runnum] [búit] höfum]

yields the construction in (22) through movement of the tensed V to C^0, the quantifier *tolf* out of its NP to [Spec, CP], and the N *runnum* to a right-adjoined position, leaving the genitive determiner *gunnelds* and the nonfinite *búit* in their underlying positions.

(22) [tolf [höfum [[gröf hjá gjalfri] [[t_{tolf}] [gunnelds t_N]] [búit] t_V] runnum]

Note in passing that Universal Grammar allows for similar sorts of movement in languages that exhibit scrambling—see Miyagawa 1989 on Japanese, for example. Skaldic poetry thus allows in part what is possible in language though impossible in everyday Icelandic.

Thus far, we have seen how the parts of a single constituent can be raised to the left and right edges of a clause, raising to the left being by far the more common. There is, moreover, no raising to the right without raising to the left as well—a modification to be incorporated into the principle given in (19).

Is it possible, then, to raise a part of one constituent to the left and a part of another to the right? There are no clear examples of this, but the inversion of adjective-noun to noun-adjective in the second *helmingr* of *Egils saga 45* (Nordal 1933, 226) and elsewhere in the poetic corpus suggests this possibility.

(23) Margr velr gestr, þars gistir,
  (A₁) Many chooses guest, (B) where "guests,"
  gjöld, finnumsk vér sjaldan,
  (A₂) rewards, (C) meet we seldom,
  Ármóði liggi, œðri,
  (D₁) Ármóðr's lie, (A₃) better,
  ölðra dregg í skeggi.
  (D₂) drinking dregs on beard.
  'Many a guest chooses better payment, there where he spends the night. We seldom meet one another. The drinking dregs lie on Ármóðr's beard.'

Taking into consideration just the clause *margr velr gestr . . . gjöld œðri*, the problem is how to account for the inverted noun-adjective order of *gjöld œðri*. It is explained if we assume that *œðri* is right-adjoined as in the following structure:

(24) [[margr [velr [[t_{margr} gestr] [[$t_{œðri}$ gjöld] [t_V]]]]] œðri]

Here the tensed V *velr* is raised to C^0, the adjective *margr* is raised out of the subject NP to [Spec, CP], and the adjective *œðri* is right-adjoined out of the object NP, the heads of these NPs being left in underlying position. Perhaps there are more convincing examples of this phenomenon, and it would not be surprising to find them, but they have yet to appear in the data that I have examined.

Finally, as Edwards points out (1983, 162), "the flexible patterning of clauses and clause parts in the helming gives the skald a means for the display of virtuosity which first and foremost serves to distinguish the poetry from the everyday language, and hence to invite the admiration and the intellectual participation of the audience." This suggests that since the "patterning of clauses and clause parts" operates on different levels, it is possible for the poet to deploy both clause intercalation and scrambling in the composition of a single *helmingr*.

We are not disappointed in this expectation. As an example of this level of complexity, see *Egils saga 23* (Nordal 1933, 148), but with Kock's parsing (1949, 29)—other suggested parsings being ill formed from the present point of view.

(25) Ókynni vensk, einnis,

    (A₁) Uncouthness is-used-to, (B₁) forehead's,

    ung, þorðak vel forðum,

    (A₂) young, (B₂) dared-I well formerly,

    hauka klifs, at hefja,

    (A₃) hawk's cliff's, (B₃) to raise,

    Hlín, þvergnípur mínar;

    (A₄) Hlín, (B₄) cross-cliffs my;

    'The young woman [hawk's cliff = arm; arm's Hlín, a

    goddess = woman] is accustomed to (my) uncouthness; I dared to

    stare at her, lit. raise my eyebrows [= forehead's cross-cliffs].'

In this verse, each of the two main clauses is partitioned into four parts, the poet then working back and forth between the two clauses. Note that the subject of the first clause is thus broken into three pieces by parts of the second clause and the object of the second clause is broken into two pieces by parts of the first clause. The first clause is not, however, unusual in its word order; if we take away the intervening pieces of the second clause, we find, ignoring the conventional figure of speech, a piece of everyday language,

(26) [ókynni [vensk [[ung hauka klifs Hlín] [t_{NP} t_V]]]]

with the tensed V raised to C^0 and its dative "object" raised to [Spec, CP], the complex subject NP remaining in place as required.

The other clause shows more complexity, the kenning for eyebrow being broken up by its genitive determiner *einnis* raising to [Spec, CP], and the movement to a right-adjoined position of its contained NP *þvergnípur mínar*.

As a final comment on this verse, note that its woman-kenning is a good example of what Edwards sees as a play both on the audience's grammatical sense and on its semantic sense:

- *ung* requires an animate N in a particular case and number further on;
- *hauka klifs*, a kenning for arm or hand—the surface on which the hawk (a hunting bird) sits—needs a person to attach to;
- *Hlín*, a goddess (wife of Óðinn), satisfies both demands.

It is possible to find verses that cannot be explained by the principle given above: *Egils saga 5* (Nordal 1933, 82), for example.

(27) Síþögla gaf söglum
(A) Ever-silent gave (to) word-quick
sárgagls þría Agli
wound-gosling's three (to) Egill
herðimeiðr við hróðri
hardy-tree with praise
hagr brimrótar gagra;
skillful furious-surf's hounds;
'The skillful man [= wound-gosling's [= weapon's] hardy-tree] gave witty Egill three snails(?) [= quiet hounds of the furious surf] as a gift [= with praise].'

In this verse, the following typical moves have taken place:

- tensed V (*gaf*) has moved to C^0;
- part of the object (*síþögla*) has moved to [Spec, CP], another part of it (*brimrótar gagra*) being adjoined at the right edge of the clause—a nice illustration, were it not in this unstructured verse, of what (23) does not strongly show;
- the quantifier *þría* of the object NP has been left in place.

But then, in addition to these normal cases of poetic movement, we find others unconstrained by principle (19).

- a piece of the indirect object (*söglum*) has been placed between the tensed V and a piece of the subject (*sárgagls*), where there is no structural position for it to be attached;

• the other parts of the subject (*herðimeiðr* and *hagr*) are themselves separated from the genitive determiner (*sárgagls*), but also from one another, by the adjunct PP *við hróðri*—again into no clear structural positions in the clause.

In short, the verse is an unstructured mess, a salad of words that cannot be explained in any principled way. Perhaps it is a case of a poet trying to move beyond the rules governing his art—although it is telling to note again that this verse is considered spurious, as was the verse (*Egils saga 4*) that went beyond Reichardt's constraint on clause intercalation.

Such unexplained verses aside, we conclude that the following principle explains the characteristics of skaldic word order that are not simply part of the everyday language:

(28) Raising proper parts of a constituent is allowed, but only to the edges of the clause, with raising to a right-adjoined position only if there is raising to [Spec, CP].

10.5 Conclusion

Returning now to the language of Hale and Nash (1997, 248), we have seen that though distinct from it in clear ways, "in a number of ways [skaldic syntax] is dependent on the 'everyday language'"—Old Icelandic. Further, we have seen that "it shows a degree of consciousness of linguistic elements for which evidence is quite poor or lacking in everyday language"—consciousness of constituent structure, for example, and of the movement of constituents. Finally, we have seen that "apart from the specific ways in which it is distinguished from the everyday language of its speakers, the special language shares its remaining regularities."

Skaldic poetry is clearly a language game that not everyone could play as either a composer or a decomposer, but with a good deal of hard work we can learn to grasp its intricacies, uncover its principles, and understand their relationship to the everyday language of the people who created it and of the audience that appreciated it.

Appendix

A comment on performance: I assume that for the audience to process skaldic verse, its presentation must have been characterized by a good deal of heavy pausing. Note, moreover, that the extensive enjambment employed by the skalds would have helped as well. In (8), for example, the first two words of the second clause (*vætti berk*) form a well-structured meaningful whole ('I bear witness'), into which, however, *þung* (in line three) must then be integrated. Similarly in (1), *mik vill menja støkkvir ... brenna ... á höndum* is complete and it is *báðum* further on that must then find an NP to be merged with. Thus, despite the clause intercalation and scrambling discussed above, enjambment must have made skaldic verse more accessible than it seems to us at this distance.

Note

Having begun this research over two decades ago (working at first with Paul Kiparsky and then by myself), I formulated the basic principles of skaldic poetic syntax in the late 1970s. At that time, I gave a number of talks on the subject: for example, at the 1978 meeting of the Society for the Advancement of Scandinavian Study ("Unscrambling Skaldic Syntax"), at NELS 1978 ("Conditions on Stylistic Movement in Old Norse Skaldic Verse"), and in the Harvard Linguistics Colloquium series for spring 1979 ("Skaldic Syntax"), a lecture that I remember Ken Hale attending. Having reached a satisfactory solution to the problem (essentially the one presented here), I set the project aside for a number of years, picking it up briefly in the late 1980s in discussions with Jay Keyser. However, despite the mention of their names, neither Kiparsky nor Keyser is to be held responsible for anything said here.

Since this study reflects some of Ken's interests in language (what doesn't?), it gives me great pleasure to present it to him here.

References

Bach, Emmon. 1972. Skaldic poetry and the mathematical theory of grammars. In *Saga og sprak: Studies in language and literature,* edited by John M. Weinstock, 179–185. Austin, Tex: Pemberton Press.

Chomsky, Noam. 1965. *Aspects of the theory of syntax.* Cambridge, Mass.: MIT Press.

Chomsky, Noam, and George A. Miller. 1963. Finitary models of language users. In *Handbook of mathematical psychology, vol. II,* edited by R. Duncan Luce, Robert R. Bush, and Eugene Galanter, 419–491. New York: John Wiley.

Edwards, Diana C. 1983. Clause arrangement in skaldic poetry. I: Clause arrangement in the *dróttkvætt* poetry of the ninth to fourteenth centuries. II: Clause arrangement in the poetry of Arnórr jarlaskáld. *Arkiv for Nordisk Filologi* 98, 123–175.

Edwards, Diana C. 1984. Clause arrangement in skaldic poetry. III: Clause arrangement in the *hrynhent* poetry of the twelfth to fourteenth centuries. *Arkiv for Nordisk Filologi* 99, 131–138.

Gibson, Edward. 2000. The dependency locality theory: A distance-based theory of linguistic complexity. In *Image, language, brain: Papers from the First Mind Articulation Project Symposium*, edited by Alec Marantz, Yasushi Miyashita, and Wayne O'Neil, 95–126. Cambridge, Mass.: MIT Press.

Hale, Ken. 1984. Remarks on creativity in Aboriginal verse. In *Problems and solutions: Occasional essays in musicology presented to Alice M. Moyle*, edited by J. Kassler and J. Stubington, 254–262. Sydney: Hale & Iremonger.

Hale, Ken, and David Nash. 1997. Damin and Lardil phonotactics. In *Boundary rider: Essays in honour of Geoffrey O'Grady*, edited by Darrell Tryon and Michael Walsh. *Pacific Linguistics* C-136, 247–259.

Helgadóttir, Guðrún P. 1961. *Skáldkonur fyrri alda I, II.* Akureyri: Kvöldvö-kuútgáfan.

Hollander, Lee M. 1965. Observations on the nature and function of the parenthetic sentence in skaldic poetry. *Journal of English and Germanic Philology* 64, 635–644.

Jónsson, Guðni, ed. 1935. *Edda Snorra Sturlusonar, með skáldatali.* Reykjavík: Bókaverzlun Sigurðar Kristjánssonar.

Jónsson, Guðni, ed. 1936. *Grettis saga Ásmundarsonar.* Reykjavík: Hið Íslenzka Fornritafélag.

Kock, Ernst A., ed. 1949. *Den norsk-isländska skaldediktningen: Första bandet.* Lund: C. W. K. Gleerups förlag.

Miyagawa, Shigeru. 1989. *Structure and case marking in Japanese.* San Diego, Calif.: Academic Press.

Nordal, Sigurður, ed. 1933. *Egils saga Skallagrímssonar.* Reykjavík: Hið Íslenzka Fornritafélag.

Nordal, Sigurður, and Guðni Jónsson, eds. 1938. *Borgfirðinga sögur.* Reykjavík: Hið Íslenzka Fornritafélag.

O'Neil, Wayne. 1977. Clause adjunction in Old English. *General Linguistics* 17, 199–211.

Reichardt, Konstantin. 1928. *Studien zu den Skalden des 9. und 10. Jahrhunderts, Palaestra 159.* Leipzig: Mayer & Müller.

Reichardt, Konstantin. 1969. A contribution to the interpretation of skaldic poetry: Tmesis. In *Old Norse literature and mythology: A symposium*, edited by Edgar C. Polomé, 200–216. Austin: University of Texas Press.

Chapter 11

T-to-C Movement: Causes and Consequences

David Pesetsky and Esther Torrego

11.1 Introduction

The research of the last four decades suggests strongly that abstract laws of significant generality underlie much of the superficial complexity of human language. Evidence in favor of this conjecture comes from two different types of facts. First, there are crosslinguistic facts. Investigation of unfamiliar and typologically diverse languages is regularly illuminated by what is already known about other languages. This could only be the case if languages shared a significant substrate of laws. This is the kind of work for which Ken Hale is best known, and which we honor with this chapter. In addition, there are facts about individual languages that closely mirror what is discovered through crosslinguistic investigation. Just as investigation of unfamiliar and diverse languages is regularly illuminated by what is already known about other languages, so the investigation of unfamiliar and diverse *structures* within a single language is regularly illuminated by what is already known about other structures within that language. Again and again, one is led to suspect that an apparent peculiarity of some particular structure is just a special case of a phenomenon characteristic of some entirely different structure. By now, many investigations of this sort have been reported, providing strong reasons to suspect that language is indeed governed by abstract laws.

Once one suspects the existence of laws governing a variety of phenomena, the next step should be a search for the laws themselves. In fact, however, "next step" research of this sort does not always happen. Often, an exciting connection is posited between apparently unconnected facts, a hypothesis is developed and investigated for a while—and then it is abandoned, not because it is disconfirmed, but because new results stop coming. The attention of the field turns elsewhere.

To pick one example, the theory of abstract case developed in the late 1970s (Rouveret and Vergnaud 1979; Chomsky 1980, 1981) provided a unified explanation for a set of contrasts between DPs and other categories, such as CP. The central observation was that the distribution of DP is restricted in a way not observed with CP (and other non-DPs). For example, English CPs generally may move to [Spec, TP] from the complement position of unaccusative and passive verbs, but are not required to do so. DPs, however, must undergo this movement.

(1) *Abstract case: DPs versus CPs as complements of passive verbs*
    a. [CP That Sue would arrive late] was expected.
    b. It was expected [CP that Sue would arrive late].
    c. [DP Sue's late arrival] was expected.
    d. *It was expected [DP Sue's late arrival].

(2) *Abstract case: DPs versus CPs as complements of unaccusative verbs*
    a. [CP That Sue would arrive late] appealed to us.
    b. It appealed to us [CP that Sue would arrive late].
    c. [DP Sue's late arrival] appealed to us.
    d. *It appealed to us [DP Sue's late arrival].

The theory of abstract case explained these contrasts as a corollary of the fact that DPs in some languages are often required to display case morphology, while (in many languages, at least) CPs do not. It was suggested that even DPs without overt case morphology must bear abstract case, and that this property is assigned (or licensed) in particular syntactic positions—for example, in [Spec, TP], but not in object position of a passive or unaccusative verb. Though this generalization, and its extension to other syntactic contexts, was important to the understanding of a range of phenomena, fundamental questions remained unanswered, including *why* DPs must bear case and move for case reasons, while CPs need not do so. What might have been an ongoing research program devoted to these and related questions did not materialize.

A similar fate met another major research topic of the late 1970s and early 1980s: the investigation of subject/nonsubject asymmetries, such as the *that*-trace effect (Perlmutter 1971). This effect is observable in many dialects of English as the obligatory absence of *that* introducing a CP from which the subject has been extracted.

(3) That-*trace effect (Perlmutter 1971)*
    a. Who do you think (that) Sue met ____?
    b. Who do you think (*that) ____ met Sue?

In research of the late 1970s and 1980s, this effect was most often attributed to a local binding requirement on subject traces—the *Empty Category Principle* (ECP). The presence of the word *that* in examples like (3b) was taken to block a crucial government relationship between the subject trace and some element in the C system. In some accounts, the relevant member of the C system was C itself (e.g., Rizzi 1990). In others, it was an intermediate trace of successive-cyclic *wh*-movement (Kayne 1980; Taraldsen 1979; Pesetsky 1982a).

As work on this effect progressed, researchers discovered other subject/nonsubject asymmetries. Attempts were made to relate these new discoveries to the *that*-trace effect, often through revisions in the formulation of the ECP. Stowell (1981; see also Kayne 1981a), for example, noted that the word *that*, which is optional in complement clauses, is obligatory in subject clauses, and he suggested an account that relates this fact to a revised ECP. The key to his proposal was the idea that when *that* is missing, an unpronounced element subject to the ECP stands in its place.

(4) That-*omission asymmetry (Stowell 1981)*
   a.   Mary thinks [that Sue will buy the book].
   b.   Mary thinks [Sue will buy the book].
   c.   [That Sue will buy the book] was expected by everyone.
   d.   *[Sue will buy the book] was expected by everyone.

In a similar vein, Koopman (1983) discussed an important asymmetry in the movement of a tensed auxiliary verb from T to C (Den Besten 1983) in English matrix *wh*-questions and suggested that this asymmetry is also due to the ECP. T-to-C movement is obligatory in questions when the nearest subject is not the phrase *wh*-moved to [Spec, CP]—and is impossible otherwise.

(5) *T-to-C movement asymmetry (Koopman 1983)*
   a.   What did Mary buy?
   b.   *What Mary bought?
   c.   *Who did buy the book?   [* unless *did* is focused][1]
   d.   Who bought the book?

Koopman proposed that the presence of T in C in (5c) blocks the government relationship between the trace of *wh*-movement in subject position and the new location of the *wh*-phrase in [Spec, CP].[2] She did not offer an account of (5b)—whose status we return to later.

The research on subject/nonsubject asymmetries of two decades ago was exciting because it promised a unification of diverse phenomena of just the sort described above. Indeed, Koopman's unification of the T-to-C movement asymmetry with the *that*-trace effect provided inspiration for our own research reported here, as will become apparent. In actual practice, however, the work of the late 1970s and early 1980s met obstacles that were not successfully overcome at the time. Some were technical. For example, it was never clear why *that* or *did* in (5c) should block government of the subject trace from [Spec, CP] (though various possibilities were explored).[3] It was also not clear why the presence of *that* should have the effect on subject traces that it does in (3), while failing to produce a similar effect on other traces plausibly in need of government— for example, adjuncts. Here too, proposals were explored (most notably by Lasnik and Saito 1984, 1992), but many questions remained. More serious, however, was the overall failure of ECP research to *explain* why subjects should have a special binding requirement in the first place—a requirement from which many or most nonsubjects were exempt. The ECP stipulated this difference, and various attempts were made to rationalize it (by Kayne (1981a), Stowell (1981), and Rizzi (1990), among many others), but a deeper explanation was never found. In the end, it is fair to say, most of the field abandoned the project. These once-central topics became peripheral, and research attention shifted to other topics.[4]

The shift to other topics was not, we think, unreasonable. We suspect that during the period when research on subject/nonsubject asymmetries flourished, the ideas and analytic tools crucial to a true understanding of their nature had not been developed. We believe, however, that the situation has changed over the past decade. We believe that the ideas and tools necessary to an understanding of the sources of subject/nonsubject asymmetries have been developed. That is the main topic of this chapter. We take up the three subject/nonsubject asymmetries just discussed, along with several related asymmetries, and offer a new explanation in light of recent work. We also argue, however, that the correct theory of subject/ nonsubject asymmetries offers new answers to other questions left open in the 1980s—including several questions about abstract case (as summarized earlier). We begin with a review of the new ideas that will be crucial to our investigation.

A particularly important development of the past decade is the hypothesis that movement is not optional (the working hypothesis of the early 1980s) but *triggered.* The version of this hypothesis most important here is Chomsky's (1995) proposal that *uninterpretable features* play a key role in the triggering process. Uninterpretable features of a lexical item are properties of the item that make no semantic contribution. Examples include person and number on T (or *wh* on C). Person and number features (the so-called φ-features) make a semantic contribution when they are found on DP or CP (McCloskey 1991), but make no semantic contribution on T.

Although it is difficult to know *why* lexical items bear uninterpretable features, their existence is a fact. Chomsky's novel conjecture amounts to the suggestion that it is an important fact. He proposed that uninterpretable features must delete and disappear by the end of a syntactic derivation—where the derivation is assumed to build structure from "bottom to top." Deletion of an uninterpretable feature F on a lexical item X can happen when another element Y also bears F, and X establishes a syntactic connection with Y. The simplest connection is the operation that Chomsky (2000) calls *Agree*.[5]

In some instances, an uninterpretable feature F on X requires that an Agree relation with F on Y be followed up with copying of material from Y into the local environment of X. This property of F is called an *EPP property*.[6] Agree that is followed up by a copy operation (motivated by an EPP property) is the composite operation called *Move*. When a feature F on X enters into an Agree or Move relation with another instance of F on Y, we will say that F on X *attracts* Y.[7] For example, *wh*-movement arises when an uninterpretable *wh*-feature on C (henceforth *u*Wh) attracts a *wh*-phrase and *u*Wh has the EPP property. *u*Wh on C enters into an Agree relation with the *wh*-phrase. The EPP property of *u*Wh then requires copying of the *wh*-phrase, forming a specifier of CP.

The hypothesis that movement is "triggered" amounts to the claim that an element Y moves *only* when attracted by a feature (of some head X) with the EPP property. More generally, heads enter into Agree and Move relations only to the extent necessary. We can summarize this as the Economy Condition in (6).

(6) *Economy Condition*

A head H triggers the minimum number of operations necessary to satisfy the properties (including EPP) of its uninterpretable features.

Another point worth noting: it will be important that EPP is a property of a *feature* of a head—not a property of the head itself. Thus, a head that bears features F and G might have the EPP property for F, but not for G. EPP is thus a "subfeature of a feature," in the sense familiar from feature geometry in phonology.

Once an uninterpretable feature F on X has attracted Y, F is said to be *deleted*. We will sometimes use the clumsier phrase *marked for deletion* because (as we will show) the final disappearance of F on X may be delayed until a later point in the derivation. For example, the final disappearance of an uninterpretable feature marked for deletion may quite regularly wait until the completion of a CP (or other category called a "phase" in Chomsky 2000, this volume). We will argue that under some circumstances, the lifespan of a feature marked for deletion can be longer.

To summarize: The three points of importance to our account of subject/nonsubject asymmetries are (1) the hypothesis that uninterpretable features must disappear by the end of the derivation, (2) the hypothesis that movement occurs only in response to an uninterpretable feature with the EPP property, and (3) the hypothesis that a feature may remain "alive" for a while after being marked for deletion. The italicized terminology presented in the preceding paragraphs indicates the concepts to keep in mind throughout this chapter.

We now begin our investigation of subject/nonsubject asymmetries in the context of these ideas about Agree and Move. The discussion of subject/nonsubject asymmetries in the 1980s took as its starting point the *that*-trace phenomenon in (3). We will start instead with the T-to-C movement asymmetry in (5), because we believe it is the key to understanding all three asymmetries. If Chomsky's hypotheses about movement are correct, then the movement of T to C in (5a) must be a response to the presence of an uninterpretable feature with the EPP property on C and the presence of a corresponding feature on T. We will make the simplest, most banal proposal about the nature of this feature that is consistent with the hypothesis about movement that we have adopted. The interest of the proposal lies not in (7) itself, but in its consequences.

(7) *Motivation for T-to-C movement (in English matrix interrogative clauses)*[8]
    C bears an uninterpretable T-feature (henceforth uT) with the EPP property.

11.2 The T-to-C Movement Asymmetry and the Nature of Nominative Case

Our most obvious task is to explain the contrast between sentences like (5c–d), in which a local nominative *wh* is moved to C—which do not show T-to-C movement—and sentences like (5a–b), in which another phrase undergoes *wh*-movement—which do show T-to-C movement. Why does T-to-C movement not take place when the local nominative subject undergoes *wh*-movement in (5c–d)? In the acceptable (5d), uWh on C is deleted by the *wh*-phrase that has been moved into its specifier.[9] But what deletes uT on C when T-to-C movement does *not* take place? It is here that we make a key new proposal. We suggest that uT on C in (5d) is deleted by the nominative *wh*-phrase itself. More generally, we propose (8).

(8) *The nature of nominative case*
Nominative case is uT on D.

Since the features of the head are shared by its projections, a nominative DP moved to [Spec, CP] can delete uT on C in the same way that T moved to C can—if (8) is true. That is why T-to-C movement is unnecessary in examples like (5d). Note that this is a situation of the type mentioned in section 11.1, in which uT on the subject DP remains "alive" and accessible to further operations at least until CP has been fully built (Chomsky's (2000) notion of "phase"), despite having been marked for deletion by T itself. At the point in the derivation at which CP is built, the nominative subject has already been attracted to [Spec, TP] by finite T, since English finite T bears uninterpretable ϕ-features ($u\phi$, realized in some cases as agreement morphology) with an EPP property.

(9) *Attraction to [Spec, TP]*
[TP[DP subject, uT̶, ϕ]ᵢ [T, $u\phi$̶] [t-subjectᵢ bought *the book*]]

The $u\phi$-features on T are marked for deletion once a syntactic relationship has been established with DP's interpretable ϕ-features. This also allows uT on DP to be marked for deletion; but, as noted, final erasure of this feature can be delayed at least as long as the CP cycle.[10]

Of course, T-to-C movement in examples like (5c–d) is not merely unnecessary, but impossible, as (5c) shows. We will suggest that the impossibility of T-to-C movement in (5c) is a consequence of the basic Economy Condition (6) that underlies the entire theory of syntactic operations adopted here. If a head has a choice among several patterns of movement that it might trigger, it picks the pattern with the fewest occurrences of movement.

To show this, however, we must first deal with an issue of locality raised by T-to-C movement in (5a–b). At first sight, T-to-C movement does not seem to obey a locality condition familiar from *wh*-movement. We know from the phenomenon called the *Superiority effect* that when a feature of C attracts *wh*, it attracts the closest instance of *wh*—a general principle that we can call *Attract Closest F* (ACF).

(10) *Attract Closest F (ACF) (simplified from Chomsky 1995, 296)*
     If a head K attracts feature F on X, no constituent that bears F is closer to K than X.

Examples that show ACF for *wh*-movement include familiar contrasts like (11).

(11) *Superiority effect*
     a.   Who C [____ bought what]?
     b.   *What did+C [who buy ____]?

If *wh*-attraction by C obeys ACF, the same should be true of T-attraction by C. If so, why is it the head T, and not its maximal projection TP, that moves to C in (5a)? After all, fewer nodes separate C from TP than separate C from T. As it happens, however, there is another natural notion of "closeness" that might be relevant to ACF. If the metric of closeness involves c-command rather than node counting (as we will argue shortly), then TP and T are equidistant from C, since domination is not a case of c-command.

(12) *Closeness*
     Y is closer to K than X if K c-commands Y and Y c-commands X.[11]

Nonetheless, something more general must be at stake, since movement of TP to C is not even an option in examples like (5a). The structure of (5a) is special in a way that might be relevant. In (5a), *u*T on C is attracting a feature of its own complement—a constituent with which C has just merged. If the entire complement of C were to be copied as [Spec, CP], C would, in effect, be merging with the same constituent twice. We suggest that it is precisely in these circumstances that the head of the complement, rather than the complement itself, is copied. In the present context, this suggestion is speculative, but it is in fact the flip side of a more familiar generalization: the Head Movement Constraint of Travis (1984). Travis's condition states that head movement is always move-ment from a complement to the nearest head. Our condition dictates that movement from a complement to the nearest head is always realized as head movement. We may call the two together the *Head Movement Generalization.*

(13) *Head Movement Generalization*
Suppose a head H attracts a feature of XP as part of a movement operation.
   a. If XP is the complement of H, copy the head of XP into the local domain of H.[12]
   b. Otherwise, copy XP into the local domain of H.

If (13) is correct, T-to-C movement in (5a) is the expected consequence of *u*T on C attracting a feature of its complement TP.

Now let us return to the impossibility of T-to-C movement in (5c) in light of the proposal that T-to-C movement results when a feature of C attracts a feature of TP, and in light of the proposal that the metric of closeness involves c-command rather than node counting. Consider the structures underlying (5a–b) and (5c–d) immediately after merger of C, assuming (8). We omit the φ-features for clarity.

(14) *Structures for (5) before movement to C and [Spec, CP]*
   a. [C, *u*T, *u*Wh] [$_{TP}$[Mary, *u*T] T [$_{VP}$ bought what]]   [(5a–b)]
   b. [C, *u*T, *u*Wh] [$_{TP}$[who, *u*T] T [$_{VP}$ bought the book]]   [(5c–d)]

In (14a), the closest element that bears *wh* is *what*. Both the nominative subject and T are closer to C than *what*. Consequently, C must delete its *u*Wh and its *u*T in two separate operations. That is why both *wh*-movement and T-to-C movement take place in (5a–b).

The situation is different in (14b). If the metric of closeness is as in (12), TP and its nominative specifier both count as the closest constituent to C. Consequently, C can (in principle) choose whether to delete its *u*T by attracting TP or by attracting the nominative [Spec, TP].[13] If C attracts TP (yielding T-to-C movement), it deletes just one of its two uninterpretable features as a consequence of this operation. A separate operation is necessary to delete its *u*Wh. If, on the other hand, C attracts the nominative [Spec, TP], both *u*T and *u*Wh can be deleted in one step, since the phrase in [Spec, TP] has nominative case and is a *wh*-phrase.[14] The more economical choice is made. Hence, in (14b), C attracts [Spec, TP] and does not attract TP itself. This accounts for the contrast in (5c–d).

Hypothesis (8), which identifies nominative case with *u*T, is crucial to our explanation of the T-to-C movement asymmetry. It is this hypothesis that helps us understand why movement of the subject to [Spec, CP] "does the same job" as T-to-C movement. Hypothesis (8) will play an important role in the explanation of the subject/nonsubject asymmetries discussed throughout this chapter. It is therefore worth pausing to consider its nature and consequences. First, we should note that (8), though new, is not radical. It amounts to the proposal that there is a close correspondence between the features of finite T and the features of nominative D. We are used to the idea that T (and its projections) bears features that are uninterpretable on it but would be interpretable were they found on D (e.g., person and number). Hypothesis (8) is simply the proposal that the reverse is also true. D and its projections bear features that are uninterpretable on it but would be interpretable were they found on T. The features proper to D are traditionally called "agreement" when borne by T, and the features proper to T are traditionally called "nominative" when borne by D; but hypothesis (8) suggests that the traditional terminology is misleading. "Agreement" is the name for the D-properties present on T, and "nominative" is the name for the T-properties present on D.

This aspect of hypothesis (8) is interesting for a more general reason. One of the most long-lasting controversies in linguistics concerns the existence of purely formal grammatical features—features utterly without semantic value. The most "minimalist" possible position would hold that such features do not exist—that the lexicon contains nothing but pairs of sounds and meanings. This position, dubbed *extreme functionalism* by Newmeyer (1998), is rarely defended, presumably because it is such an obvious nonstarter. Lexical items often bear features that have no evident semantic import, and, it would seem, there is no getting around this fact. Nonetheless, one must ask how much of a counterexample to extreme functionalism such facts really are.[15]

Chomsky's (1995) focus on the interpretability of features suggests an interesting new answer to this question: a minimal retreat from extreme functionalism that we can call *relativized extreme functionalism*. Relativized extreme functionalism agrees with its nonrelativized predecessor that all grammatical features have a semantic value, but recognizes that they do not get a chance to express their semantic value in every context in which they occur. Of course, even *relativized extreme functionalism* is untenable if there exist grammatical features that have no semantic value in *any* environment. If, for example, there is a feature called "nominative" whose only function is to mark certain Ds and DPs as capable of being attracted by finite T (as Chomsky (2000) argues),[16] then even relativized extreme functionalism is untenable. On the other hand, if nominative is simply an uninterpretable T-feature on D or DP, then the existence of nominative case is consistent with relativized extreme functionalism. Hypotheses like (8) thus have an interest beyond their role in explaining phenomena like the distribution of T-to-C movement. They bear on central issues of linguistics.[17]

Although our unification of nominative case on DP and agreement on T may have conceptual appeal, from a morphological perspective it is not (perhaps) the most obvious proposal. The idea that agreement morphology on T realizes uninterpretable features otherwise found on DP makes sense, since the actual shape of agreement morphology often covaries with the particular feature values borne by the nominative DP that T attracts. That is why this morphology is called "agreement." Comparable covariation is not generally found between the shape of nominative case morphology and particular feature values borne by the T that attracts the nominative phrase. For example, the morphology of nominative case does not often covary with choice of present, past, or future tense. This mismatch may reflect an inherent morphological asymmetry between attractor and attractee,[18] or it might indicate that the features we are calling "T" are more properly analyzed as some other member of the tense-mood-aspect system. We will not attempt to explain the mismatch, instead leaving it as an open problem. We do, however, know of two instances in which nominative case morphology reflects T in a more direct way than it does in languages like English. We mention them briefly here.

The first case, brought to our attention by Ken Hale (personal communication), comes from Pitta-pitta, a language of western Queensland, Australia (Blake and Breen 1971; Hale 1998a,b). In this language, future tense is marked on the nominative subject DP.

(15) *Pitta-pitta future tense marked on nominative DP*
　　a. Ngapiri-ngu thawa paya-nha.
　　　 father-FUT　kill　bird-ACC
　　　 'Father will kill the bird (with missile thrown).'
　　b. Thithi-ngu　　　　karnta pathiparnta.
　　　 elder brother-FUT go　　morning
　　　 'My elder brother will go in the morning.'

In other tenses, no tense is marked on any nominal. Tense is not generally marked on nonsubject nominals (a feature that distinguishes Pitta-pitta from neighboring languages that display extensive "case spreading"), though apparently older stages of the language did mark future tense on object nominals as well (Roth 1897), as Claire Bowern (personal communication) has pointed out to us.

(16) a. Ngathu manhakurri-nya puri-nha.
      1SG.ERG mishandle-PAST money-ACC
      'I lost (my) money.'
    b. Ngamari-lu takuku-nha wajama-ya.
      mother-ERG child-ACC   wash-PRES
      'Mother is washing the baby.'

Classical Arabic represents an interesting case of a different sort. It does not exhibit covariation between the tense of the sentence and the morphology of the nominative subject, but it displays something else of interest. The suffixes that mark nominative case are identical to the "mood" morphology of the imperfective indicative verb across all three numbers and have traditionally been viewed as one system by the Arab grammarians (Benmamoun 1992, 2000).[19]

(17) *Classical Arabic*

Singular	Dual	Plural
ṭ-ṭaalib-u	ṭ-ṭaalib-aan	l-muʕallim-uun
the-student-NOM	the-student-DUAL.NOM	the-teacher-PL.NOM
ya-ktub-u	ya-ktub-aan	yu-ʕallim-uun
3M-write-IND	3M-write-DUAL.IND	3M-teach-PL.IND

Thus, though we do not explain the overall asymmetry between the morphology of uninterpretable nominal features on T and uninterpretable T-features (uT) on nominals, there is some evidence from overt morphology that supports our hypothesis that these features are fundamentally the same.

What about structural case more generally—in particular, accusative case? In this chapter, we focus on nominative and do not argue for any particular hypothesis about accusative. It is clear, however, that plausible hypotheses in the spirit of (8) can be formulated (and should be investigated, if we are to maintain relativized extreme functionalism as a working hypothesis). For example, it is quite possible that accusative case is also uT on D—in which case, uT is the proper characterization of "structural case" in general.[20] If accusative case is also uT on D, finite T must be capable of Agree and Move relations with more than one DP, to allow for sentences containing both nominative and accusative DPs. T would then resemble the C used in multiple questions, which seems to enter into such relations with more than one *wh* (Pesetsky 2000). In languages that make a morphological distinction between nominative and accusative, the choice of case morphology would be taken to reflect the order in which the DPs enter into an attract relation with T.[21] Alternatively, we might suppose that accusative case is an uninterpretable version of a different feature—perhaps an uninterpretable version of some feature associated with the *v* of Hale and Keyser (1993) and Chomsky (1995), which assigns external thematic roles (or the aspectual projections proposed in Borer 1998). We leave the matter open.[22]

11.3 The *That*-Trace Effect and the Nature of English *That*

Is *u*T on C limited to interrogative clauses, or do other types of C also bear *u*T? The question is natural, particularly since *u*T on D (i.e., nominative case) is certainly not restricted to DPs with an interrogative interpretation. In fact, there might be good reason to find *u*T on noninterrogative C, especially when C attracts a *wh*-phrase as part of the phenomenon of successive-cyclic *wh*-movement. If our analysis of the T-to-C movement asymmetry is correct, the acceptable examples in (5) have an interesting property in addition to those already discussed. In every matrix question in which *wh*-movement was observed, some instance of movement to C took place from a position that is maximally close to C. When a phrase other than the nominative subject underwent *wh*-movement, the movement observed from a maximally close position was T-to-C movement. When the nominative subject itself underwent *wh*-movement, it was *wh*-movement itself that involved the maximally close position. This fact about (5) might hint at a more general law. Such a law might require one instance of any sort of movement to a head H to be strictly local, less local instances of movement to H being tolerated only when strictly local movement has also occurred. This possibility strongly recalls work by Richards (1997, 1998), who argues that "closeness" conditions like ACF in (10) obey a Principle of Minimal Compliance.[23]

(18) *Principle of Minimal Compliance (PMC) (simplified from Richards 1997)*
Once an instance of movement to α has obeyed a constraint on the distance between source and target, other instances of movement to α need not obey this constraint.

Let us examine how the PMC works. One of the most straightforward demonstrations offered by Richards concerns the distribution of Superiority effects in Bulgarian. Recall that the Superiority effect in English (illustrated in (11)) is an effect of ACF. This effect shows up in Bulgarian as an ordering restriction on multiple overt *wh*-movement to [Spec, CP] (Koizumi 1995). In multiple questions with two *wh*-phrases, the closest *wh*-phrase to C moves to form a [Spec, CP]; the next-closest *wh*-phrase "tucks in" underneath this first phrase to form an inner [Spec, CP].

(19) *Superiority effect in Bulgarian multiple questions with two*
     wh-*phrases (Rudin 1988)*
     a. Koj kakvo vižda?
         who what   sees
         (cf. Who sees what?)
     b. *Kakvo koj vižda?
         what   who sees
         (cf. *What does who see?)

Strictly speaking, ACF should block sentences like (19a). Why can C attract the second *wh*-phrase at all, given that the second *wh*-phrase is not the closest *wh*-phrase to C? The answer to this question, according to Richards, falls together with the explanation of an even more surprising phenomenon: the behavior of multiple questions in which three or more *wh*-phrases move overtly. As before, the *wh*-phrase that starts highest must move first and ends up leftmost. The order of the other two *wh*-phrases, however, is free (as discussed by Bošković (1995)).

(20) *Superiority effect in Bulgarian multiple questions with three*
     wh-*phrases*
     a. Koj kogo kakvo e   pital? [wh_1 wh_2 wh_3]
         who whom what AUX asked
     b. Koj kakvo kogo e pital? [wh_1 wh_3 wh_2]

The ordering options displayed in (20), combined with the issues raised by (19), suggest that the interrogative C of a multiple question—after attracting the nearest *wh*-phrase (wh_1)—must be free to disregard ACF thereafter. This is what the PMC allows. The PMC explains why C can attract other *wh*-phrases from further away, and why it can attract them in any order.[24]

(21) *Derivation of (20b)*
     a. Structure before *wh*-movement
         C [koj pital kogo kakvo]

b. Step 1
   C attracts the *wh*-feature of *koj*.
   koj C [_____ e pital kogo kakvo]
c. Step 2
   The PMC now allows C to attract either of the two remaining
   wh-phrases without regard to ACF. It tucks in under *koj*.
   [koj kakvo C [_____ e pital kogo _____]
d. Step 3
   C attracts the other *wh*-phrase, which tucks in under *kakvo*.
   koj kakvo kogo C [_____ e pital _____ _____]

If the similarity between this scenario and the one observed in (5) is not an
accident, then in addition to Attract Closest F (ACF), which prevents a
head in search of a feature F from looking past the closest instance of F,
there must be an independent, tighter constraint, *Attract Closest X*
(ACX), which prevents Attract operations from looking past the closest
instance of *anything*.

(22) *Attract Closest X (ACX)*
     If a head K attracts X, no constituent Y is closer to K than X.

Left to its own devices, ACX should prevent all but maximally local
instances of movement,[25] but if ACX is subject to Richards's PMC,
nonlocal movement to K will be possible when preceded by an instance of
local movement to K. This is the case when T-to-C movement precedes
wh-movement from inside VP.

(23) *Object* wh-*movement*
     a. Structure before T-to-C movement and *wh*-movement
        [C, uT, uWh] [Mary [$_T$ will] buy what]
     b. Step 1
        uT on C attracts TP; the resultant T-to-C movement satisfies
        ACX.
        [$_T$ will] + [C, $u\text{T}$, uWh] C [Mary _____ buy what]
     c. Step 2
        uWh on C attracts *what*, which would be blocked by ACX if
        step 1 had not occurred first.
        what [$_T$ will] + [C, $u\text{T}$, $u\text{Wh}$] [Mary _____ buy _____]

If ACX is correct, then any C capable of attracting a *wh*-phrase from a
position other than [Spec, TP] must bear uT in addition to uWh. This may
be true. Consider long-distance *wh*-movement from an embedded finite

declarative clause to a higher interrogative CP. We begin with cases where the moved *wh*-phrase is an object, like (28), where we focus on the embedded clause.

(24) What did John say [$_{CP}$ that Mary will buy ____]?

Let us take it as established that movement of this sort must pass through the specifier of the embedded declarative CP.[26] In a feature-based theory of movement, this means that the embedded C must bear *u*Wh (with the EPP property) so as to attract the *wh*-phrase.[27] The problem is that movement of a *wh*-phrase from anywhere other than [Spec, TP] violates ACX. If ACX is correct, we must assume that the embedded C in structures like (24) (i.e., the C of matrix interrogatives) bears *u*T. Consequently, we expect movement of T to C to accompany successive-cyclic *wh*-movement. (Alternatively, movement of the nominative subject to [Spec, CP] accompanies the *wh*-movement, a topic to which we return.)

In fact, T-to-C movement is found in just this environment in a variety of languages. One particularly clear example is Belfast English, as discussed by Henry (1995, 108–109). Belfast English shares with other dialects obligatory T-to-C movement in *wh*-interrogatives (and also allows inversion in embedded questions, as we discuss below). In addition, however, obvious cases of T-to-C movement are found in clauses through which successive-cyclic interrogative *wh*-movement has passed.[28]

(25) *Belfast English*
   a. Who did John hope [would he see ____]?
   b. What did Mary claim [did they steal ____]?
   c. I wonder what did John think would he get ____?
   d. Who did John say [did Mary claim [had John feared [would Bill attack ____]]]?

Very similar data are found in Spanish[29] (Torrego 1983, 1984) and in French (Kayne and Pollock 1978), where the phenomenon is called *stylistic inversion*.[30]

(26) *Spanish*
   a. A quién prestó Juan el   diccionario?
      to whom lent   Juan the dictionary
      'To whom did Juan lend the dictionary?'
   b. Con quién podrá   Juan ir   a Nueva York?
      with whom will-be-able Juan to-go to New York
      'With whom will Juan be able to go to New York?'

    c. Qué pensaba Juan [que le   había dicho Pedro [que había
       what thought Juan that him had   told   Pedro that had
       publicado la   revista]]]?
       published the journal
       'What did Juan think that Pedro had told him that the journal
       had published?'

(27) *French stylistic inversion*
    a. Qui a-t-elle dit qu'avait vu   Paul?
      who did she say that had seen Paul
    b. l'homme avec lequel je crois   qu'a   soupé Marie
      the man with whom I believe that has dined Marie

One might think that Standard English poses a threat to our expectation that T-to-C movement may always accompany successive-cyclic *wh*-movement in questions. We will now show that this is not the case. It is at this point that we can begin to provide a unified explanation of the subject/nonsubject asymmetries presented in section 11.1.

The argument comes from examples identical to (24), except that the nominative subject, rather than another phrase, has been *wh*-moved from the embedded clause. Here, as we have already noted, the so-called *that*-trace effect is observed. The word *that* may introduce the embedded clause when a nonsubject is *wh*-moved from it, but may not introduce the same clause when the nominative subject is *wh*-moved from it.

(28) a.   Who did John say _____ will buy the book?
     b. *Who did John say that _____ will buy the book?

The *that*-trace effect is strikingly similar to the T-to-C movement asymmetry discussed in the previous section. In both cases, subject *wh*-extraction prevents a word from occurring in C that is found there otherwise. In the case of the T-to-C movement asymmetry in English, the element barred from C with subject *wh*-movement is the tensed auxiliary verb, which we analyze as an instance of T that has moved to C. In the case of the *that*-trace effect, the element barred from C with subject *wh*-movement is the word *that*, which one is accustomed to thinking of as the complementizer itself, inserted as the sister of TP by Merge.

Suppose, however, that this traditional view of *that* is wrong. In particular, suppose that *that* in the examples under discussion is not C at all, but an instance of T that has moved to C. If this is true, the obligatory absence of *that* in C when the local subject has been extracted can be viewed as just another instance of the T-to-C movement asymmetry. If this is the case, *that* in examples like (24) is in C because it has *moved* there—just like the auxiliary verbs that move to C in Belfast English examples like (25a–d).

Of course, there is a difference between the two cases. In Belfast English, when T moves to C, T is overtly realized in C in the form of an auxiliary verb, and a gap is left in the original T position. If *that* is also an instance of T moved to C, it represents a different realization of T-to-C movement—one in which both the new and the original positions are pronounced. In this respect, Standard English embedded T-to-C movement resembles instances of *wh*-movement that leave resumptive pronouns. For resumptive pronouns, it has been argued (Engdahl 1985; Demirdache 1991; Fox 1994) that the pronoun is linked to its *wh*-antecedent by movement, even though both positions are pronounced. We make a very similar proposal for the relation between *that* and the original position of T.[31] We will not attempt to explain why T-to-C movement is realized as a "traditional" instance of auxiliary verb movement in some environments in some dialects, and as *that* doubling a tensed verb in others. That is an important question, of course, and our failure to offer an account constitutes a gap in our proposal. We will, however, give a more complete characterization of the facts in the following sections, which can (we hope) serve as a foundation for further investigation of the matter.

Putting these questions aside, let us see how our hypothesis accounts for the facts under discussion. Declarative C, when it hosts successive-cyclic *wh*-movement, bears both *u*T and *u*Wh. Both features have the EPP property. Suppose the nearest *wh*-phrase to C is a nonsubject. In such a structure, *u*T on C may be deleted by T-to-C movement, while *u*Wh on C is deleted by movement of the *wh*-phrase. In Standard English, T in C is pronounced as *that* in this environment. C itself, we assume, is null in English. The result is (29).

(29) *Nonsubject extraction from a declarative CP*
    What$_i$ did John say [$_{CP}$ *t-what$_i$* [$_T$ that]$_j$ + [C, *u*T̶, *u*W̶h̶] [$_{IP}$ Mary will$_j$ buy *t-what$_i$*]]?

Now consider the case in which the nearest *wh*-phrase to C is the nominative subject. In this situation, movement of the nominative subject to [Spec, CP] can simultaneously delete both *u*T and *u*Wh on C. By the Economy Condition (6), this possibility excludes the less economical derivation in which uWh is deleted by *wh*-movement and uT by T-to-C movement. Since T in C is pronounced *that* in Standard English embedded declaratives, the result is the obligatory absence of *that*.

We thus predict the *that*-trace effect, illustrated in (30), where the crossed-out material is the trace of successive-cyclic *wh*-movement.

(30) *Subject extraction from a declarative CP: the* that-*trace effect*
    a. *Who$_i$ did John say [$_{CP}$ t-[who, +wh, uT]$_i$ [$_T$ that]$_j$ + [C, uT, uWh]
        [$_{IP}$ t-who$_i$ will$_j$ buy the book]]?
    b. Who$_i$ did John say [$_{CP}$ t-[who, +wh, uT]$_i$ [C, uT, uWh]
        [$_{IP}$ t-who$_i$ will$_j$ buy the book]]?

If this analysis of the *that*-trace effect is correct, there is indeed T-to-C movement in every clause in which a nonsubject has undergone *wh*-movement, as we expect if ACX is correct.[32] We have not, of course, proven that ACX is correct—merely that it predicts the presence of uT on any C that attracts nonsubject *wh*-phrases. We return to more affirmative arguments for ACX in section 11.5 and especially in section 11.11. At this point, ACX is a heuristic that led us to our account of the *that*-trace effect. That account is the main result of this section, vindicating Koopman's (1983) idea that the T-to-C movement asymmetry and the *that*-trace effect are two aspects of the same phenomenon.

11.4 Movement of the Nominative Subject to [Spec, CP] in Embedded Declarative Clauses

Once we analyze English *that* as T moved to C in clauses that host successive-cyclic *wh*-movement, we should view English *that* as T-in-C movement in *all* clauses, not just those from which *wh*-movement has taken place. This means that *that* is T moved to C even in simple sentences like (31).

(31) Mary thinks that Sue will buy the book.

If this is the case, all instances of finite C bear uT in English, not just cases in which C also bears uWh.

(32) Mary expects [$_{CP}$[$_T$ that]$_j$ + [C, uT] [$_{IP}$ Sue will$_j$ buy the book]].

We are now in a position to also discuss the syntax of embedded declarative clauses like (33) that are *not* introduced by *that*.

(33) Mary thinks Sue will buy the book.

In (33), the C of the embedded declarative should be no different from the C of the embedded declarative of (31), as analyzed in (32). C in (33), like C in (32), presumably bears an instance of uT that must be deleted. Clearly, uT is not deleted here by T-to-C movement, since the embedded clause is not introduced by *that*. What does delete uT on C in (33)? We once again suggest that the nominative subject does this job. The nominative subject moves to [Spec, CP], attracted by uT on C, satisfying the EPP property of C's uT.

(34) Mary expects [$_{CP}$[Sue, $u\text{T}$]$_j$ [C, $u\text{T}$] [$_{IP}$ *t-Sue$_j$* will buy the book]].

Why are both (32) and (34) possible? In embedded declarative clauses, C seems able to choose freely between TP and [Spec, TP] when it looks for a way to delete its uT. This is expected, since both TP and its specifier bear a T-feature (interpretable on TP, uninterpretable on its specifier), and both are equally close to C by the definition of closeness in (12). The freedom seen in embedded declaratives like (32) and (34) contrasts with the lack of freedom in the interrogative and declarative clauses that we have been discussing until now. In the previous sections, we examined interrogative clauses and those embedded declaratives whose C bears uWh. In such clauses, when the nominative subject is a *wh*-phrase, the Economy Condition in (6) forces C to pick [Spec, TP] over TP itself as the element that deletes uT on C. The Economy Condition makes this choice because a nominative *wh*-phrase in [Spec, TP] can delete uWh on C in addition to uT. In declaratives like (32) and (34), from which *wh*-movement does not take place, C does not bear uWh in addition to uT. Consequently, economy considerations play no role here in deciding whether uT on C will be deleted by T-to-C movement or by movement of the subject to [Spec, CP]. C is free to choose either method for deleting its uT.

The same freedom should be available to C even when C bears uWh —so long as the nominative subject is not a *wh*-phrase. Example (24) showed a nonsubject *wh*-phrase extracted from an embedded declarative. This declarative clause was introduced by *that*, which meant that uT on C was deleted by T-to-C movement, as analyzed in (29). At that time, we did not address the analysis of examples that differ from (24) only in the absence of the word *that*.

(35) What did Sue say [$_{CP}$ Mary will buy ____]?

In fact, the absence of *that* in (35) receives the same analysis as the absence of *that* in (33) (see (34)). Either uT on the embedded C can be deleted by T-to-C movement, as in (32), or it can be deleted by movement of the nominative subject to [Spec, CP], as in (34). This yields the variant without *that* seen in (35). Example (35) is thus analyzed as in (36).[33]

(36) What$_i$ did Sue say [$_{CP}$ *t*-[what, +wh]$_i$ [Mary, ~~*u*T~~]$_j$ [C, ~~*u*T~~, ~~*u*Wh~~]
     [$_{TP}$ *t*-Mary$_j$ will buy *t*-what$_i$]].

One interesting property of embedded declarative clauses without *that* may provide two arguments of interest here: first, an argument in favor of our proposal that such clauses involve movement of the subject to [Spec, CP], and second, an argument in favor of ACX. As observed by Doherty (1993; see also Grimshaw 1997), the presence of *that* is nearly obligatory in embedded declarative clauses in which an adverbial or topicalized phrase has been fronted.

(37) a. Mary is claiming that [for all intents and purposes] John is the mayor of the city.
     b. ??Mary is claiming [for all intents and purposes] John is the mayor of the city.

(38) a. Mary knows that [books like this] Sue will enjoy reading.
     b. ??Mary knows [books like this] Sue will enjoy reading.

We cannot provide a detailed account of adverb fronting or topicalization. Let us suppose, however, that the fronted adverbial in (37) and the topicalized phrase in (38) are dominated by TP—perhaps as specifiers external to the nominative subject.[34] The presence of these phrases has an effect on what may delete *u*T on C, if ACX is correct. The nominative subject and TP are no longer equally close to C under the definition of closeness in (12), because of the presence of the outer specifier that c-commands the subject.[35]

(39) [C, *u*T] [$_{TP}$ topic [$_{T'}$ subject [$_{T'}$ T . . .]]]

Only TP counts as maximally close to C. Consequently, given ACX, C must choose TP rather than the nominative subject to delete its *u*T. This yields the obligatory *that* (the realization of T-to-C movement) observed in these examples. (Remember that attraction of TP by *u*T on C is realized as T-to-C head movement, as a result of the Head Movement Generalization in (13).)

A further consequence is also expected. Consider a configuration like (39) in which C bears *u*Wh in addition to *u*T, and in which the subject is a *wh*-phrase— for example, (40).

(40) [C, uT, uWh] [$_{TP}$ topic [$_{T'}$ who [$_{T'}$ T ...]]]

Here too the nominative subject is farther from C than TP. If (40) is an embedded declarative clause from which nominative *who* is being extracted, we expect an "anti-*that*-trace" effect.[36] Even though the nominative subject is being extracted, *that* should be possible (in fact, obligatory). As observed by Bresnan (1977, 194, fn. 6; see also Culicover 1993; Browning 1996), *that* is indeed possible in configurations like (40).[37]

(41) *Anti*-that-*trace effect*[38]

    a. Sue met the man who Mary is claiming that [for all intents and purposes] ____ was the mayor of the city.

    b. Bill, who Sue said that [to the rest of us] ____ might seem a bit strange, turned out to be quite ordinary.

11.5   T-to-C Movement versus Subject Movement in Matrix Questions

If non-*wh* nominative subjects can move to [Spec, CP] and delete uT on declarative C, we must ask how general this possibility is. When we discussed the T-to-C movement asymmetry in matrix *wh*-questions, we talked as if the presence of uT on C forced T-to-C movement in all cases except those in which the subject of the clause is a nominative *wh*-phrase. In fact, however, we must ask whether movement of a nominative subject to [Spec, CP] could delete uT even when the *wh*-phrase of the clause is not the nominative subject. One important case is the contrast between (5a) and the unacceptable (5b), repeated here.

(42) *T-to-C movement obligatory in matrix* wh-*questions*

    a.   What did Mary buy?

    b.   *What Mary bought?

The obligatoriness of T-to-C movement here might lead us to search for a factor that favors T-to-C over subject movement in matrix clauses where C bears uT and uWh. We suspect that this is not the right approach. If we replace the interrogative *wh*-phrase in (42) with one that supports an exclamative interpretation (Elliott 1971; Grimshaw 1979), the judgments reverse. Compare (42) with (43).

(43) *T-to-C movement impossible in matrix* wh-*exclamatives*

    a.   *What a silly book did Mary buy!

    b.   What a silly book Mary bought!

This suggests that in general, matrix *wh*-clauses indeed have two options for deleting uT on C when the *wh*-phrase is not the nominative subject. In addition to T-to-C movement, the option of nominative subject movement to [Spec, CP] is available.

(44) [$_{CP}$[What a silly book]$_i$ [Mary, uT̶]$_j$ [C, uT̶, uW̶h̶] [$_{TP}$ *t-Mary*$_j$ T bought *t-what a silly book*$_i$]]!

What is interesting is the fact that the choice among these options has a consequence for interpretation. The facts seem to be as described in (45).

(45) *Exclamative versus interrogative interpretation*
     A matrix CP whose head bears uWh is interpreted as an
     exclamative if a non-*wh*-phrase appears as one of its specifiers.
     Otherwise, it is interpreted as a question.[39]

Semantic conditions on the nature of the *wh*-phrase further filter the class of available structures, so that *who* and *what* support only interrogatives, while phrases like *what a silly book* support only exclamatives.

   If (45) is the correct description of the facts, it should be impossible to form a *wh*-exclamative whose moved *wh*-phrase is the nominative subject. When the nearest bearer of uT and uWh is the same phrase, no non-*wh*-phrase will move to [Spec, CP]. Speakers, judgments confirm the prediction. The type of *wh*-phrase seen in (46) supports only an exclamative interpretation—but that interpretation is unavailable, since no non-*wh*-phrase has moved to [Spec, CP].[40]

(46) *What a silly person just called me on the phone!

We will not investigate (45) in any depth, but leave it as an observation to be explored in further research. For our purposes, it is sufficient to note what matrix *wh*-exclamatives show: that movement of the nominative subject to C is available as an alternative to T-to-C movement—even in matrix clauses headed by a C that contains uWh.

11.6   EPP and Embedded Questions

A similar issue arises with embedded questions in Standard English. Here too, we do not find overt T-to-C movement, either in the form of *that* or in the form of a fronted auxiliary verb.

(47) *Standard English: no embedded T-to-C movement*
    a. Bill asked what Mary bought.
    b. *Bill asked what did Mary buy.
    c. *Bill asked what that Mary bought.

The fact displayed in (47c) is one of the standard cases of the Doubly Filled Comp Filter, which bars the co-occurrence of *that* and a *wh*-phrase in [Spec, CP]. The traditional implementations of this filter posit an analysis for (47a) in which *that* appears in C in the syntax, but is unpronounced owing to a phonological deletion rule (Chomsky and Lasnik 1977; Pesetsky 1998). The view of movement that we are adopting, along with the proposals made here, suggests a different approach. Here there is no contrast between embedded interrogatives and exclamatives, so we would not wish to analyze the contrast between (47a) and (47b–c) as related to interpretation. There is, however, a contrast among dialects of English.

In particular, sentences like (47b–c) are acceptable in Belfast English, as discussed by Henry (1995). The co-occurrence of *that* with the *wh*-phrase seen in (49) is limited to embedded questions in Belfast English, much as *that* in declarative sentences is limited to embedded contexts in Standard English.[41]

(48) *Belfast English embedded T-to-C movement (auxiliary verbs)*
    a. She asked who had I seen.
    b. They wondered what had John done.
    c. They couldn't understand how had she had time to get her hair done.
    d. I wondered where were they going.
        (Henry 1995, 106, 116)

(49) *Belfast English embedded T-to-C movement (that)*
    a. I wonder which dish that they picked.
    b. They didn't know which model that we had discussed.
        (Henry 1995, 107)

Belfast English thus displays embedded questions whose syntax resembles the syntax of other (Standard English) clause-types considered so far. Thus, the examples in (48) and (49) show *u*T on the embedded C deleted by T-to-C movement. Examples like (47a), when used in Belfast English, may display the subject movement option.

Evidence that Belfast English *that* is an instance of T moved to C (just like Standard English *that*) comes from the fact that, just like *do* in Standard (and Belfast) English, *that* in constructions like (49a–b) is impossible in embedded interrogative clauses whose nominative subject is the *wh*-word of the clause. We can view this phenomenon as the T-to-C movement asymmetry with *that* rather than the auxiliary, or as a short-distance case of the *that*-trace effect. Either way, the phenomenon reinforces our claim (inherited from Koopman 1983) that the phenomena are fundamentally identical.[42]

(50) *Belfast English: T-to-C asymmetry recapitulated with* that
    a. *I wonder who did go to school?   [* unless *do* is emphatic]
       (Alison Henry, personal communication)
    b. *I wonder which author that wrote this book.
       (Henry 1995, 141, fn. 2)

As expected, given (50), Belfast English also displays a *that*-trace effect in embedded declarative clauses identical to that found in Standard English. Since embedded T-to-C movement in Belfast English takes the form of a moved auxiliary in addition to the form of *that*, the effect is found both with *that* and with fronted auxiliaries.

(51) *Belfast English:* that-*trace effect*
    a. *Who did John say [did ____ go to school]?   [* unless *do* is
       emphatic]
       (Alison Henry, personal communication)
    b. *Who do you think [that ____ left]?
       (Henry 1995, 128)

We can thus be reasonably certain that Belfast English differs from Standard English in using T-to-C movement to delete uT on C in embedded *wh*-questions.

What lies behind this difference between Belfast English and Standard English? We suggest that the dialects differ on one simple point: whether or not *movement* is the strategy adopted to delete uT on C. As we noted earlier, deletion of uninterpretable features is not always accomplished by movement, but is sometimes accomplished by the simpler operation of Agree—one of the components of movement. In these cases, a connection is established between the uninterpretable feature and another occurrence of that feature. This connection suffices to delete the uninterpretable feature, but does not motivate movement. In these cases, we say that the uninterpretable feature lacks the "EPP property." Languages and dialects differ precisely on the question of which uninterpretable features have the EPP property.

We suggest that Standard English embedded interrogative C lacks the EPP property for uT, while Belfast English C in the same context has the EPP property.[43] That is why no form of T-to-C movement (involving either *that* or a fronted auxiliary verb) is observed in Standard English embedded interrogatives. In attributing the contrast between Belfast English and Standard English to a difference in the EPP property of embedded interrogative C, we are suggesting that this difference is fairly trivial. It may, of course, turn out that deeper factors are involved, but at present all we can say is that the dialects differ and that it is possible to localize the difference in the grammar.

11.7   Summary

In this section, we summarize our account of the T-to-C movement asymmetry, the *that*-trace effect, and related phenomena. So far, we have considered four types of clauses.

(52) *Matrix* wh-*clause*[44]

Features of C:	uT (+EPP), uWh (+EPP)
Deletion of uT:	by T-to-C movement or subject movement
Deletion of uWh:	by *wh*-movement
Note 1:	By the Economy Condition (6), if the nominative subject is *wh*, no T-to-C movement occurs (the "T-to-C movement asymmetry").
Note 2:	If subject movement deletes uT, exclamative interpretation results; otherwise, interrogative interpretation.

(53) *Embedded* wh-*clause*

	Standard English	Belfast English
Features of C:	uT (−EPP), uWh (+EPP)	uT (+EPP), uWh (+EPP)
Deletion of uT:	by Agree (no movement)	by T-to-C movement or subject movement
Deletion of uWh:	by *wh*-movement	by *wh*-movement

(54) *Embedded declarative with no* wh-*extraction*
Features of C: uT (+EPP)
Deletion of uT: by T-to-C movement or subject movement
                      (looks like *that*-deletion)

(55) *Embedded declarative with* wh-*extraction*
Features of C: uT (+EPP), uWh (+EPP)
Deletion of uT: by T-to-C movement or subject movement
                      (looks like *that*-deletion)
Deletion of uWh: by *wh*-movement
Note: By the Economy Condition (6), if the
                      nominative subject is *wh*, no T-to-C
                      movement occurs (the *that*-trace effect).

In addition, though we do not offer an explanation for the different forms that T-to-C movement takes in Standard and Belfast English, we can describe the facts as follows:

(56) *Realization of T-to-C movement*
a. Standard English
   T-to-C movement is realized as auxiliary verb movement in main clauses where C has uWh. Otherwise, T-to-C movement is realized as *that* doubling T.
b. Belfast English
   T-to-C movement is always realized as auxiliary verb movement in main clauses and is optionally realized as auxiliary verb movement in embedded clauses, where C has uWh. Otherwise, T-to-C movement is realized as *that* doubling T.

We should also note at this point a cautionary lesson from our findings. English C, if we are correct, is phonologically null. Morphemes pronounced in C are pronounced there as a consequence of movement. We do not expect to find this pattern of data in every language. As far as we know, C does not have to be a zero morpheme. Consequently, it becomes necessary to establish whether the "clause introducer" of a given language is C or an element moved to C. In Spanish, for instance, if examples like (26a–c) studied by Torrego (1983, 1984) show T-to-C movement, the presence of *que* to the left of the fronted tensed verb suggests that *que* is an instance of C—not an element moved to C.[45] In Yiddish, on the other hand, the morpheme *az* that introduces finite clauses is probably an instance of T moved to C, like English *that*. As noted by Diesing (1990), Yiddish does show an *az*-trace effect.

(57) *Yiddish az-trace effect*
    Ver hot er moyre (*az)   vet kumen?
    who has he fear   (*that) will come
    'Who is he afraid will come?'
    (Diesing 1990, 75)

Yiddish also shows T-to-C movement of the more traditional sort accompanying successive-cyclic *wh*-movement just as in Spanish. Unlike Spanish *que*, however, *az* does not co-occur with the fronted verb—a further argument that *az*, unlike *que*, is not C, but a realization of T moved to C. *Az* does not co-occur with the fronted verb because *az*-fronting and verb fronting are two different realizations of the same operation: T-movement to C.[46]

(58) *Yiddish T-to-C movement accompanying successive-cyclic*
    wh-*movement*
    a. Vos hot er nit gevolt az mir zoln   leyenen?
        what has he not wanted that we should read
        'What did he not want us to read?'
    b. Vos hot er nit gevolt zoln   mir leyenen?
        what has he not wanted should we read
    c. *Vos hot er nit gevolt az zoln   mir leyenen?
        what has he not wanted that should we read
        (Diesing 1990, 71–72)

11.8   The *That*-Omission Asymmetry

Let us now turn to a difference between embedded declarative clauses with and without *that*. We analyzed this alternation in (32) and (34) as the consequence of *u*T on C attracting TP or attracting its specifier. We repeat the embedded clauses of (32) and (34) as (59a–b).

(59) a. ... [$_{CP}$[$_T$ that]$_j$ + [C, uT̶] [$_{IP}$ Sue will$_j$ buy the book]]
    b. ... [$_{CP}$ [Sue, uT̶]$_j$ [C, uT̶] [$_{IP}$ t-Sue$_j$ will buy the book]]

In (59b), the nominative subject has been attracted to [Spec, CP] by *u*T on C. This means, as we noted earlier, that *u*T on the subject did not disappear while still in [Spec, TP]—even though T entered an Agree relation with *u*T on the subject that marked *u*T on the subject for deletion.

Nevertheless, uninterpretable features that have been marked for deletion (like uT on *Sue*) must finally disappear once the embedded CP has been built. Otherwise, we might expect the nominative subject to be attracted out of [Spec, CP] by a higher functional head. For example, if the embedded clause in (59b) is the object of a passive verb, we might expect *Sue* to be attracted into the higher subject position by the matrix T.[47]

(60) *Sue was expected [____ will buy the book].

We can exclude (60) if uT on *Sue* is erased once and for all after the embedded CP is fully built, and if the presence of uT on DP is crucial to the attraction of DP by matrix T. We propose that this is the case. The assumption that uninterpretable features marked for deletion disappear completely at the end of the CP cycle is the proposal that Chomsky (2000, this volume) also argues for in discussing the notion "phase."[48] The observation that erasure of uT on *Sue* at the conclusion of the CP cycle prevents attraction by the higher T arises, we suggest, from a different fact about the grammar: a requirement that *all* the features of an attractor be present (in interpretable or uninterpretable form) on the elements that it attracts.[49]

(61) *Match Condition*
    If a head H enters an Agree relation with a set of phrases K, each syntactic feature of H must be present on some member of K[50] (not neccessarily with the same value, including value for EPP).

The Match Condition is asymmetric, in that it allows the attracted element to bear features not present on the attractor—as is the case, for example, when T happens to attract a nominative *wh*-phrase. In such an instance, the attracted element bears uT and ϕ-features also present on T, but bears a *wh*-feature not present on T. In (60), by contrast, since uT on *Sue* has completely disappeared once the embedded CP is built, it cannot be attracted by the matrix T, even though it bears ϕ-features capable of deleting the uninterpretable ϕ-features of the matrix T. By the Match Condition, the higher T cannot attract *Sue*.

Now consider in this light the embedded CPs in (59a–b). In (59a), head-to-head movement has taken place, with the result that C includes an instance of T. Since T here is the actual Tense of the sentence, its tense property is, of course, interpretable and does not delete. The presence of interpretable T in C in examples like (59a) has important syntactic consequences. To illustrate this, we consider the contrast between (59a) and (59b). Here, instead of T moving to C, the nominative subject has moved to [Spec, CP]. Like T, the nominative subject is able to delete uT on C. Unlike the tense properties of T itself, the T-feature of the nominative subject is uninterpretable. As a consequence, there is no instance of interpretable T in the C system of (59b).

Suppose one of the CPs seen in (59) is merged into a higher clause that contains finite T. As we indicated in (9), finite T in English bears $u\phi$ with an EPP property and therefore should attract the closest bearer of ϕ-features into its specifier, in accordance with ACF (10). Suppose the closest bearer of ϕ-features is the merged CP[51]—either because CP is a direct object of a passive or unaccusative verb, or because CP has been merged into an external argument position below T. By the Match Condition, this CP must bear T-features of some sort in addition to its ϕ-features; otherwise, the higher T cannot attract it into its specifier and delete $u\phi$ on T. In other words, this CP must be of the type seen in (59a), where CP is headed by a C that has incorporated T (realized as *that*); it cannot be of the type seen in (59b), where uT on C has been deleted by the nominative subject and has been erased at the end of the CP cycle. In fact, this is the case. We have just provided an account of the *that*-omission asymmetry presented in section 11.1. As we noted there, a finite CP functioning as the subject of a higher clause must be introduced by *that*.[52]

(62) a. [That Sue will buy the book] was expected by everyone.
     b. *[Sue will buy the book] was expected by everyone.

(63) a. [That Sue will buy the book] proves that she's rich.
     b. *[Sue will buy the book] proves that she's rich.

Let us see how our explanation of these contrasts works. At the point at which the higher T has been merged, the structures of (62a–b) are as shown in (64a–b), respectively.

(64) *(62a–b) midway in the derivation*
     a. [T, $u\phi$ (+EPP)] was expected [$_{CP}$[$_T$ that]$_j$ + [C, uT̶, ϕ] [$_{IP}$ Sue will$_j$ buy the book]]] . . .
     b. [T, $u\phi$ (+EPP)] was expected [$_{CP}$[Sue, uT̶]$_j$ [C, uT̶, ϕ] [$_{IP}$ t-Sue_j will buy the book]] . . .

The higher T must attract an element that has ϕ- and T-features of its own (interpretable or uninterpretable) and merge this element as a specifier. In (64a), because T-to-C movement has taken place in the embedded clause, the head of CP (hence CP itself) bears the necessary features to be attracted by the higher T and become its specifier. The result is (62a). In (64b), where uT on the lower C has been marked for deletion by the nominative subject *Sue*, no instance of uT remains on C once the CP cycle is completed. Since the nearest bearer of ϕ-features is the CP, ACF will not allow C to attract any lower phrase. Since the embedded CP lacks a T-feature at this point in the derivation, the Match Condition prevents T from attracting this CP.[53] Since the Match Condition prevents C from attracting the only phrase that ACF allows it to attract, T is unable to delete its uϕ-features in a way that satisfies their EPP property.

Our discussion has been fairly technical, but it actually amounts to a simple, traditional idea, which is worth noting at this point. The key to our hypothesis about the *that*-omission effect is the idea that a clause may become a specifier of finite T only if its head bears a T-feature. We identified the uninterpretable variant of the T-feature with the more familiar notion "nominative case," but we could as well have generalized this proposal to phrases bearing any sort of T-feature, interpretable or uninterpretable. If one thinks of the predicate "bearing nominative case" as equivalent to the predicate "bearing a T-feature," then our proposal concerning the *that*-omission asymmetry amounts to the simple statement that the subject of T is nominative. The novelty of our proposal lies mainly in the claim that declarative clauses introduced with *that* are nominative, while declarative clauses without *that* are not.[55]

11.9   Subject Questions and the Lifespan of Deleted Features

Embedded *wh*-questions in Standard English raise a problem for our proposal, since they can function as subjects of finite T.[56]

(65) [Which book Mary read yesterday] is not known.

This problem arises if, as we have suggested, uT on interrogative C lacks the EPP property in Standard English embedded questions. If uT on the embedded C in (65) lacks the EPP property, then T has not moved to C. Instead, uT on C has entered an Agree relation with the embedded TP (or with the nominative subject). Since C in (65) does not actually contain T, the subject clause in (65) should have the same status as the subject declarative clauses without *that* that we examined in the previous section; that is, it should be unacceptable. Obviously, this prediction is false.

One might attempt to avoid this problem by proposing that—instead of Agree—some type of "feature movement" from T to C (like that proposed in Chomsky 1995) may take place when uT on C lacks the EPP property. On this view, C in (65) could acquire an interpretable T-feature by feature movement. This alternative will fail, however, for embedded *wh*-questions whose *wh*-phrase is the nominative subject.

(66) [Which person read the book] is not known.

In (66), if our previous discussion is correct, uT on C has made no contact whatsoever with TP. Instead, C has attracted the nominative *wh*-phrase (for reasons already discussed). Thus, even if the proper analysis of (65) should turn out to involve feature movement rather than Agree, (66) would remain a problem.

Although we do not have a conclusive solution to this problem, we can offer a reasonable (but not inevitable) proposal that works well with the discussion so far and has consequences for other phenomena discussed below. Further work will be necessary to establish whether our proposal has independent support outside the domain of facts investigated here.

The problem in (65) and (66) arises only if uT on interrogative C (in embedded questions) must disappear at the end of the CP cycle (once marked for deletion), as is the case in embedded declaratives. If uT on C of an embedded question could stay "alive" after the CP cycle, despite being marked for deletion, then the matrix T would be able to attract the embedded question without violating the Match Condition. The embedded question would still bear an instance of uT in addition to its φ-features, even though uT would have been marked for deletion on the lower CP cycle. Thus, it is possible that embedded questions in Standard English differ from embedded declaratives in not requiring that features marked for deletion disappear at the end of the CP cycle.

This difference between embedded declarative and interrogative clauses might then be related to the EPP difference between uT on C in an embedded declarative and uT on C in an embedded question. In Standard English, as we have observed, uT on C in the embedded declarative has the EPP property, but uT on C in the embedded question does not. More generally (and speculatively), we propose (67).

(67) *Feature lifespan*
    A feature F on α marked for deletion disappears at the end of the CP cycle unless F on α is an attractor (see note 7) and is [−EPP].

As a consequence of (67), uT on the embedded declarative C in (64b) must disappear before the embedded clause is merged with the higher verb, but uT on C of the embedded question in (66) remains and is therefore eligible for attraction when the higher T is merged. This difference is illustrated in (68) and (69).

(68) *Disappearance of features in subject declarative clauses without* that
     The embedded clause of (64b)—

   a. [$_{CP}$[Sue, $u\text{T}$]$_j$ [C, $u\text{T}$, ϕ] [$_{IP}$ t-Sue_j will buy the book]] . . .
      —*looks like this when merged with the higher verb because* uT *on C has the EPP property.*

   b. expected [$_{CP}$[Sue]$_j$ [C, ϕ] [$_{IP}$ t-Sue_j will buy the book]] . . .
      When T merges, it cannot attract the lower CP.

   c. [T, $u\phi$ (+EPP)] was expected [$_{CP}$[Sue]$_j$ [C, ϕ] [$_{IP}$ t-Sue_j will buy the book]] . . .

(69) *Nondisappearance of features in embedded* wh-*questions*
     The embedded clause of (66)—

   a. [$_{CP}$[which person, $u\text{T}$, ϕ, wh]$_j$ [C, $u\text{T}$, ϕ wh] [$_{IP}$ t-$which\ person_j$ read the book]] . . .
      —*looks the same when merged with the higher verb because* uT *on C lacks the EPP property.*

   b. known [$_{CP}$[which person, $u\text{T}$, ϕ, wh]$_j$ [C, $u\text{T}$, ϕ, wh]
      [$_{IP}$ t-$which\ person_j$ read the book]] . . .
      When T merges, it does attract the lower CP.

   c. [$_T$ is, $u\phi$ (+EPP)] not known
      [$_{CP}$[which person, $u\text{T}$, ϕ, wh]$_j$ [C, $u\text{T}$, ϕ, wh] [$_{IP}$ t-$which\ person_j$ read the book]] . . .

The correlation suggested in (67) may also provide a reason for the existence of pied-piping (as originally described in Ross 1967) in *wh*-movement and similar constructions. Consider a situation in which a *wh*-phrase proceeds successive-cyclically through the specifiers of a number of categories whose heads bear uWh, on the way to its final landing site in the specifier of an interrogative C. On this scenario, the interrogative C bears uWh with the EPP property; if it did not, *wh*-movement would not be overt. Suppose, however, that one of the embedded heads bearing uWh—for example, P—bears a version of uWh that lacks the EPP property. The situation we have in mind is the one schematized in (70), where *who* bears the *wh*-feature and is the object of a P with uWh lacking the EPP property. *Wh*-movement has not yet taken place.

(70) $[_{CP}[C, u\text{Wh} (+\text{EPP}), \ldots] \ldots [_{PP}[P, u\text{Wh} (-\text{EPP})] \text{ who}] \ldots]$

A relation is established between uWh on P and the *wh*-feature of *who*. Since uWh on P lacks the EPP property, this relation has to be Agree, not Move. If (67) is correct, this means that uWh on P will not disappear just because a CP cycle might come to an end in the course of the derivation. Consequently, we expect PP in (70) to be able to undergo *wh*-movement —the phenomenon known as *pied-piping*. Notice that PP can be attracted by a higher uWh whether it is in its original position (e.g., as a complement to a verb) or in the specifier of some intermediate CP (as a step in successive-cyclic movement).

The standard description of pied-piping in *wh*-constructions relies on a mechanism of "percolation" that copies the *wh*-feature of a *wh*-word (in uninterpretable form, presumably) onto a constituent that dominates it. The *wh*-word remains in situ within the larger constituent and the larger constituent undergoes *wh*-movement. Our account reverses this logic. uWh is present on the larger constituent from the start (because otherwise an island condition would be violated by movement out of the larger constituent). The connection between the *wh*-word and uWh on P does not result from a special percolation mechanism, but from the normal rule of Agree. The reason a pied-piped *wh*-phrase can exit CP is (67). Although it is premature to regard this account as established, we suspect that the phenomenon of pied-piping will turn out to provide further support for (67).[57]

11.10   The Irrelevance of Emptiness

We have now offered a unified explanation of the three subject/nonsubject asymmetries introduced in section 11.1. As we pointed out, the prospect of a unified explanation of these phenomena was anticipated by researchers of the 1980s, who attributed the phenomena to various versions of the Empty Category Principle (ECP). We have argued that these effects do have a common origin, but have offered an entirely different account. It is worth comparing the central points of our account with the ECP proposals of the 1980s, in part because the comparison highlights important differences between our overall approach to movement and structure building and the Government-Binding approaches of the 1980s.

First, let us consider our account of the T-to-C movement asymmetry and the *that*-trace effect. The accounts of the 1980s took both effects to be consequences of a representational condition on traces of movement. Traces showed the effects of this condition because they were "empty categories"—unpronounced phrases in need of special licensing because of their absence from the phonetic signal. Many versions of this condition were offered. Chomsky's (1981) proposal is shown in (71).

(71) *Empty Category Principle (Chomsky 1981)*
    a. *ECP:* $[_\alpha \ e]$ must be properly governed,
    b. *Proper government:* α properly governs β if and only if α governs β [and $\alpha \neq$ Agr].
    c. *Government:* Consider the structure $[_\beta \ldots \gamma \ldots \alpha \ldots \gamma \ldots]$, where
        i. $\alpha = X^0$ [*head government*] or is coindexed with γ [*antecedent government*],
        ii. where ϕ is a maximal projection, if ϕ dominates γ, then ϕ dominates α, and
        iii. α c-commands γ.
    In this case, α governs γ.

A trace of *wh*-movement in [Spec, Agr] (i.e., T) could satisfy the ECP only by antecedent government, while a trace in object position required government by V. The *that*-trace effect arose because the presence of *that* somehow blocked antecedent government. In Koopman's (1983) account of the T-to-C movement asymmetry, a fronted auxiliary verb was taken to have the same blocking property. These accounts had a strongly "representational" character. At the point at which the ECP matters, *wh*-movement has taken place, *that* is present in C, any auxiliary verbs have raised, and the question is, is the structure legitimate? A proposal of this sort was quite natural in the Government-Binding framework of the times, in which movement was taken to be a free option, restricted mainly by conditions on its output. Yet, as the wisdom of hindsight makes clear, the specific proposal is unpromising from the start. It stipulates too much that is particular to the constructions being explained: for example, that antecedent government and head government have the same licensing effect, that Agr does not count as a governor, and that elements like *that* that should not block government, given (71), nonetheless do.

Our explanation of the *that*-trace effect and T-to-C movement asymmetry depends crucially on the new view of movement developed in the late 1980s and 1990s[58]—namely, that movement is not a free option, but occurs only to resolve the very particular problems of heads that bear uninterpretable features (with an EPP property). It is only in this context that our identification of *that* as T moved to C is significant, since it allows us to view the *that*-trace effect as the result of competition between T and its specifier to solve the "Tense problems" of C. Only a theory in which movement is a last-resort problem-solving strategy gives meaning to competition of this sort. If our proposals are correct, traces need no special licensing. Likewise, the fact that traces are "empty categories" plays no particular role in our account.[59]

These differences between ECP proposals and our own have particularly important empirical consequences for the *that*-omission asymmetry. The ECP account of this asymmetry relied on the idea that an unpronounced head of a category XP counts as properly governed if XP itself is properly governed (Belletti and Rizzi 1981; Stowell 1981). An unpronounced C that is not antecedent-governed could satisfy the ECP only if its maximal projection was governed by a head other than Agr. The word *that* was, of course, taken to be a pronounced instance of C. Finite embedded clauses without *that* were taken to have an unpronounced version of *that*—that is, an "empty" C. The *that*-omission asymmetry introduced in (4) followed from the ECP under an analysis like that sketched in (72), where the fact that C is null in (72d) is crucial.

(72) That-*omission asymmetry as analyzed by Stowell (1981)*
   a.   Mary thinks [[$_C$ that] Sue will buy the book].
   b.   Mary thinks [[$_C$ ∅]   Sue will buy the book].
   c.   [[$_C$ That] Sue will buy the book] was expected by everyone.
   d.   *[[$_C$ ∅]   Sue will buy the book] was expected by everyone.

Once again, the ECP account was crucially representational. English finite C was taken to come in two varieties: pronounced and "empty." In a structure with a subject CP whose head is unpronounced, the ECP was taken to filter out the unpronounced variant when it was not properly governed.

By contrast, our account has no filter that excludes heads of subject sentences if they fail to meet some criterion. Instead, the laws of movement determine whether a CP whose head has a particular featural composition can become a subject in the first place. This account once again relies on the idea that movement occurs only when it can solve a problem. It also relies on a finding more recent than the early ECP literature: the discovery that when an argument occupies [Spec, TP], it moves there from a lower position (Ken Hale, class lectures, 1980; Kitagawa 1986; Kuroda

1988; Koopman and Sportiche 1991). This finding is significant, since the effect seen in (72) is found with subjects of active transitive verbs as well as with subjects that were taken to be derived by movement even in 1981. What is important in our account is whether T of the higher clause bears any features not borne by C of the embedded clause—that is, whether the Match Condition (i.e., the requirement that the element attracted by T also bear some type of T-feature) may be satisfied by movement of the embedded CP to the specifier of the higher TP. This, in turn, depends on the movement patterns within the lower clause—in particular, whether T moved to C. Interestingly, "emptiness" is irrelevant. In English embedded finite declarative clauses, it so happens that the CP with the more restricted distribution contains an unpronounced C and the freer CP contains phonological material in C; but that is simply because the English declarative complementizer is null, while T (in the form of *that*) is not. If our account is correct, "emptiness" as a factor in the *that*-omission asymmetry was a red herring.

The case of embedded questions in subject position examined in the previous section already demonstrated this quite nicely.[60] Such questions are acceptable despite the absence of pronounced material in C. We attributed this state of affairs to the fact that C is null in English, and to the conjecture that uninterpretable features marked for deletion do not disappear at the end of the CP cycle if they lack the EPP property. More generally, we expect no general correlation between emptiness of C and acceptability of CP as a subject in a higher clause. We would thus not be surprised to find a wide range of phenomena like (72), including contrasts in which only the *un*acceptable member of the pair has pronounced material in C and cases in which both members of the contrasting pair have pronounced material in C. Cases like these may in fact exist.

Nakajima (1996) has discovered a case of the first kind: a contrasting pair that exhibits an effect akin to the *that*-omission asymmetry, except that the acceptable member of the pair has unpronounced C while the unacceptable member of the pair has pronounced C. His examples involve the two ways of introducing embedded yes/no questions in Standard English: with *whether* and with *if*. We will assume that *whether* is a *wh*-phrase in [Spec, CP] (with C null as always in embedded questions), while *if* occupies C. This assumption is supported by the fact that *whether*, unlike *if*, shows the morphology and behavior of a *wh*-phrase (as observed by Emonds (1985, 286–287), Larson (1985), and Kayne (1991)). For example, *whether* may form part of the larger phrase *whether or not*, but nothing comparable is available for *if*. While it is possible that *if*, like *that*, has raised to C from a lower position, we will assume that it is a complementizer.

(73) a. Mary asked me [whether $\emptyset_C$ Bill was happy].
     b. Mary asked me [if$_C$ Bill was happy].

Nakajima observes that *if*-questions may not function as subjects, while *whether*-questions may. This fact strongly resembles a mirror image of the *that*-omission asymmetry.

(74) *Nakajima's* whether/if *asymmetry*
     a. i.   [Whether Bill was happy] was the main topic of discussion at our dinner.
        ii. *[If Bill was happy] was the main topic of discussion at our dinner.
     b. i.   [Whether the election was fair] will be determined by the commission.
        ii. *[If the election was fair] will be determined by the commission.

The existence of contrasts like these is not surprising if attraction by finite T obeys the Match Condition. If the complementizer *if* lacks either uT or ϕ-features, the CP headed by *if* will not be attracted by T and will not surface in subject position. The complementizer found when *whether* occupies [Spec, CP] is presumably the normal null complementizer found in embedded questions. It bears both uT and ϕ-features, just as in the examples already examined.[61] Needless to say, if the ECP predicts any contrast between the (i) and (ii) examples of (74a) and (74b), it predicts a contrast opposite to the one we find.

Polish may display a case of the second kind (as was brought to our attention by Barbara Citko): a contrasting pair of subject CPs in which both members of the pair contain pronounced C. Polish embedded clauses may be introduced by *że* on its own, or by the sequence *to że*, where *to* is found elsewhere in Polish functioning as a demonstrative pronoun (and also as a copula). Only the *to że* variant can introduce a subject clause.

(75) *Polish* to-*omission asymmetry*
     a. [To że tu   jesteśmy] jest wszystkim   wiadome.
        TO C here we are   is   to-everyone known
        'That we are here is known to everyone.'
     b. *[Że tu jesteśmy] jest wszystkim wiadome.

We have not investigated these structures carefully enough to determine exactly what feature *to* adds to *że* that allows CP to function as a specifier of the higher TP. Perhaps Polish is like English, except that it has an overt complementizer *że*, and *to* is a realization of (interpretable) T moved to C, like English *that*. Or perhaps *to że* is a form of *że* that contains T-features or φ-features otherwise missing from *że*.[62] For present purposes, what matters is the apparent existence of a contrast similar to the *that*-omission asymmetry that does not involve an empty C. We conclude that "emptiness" was indeed a red herring in the ECP discussion of the 1980s.

11.11 Infinitival Clauses: Evidence for ACX

The distribution and interpretation of Standard English infinitival clauses provides another argument that the "emptiness" of C does not determine the distribution of CP. Like Standard English embedded questions, infinitival clauses present a case in which C may be phonologically null and yet head a CP that occupies the subject position of a higher clause. We will, in fact, argue that such infinitival clauses share a significant property—uT on C without the EPP property—with embedded questions. Infinitival clauses are interesting for another reason, however: they offer a new argument that ACX plays a role in the internal syntax of CP. We return to this point once we have sketched our basic analysis of infinitival CPs.

We begin with infinitival CPs whose subject is overt (not PRO). As noted by Bresnan (1972; see also Carstairs 1973; Stowell 1982; Pesetsky 1991), such CPs have a particular interpretation. Either they are understood as containing an irrealis modal, or they receive a generic interpretation.

(76) *Irrealis/generic infinitival clauses*
    a.   I would like (very much) for Sue to buy this book.   [irrealis]
    b.   I always prefer for my students to buy this book.   [generic]
    c.   *I liked (very much) for Sue to buy this book yesterday.
                                 [non-irrealis, nongeneric]
       'I liked it that Sue bought this book yesterday.'
    d.   *I preferred for Sue to buy this book yesterday.
                                   [non-irrealis, nongeneric]

The distribution of CPs introduced by *for* parallels quite closely the distribution of CPs headed by *that*.[63] *For* is optionally omitted in object infinitives, just like *that*.

(77) *Omission of* for
   a. I would like [Sue to buy this book].
   b. I would prefer [my students to buy this book].

When the subject of an infinitival clause is extracted by *wh*-movement, *for* may not appear in Standard English, just as *that* may not appear in comparable finite clauses. In other words, there is a *for*-trace effect exactly parallel to the *that*-trace effect (as observed by Bresnan (1977)).[64]

(78) *The* for-*trace effect*
   a. Who would you like [____ to buy the book]?
   b. *Who would you like [for ____ to buy the book]?

For is obligatory when infinitival clauses like those in (76)–(77) are used as subjects of a higher clause.

(79) *The* for-*omission asymmetry*
   a. I would prefer [for Sue to buy the book].
   b. I would prefer [Sue to buy the book].
   c. [For Sue to buy the book] would be preferable.
   d. *[Sue to buy the book] would be preferable.

The similarities between the distribution of *for* and the distribution of *that* suggest an analysis of *for* modeled closely on our analysis of *that*. We therefore suggest that *for* in Standard English is a form of T that doubles infinitival *to*—just as *that* is a form of T that doubles the tense of the finite verb. We take C in the infinitival clauses of (75)–(79) to be identical with the C that introduces finite clauses. It bears uT and ϕ. Its uT can be deleted by movement of T to C (realized as *for* in C) or by movement of the (overt) subject to [Spec, CP] (which yields the infinitival clauses that lack *for*).[65]

(80) *Analysis of irrealis/generic infinitives*
   a. ... [$_{CP}$[$_T$ for]$_j$ + [C, uT̶] [$_{IP}$ Sue to$_j$ buy the book]] ...
   b. ... [$_{CP}$[Sue, uT̶]$_j$ [C, uT̶] [$_{IP}$ *t-Sue*$_j$ to buy the book]] ...   [compare (59)]

The *for*-trace effect arises because it is less costly to move a *wh*-subject when C bears both uT and uWh than it is to move T to C and separately move a *wh*-phrase to C. The *for*-omission effect arises because when *for* is missing, the subject has raised to delete uT on C. Interpretable T has not moved to C, and uT on C disappears once the CP cycle is complete.

English infinitives differ from finite clauses in allowing PRO as subject. In Standard English, *for* is excluded in such infinitives. This is the so-called *For-To* Filter of Chomsky and Lasnik (1977).

(81) *for-to
    a. Sue would like [PRO to buy the book].
    b. *Sue would like [for PRO to buy the book].

If *for* is the realization of nonfinite T moved to C, the exclusion of *for* can be explained if movement of T to C is impossible in an infinitival clause whose subject is PRO. Why should T-to-C movement be incompatible with PRO? There are several possibilities. One might imagine that the uT problem of C must be solved by subject movement to [Spec, CP] when the subject is PRO. But this would predict that an irrealis/generic infinitival CP could not function as a subject of a higher clause when its own subject is PRO. This is not the case. Such infinitives function perfectly well as subjects of a higher clause.

(82) *Infinitival subject clauses with PRO*
    [PRO to buy the book] would be preferable.

One might also imagine that C lacks uT entirely when the subject of TP is PRO. Though such instances of C exist (a topic to which we return shortly), this is not a viable hypothesis about irrealis/generic infinitives. If C with such infinitives lacks uT entirely, *for* would be excluded, but so would (82).

Our approach provides one other possible reason for the exclusion of *for* in irrealis/generic clauses with PRO. If C in such clauses bears an instance of uT that lacks the EPP property, C will mark uT for deletion by Agree, rather than Move—just as we noted in the case of Standard English embedded questions. The absence of T-to-C *movement* will account for the absence of *for*. Furthermore, if our proposal about embedded questions is correct, uT that lacks the EPP property remains "alive" even after it is marked for deletion in the lower clause. This allows an infinitival CP with PRO to be attracted by a higher instance of T, accounting for the acceptability of examples like (82). This analysis entails a correlation between the EPP status of uT on C and the presence of PRO in TP. We will not attempt to explain the correlation or investigate it further here. Obviously, if the correlation is true, one wants to learn why it holds.[66]

(83) *C-PRO correlation*
    uT on C does not have the EPP property in a declarative clause whose subject is PRO.

There are, however, other infinitival clauses whose subject is PRO that are excluded from the subject position of a higher clause. These are infinitival clauses that do *not* receive an irrealis or generic interpretation, but receive a realis (and typically factive or implicative) interpretation. Such clauses are found in object position.

(84) *Realis infinitives in object position*
    a. Sue hated [PRO to learn the election results from the Internet].
    b. Sue managed [PRO to lose the game].

Once again, *for* is impossible.

(85) *Sue hated [for PRO to learn the election results from the Internet].

But realis infinitives are impossible as subjects, as discussed by Stowell (1982). For some speakers, this is a subtle effect, but others find the effect strong. It helps to contrast realis infinitives with their irrealis counterparts.

(86) *Irrealis/generic infinitives versus realis infinitives in subject position*
    a. i. ??[PRO to learn the election results] shocked me.
                                          [realis/factive]
       ii. [PRO to learn the election results] would shock me.
                                             [irrealis]
      iii. [PRO to learn the election results early] is a crime.
                                          [generic]
    b. i. ??[PRO to lose the game] proved they were idiots.
                                         [realis/factive]
       ii. [PRO to lose the game] would prove they are idiots.
                                           [irrealis]
      iii. [PRO to lose games like this] annoys the public. [generic]

Realis infinitival clauses are thus good candidates for one of the two analyses that we rejected when discussing irrealis/generic infinitival clauses. Either C bears uT with the EPP property, and for some reason PRO, rather than T, moves to delete uT (in which case (83) is false), or else C lacks uT entirely.[67] If realis C in infinitives lacks uT entirely, the absence of *for* is explained by the absence of any need to check T-features on C. The impossibility of such infinitives as subjects follows from the fact that a clause without a T-feature on C cannot move to [Spec, TP] (by the Match Condition).

In fact, the second possibility seems to be correct. C in realis infinitival clauses seems to lack uT entirely.[68] The argument in favor of this view is simultaneously an argument in favor of the existence of ACX as an overarching condition on movement, in a framework that also contains the PMC. Recall that ACX requires movement to be absolutely local. The PMC allows attraction to violate ACX once the attractor has entered into an Agree or Move relation with some other element that has obeyed ACX. For this reason, if ACX is true, no instance of movement to [Spec, CP] can take place from anywhere lower than [Spec, TP] unless C has already attracted T or its specifier (by Move or Agree). In a feature-driven theory of movement, this means that a nonsubject cannot move to [Spec, CP] unless C bears uT.

This leads us to expect something surprising if C of realis clauses lacks uT. Nonsubjects should be unable to move to [Spec, CP] *inside* a clause whose head C has uT. That is, we expect a correlation between the external syntax of an infinitive (ability/inability to move to a higher [Spec, TP]) and its internal syntax (ability/inability to allow nonsubject movement to [Spec, CP]). In fact, in a range of cases, we observe exactly this correlation. The relevant cases involve infinitives whose [Spec, CP] is the final landing site for operator movement. For reasons we cannot explain, the operators in these constructions are typically unpronounced in English, but have been convincingly argued to exist nonetheless by Chomsky (1977b). Infinitival arguments of degree expressions like *too* and *enough* provide a particularly clear case. Operator movement takes place within these infinitives. When the infinitive has an irrealis (modal) interpretation, the gap left by operator movement may be a subject or a nonsubject.

(87) *Irrealis infinitives: movement to [Spec, CP] of subject or nonsubject (in the* too-*construction)*
  a. Bill is too short [Op C [____ to see Mary over the fence]].
     'Bill's height is such that he cannot see Mary over the fence.'
  b. Bill is too short [Op C [PRO to see ____ over the fence]].
     'Bill's height is such that one cannot see him over the fence.'

A realis reading of the infinitive is also possible and can be forced if the infinitive bears perfect tense. Strikingly, the nonsubject gap becomes impossible.

(88) *Realis infinitives: no movement to [Spec, CP] of nonsubject (in the* too-*construction)*
  a. Bill is too short [Op C [____ to have seen Mary over the fence]].
     'Bill's height is such that he did not see Mary over the fence.'
  b. *Bill is too short [Op C [PRO to have seen ____ over the fence]].

ACX accounts for the contrast in (88) if C lacks uT. Since neither PRO nor T is attracted by C in (88b), movement of the direct object to [Spec, CP] is not movement of the closest possible element, nor is it movement that has been preceded by an Agree or Move operation involving the closest possible element. In (88a), by contrast, if operator movement to [Spec, CP] is taking place, it *is* taking place from one of the positions that counts as maximally close to C: the subject position.[69]

Another example of the same sort is provided by infinitival relative clauses. Infinitival relative clauses may have an irrealis interpretation.[70] In fact, this is their typical interpretation in English.

(89) *Irrealis infinitives: movement to [Spec, CP] of subject or nonsubject (in relative clauses)*

    a. [A person [Op C [_____ to talk to Bill]]] is Sue.
       'A person who might (profitably) talk to Bill is Sue.'
    b. [A person [Op C [PRO to talk to _____]]] is Sue.
       'A person who one might (profitably) talk to is Sue.'

As noted by Kjellmer (1975; see also Bhatt 1999), infinitival relative clauses may also receive a realis interpretation if the head of the relative contains an assertion of uniqueness. We will not address the uniqueness requirement here, but we do wish to note another observation of Kjellmer's: that the realis interpretation is unavailable when the trace of relativization is a nonsubject.[71]

(90) *Realis infinitives: no movement to [Spec, CP] of nonsubject (in relative clauses)*

    a. [The last person [Op C [_____ to talk to Sue]]] was contacted by the police.
       'The last person who talked to Sue was contacted by the police.'
    b. *[The last person [Op C [PRO to talk to _____]]] was contacted by the police.

If (90b) is acceptable at all, the infinitival relative clause has only the irrealis (modal) reading that is disfavored by the context: 'The last person who one might (profitably) talk to was contacted by the police'.[72]

Questions remain in this complex domain of data, ranging from the nature of the uniqueness requirement to the apparent absence of detectable contrasts between irrealis and realis interpretation in some infinitives with nonsubject gaps (e.g., *tough*-movement). Nonetheless, the correlation between the inability of realis infinitival CPs to serve as subjects of higher clauses and their inability to host nonsubject operator movement is just the correlation between the external and internal syntax of these clauses that we expect if their C lacks uT and ACX is correct. We therefore take the data in (87)–(90) as support for both these claims, though we recognize the need for further investigation.

11.12 Bottom-to-Top Syntax and the Distinction between C and D

Let us return to those CPs whose C bears uT. Our account of the subject/ nonsubject asymmetries that arise with such clauses has relied on a property of the overall model that we have left implicit so far. The asymmetries that we have discussed arise from the fact that an instance of C that bears uT "has a Tense problem": uT must be marked for deletion so that it may eventually disappear from the structure. Consider in this light our account of the *that*-omission asymmetry (and its "*for*-omission" counterpart in irrealis infinitives). We observed that an embedded declarative CP whose C solves its Tense problem by attracting T ends up with T incorporated in C. As a consequence, the embedded CP may be attracted by a higher T. If C solves its Tense problem by attracting the nominative subject, T is not incorporated in C, and the embedded CP may not be attracted by a higher T.

There is a third possibility that we did not consider. In sketching the two possible outcomes when C of an embedded declarative bears uT, we limited our discussion to the two ways that the problem could be solved internal to CP. Suppose, however, that a CP whose head bears uT could wait until it is merged with higher structure to solve its Tense problem. In other words, consider a derivation in which a CP is built whose head contains uT, where neither T nor its specifier enters into any sort of Agree or Move relationship with uT on C. If such a derivation were possible, we would have an unwanted way of allowing declarative clauses in subject position that are introduced by neither *that* nor *for*. C could solve its Tense problem in the higher clause, if the CP that it heads is attracted by a higher occurrence of T.

(91) *Unwanted derivation of subject declarative without* that
[T, $u\phi$ (+EPP)] was expected [$_{CP}$C, uT, ϕ] [$_{IP}$ Sue will buy the book]] $\Rightarrow$ [$_{CP}$[C, $u\text{T}$, ϕ] [$_{IP}$ Sue will buy the book]]$_i$ [T, $u\phi$ (+EPP)] was expected t-CP$_i$

The derivation in (91) is excluded if the syntax has a crucially "bottom-to-top" character, as suggested in much recent work (especially Epstein et al. 1998). What (91) shows is that uninterpretable features must be marked for deletion (and actually eliminated) as soon as possible. Since uT on C could be marked for deletion in the lower CP of (91), it had to be. This is essentially a version of Pesetsky's (1989) Earliness Principle.

(92) *Earliness Principle*
An uninterpretable feature must be marked for deletion as early in the derivation as possible.[73]

If our discussion of embedded questions and realis infinitives is on the right track, it is important to distinguish "marking a feature for deletion" from the actual disappearance of the feature itself when thinking about the Earliness Principle. The former must happen as early as possible. The latter may be delayed, under the EPP-related circumstances discussed earlier. A CP whose head bears an instance of uT that has been marked for deletion but has not disappeared may *behave* as if uT had not been marked for deletion at all. This was the case with embedded questions and irrealis infinitives. In the case of irrealis infinitives, we have just given evidence (the possibility of nonsubject movement to [Spec, CP] that uT on C is indeed marked for deletion on the lower cycle (just as required by the Earliness Principle), even though it does not disappear on that cycle.

The CPs whose head bears a T-feature after the CP cycle is complete are the CPs that can be attracted by T. We have noted two ways for C to bear a T-feature after the end of the CP cycle, and two ways for it to lack such a feature.

(93) *T-features on C*
a. C bears a T-feature after the CP cycle is complete if[74]
    i. C has uT (+EPP) and T moves to C (declarative *that*-clauses and *for*-clauses), or
    ii. C has uT (−EPP) (indirect questions and irrealis/generic infinitives whose subject is PRO).
b. C lacks a T-feature after the CP cycle is complete if
    i. C has uT (+EPP) and the nominative subject moves to C (declarative clauses without *that* and *for*), or
    ii. C does not bear uT (*if*-interrogatives and realis infinitival clauses).

In more traditional terminology, the CPs in (93a) are the CPs that can move to [Spec, TP] "for case reasons." Although these CPs may (and do) move to [Spec, TP] when necessary in order to satisfy the featural (including EPP) requirements of T, they have no need of their own forcing them to move to [Spec, TP]. This is because in the first case of (93a), the T present on C is interpretable, and in the second case, the T-feature present on C, though uninterpretable, has already been marked for deletion in the CP cycle.

We could imagine a third case of (93a), in which a T-feature on C is uninterpretable but has not yet been marked for deletion within the CP cycle. As we have just noted, when it is possible for uT on C to be marked for deletion within the CP cycle, it must be marked for deletion at that time—by the same Earliness Principle that ruled out the unwanted derivation in (91). What if uT on C cannot be marked for deletion, because C contains no local occurrence of a head or phrase that can do the job? This will never be the case in CPs of the type we have examined so far, whose heads take TP as a complement. TP, by definition, is capable of deleting uT on C.

One might, however, imagine a head that is identical to C in bearing uT and ɸ-features, but different from C in taking a category other than TP as its complement. Such a head would be unable to delete uT within its maximal projection and therefore would always need some external head to delete its uT. If we are correct in identifying nominative case (and possibly structural case more generally) with uT, a head of just this sort exists. It is the category usually called D.[75] C and D are very similar. Both bear ɸ-features. Both bear T-features (with a few exceptions for C noted above—and putting aside the analysis of inherent case on DP). C and D do differ in the type of complement that they take. We wish to end our discussion of C with the tentative suggestion that this is the *only* difference between C and D, as argued on independent grounds by Szabolcsi (1987).[76] Szabolcsi notes that C, like D, "turns a proposition into something that can act as an argument" (p. 180).[77]

Let us consider how the differences between CP and DP follow from the selectional differences between C and D. Consider a D bearing uT (i.e., D that heads a structurally case-marked DP). On a traditional analysis (Abney 1987), an article like *the* is D and the complement of D is NP. (We will shortly suggest a slight revision of this traditional view.)

(94) [$_{DP}$[$_D$ the, uT, ɸ] [$_{NP}$ picture [of Sue]]]

In (94), uT on D cannot be marked for deletion internal to DP. NP, we assume, lacks a T-feature. (The DP *Sue* may bear uT, but is inaccessible to D by ACX.) Consequently, uT on D simply fails to be marked for deletion on the DP cycle. For the derivation to converge, DP must be merged into a higher structure where uT on D can be deleted. An example is the passive structure of (95), where the object DP is attracted by T. The main difference between the acceptable derivation in (95) and the unacceptable derivation in (91) is the fact that uT on the embedded C of (91) could have been deleted on the lower CP cycle, while uT on the embedded D of (95) could not have been. This is why the DP in (95), but not the CP in (91), is attracted to the specifier of the higher TP. Note that uT on D must lack the EPP property if it is allowed to delete external to DP. This will be important shortly.

(95) *DP with undeleted* u*T on its head*

[T, uφ (+EPP)] was praised [$_{DP}$[$_D$ the, uT, φ] [$_{NP}$ picture [of Sue]]] ⇒ [$_{DP}$[$_D$ the, ~~uT~~, φ] [$_{NP}$ picture [of Sue]]] [T, ~~uφ~~ (+EPP)] was praised

Our proposals, however, conflict with a standard syntax for English possessive DPs. A DP that contains a possessor is perfectly acceptable both as the subject of a sentence and as the possessor of a larger DP. The question we must ask is why the internal syntax of English DPs that contain a possessor does not affect the external syntax of such DPs—as was the case for CPs.[78]

(96) a. [Mary's criticism of Sue] was praised.

b. [Mary's cousin's criticism of Sue]

The expectation that the presence of a possessor inside DP might affect its external syntax arises if the possessor phrase is the specifier of the highest head of the larger DP—that is, if it is the specifier of D, as proposed by Abney (1987) and others. According to this view, possessive *'s* belongs to the same category as *the* and *a*, thus explaining the fact that they are in complementary distribution. The fact that *'s* follows the entire possessor DP (as in *the king of England's throne*) is explained if the possessor is the specifier of *'s* (as the result of either movement from NP or direct merger). These are results that we do not wish to lose. On the other hand, if *'s* (along with *the* and *a*) is the highest head of DP, problems arise.

In particular, the assumption that *'s* is the highest head of DP (i.e., D) conflicts with our view that movement is feature-driven. Let us consider what feature of *'s* might cause the possessor DP to move to its specifier position, and what consequences this has for the external syntax of DP, if *'s* is an instance of D. If the feature driving movement to the specifier of *'s* is uT, we must then posit an instance of uT on *'s* that has the EPP property. (By the Match Condition, the possessor DP must also bear uT.) As a result, uT on *'s* would be marked for deletion within DP by the raising of the possessor. If D and C are the same category, we expect the deleted uT on D to disappear once DP is complete. Consequently, if *'s* is an instance of D, DP should not behave like a category whose head bears uT once DP is merged into a higher structure. Movement of this DP to [Spec, TP] should be impossible. This is an incorrect result, as (96a) shows. Suppose alternatively that the possessor is attracted by some other feature on *'s*— call it uF. If this were the case, we would not have to assume that uT on D has the EPP property. Consequently, even if the possessor were to mark uT on D for deletion, uT would be able to remain "alive" after the DP cycle is complete. However, uF would not remain alive, since uF, by hypothesis, would have the EPP property. This too leads to an incorrect result if *'s* an instance of D. A DP containing a possessor would be a DP that does not bear uF on D once the DP cycle is finished. Consequently, a DP containing a possessor should be unable to function as a possessor of a higher DP. Example (96b) shows that this result is also wrong.

We therefore tentatively drop the assumption that *'s*, *the*, and *a* are the highest head of DP. We propose that *'s*, *the*, and *a* are not instances of D, but belong to a category that we may call R ("*ar*ticle"). RP is the complement of D, which is null in English. We maintain the common view that possessors occupy the specifier of *'s*—now understood as the specifier of RP. The possessor is attracted to *'s* by some feature on *'s* with the EPP property. Whether this feature is uT or uF remains unclear. In (97a), we adopt uF for ease of presentation.

(97) a. [$_{DP}$[D, uT (−EPP), ϕ] [$_{RP}$[$_{DP}$ Mary, uT, F]$_i$ [R 's, $u\cancel{F}$ (+EPP)] [$_{NP}$ t_i criticism [of Sue]]]]]

  b. [$_{DP}$[D, uT (−EPP), ϕ] [$_{RP}$[$_R$ the] [$_{NP}$ criticism [of Sue]]]]

  c. [$_{DP}$[D, uT (−EPP), ϕ] [$_{RP}$[$_R$ a] [$_{NP}$ picture [of Sue]]]]

The fact that English D is phonologically null in DPs like those of (97), of course, is yet another respect in which English C and D are alike. At the same time, the existence of DPs like *all Sue's pictures of Mary* and *all the pictures of Sue* may suggest variants of D that are not phonologically null. It is also worth noting that the structures we propose in (97) are close to those proposed for Hungarian DPs by Szabolcsi (1983, 1987), whose proposals were further developed by Kayne (1993)—and it is worth noting that possessors in Hungarian and other languages are often morphologically nominative.

We began this chapter with several classic observations about asymmetries in the theory of case and in the behavior of the English complementizer system. If we are correct, the proper treatment of one of these asymmetries—the T-to-C movement asymmetry—leads immediately to an understanding of a wide range of other phenomena, including (but not limited to) those with which we began.

Notes

It is with equal amounts of pleasure and humility that we dedicate this chapter to Ken Hale, our colleague, teacher, and friend for many years. We are also grateful to him for discussing this work with us, and especially for offering the marvelous example of Pitta-pitta.

In addition, we wish to thank Elena Anagnostopoulou, Joseph Aoun, Abbas Benmamoun, Jonathan Bobaljik, Cedric Boeckx, Lisa Cheng, Noam Chomsky, Barbara Citko, Sam Epstein, Danny Fox, Hubert Haider, Sabine Iatridou, Richard Kayne, Howard Lasnik, James McCloskey, Alan Munn, Martin Prinzhorn, Norvin Richards, and Koldo Sainz for useful conversations about this work. We also wish to thank the students and visitors at MIT who improved the work with their questions and comments, as well as audiences at New York University, WCCFL (University of Arizona), the University of Vienna, the LSA Summer Institute at the University of Illinois, SUNY Stony Brook, and the Instituto Universitario "Ortega y Gasset" (Madrid). Thanks also to Michael Kenstowicz for helpful comments on an earlier draft and for generous editorial patience. We are also grateful to Jon Nissenbaum for a very thorough reading of the manuscript and for many insightful comments and suggestions.

As we were writing this chapter, we learned of the research of Haeberli (1999), who, like us, argues that nominative case (and structural case more generally) is an uninterpretable T-feature on D. He develops this idea in a different way than we do here. We hope to compare his work with ours in the near future, with a view to integrating the two bodies of research.

The authors' names are listed alphabetically.

1. The possibility of focused *did* is independent of *wh*-movement and thus irrelevant to our concerns: compare *Mary did buy the book!* We assume, with Chomsky (1957) and Laka (1990), that *do*-support is triggered by an affirmative counterpart to *not* (Chomsky's morpheme A, Laka's Σ) whose phonological content is stress or high pitch.

2. A similar proposal was advanced by Rizzi (1996, 68).

3. In Rizzi's (1990) account of the *that*-trace effect, English clauses without *that* were taken to be headed by an unpronounced complementizer containing agree-

ment morphology that properly governed the subject position. In such a theory, it becomes puzzling why an overtly agreeing auxiliary verb like *did* does not also govern the subject position once moved to C.

4. Huang (1982) suggested that the island sensitivity of adjunct extraction was a consequence of the ECP effect akin to the *that*-trace effect. This suggestion, as developed by Lasnik and Saito (1984, 1992) and others, led to a vigorous "afterlife" for ECP research, some of which, oddly enough, failed to take into account the subject/nonsubject asymmetries that had motivated the ECP in the first place. We will not discuss adjunct extraction here.

5. Chomsky (1995) suggested that this operation involves literal movement (copying) of features of the attractee to the attractor ("feature movement"). It will be of some importance to our proposals that this hypothesis is incorrect, and that Chomsky's later (2000) proposal, in which Agree does not involve any copying of features, is correct.

6. The term *EPP* derives from the Extended Projection Principle of Chomsky 1981, which required that T (then called "Infl") have a specifier. In Chomsky 2000, it is suggested that other heads have versions of the same requirement. We suggest below that the choice between phrasal and head movement is predictable and that a unified "EPP property" can therefore be taken to be the motivation for movement of all sorts. Our suggestion that both head movement and XP-movement may satisfy an EPP property of a feature is similar to recent proposals by Alexiadou and Anagnostopoulou (1998).

7. This use of the term *attract* is slightly nonstandard. It follows terminology used in Chomsky 1995, where the operation that we call Agree (following Chomsky 2000) was viewed as actual movement of a feature.

8. The parenthesized restriction to English matrix questions is for expository purposes only. We discuss other instances of C (and other instances of T-to-C movement) below.

9. The literature contains some skepticism about whether nominative *wh*-phrases really do move to [Spec, CP] in questions like (5d) (Gazdar 1981; Chung and McCloskey 1983; Chomsky 1986). One argument that they do can be found in the distribution of expressions like *the hell* (Pesetsky 1987) that attach to *wh*-phrases. As Pesetsky notes, these phrases are allowed only on *wh*-phrases that have overtly moved to [Spec, CP].

(i) a. What the hell did Sue give to whom?
     b. Who the hell did Bill meet where?

(ii) a. *What did Sue give to whom the hell?
     b. *Who did Bill meet where the hell?

As Ginzburg and Sag (to appear) point out, they are quite possible on nominative *wh*-phrases in the interrogative clauses under consideration, as in (iii). This seems to argue that they have moved to [Spec, CP].

(iii) Who the hell bought what?

It is also fairly certain that the presence of *the hell* on fronted *wh*-phrases is not just a second-position effect, since *the hell* occurs freely with a nominative *wh*-phrase that introduces an embedded question, as in (iv), but not with a nominative *wh*-phrase at the left edge of an embedded declarative that is clearly not in [Spec, CP], as in (v).

(iv) Who wondered who (the hell) bought this book?

(v)   Who believed who (*the hell) bought this book?

Another argument making the same point is implied by Lasnik and Saito (1992, 101–102).

10. By claiming that nominative case is *u*T on D, but that the association of a nominative DP with T is driven by *u*ϕ on T, we unite both sides of an old debate about whether nominative is "really" assigned by tense or by agreement (e.g., George and Kornfilt 1981, Chomsky 1981, Raposo 1987, Raposo and Uriagereka 1990 for agreement vs. Rouveret and Vergnaud 1980, Chomsky 1980, Guéron and Hoekstra 1988 for tense). There is also a point of similarity between our proposal that *u*T is present on finite C and Bittner and Hale's (1996) proposal that C is crucially involved in case assignment more generally.

11. We use *closeness* and *closer* as technical terms somewhat differently from the way they are used in ordinary language. In particular, the relation is not transitive, since (for example) in a simple clause of the form in (i),

(i) [C [[Spec, TP] T [V ...]]]

both TP and [Spec, TP] count as equally close to C, but only [Spec, TP] is closer to C than V. TP is not closer to C than V because it dominates V. We thank Iris Mulders (personal communication) for noting this possible source of confusion.

12. We assume that head movement yields an adjunction structure, though other possibilities are conceivable.

13. We take up the possibility that the nominative subject *Mary* might be attracted by *u*T on C even in (14a) (forming a second specifier of CP) in section 11.4.

14. The EPP property of two distinct uninterpretable features is satisfied by a single instance of movement here. The presence of the EPP property on an uninterpretable feature *u*F must therefore be nothing more than the requirement that the element with which *u*F enters an Agree relation must be copied into the very local domain of the bearer of *u*F. It does not matter which feature actually triggers the copying.

15. Some of the diverse research that goes by the name of "functionalist" can be seen as alternative attempts to rescue as much of the extreme functionalist hypothesis as is consistent with the actual facts of human language. For example, some research in this tradition acknowledges the existence of morphemes with no semantic content, but suggests that such morphemes always arise historically from morphemes that do have semantic content—a process called "grammaticalization." (See Newmeyer 1998 for a critique of this notion.) Other work argues that

purely grammatical morphemes only occur synchronically insofar as they belong to larger units with designated semantic content, often called "constructions" (Goldberg 1995). In contrast, the nonfunctionalist literature has largely turned its back on the entire issue, taking as fact the observation that some grammatical features have a semantic value and others do not. In this sense, our proposal is closer to the functionalist tradition than to the nonfunctionalist tradition.

16. Strictly speaking, Chomsky suggests that the relevant feature is "structural case," unspecified for nominative or accusative, but he does take this feature to lack semantic value in every context.

17. We take it for granted that actual nominative case lacks semantic content entirely. This view was challenged by Jakobson (1936/1984). He agreed that a unitary meaning for nominative cannot be detected, but argued that nominative does have semantic content, which derived from its status as the unmarked member of the pair nominative-accusative. The meaning of nominative is, for Jakobson, the complement set of the meanings associated with the other cases (including accusative), hence the absence of a unitary characterization. The results we present here, if correct, constitute an argument against this view.

Still, the dichotomy "interpretable"/"uninterpretable" may in the end turn out to be too crude. While agreement on T is plausibly devoid of semantics, DP does have tense properties of some subtlety and complexity, studied by Enç (1981), Musan (1995), and others. Furthermore, DPs in Somali (Lecarme 1997) and in languages of the Salishan group (Demirdache 1997) overtly express tense on DP in a variety of ways. (In Somali, a present/past interpretation is accorded to the proximate/distal system.) Thus, the presence of T-features on DP in a language like English, while "uninterpretable" in some sense, might have some roots in the semantics of DP after all. We have not investigated these matters, and we will treat the T-features of DP as strictly uninterpretable in this chapter. We are aware that future work may cause us to qualify this view.

18. Chomsky (2000) argues from the existence of "defective intervention effects" that uninterpretable features are initially unvalued and that they receive values (e.g., specific values for person, number, etc.) as a by-product of the rule Agree (either on its own or as a subcomponent of Move). It is possible that only the features of the attractor in an Agree operation receive values in this manner. The features of the attracted element might remain unvalued, in which case the observed asymmetry is accounted for. This, of course, would make Pitta-pitta (discussed below), rather than English, the surprising case.

19. We are grateful to Abbas Benmamoun and Joseph Aoun for bringing these facts to our attention.

20. More to the point, argumental locative PPs in languages like English must be viewed as bearers of uT, especially in the construction known as locative inversion (*In the center of the room sat a frog*). This is not unreasonable, especially given the fact that in Chichewa (Bresnan and Kanerva 1989), locatives behave in this construction entirely like nominative DPs in Indo-European languages, triggering verbal agreement and other processes characteristic of subjects. In English, they

behave like nominative subjects for the T-to-C movement asymmetry (*In the center of which room sat/*did sit a frog?*) and for the *that*-trace effect (*In the center of which room do you think (*that) sat a frog?*; Bresnan 1977). In Dutch (Mulder and Sybesma 1992), argumental locative PPs are obligatorily preverbal in embedded clauses, like structurally case-marked accusative DPs, while other PPs may occur postverbally. Space limitations prevent us from pursuing this extension of our proposals here.

21. This proposal is a version of Marantz's (1991) "dependent case" theory. Compare also Richards's (1997) hypothesis that nominative and accusative case depend on a link to an AgrP common to the two cases. These proposals can be naturally extended to ergative/absolutive languages, as Marantz shows.

22. We also put aside occurrences of nominative case morphology that may arise by agreement with a nominative DP (e.g., nominative adjectives and predicate nominals), as well as occurrences that might represent "default case," in the sense proposed by Schütze (1997).

23. The connection between (5) and Richards's Principle of Minimal Compliance has been independently noted by Platzack (to appear).

Jon Nissenbaum (personal communication) points out that Richards's constraint has a derivational character not motivated by the phenomena that we have discussed so far. No fact so far has indicated whether T-to-C movement precedes or follows *wh*-movement in the derivation of a sentence like *What did Mary buy?*

24. The PMC is incompatible with Rizzi's (1996) claim that T that moves to C in an interrogative clause bears uWh. If T were to bear uWh, then movement of T to C would satisfy ACF for uWh on C, and no Superiority effect would arise, contrary to fact.

25. ACX is in this respect quite similar to Chomsky's (2000) Phase-Impenetrability Condition, except that TP for Chomsky (and, ultimately, for us) cannot be regarded as a phase elsewhere. There is also a strong similarity to much earlier proposals by Koster (1978a), whose Bounding Condition stipulated that all maximal projections should be regarded as islands for extraction, with their specifiers functioning as "escape hatches."

26. This requirement might be motivated by ACX, depending on what other movement takes place to other possible landing sites. Otherwise, we assume that other constraints force successive-cyclic *wh*-movement.

27. It is important to remember that the head of a declarative clause may perfectly well bear uWh, since uWh is an *uninterpretable* instance of the *wh*-feature. The *wh*-feature is the property that is interpretable on *wh*-phrases. We assume that there is a distinct interpretable feature Q on interrogative complementizers, which (by the Match Condition presented later in (61)) entails the presence of uQ on *wh*-phrases, but this detail will not be important here.

28. Both in Belfast English and in Spanish, movement of a relative pronoun does not trigger (overt) T-to-C movement of the sort demonstrated here. By contrast, in French, relative-pronoun movement does trigger successive-cyclic T-to-C move-

ment (Marie Claude Boivin, personal communication). We do not have an account of this asymmetry—though our overall proposal will make it possible to analyze relative clauses as involving successive-cyclic *wh*-movement without necessarily triggering overt T-to-C movement. See the discussion of English embedded questions in section 11.6.

29. There is controversy about the analysis of (26) as T-to-C movement. For alternative proposals, see Suñer 1994, Ordoñez 1997, and Barbosa 1999, among others. For dialect variation, see Baković 1998.

If we are correct to group the Belfast English data in (25) with the Spanish data in (26) (in agreement with Henry (1995)), then the phenomenon in question cannot be seen as a way of avoiding barriers to *wh*-movement that are (allegedly) created by overt specifiers—the hypothesis advanced by Uriagereka (1999).

30. For present purposes, we assume that the Spanish and French data display adjunction of the moved finite verb (pied-piped by T) to the right side of C. Right-adjunction of this sort is sometimes argued to be impossible, since it falls outside the range of possibilities allowed under Kayne's (1994) antisymmetry hypothesis and similar proposals. We hope to return to this matter in subsequent work.

31. Our treatment of *that* also recalls clitic-doubling constructions in Romance and elsewhere, as well as "partial *wh*-movement" constructions in German and other languages. These are cases in which some features of an element left in situ appear in a position arguably created by movement.

(i) Juan *la*   vió a *Mafalda.*
     Juan her-ACC saw to Mafalda
     'Juan saw Mafalda.'
     (Jaeggli 1982)

(ii) *Was* glaubt Hans *mit wem*   Jakob jetzt spricht?
     what believes Hans with whom Jakob now talks
     'With whom does Hans believe that Jakob is now talking?'
     (McDaniel 1989, 569)

The treatment of both of these constructions is an open issue. If these constructions are instances of doubling akin to our treatment of *that*, it may be possible to develop a wider theory of doubling constructions. In this light, the research of Anagnostopoulou (1999, to appear) on clitic doubling in Greek is particularly interesting, since it appears to show local clitic doubling of indirect object DPs licensing longer-than-expected A-movement of the direct object—an interaction reminiscent of ACX, if clitic doubling (at least in Greek) is a realization of movement.

32. It is crucial to our explanation of the *that*-trace effect that long-distance *wh*-movement must proceed via [Spec, CP] (as a consequence of the Subjacency Condition or whatever derives its effects). Because *wh*-movement must proceed successive-cyclically, the nearest C must bear *u*Wh. If the nearest C lacks *u*T, there will be no *that*-trace effect, but the *wh*-phrase will leave CP without passing through its specifier.

33. The analysis in (36) shows two specifiers of CP. English, of course, does not permit more than one overt *wh*-specifier of CP (as illustrated in multiple questions), but that is not the situation in (36). See our discussion of exclamatives (example (44) below) for another example of multiple [Spec, CP] in English. We are grateful to Jon Nissenbaum (personal communication) for this observation.

34. Our results, as reported here, depend on TP's being the complement of C. Recent proposals by Rizzi (1997) and Cinque (1999) that argue for functional heads between T and C are incompatible with these results. If the structures proposed by Rizzi and Cinque are correct, we believe that our core results can be recast in their terms, once one allows for T-movement to these higher functional heads preceding attraction of T to C.

35. It has, of course, been argued that multiple specifiers count as equidistant from higher nodes (e.g., by Chomsky (2000), whose concern is the ability of the external argument generated as a specifier of *v*P to be attracted to [Spec, TP] over a higher specifier of *v*P).

36. As Jon Nissenbaum (personal communication) has pointed out, the logic of the situation requires ACX to outrank the Economy Condition, in that an attractor picks the attraction pattern that involves the fewest operations (Economy) from the set of attraction patterns that satisfy ACX.

37. The existence of alternative parses for crucial examples makes it hard to determine whether *that* is obligatory, as predicted. If we drop the *that* in (41a–b), the result is not terribly unacceptable, which might seem to contradict our proposals. The problem is that the phrases *for all intents and purposes* and *to the rest of us*, which clearly precede [Spec, TP] in (37)–(38) and arguably may precede [Spec, TP] in (41a–b) (allowing *that*), can be analyzed as parentheticals that follow [Spec, TP] in the counterparts to (41a–b) without *that*. On this parse, we expect a *that*-trace effect, rather than an anti-*that*-trace effect.

(i)   Sue met the man who Mary is claiming ____ [for all intents and purposes] was the mayor of the city.

(ii) Bill, who Sue said ____ [to the rest of us] might seem a bit strange, turned out to be quite ordinary.

An issue also arises in matrix questions, where topicalization does not obviate the T-to-C movement asymmetry, which otherwise tracks the *that*-trace effect, as we have seen.

(iii) *Who [for all intents and purposes] did buy the book?   [* except if *did* is focused]

(iv) *Who [to the rest of us] did seem strange?   [* except if *did* is focused]

Here, the interfering factor is not only the availability of a postsubject position for *for all intents and purposes* and *to the rest of us*, but also the fact that topicalization (and fronting more generally) is not permitted between C and the nominative subject in matrix questions. Instead, the landing site seems to precede CP.

(v)   *What did [for all intents and purposes] Mary but ____?

(vi)   *How strange did [to the rest of us] Bill seem ____?

(vii) [For all intents and purposes], what did Mary buy?

(viii) [To the rest of us], how strange did Bill seem ____?

The acceptable counterparts to (iii) and (iv) without *did* (presented in (ix) and (x)) once again probably show the bracketed phrase in a position after the nominative subject.

(ix) Who [for all intents and purposes] bought the book?

(x)   Who [to the rest of us] seemed strange?

38. Another "anti-*that*-trace effect" is found in English relative clauses, where subject extraction requires an overt *wh* or *that* and disallows the absence of both. We will not discuss these facts here.

39. Possibly the near obligatoriness of interjections like *boy* in non-*wh* exclamatives with T-to-C movement like *Boy, is syntax easy!* (McCawley 1973) might arise from the need to supply a non-*wh* [Spec, CP]. While McCawley offers many examples of exclamatives that lack an initial interjection, they all seem to us to require something preceding the fronted auxiliary, even if it is only a whistle or a sharp intake of breath. Perhaps one could argue that the whistle or intake of breath occupies [Spec, CP], in conformity with (45).

40. The judgment in (46) seems to be extremely secure, but judgments waver with unaccusative verbs: for example (?)*What a strange package just arrived!*

41. This fact may be of deeper significance, if the realization of T on C as *that* is tied in some way to the anaphoric function of *that* in its other capacity as a (demonstrative) pronoun. It could be that *that* is available as a realization of T only when in the c-command domain of another occurrence of T, possibly with consequences for sequence-of-tense interpretation. Remarks about the semantics of *that*-omission in Swedish by Platzack (1998) may reinforce this view (see also Ippolito 1999), as do suggestive observations about English by Ritter and Szabolcsi (1985). This property would also prevent *that* from occurring in matrix clauses more generally—assuming that root declarative sentences are CP rather than TP. See Szabolcsi 1987 for an alternative view.

42. Much the same facts were observed by Keyser (1975) in Middle English relative clauses. Nominative *who* (an innovation of the Middle English period) was never followed by *that*, while nonnominative *whom* often was.

43. Obviously, one wants the reference to "embedded" versus "matrix" clauses to follow from other properties of the theory, but we will not explore this area here.

44. We leave open whether matrix *declarative* clauses are CPs or TPs, as discussed in note 41. If they are CPs, it is quite possible that matrix declarative C also bears *u*T. If this occurrence of *u*T has the EPP property, then perhaps some factor like the one discussed in note 41 requires the nominative subject, rather than T, to delete *u*T on C.

45. This might explain the apparent absence of a *que*-trace effect in Spanish (Perlmutter 1971). It has, however, been argued that counterparts to this effect do

exist in the area of scope (Kayne 1981b; Rizzi 1982; Picallo 1984). Jaeggli (1982, 1984) made this argument for Spanish. We assume for the purposes of this chapter that restrictions on wide scope do not follow from the same factors that yield the *that*-trace effect. A fuller investigation of these matters would also take up the phenomenon of *que/che* omission in pro-drop Romance languages, which has also not been fully investigated.

46. Subject movement to [Spec, CP] is not possible in these examples (i.e., the embedded clause must be introduced either by *az* or by the fronted verb). Perhaps multiple specifiers of CP are not allowed in Yiddish.

47. Example (60) raises the possibility that the ban on movement from an Ā- to an A-position (so-called improper movement) might be explained as a consequence of the lifespan of features marked for deletion. Traditional accounts, in which movement for "case reasons" is always movement to an A-position, are undermined by our argument that movement to [Spec, CP] takes place to delete uT—that is, for "case reasons."

48. Chomsky argues that both CP and vP are "phases." We take no stand here on whether vP is a phase akin to CP. For some evidence in favor of this view, see Nissenbaum, in preparation.

49. The observation that uT must be present on DP for T to successfully attract it is the counterpart in our system to Chomsky's (2000) proposal that a case feature must be present on DP if T is to attract it. For Chomsky, this requirement is a special case of a more general requirement that a phrase must contain some uninterpretable feature in order to be attracted. The key example involves case, where it is assumed that the absence of a case feature on a potential attractee makes it ineligible for attraction by T but capable of preventing T from attracting other phrases. The Match Condition may have this effect as well, except that it relies on the idea that case on DP is not a sui generis uninterpretable feature, but an instance of a feature present on T.

50. The word *some* is important, since a C bearing uWh and uT may attract a phrase bearing T that lacks *wh* (e.g., TP) and may attract a phrase bearing *wh* that does not bear T (e.g., *how* or *with whom*)—in two distinct operations.

It is important that T not bear uWh (at least in English); if it did, movement of T to C could obviate the Superiority Condition, given the Principle of Minimal Compliance that allows interrogative C to attract a *wh*-phrase that is not the closest once it has attracted an instance of the *wh*-feature that does count as closest.

51. As noted in passing in section 11.1, we assume that CP bears φ-features— third person singular in the languages familiar to us, though under certain conditions conjoined CPs behave as plurals. We do not explain the intriguing fact that CP in a variety of languages cannot be the antecedent for a null pronoun (Iatridou 1991; Iatridou and Embick 1997), a fact that Iatridou and Embick link to a claim that CP does not bear φ-features at all.

52. Koster (1978b) argued that CPs introduced by *that* are never subjects, but occupy a topic position with distinct properties. Some of the evidence adduced in favor of this claim seems incorrect to us. For example, Koster claims that auxil-

iary verbs cannot be fronted over a putative subject *that*-clause; however, it seems to us that an intonational effect is at work in these cases. Examples such as *Did that Sue bought the book really bother you?* are hard to parse unless the *that*-clause is destressed but seem acceptable otherwise. We therefore assume that subject CPs do exist and that subject *that*-clauses do not necessarily have the syntax of topics. See Piera 1979 for other arguments to this effect from English, French, and Spanish. On the other hand, if topics are specifiers of TP, as we cautiously suggested in section 11.4, one might accept Koster's proposal without giving up the claim that the *that*-omission asymmetry is due to the ability of CP to be attracted by T.

53. Our Match Condition plays much the same empirical role as Chomsky's (2000) requirement that attracted phrases bear an uninterpretable feature (that they be "active," in his terminology), while differing from his proposal conceptually. Our Match Condition can generate "defective intervention effects" of the sort discussed by Chomsky if the nearest bearer of a feature F sought by an attractor X fails to bear some other feature of X. In languages (e.g., Spanish; Torrego 1986) in which a dative DP blocks an Agree relation between a lower nominative DP and T (even though the dative cannot move to T itself), we would speculate that the dative DP lacks uT (though it has ϕ-features).

54. Movement of T to C would, of course, delete $u\phi$ on T just as effectively as movement of the subject to [Spec, TP], but would not satisfy the EPP property of $u\phi$ on T. When a feature uF on X has the EPP property, some element that bears F (interpretable or uninterpretable) must merge with X or a projection of X.

55. We suggested in section 11.4 that topicalized phrases are outer specifiers of TP, which probably means they are attracted by some uninterpretable feature of T with the EPP property. In this connection, it is interesting to note that topicalized object CPs behave like subjects in requiring the presence of *that*, which suggests that Topics might bear uT.

(i) a. [That Sue bought the book] we all know.
    b. *[Sue bought the book] we all know.

If this is so, we might ask why the topic cannot raise to [Spec, CP] instead of the subject, yielding embedded clauses with topicalization, but without *that*—undermining our account of (62)–(63). Perhaps the answer is that the topic can be attracted to [Spec, CP] (as an alternative to attraction of TP by uT on C) in these examples, but that the result violates an independent condition that prevents scope-bearing elements from raising out of their scope position. This would be the condition that prevents English *wh*-phrases, for example, from undergoing $\bar{A}$-movement to positions higher than their scope position. We leave this as an open issue. See also note 52.

56. We use *which book* rather than *what* to exclude a free relative reading of the main-clause subject: compare *I read which book Mary read yesterday.

57. It is crucial that the instance of F on a moved element deletes at the end of the CP cycle—so that, for example, *Sue* in (60) (*Sue was expected [____ will buy the

book]) no longer bears uT once the lower CP is complete. That is why the exception clause in (67) makes important reference to F as an "attractor" (cf. Chomsky's (2000) notion of "probe"). Our formulation of (67) suggests an interesting connection between movement and feature lifespan. We hope to explore this connection in future work. We wish to thank Jonathan Bobaljik and the other participants of the McGill University syntax reading group for bringing this issue to our attention.

Condition (67) also correctly excludes an ungrammatical counterpart to (60) with an embedded question as subject (cf. (65)).

(i) *[Which person will read the book] is expected [$_{CP}$· C ____ is unknown].

If uT on C of the embedded question is still alive not only at the end of the embedded question cycle (necessary to allow (65)) but even at the end of the cycle labeled CP*, we might expect it to be attractable by the matrix T, yielding (i). Note, however, that once uT on the embedded question has participated in the movement operation triggered by T of CP*, it disappears at the end of the CP* cycle. We thank Jon Nissenbaum for pointing out the importance of these cases.

A problem arises in this context, however, for the view of pied-piping that we advanced in the text, because *wh*-movement appears to show a pattern distinct from (i). Once the PP in (70) has undergone *wh*-movement (to an intermediate [Spec, CP], for example), uWh on P is expected to disappear, given (67), making further *wh*-movement of the PP impossible. The fact that the PP occupies the structural periphery of CP in such cases, but not in (i), may be relevant to the solution of this problem (see Chomsky 2000 for other special properties of the periphery of a "phase").

58. We owe this approach to subject/nonsubject contrasts to discussions with Marie Claude Boivin. In Boivin 1999a,b, she proposes that a contrast in French *en*-cliticization be attributed, not to the ECP, as in Pollock 1986, but to the inability of a clause from which *en* has been extracted to raise to subject position. This logic inspired our proposal, though Boivin's development of this idea differs from ours in several details.

59. An echo of the ECP can be found in ACX, which, like the ECP, attributes the specialness of subject *wh*-movement to the strictly local relation between the subject position and [Spec, CP].

60. Pesetsky (1998), assuming an ECP account of the *that*-omission asymmetry (and structures like those in (72)), suggests that embedded questions in subject position escape the effects of the ECP because the constraints that give rise to the obligatory absence of *that* in embedded questions outrank the ECP (in the sense of Optimality Theory). The ECP account may in the end turn out to be more principled, though (as noted above) more evidence in its favor is necessary before we can draw this conclusion. If the phonological "emptiness" of C is irrelevant, as argued here, the overall account offered in Pesetsky 1998 must be rejected in any case.

60. Probably the features missing from *if*-clauses are the φ-features, rather than uT. The evidence comes from the "*wh*-trace effect," often grouped with the *that*-trace effect in ECP accounts (Chomsky 1980, 1981).

(i) a. ??What passage do you not know how Sue translated ____?
   b. *Who do you not know how ____ translated this passage?

The contrast between (ia) and (ib) does not fall together with our account of the *that*-trace effect, but is an instance of a "nested dependency effect" (Kuno and Robinson 1972; Pesetsky 1982b; Richards 1997). *How* moves from a position lower than *who*, crosses *who*, and ends up in a position lower than *who*. Much the same analysis can be given for this effect in a *whether*-question, if *whether* originates lower than the subject (perhaps in the specifier of Laka's (1990) head Σ, the generalized version of Pollock's (1989) NegP) and undergoes *wh*-movement from there.

(ii) a. ??What passage do you not know whether Sue translated ____?
    b. *Who do you not know whether ____ translated this passage?

The point of interest now is the fact that these effects are also observed in *if*-questions.

(iii) a. ??What passage do you not know if Sue translated ____?
     b. *Who do you not know if ____ translated this passage?

We may view this contrast too as a nested dependency effect if *if*-interrogatives involve *wh*-movement of a null version of *whether* to [Spec, *if*]. If ACX is true, as we argue below, this means that *if* must bear not only *u*Wh (which triggers *wh*-movement), but also *u*T (without the EPP property); if it did not, movement of the null version of *whether* from below TP would violate ACX. The presence of *u*T on *if* allows it to attract TP or its specifier. The absence of φ-features on *if* does not prevent it from attracting a lower occurrence of T, but does prevent it from being attracted by a higher occurrence of T because of the asymmetry in the Match Condition: the attractee may have features missing from the attractor, but the attractor must not have features missing from the attractee.

62. *To że* is not freely available as an alternative to *że* in object position. It is most commonly available when a DP in object position would show a case other than accusative (Barbara Citko, personal communication). In this respect, it differs from English *that*.

63. The possibility of subjunctive clauses introduced by *that* in many of the environments where irrealis *for*-clauses are found (especially as complements of jussive and volitional verbs) is in keeping with this generalization (*I would prefer that Sue buy this book*/*I demanded that Sue buy this book*). The fact that *that*-omission (*che*-omission, *que*-omission, etc.) is possible in some Romance languages but limited to the subjunctive might suggest that in these languages, subjunctive clauses, rather than indicatives, are the counterparts to the English indicative.

64. See Browning 1996, 238, fn. 2, for reasons why *for*-trace effects are not ameliorated by the intervention of adverbs, as is the case with the *that*-trace effects of (example (41)).

65. We treat the subject of these infinitives as nominative, even though pronominal subjects appear as *me, him, her,* and so on, rather than *I, he, she,* and so on. We assume, with Emonds (1986), that the *I*/*me* distinction is not a nominative/

accusative distinction, but a low-level rule that assigns the *I* form to pronouns standing alone as subject of finite T. This is supported by the widespread use of the *me* series in positions where other languages would show nominative case. If, however, we extend our theory of *u*T to accusative, we might be able to treat these subject pronouns as accusative, if that should turn out to be correct.

66. One other possibility: T-to-C movement does take place, but *to* moves directly rather than being doubled by *for*—analogous to Belfast embedded aux-to-C movement versus Standard English *that*. This is unlikely since *to* appears to be just as low in clauses with PRO as elsewhere. It can be preceded by *not*, adverbs, and similar elements.

67. Instead of lacking *u*T, C might lack ϕ. This would raise the question of why *for* fails to occur (if C has *u*T with the EPP property), but it also fails to explain the effects in the text below.

68. In a sense, our analysis is quite similar to Stowell's (1982) proposal. He suggested that irrealis infinitives differ from realis infinitives in having T in C. For him, the T in question was assumed to be interpretable, with irrealis interpretation somehow following from the presence of T in C. He also suggested that T in C, though null, suffices to classify C as a nonempty category, hence exempt from the ECP. For us, it is the T in C itself—whether interpretable or uninterpretable, empty or nonempty—that licenses CP as a subject.

69. It is not completely clear that the subject gaps are syntactically bound by an operator moved to [Spec, CP]. This option appears unavailable in infinitival questions (**I wonder who to solve this problem*).

70. More precisely, the interpretation of infinitival relatives involves modality, often either *should* or *could.* See Hackl and Nissenbaum, forthcoming, for an interesting account of the distribution of these readings. We have not investigated how these distinctions interact with the data discussed here.

71. We are grateful to Rajesh Bhatt for bringing Kjellmer's work to our attention. Bhatt (1999) argues that the realis infinitives in (90) are reduced relatives that lack a CP projection and do not involve operator movement at all. This claim is logically consistent with our proposal, though (if true) it would remove (90) as an example of short-distance movement to [Spec, CP]. It seems difficult to give a reduced relative analysis to (88a), however.

72. Long-distance *wh*-movement of a nonsubject out of a realis infinitive should be impossible if the *wh*-phrase must stop in the specifier of the infinitive. An example like *Which election results did Mary hate to learn from the Internet?* is awkward, but not impossible. Consequently, it must not be obligatory for *wh*-movement to land in [Spec, CP] of a realis infinitival, though it must be obligatory in other clause types, or else the *that*-trace and *for*-trace effects would not be observed. This suggests that the presence of a T-feature, including *u*T, creates an island, much as in earlier works that proposed the Tensed-S Condition (Chomsky 1977a).

73. The Earliness Principle in the form given here can replace the carefully worded Economy Condition in (6) as the reason for the T-to-C movement asym-

metry, the *that*-trace effect, and the other effects grouped with these in our proposal. When a C bearing *u*T and *u*Wh can mark both features for deletion with a single operation, the Earliness Principle requires it to do so, and it rejects alternatives in which it deletes one of the features later than the other.

An interesting difference between the two approaches arises from the possibility that a C with *u*T and *u*Wh in a question like *Who bought the book?* might enter a second Agree (or Move) relation with TP after it has attracted the nominative *wh*-phrase. This is a possibility made available by our proposals concerning the lifespan of uninterpretable features (section 11.6). Multiple Agree and multiple Move operations triggered by a single uninterpretable feature are attested and are consistent with the proposal that uninterpretable features marked for deletion do not disappear instantly.

For example, *u*Wh on C in multiple questions seems to enter multiple Agree and multiple Move relationships with several *wh*-phrases (as argued by Koizumi (1995) for Bulgarian; see also Pesetsky 2000). In section 11.2, we speculated that *u*ϕ on finite T might enter into an Agree or Move relation with both nominative subject and accusative object, with the nominative/accusative distinction on DPs reflecting whether its link to T was established first or second in the derivation.

The possibility that *u*T on C might also enter into multiple Agree or Move relations might help to account for a well-known alternation in French. French finite clauses are normally introduced by *que*, which we might analyze as an instance of T moved to C (like English *that*). (This analysis would conflict with the assumption that the stylistic inversion seen in (27) is an instance of T-to-C movement, since *que* and an arguably fronted verb co-occur in this construction. Conceivably, the proper analysis of French stylistic inversion should view the construction as an instance of (apparently) rightward subject movement rather than leftward T-to-C movement. For an analysis along these lines, see Kayne and Pollock 1999.)

When a subject *wh*-phrase has been extracted from a clause, the clause is introduced by *qui* instead of *que* (Kayne 1977; Chomsky and Lasnik 1977), as the contrast between (ia) and (ib) illustrates.

(i) a. Quelle femme crois-tu   [que Pierre a   rencontrée ____]?
       which woman believe-you *que* Pierre has met
       'Which woman do you believe that Pierre met?'
    b. Quelle femme crois-tu   [qui ____ a   rencontré Pierre]?
       which woman believe-you *qui*   has met   Pierre
       'Which woman do you believe met Pierre?'

If *qui* is in C, it might represent the form taken by T when it is the second element attracted by *u*T on C. In a certain sense, if this proposal and our speculation about accusative case are both correct, *qui* is the "accusative" form of *que*. Movement of the nominative subject to [Spec, CP] might be represented by constructions such as (ii).

(ii) J'ai   vu [Marie qui sortait du cinéma].
     I have seen Marie *qui* left the movie theater
     'I saw Marie leaving the movie theater.'

Unexplained would be the fact that the bracketed phrase in (ii) is limited to the complement of perception verbs and existential verbs, and receives the "direct perceptual report" interpretation discussed by Higginbotham (1983)—unlike its counterpart in English, under this analysis.

A similar analysis might be accorded to West Flemish *die*, which alternates with *da* in a manner reminiscent of the *que/qui* alternation of French (Haegeman 1983; Rizzi 1990).

Standard and Belfast English would presumably have no second attraction of T by uT on C, or second attraction that is covert in one of the senses discussed by Pesetsky (2000). The dialects of the American Midwest, discussed by Sobin (1987), might differ on precisely this point. They show no *that*-trace effect (or at most a very weak effect). In these dialects, second attraction of T by uT on C might be overt, as in French, but without the morphological reflex.

74. The Earliness Principle precludes (91), which would otherwise constitute a third case under (93a).

75. The Portuguese clause type called the "inflected infinitive" might also have the character we attribute to DP, given Raposo's (1987) observation that these infinitival clauses—whose subjects may be nominative—need "case licensing" from outside. This suggests that the counterpart to TP in an inflected infinitive CP might not be TP, but some other category that leaves uT on C unmarked for deletion.

76. Szabolcsi's arguments concern parallels between the internal structure of DP and the internal structure of CP. Similar results are reached by Torrego (1985), who argues for a position in DP with the properties of [Spec, CP].

77. A question left open by our work is the *reason* for the obligatory presence of uT on instances of C and D. Were it not for the existence of realis infinitives whose C seems to lack uT, we might speculate that the presence of uT on CP and DP is related in some way to their ability to serve as arguments. Alternatively, we might ask whether the presence of uT on C reflects the status of C as an "extended projection" of T in the sense of Grimshaw (1991) (cf. Abney 1987). The difficulty with this proposal is precisely the presence of uT on D, which does not take TP as its complement—but see note 17 for a possible avenue to pursue.

78. See Krause 2000 for a phenomenon of just this sort in German.

References

Abney, Steven. 1987. The English noun phrase in its sentential aspect. Doctoral dissertation, MIT.

Alexiadou, Artemis, and Elena Anagnostopoulou. 1998. Parametrizing AGR: Word order, V-movement and EPP-checking. *Natural Language & Linguistic Theory* 16, 491–539.

Anagnostopoulou, Elena. 1999. On clitics, feature movement and double object alternations. In Pius Ngwa Tamanji, Masako Hirotani, and Nancy Hall, eds., *NELS* 29. GLSA University of Massachusetts, Amherst.

Anagnostopoulou, Elena. To appear. *On double object alternations and clitics.* The Hague: Mouton.

Baković, Eric. 1998. Optimality and inversion in Spanish. In Pilar Barbosa, Danny Fox, Martha McGinnis, Paul Hagstrom, and David Pesetsky, eds., *Is the best good enough?* Cambridge, Mass.: MITWPL and MIT Press.

Barbosa, Pilar. 1999. On inversion in *wh*-questions in Romance. Ms., Universidade do Minho, Portugal.

Belletti, Adriana, and Luigi Rizzi. 1981. The syntax of *ne*: Some theoretical implications. *The Linguistic Review* 1, 117–154.

Benmamoun, Elabbas. 1992. Functional and inflectional morphology: Problems of projection, representation, and derivation. Doctoral dissertation, University of Southern California.

Benmamoun, Elabbas. 2000. *The feature structure of functional categories: A comparative study of Arabic dialects.* Oxford: Oxford University Press.

Besten, Hans den. 1983. On the interaction of root transformations and lexical deletive rules. In Werner Abraham, ed., *On the formal syntax of the West-germania.* Amsterdam: John Benjamins.

Bhatt, Rajesh. 1999. Covert modality in non-finite contexts. Doctoral dissertation, University of Pennsylvania.

Bittner, Maria, and Ken Hale. 1996. The structural determination of Case and agreement. *Linguistic Inquiry* 27, 1–68.

Blake, Barry J., and J. Gavan Breen. 1971. The Pitta-pitta dialects. Linguistic Communications 4. Melbourne: Monash University.

Boivin, Marie Claude. 1999a. Case feature checking and its consequences: Evidence from *en*-cliticization in French. In J.-Marc Authier, Barbara E. Bullock, and Lisa A. Reed, eds., *Formal perspectives on Romance linguistics.* Amsterdam: John Benjamins.

Boivin, Marie Claude. 1999b. Split noun phrases and the theory of Case. Doctoral dissertation, MIT.

Borer, Hagit. 1998. Deriving passive without theta roles. In Steven D. Lapointe, Diane Brentari, and Patrick Farrell, eds., *Morphology and its relations with phonology and syntax.* Stanford, Calif.: CSLI Publications.

Bošković, Željko. 1995. On certain violations of the Superiority Condition, AgrO, and economy of derivation. *Journal of Linguistics* 33, 227–254.

Bresnan, Joan. 1972. Theory of complementation in English syntax. Doctoral dissertation, MIT.

Bresnan, Joan. 1977. Variables in the theory of transformations. In Peter W. Culicover, Thomas Wasow, and Adrian Akmajian, eds., *Formal syntax.* New York: Academic Press.

Bresnan, Joan, and Jonni Kanerva. 1989. Locative inversion in Chicheŵa: A case study of factorization in grammar. *Linguistic Inquiry* 20, 1–50.

Browning, M. A. 1996. CP recursion and *that-t* effects. *Linguistic Inquiry* 27, 237–256.

Carstairs, Andrew. 1973. *For-to* complements and *if*-clauses. In *Quarterly Progress Report 109*, 147–153. Research Laboratory of Electronics, MIT.

Chomsky, Noam. 1957. *Syntactic structures.* The Hague: Mouton.

Chomsky, Noam. 1977a. *Essays on form and interpretation.* Amsterdam: Elsevier North-Holland.

Chomsky, Noam. 1977b. On *wh*-movement. In Peter W. Culicover, Thomas Wasow, and Adrian Akmajian, eds., *Formal syntax.* New York: Academic Press.

Chomsky, Noam. 1980. On binding. *Linguistic Inquiry* 11, 1–46.

Chomsky, Noam. 1981. *Lectures on government and binding.* Dordrecht: Foris. [Reprint, Dordrecht: Mouton de Gruyter (1993).]

Chomsky, Noam. 1986. *Barriers.* Cambridge, Mass.: MIT Press.

Chomsky, Noam. 1995. Categories and transformations. In *The Minimalist Program.* Cambridge, Mass.: MIT Press.

Chomsky, Noam. 2000. Minimalist inquiries: The framework. In Roger Martin, David Michaels, and Juan Uriagereka, eds., *Step by step.* Cambridge, Mass.: MIT Press.

Chomsky, Noam, and Howard Lasnik. 1977. Filters and control. *Linguistic Inquiry* 8, 425–504.

Chung, Sandra, and James McCloskey. 1983. On the interpretation of certain island facts in GPSG. *Linguistic Inquiry* 14, 704–713.

Cinque, Guglielmo. 1999. *Adverbs and functional heads.* Oxford: Oxford University Press.

Culicover, Peter. 1993. Evidence against ECP accounts of the *that-t* effect. *Linguistic Inquiry* 24, 557–561.

Demirdache, Hamida. 1991. Resumptive chains in restrictive relatives, appositives and dislocation structures. Doctoral dissertation, MIT.

Demirdache, Hamida. 1997. A cross-linguistic asymmetry in the temporal interpretation of DPs. In Anthony Green and Virginia Motapanyane, eds., *Proceedings of ESCOL '96.* Cornell Linguistics Circle, Cornell University.

Diesing, Molly. 1990. Verb movement and the subject position in Yiddish. *Natural Language & Linguistic Theory* 8, 41–80.

Doherty, Cathal. 1993. Clauses without *that*: The case for bare sentential complementation in English. Doctoral dissertation, University of California, Santa Cruz.

Elliott, Dale. 1971. The grammar of emotive and exclamatory sentences in English. Doctoral dissertation, Ohio State University. [Reproduced in *Working papers in linguistics no. 8.* Ohio State University.]

Emonds, Joseph. 1985. *A unified theory of syntactic categories.* Dordrecht: Foris.

Emonds, Joseph. 1986. Grammatically deviant prestige constructions. In Michael Brame, Heles Contreras, and Frederick J. Newmeyer, eds., *A festschrift for Sol Saporta.* Seattle, Wash.: Noit Amrofer.

Enç, Mürvet. 1981. Tense without scope: An analysis of nouns as indexicals. Doctoral dissertation, University of Wisconsin, Madison.

Engdahl, Elisabet. 1985. Parasitic gaps, resumptive pronouns and subject extractions. *Linguistics* 23, 3–44.

Epstein, Samuel D., Erich M. Groat, Ruriko Kawashima, and Hisatsugu Kitahara. 1998. *A derivational approach to syntactic relations.* Oxford: Oxford University Press.

Fox, Danny. 1994. Relative clauses and resumptive pronouns in Hebrew: An optimality theoretic approach. Ms., MIT.

Gazdar, Gerald. 1981. Unbounded dependencies and coordinate structure. *Linguistic Inquiry* 12, 155–184.

George, Leland, and Jaklin Kornfilt. 1981. Finiteness and boundedness in Turkish. In Frank Heny, ed., *Binding and filtering.* Cambridge, Mass.: MIT Press.

Ginzburg, Jonathan, and Ivan A. Sag. To appear. *English interrogative constructions.* Stanford, Calif.: CDLI Publications.

Goldberg, Adele. 1995. *Constructions: A construction grammar approach to argument structure.* Chicago: University of Chicago Press.

Grimshaw, Jane. 1979. Complement selection and the lexicon. *Linguistic Inquiry* 10, 279–326.

Grimshaw, Jane. 1991. Extended projection. Ms., Brandeis University.

Grimshaw, Jane. 1997. Projection, heads, and optimality. *Linguistic Inquiry* 28, 373–422.

Guéron, Jacqueline, and Teun Hoekstra. 1988. T-chains and the constituent structure of auxiliaries. In Anna Cardinaletti, Guglielmo Cinque, and Giuliana Giusti, eds., *Annali di Cà Foscari—Constituent structure: Papers from the 1987 GLOW Conference.* Venice: Editoriale Programma.

Hackl, Martin, and Jon Nissenbaum. Forthcoming. Toward a semantics of *for*-infinitivals. In Alessandra Giorgi, James Higginbotham, and Fabio Pianesi, eds., *Proceedings of the Bergamo Conference on the Syntax and Semantics of Tense and Mood Selection.* Oxford: Oxford University Press.

Haeberli, Eric. 1999. Features, categories and the syntax of A-positions: Synchronic and Diachronic variation in the Germanic languages. Thèse de doctorat, University of Geneva.

Haegeman, Liliane. 1983. *Die* and *dat* in West-Flemish relative clauses. In Hans Bennis and W. U. S. van Lessen-Kloeke, eds., *Linguistics in the Netherlands.* Dordrecht: Foris.

Hale, Ken. 1998a. A note on the Pittapitta nominative case and the future tense. Ms., MIT.

Hale, Ken. 1998b. On endangered languages and the importance of linguistic diversity. In Lenore A. Grenoble and Lindsay J. Whaley, eds., *Endangered languages: Language loss and community response.* Cambridge: Cambridge University Press.

Hale, Kenneth, and Samuel Jay Keyser. 1993. On argument structure and the lexical expression of syntactic relations. In Kenneth Hale and Samuel Jay Keyser, eds., *The view from Building 20.* Cambridge, Mass.: MIT Press.

Henry, Alison. 1995. *Belfast English and Standard English.* Oxford: Oxford University Press.

Higginbotham, James. 1983. The logic of perceptual reports: An extensional alternative to situation semantics. *Journal of Philosophy* 80, 100–127.

Huang, C.-T. James. 1982. Logical relations in Chinese and the theory of grammar. Doctoral dissertation, MIT.

Iatridou, Sabine. 1991. Topics in conditionals. Doctoral dissertation, MIT.

Iatridou, Sabine, and David Embick. 1997. Apropos *pro. Language* 73, 58–78.

Ippolito, Michela. 1999. The syntax of temporal subordinate clauses. Ms., MIT.

Jaeggli, Osvaldo. 1982. *Topics in Romance syntax.* Dordrecht: Foris.

Jaeggli, Osvaldo. 1984. Subject extraction and the null subject parameter. In Charles Jones and Peter Sells, eds., *Proceedings of NELS 14.* GLSA, University of Massachusetts, Amherst.

Jakobson, Roman. 1936/1984. Beitrag zur allgemeinen Kasuslehre: *Gesamtbedeutung der russischen Kasus.* Translated as: General meanings of the Russian cases. In *Russian and Slavic grammar: Studies 1931–1981.* Berlin: Mouton de Gruyter.

Kayne, Richard S. 1977. French relative *que.* In Marta Luján and Fritz Hensey, eds., *Current studies in Romance linguistics.* Washington, D.C.: Georgetown University Press.

Kayne, Richard S. 1980. Extensions of binding and Case-marking. *Linguistic Inquiry* 11, 75–96. [Reprinted in Kayne 1984.]

Kayne, Richard S. 1981a. ECP extensions. *Linguistic Inquiry* 12, 93–133. [Reprinted in Kayne 1984.]

Kayne, Richard S. 1981b. Two notes on the NIC. In Adriana Belletti, Luciana Brandi, and Luigi Rizzi, eds., *Theory of markedness in generative grammar: Proceedings of the 1979 GLOW Conference.* Pisa: Scuola Normale di Pisa. [Reprinted in Kayne 1984.]

Kayne, Richard S. 1984. *Connectedness and binary branching.* Dordrecht: Foris.

Kayne, Richard S. 1991. Romance clitics, verb movement, and PRO. *Linguistic Inquiry* 22, 647–686.

Kayne, Richard S. 1993. Toward a modular theory of auxiliary selection. *Studia Linguistica* 47, 3–31.

Kayne, Richard S. 1994. *The antisymmetry of syntax.* Cambridge, Mass.: MIT Press.

Kayne, Richard S., and Jean-Yves Pollock. 1978. Stylistic inversion, successive cyclicity, and Move NP in French. *Linguistic Inquiry* 9, 595–621.

Kayne, Richard S., and Jean-Yves Pollock. 1999. New thoughts on stylistic inversion. Ms., New York University, and UPR-9075, CNRS Lyons, France.

Keyser, Samuel Jay. 1975. A partial history of the relative clause in English. In Jane Grimshaw, ed., *Papers in the history and structure of English: University of Massachusetts occasional papers in linguistics 1.* GLSA, University of Massachusetts, Amherst.

Kitagawa, Yoshihisa. 1986. Subjects in Japanese and English. Doctoral dissertation, University of Massachusetts, Amherst.

Kjellmer, Göran. 1975. Are relative infinitives modal? *Studia Neophilologica* 47, 323–332.

Koizumi, Masatoshi. 1995. Phrase structure in minimalist syntax. Doctoral dissertation, MIT.

Koopman, Hilda. 1983. ECP effects in main clauses. *Linguistic Inquiry* 14, 346–350.

Koopman, Hilda, and Dominique Sportiche. 1991. The position of subjects. *Lingua* 85, 211–258.

Koster, Jan. 1978a. *Locality principles in syntax.* Dordrecht: Foris.

Koster, Jan. 1978b. Why subject sentences don't exist. In Samuel Jay Keyser, ed., *Recent transformational studies in European languages.* Cambridge, Mass.: MIT Press.

Krause, Cornelia. 2000. On possession and inherent case. Ms., MIT.

Kuno, Susumu, and Jane J. Robinson. 1972. Multiple WH-questions. *Linguistic Inquiry* 3, 463–487.

Kuroda, S.-Y. 1988. Whether we agree or not: A comparative syntax of Japanese and English. In William Poser, ed., *Papers from the Second International Workshop on Japanese Syntax.* Stanford, Calif.: CSLI Publications.

Laka, Itziar. 1990. Negation in syntax: On the nature of functional categories and projections. Doctoral dissertation, MIT.

Larson, Richard. 1985. On the syntax of disjunction. *Natural Language & Linguistic Theory* 3, 217–264.

Lasnik, Howard, and Mamoru Saito. 1984. On the nature of proper government. *Linguistic Inquiry* 15, 235–290.

Lasnik, Howard, and Mamoru Saito. 1992. *Move α: Conditions on its application and output.* Cambridge, Mass.: MIT Press.

Lecarme, Jacqueline. 1997. Nominal tense and tense theory. In Francis Corblin, Carmen Dobrovie-Sorin, Jean-Marie Marandin, eds., *Empirical issues in formal syntax and semantics 2: Selected papers from the Colloque de Syntaxe et Sémantique, Paris (CSSP).* The Hague: Holland Academic Graphics.

Marantz, Alec. 1991. Case vs. licensing. In German Westphal, Benjamin Ao, and Hee-Rahk Chae, eds., *Proceedings of ESCOL '91*. Cornell Linguistics Circle, Cornell University.

McCawley, Noriko Akatsuka. 1973. Boy! Is syntax easy! In Claudia Corum, T. Cedric Smith-Stark, and Ann Weiser, eds., *Papers from the Ninth Regional Meeting, Chicago Linguistic Society*. Chicago Linguistic Society, University of Chicago.

McCloskey, James. 1991. *There, it*, and agreement. *Linguistic Inquiry* 22, 563–567.

McDaniel, Dana. 1989. Partial and multiple *wh*-movement. *Natural Language & Linguistic Theory* 7, 565–604.

Mulder, René, and Rint Sybesma. 1992. Chinese is a VO language. *Natural Language & Linguistic Theory* 10, 439–476.

Musan, Renate. 1995. On the temporal interpretation of noun phrases. Doctoral dissertation, MIT. [Reprint, New York: Garland (1997).]

Nakajima, Heizo. 1996. Complementizer selection. *The Linguistic Review* 13, 143–164.

Newmeyer, Frederick J. 1998. *Language form and language function*. Cambridge, Mass.: MIT Press.

Nissenbaum, Jonathan. 2000. Doctoral dissertation, MIT.

Ordoñez, Francisco. 1997. Word order and clause structure in Spanish and other Romance languages. Doctoral dissertation, City Universtity of New York.

Perlmutter, David. 1971. *Deep and surface structure constraints in syntax*. New York: Holt, Rinehart and Winston.

Pesetsky, David. 1982a. Complementizer-trace phenomena and the Nominative Island Condition. *The Linguistic Review* 1, 297–344.

Pesetsky, David. 1982b. Paths and categories. Doctoral dissertation, MIT.

Pesetsky, David. 1987. *Wh*-in-situ: Movement and unselective binding. In Eric Reuland and Alice ter Meulen, eds., *The representation of (in)definiteness*. Cambridge, Mass.: MIT Press.

Pesetsky, David. 1989. Language-particular processes and the Earliness Principle. Ms., MIT. [Available at: http://web.mit.edu/linguistics/www/pesetsky/earliness.pdf]

Pesetsky, David. 1991. Zero syntax. Ms., MIT. [Available at http://web.mit.edu/linguistics/www/pesetsky/infins.pdf]

Pesetsky, David. 1998. Some optimality principles of sentence pronunciation. In Pilar Barbosa, Danny Fox, Martha McGinnis, Paul Hagstrom, and David Pesetsky, eds., *Is the best good enough?* Cambridge, Mass.: MITWPL and MIT Press.

Pesetsky, David. 2000. *Phrasal movement and its kin*. Cambridge, Mass.: MIT Press.

Picallo, M. Carme. 1984. The Infl node and the null subject parameter. *Linguistic Inquiry* 15, 75–102.

Piera, Carlos. 1979. Some subject sentences. *Linguistic Inquiry* 10, 732–734.

Platzack, Christer. To appear. Multiple interfaces. In Urpo Nikanne and Emile van der Zee, eds., *Conceptual structure and its interfaces with other modules of representation.* Oxford: Oxford University Press.

Platzack, Christer. 1998. A visibility condition for the C-domain. *Working Papers in Scandinavian Syntax* 61, 53–99.

Pollock, Jean-Yves. 1986. Sur la syntaxe de *en* et le paramètre du sujet nul. In Mitsou Ronat and Daniel Couqaux, eds., *La grammaire modulaire.* Paris: Editions de Minuit.

Pollock, Jean-Yves. 1989. Verb movement, Universal Grammar, and the structure of IP. *Linguistic Inquiry* 20, 365–424.

Raposo, Eduardo. 1987. Case theory and Infl-to-Comp: The inflected infinitive in European Portuguese. *Linguistic Inquiry* 18, 85–109.

Raposo, Eduardo, and Juan Uriagereka. 1990. Long-distance Case assignment. *Linguistic Inquiry* 21, 505–538.

Richards, Norvin. 1997. What moves where when in which language? Doctoral dissertation, MIT.

Richards, Norvin. 1998. The Principle of Minimal Compliance. *Linguistic Inquiry* 29, 599–629.

Ritter, Elizabeth, and Anna Szabolcsi. 1985. Let's take the *that*-trace effect seriously. Ms., MIT.

Rizzi, Luigi. 1982. *Issues in Italian syntax.* Dordrecht: Foris.

Rizzi, Luigi. 1990. *Relativized Minimality.* Cambridge, Mass.: MIT Press.

Rizzi, Luigi. 1996. Residual verb second and the *Wh*-Criterion. In Adriana Belletti and Luigi Rizzi, eds., *Parameters and functional heads: Essays in comparative syntax.* Oxford: Oxford University Press.

Rizzi, Luigi. 1997. The fine structure of the left periphery, In Liliane Haegeman, ed., *Elements of grammar: Handbook of generative syntax.* Dordrecht: Kluwer.

Ross, John R. 1967. Constraints on variables in syntax. Doctoral dissertation, MIT.

Roth, Walter Edmund. 1897. *Ethnological studies among the north-west central Queensland aborigines.* Brisbane: Government Printer.

Rouveret, Alain, and Jean-Roger Vergnaud. 1980. Specifying reference to the subject: French causatives and conditions on representations. *Linguistic Inquiry* 11, 97–202.

Rudin, Catherine. 1988. On multiple questions and multiple WH fronting. *Natural Language & Linguistic Theory* 6, 445–502.

Schütze, Carson. 1997. INFL in child and adult language: Agreement, Case and licensing. Doctoral dissertation, MIT.

Sobin, Nicholas. 1987. The variable status of Comp-trace phenomena. *Natural Language & Linguistic Theory* 5, 33–60.

Stowell, Tim. 1981. Origins of phrase structure. Doctoral dissertation, MIT.

Stowell, Tim. 1982. The tense of infinitives. *Linguistic Inquiry* 13, 561–570.

Suñer, Margarita. 1994. Verb movement and the licensing of argumental *wh*-phrases in Spanish. *Natural Language & Linguistic Theory* 12, 335–372.

Szabolcsi, Anna. 1983. The possessor that ran away from home. *The Linguistic Review* 3, 89–102.

Szabolcsi, Anna. 1987. Functional categories in the noun phrase. In István Kenesei, ed., *Approaches to Hungarian. Vol. 2, Theories and analyses.* Szeged: Jate Szeged.

Taraldsen, Knut Tarald. 1979. On the NIC, vacuous application and the *That-Trace Filter.* Indiana University Linguistics Club, Bloomington.

Torrego, Esther. 1983. More effects of successive cyclic movement. *Linguistic Inquiry* 14, 561–565.

Torrego, Esther. 1984. On inversion in Spanish and some of its effects. *Linguistic Inquiry* 15, 103–130.

Torrego, Esther. 1985. On empty categories in nominals. Ms., University of Massachusetts, Boston.

Torrego, Esther. 1986. Experiencers and raising verbs. In Robert Freidin, ed., *Current issues in comparative grammar.* Dordrecht: Kluwer.

Travis, Lisa. 1984. Parameters and effects of word order variation. Doctoral dissertation, MIT.

Uriagereka, Juan. 1999. Minimal restrictions on Basque movements. *Natural Language & Linguistic Theory* 17, 403–444.

Chapter 12

Segmental Phonology in Yawelmani

Cheryl Zoll

12.1 Introduction

Zoll 1998 provides several arguments against the traditional dichotomy between latent segments and floating features, demonstrating that the traditional roles associated with the root node (Clements and Keyser 1983) do not correlate with the presence or absence of a root node underlyingly. This chapter, a case study of the three kinds of latent segments in Yawelmani, further supports the view that latent segments have the same underlying representation as floating features (1). The analysis provides for the first time a unified explanation for the special ability of these latent segments to resist regular parsing as well as for the fact that only a small but nonrandom part of the segment inventory has latent counterparts.

(1) *Segments*   *Latent Segments and*
                         Floating Features

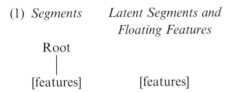

The representational distinction in (1) accounts for the primary difference between segmental and subsegmental units: namely, segments are immediately syllabifiable while subsegments require the addition of a root node in order to be parsed (2). The differences among subsegments derive from the source of the inserted root node. In the case of surface-dependent features, an existing segment provides the appropriate anchor (2b), while for latent segments, high-ranking constraints compel epenthesis of a new root node (2c).

(2) a. *Unsyllabifiable floating f₃*

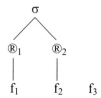

b. *f₃ parsed as a dependent feature*

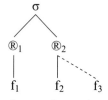

c. *f₃ parsed as a latent segment*

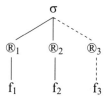

In section 12.2, I present data that illustrate the variety of segment types in Yawelmani. In section 12.3, I provide an analysis of the behavior of the glottal quasi-segment, which is subsequently extended to the latent consonants and vowel. In section 12.4, I show how the representations in (1) provide an explanation for the limited number of defective consonants that are found.

12.2 Data

12.2.1 Glottal Quasi-segments
The Yawelmani floating glottalization (Newman 1944; Kuroda 1967; Kisseberth 1970; Archangeli 1983, 1984, 1991; Noske 1984; Archangeli and Pulleyblank 1994) constitutes an example of a subsegment difficult to classify as either segment or floating feature. Depending on context, it either moves to find a suitable docking site in the base or projects its own root node. I refer to elements that have this kind of mixed behavior as *quasi-segments*. (3) shows the central examples (where *(ʔ)aa* is the durative suffix and *(ʔ)* = [constricted glottis]). Suffix-induced glottalization

targets the rightmost postvocalic sonorant in the base (3a). Otherwise, in a biconsonantal root, it manifests itself as a suffix-initial glottal stop (3b). Note that in (3a), vowel shortening is unnecessary since the floating feature can dock as a secondary feature on the preceding sonorant, whereas in (3b), a biconsonantal stem with no glottalizable sonorant, vowel length is sacrificed to the parsing of the full glottal. In the triconsonantal root in (3c), there is no way to parse the feature since there is no postvocalic sonorant, nor is there space for a full glottal stop without epenthesizing a vowel, so the glottalization is not expressed. Other glottalizing suffixes are shown in (4).

(3) *Glottal quasi-segments in Yawelmani*
    a. Glottalize rightmost postvocalic sonorant
       /caaw-(ʔ)aa/   caaw̲ʔaa-   'shout'
       /ʔiilk-(ʔ)aa/   ʔel̲ʔkaa-   'sing'
    b. Otherwise, full glottal root-finally if room
       /maax-(ʔ)aa/   max̲ʔaa-   'procure'
    c. Otherwise, fail to surface (*CCC)
       /hogn-(ʔ)aa/   hognaa-   'float'

(4) *Suffixes with glottal quasi-segment (Archangeli 1983, 379)*
    (ʔ)iixoo consequent auxiliary (ʔ)aas   habitual genitive
    (ʔ)aa   continuative   (ʔ)inʔay contemporaneous gerundial
    (ʔ)ic   agentive   (ʔ)anaa desiderative agentive

The absence of epenthesis to rescue the glottal in (3c) sets the glottal quasi-segment apart from regular segments. As shown in (5), a full segment in the same triconsonantal context does trigger vowel insertion to save itself.

(5) a. *Full segment: epenthesis into CCC cluster*
       /woʔy-hin/   *woy.hin   wo.ʔU̲y.hin   'sleep (passive aorist)'
    b. *Glottal quasi-segment: no epenthesis*
       /hogn-(ʔ)aa-/   hog.naa-   *ho.gI̲n.ʔaa-   'float'

Finally, observe that not all suffix-initial glottals are quasi-segmental. Some appear consistently as glottal stops even when a glottalizable sonorant is present in the stem. In (6), for instance, example (i) of each affix has no glottalizable sonorant, so the glottal appears as the expected glottal stop. But in examples (ii) and (iii), which contain postvocalic sonorants, a glottal quasi-segment would surface as a dependent feature. Here it does not, indicating that the special behavior of the glottal quasi-segment is a function of the segment itself, and not a special vulnerability of all suffix-initial glottals.

(6) *Nonfloating suffix-initial glottal stops*
    a. /-ʔan/ durative present (Newman 1944, 101)
        i. /put'put'wa:-ʔan/   put'put'wa:ʔan   'whirl about in the air repeatedly'
        ii. /ileew-ʔan/   ilewʔan   'bloom'
        iii. /cuma:-ʔan/   cuma:ʔan   'devour, destroy'
    b. /-ʔat/ passive durative aorist (Newman 1944, 102)
        i. /ʔuko:c-ʔat/   ʔukocʔat   'depend on, desire'
        ii. /bine:t-ʔat/   binetʔat   'ask'
        iii. /t'uya:-ʔat/   t'uya:ʔat   'shoot at, shoot'
    c. /-ʔa:nit/ durative passive future or present (Newman 1944, 102)
        i. /ʔuko:c-ʔa:nit/   ʔukocʔa:nit   'depend on, desire'
        ii. /bilees-ʔa:nit/   biles?a:nit   'finish'
        iii. /xaya:-ʔa:nit/   xaya:ʔa:nit   'place, put'

12.2.2   Latent Consonants

A list of the suffixes containing other latent consonants, shown in parentheses, is provided in (7).

(7) *Yawelmani suffixes with latent segments (Archangeli 1984)*
    (ʰ)nel   passive adjunctive
    (ᵐ)aam   decedent
    (ˡ)saa   causative repetitive
    (ⁿ)iit   decedent

Like the floating glottal, these latent segments are distinguished from regular consonants in that they delete rather than trigger epenthesis to avoid forming an illicit cluster. The data in (8) illustrate this contrast. The suffix-initial *h* in *hin* is a full segment. In (8a), suffixation results in a tri-consonantal *gnh* cluster that must be resolved, since the maximal syllable in Yawelmani is CVX. Because all three consonants are full segments, they must all be parsed, and therefore a vowel is epenthesized.[1] In (8b), suffixation of *(h)nel* likewise has the potential to produce a triconso-nantal cluster, but since here *h* is a latent segment, like the glottal above, it fails to appear rather than force epenthesis. It is the hallmark of these latent segments as well as the glottal stop that they never trigger epen-thesis of a vowel to save themselves, although as we see again in (8c), vowel length is sacrificed to spare a latent segment. What distinguishes these latent consonants from the glottal is that they never manifest themselves by docking onto an existing segment as secondary articulations.

(8) *Behavior of latent segments (Archangeli 1991)*
  a. -hin   /hogn-hin/   ho.gIn-hin
  b. -(h)nel /hogon-(h)nel/ ho.gon.··nel *ho.gʰon.-nel
  c. cf.   /maxaa-(h)nel/ ma.xa-h.nel

12.2.3 Latent Vowels

Yet a third kind of behavior is exhibited by latent vowels, exemplified in (9). Like latent consonants, latent vowels sometimes fail to surface. Unlike the consonants, however, these vowels are parsed only when necessary. In (9a), the final vowel is required to facilitate syllabification of *m* in the precative suffix -*m(i)*. In (9b), on the other hand, this *m* becomes the coda of the preceding open syllable. There is room for the vowel; but as it is not necessary for any other reason, it does not materialize.

(9) *Vowel/∅ alternation: latent vowels surface only when they are*
  necessary (Newman 1994, 135)
  a. /amic-m(i)/ amic-mi *amic-m· 'having approached'
  b. /panaa-m(i)/ panam· *panaa-mi 'having arrived'

This is not simply a vowel deletion rule, since it is not the case that all expendable final vowels are deleted (Noske 1984). As shown in (10), for example, the indirect object suffix *ni* holds on to its final vowel even though suffixed to a vowel-final root.

(10) *No final vowel deletion (Newman 1944, 201)*
  a. /talaap-ni/ talapni   'bow-IO'
  b. /xataa-ni/ xataani *xatan· 'food-IO'

12.2.4 Summary

Superficially, it appears that there are three kinds of latent segments in Yawelmani: (1) glottal quasi-segments that appear wherever they can, (2) other latent consonants that appear only when there is room for them, and (3) latent vowels that appear only when they are absolutely necessary. The first type appear either as full segments or as secondary features, the latter two always as independent segments. All three of these contrast with full segments, which are always parsed even if epenthesis is required to do so.

How many representations are needed to distinguish the four segment types? Assuming the standard representation for full segments, Archangeli (1984) and Archangeli and Pulleyblank (1994) argue that the glottal quasi-segment should be represented as a floating glottal feature. In the next section, I will show that likewise all of the exceptional segments are represented as underlying floating features. The surface differences between them will follow from different constraints on output.

(11) *Exceptional parsing* ⇒ *No root node*

	Full segments	Quasi-segments and latent segments
Underlying	Root | [features]	[features]

12.3   Analysis

12.3.1   Overview

Before I launch into the full story, it is possible to convey the basic idea of the irrelevance of underlying distinctions between the quasi-segments and latent segments by comparing the behavior of the glottal quasi-segment and the latent [h]. For these, I propose the underlying representations in (12).

(12)   ʔ (quasi-segment)   h (latent segment)
         Underlying   [constricted glottis]   [spread glottis]

The only thing that sets the behavior of the glottal apart from the behavior of [h] is that glottalization sometimes docks secondarily on an existing segment. This restriction does not require a wholly different kind of underlying representation for the two kinds of segments, but follows from the general notion of structure preservation. Glottalized segments are among the possible segment types in Yawelmani (13), so it is no surprise that a floating glottal feature will associate to an existing plain segment. Glottalization constitutes the only contrastive secondary articulation in Yawelmani, however, so [spread glottis] is precluded from docking onto existing segments by segment structure constraints that prohibit the creation of phonologically aspirated consonants.[2] Therefore, the feature [spread glottis] can only be realized as the primary articulation on an inserted root node.

(13) *Yawelmani inventory (Archangeli 1984, 60, from Newman 1944)*

Labial	Dental	Alveolar	Dorsal
b, p, p$^?$	d, t, t$^?$	D, T, T$^?$	g, k, k$^?$
	3, c, c$^?$	z, C, c$^?$	
	s	s	
m, m$^?$	n, n$^?$		
w, w$^?$	y, y$^?$		h, ?
	l, l$^?$		

A small part of the analysis, given in (14), provides a simple illustration of this point. A constraint against epenthesis of a root node, DEP(ROOT), is outranked by a markedness constraint, *C^h, that penalizes phonologically aspirated consonants.

(14) *Constraints*
 DEP(ROOT)   A root node in the output has a correspondent in the input. (after McCarthy and Prince 1995)
 *C^h A consonant is not aspirated.

The tableau in (15) illustrates the fate of an underlying [spread glottis] feature from the hypothetical input /caw-(^{h})aa/. In (15a), it has docked on the root-final consonant. As this fatally violates the high-ranking markedness constraint against aspirated consonants *C^h, the winning candidate in (15b) rescues the floating feature by inserting a root node, violating only the lower-ranked faithfulness constraint DEP(ROOT). Contrast this with the tableau in (16). Here, no markedness constraint rules out dependent [constricted glottis] on the root-final sonorant (16a), since *C$^?$ is ranked below DEP(ROOT). Nothing forces violation of DEP(ROOT), so the candidate in (16a) prevails.

(15) */caw, aa/ [spread glottis]*

Candidates	*C^h	DEP-(ROOT)	Comments
a. caw^h-aa	*!		• feature docks to segment
b. ☞ caw-haa		*	• root node inserted to host feature

(16) /caw, aa/ [constricted glottis]

Candidates	*C^h	DEP-(Root)	Comments
a. ☞ caw$^?$-aa			• feature docks to segment
b. caw-?aa		*!	• root node inserted to host feature

Therefore, the difference between the glottal and the other latent segments need not reflect distinct underlying configurations; instead, it depends on the nature of the features involved. The bottom line is that structure preservation, implemented as markedness constraints on surface forms, determines whether or not a feature surfaces as an independent segment or a dependent feature, making underlying representational distinctions between them irrelevant. In the following sections, we will see how this fits into a larger hierarchy. It will transpire that the only representational difference necessary is between full segments and subsegments (which comprise quasi-segments and latent segments). The grammar dictates the optimal target for each floating feature. Latent segments differ from quasi-segments (and prototypical floating features) only in that their target is an inserted root node rather than a consonant or vowel present elsewhere in the string.

12.3.2 The Dual Behavior of the Quasi-segment

The first task is to account for the behavior of the glottal quasi-segment. Since this appears sometimes as an independent segment and sometimes as a feature, once its behavior is accounted for we will have everything necessary to deal with the other latent segments. (17) summarizes the necessary constraints. Notice that the solution uses only constraints that have been independently motivated for other phenomena. These will be discussed further as ranking arguments are introduced.

(17) *Constraints*

Faithfulness

(McCarthy and Prince 1995)

MAX(Segment)   A segment in the input has a
                 correspondent in the output.

MAX(Feature)   A feature in the input has a
                 correspondent in the output.

IDENT(Place)   The place feature of a segment in
                   the input is the same as that of its
                   correspondent in the output.
IDENT(Length)   The length of a segment in the input
                   is identical to its length in the
                   output. (see Urbanczyk 1995)
DEP(Root)   A root node in the output has a
                   correspondent in the input.
CONTIGUITY   Segments that are contiguous in the
                   input are contiguous in the output.

Markedness

*STRUC(σ) (Zoll 1993)   No syllables
Syllable structure constraints   The maximal syllable is CVC (see
                                      below).
Segment structure constraints   (see below)

Alignment

(McCarthy and Prince 1993)

ALIGN-RIGHT(Affix, PWd)   The rightmost element in the affix
                                      coincides with the rightmost
                                      element in the word.
ALIGN-RIGHT(Base, Syllable)   The rightmost element in the base
                                      coincides with the rightmost
                                      element in a syllable.

12.3.2.1 Segment Structure Constraints   The claim that the difference
between dependent features and latent segments derives primarily from
target availability requires first explaining why suffix-induced glottalization is restricted to postvocalic sonorants, particularly in light of the
fact that the Yawelmani inventory also includes glottalized obstruents.
Steriade (1997) argues, however, that glottalized obstruents and sonorants
do not mark glottalization with the same feature, since in fact their
behavior varies in several ways. First, in Yawelmani, although both
obstruents and sonorants are described as glottalized, their actual manifestation of glottalization differs. Newman (1944, 14) states that "the glottalized stops and affricates are articulated with a light degree of glottal
plosion. Glottalized stops are pronounced with a simultaneous release of
the glottis and the stop closure." The glottalized sonorants, on the other
hand, "are pronounced with a slight glottal break, as [mˀm] or [ˀm] etc."
(Newman 1944, 16).

More importantly, the two sets of segments are treated differently by the phonology. As we have seen, the floating glottalization does not treat these as a natural class of targets. In addition, while glottalized sonorants are licensed only in postvocalic positions, glottalized obstruents have a completely free distribution (18).

(18) *Distribution of glottalized obstruents and sonorants (Newman 1944)*

	Obstruents		Sonorants	
Initial	TˀayTˀay	'bluejay'		
Postvocalic	ʔɔTˀɔw	'head'	nɔːnˀɔ	'man'
	ʔusokˀway	'hearts'	tˀɔnˀTim	'transvestites'
Postconsonantal	hidiscˀeː	'woodrat'		

The proposed distinction between the two types of glottalization readily finds crosslinguistic support. A similar separation between glottalized obstruents and sonorants can be found in other languages. Klamath (Penutian), for example, is described as having both. Blevins (1993, 238) points out, however, that glottalized obstruents are in reality ejectives with a distinct laryngeal airstream mechanism. Likewise, Klamath phonology does not always treat glottalized sonorants and obstruents as a natural class. The glottalized sonorants have special distributional limitations, just as in Yawelmani.

Moreover, it is not unusual to find glottalization that solely targets sonorants. Nichols (1971) gives a number of such cases of diminutive glottalization. In Kalispel and Coeur D'Alene (19), for example, diminutivization targets all root sonorants (except sometimes the final one). Although both languages have ejectives, obstruents are not glottalized in this process.

(19) *Diminutive glottalization (Nichols 1971, 844)*

    a. Kalispel (Salish)

       i. iləmixum   'chief'

          ł-ilˀəmˀixum   'little chief'

       ii. suyapi

          s-ł-uyˀapi   'American'

    b. Coeur D'Alene (Salish)

       i. mar-marim-əntəm-ilš   'they were treated one by one'

          mˀ-mˀarˀ-mˀarˀimˀ-ənˀtəmˀ-   'they little ones were treated

          ilš   one by one'

ii. yær-yær-p   'wagon'

y$^?$-y$^?$ær$^?$-y$^?$ær-p   'cart'

I assume, therefore, following Steriade (1997, 79), that glottalization of obstruents and sonorants corresponds phonologically to different privative glottal features, as shown in (20). To the extent that glottalized obstruents and glottalized sonorants *are* a natural class, it is because both employ glottal constriction, which is captured by positing that the feature [constricted glottis] dominates both [creak] and [ejective].

(20)   *On sonorants*   *On obstruents*

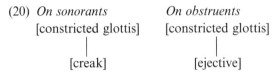

For Yawelmani, then, the glottal quasi-segment must contain the feature [constricted glottis/creak], which I will continue to represent as the superscript glottal stop (ʔ). The failure of the floating glottal to target obstruents results from the simple fact that [creak] is not a possible feature on obstruents. This is expressed straightforwardly by the segment structure constraint *T/creak (21). In a word with no glottalizable sonorant (22), the feature surfaces as a glottal stop if possible (22c) and otherwise deletes. *T/creak is essentially an inviolable constraint, since it prohibits incompatible feature specifications. Henceforth, candidates with [creak]-marked obstruents will not be considered.

(21) *T/creak   An obstruent is not marked with the feature [creak].

(22) *xat-ʔa 'one who is always eating' (Newman 1944, 156)*[3]

	Candidates	*T/CREAK
a.	xˀata	*!
b.	xatˀa	*!
c. ☞	xatʔa	

The additional restriction of glottalization in Yawelmani to postvocalic sonorants reflects general distributional limitations on glottalized sonorants in the language, as illustrated above. According to Newman (1944, 15), "Each of the simple nasals, semivowels, and laterals is balanced with a glottalized consonant which is treated as a distinct phoneme with the following limitation: it can never appear initially in a word or in a syllable that follows a closed syllable." This sort of restriction is not limited to Yawelmani. In Shuswap (Kuipers 1974), for example, glottalized sonorant consonants can only appear postvocalically, and in Kashaya (Buckley 1994), they are found only in codas. Steriade (1997) captures these facts with the hierarchy shown in (23), grounded in a framework where glottalization is more likely to be found in environments with more robust phonetic cues.[4] In the case of Yawelmani, glottalization is especially salient postvocalically, since the glottalized consonants lend a "rasping timbre" to the preceding vowel (Newman 1944, 19).

(23) $*{}^{?}R/C\_\_ \gg *{}^{?}R/\#\_\_ \gg$ Max(Feature) $\gg *{}^{?}R/V\_\_$
       (R = a sonorant C)

The tableau in (24) considers possible outputs for glottalization of a base that contains three sonorants. The high-ranking positional markedness constraints eliminate the initial (24c) and postconsonantal (24a) glottalized sonorants. Candidate (24b) is optimal since it manages to parse the glottal feature on a postvocalic sonorant. Although this violates the low-ranked contextual markedness constraint, it is superior to (24d), which fails to parse [constricted glottis/creak], thereby violating Max(Feature) (Max(F)).

(24) $/l\text{ɔ}wn\text{-}({}^{?})a\text{ː}/ \rightarrow l\text{ɔ}w^{?}n\text{ɔ}$ 'attendant to a feast' (lit. 'attend a feast-agentive') (Newman 1944, 157)

Candidates	$*^{?}R/C\_\_$	$*^{?}R/\#\_\_$	Max(F)	$*^{?}R/V\_\_$
a. lɔwn${}^{?}$ɔ	*!			
b. ☞ lɔw${}^{?}$nɔ				*
c. l${}^{?}$ɔwnɔ		*!		
d. lɔwnɔ			*!	

12.3.2.2 Syllable Structure Constraints Having established the possible targets for glottalization, I turn to the role of syllable structure constraints in determining the surface form of the glottal quasi-segment. The maximal syllable in Yawelmani is CVX. This is enforced by the constraints in (25) against complex onsets and codas, as well as by a constraint limiting a syllable to two moras. These syllable structure constraints always trigger some kind of repair. Potential violations are repaired either by epenthesis of a vowel, by deletion of a latent segment, or by vowel shortening (26). Subsequent sections will deal with the interactions of lower-ranked constraints that determine the specific repair in a particular context.

(25) *Syllable structure constraints (SYLL-STRUC)*

*Complex Onset	An onset consists of a single consonant.
*Complex Coda	A coda consists of a single consonant.
Bimoraic	A syllable is maximally bimoraic.

(26) *Repair of ill-formed syllables*

Epenthesis	/woʔy-hin/ → wo.ʔu̲y.hin	'sleep (passive aorist)'
Deletion	/hogn-(ʔ)aa-/ → hog.naa-	'float'
V Shortening	/ma̲a̲x-(ʔ)aa/ → max.ʔaa	'procure'

12.3.2.3 The Difference between Full Segments and Subsegments Now consider that full segments trigger epenthesis to facilitate parsing into well-formed syllables while the glottal quasi-segment does not. The parsing constraints that make the necessary distinctions between floating features and full segments are shown in (27)–(28) (repeated from (17)). MAX(F) violations accrue when an input feature does not appear in the output, while MAX(Segment) (MAX(Seg)) is violated only by the deletion of an entire segment.

(27) MAX(Seg)   A segment in the input has a correspondent in the output. (McCarthy and Prince 1995)

(28) MAX(F)   A feature in the input has a correspondent in the output. (McCarthy and Prince 1995)

Because only potentially unparsable *full* segments trigger vowel insertion, some constraint against epenthesis must come between the two parsing constraints. Elsewhere (Zoll 1993) I have proposed *STRUC(σ), a constraint that minimizes the number of syllables in a word (29). This is an Optimality Theory implementation of Selkirk's (1981) Syllable Minimization Principle. (See also Broselow 1995, fn. 19, and Noske 1984.)

(29) *STRUC(σ)   No syllables. (Zoll 1993)

a. ¬∃x(Syllable(x))

b. Assess one mark for each value of x for which (a) is false.

Max(Seg) must outrank *Struc(σ) in Yawelmani, because a vowel will be inserted to facilitate parsing of an input segment. The tableau in (30) takes as its input a word with an unsyllabifiable sequence of three full consonants, ʔyh. Candidate (30a) is optimal because it best satisfies Max(Seg). It prevails over (30b), despite the greater number of *Struc(σ) violations, because *Struc(σ) stands below Max(Seg) in the hierarchy.

(30) /woʔy-hin/ → wo.ʔuy.hin 'sleep (passive aorist)'

	Candidates	Max(Seg)	*Struc(σ)	Comments
a. ☞	wo.ʔuy.hin		***	• u is epenthetic
b.	woy.hin	*	**	• ʔ is deleted

By the same reasoning, *Struc(σ) must outrank Max(F) since a floating [constricted glottis/creak] feature deletes rather than trigger epenthesis (31).

(31) Rankling: *Struc(σ) ≫ Max(F)
Rationale: Input floating features are not rescued by insertion of an epenthetic vowel.

For /hogn-ʔaa/, in the tableau in (32), for example, no sonorants in the base attract the glottalization since none are postvocalic.[5] Yet unlike in the example in (30), the floating [constricted glottis/creak] also fails to emerge as an independent segment. This is because the CVX maximal syllable limit in Yawelmani keeps the floating feature from turning up as a full glottal stop without vowel epenthesis, but epenthesis would lead to a fatal violation of *Struc(σ) (32a). The most harmonic candidate (32b) fails to parse [constricted glottis/creak], thereby avoiding the more serious *Struc(σ) violations that would otherwise ensue.

(32) Segment structure, *Struc(σ) ≫ Max(F) from /hogn, ʔaa/

	Candidates	*Struc(σ)	Max(F)
a.	ho.gIn.ʔaa	***!	
b. ☞	hog.naa	**	*

Another logically possible candidate in (32) is hognaʔ, with a glottal stop at the end of the word. This form satisfies both syllable structure and Contiguity while preserving the floating feature. The absence of this form is probably due to a constraint against final glottal stops (Newman 1944, 17). As shown in (33), this constraint outranks MAX(F) and thus blocks the appearance of a glottal stop at the end of the word.

(33) /hogn, ʔaa/

	Candidates	*ʔ]ᵥₒᵣd	MAX(F)
a.	hognaʔ	*!	
b. ☞	hognaa		*

This results in the hierarchy in (34). The domination of *STRUC(σ) by MAX(Seg) accounts for the triggering of epenthesis to avoid deletion of stray full consonants. The low ranking of MAX(F) captures the fact that floating features will delete rather than prompt life-saving insertion of an additional vowel.

(34) *ʔ]ᵥₒᵣd, MAX(Seg) ≫ *STRUC(σ) ≫ MAX(F)

There are of course a number of other possible ways to keep a floating feature from manifesting itself as a full segment. A FILL (Prince and Smolensky 1993) or DEP (McCarthy and Prince 1995) constraint could proscribe insertion of a new root node, or we could count additional segments rather than syllables as extra structure violations. However, of these only *STRUC(σ) correctly predicts an asymmetry that exists between the behavior of floating consonantal features and the behavior of floating vocalic features (35).[6] Namely, since extra consonants can be an onset or coda to an already existing syllable, they will not necessarily violate the constraint when they surface as independent segments. In a language without diphthongs, however, an inserted vowel inevitably adds a new syllable and thus violates *STRUC(σ). It follows from this that latent consonants will surface more readily than latent vowels. This prediction is confirmed below in Yawelmani.

(35) *Prediction of *STRUC(σ): a symmetry between C and V epenthesis*
    (® = inserted root node)
    a. Inserted V violates *STRUC(σ)   b. Inserted C does not

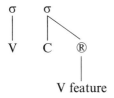

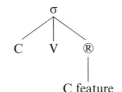

12.3.2.4 Affix Placement The previous sections have accounted for the absence of epenthesis to rescue the glottal quasi-segment, as well as the restriction of glottalization to postvocalic sonorants. When the glottal stop appears, however, other constraints govern its position. First, the placement of each suffix is determined by the alignment constraint in (36). This constraint refers to the right edge and demands that the final segment in the suffix also be the final segment of the word.

(36) *Constraint on affix placement*
    ALIGN-RIGHT(Affix, PWd)   The rightmost segment in the affix is
                                   the rightmost segment in the PWd.
                                   (McCarthy and Prince 1993)

In addition, a CONTIGUITY constraint (37) prevents the intermingling of base and affix segments. Where no glottalizable sonorant exists, [constricted glottis/creak] will emerge as a full segment if its presence does not entail insertion of another vowel for syllable well-formedness. The tableau in (38) provides a demonstration. There is no glottalizable (postvocalic) sonorant in *maax*, so secondary glottalization is impossible. The only way MAX(F) can be satisfied is by insertion of a full glottal stop (38b). Note that CONTIGUITY operates here to make sure that the resulting glottal stop surfaces between root and affix, since there is no inherent contiguity between the segments in two different morphemes. The logically possible candidates in (38b) and (38c), where the suffixal glottal precedes a segment that corresponds to the base, will never be optimal in Yawelmani because they result in CONTIGUITY violations.

(37) CONTIGUITY   Segments that are contiguous in the input are
                         contiguous in the output. (McCarthy and Prince
                         1995)

(38) *The role of* CONTIGUITY */maax, ˀaa/*

Candidates	CONTIGUITY	Comments
a. ☞ maxˀaa		
b. maˀxaa	*!	• ˀ interrupts contiguity of root segments
c. maxaˀa	*!	• ˀ interrupts contiguity of affix segments

CONTIGUITY must outrank MAX(F). Consider a form with no glottalizable sonorant in the base, where a suffix-initial glottal stop is prohibited by syllable structure constraints that limit clusters (39a). Although a form with a suffix-internal glottal is consistent with syllable structure constraints (39b), it incurs a fatal violation of CONTIGUITY. In the optimal candidate (39c), the glottal feature fails to appear, violating only the low-ranked MAX(F).

(39) $/hogn,\ ^{?}aa/$

Candidates	SYLL-STRUC	CONTIGUITY	MAX(F)
a. hogn?a͟a	*! (cluster)		
b. hogna͟?a͟		*!	
c. ☞ hogna͟a͟			*

On the other hand, the infixation of a dependent feature does not violate CONTIGUITY, since intersegmental contiguity relations are not altered. Consider the tableau in (40). A suffix-initial full glottal stop is impossible here owing to unviolated syllable structure considerations (40a). A suffix-internal glottal stop fatally violates CONTIGUITY, while nonparsing of the feature violates MAX(F). In the optimal form [constricted glottis/creak] docks onto the available postvocalic sonorant base-internally (40d). If CONTIGUITY included infixed dependent features as violations, then the analysis would wrongly eliminate glottalization in cases like these. CONTIGUITY refers exclusively to segments.

(40) $/?elk,\ ^{?}aa/$

Candidates	SYLL-STRUC	CONTIGUITY	MAX(F)
a. ?elk?a͟a	*! (cluster)		
b. ?elka͟?a͟		*!	
c. ?elka͟a͟			*!
d. ☞ ?el?ka͟a͟			

(41) summarizes the rankings that have been established so far.

(41) *Rankings*
     a. MAX(Seg) ≫ *STRUC(σ) ≫ MAX(F)
     b. *?]$_{word}$, syllable structure constraints, ALIGN-RIGHT(Affix, PWd), CONTIGUITY ≫ MAX(F)

12.3.2.5   MAX(F) and IDENT(Length)   Finally, it is necessary to account for the case where vowel shortening occurs to accommodate a full glottal stop. We saw above that the surface form of /maax, ʔaa/ is *maxʔaa*, with a full glottal stop and subsequent shortening of the root vowel. The constraint in (42) that penalizes vowel shortening, IDENT(Length), must therefore rank below MAX(F), since parsing of the floating feature can force the nonidentity of vowel length between input and output.

(42) IDENT(Length)   Corresponding vowels have identical length.
                         (after Urbanczyk 1995)

The tableau in (43) provides a demonstration. Since *maax* has no glottalizable (postvocalic) sonorant, secondary glottalization is impossible. The only way MAX(F) can be satisfied here is by insertion of a full glottal stop (43b), despite the resulting shortening of the long vowel. The need to parse the feature outweighs any cost incurred by shortening (as reflected by violation of IDENT(Length)).[7]

(43) /maax, ʔaa/

Candidates	SYLL-STRUC	CONTI-GUITY	MAX(F)	IDENT-(Length)
a. maaxʔaa	*!			
b. maʔaxaa		*!		
c. maaxaa			*!	
d. ☞ maxʔaa				*

The tableau in (44) shows, however, that IDENT(Length) does serve a crucial function in the hierarchy. From /caaw, ʔaa/, either *caw.ʔaa* or *caa.wʔaa* would be acceptable with respect to syllable structure, CONTI-GUITY, and MAX(F). IDENT(Length) makes the pivotal decision, favoring the form in (44d) without unnecessary vowel shortening.

(44) /caaw, ˀaa/

	Candidates	SYLL-STRUC	CONTI-GUITY	MAX(F)	IDENT-(Length)
a.	caaw.ˀaa	*!			
b.	caa.waa			*!	
c.	caw.ˀaa				*!
d. ☞	caa.wˀaa				

12.3.2.6 Summary The mixed behavior of the Yawelmani glottal quasi-segment follows from the interaction of a hierarchy of general constraints with the floating glottal feature [constricted glottis/creak]. The ranking of the constraints is given in (45). The constraints in the top row are never violated. ALIGN-RIGHT(Affix, PWd) guarantees that the affix is a suffix. It has no crucial interactions with the other constraints, so its ranking is indeterminate. Next, the ranking MAX(Seg) ≫ *STRUC(σ) ≫ MAX(F) ≫ IDENT(Length) determines the basic difference between the full segments and the floating glottal. Here, topmost MAX(Seg) forces epenthesis to save potentially stray consonants, while *STRUC(σ) ≫ MAX(F) favors deletion of an input floating feature over vowel epenthesis. Finally, the *ˀ]word, SEGMENT STRUCTURE, SYLLABLE STRUCTURE, and CONTIGUITY constraints crucially dominate MAX(F) and thus influence whether and how the floating glottal will appear in a surface form. In sections 12.3.3 and 12.3.4, I will show how this hierarchy accounts for the diverse behavior of Yawelmani's other latent consonants and vowels as well.

(45) *Summary of the analysis*

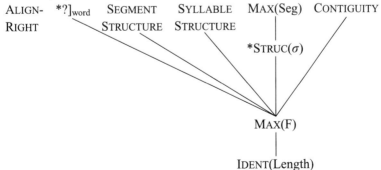

12.3.3   Other Latent Segments

12.3.3.1   Analysis of Latent Consonants   In (46), I have repeated the list of suffixes with latent consonants, along with a sketch of their proposed underlying representations.[8]

(46)   *Yawelmani suffixes with latent C*[9]

Suffix	Underlying representation of latent C
(^{h})nel passive adjunctive	Lar | [spread glottis]
(^{l})saa causative repetitive	CPlace | coronal | [lateral]
(^{m})aam decedent	CPlace | [labial]
(^{n})iit decedent	[nasal]

Once this distinction between full segments (which have a root node) and latent segments (which lack a root node) has been made, the diversified behavior of the different latent features follows from the Yawelmani hierarchy developed in the previous section. Their surface patterns result directly from structure preservation. The only thing that sets the behavior of the other latent consonants apart from the glottal is that they never dock secondarily onto an existing segment, since glottalization is the only contrastive secondary articulation in Yawelmani. The other floating features are precluded from docking onto existing segments by segment structure constraints that prohibit the creation of elements like phonologically aspirated consonants or doubly articulated stops. The floating features in (46) therefore can only be realized as the primary articulation on an inserted root node; that is, they will act like latent segments.

The same hierarchy that derived the glottal pattern yields the correct outputs for the other latent consonants as well. First, the ranking of *STRUC(σ) above MAX(F) entails that when there is no available spot in an existing syllable, the features will fail to appear. This is illustrated by the tableaux in (47)–(48). For the triconsonantal root *hogon-* in (47), the only way for the suffix's latent (*h*) to surface would be through CONTIGUITY-violating metathesis (47b) or epenthesis of a syllable nucleus vowel (47c). The consequent addition of a syllable fatally violates *STRUC(σ), so instead the best choice is to let the feature go (47d).

(47) *hogonnel, from |hogon, (ʰ)nel|*

Candidates	SEG-STRUC	CONTI-GUITY	*STRUC-(σ)	MAX(F)
a. ho.gʰon.nel	*!			
b. hog.hon.nel		*!		
c. ho.gon.hI.nel			****!	
d. ☞ ho.gon.nel			***	*

Compare that result with the result for the biconsonantal root *maxaa*. Here, with vowel shortening, the optimal candidate (48c) has room for the latent feature to surface as an independent segment. This candidate outdoes (48b), where the feature is left unparsed. CONTIGUITY ensures that when there is room for the epenthetic root node, it will be inserted between the root and the affix, so we need not depend on underlying root nodes to keep latent features in place. The candidate in (48a), which differs from the winner only in that the inserted root appears further to the left, loses on the grounds that it violates CONTIGUITY.

(48) *maxahnel, from |maxaa, (ʰ)nel|*

Candidates	CONTI-GUITY	*STRUC-(σ)	MAX(F)	IDENT-(Length)
a. mah.xaa.nel	***!	***		
b. ma.xaa.nel		***	*!	
c. ☞ ma.xah.nel		***		*

What differentiates the so-called floating glottal from the other latent consonants, then, is that the only contrastive secondary articulation possible in Yawelmani is glottalization. Other potentially floating features can only occur as independent segments whose position is fixed by CONTIGUITY. Therefore, the behavior of the latent consonants does not entail that they have an underlying root node, since their form and position are completely predictable from the grammar.

12.3.3.2 Analysis of Latent Vowels Finally, we return to the latent vowels. The relevant data involving the precative suffix -*m(i)* are shown again in (49). The behavior of the latent vowels differs from that of the latent consonants, including the glottal, in that they do not surface every time there is room for them. Rather, they appear only when called upon to rescue an otherwise unparsable consonant, as in (49a).

(49) *Vowel/∅ alternation: Latent vowels surface only when they are necessary (Newman 1944, 135)*
      a. /amic-m(i)/   amic-mi   *amic-m·   'having approached'
      b. /panaa-m(i)/   panam·   *panaa-mi   'having arrived'

The behavior of the latent vowel, analyzed as a floating V-place feature [high], also follows from the constraint hierarchy already established. It is *STRUC(σ), which militates against superfluous syllable building, that distinguishes the behavior of the latent vowels from the latent consonants. This constraint has no impact on the consonants themselves, since they emerge by simply slipping into existing syllable structure. The constraint functions there only to exclude an epenthetic vowel whose sole purpose is to rescue an otherwise doomed latent feature. By contrast, *STRUC(σ) limits the realization of latent vowels themselves, because a vowel always heads its own syllable in Yawelmani. Every time a vowel appears, it triggers a violation of *STRUC(σ), so latent vowels show up only when violation of *STRUC(σ) is forced by some higher constraint, in this case MAX(Seg) as argued above. Since the language has no secondary vocalic articulations, segment structure constraints will prevent them from otherwise docking on existing full segments.

This state of affairs is illustrated by the tableaux in (50)–(51). The winner in (50a) succeeds in parsing all the full segments into only two syllables, violating *STRUC(σ) only twice, while parsing the latent vowel in the nonoptimal (50b) requires three syllables.

(50) *panam, from* $|panaa\text{-}m^{(i)}|$

Candidates	Max(Seg)	*Struc(σ)	Max(F)
a. ☞ pa.na.<u>m</u>		**	*
b. pa.naa.<u>mi</u>		***!	

In the tableau in (51), on the other hand, the latent vowel is needed to rescue the otherwise unparsable *m*. This causes an additional *Struc(σ) violation but is necessary in order to avoid deleting a full segment. Therefore, (51b) is optimal.

(51) *amicmi, from* $|amic\text{-}m^{(i)}|$

Candidates	Max(Seg)	*Struc(σ)	Comments
a. a.mic	*!	**	• *m* deleted
b. ☞ a.mic.<u>mI</u>		***	• latent *I* saves *m*

This case requires an additional constraint to make sure that the vowel appears word-finally, since *amic-im* and *amic-mi* are equivalent with respect to the constraint hierarchy motivated above. Elsewhere (Zoll 1993) I have proposed a constraint, Align-Right(Base, Syllable), necessary to determine the position of an epenthetic vowel with respect to a template, that also places the latent vowel in the right position (52). In the tableau in (53), the right edge of the base is marked with a bracket. This coincides with the right edge of a syllable only in (53b), where the latent vowel emerges at the end of the word.

(52) Align-Right(Base, Syllable) The right edge of the base coincides with the right edge of a syllable.

(53) $|amic\text{-}m^{(i)}|$

Candidates	Align-Right(Base, Syllable)
a. a.mi.c]<u>I</u>m	*!
b. ☞ a.mic].<u>mI</u>	

The tableau in (54) shows that Align-Right(Base, Syllable) must rank below Max(F), because it will be violated in order to preserve even an underlying floating feature. In this tableau, the candidate that parses the floating [spread glottis] feature in the input (54b) violates the alignment constraint. It is optimal because the competitor in (54a), while satisfying ALIGN-RIGHT (Base, Syllable), does so by eliminating [spread glottis] in the output. This incurs a violation of the higher-ranking faithfulness constraint.

(54) *maxahnel, from |maxaa, (^{h})nel|*

Candidates	MAX(F)	ALIGN-RIGHT- (Base, Syllable)
a. ma.xaa.]nel	*!	
b. ☞ ma.xa]h.nel		*

Thus, in Yawelmani there is no need to distinguish the variety of latent segments representationally, since both their movement and/or possible segmenthood is predictable from the interaction of segment structure restrictions with a grammar that consists of ranked and violable constraints.

12.4 Fill-In of Missing Features

Table (55) summarizes the proposed underlying representations for the latent segments and the glottal quasi-segment in Yawelmani. In previous sections, I have demonstrated that from these inputs the hierarchy of ranked and violable constraints correctly determines whether the surface form will be an independent segment or a dependent feature. It remains now only to show how the rest of the features are filled in when these floating features do surface as independent segments. The assignment of these features is straightforward, since it turns out that the missing values are the unmarked ones, and these follow from independent markedness constraints (Prince and Smolensky 1993). This is immediately obvious for the latent vowel *i*, since *i* is the unmarked vowel in many languages, and, indeed, it is also the epenthetic vowel in Yawelmani. I will show that likewise the consonants are the unmarked members of their respective classes.

(55) *Representation of latent segments*

Latent segment	Representation
m	CPlace | [labial]
l	CPlace | [coronal] | [lateral]
n	[nasal]
ʔ	Lar | [constricted glottis] | [creak]
h	Lar | [spread glottis]
i	V-Place | [high]

The full consonant inventory is repeated here in (56). The consonants that occur as latent segments in some contexts are underlined. Observe that the set of latent segments is a highly asymmetric portion of the total inventory of Yawelmani. Only sonorants have latent counterparts—in particular, only the sonorants lacking glottalization.

(56) *Yawelmani inventory (Archangeli 1984, 60, from Newman 1944)*

Labial	Dental	Alveolar	Dorsal
b, p, $p^{\textipa{?}}$	d, t, $t^{\textipa{?}}$	D, T, $T^{\textipa{?}}$	g, k, $k^{\textipa{?}}$
	ʒ, c, $c^{\textipa{?}}$	z, C, $c^{\textipa{?}}$	
	s	s	
<u>m</u>, $m^{\textipa{?}}$	<u>n</u>, $n^{\textipa{?}}$		
w, $w^{\textipa{?}}$	y, $y^{\textipa{?}}$		<u>h</u>, <u>ʔ</u>
	<u>l</u>, $l^{\textipa{?}}$		

Since only unpredictable information is included in the input, the remaining features must be supplied by language-specific defaults and universal markedness conventions, in the tradition of underspecification, and following more recently Prince and Smolensky 1993 and Smolensky 1993.[10] The more familiar universal markedness statements are given in (57) along with their corresponding constraints.

(57) *Universal markedness statements*

Markedness rules	Constraints
[+sonorant] → [+voice]	*[+sonorant] | [−voice]
[CPlace] → [+consonantal]	*[−consonantal] | CPlace
[constricted glottis] → [+consonantal]	*[−consonantal] | [constricted glottis]
[+spread glottis] → [+consonantal]	*[−consonantal] | [spread glottis]
[nasal] → [+consonantal]	*[−consonantal] | [nasal]
[∅ CPlace → [coronal]	*CPlace *CPlace | | labial dorsal

In addition, since the Yawelmani latent consonants are all [+sonorant], one language-particular ranking of the sonorant markedness constraints is needed (58).[11]

(58) *Language-particular ranking*

Language-particular default	Constraint
∅ → [+sonorant]	*[−sonorant] ≫ *[+sonorant]

The tableau in (59) illustrates how these constraints produce the desired optimal [n] output for an underlying floating [nasal]. Note that none of these constraints can be ranked with respect to each other here since the output violates none of them.

(59) *[nasal]* → *n*

Candidates	*[−son]	*[+son] | [−voice]	*[−cons] | [nasal]	*CPlace | labial	*CPlace | dorsal
a. ☞ n					
b. ŋ					*!
c. m				*!	
d. ĩ			*!		
e. n̥		*!			
f. ⁿt	*!				

Given that default specification involves minimal feature addition, it follows that the plain sonorants rather than their glottalized counterparts serve as the latent segments. Although it is logically possible to assign [+constricted glottis] by default to every segment underlyingly unspecified for that feature, no theory of universal markedness or language-specific defaults that I know of would posit such a rule. If on the other hand the latent segments were not melodically defective, the absence of glottalized latent consonants and other contrasts would not follow from the representation. These sorts of asymmetries are merely accidental in other theories of latent segments that maintain a configurational distinction between the latent segments and floating features, all of which leave the segment itself intact.

12.5 Conclusion

This case study of defective segments in Yawelmani has provided further support for the position taken in Zoll 1998 that special representational distinctions between latent segments and floating features are unnecessary. I have shown that although Yawelmani has four different segment types, the only distinction required is between the full segments and the defective ones (including latent consonants and vowels as well as the glottal quasi-segment). Whether or not an input floating feature surfaces as an independent segment or dependent feature, as well as the contexts in which it appears, is straightforwardly derived from a grammar that consists of a hierarchy of ranked and violable constraints.

Notes

I am grateful to Michael Kenstowicz for comments and suggestions.

1. See Noske 1984, Zoll 1993, Broselow 1995, and Archangeli 1991 for choice of epenthesis site in a cluster.

2. The voiceless series is pronounced with aspiration (see Newman 1944, 14). Aspiration is not a contrastive feature in Yawelmani, however, so I follow Archangeli in classifying obstruent stops as voiced versus voiceless.

3. This word is actually from the Chukchansi dialect of Yokuts, where the affix has a short vowel. The rules governing the glottalization are the same as in Yawelmani.

An unviolated constraint against final glottal stop rules out *xata?*. See below.

4. The details of these constraints differ somewhat from those of Steriade's (1997) constraints, which are formulated with specific reference to phonetic cues.

5. A high-ranking CONTIGUITY constraint keeps the glottal from surfacing suffix-internally as *a?a* (as proposed in Kenstowicz 1994 for a similar restriction on schwa epenthesis in Chukchee).

6. The FILL(Nuc) constraint (Prince and Smolensky 1993) makes the same prediction, but requires reference to the nucleus as a constituent not reducible to a mora, since it does not refer to both nuclei and moraic codas. Another alternative would be to posit separate DEP(C) and DEP(V) constraints. The ranking DEP(V) ≫ MAX(F) ≫ DEP(C) would make the same prediction as *STRUC(σ) ≫ MAX(F). However, *STRUC(σ) is independently necessary for vowel syncope. In addition, I have not found any cases that would require the opposite ranking (DEP(C) ≫ MAX(F) ≫ DEP(V)). At this point, therefore, the *STRUC(σ) hypothesis appears to be superior.

7. For discussion of the function of template integrity in Yawelmani, the source of vowel length, see Zoll 1993, Broselow 1995.

8. See section 12.4 for the filling in of the remaining features.

9. I assume the geometry of features in (i) (Clements 1985; Sagey 1986; McCarthy 1988; Selkirk 1988; Hume 1992; Padgett 1995), with a separation between consonantal place features and vocalic place features, following Clements (1991), Clements and Hume (1995), and Ní Chiosáin and Padgett (1993). For the purposes of this chapter, it does not matter whether this separation is effected through independent place nodes or by using different names for the consonantal and vocalic features. Here, for clarity of exposition, I will use the traditional vowel features {high, low, back, round, ATR, RTR} for vowels and reserve place-of-articulation names {coronal, dorsal, labial, pharyngeal} for consonants.

(i)

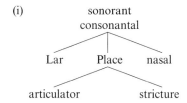

10. It is important to stress that these conditions are necessary independently of whether or not one adopts a theory of input underspecification in general. The same constraints that fill in default features in an underspecification framework are necessary to derive the "emergence of the unmarked" (McCarthy and Prince 1994) in a theory where inputs are fully specified.

11. Since this is not a statement of universal markedness, we expect to find the opposite ranking in some other language. This is the case in French, where all of the latent consonants (except the nasal) surface as obstruents. See Zoll 1998.

References

Archangeli, D. 1983. The root CV-template as a property of the affix: Evidence from Yawelmani. *Natural Language & Linguistic Theory* 1, 348–384.

Archangeli, D. 1984. *Underspecification in Yawelmani phonology and morphology.* New York: Garland.

Archangeli, D. 1991. Syllabification and prosodic templates in Yawelmani. *Natural Language & Linguistic Theory* 9, 231–284.

Archangeli, D., and D. Pulleyblank. 1994. *Grounded Phonology.* Cambridge, Mass.: MIT Press.

Blevins, J. 1993. Klamath laryngeal phonology. *International Journal of American Linguistics* 59, 237–279.

Broselow, E. 1995. Skeletal positions and moras. In J. Goldsmith, ed., *The handbook of phonological theory*, 175–205. Oxford: Blackwell.

Buckley, E. 1994. *Theoretical aspects of Kashaya phonology and morphology.* Stanford, Calif.: CSLI Publications.

Clements, G. N. 1985. The geometry of phonological features. *Phonology* 2, 225–252.

Clements, G. N. 1991. Place of articulation in consonants and vowels: A unified theory. In *Working papers of the Cornell Phonetics Laboratory 5*, 77–123. Department of Linguistics, Cornell University, Ithaca, N.Y.

Clements, G. N., and E. V. Hume. 1995. The internal organization of speech sounds. In J. Goldsmith, ed., *The handbook of phonological theory*, 245–306. Oxford: Blackwell.

Clements, G. N., and S. J. Keyser. 1983. *CV phonology: A generative theory of the syllable.* Cambridge, Mass.: MIT Press.

Hume, E. V. 1992. Front vowels, coronal consonants, and their interaction in nonlinear phonology. Doctoral dissertation, Cornell University, Ithaca, N.Y.

Kenstowicz, M. 1994. Syllabification in Chukchee: A constraints-based analysis. Rutgers Optimality Archive ROA-30-1094, Rutgers University, New Brunswick, N.J.

Kisseberth, C. W. 1970. On the functional unity of phonological words. *Linguistic Inquiry* 1, 291–306.

Kuipers, A. 1974. *The Shuswap language*. The Hague: Mouton.

Kuroda, S.-Y. 1967. *Yawelmani phonology*. Cambridge, Mass.: MIT Press.

McCarthy, J. 1988. Feature geometry and dependency: A review. *Phonetica* 43, 84–108.

McCarthy, J., and A. Prince. 1993. Generalized Alignment. Ms., University of Massachusetts, Amherst, and Rutgers University, New Brunswick, N.J.

McCarthy, J., and A. Prince. 1994. The emergence of the unmarked: Optimality in Prosodic Morphology. In M. Gonzàlez, ed., *NELS 24*, 333–379. GLSA, University of Massachusetts, Amherst.

McCarthy, J., and A. Prince. 1995. Faithfulness and reduplicative identity. In J. N. Beckman, L. W. Dickey, and S. Urbanczyk, eds., *Papers in Optimality Theory*, 249–384. GLSA, University of Massachusetts, Amherst.

Newman, S. 1944. *Yokuts language of California*. New York: Viking Fund Publications.

Ní Chiosáin, M., and J. Padgett. 1993. Inherent VPlace. LRC-93-09. Linguistics Research Center, University of California, Santa Cruz.

Nichols, J. 1971. Diminutive consonant symbolism in western North America. *Language* 47, 826–848.

Noske, R. 1984. Syllabification and syllable changing processes in Yawelmani. In H. van der Hulst and N. Smith, eds., *Advances in nonlinear phonology*, 257–310. Dordrecht: Foris.

Padgett, J. 1995. *Stricture in feature geometry*. Stanford, Calif.: CSLI Publications.

Prince, A., and P. Smolensky. 1993. Optimality Theory: Constraint interaction in generative grammar. Ms., Rutgers University, New Brunswick, N.J., and University of Colorado, Boulder.

Sagey, E. 1986. *The representation of features and relations in nonlinear phonology*. New York: Garland.

Selkirk, E. 1981. Epenthesis and degenerate syllables in Cairene Arabic. In H. Borer and J. Aoun, eds., *Theoretical issues in the grammar of Semitic languages*, 209–232. MIT Working Papers in Linguistics 3. MITWPL, Department of Linguistics and Philosophy, MIT, Cambridge, Mass.

Selkirk, E. 1988. Dependency, place, and the notion "tier." Ms., University of Massachusetts, Amherst.

Smolensky, P. 1993. Harmony, markedness, and phonological theory. Rutgers Optimality Archive ROA 87-0000. Rutgers University, New Brunswick, N.J.

Steriade, D. 1997. Phonetics in phonology: The case of laryngeal neutralization. Ms., UCLA, Los Angeles, Calif.

Urbanczyk, S. 1995. Double reduplication in parallel. In J. N. Beckman, L. W. Dickey, and S. Urbanczyk, eds., *Papers in Optimality Theory*, 499–532. University of Massachusetts Occasional Papers 18. GLSA, University of Massachusetts, Amherst.

Zoll, C. 1993. Directionless syllabification in Yawelmani. Rutgers Optimality Archive ROA 28-0000. Rutgers University, New Brunswick, N.J.

Zoll, C. 1998. *Parsing below the segment in a constraint-based framework*. Stanford, Calif.: CSLI Publications.

Publications of Ken Hale: 1958–2000

compiled by Marilyn Goodrich

1958 Internal diversity in Uto-Aztecan: I. *International Journal of American Linguistics* 24, 101–107.

1959 Internal diversity in Uto-Aztecan: II. *International Journal of American Linguistics* 25, 114–121.

1962 (with C. F. and F. M. Voegelin) *Typological and comparative grammar of Uto-Aztecan: I (Phonology)*. Indiana University Publications in Anthropology and Linguistics, Memoir 17 of the *International Journal of American Linguistics*.

1962 Jemez and Kiowa correspondences in reference to Kiowa-Tanoan. *International Journal of American Linguistics* 28, 1–5.

1962 *Internal relationships of Arandic, Central Australia, in some linguistic types in Australia*. Oceania Linguistic Monographs 7. Sydney.

1964 The sub-grouping of Uto-Aztecan languages: Lexical evidence for Sonoran. In *Actas y Memorias del XXXV Congreso Internacional de Americanistas, Mexico*, 511–517.

1964 Classification of Northern Paman languages, Cape York Peninsula, Australia: A research report. *Oceanic Linguistics* 3, 248–264.

1965 Review of Fodor and Katz, *The structure of language: Readings in the philosophy of language. American Anthropologist* 67, 1011–1020.

1965 Review of Bach, *An introduction to transformational grammars. International Journal of American Linguistics* 21, 265–270.

1965 On the use of informants in field-work. *Canadian Journal of Linguistics* 10(2–3), 108–119.

1965 Australian languages and transformational grammar. *Linguistics* 16, 32–41.

1965 Some preliminary observations on Papago morphophonemics. *International Journal of American Linguistics* 31, 295–305.

1966 Kinship reflections in syntax: Some Australian languages. *Word* 22, 318–324.

1967 (with Joseph B. Casagrande) Semantic relationships in Papago folk-definitions. In D. Hymes and W. Bittle, eds., *Studies in Southwestern ethnolinguistics: Meaning and history in the languages of the American Southwest*, 165–193. The Hague: Mouton.

1967 Review of G. H. Matthews, *Hidatsa syntax. International Journal of American Linguistics* 33, 329–341.

1967 Some productive rules in Lardil (Mornington Island) syntax. In C. G. von Brandenstein, A. Capell, and K. Hale, eds., *Papers in Australian linguistics no. 2*, 63–73. Pacific Linguistics, Series A, No. 11. Canberra: Australian National University.

1967 Toward a reconstruction of Kiowa-Tanoan phonology. *International Journal of American Linguistics* 33, 112–120.

1969 Review of P. W. Hohepa, *A profile generative grammar of Maori. The Journal of the Polynesian Society* 77(1).

1969 Papago /cim/. *International Journal of American Linguistics* 35, 203–212.

1969 American Indians in linguistics. *The Indian Historian* 2.

1970 Papago laryngeals. In E. Swanson, ed., *Languages and cultures of western North America*, 54–60. Pocatello: Idaho State University.

1970 (with Albert Alvarez) Toward a manual of Papago grammar: Some phonological terms. *International Journal of American Linguistics* 36 (Memorial issue for Hans Wolff, fascicle II), 83–97.

1970 The passive and ergative in language change: The Australian case. In S. A. Wurm and D. C. Laycock, eds., *Pacific linguistic studies in honour of Arthur Capell*, 751–781. Canberra: Australian National University.

1971 A note on a Warlpiri tradition of antonymy. In D. Steinberg and L. A. Jakobovits, eds., *Semantics*, 472–482. Cambridge: Cambridge University Press.

1972 A new perspective on American Indian linguistics. With appendix by A. Alvarez. In A. Ortiz, ed., *New perspectives on the pueblos*, 87–133. Albuquerque: University of New Mexico Press.

1972 Some questions about anthropological linguistics: The role of native knowledge. In D. Hymes, ed., *Reinventing anthropology*, 382–397. New York: Pantheon.

1973 The role of American Indian linguistics in bilingual education. In P. Turner, ed., *Bilingualism in the Southwest*, 203–225. Tucson: University of Arizona Press.

1973 A note on subject-object inversion in Navajo. In B. B. Kachru et al., eds., *Issues in linguistics: Papers in honor of Henry and Renée Kahane*, 300–309. Urbana: University of Illinois Press.

1973 Deep-surface canonical disparities in relation to analysis and change: An Australian example. In T. A. Sebeok, ed., *Current trends in linguistics*, 401–458. The Hague: Mouton.

1973 Person marking in Warlpiri. In S. Anderson and P. Kiparsky, eds., *A festschrift for Morris Halle*, 308–344. New York: Holt, Rinehart & Winston.

1974 (with Paul Platero) Aspects of Navajo anaphora: Relativization and pronominalization. *Diné Bizaad Náníl'įįh/Navajo Language Review* 1, 9–28.

1974 (with Lorraine Honie) Ał'ąą dine'é bizaad ałhąąh naha'níłígíí. *Diné Bizaad Náníl'įįh/Navajo Language Review* 1, 85–94.

1974 Counterexamples and explanations in Navajo linguistics: Phonology. *Diné Bizaad Náníl'įįh/Navajo Language Review* 1, 175–203.

1975 Counterexamples and explanations in Navajo linguistics: Syntax. *Diné Bizaad Náníl'įįh/Navajo Language Review* 2, 29–60.

1975 (with Lorraine Honie) Diné bizaad yá'áti' bee diits'a'ígíí: áłtsé bíhoo'aahígíí (The sounds of Navajo: First lesson). *Diné Bizaad Náníl'įįh/ Navajo Language Review* 2, 61–82.

1975 Gaps in grammars and cultures. In M. D. Kinkade, K. L. Hale, and O. Werner, eds., *Linguistics and anthropology: In honor of C. F. Voegelin*, 295–315. Lisse: Peter de Ridder Press.

1976 Theoretical linguistics in relation to American Indian communities. In W. L. Chafe, ed., *American Indian languages and American linguistics*, 35–50. Lisse: Peter de Ridder Press.

1976 Phonological developments in particular Northern Paman languages. In P. Sutton, ed., *Languages of Cape York*, 7–40. Canberra: Australian Institute of Aboriginal Studies.

1976 Phonological developments in a Northern Paman language: Uradhi. In P. Sutton, ed., *Languages of Cape York*, 41–50. Canberra: Australian Institute of Aboriginal Studies.

1976 Wik reflections of Middle Paman phonology. In P. Sutton, ed., *Languages of Cape York*, 50–60. Canberra: Australian Institute of Aboriginal Studies.

1976 Tya:pukay (Djaabugay). In P. Sutton, ed., *Languages of Cape York*, 236–242. Canberra: Australian Institute of Aboriginal Studies.

1976 The adjoined relative clause in Australia. In R. M. W. Dixon, ed., *Grammatical categories in Australian languages*, 78–105. Canberra: Australian Institute of Aboriginal Studies.

1976 Dja:bugay. In R. M. W. Dixon, ed., *Grammatical categories in Australian languages*, 321–326. Canberra: Australian Institute of Aboriginal Studies.

1976 On ergative and locative suffixal alternations in Australian languages. In R. M. W. Dixon, ed., *Grammatical categories in Australian languages*, 414–417. Canberra: Australian Institute of Aboriginal Studies.

1976 Linguistic autonomy and the linguistics of Carl Voegelin. *Anthropological Linguistics* 18, 120–128.

1976–77 (with Chisato Kitagawa)   A counter to Counter-Equi. *Papers in Japanese Linguistics* 5, 41–61.

1977 (with LaVerne Masayesva Jeanne and Paul Platero)   Three cases of overgeneration. In P. Culicover, T. Wasow, and A. Akmajian, eds., *Formal syntax*, 397–416. New York: Academic Press.

1979 The problem of psychological reality in the phonology of Papago. In Eli Fischer-Jørgensen et al., *Proceedings of the Ninth International Congress of Phonetic Sciences*, vol. II, 108–113. Institute of Phonetics, University of Copenhagen.

1979 (with David Harris)   Historical linguistics and archeology in the Southwest. In A. Ortiz, ed., *Handbook of North American Indians*, vol. 9, 170–177. Washington, D.C.: Smithsonian Institution.

1980 Remarks on Japanese phrase structure: Comments on the papers on Japanese syntax. In Y. Otsu and A. Farmer, eds., *Theoretical issues in Japanese linguistics*, 185–203. MIT Working Papers in Linguistics 2. MITWPL, Department of Linguistics and Philosophy, MIT.

1980 (with Josie White Eagle) A preliminary metrical account of Winnebago accent. *International Journal of American Linguistics* 46, 117–132.

1980 Warlpiri: Traditional Aboriginal owners. *ARC Newsletter* 4, 5.

1981 On the position of Warlpiri in a typology of the base. Indiana University Linguistics Club, Bloomington.

1981 Preliminary remarks on the grammar of part-whole relations in Warlpiri. In J. Hollyman and A. Pawley, eds., *Studies in Pacific languages and cultures in honor of Bruce Biggs*, 333–344. Auckland: Linguistic Society of New Zealand.

1982 Some essential features of Warlpiri verbal clauses. In S. Swartz, ed., *Papers in Warlpiri grammar in memory of Lothar Jagst*. Work Papers of SIL-AAB. Darwin.

1982 The logic of Damin kinship terminology. In J. Heath, F. Merlan, and A. Rumsey, eds., *Languages of kinship in Aboriginal Australia*. Oceania Linguistic Monographs 24. University of Sydney.

1983 Warlpiri and the grammar of non-configurational languages. *Natural Language & Linguistic Theory* 1, 5–47.

1983 (with James McCloskey) The syntax of inflection in Modern Irish. In P. Sells and C. Jones, eds., *Proceedings of ALNE 13/NELS 13*, 173–190. GLSA, University of Massachusetts, Amherst.

1983 A lexicographic study of some Australian languages: Project description. In P. Austin, ed., *Papers in Australian linguistics no. 15: Australian Aboriginal lexicography*, 71–107. Pacific Linguistics, Series A, No. 66. Canberra: University of Australia.

1983 Papago (k)c. *International Journal of American Linguistics* 49, 299–327.

1984 Remarks on creativity in Aboriginal verse. In J. Kassler and J. Stubington, eds., *Problems and solutions: occasional essays in musicology presented to Alice M. Moyle*, 254–262. Sydney: Hale & Iremonger.

1985 A note on Winnebago metrical structure. *International Journal of American Linguistics* 51, 427–429.

1985 On nonconfigurational structures. In S. Kuno et al., eds., *Harvard studies in Korean linguistics: Proceedings of the 1985 Harvard Workshop on Korean Linguistics, July 12–13, 1985*. Seoul: Hanshin.

1985 (with Viviane Déprez) Resumptive pronouns in Irish. In P. Jefferiss and W. J. Mahon, eds., *Proceedings of the Harvard Celtic Colloquium (May 3–4, 1985)*, vol. V, 38–48.

1986 (with Paul Platero) Parts of speech. In P. Muysken and H. van Riemsdijk, eds., *Features and projections*, 31–40. Studies in Generative Grammar 25. Dordrecht: Foris.

1986 Notes on world view and semantic categories: Some Warlpiri examples. In P. Muysken and H. van Riemsdijk, eds., *Features and projections*, 233–254. Studies in Generative Grammar 25. Dordrecht: Foris.

1986 On nonconfigurational structures. *Anuario del Seminario de Filología Vasca "Julio de Urquijo"* ASJU XX-2. Donostia-San Sebastian.

1986 (with Samuel Jay Keyser) Some transitivity alternations in English. Lexicon Project Working Papers 7. Center for Cognitive Science, MIT, Cambridge, Mass., and *Anuario del Seminario de Filología Vasca "Julio de Urquijo"* ASJU XX-3, 605–638. Donostia-San Sebastian.

1987 (with Danilo Salamanca) La naturaleza de la lengua miskita y las principales dificultades para aprenderla (with Miskitu version). *Wani*, 6, 16–30.

1987 (with Samuel Jay Keyser) A view from the middle. Lexicon Project Working Papers 10. Center for Cognitive Science, MIT, Cambridge, Mass.

1987 (with Elisabeth Selkirk) Government and tonal phrasing in Papago. In C. Ewen and J. Anderson, eds., *Phonology yearbook 4*, 151–183. Cambridge: Cambridge University Press.

1987 (with LaVerne Masayesva Jeanne) Argument obviation and switch-reference in Hopi: *Anuario del Seminario de Filología Vasca "Julio de Urquijo"* ASJU XXI-1, 3–11. Donostia-San Sebastian.

1988 (with Colette Craig) Relational preverbs in some languages of the Americas: Typological and historical perspectives. *Language* 64, 312–344.

1988 Linguistic theory: Generative grammar. In S. Flynn and W. O'Neil, eds., *Linguistic theory in second language acquisition*. Dordrecht: Kluwer.

1988 Review of "Cry, Sacred Ground: Big Mountain U.S.A." *Resist Newsletter* 211(3–5), 9.

1988 (with Abanel Lacayo Blanco) Vocabulario preliminar del ulwa (sumu meridional). Centro de Investigaciones y Documentacion de la

Costa Atlantica (CIDCA) and Lexicon Project of the Center for Cognitive Science, MIT.

1989   The causative construction in Miskitu. In D. Jaspers ed., *Sentential complementation and the lexicon: Studies in honour of Wim de Geest*, 189–205. Dordrecht: Foris.

1989   The syntax of lexical word formation. In R. Carlson et al., eds., *Proceedings of the Fourth Meeting of the Pacific Linguistics Conference*, 190–217. Department of Linguistics, University of Oregon, Eugene.

1989 (with Andrew Barss, Ellavina Tsosie Perkins, and Margaret Speas) Aspects of Logical Form in Navajo. In E.-D. Cook and K. D. Rice, eds., *Athapaskan linguistics: Current perspectives on a language family*, 317–334. Trends in Linguistics, State-of-the-Art Reports 15. Berlin: Mouton de Gruyter.

1989 (with LaVerne Masayesva Jeanne)   Argument obviation and switch-reference in Hopi. In M. R. Key and H. M. Hoenigswald, eds., *General and Amerindian ethnolinguistics: In remembrance of Stanley Newman*, 201–211. Contributions to the Sociology of Language 55. Berlin: Mouton de Gruyter. [same as Jeanne and Hale 1987]

1989 (with CODIUL/UYUTMUBAL, Ulwa Language Committee of Karawala, RAAS, Nicaragua)   *Diccionario elemental del ulwa (sumu meridional)*. Centro de Investigaciones y Documentacion de la Costa Atlantica (CIDCA) and Lexicon Project of the Center for Cognitive Science, MIT.

1989   Remarks on lexicography in relation to Uto-Aztecan ethnolinguistic research. *Tlalocan* 11, 15–24. Instituto de Investigaciones Históricas e Filológicas, Universidad Nacional Autónoma de México.

1990 (with Mark Baker)   Relativized Minimality and pronoun incorporation. *Linguistic Inquiry* 21, 289–297.

1990   Some remarks on agreement and incorporation. *Studies in Generative Grammar* 1, 117–144.

1991 (with LaVerne Masayesva Jeanne and Paula Pranka)   On suppletion, selection, and agreement. In C. Georgopoulos and R. Ishihara, eds., *Essays in honor of S.-Y. Kuroda*, 255–270. Dordrecht: Kluwer.

1991 (with Andrew Barss, Ellavina Tsosie Perkins, and Margaret Speas)   Logical Form and barriers in Navajo. In C.-T. J. Huang and R. May, eds., *Logical structures and linguistic structure*, 25–47. Studies in Linguistics and Philosophy 40. Dordrecht: Kluwer.

1991 El ulwa, sumu meridional: Un idioma distinto? *Wani* 11. Managua, Nicaragua.

1992 (with Samuel Jay Keyser) The syntactic character of thematic structure. In I. M. Roca, ed., *Thematic structure: Its role in grammar*, 107–144. Berlin: Foris.

1992 (with Samuel Jay Keyser) Lexical categories and the projection of argument structure. In J. A. Lakarra and J. Ortiz de Urbina, eds., *Syntactic theory and Basque syntax*, 147–173. Supplements of the *Anuario del Seminario de Filología Vasca "Julio de Urquijo" International Journal of Basque Linguistics and Philology* XXVII, 147–173.

1992 (with Colette Craig, Nora England, LaVerne Masayesva Jeanne, Michael Krauss, Lucille Watahomigie, and Akira Yamamoto) Endangered languages. *Language* 68, 1–42.

1992 Basic word order in two "free word order" languages. In D. L. Payne, ed., *Pragmatics of word order flexibility*, 63–82. Typological Studies in Language 22. Amsterdam: John Benjamins.

1992 Dangerous memories. *Resist Newsletter* 248(1), 9–10.

1992 Subject obviation, switch reference, and control. In R. K. Larson, S. Iatridou, U. Lahiri, and J. Higginbotham, eds., *Control and grammar*, 51–77. Dordrecht: Kluwer.

1993 Language endangerment essays. In André Chrochetière, Jean-Claude Boulanger, and Conrad Ouellon, eds., *Proceedings of the 15th International Congress of Linguists, Québec, Université Laval, 9–14 August 1992, vol. 1*, 17–31. Québec: Les Presses de l'Université Laval.

1993 (with Samuel Jay Keyser) (eds.) *The view from Building 20: Essays in linguistics in honor of Sylvain Bromberger*. Cambridge, Mass.: MIT Press.

1993 (with Samuel Jay Keyser) On argument structure and the lexical expression of syntactic relations. In Hale and Keyser 1993, 53–108.

1993 Prólogo. [Prologue to] W. R. Miller, *Guarijío de Arechuyvo, Chihuahua*. Archivo de Lenguas Indígenas de México. México D.F.: El Colegio de México.

1994 Core structures and adjunctions in Warlpiri syntax. In N. Corver and H. van Riemsdijk, eds., *Studies on scrambling: Movement and non-movement approaches to free word-order phenomena*. Studies in Generative Grammar 41. Berlin: Mouton de Gruyter.

1994 La naturaleza sintáctica de la estructura argumental. In Z. Estrada Fernández, ed., *Memorias del II Encuentro de Lingüística en el Noroeste, tomo I*, 227–247. Hermosillo: Universidad de Sonora.

1994 (with Samuel Jay Keyser) Constraints on argument structure. In B. Lust, M. Suñer, and J. Whitman, eds., *Syntactic theory and first language acquisition: Cross-linguistic perspectives*. Vol. 1, *Heads, projections, and learnability*, 53–71. Hillsdale, N.J.: Lawrence Erlbaum Associates.

1994 (with Samuel Jay Keyser) A uniqueness condition on argument structure. In Y.-S. Kim, B.-C. Lee, K.-J. Lee, H.-K. Yang, and J.-Y. Yoon, eds., *Explorations in generative grammar: A festschrift for Dong-Whee Yang*. Seoul: Hankuk.

1995 (with Maria Bittner) Remarks on definiteness in Warlpiri. In E. Bach, E. Jelinek, A. Kratzer, and B. Partee, eds., *Quantification in natural languages*, 81–105. Dordrecht: Kluwer.

1995 (with Peter Ihionu and Victor Manfredi) Ìgbo bipositional verbs in a syntactic theory of argument structure. In A. Akinlabi, ed., *Theoretical approaches to African linguistics*, 83–107. Trenton, N.J.: Africa World Press.

1995 *An elementary Warlpiri dictionary*. Alice Springs: IAD Press.

1995 (with Mary Laughren and Jane Simpson). Warlpiri. In J. Jacobs, A. von Stechow, W. Sternefeld, and T. Vennemann, eds., *Syntax: An international handbook of contemporary research, vol. 2*, 1430–1451. Berlin: Walter de Gruyter.

1996 (with Mary Laughren, Robert Hoogenraad, and Robin Granites) *A learner's guide to Warlpiri*. Alice Springs: IAD Press.

1996 (with Chunyan Ning) Raising in Dagur relative clauses. In B. Agbayani, K. Takeda, and S.-W. Tang, eds., *UCI working papers in linguistics 1*. Department of Linguistics, University of California, Irvine.

1996 (with Maria Bittner) The structural determination of Case and agreement. *Linguistic Inquiry* 27, 1–68.

1996 Can UG and L1 be distinguished in L2 acquisition? *Behavioral and Brain Sciences* 19(4) (commentary on target article).

1996 (with Paul Platero) Navajo reflections of a general theory of lexical argument structure. In E. Jelinek, S. Midgette, K. Rice, and L. Saxon, eds., *Athabaskan language studies: Essays in honor of Robert W. Young*. Albuquerque: University of New Mexico Press.

1996 (with Maria Bittner)   Ergativity: Toward a theory of a heterogeneous class. *Linguistic Inquiry* 27, 531–604.

1996   Universal Grammar and the roots of linguistic diversity. In J. D. Bobaljik, R. Pensalfini, and L. Storto, eds., *Papers on language endangerment and the maintenance of linguistic diversity*, 137–161. MIT Working Papers in Linguistics 28. MITWPL, Department of Linguistics and Philosophy, MIT.

1997   Some observations on the contributions of local languages to linguistic science. *Lingua* 100, 71–89.

1997 (with Luciana Storto)   Agreement and spurious antipassives. *ABRALIN—Boletim da Associação Brasileira de Lingüística, Nº 20, Homenagem a Aryon Dall-Igna Rodrigues.* January 1997, 61–89.

1997 (with Samuel Jay Keyser)   On the complex nature of simple predicators. In A. Alsina, J. Bresnan, and P. Sells, eds., *Complex predicates*, 29–65. CSLI Lecture Notes 64. Stanford, Calif.: CSLI Publications.

1997 (with David Nash)   Damin and Lardil phonotactics. In D. Tryon and M. Walsh, eds., *Boundary rider: Essays in honour of Geoffrey O'Grady*, 247–259. Pacific Linguistics C-136. Canberra: Australian National University.

1997   A Linngithigh vocabulary. In D. Tryon and M. Walsh, eds., *Boundary rider: Essays in honour of Geoffrey O'Grady*, 209–246. Pacific Linguistics C-136. Canberra: Australian National University.

1997   The Misumalpan causative construction. In J. Bybee, J. Haiman, and S. A. Thompson, eds., *Essays on language function and language type dedicated to T. Givón*, 200–215. Amsterdam: John Benjamins.

1997 (with Samuel Jay Keyser)   *Have*: Linguistic diversity in the expression of a simple relation. In D. van der Meij, ed., *India and beyond, aspects of literature, meaning, ritual, and thought: Essays in honor of Frits Staal*, 194–206. International Institute for Asian Studies, Leiden and Amsterdam. London: Kegan Paul International.

1997 (with Samuel Jay Keyser)   The limits of argument structure. In A. Mendikoetxea and M. Uribe-Etxebarria, eds., *Theoretical issues at the morphology-syntax interface*, 203–230. Bilbao/Donostia-San Sebastian: Universidad del País Vasco/Diputación Foral de Gipuzkoa.

1997   On Campbell's *American Indian languages. Mother Tongue: Journal of the Association for the Study of Language in Prehistory* 3, 145–158.

1997 Grammatical preface. In Kubarikun, compiler, *Lardil dictionary: A vocabulary of the language of the Lardil people of Mornington Island, Gulf of Carpenteria, Queensland*, 12–56. Ngakulmungan Kangka Lewanl Language Projects Steering Committee, Mornington Shire Council, Gunana, Queensland.

1998 On endangered languages and the importance of linguistic diversity. In L. A. Grenoble and L. J. Whaley, eds., *Endangered languages: Language loss and community response*, 192–216. Cambridge: Cambridge University Press.

1998 L'antipassif de focalisation du k'ichee' et la forme inversée du chukchi: Une étude de l'accord excentrique. *Recherches Linguistiques de Vincennes* 27, 95–114.

1998 El antipasivo de enfoque del k'ichee' y el inverso del chukchi: Un estudio de la concordancia excéntrica. In Z. Estrada Fernández et al., eds., *IV Encuentro Internacional de Lingüística en el Noroeste.* Tomo I, *Lenguas indígenas, volumen I.* Hermosillo, Sonora: Editorial Unison, Universidad de Sonora.

1998 (with Thomas Green) Ulwa, the language of Karawala, eastern Nicaragua: Its position and prospects in modern Nicaragua. *International Journal of the Sociology of Language: Indigenous Language Use and Change in the Americas* 132, 185–201.

1998 (with Samuel Jay Keyser) The basic elements of argument structure. In H. Harley, ed., *Papers from the UPenn/MIT Roundtable on Argument Structure and Aspect*, 73–118. MIT Working Papers in Linguistics 32. MITWPL, Department of Linguistics and Philosophy, MIT.

1999 Conflicting truths. In M. Darnell, E. Moravcsik, F. Newmeyer, M. Noonan, and K. Wheatley, eds., *Functionalism and formalism in linguistics.* Vol. I: *General papers*, 167–175. Amsterdam: John Benjamins.

1999 Review of *Políticas lingüísticas en México*, B. Cuarón, ed., Colección: La democracia en México. *Anthropological Linguistics* 41, 127–134.

1999 (with Samuel Jay Keyser) A response to Fodor and Lepore, "Impossible words?" *Linguistic Inquiry* 30, 453–466.

1999 (with Samuel Jay Keyser) Bound features, Merge, and transitivity alternations. In L. Pylkkänen, A. van Hout, and H. Harley, eds., *Papers from the UPenn/MIT Roundtable on the Lexicon*, 49–72. MIT Working Papers in Linguistics 35. MITWPL, MIT, Cambridge, Mass.

2000 (with Samuel Jay Keyser) Conflation. In A. Bravo Martín, C. Luján Berenguel, and I. Pérez Jiménez, eds., *Cuadernos de lingüística VII 2000: Documentos de trabajo. Lingüística theórica*, 39–76. Madrid: Instituto Universitario Ortega y Gasset.

2000 Ulwa (Southern Sumu): The beginnings of a language research project. In P. Newman and M. Ratliff, eds., *Linguistic fieldwork*. Cambridge: Cambridge University Press.

Index

Current Studies in Linguistics
Samuel Jay Keyser, general editor